THE
ART OF COOKERY,
MADE
PLAIN and EASY;

Which far excels any Thing of the Kind yet publiſhed.

CONTAINING,

I. A Liſt of the various Kinds of Meat, Poultry, Fiſh, Vegetables, and Fruit, in Seaſon, in every Month of the Year.
II. Directions for Marketting.
III. How to Roaſt and Boil to Perfection.
IV. Sauces for all plain Diſhes.
V. Made Diſhes.
VI. To dreſs Poultry, Game, &c.
VII. How expenſive a French Cook's Sauce is.
VIII. To make a Number of pretty little Diſhes for Suppers, or Side or Corner Diſhes.
IX. To dreſs Turtle, Mock-turtle, &c.
X. To dreſs Fiſh.
XI. Sauces for Fiſh.
XII. Of Soups and Broths.
XIII. Of Puddings and Pies.
XIV. For a Lent Dinner; a Number of good Diſhes, which may be made uſe of at any other Time.
XV. Directions for the Sick.
XVI. For Captains of Ships; how to make all uſeful Diſhes for a Voyage; and ſetting out a Table on board.
XVII. Of Hog's Puddings, Sauſages, &c.
XVIII. To pot, make Hams, &c.
XIX. Of Pickling.
XX. Of making Cakes, &c.
XXI. Of Cheeſecakes, Creams, Jellies, Whipt Syllabubs.
XXII. Of Made Wines, Brewing, Baking, French Bread, Muffins, Cheeſe, &c.
XXIII. Jarring Cherries, Preſerves, &c.
XXIV. To make Anchovies, Vermicelli, Catchup, Vinegar, and to keep Artichokes, French Beans, &c.
XXV. Of Diſtilling.
XXVI. Directions for Carving.
XXVII. Uſeful and valuable Family Receipts.
XXVIII. Receipts for Perfumery, &c.

IN WHICH ARE INCLUDED,

One Hundred and Fifty new and uſeful Receipts, not inſerted in any former Edition.

WITH A COPIOUS INDEX.

By Mrs. GLASSE.

A NEW EDITION,

With all the Modern Improvements:

And alſo the Order of a Bill of Fare for each Month; the Diſhes arranged on the Table in the moſt faſhionable Style.

LONDON:

Printed for T. Longman, B. Law, J. Johnſon, G. G. and J. Robinſon, H. Gardner, T. Payne, F. and C. Rivington, J. Sewell, W. Richardſon, W. Lane, W. Lowndes, G. and T. Wilkie, W. Nicoll, W. Fox, Ogilvy and Speare, J. Debrett, J. Scatcherd, Vernor and Hood, Clarke and Son, J. Nunn, J. Barker, B. Croſby, Cadell and Davies, and E. Newbery.

1796.

TO THE READER.

I Believe I have attempted a branch of Cookery, which nobody has yet thought worth their while to write upon: but as I have both seen, and found by experience, that the generality of servants are greatly wanting in that point, therefore I have taken upon me to instruct them in the best manner I am capable; and, I dare say, that every servant who can but read, will be capable of making a tolerable good cook, and those who have the least notion of Cookery cannot miss of being very good ones.

If I have not wrote in the high polite style, I hope I shall be forgiven; for my intention is to instruct the lower sort, and therefore must treat them in their own way. For example, when I bid them lard a fowl, if I should bid them lard with large lardoons, they would not know what I meant; but when I say they must lard with little pieces of bacon, they know what I mean. So in many other things in Cookery, the great cooks have such a high way of expressing themselves, that the poor girls are at a loss to know what they mean: and in all Receipt Books yet printed, there are such an odd jumble of things as would quite spoil a good dish; and indeed some things so extravagant, that it would be almost a shame to make use of them, when a dish can be made full as good, or better, without them. For example: when you entertain ten or twelve people, you shall use for a cullis, a leg of veal and a ham; which, with the other ingredients, makes it very expensive, and all this only to mix with other sauce. And again, the essence of ham for sauce to one dish; when I will prove it, for about three shillings I will make as

To the READER.

rich and high a sauce as all that will be, when done. For example:

Take a large deep stew-pan, half a pound of ham, fat and lean together, cut the fat and lay it over the bottom of the pan; then take a pound of veal, cut it into thin slices, beat it well with the back of a knife, lay it all over the ham; then have six-penny-worth of the coarse lean part of the beef cut thin, and well beat, lay a layer of it all over, with some carrot, then the lean of the ham cut thin and laid over that; then cut two onions and strew over, a bundle of sweet herbs, four or five blades of mace, six or seven cloves, a spoonful of all-spice or Jamaica pepper, half a nutmeg beat, a pigeon beat all to pieces, lay that all over, half an ounce of truffles and morels, then the rest of your beef, a good crust of bread toasted very brown and dry on both sides: you may add an old cock beat to pieces; cover it close, and let it stand over a slow fire two or three minutes, then pour on boiling water enough to fill the pan, cover it close, and let it stew till it is as rich as you would have it, and then strain off all that sauce. Put all your ingredients together again, fill the pan with boiling water, put in a fresh onion, a blade of mace, and a piece of carrot; cover it close, and let it stew till it is as strong as you want it. This will be full as good as the essence of ham for all sorts of fowls, or indeed most made dishes, mixed with a glass of wine, and two or three spoonfuls of catchup. When your first gravy is cool, skim off all the fat, and keep it for use.——*This falls far short of the expence of a leg of veal and ham, and answers every purpose you want.*

If you go to market, the ingredients will not come to above half a crown; or for about eighteen-pence you may make as much good gravy as will serve twenty people.

Take twelve-penny-worth of coarse lean beef, which will be six or seven pounds, cut it all to pieces, flour it well; take a quarter of a pound of good butter, put it into a little pot or large deep stew-pan, and put in your beef: keep stirring it, and when it begins to look a little brown, pour in a pint of boiling water; stir it all together, put in a large onion, a bundle of sweet herbs, two or three blades of mace, five or six cloves, a spoonful of all-spice, a crust of bread toasted, and a piece of carrot; then pour in four or five quarts of water, stir all together, cover close, and let it stew till it is as rich as you would have it; when enough, strain it off, mix it with two or three spoonfuls of catchup, and half a pint of white wine; then put all the ingredients together again, and put in two quarts of boiling water, cover it close, and let it boil till there is about a pint; strain it off well, add it to the first, and give it a boil together. This will make a great deal of good rich gravy.

You may leave out the wine, according to what use you want it for; so that really one might have a genteel entertainment for the price the sauce of one dish comes to; but if gentlemen will have French *cooks, they must pay for* French *tricks.*

A Frenchman *in his own country will dress a fine dinner of twenty dishes, and all genteel and pretty, for the expence he will put an* English *lord to for dressing one dish. But then there is the little petty profit. I have heard of a cook that used six pounds of butter to fry twelve eggs; when every body knows (that understands cooking) that half a pound is full enough, or more than need be used: but then it would not be* French. *So much is the blind folly of this age, that they would rather be imposed on by a* French *booby, than give encouragement to a good* English *cook!*

I doubt I shall not gain the esteem of those gentlemen; however, let that be as it will, it little concerns me; but should I be so happy as to gain the good opinion of my own sex, I desire no more; that will be a full recompence for all my trouble: and I only beg the favour of every lady to read my Book *throughout before they censure me, and then I flatter myself I shall have their approbation.*

I shall not take upon me to meddle in the physical way farther than two receipts, which will be of use to the public in general, one is for the bite of a mad dog; and the other, if a man should be near where the plague is, he shall be in no danger; which, if made use of, will be found of very great service to those who go abroad.

Nor shall I take upon me to direct a lady in the œconomy of her family; for every mistress does, or at least ought to know, what is most proper to be done there; therefore I shall not fill my Book *with a deal of nonsense of that kind, which I am very well assured none will have regard to.*

I have indeed given some of my dishes French *names to distinguish them, because they are known by those names: and where there is a great variety of dishes, and a large table to cover, so there must be a variety of names for them; and it matters not whether they be called by a* French, Dutch, *or* English *name, so they are good, and done with as little expence as the dish will allow of.*

I shall say no more, only hope my Book *will answer the ends I intend it for; which is to improve the servants, and save the ladies a great deal of trouble.*

PREFACE

TO THE

PRESENT EDITION.

Notwithstanding the vast number of books on the subject of Cookery, which are every day presented to the public, Mrs. Glasse's Work has continued to maintain a decided preference: The reason of this must be obvious to every one on comparison, when they observe that, in point of quantity, her Book exceeds every one in print, by at least one half, and in point of usefulness, beyond all comparison; insomuch that many persons who have been induced for the sake of novelty, or by the sound of a name, to try other publications, have on experiment laid them on the shelf, and returned to their old director, as more easy, comprehensible, and useful.

But, as there is a fashion in Cookery, as well as every thing else; and it is as well to know nothing, as not to know the most modern improvements in the art, this edition has been undertaken to give all the additional information which can be communicated; and so to improve the established receipts, as to make them of general use, and entitle them to increased approbation: For this purpose, upwards of one hundred and fifty new Receipts are given in this Book, all of them useful, and highly genteel and ornamental.

That some few of these have been taken from other publications, the Editor does not pretend to deny; but the greater part are original, collected and improved during a service of eighteen years in the most respectable families: If those taken for this edition from other printed books were to be restored, it would only diminish the size of the volume by a very few pages; but if all they have borrowed from our book, and put into theirs, in a worse form, were to be taken away, many a large and high-priced publication would shrink to a bulk no greater than a child's spelling book.

In this edition, the greatest care has been taken to unite elegance with œconomy, and to enable the Housekeeper to make a fashionable appearance at as small an expence as possible; an object highly desireable in all classes of life, as unnecessary profusion is a mark of folly rather than generosity.

Great pains have also been taken to arrange the subjects, so as to introduce one by another, and to enable people to find what they want without much difficulty; and the care bestowed on the Index and table of Contents, will render it easy to find whatever is wanted in a moment's search.

CONTENTS.

CHAP. I.
Containing a List of the various Kinds of MEAT, POULTRY, FISH, VEGETABLES, *and* FRUIT, *in Season, in every Month of the Year.*

CHAP. II.
Directions for Marketting.

PIECES in a bullock,	6	Heath and pheasant poults,	12
In a sheep,	7	Heath cock and hen,	ib.
In a calf,	ib.	Woodcock and snipe,	ib.
In a lamb,	ib.	Partridge,	ib.
In a hog,	ib.	Doves, &c.	ib.
In a bacon hog,	ib.	Teal and widgeon,	ib.
To choose beef,	8	A hare,	ib.
Mutton and lamb,	ib.	A leveret,	13
Veal,	9	Rabbit,	ib.
Pork,	ib.	To choose salmon, trout, &c.	ib.
Brawn,	ib.	Turbot,	ib.
Dried hams and bacon,	ib.	Soals,	ib.
Venison,	10	Plaice and Flounders,	ib.
To know if a capon be young or old, &c.	ib.	Cod and codling,	ib.
		Fresh herrings and mackarel,	ib.
To choose a turkey,	ib.	Pickled salmon,	14
A cock, hen, &c.	ib.	Pickled and red herrings,	ib.
To know if chickens are new or stale,	11	Dried ling,	ib.
		Pickled sturgeon,	ib.
To choose a goose, wild-goose, &c.	ib.	Lobsters,	ib.
		Crab-fish, great and small,	ib.
Wild and tame ducks,	ib.	Prawns and shrimps,	ib.
Bustard,	ib.	Butter and eggs,	15
Shufflers, goodwits, &c.	ib.	Cheese,	ib.
Pheasant,	ib.		

CHAP. III.
Roasting, Boiling, &c.

GENERAL directions for ROASTING,	16	To kill a pig and prepare it for roasting,	18
To roast beef,	ib.	To roast a pig,	ib.
Mutton,	ib.	Another way,	19
Lamb,	17	To roast the hind-quarter of a pig lamb-fashion,	ib.
Veal,	ib.		
Pork,	ib.	To bake a pig,	ib.

To

CONTENTS.

To roast venison,	19	BOILING.	
To dress a haunch of mutton,	20	General directions,	26
To dress mutton venison-fashion,		To boil a ham,	ib.
	ib.	Tongue,	ib.
To keep venison or hares sweet,		Round of beef,	ib.
	ib.	Brisket of beef,	ib.
To roast a tongue and udder,	ib.	Calf's head,	27
To roast geese, turkies, &c.	ib.	Lamb's head,	ib.
To roast a fowl pheasant-fashion,		Boiled leg of lamb, and the loin fried round it,	ib.
	21		
To roast a fowl,	ib.	To boil a leg of pork,	28
Pigeons,	ib.	Pickled pork,	ib.
Partridges,	ib.	POULTRY.	
Larks,	22	To boil a turkey,	ib.
Woodcocks and snipes,	ib.	Young chickens,	ib.
Another way,	ib.	Fowls and house lamb,	29
Hare,	ib.	GREEN ROOTS, &c.	
Rabbits,	23	To dress spinage,	ib.
Rabbit hare-fashion,	ib.	Cabbages, &c.	ib.
To keep meat hot,	ib.	Carrots,	ib.
BROILING.		Turnips,	30
General directions,	ib.	Parsnips,	ib.
To broil beef steaks,	24	Brocoli,	ib.
Mutton chops,	ib.	Potatoes,	ib.
Pork steaks,	ib.	Cauliflowers,	ib.
Chickens,	ib.	Common way,	31
Pigeons,	25	French beans,	ib.
FRYING.		Artichokes,	ib.
To fry beef steaks,	ib.	Asparagus,	ib.
A second way,	ib.	Green Pease,	32
Tripe,	ib.	Beans and bacon,	ib.
Sausages,	ib.		

CHAP. IV.

Sauces for all the Dishes mentioned in the foregoing Chapter.

To melt butter,	32	To make hot poivrade-sauce,	34
To make veal, mutton, or beef gravy,	ib.	Cold poivrade-sauce,	ib.
		Sauce for a hare,	35
To make gravy,	33	Gravy for a turkey, or any sort of fowls,	ib.
Different sorts of sauce for a pig,	ib.		
		Turkies, pheasants, &c. may be larded,	ib.
Different sorts of sauce for venison,	ib.		
		Sauce for steaks,	ib.
Sauce for a goose,	34	Sauce for a boiled turkey,	ib.
Apple-sauce,	ib.	Sauce for a boiled goose,	36
Sauce for a turkey,	ib.	Sauce for boiled ducks or rabbits,	ib.
Sauce for ducks,	ib.		
Sauce for fowls,	ib.	To bake a leg of beef,	ib.
Sauce for pheasants and partridges,	ib.	To bake an ox's head,	ib.

CHAP.

CHAP. V.
Made Dishes.

RULES to be observed in all made-dishes,	37
To make lemon-pickle,	ib.
Browning for made-dishes,	38
To dress Scotch collops,	ib.
To dress white collops,	39
To dress fillet of veal with collops,	ib.
Collops à la Françoise,	ib.
Savoury dish of veal,	ib.
Italian collops,	40
To do them white,	ib.
Beef collops,	ib.
Force-meat balls,	ib.
Truffles and morels, good in sauces, &c.	41
To stew ox palates,	ib.
To ragoo ox palates,	ib.
To fricassee ox palates,	ib.
To roast ox palates,	42
To fricando ox palates,	ib.
To make a brown fricassee,	ib.
To make a white fricassee,	43
To fricassee rabbits, lamb, or veal,	ib.
A second way to make a white fricassee,	ib.
A third way of making a white fricassee,	ib.
To fricassee rabbits, lamb, sweetbreads, or tripe,	44
Fricassee tripe, another way,	ib.
Fricassee calves' feet and chaldron, after the Italian way,	ib.
Fricassee pigeons,	ib.
Fricassee lamb-stones, and sweetbreads,	45
Fricassee lamb cutlets,	ib.
To hash a calf's head,	ib.
To hash a calf's head white,	46
Another way less expensive and troublesome,	ib.
To hash venison,	47
To hash beef,	ib.
To hash mutton,	ib.
To hash veal,	ib.
To hash turkey,	ib.
To hash a fowl,	48
To hash a woodcock or partridge,	ib.
To hash a wild duck,	ib.
To hash a hare,	ib.
To bake a calf's head,	49
To bake a sheep's head,	ib.
To dress a lamb's head,	ib.
Calf's head surprize,	50
Calf's head dressed after the Dutch way,	ib.
To stew a lamb's or calf's head,	ib.
To grill a calf's head,	51
Breast of veal in hodge-podge,	ib.
To collar a breast of veal,	52
To collar a breast of mutton,	ib.
Another good way to dress a breast of mutton,	53
To ragoo a leg of mutton,	ib.
To ragoo hog's feet and ears,	ib.
To ragoo a neck of veal,	ib.
To ragoo a breast of veal,	54
To ragoo another way,	ib.
To ragoo a fillet of veal,	55
To ragoo sweetbreads,	ib.
To ragoo lamb,	ib.
To ragoo a piece of beef,	ib.
To force the inside of a sirloin of beef,	56
Another way,	ib.
Sirloin of beef en epigram,	57
To force the inside of a rump of beef,	ib.
To force a round of beef,	ib.
To force a leg of lamb,	ib.
Another way,	58
To force a large fowl,	ib.
To roast a turkey the genteel way,	ib.
To stew a knuckle of veal,	59
Another way,	ib.
To stew a fillet of veal,	ib.
Beef tremblant,	ib.
Beef à la daub,	60
Beef alamode,	ib.

Beef

CONTENTS.

Beef alamode in pieces,	61
To stew beef-steaks,	ib.
Beef-steaks after the French way,	ib.
A pretty side-dish of beef,	ib.
To stew a rump of beef,	62
Another way,	ib.
Portugal beef,	ib.
To stew a rump of beef, or brisket, the French way,	63
To stew beef-gobbets,	ib.
Beef royal,	ib.
To stew an ox-cheek,	64
To stew a shank of beef,	ib.
To stew a turkey or fowl,	ib.
A rolled rump of beef	65
To boil a rump of beef the French fashion,	ib.
Beef-escarlot,	66
Fricando of beef,	ib.
Beef olives,	ib.
To dress a fillet of beef,	ib.
Beef-steaks rolled,	67
To dress the inside of a cold sirloin of beef,	ib.
Boullie-beef,	ib.
To make mock-hare of a beast's heart,	68
Tripe à la Kilkenny,	ib.
Tongue and udder forced,	ib.
To fricassee neats' tongues brown,	ib.
To force a tongue,	69
To stew neats' tongues whole,	ib.
To dress a leg of mutton à la royale,	ib.
A leg of mutton à la haut goût,	70
To roast a leg of mutton with oysters,	ib.
A second way,	ib.
To roast a leg of mutton with cockles,	ib.
A shoulder of mutton en epigram,	ib.
Harrico of mutton,	ib.
To French a hind saddle of mutton,	71
Another way, called St. Menehout,	ib.
Cutlets à la Mainténon,	72
Mutton-chops in disguise,	ib.
To dress a leg of mutton to eat like venison,	ib.
To dress mutton the Turkish way,	ib.
Hodge-podge of mutton,	73
Shoulder of mutton with a ragoo of turnips,	ib.
To stuff a leg or shoulder of mutton,	74
Oxford John,	ib.
Mutton-rumps à la braise,	ib.
Sheeps' rumps with rice,	75
Mutton kebobbed,	ib.
A neck of mutton, called the Hasty Dish,	76
To bake lamb and rice,	ib.
To fry a loin of lamb,	ib.
Another way,	77
Lamb chops larded,	ib.
Lamb chops en caserole,	ib.
To dress a dish of lambs' bits,	ib.
To dress veal à la Bourgeoise,	78
Disguised leg of veal and bacon,	ib.
Loin of veal en epigram,	ib.
To make a porcupine of a breast of veal,	79
A pillaw of veal,	ib.
A fricando of veal,	80
Bombarded veal,	ib.
Veal rolls,	ib.
Veal olives,	81
Veal olives the French way,	ib.
Veal blanquets,	ib.
Shoulder of veal à la Piedmontoise,	82
Sweetbreads of veal à la Dauphiné,	ib.
Another way,	ib.
Sweetbreads en Cordonnier,	83
Calf's chitterlings, or andouilles,	ib.
To dress calf's chitterlings curiously,	84
To dress a calf's liver in a caul,	ib.
To roast a calf's liver,	ib.
Calves' feet stewed,	ib.
To make fricandillas,	85

To

To make a Scotch haggafs, 85	To drefs a pig the French way, 89
To make it fweet with fruit, ib.	To drefs a pig au pere Douiller, ib.
To drefs a ham à la braife, ib.	Pig matelote, 90
To roaft a ham or gammon, 86	To drefs a pig like a fat lamb, ib.
To make effence of ham, ib.	Barbecued pig, ib.
To ftuff a chine of pork, ib.	To drefs pig's pettitoes, 91
To barbecue a leg of pork, 87	To make a pretty difh of a breaft of venifon, ib.
Various ways of dreffing a pig, ib.	To boil a haunch or neck of venifon, ib.
Pig in jelly, 88	
Collared pig, ib.	

CHAP. VI.
To drefs Poultry, Game, &c.

To roaft a turkey, 92	Fowl à la braife, ib.
A white fauce for fowls or chickens, 93	Capon French way, 99
To make mock oyfter-fauce, ib.	To roaft a fowl with chefnuts, ib.
To make mufhroom-fauce, ib.	To marinate fowls, ib.
To make ditto, ibid.	To make a frangas incopades, 100
To make celery-fauce, ib.	Pullets à la Sainte Menehout, ib.
To make brown celery-fauce, 94	Chicken-furprize, ib.
To ftew a turkey or fowl in celery-fauce, ib.	Chickens in favoury jelly, 101
To make egg-fauce, ib.	Chickens roafted with forcemeat and cucumbers, ib.
To make fhalot-fauce, ib.	Chickens à la braife, 102
To make carrier-fauce, ib.	Chickens to broil, ib.
To make fhalot-fauce, 95	Chickens pulled, 103
To drefs livers with mufhroom-fauce, ib.	Chickens chiringrate, ib.
A pretty little fauce, ib.	Chickens French way, 104
Lemon-fauce, ib.	Chickens boiled with bacon and celery, ib.
A German way of dreffing fowls, ib.	Chickens with tongues, a good difh for a great deal of company, ib.
To drefs a turkey or fowl to perfection, ib.	Scotch chickens, ib.
To ftew a turkey brown, 96	To ftew chickens the Dutch way, 105
Another way. ib.	To ftew chickens, ib.
Turkies and chickens Dutch way. 97	A pretty way of ftewing chickens, ib.
Turkey ftuffed Hamburgh way, ib.	Ducks alamode, ib.
Turkey à la daub, to be fent up hot, ib.	To ftew ducks with green peafe, 106
Turkey à la daub to be fent up cold, ib.	To drefs a wild duck the beft way, ib.
Turkey in jelly, 98	Another way, ib.

To

CONTENTS

To boil a duck or rabbit with onions, 106
To dress a duck with green peas, 107
To dress a duck with cucumbers, ib.
To dress a duck à la braise, ib.
To boil ducks the French way, 108
To dress a goose with onions or cabbage, ib.
Directions for roasting a goose, 109
A green goose, ib.
To dress a stubble goose, ib.
To dry a goose, ib.
To dress a goose in ragoo, 110
To dress a goose alamode, ib.
To stew giblets, 111
Giblets à la turtle, ib.
To roast pigeons, 112
To boil pigeons, ib.
To à la daub pigeons, ib.
Pigeons au poire, 113
Pigeons stoved, 114
Pigeons surtout, ib.
Pigeons compote, ib.
Pigeons, a French pupton, 115
Pigeons boiled with rice, ib.
Pigeons transmogrified, ib.
A second way, 116
Pigeons in fricando, ib.
To roast pigeons with a farce, ib.
Pigeons in savoury jelly, ib.
Pigeons à la Souffel, 117
Pigeons in Pimlico, ib.
Pigeons in a hole, ib.
To jug pigeons, 118
To stew pigeons, ib.
Another way, ib.
To fricassee pigeons the Italian way, 119
To make force-meat for pigeons, 119
To boil partridges, ib.
Partridges à la braise 120
Partridge panes, ib.
To stew partridges, 121
A second way, ib.
To stew partridges or pigeons with red or white cabbage, ib.
To roast pheasants, 122
A stewed pheasant, ib.
To dress pheasant à la braise, ib.
To boil a pheasant, 123
To salmec a snipe or woodcock, ib.
Snipes or woodcocks in surtout, ib.
To boil snipes or woodcocks, 124
To dress Ortolans, ib.
To dress ruffs and rees, ib.
To dress larks, 125
To dress larks pear fashion, ib.
To dress plovers, ib.
Jugged hare, 126
Another way, ib.
Florendine hare, ib.
To scare a hare, 127
To stew a hare, ib.
To hodge-podge a hare, ib.
A hare civet, 128
Portuguese rabbits, ib.
Rabbits surprise, ib.
Rabbits in casserole, 129
To make a curry the Indian way, ib.
To boil the rice, ib.
Another way, ib.
To boil the rice, 130
To make a pillaw the Indian way, ib.
Another way, ib.

CHAP.

CONTENTS.

CHAP. VII.
Shewing how expensive a French Cook's Sauce is.

FRENCH way of dreſſing partridges, 131
To make eſſence of ham, ib.
Cullis for all ſorts of ragoo, 132
Cullis for all ſorts of butchers' meat, ib.
Cullis the Italian way, 133
Cullis of Craw-fiſh, ib.
A white cullis, ib.
Sauce for a brace of partridges, &c. 134

CHAP. VIII.
Pretty little Diſhes.

HOGS' ears forced, 134
To force cock's-combs, 135
To force cabbage, ib.
Savoys forced and ſtewed, ib.
Forced eggs, 136
Forced cucumbers, ib.
To preſerve cock's-combs, ib.
To preſerve or pickle pig's feet and ears, ib.
Another way, 137
To pickle ox palates, ib.
To ſtew cucumbers, ib.
To ſtew red cabbage, ib.
To ſtew peaſe and lettuce, 138
Another way, ib.
To ſtew ſpinage and eggs, ib.
To ſtew muſhrooms, ib.
Another way, 139
To ſtew chardoons, ib.
To dreſs Windſor-beans, ib.
To make jumballs, ib.
To ragoo cucumbers, ib.
To ragoo onions, 140
To ragoo oyſters, ib.
To ragoo aſparagus, ib.
To ragoo livers, 141
To ragoo cauliflowers, ib.
Fried ſauſages, ib.
Collops and eggs, ib.
To dreſs cold fowl or pigeon, ib.
To fry cold veal, 142
To toſs up cold veal white, ib.
To haſh cold mutton, ib.
To haſh mutton like veniſon, ib.
To make collops of cold beef, 143
To mince veal, ib.
To make a florentine of veal, ib.
Salmagundy, ib.
Another way, 144
To make little paſties, ib.
Petit paſties for garniſhing diſhes. ib.

CHAP. IX.
Turtle, Mock Turtle, &c.

TO dreſs a turtle the Weſt-India way, 145
Another way, 146
To make a mock-turtle, 147
To make mock-turtle ſoup, 148

CHAP. X.
Fiſh.

TO boil a turbot, 148
To bake a turbot, 149
To dreſs a brace of carp, ib.
To dreſs carp au bleu, 150
To ſtew a brace of carp, ib.
To fry carp, 151
To bake carp, 151
To ſtew carp or tench, ib.
To fry tench, 152
To roaſt a cod's head, ib.
To boil a cod's head, 153
To ſtew cod, ib.

CONTENTS.

To fricassee cod,	153
To bake a cod's head,	154
To crimp cod the Dutch way,	ib.
To broil cod-sounds,	ib.
Cod-sounds broiled with gravy,	155
To fricassee cod-sounds,	ib.
To broil crimp-cod, &c.	ib.
To dress little fish,	ib.
To broil mackarel,	ib.
To broil mackarel whole,	156
Mackarel à la maitre d'hotel,	ib.
To boil mackarel,	ib.
To broil weavers,	ib.
To dress a jowl of pickled salmon,	157
To broil salmon,	ib.
Baked salmon,	ib.
Salmon au court Bouillon,	ib.
Salmon à la braise,	158
Salmon in cases,	ib.
To boil salmon-crimp,	159
To broil herrings,	ib.
To fry herrings,	ib.
To bake herrings,	ib.
To make water-sokey,	ib.
To dress flat fish,	160
To dress salt fish,	ib.
The manner of dressing various sorts of dried fish,	ib.
Dried salmon,	161
Dried herring,	ib.
Stock-fish,	ib.
To stew eels,	162
To stew eels with broth,	ib.
To stew eels excellently,	ib.
To dress lampreys,	ib.
To fry lampreys,	163
To pitchcock eels,	ib.
To fry eels,	ib.
To broil eels,	ib.
To farce eels with white sauce,	164
To dress eels with brown sauce,	164
To dress a pike,	ib.
To broil haddocks when they are in high season,	165
To dress haddocks after the Spanish way,	ib.
To dress haddocks the Jews way,	ib.
To roast a piece of fresh sturgeon,	ib.
To roast a fillet or collar of sturgeon,	166
To boil sturgeon,	ib.
To crimp skate,	ib.
To fricassee skate or thornback white,	167
To fricassee it brown,	ib.
To fricassee soals white,	ib.
To fricassee soals brown,	168
To boil soals,	ib.
Another way,	ib.
To make a collar of fish in ragoo,	ib.
To butter crabs or lobsters,	169
Another way,	ib.
To roast lobsters,	170
To make a fine dish of lobsters,	ib.
To dress a crab,	ib.
To stew prawns, shrimps, or crawfish,	ib.
Scolloped oysters,	171
To ragoo oysters,	ib.
To fry oysters,	ib.
To stew oysters, &c.	172
Oyster loaves,	ib.
To stew muscles,	ib.
Another way,	ib.
A third way,	173
To stew scollops,	ib.
To grill shrimps,	ib.
Buttered shrimps,	ib.
To fry smelts,	ib.
To dress white-bait,	ib.

CHAP.

CHAP. XI.
Sauces for Fish.

To make Quin's sauce,	174	Anchovy-sauce,	175
Another way,	ib.	Dutch sauce,	ib.
Lobster-sauce,	ib.	Sauce for cod's head,	ib.
Shrimp-sauce,	ib.	Sauce for most sorts of fish,	176
Oyster-sauce,	175	White sauce,	ib.

CHAP. XII.
Soups and Broths.

Rules to be observed in making soups and broths,	176	A green peas soup,	180
		Another way,	181
		A peas soup for winter,	ib.
To make strong broth for soup or gravy,	177	Another way,	182
		A chesnut soup,	ib.
Gravy for white sauce,	ib.	Hare-soup,	ib.
Gravy for turkey, fowl, or ragoo,	ib.	Soup à la reine,	ib.
		Mutton-broth,	183
Gravy for a fowl when you have no meat or gravy ready,	ib.	Beef-broth,	ib.
		Scotch barley-broth,	ib.
Vermicelli-soup,	178	Hodge-podge,	184
Macaroni-soup,	ib.	Hodge-podge of mutton,	ib.
Soup-cressu,	ib.	Partridge-soup,	185
Mutton or veal gravy,	ib.	Portable soup,	ib.
To make strong fish gravy,	ib.	Ox-cheek soup,	186
Plumb-porridge for Christmas,	179	Almond soup,	ib.
		Transparent soup,	ib.
To make strong broth to keep for use,	ib.	Brown pottage,	ib.
Craw-fish soup,	ib.	White barley pottage, with a chicken in the middle,	ib.
Soup-santé, or gravy-soup,	180		

CHAP. XIII.
Puddings, Pies, &c. which are not included in the Lent Chapter, on account of their being made with Meat, Suet, &c.

Rules to be observed in making puddings, &c.	188	Suet dumplings,	191
		An Oxford pudding,	ib.
An oat-pudding to bake,	ib.	Observations on pies,	ib.
Calf's-foot pudding,	ib.	To make a very fine sweet lamb or veal pie,	ib.
Pith-pudding,	189		
Marrow-pudding,	ib.	A savoury veal pie,	192
Boiled suet-pudding,	ib.	A savoury lamb or veal pie,	ib.
Boiled plum-pudding,	190	A calf's-foot pie,	ib.
Hunting-pudding,	ib.	An olive pie,	193
Yorkshire pudding,	ib.	To season an egg-pie,	ib.
Vermicelli-pudding,	ib.	To make a mutton-pie,	ib.
A steak-pudding,	191	A beef-steak pie,	ib.

a A ham-

A ham-pie,	193	Paste for tarts,	201
A pigeon pie,	194	Another paste for tarts,	ib.
A giblet-pie,	ib.	Puff-paste,	ib.
A duck-pie,	ib.	A good crust for great pies,	ib.
A chicken-pie,	195	A standing crust for great pies,	ib.
A Cheshire pork-pie,	ib.		
A Devonshire squab-pie,	ib.	A cold crust,	202
An ox-cheek-pie,	ib.	A dripping crust,	ib.
A Shropshire pie,	196	A crust for custards,	ib.
A Yorkshire Christmas-pie,	ib.	Paste for crackling crust,	ib.
A goose-pie,	197	An Hottentot pie,	ib.
A venison-pasty,	ib.	A bride's pie,	ib.
A calf's-head pie,	198	A thatched-house pie.	203
To make a tort,	ib.	A French pie,	ib.
Mince pies,	199	A savoury chicken pie,	204
Another way,	ib.	Egg and bacon pie,	ib.
Tort de Moy,	ib.	Pork pie,	ib.
To make orange or lemon tarts,	200	To make savoury patties,	ib.
		Common patties,	ib.
To make different sorts of tarts,	ib.	Fine patties,	ib.

CHAP. XIV.

For Lent, or a Fast Dinner, a Number of good Dishes, which may be made use of for a Table at any other Time.

A Peas-soup,	205	Furmity,	213
Green peas-soup,	206	Plum-porridge, or barley-gruel,	ib.
Another green peas-soup,	ib.		
Soup meagre,	ib.	Buttered wheat,	ib.
Onion-soup,	207	Plum gruel,	ib.
Eel-soup,	ib.	Flour hasty-pudding,	ib.
Craw-fish soup,	ib.	Oatmeal hasty-pudding,	214
Muscle-soup,	208	Fine oatmeal hasty-pudding,	ib.
Scate or thornback soup,	209	To make an excellent sack-posset,	ib.
Oyster-soup,	ib.		
Almond-soup,	ib.	Another way,	ib.
Rice-soup,	210	Or make it thus,	ib.
Barley-soup,	ib.	To make hasty fritters,	215
Turnip-soup,	ib.	Fine fritters,	ib.
Egg-soup,	ib.	Apple-fritters,	ib.
Peas-porridge,	211	Curd-fritters,	ib.
Spanish peas-soup,	ib.	Royal fritters,	ib.
Onion-soup the Spanish way,	ib.	Skirret-fritters,	216
Milk-soup the Dutch way,	ib.	White fritters,	ib.
A white-pot,	ib.	Syringed fritters,	ib.
Rice white-pot,	212	Vine-leaf fritters,	ib.
Rice-milk,	ib.	Clary-fritters,	217
An orange-fool,	ib.	Spanish fritters,	ib.
Westminster-fool,	ib.	Plum-fritters with rice,	ib.
Gooseberry-fool,	ib.	Apple frazes,	ib.

Almond

CONTENTS

Almond frazes,	218	To fricassee artichoke bottoms,	229
German puffs,	ib.		
Pancakes,	ib.	To fricassee mushrooms white,	ib.
Fine pancakes,	ib.		
Second sort,	219	Chardoons fried and buttered,	230
Third sort,	ib.	Chardoons à la fromage,	ib.
Fourth sort called quire of paper,	ib.	To make a Scotch rabbit,	ib.
		To make a Welch rabbit,	ib.
Rice pancakes,	ib.	To make an English rabbit,	ib.
Wafer pancakes,	ib.	Or thus,	ib.
Tansey pancakes,	ib.	To fry artichokes,	231
Pink-coloured pancakes,	220	Artichoke-suckers, Spanish way,	ib.
Pupton of apples,	ib.		
Black-caps,	ib.	Brocoli and sallad,	ib.
To bake apples whole,	ib.	Potatoe cakes,	ib.
To make a dish of roasted apples,	ib.	A pudding,	ib.
		To make potatoes like collar of veal or mutton,	ib.
To stew pippins whole,	221		
To stew pears,	ib.	To broil potatoes,	232
To stew pears in a sauce-pan,	ib.	To fry potatoes,	ib.
To stew pears purple,	ib.	Mashed potatoes,	ib.
A pretty made-dish,	ib.	To dress spinage,	ib.
Kickshaws,	222	Asparagus forced in French rolls,	ib.
Pain perdu, &c.	ib.		
Salmagundy,	ib.	Asparagus dressed the Italian way,	233
To make a tansey,	223		
Another way,	ib.	To stew parsnips,	ib.
A bean tansey,	ib.	To mash parsnips,	ib.
A water tansey,	ib.	Sorrel with eggs,	ib.
A hedge-hog,	224	Brocoli and eggs,	ib.
Or thus,	ib.	Asparagus and eggs,	234
To ragoo endive,	225	A pretty dish of eggs,	ib.
To ragoo French beans,	ib.	Eggs à la tripe,	ib.
Another way,	226	A fricassee of eggs,	ib.
A ragoo of beans, with a force,	ib.	A ragoo of eggs,	235
		To broil eggs,	ib.
Beans ragooed with cabbage,	ib.	To dress eggs with bread,	ib.
		To farce eggs,	ib.
Beans ragooed with parsnips,	227	Eggs with lettuce,	236
Beans ragooed with potatoes,	ib.	To fry eggs as round as balls,	ib.
		To make an egg as big as twenty,	ib.
To dress beans in ragoo,	ib.		
An amlet of beans,	ib.	To make a grand dish of eggs,	ib.
Carrots and French beans Dutch way,	228	To make a pretty dish of whites of eggs,	237
Beans German way,	ib.	To stew cucumbers,	ib.
To ragoo celery,	ib.	To farce cucumbers,	238
To ragoo mushrooms,	ib.	To stew cucumbers,	ib.
To make good brown gravy,	229	Fried celery,	239
		Celery with cream,	ib.
To fricassee skirrets,	ib.	Peas Françoise,	ib.

Green

CONTENTS.

Green peas with cream, 240	Ipswich almond pudding, 251
A farce-meagre cabbage, ib.	Transparent pudding, ib.
Red cabbage, Dutch way, ib.	Puddings for little dishes, ib.
Cauliflowers, Spanish way, ib.	Sweetmeat pudding, 252
Cauliflowers fried, 241	Fine plain pudding, ib.
To make an oatmeal pudding, ib.	Ratafia pudding, ib.
	Bread and butter pudding, ib.
To make a potatoe pudding, ib.	Boiled rice-pudding, 253
Second way, ib.	Cheap rice-pudding, ib.
Third way, ib.	Cheap plain rice-pudding, ib.
Buttered loaves, 242	Cheap baked rice-pudding, ib.
Orange pudding, ib.	A Hanover cake or pudding, ib.
Second orange pudding, ib.	
Third orange pudding, ib.	A yam pudding, 254
Fourth orange pudding, 243	A vermicelli pudding, ib.
Lemon pudding, ib.	A red sago, ib.
Another way, ib.	A spinage pudding, ib.
To bake an almond pudding, ib.	A quaking pudding, 255
To boil an almond pudding, 244	Cream pudding, ib.
	Prune pudding, ib.
To make a sago pudding, ib.	Spoonful pudding, ib.
To make a millet pudding, ib.	Lemon tower or pudding, ib.
To make a carrot pudding, ib.	Yeast dumplings, 256
A second way, 245	Norfolk dumplings, ib.
A cowslip pudding, ib.	Hard dumplings, ib.
Quince, apricot, or white pear plum-pudding, ib.	Another way, ib.
	Apple dumplings, ib.
Pearl-barley pudding, ib.	Another way, 257
French barley pudding, ib.	Raspberry dumplings, ib.
Apple pudding, 246	Citron puddings, ib.
Another way, ib.	Cheese-curd florendine, ib.
Baked pudding, ib.	Florendine of oranges or apples, ib.
Italian pudding, ib.	
Rice pudding, ib.	Artichoke pie, 258
Second pudding, 247	Sweet egg pie, ib.
Third pudding, ib.	Potatoe pie, ib.
Carolina rice pudding, ib.	Onion pie, 259
To boil custard pudding, ib.	Orangeado pie, ib.
Flour pudding, 248	Vegetable pie, ib.
Batter pudding, ib.	Skirret pie, ib.
Batter pudding without eggs, ib.	Apple pie, 269
Grateful pudding, ib.	Green codling pie, ib.
Bread pudding, ib.	Cherry pie, 261
Fine bread pudding, 249	Salt fish pie, ib.
Ordinary bread pudding, ib.	Carp pie, ib.
Baked bread pudding, ib.	Soal pie, ib.
Boiled loaf, 250	Eel pie, 262
Chesnut pudding, ib.	Flounder pie, ib.
Fine plain baked pudding, ib.	Herring pie, ib.
Cheese-curd pudding, ib.	Salmon pie, ib.
Apricot pudding, 251	Lobster pie, 263

Muscle-

CONTENTS.

Muscle pie, 263
Lent mince-pies, ib.
Fish pasties the Italian way, 263
To roast a pound of butter, 264

CHAP. XV.
Directions for the Sick.

To make mutton-broth, 264
To boil a scrag of veal, ib.
Beef or mutton broth for very weak people, ib.
Beef drink, 265
Beef tea, ib.
Pork broth, ib.
To boil a chicken, 265
To boil pigeons, ib.
To boil partridge, or any wild fowl, ib.
To boil place or flounder, ib.
Mince veal or chicken, ib.
Pull a chicken, 267
Chicken broth, ib.
Chicken water, ib.
White caudle, ib.
Brown caudle, ib.
Water-gruel, 268
Panado, ib.
To boil sago, 268
Saloop, ib.
Isinglass jelly, ib.
To make pectoral drink, ib.
To make buttered water, 269
Seed-water, ib.
Bread soup, ib.
Artificial ass's milk, ib.
Cow's milk next to ass's milk, ib.
To make a good drink, ib.
To make barley water, 270
Sago tea, ib.
Sago tea for a child, ib.
Liquor for a child that has the thrush, ib.
To boil comfrey-roots, ib.
To make knuckle broth, ib.
A medicine for a disorder in the bowels, 271

CHAP. XVI.
For Captains of Ships.

To make catchup to keep for twenty years, 271
To make fish-sauce to keep the whole year, ib.
To pot dripping to fry fish, &c. 272
To pickle mushrooms for the sea, ib.
To make mushroom powder, ib.
To keep mushrooms without pickle, 273
To keep artichoke-bottoms dry, ib.
To fry artichoke-bottoms, ib.
To ragoo artichoke-bottoms, ib.
To dress fish, ib.
To bake fish, 274
To make gravy-soup, ib.
To make peas-soup, ib.
To make a pork pudding, or beef, &c. ib.
To make a rice-pudding, 275
To make a suet-pudding, ib.
To make a liver-pudding boiled, ib.
To make an oatmeal-pudding, ib.
To bake an oatmeal-pudding, ib.
A rice-pudding baked, ib.
To make peas-pudding, 276
To make a harrico of French beans, ib.
To make a fowl pie, ib.
To make a Cheshire pork pie for sea, 277
To make sea venison, ib.
To make dumplings when you have white bread, ib.
To make chouder; a sea dish, 278

a 3   CHAP.

CHAP. XVII.
Hogs' Puddings and Sausages.

To make almond hogs'-puddings,	278	Savoloys,	280
Another way,	279	To make fine sausages,	ib.
A third way,	ib.	To make common sausages,	281
To make hogs'-puddings with currants,	ib.	Oxford sausages,	ib.
		Bologna sausages,	ib.
		Hamburgh sausages,	ib.
To make black puddings,	ib.	Sausages the German way,	282

CHAP. XVIII.
To Pot, make Hams, &c.

Observations on preserving salt meat, &c.	282	To collar a pig,	289
To pot pigeons or fowls,	283	To collar swine's face,	290
To pot a cold tongue, beef, or venison,	ib.	To collar salmon,	ib.
		To collar eels,	ib.
To pot venison,	ib.	To collar mackarel,	291
To pot a hare,	ib.	To make Dutch beef,	ib.
To pot tongues,	284	To make sham brawn,	ib.
A fine way to pot a tongue,	ib.	To souse a turkey in imitation of sturgeon,	292
To pot beef like venison,	285	To pickle pork,	ib.
To pot Cheshire cheese,	ib.	A pickle for pork which is to be eat soon,	ib.
To pot ham with chickens,	ib.		
To pot woodcocks,	286	The Jews way to pickle beef,	ib.
To pot red and black moor-game,	ib.	Pickled beef for present use,	293
To pot all kinds of small birds,	ib.	To preserve tripe to go to the East Indies,	ib.
To save potted birds that begin to be bad,	ib.	The Jews way of preserving salmon, and all sorts of fish,	ib.
To pot chars,	287	To pickle oysters, cockles, and muscles,	294
To pot pike,	ib.		
To pot salmon,	ib.	To pickle mackarel, called caveach,	295
Another way,	ib.		
To pot a lobster,	288	To make veal hams,	ib.
To pot eels,	ib.	To make beef hams,	ib.
To pot lampreys,	ib.	To make mutton hams,	296
To collar a breast of veal,	289	To make pork hams,	ib.
To make marble veal,	ib.	To make bacon,	297
To collar beef,	ib.		

CHAP. XIX.
Pickling.

Rules to be observed in pickling,	297	To pickle walnuts white,	298
		To pickle walnuts black,	ib.
To pickle walnuts green,	ib.	To pickle gerkins,	299

CONTENTS.

To pickle gerkins another way, 300
To pickle large cucumbers in slices, ib.
To pickle afpargus, ib.
To pickle peaches. ib.
To pickle radifh-pods, 301
To pickle French beans, ib.
To pickle cauliflowers, ib.
To pickle beet-root, 302
To pickle white plums, ib.
To pickle onions, ib.
Another way, ib.
To pickle lemons, ib.
To pickle mufhrooms white, 303
To make pickle for mufhrooms, ib.
To pickle codlings, ib.
To pickle fennel, ib.
To pickle grapes, 304
To pickle barberries, 304
To pickle red cabbage, 305
To pickle golden pippins, ib.
To pickle nafterttum berries and limes, ib.
To pickle young fuckers or artichokes, ib.
To pickle artichoke bottoms, 306
To pickle famphire, ib.
To pickle mock ginger. ib.
To pickle melon mangoes, ib.
To pickle elder-fhoots, in imitation of bamboo, 307
To make Paco-lilla, or Indian pickle, ib.
To pickle the fine purple cabbage, so much admired at great tables, 308
To make the pickle, ib.
To make Indian pickle, ib.

CHAP. XX.
Of making Cakes, &c.

To make a rich cake, 309
To ice a great cake, ib.
To make a pound cake, ib.
To make a cheap feed-cake, 310
To make a butter-cake, ib.
To make gingerbread cakes, ib.
To make feed or faffron cake, ib.
To make a rich feed cake called nun's cake, 311
To make pepper cakes, ib.
To make Portugal cakes, ib.
To make a pretty cake, ib.
To make gingerbread, 312
To make fine little cakes, ib.
Another fort of little cakes, ib.
To make drop bifcuits, ib.
To make common bifcuits, 313
To make French bifcuits, ib.
To make mackeroons, 313
To make Shrewfbury cakes, ib.
To make madling cakes, 314
To make wigs, ib.
To make light wigs, ib.
To make very good wigs. ib.
To make buns, 315
To make a cake the Spanifh way, ib.
Another way, ib.
Uxbridge cakes, ib.
To make bifcuit bread, ib.
To make carraway cakes, 316
To make bride cake, ib.
To make Bath cakes, 317
To make queen cakes, ib.
To make ratafia cakes, ib.
To make little plum cakes, ib.

CHAP. XXI.
Of Cheefecakes, Creams, Jellies, Whipt Syllabubs, &c.

To make fine cheefecakes, 318
To make lemon cheefecakes, ib.
A fecond fort, 318
Almond cheefecakes, 319
Cheefecakes without currants, ib.

Citron

CONTENTS.

Citron cheesecakes,	319	Pippin jelly,	330
Lemon custards,	ib.	China orange jelly,	ib.
Orange custards,	320	Raspberry jam,	ib.
Beest custard,	ib.	To make a hedge-hog,	ib.
Almond custards,	ib.	Moon-shine,	331
Baked custards,	ib.	A floating island,	ib.
Plain custards,	ib.	A fish-pond,	332
Orange butter,	321	A hen's nest,	ib.
Fairy butter,	ib.	A mouse trap,	333
Almond butter,	ib.	Moon and stars in jelly,	ib.
Steeple cream,	ib.	Hen and chickens in jelly,	ib.
Lemon cream,	322	A desert island,	ib.
A second lemon cream,	ib.	Gilded fish in jelly,	334
Jelly of cream,	ib.	Hartshorn flummery,	ib.
Orange cream,	ib.	A second way,	ib.
Gooseberry cream,	323	Oatmeal flummery,	335
Barley cream,	ib.	Blanc-mange,	ib.
Another way,	ib.	Dutch blanc-mange,	ib.
Ice cream,	ib.	A buttered tort,	336
Pistachio cream,	324	Fruit wafers, of codlings, plums, &c.	ib.
Hartshorn cream,	ib.	White wafers,	ib.
Almond cream,	ib.	Brown wafers,	ib.
A fine cream,	ib.	Gooseberry wafers,	ib.
Ratafia cream,	ib.	Orange wafers,	337
Whipt cream,	325	Orange cakes,	ib.
Clear lemon cream,	ib.	Orange loaves,	338
Sack cream like butter,	ib.	Orange biscuits,	ib.
Barley cream,	ib.	White cakes like china dishes,	ib.
Clouted cream,	ib.		
Quince cream,	ib.	Lemon honeycomb,	339
Citron cream,	ib.	Sugar of pearl,	ib.
Cream of apples, quinces, gooseberries, &c.	326	Almond rice,	ib.
Sugar loaf cream,	ib.	Almond knots,	ib.
Whipt syllabubs,	327	Almond cakes,	340
Everlasting syllabubs.	ib.	Sugar cakes,	ib.
Solid syllabub,	ib.	Another way,	ib.
A fine syllabub from the cow,	328	Cracknels,	ib.
		German puffs,	ib.
A trifle,	ib.	Carolina snow balls,	341
To make hartshorn jelly,	ib.	Ginger tablet,	ib.
Orange jelly,	329	Thin apricot chips,	ib.
Ribband jelly,	ib.	Sham chocolate,	ib.
Calves feet jelly,	ib.	To make chocolate,	ib.
Currant jelly,	330	Another way,	342

CHAP. XXII.

Of Made-Wines; Brewing; Baking French Bread and Muffins; Cheese, &c.

To make raisin wine,	342	Rules for brewing,	348
The best way,	ib.	The best thing for rope,	350
To make blackberry wine,	343	When a barrel of beer has turned sour,	ib.
To make alder wine,	ib.		
To make orange wine,	344	To make cyder,	ib.
To make orange wine with raisins,	ib.	For fining cyder,	ib.
		After it has fined,	351
Alder-flower wine, very like Frontiniac,	ib.	To make white bread the London way,	ib.
Gooseberry wine,	345	French bread,	ib.
Currant wine,	ib.	Muffins and oat-cakes,	352
White currant wine,	ib.	Bread without barm,	353
Cherry wine,	ib.	To preserve a large stock of yeast,	ib.
Birch wine,	346		
Quince wine,	ib.	Slip-coat cheese,	354
Cowslip or clary wine,	ib.	Brick-bat cheese,	ib.
Turnip wine,	347	Cream cheese,	ib.
Raspberry wine,	ib.	Bullace cheese,	355
Mead,	ib.	Stilton cheese,	ib.
White mead,	ib.		

CHAP. XXIII.

Jarring Cherries, Preserves, &c.

To jar cherries, Lady North's way,	355	To make quince cakes,	360
		To preserve apricots,	ib.
To dry cherries,	356	Another way,	361
Another way,	ib.	To preserve damsons whole,	ib.
To preserve cherries, the leaves and stalks green,	ib.	To preserve gooseberries whole,	ib.
To preserve cherries in brandy,	357	To preserve white walnuts,	362
		To preserve green walnuts,	ib.
To preserve cherries	ib.	To preserve large green plums,	363
Another way,	ib.		
To barrel Morello cherries,	ib.	To preserve peaches,	ib.
Orange marmalade,	ib.	To preserve golden pippins,	ib.
Marmalade of eggs the Jews way,	358	To preserve grapes,	ib.
		To preserve green codlings,	ib.
Marmalade of cherries,	ib.	To preserve apricots or plums green,	364
White marmalade of quinces,	ib.		
		To preserve barberries,	ib.
Another way,	ib.	To preserve white pear plums,	ib.
To make red marmalade,	ib.		
To preserve oranges whole,	359	To preserve currants,	365
Quinces whole,	360	To preserve raspberries,	ib.
To preserve white quinces whole,	ib.	To preserve pippins in slices,	ib.

To

CONTENTS.

To preserve cucumbers equal to any Italian sweetmeat,	365	To candy cherries, or green gages,	368
Conserve of roses boiled,	ib.	To candy angelica,	ib.
Conserve of red roses, or any other flowers,	366	To candy cassia,	ib.
		To dry pears without sugar,	ib.
Conserve of hips,	ib.	To dry plums	369
Syrup of roses,	ib.	To dry peaches,	ib.
Syrup of citron,	367	To dry damsons,	ib.
Syrup of clove-gilliflowers,	ib.	To dry pear-plums,	ib.
Syrup of peach-blossoms,	ib.	The filling for the aforesaid plums,	370
Syrup of quinces,	ib.		
To candy any sort of flowers,	ib.	To clarify sugar the Spanish way,	ib.
To make citron,	368		

CHAP. XXIV.
To make Anchovies, Vermicelli, Catchup, Vinegar; and to keep Artichokes, French Beans, &c.

TO make anchovies,	370	Another way to preserve green peas,	373
To pickle smelts where you have plenty,	371	To keep green peas, &c. and fruit fresh till Christmas,	ib.
To make vermicelli,	ib.		
To make catchup,	ib.	To keep green gooseberries till Christmas,	ib.
Another way,	ib.		
Artichokes to keep all the year,	372	To keep red gooseberries,	374
		To keep walnuts all the year,	ib.
Artichokes preserved the Spanish way,	ib.	Another way to keep lemons,	ib.
To keep French beans all the year,	ib.	To keep white bullace, &c.	ib.
		To make sour crout,	375
To keep green peas till Christmas,	373	To raise mushrooms,	ib.
		To make vinegar,	ib.

CHAP. XXV.
Distilling.

TO distil walnut-water,	376	To make hysterical water,	378
To distil red rose buds,	ib.	To make plague water,	ib.
How to use this ordinary still,	377	To make surfeit water,	379
		To make milk water,	ib.
To make treacle water,	ib.	Another way,	380
To distil treacle-water Lady Monmouth's way,	ib.	To make stag's heart water,	ib.
		To make Angelica water,	ib.
Prepare all these simples thus,	ib.	To make cordial poppy water,	381
To make black cherry water,	378		

CONTENTS.

CHAP. XXVI.

NECESSARY DIRECTIONS *whereby the Reader may easily attain the* ART OF CARVING.

To cut up a turkey, 381	To allay a pheasant or teal, 382
To rear a goose, ib.	To dismember a hern, ib.
To unbrace a mallard or duck, ib.	To thigh a woodcock, ib.
	To display a crane, ib.
To unlace a coney, 382	To lift a swan, ib.
To wing a partridge or quail, ib.	

CHAP. XXVII.

Useful and valuable Family Receipts.

A Certain cure for the bite of a mad dog, 383
Another, ib.
Receipt against the plague, ib.
To make a fine bitter, 384
For a consumption; an approved receipt, by a lady at Paddington, ib.
To stop a violent purging or flux, 385
For obstructions in females, ib.
Another, ib.
For a hoarseness, ib.
Lozenges for the heart-burn, ib.
Lozenges for a cold, ib.
The genuine receipt for Turlington's balsam, 386
How to keep clear from bugs, ib.
An effectual way to clear your bedstead, 387
Directions to the housemaid, 387
How to make yellow varnish, ib.
To make a pretty varnish to colour little baskets, bowls, &c. ib.
To clean gold and silver lace, 388
To clean white sattins, flowered silks with gold and silver in them, ib.
To keep arms, iron, or steel from rusting, ib.
To take iron-moulds out of linen, ib.
To take iron-moulds out of linen, and grease out of woollen—One Shilling a bottle, ib.
To prevent infection among horned cattle, ib.

CHAP. XXVIII.

Receipts for Perfumery, &c.

To make red, light, or purple wash-balls, 391
To make blue, red, or purple, or to marble wash-balls, ib.
White almond wash-balls, 392
Brown almond wash-balls, ib.
Windsor soap—Two shillings a pound, ib.
To make lip salve, ib.
To make white lip salve for chopped hands and face—Six shillings and threepence per pot, 393
French rouge—Five shillings per pot, 393
Opiate for the teeth.—Two shillings and sixpence per pot, ib.
Delescot's opiate, ib.
Tooth-powder—One shilling per bottle, ib.
Shaving oil—One shilling per bottle, ib.
Shaving-powder, ib.
Soap to fill shaving-boxes, 394
Wash for the face, ib.
Almond milk for a wash, ib.

An

CONTENTS.

An approved method to preserve hair and make it grow thick, 394
A stick to take hair out, ib.
Liquid for the hair—Two shillings a quarter of a pint, ib.
White almond-paste, 395
Brown almond paste, ib.
Sweet-scented bags to lay with linen, at one shilling and sixpence, two shillings and sixpence, &c. &c. each bag, ib.
Orange-butter, ib.
Lemon-butter, ib.
Marechalle - powder — Sixteen shillings per pound, ib.
Virgin's milk—Two shillings per bottle, ib.
Honey-water—One shilling per bottle, 396
Pearl-water, ib.
Milk flude water, ib.
Beautifying-water, ib.
Miss in her teens, ib.
Lady Lilley's ball, ib.
Nun's cream, ib.
Cold cream, ib.
The ambrosia nosegay, ib.
Eau de bouquet, 397
Eau de luce, ib.
Eau sans pareil, ib.
Hard pomatum, ib.
Soft pomatum, ib.
Sirop de capillaire, ib.
Dragon-roots, 398

[xxix]

The ORDER *of a* MODERN BILL *of* FARE, *for each Month, in the* MANNER *the* DISHES *are to be placed upon the* TABLE.

―――――

JANUARY.

FIRST COURSE.

	Chesnut Soup.	
Small Leg of House Lamb.	Petit Patties.	Boiled Chickens.
Chicken and Veal Pie.	Cod's Head.	Tongue.
Rabbits smothered with Onions.	Raisolds.	Porcupine Beef.
	Vermicelli Soup.	

SECOND COURSE.

	Roast Turkey.	
Marinated Smelts.	Tartlets.	Mince Pies.
Roast Sweetbreads.	Stands of Jellies.	Larks.
Almond Tort.	Maids of Honour.	Lobsters.
	Woodcocks.	

THIRD COURSE.

	Morels.	
Artichoke Bottoms.	Dutch Beef scraped.	Macaroni.
Custards.	Cut Pastry.	Black Caps.
Scolloped Oysters.	Potted Chars.	Stewed Celery.
	Rabbit Fricasseed.	

FE‑

FEBRUARY.

FIRST COURSE.

	Peas Soup.	
Curry.	Chicken Patty.	Veal Blanquets.
Small Ham.	Salmon and Smelts.	Chickens.
Pork Cutlets Sauce Robert.	Oyster Patties.	Harrico.
	Soup Santè.	

SECOND COURSE.

	Wild Fowl.	
Cardoons.	Dish of Jelly.	Stewed Pippins.
Scolloped Oysters.	Epergne.	Ragout Mele.
Comport Pears.	Caromel.	Artichoke Bottoms.
	Hare.	

THIRD COURSE.

	Two Woodcocks.	
Craw-fish.	Asparagus.	Preserved Cherries.
Pigs' Ears.	Crocant.	Lamb Chops larded.
Blanched Almonds and Raisins.	Mushrooms.	Prawns.
	Larks à la Surprise.	

MARCH.

MARCH.

FIRST COURSE.

Soup à la Reine.

Beef Olives. Almond Pudding. Fillet of Pork.
Boiled Turkey. Stewed Carp or Tench. Small Ham.
Veal Collops. Beaf Steak Pie. Calves' Ears forced.

Gravy Soup.

SECOND COURSE.

A Poulard larded and roasted.

Asparagus. Blanc-mange. Prawns.
Ragooed Sweetbreads. A Trifle. Fricassee of Rabbits.
Craw-fish. Cheesecakes. Fricassee of Mushrooms.

Tame Pigeons roasted.

THIRD COURSE.

Ox Palates shivered.

Tartlets. Potted Larks. Stewed Pippins.
Cardoons. Jellies. Spanish Peas.
Black Caps. Potted Partridge. Almond Cheesecakes.

Cocks'-Combs.

APRIL.

APRIL.

FIRST COURSE.

Crimp Cod and Smelts.

Chickens.   Marrow Pudding.   Cutlets à la Maintenon.

Breast of Veal in Rolio.   Spring Soup.   Beef Tremblant.

Lambs' Tails à la Bashemel.   Pigeon Pie.   Tongue.

Roast Beef.

SECOND COURSE.

Ducklings.

Asparagus.   Tartlets.   Black Caps.

Roast Sweetbreads.   Jellies and Syllabubs.   Oyster Loaves.

Stewed Pears.   Tansey.   Mushrooms.

Ribs of Lamb.

THIRD COURSE.

Petit Pigeons.

Mushrooms.   French Plums.   Pistachio Nuts.

Marinated Smelts.   Sweetmeats.   Oyster Loaves.

Blanched Almonds.   Raisins.   Artichoke Bottoms.

Calves' Ears à la Braise.

MAY.

MAY.

FIRST COURSE.

Calvert's Salmon broiled
with Smelts round.

Rabbits with Onions.   Veal Olives.   Collared Mutton.
Pigeon Pie raised.   Vermicelli Soup.   Macaroni Tort.
Patties.   Ox Palates.   Matelot of Tame Duck.
Chine of Lamb.

SECOND COURSE.

Fricasseed Chickens.

Asparagus.   Custards.   Cocks' Combs.
Green Gooseberry Tarts.   Epergne.   Green Apricot Tarts.
Lamb Cutlets.   Blanc-mange.   Stewed Celery.
Green Goose.

THIRD COURSE.

Lambs' Sweetbreads.

Stewed Lettuce.   Rhenish Cream.   Raspberry Puffs.
Lobsters ragooed.   Compost of Green Apricots.   Buttered Crab.
Lemon Cakes.   Orange Jelly.   French Beans.
Ragout of fat Livers.

JUNE.

JUNE.

FIRST COURSE.

	Green Peas Soup.	
Chickens.	Haunch of Venison.	Harrico.
Lamb Pie.	Turbot.	Ham.
Veal Cutlets.	Neck of Venison.	Orange Pudding.
	Lobster Soup.	

SECOND COURSE.

	Turkey Poults.	
Peas.	Apricot Puffs.	Lobsters.
Fricassee of Lamb.	Half Moon.	Roasted Sweetbreads.
Pickled Sturgeon.	Cherry Tart.	Artichokes.
	Roasted Rabbits.	

THIRD COURSE.

	Sweetbreads à la Blanche.	
Fillets of Soals.	Potted Wheat Ears.	Ratafia Cream.
Peas.	Green Gooseberry Tart.	Forced Artichokes.
Preserved Oranges.	Potted Ruff.	Matelot of Eels.
	Lambs' Tails à la Braise.	

JULY.

JULY.

FIRST COURSE.

Mackerel, &c.

Breast of Veal à la Braise. Tongue and Turnips. Pulpeton.

Venison Pasty. Herb Soup. Neck of Venison.

Chickens. Boiled Goose and stewed red Cabbage. Mutton Cutlets.

Trout boiled.

SECOND COURSE.

Roast Turkey.

Stewed Peas. Apricot Tart. Blanc-mange.

Sweetbreads. Jellies. Fricassee of Rabbits.

Custards. Green Codlin Tart. Blaized Pippins.

Roast Pigeons.

THIRD COURSE.

Fricassee of Rabbits.

Apricots. Pains à la Duchesse. Forced Cucumbers.

Crawfish ragooed. Morello Cherry Tart. Lobsters à la Braise.

Jerusalem Artichokes. Apricot Puffs. Green Gage Plums.

Lamb Stones.

AUGUST.

FIRST COURSE.

	Stewed Soals.	
Fillets of Pigeons.	Ham.	Turkey à la Daube.
French Patty.	Crawfish Soup.	Petit Patties.
Chickens.	Fillet of Veal.	Rofard of Beef Palates.
	Whitings.	

SECOND COURSE.

	Roaft Ducks.	
Macaroni.	Tartlet.	Fillets of Soals.
Cheefecakes.	Jellies.	Apple Pie.
Matelot of Eels.	Orange Puffs.	Fricaffee of Sweetbreads.
	Leveret.	

THIRD COURSE.

	Wheat Ears.	
Stewed Peas.	Potted Lampreys.	Crawfish.
Apricot Tart.	Fruit.	Cut Paftry.
Prawns.	Scraped Beef.	Blanched Celery.
	Ruffs and Rees.	

SEP-

SEPTEMBER.

FIRST COURSE.

Dish of Fish.
Chickens.   Stewed Giblets.   Veal Collops.
Pigeon Pie.   Gravy Soup.   Almond Tort.
Harrico of Mutton.   Partridge panes.   Ham.
Roast Beef.

SECOND COURSE.

Wild Fowls.
Peas.   Damson Tarts.   Ragooed Lobsters.
Sweetbreads.   Crocant.   Fried Piths.
Crawfish.   Maids of Honour.   Fried Artichokes.
Ducks.

THIRD COURSE.

Ragooed Palates.
Comport of Biscuits.   Tartlets.   Fruit in Jelly.
Green Truffles.   Epergne.   Cardoons.
Blanc-mange.   Cheesecakes.   Ratafia Drops.
Calves' Ears à la Braise.

OCTOBER.

FIRST COURSE.

Cod and Oyster Sauce.
Jugged Hare.   Neck of Veal   Small Puddings.
à la Braise.
French Patty.   Almond Soup.   Stewed Pigeons.
Chickens.   Tongue.   Torrent de Veau.
Fillet of Beef, &c.

SECOND COURSE.

Pheasant.
Stewed Pears.   Apple Tarts.   Mushrooms.
Roast Lobsters.   Jellies.   Oyster Loaves.
White Fricassee.   Custards.   Pippins.
Turkey.

THIRD COURSE.

Sweetbread à la Braise.
Fried Artichokes.   Potted Eels.   Pigs' Ears.
Almond Cheesecakes.   Fruit.   Apricot Puffs.
Amulet.   Potted Lobsters.   Forced Celery.
Larks.

NOVEMBER.

FIRST COURSE.

	Dish of Fish.	
Veal Cutlets.	Roasted Turkey.	Ox Palates.
Two Chickens and Broccoli.	Vermicelli Soup.	Gammon of Bacon.
Beef Collops.	French Pye.	Harrico.
	Chine of Pork.	

SECOND COURSE.

	Woodcocks.	
Sheeps' Rumps.	Apple Puffs.	Dish of Jelly.
Oyster Loaves.	Crocant.	Ragooed Lobsters.
Blanc-mange.	Lemon Tort.	Lambs' Ears.
	Hare.	

THIRD COURSE.

	Petit Patties.	
Stewed Pears.	Potted Chars.	Fried Oysters.
Gallantine.	Ice Cream.	Collared Eel.
Fillets of Whitings.	Potted Crawfish.	Pippins.
	Lambs' Ears à la Braise.	

MODERN BILL OF FARE.

DECEMBER.

FIRST COURSE.

Cod's Head.

Chickens.   Stewed Beef.   Fricando of Veal.
Almond Puddings.   Soup Santé.   Calves' Feet Pie.
Very small Fillet of Pork, with sharp Sauce.   Currey.   Tongue.

Chine of Lamb.

SECOND COURSE.

Wild Fowls.

Lambs' Fry.   Orange Puffs.   Sturgeon.
Gallantine.   Jellies.   Savoury Cake.
Prawns.   Tartlets.   Mushrooms.

Partridges.

THIRD COURSE.

Ragooed Palates.

Savoy Cakes.   Dutch Beef scraped.   China Oranges.
Lambs' Tails.   Half Moon.   Calves' Burs.
Jargonel Pears.   Potted Larks.   Lemon Biscuits.

Fricassee of Crawfish.

N. B. In your first Course always observe to send up all Kinds of Garden Stuff suitable to your Meat, &c. in different Dishes, on a Water-dish filled with hot Water on the Side-Table; and all your Sauce in Boats or Basons, to answer one another at the Corners.

THE ART of COOKERY MADE PLAIN AND EASY.

CHAP. I.

Containing a List of the various Kinds of MEAT, POULTRY, FISH, VEGETABLES, *and* FRUIT, *in Season in every* MONTH *of the* YEAR.

BEFORE any instructions are given for dressing and preparing a dinner, it is certainly necessary to inform the reader what is to be had; for that reason I have, in this edition, altered the order observed in former ones, by treating of this subject first, which has been always hitherto placed at the end, or in the middle of books, so as to escape attention, or be difficult to find. The following list is greatly enlarged and improved.

JANUARY.

MEAT. Beef, mutton, veal, house-lamb, pork, doe-venison.—N. B. The three first articles, being in season all the year, will not be repeated in the future months.

POULTRY and GAME. Pheasant, partridge, hares, rabbits, woodcocks, snipes; hen-turkeys, capons, pullets, fowls, chickens, tame pigeons; and all sorts of wild fowl.

FISH. Carp, tench, perch, lampreys, eels, crawfish, cod, soles, flounders, plaice, turbot, thornback, skate, sturgeon, smelts, whitings, lobsters, crabs, prawns, oysters, dorey, brill, gudgeons, cockles, muscles, sprats, &c.

VEGETABLES. Cabbage, savoys, coleworts, sprouts, brocoli purple and white, cauliflowers (by art) and artichokes in sand, spinage, cardoons, beets, turnips, potatoes, carrots, parsnips, parsley, endive, lettuces, cresses, mustard, radish, rape, sorrel, celery, chervil, tarragon, cucumbers in hot-houses, mint, thyme, savory, pot-marjoram, sage, hyssop, skirrets, salsifie, scorzonera. *To be had though not in season*, Jerusalem artichokes, asparagus, mushrooms.

FRUIT. Nuts, almonds, services, grapes, medlars, golden-pippins, and various other fine eating and boiling apples, bergamot, bon-chretien and other pears, foreign grapes, and oranges.

FEBRUARY.

MEAT. House-lamb and pork.

POULTRY and GAME. Pheasants, partridges, hares, tame rabbits, woodcocks, snipes, turkeys, pullets with eggs, capons, chickens, tame and wild pigeons, and all sorts of wild fowl, (which in this month begin to decline.)

FISH. Cod, soles, turbot, carp, tench, sturgeon, thornback, flounders, plaice, smelts, whitings, skate, perch, eels, lampreys, gollin, sprats, dorey, hollebet, anchovy, lobsters, crabs, prawns, oysters, crawfish.

VEGETABLES. Cabbage, savoys, sprouts, coleworts, brocoli purple and white, lettuces, endive, celery, onions, leeks, garlick, shalots, rocambole, cardoons, beets, sorrel, chervil, chardbeets, parsley, cresses, mustard, rape, tarragon, burnet, tansey, mint, thyme, marjoram, savory, turnips, carrots, potatoes, parsnips; *also may be had* forced radishes, cucumbers, asparagus, kidney beans, salsifie, scorzonera, skirret, and Jerusalem artichokes.

FRUIT. Golden and Dutch pippins, with various other kinds of apples, winter bon-chretien pear, winter mask and winter Norwich, &c. &c. grapes, and oranges.

MARCH.

MEAT. House-lamb and pork.

POULTRY. Turkeys, fowls, pullets, capons, chickens, ducklings, tame rabbits, pigeons.

FISH. Turbot, thornback, skate, carp, tench, mullets, eels, whitings, soles, flounders, plaice, bream, barbel, mackerel, dace, bleak, roach, crabs, prawns, lobsters, crawfish, and oysters.

VEGETABLES. Carrots, potatoes, turnips, parsnips, Jerusalem artichokes, garlick, onions, shalots, coleworts, borecole, cabbages, savoys, spinage, brocoli, beets, cardoons, parsley, fennel, celery, endive, tansey, mushrooms, lettuces, chives, cresses, mustard, rape, radishes, turnips, tarragon, mint, burnet, thyme, winter-savory, pot-marjoram, cucumbers, and kidney-beans.

FRUIT. Golden pippins, rennetings, loves pearmain, and john-apples, the latter bon-chretien and double-blossom pear, oranges, and forced strawberries.

APRIL.

APRIL.

MEAT. Grass-lamb.

POULTRY. Pullets, spring fowls, chickens, pigeons, ducklings, young geese, turkey poults, wild rabbits, leverets.

FISH. Mullets, carp, tench, soles, turbot, chub, trout, crawfish, salmon, skate, smelts, herrings, crabs, lobsters, prawns, oysters, lamprey or lampor eels, and mackerel.

VEGETABLES. Sprouts, coleworts, brocoli, spinage, asparagus, young radishes, parsley, chervil; Dutch brown lettuce, and cresses, young onions, celery, endive, sorrel, burnet, tarragon; all sorts of small salad, and early kidney-beans.

FRUIT. Forced cherries, green apricots, and gooseberries for tarts, pippins, Westbury apple, russeting, gilliflower; the latter bon-chretien, oak pear, and oranges.

MAY.

MEAT. Buck venison, and grass lamb.

POULTRY. The same as in April.

FISH. Salmon, carp, tench, eels, trout, chub, soles, turbot, herrings, lobsters, crawfish, crabs, prawns, smelts.

VEGETABLES. Lettuces, cresses, mustard, all sorts of small sallad herbs, early potatoes, carrots, turnips, radishes, early cabbages, cauliflowers, artichokes, spinage, parsley, sorrel, asparagus, peas, beans, kidney-beans, cucumbers, thyme, savory and all other sweet herbs, purslane, fennel, mint, and balm. Now is the proper time to distil herbs, which are in their greatest perfection.

FRUIT. May cherries, May dukes, apples, pears, strawberries, melons, green apricots, gooseberries, currants for tarts; and oranges.

JUNE.

MEAT. The same as in May.

POULTRY. Ducklings, green geese, turkey-poults, fowls, pullets, chickens, plovers, wheat-ears, leverets, rabbits.

FISH. Turbot, trout, tench, pike, eels, salmon, soles, mullets, mackerel, herrings, smelts, skate, chub, grigs, lobsters, crawfish, prawns, sturgeon; this fish is commonly found in the Northern seas, but now and then we find them in our great rivers, the Thames, the Severn, and the Tyne. This fish is of a very large size, and will sometimes measure eighteen feet in length. They are much esteemed when fresh, cut in pieces, roasted, baked or pickled, for cold treats. The caviare is esteemed a dainty, which is the spawn of this fish.

VEGETABLES. Beans, peas, carrots, turnips, potatoes, parsnips, rape, cresses, and all other small sallading, Battersea and

THE ART OF COOKERY

Dutch cabbage, cauliflowers, artichokes, radishes, onions, cucumbers, spinage, purslane, parsley; all sorts of pot-herbs, borage, burnet, and endive.

FRUIT. Green gooseberries, strawberries, some raspberries, currants white and black; duke cherries, red hearts, the Flemish and carnation cherries, codlins, jannatings, the masculine apricot, pears, and oranges.

JULY.

MEAT. The same.

POULTRY. The same; with young partridges, pheasants, and wild ducks, called flappers or moulters.

FISH. Cod haddocks, mullets, mackerel, herrings, soles, plaice, flounders, skate, thornback, salmon, carp, tench, pike, eels, lobsters, prawns, shrimps, crawfish, and sturgeon.

VEGETABLES. Carrots, turnips, potatoes, cabbages, sprouts, artichokes, celery, radishes, endive, onions, garlick, finocha, chervil, sorrel, purslane, lettuce, cresses, and all sorts of sallad-herbs, rocombole, scorzonera, salsifie, mushrooms, cauliflowers, mint, balm, thyme, and all other pot-herbs, pease of various kinds, beans, kidney-beans, cucumbers.

FRUIT. Musk-melons, wood-strawberries, currants, gooseberries, raspberries, red and white jannatings, and several early apples and pears, morella and other cherries, peaches, nectarines, apricots, plumbs, figs, and grapes. Walnuts in high season to pickle, and rock samphire. The fruit yet lasting of last year, is the deuxans, winter russeting, and some oranges.

AUGUST.

MEAT. The same.

POULTRY. Green geese, turkey-poults, ducklings, pullets, fowls, chickens, leverets, rabbits, pigeons, young pheasants, wild ducks, wheat-ears, plovers.

FISH. Cod, haddock, plaice, skate, flounders, thornback, mullets, mackerel, eels, herrings, pike and carp, trout, turbot, soles, grigs, salmon, sturgeon, chub, lobsters, crabs, crawfish, prawns, oysters, and shrimps.

VEGETABLES. Beans and pease of some kinds, cabbages, sprouts, cauliflowers, artichokes, cabbage-lettuce, beets, carrots, potatoes, turnips, kidney-beans, all sorts of kitchen herbs, radishes, horse-radish, cucumbers, cresses and small sallad, onions, garlick, shalots, rocomboles, mushrooms, celery, endive, finocha, cucumbers for pickling.

FRUIT. Gooseberries, raspberries, currants, figs, mulberries, filberts, apples; bergamot, Windsor and other pears; Bourdeaux and other peaches, nectarines, plumbs, cluster, muscadine, and Cornelian grapes, melons, and pine-apples.

SEPTEMBER.

SEPTEMBER.

MEAT. Grafs-lamb, pork, buck-venifon.

POULTRY. Geefe, turkies, pullets, fowls, chickens, ducks, teal, pigeons, larks, hares, rabbits, pheafants, partridges.

FISH. Cod, haddock, flounders, herrings, plaice, thornbacks, fkate, carp, tench, foles, fmelts, falmon, pike, gudgeons, chub, trout, fturgeon, lobfters, crabs, prawns, fhrimps, oyfters, &c.

VEGETABLES. Carrots, turnips, potatoes, garden and fome kidney-beans, rounceval peas, artichokes, radifhes, cauliflowers, cabbage-lettuce, fmall fallad, chervil, onions, garlick, fhalots, and leeks; tarragon, burnet, celery, endive, mufhrooms, fkirrets; beets, fcorzonera, falfifie, cardoons, horfe-radifh, rocombole, cabbage and fprouts, favoys.

FRUIT. Peaches, grapes, figs, pears, plumbs, walnuts, filberts, nectarines, morella cherries, melons, pine-apples, almonds, quinces.

OCTOBER.

MEAT. Pork, doe-venifon.

POULTRY. Turkies, geefe, pullets, fowls, chickens, pigeons, rabbits, wild ducks, teal, widgeons, woodcocks, fnipes, dottrels, larks, hares, pheafants, partridges.

FISH. Cod, haddock, ling, mullet, dories, holobert, herrings, fprats, barbel, foles, flounders, plaice, dabs, eels, chars, pike, tench and fea-tench, oyfters and fcollops, thornback, gudgeons, falmon-trout, brill, perch, cockles, mufcles.—N. B. Skate maids are black, and thornback maids white; grey bafs come with the mullet; there are two forts of mullets, the fea-mullet and river-mullet, both equally good.

VEGETABLES. Some cauliflowers, artichokes, beans, peas, cucumbers; alfo July-fown kidney-beans, turnips, carrots, parfnips, potatoes, fkirrets, fcorzonera, beets, onions, garlick, fhalots, rocombole, chardoons, creffes, chervil, muftard, radifh, rape, fpinage, lettuce fmall and cabbaged, burnet, tarragon, blanched celery and endive, cabbages and fprouts.

FRUIT. Late peaches and plumbs, grapes and figs, mulberries, filberts and walnuts; bullace, pines, and great variety of pears and apples, medlars, fervices, quinces, hazle-nuts.

NOVEMBER.

MEAT. Houfe-lamb, and doe-venifon.

POULTRY. Geefe, turkies, fowls, chickens, pullets, pigeons, woodcocks, fnipes, larks, wild ducks, teal, widgeon, hares, rabbits, dottrels, partridges, pheafants.

FISH. The fame as laft month.

VEGETABLES. Cauliflowers in the green-house, and some artichokes, carrots, parsnips, turnips, beets, skirrets, scorzonera, horse-radish, potatoes, onions, garlick, shalots, rocombole, celery, parsley, sorrel, thyme, savory, sweet-marjoram, dry and clary cabbages and their sprouts, savoy cabbage, spinage, late cucumbers, hot-herbs on the hot-bed, burnet, cabbage, lettuce, endive, blanched Jerusalem artichokes; and all sorts of pot-herbs.

FRUIT. Bullace, medlars, walnuts, hazel-nuts, chesnuts, pears, apples, services, grapes, oranges.

DECEMBER.

MEAT. House-lamb, pork, doe-venison,

POULTRY. The same as last month.

FISH. Turbot, sturgeon, gurnets, dorees, holoberts, barbel, smelts, cod, codlings, soles, carp, gudgeons, eels, perch, anchovy, perriwinkles, cockles, muscles, oysters, brill, and scollop.

VEGETABLES. Many sorts of cabbages and savoys, spinage, and some cauliflowers in the conservatory, and artichokes in the sand, roots as in last month, small sallading on hot-beds, also mint, tarragon, and cabbage-lettuce under glasses, chervil, celery, and endive blanched; sage, thyme, savory, beet-leaves, tops of young beets, parsley, sorrel, spinage, leeks and sweet-marjoram, marigold flowers, and mint dried; asparagus on the hot-bed, and cucumbers on the plants sown in July and August; onions, garlick, shalots, and rocombole.

FRUIT. Apples, pears, medlars, chesnuts, walnuts, services, grapes, hazel-nuts, and oranges.

CHAP. II.

DIRECTIONS FOR MARKETING; *containing the Names of all the Joints of every Beast; and Instructions how to chuse all Kinds of Butcher's Meat, Poultry, Fish, Butter, Eggs, and Cheese.*

OF BUTCHER'S MEAT.—*Pieces in a Bullock.*

THE head, tongue, palate; the entrails are the sweetbreads, kidneys, skirts, and tripe; there is the double, the roll, and the reed tripe.

The Fore-Quarter.

FIRST is the haunch, which includes the clod, marrow-bone, skin, and the sticking piece, that is, the neck end; the next is the leg of mutton piece, which has part of the bladebone; then the chuck,

chuck, the brisket, the fore ribs, and middle rib, which is called the chuck rib.

The Hind-Quarter.

First sirloin and rump, the thin and thick flank, the veiny-piece, then the isch-bone, or chuck-bone, buttock, and leg.

In a Sheep.

The head and pluck; which includes the liver, lights, heart, sweetbreads, and melt.

The Fore-Quarter.

The neck, breast, and shoulder.

The Hind Quarter.

The leg and loin. The two loins together is called a chine or saddle of mutton, which is a fine joint when it is the little fat mutton.

In a Calf.

The head and inwards are the pluck; which contains the heart, liver, lights, nut, and melt, and what they call the skirts, (which eat finely broiled,) the throat-sweetbread, and the wind-pipe-sweetbread, which is the finest.

The fore-quarter is the shoulder, neck, and breast.

The hind quarter is the leg, which contains the knuckle and fillet, then the loin.

In a Lamb.

The head and pluck, that is, the liver, lights, heart, nut, and melt. Then there is the fry, which is the sweetbreads, lamb-stones, and skirts, with some of the liver.

The fore-quarter is the shoulder, neck, and breast together.

The hind-quarter is the leg and loin.

In a Hog.

The head and inwards; and that is the haslet, which is the liver and crow, kidney and skirts. It is mixed with a great deal of sage and sweet herbs, pepper, salt, and spice, so rolled in the caul and roasted; then there are the chitterlins and the guts, which are cleaned for sausages.

The fore-quarter is the fore-loin and spring; if a large hog, you may cut a spare-rib off.

The hind-quarter only leg and loin.

A Bacon Hog.

This is cut different, because of making hams, bacon, and pickled pork. Here you have fine spare-ribs, chines, and griskins, and fat for hog's-lard. The liver and crow is much admired

mired fried with bacon; the feet and ears are both equally good souſed.

To chooſe Beef.

IF it be true ox-beef, it will have an open grain, and the fat, if young, of a crumbling, or oily ſmoothneſs, except it be the briſket and neck pieces, with ſuch others as are very fibrous. The colour of the lean ſhould be of a pleaſant carnation red, the fat rather inclining to white than yellow, (which ſeldom proves good,) and the ſuet of a fine white.

Cow-beef is of a cloſer grain, the fat whiter, the bones leſs, and the lean of a paler colour. If it be young and tender, the dent you make with your finger by preſſing it, will, in a little time, riſe again.

Bull-beef is of a more duſky red, a cloſer grain, and firmer than either of the former; harder to be indented with your finger, and riſing again ſooner. The fat is very groſs and fibrous, and of a ſtrong rank ſcent. If it be old it will be ſo very tough, that if you pinch it you will ſcarce make any impreſſion in it. If it be freſh, it will be of a lively freſh colour; but if ſtale, of a dark duſky colour, and very clammy. If it be bruiſed, the part affected will look of a more duſky or blackiſh colour than the reſt.

Mutton and Lamb.

TAKE ſome of the fleſh between your fingers and pinch it; if it feels tender, and ſoon returns to its former place, it is young; but if it wrinkles, and remains ſo, it is old. The fat will alſo eaſily ſeparate from the lean, if it be young; but if old, it will adhere more firmly, and be very clammy and fibrous. If it be ram mutton, the fat will be ſpongy, the grain cloſe, the lean rough, and of a deep red, and when dented by your finger will not riſe again. If the ſheep had the rot, the fleſh will be paliſh, the fat a faint white, inclining to yellow; the meat will be looſe at the bone, and, if you ſqueeze it hard, ſome drops of water, reſembling a dew or ſweat, will appear on the ſurface. [If it be a fore-quarter, obſerve the vein in the neck, for if it look ruddy, or of an azure colour, it is freſh; but if yellowiſh, it is near tainting, and if green, it is already ſo. As for the hind-quarter, ſmell under the kidney, and feel whether the knuckle be ſtiff or limber; for if you find a faint or ill ſcent in the former, or an unuſual limberneſs in the latter, it is ſtale.] The ſentences included in crotchets, will likewiſe be the marks for chooſing lamb; and for chooſing a lamb's head, mind the eyes; if they be ſunk or wrinkled, it is ſtale; if plump and lively, it is new and ſweet.

Veal,

Veal.

OBSERVE the vein in the shoulder; for if it be of a bright red, or looks blue, it is newly killed; but if greenish, yellowish, or blackish, or more clammy, soft, and limber than usual, it is stale. Also, if it has any green spots about it, it is either tainting, or already tainted. If it be wrapped in wet cloths, it is apt to be musty; therefore always observe to smell to it. The loin taints first under the kidney, and the flesh, when stale, will be soft and slimy. The neck and breast are first tainted at the upper end, and when so, will have a dusky, yellowish, or greenish appearance, and the sweetbread on the breast will be clammy. The leg, if newly killed, will be stiff in the joint; but if stale, limber, and the flesh clammy, intermixed with green or yellowish specks. The flesh of a bull-calf is firmer grained and redder than that of a cow-calf, and the fat more curdled. In choosing the head, observe the same directions as above given for that of the lamb.

Pork.

PINCH the lean between your fingers; if it breaks, and feels soft and oily, or if you can easily nip the skin with your nails, or if the fat be soft and oily, it is young; but if the lean be rough, the fat very spongy, and the skin stubborn, it is old. If it be a boar, or a hog gelded at full growth, the flesh will feel harder and rougher than usual, the skin thicker, the fat hard and fibrous, the lean of a dusky red, and of a rank scent. To know if it be fresh or stale, try the legs and hands at the bone, which comes out in the middle of the fleshy part, by putting in your finger; for as it first taints in those places, you may easily discover it by smelling to your finger; also the skin will be clammy and sweaty when stale, but smooth and cool when fresh.

Brawn.

THE best method of knowing whether brawn be young or old, is by the extraordinary or moderate thickness of the rind, and the hardness or softness of it; for the thick and hard is old, but the moderate and soft is young. If the rind and fat be remarkably tender, it is not boar brawn, but barrow or sow.

Dried Hams and Bacon.

TAKE a sharp-pointed knife, run it into the middle of the ham, on the inside, under the bone, draw it out quickly and smell to it; if its flavour be fine and relishing, and the knife little daubed, the ham is sweet and good; but if, on the contrary, the knife be greatly daubed, has a rank smell, and a ho-
goo

goo issues from the vent, it is tainted. Or you may cut off a piece at one end to look on the meat; if it appear white and be well scented, it is good; but if yellowish, or of a rusty colour, not well scented, it either is tainted or rusty, or at least will soon be so. A gammon of bacon may be tried in the same manner, and be sure to observe that the flesh sticks close to the bones, and the fat and lean to each other; for if it does not, the hog was not sound. Take care also that the extreme part of the fat near the rind be white, for if that be of a darkish or dirty colour, and the lean pale and soft, with some streaks of yellow, it is rusty, or will soon be so.

Venison.

Try the haunches, shoulders, and fleshy parts of the sides with your knife, in the same manner as before directed for ham, and in proportion to the sweet or rank smell it is new or stale. With relation to the other parts, observe the colour of the meat; for if it be stale or tainted, it will be of a black colour, intermixed with yellowish or greenish specks. If it be old, the flesh will be tough and hard, the fat contracted, the hoofs large and broad, and the heel horny and much worn.

Of POULTRY.

To know if a Capon be a true one or not, or whether it be young or old, new or stale.

If a capon be young, his spurs will be short and blunt, and his legs smooth: if a true capon, it will have a fat vein on the side of the breast, a thick belly and rump, and its comb will be short and pale. If it be new, it will have a close hard vent; but if stale, an open loose vent.

To choose a Cock or Hen Turkey, Turkey-Poults, &c.

If the spurs of a turkey-cock are short, and his legs black and smooth, he is young; but if his spurs be long, and his legs pale and rough, he is old. If long killed, his eyes will be sunk into his head, and his feet feel very dry; but if fresh, his feet will be limber, and his eyes lively. For the hen, observe the same signs. If she be with egg, she will have an open vent; but if not, a close, hard vent. The same signs will serve to discover the newness or staleness of turkey-poults; and, with respect to their age, you cannot be deceived.

A Cock, Hen, &c.

If a cock be young, his spurs will be short and dubbed; (be sure to observe that they are not pared or scraped to deceive you;)

you;) but if sharp and standing out, he is old. If his vent be hard and close, it is a sign of his being newly killed; but if he be stale, his vent will be open. The same signs will discover whether a hen be new or stale; and if old, her legs and comb will be rough; but if young, smooth.

To know if Chickens are new or stale.

If they are pulled dry, they will be stiff when new; but when stale, they will be limber, and their vents green. If they are scalded, or pulled wet, rub the breast with your thumb or finger, and if they are rough and stiff, they are new; but if smooth and slippery, stale.

To choose a Goose, Wild-Goose, and Bran-Goose.

If the bill and foot be red, and the body full of hairs, she is old; but if the bill be yellowish, and the body has but few hairs, she is young. If new, her feet will be limber; but if stale, dry. Understand the same of a wild-goose, and bran-goose.

Wild and tame Ducks.

These fowls are hard and thick on the belly, when fat, but thin and lean, when poor; limber-footed when new; but dry-footed when stale. A wild duck may be distinguished from a tame one, by its foot being smaller and reddish.

Bustard.

Observe the same rules in choosing this curious fowl, as those already given for the turkey.

The Shuffler, Godwits, Marle, Knots, Gulls, Ruffs, Dotters, and Wheat-Ears.

These birds, when new, are limber-footed; when stale, dry-footed: when fat, they have a fat rump; when lean, a close and hard one; when young, their legs are smooth; when old, rough.

Pheasant Cock and Hen.

The spurs of the pheasant cock, when young, are short and dubbed; but long and sharp when old; when new, he has a firm vent, when stale, an open and flabby one. The pheasant hen, when young, has smooth legs, and her flesh is of a fine and curious grain; but when old, her legs are rough, and her flesh hairy when pulled. If she be with egg, her vent will be open; if not, close. The same signs, as to newness or staleness, are to be observed as were before given for the cock.

Heath

Heath and Pheasant Poults.

The feet of these, when new, are limber, and their vents white and stiff; but when stale, are dry-footed, their vents green, and if you touch it hard, will peel.

Heath Cock and Hen.

The newness or staleness of these are known by the same signs as the foregoing; but when young, their legs and bills are smooth; when old, both are rough.

Woodcock and Snipe.

These fowls are limber-footed when new; when stale, dry-footed: if fat, thick and hard; but if their noses are snotty, and their throats moorish and muddy, they are bad. A snipe, particularly, if fat, has a fat vein in the side under the wing, and in the vent feels thick.

Partridge Cock or Hen.

These fowls, when young, have black bills, and yellowish legs; when old, white bills and blueish legs; when new, a fast vent; when stale, a green and open one, which will peel with a touch; if they had fed lately on green wheat, and their crops be full, smell to their mouths, lest their crops be tainted.

Doves or Pigeons, Plovers, &c.

The turtle-dove is distinguished by a blueish ring round its neck, the other parts being almost white. The stock-dove exceeds both the wood-pigeon and ring-dove in bigness. The dove-house pigeons are red-legged when old: if new and fat, limber-footed, and feel full in the vent; but when stale, their vents are green and flabby.

After the same manner you may choose the grey and green plover, fieldfare, thrush, mavis, lark, blackbird, &c.

Teal and Widgeon.

These, when new, are limber-footed; when stale, dry-footed; thick and hard on the belly, if fat; but thin and soft, if lean.

Hare.

If the claws of a hare are blunt and rugged, and the clift in her lip spread much, she is old; but the opposite, if young: if new and fresh killed, the flesh will be white and stiff; if stale, limber and blackish in many places. If the hare be young, the ears will tear like a sheet of brown paper; if old, they are dry and tough.

Leveret.

Leveret.

THE newness or staleness may be known by the same signs as the hare; but in order to discover if it be a real leveret, feel near the foot on its fore leg; if you find there a knob or small bone, it is a true leveret; but if not, a hare.

A Rabbit.

IF a rabbit be old, the claws will be very long and rough, and grey hairs intermixed with the wool; but if young, the claws and wool smooth; if stale, it will be limber, and the flesh will look blueish, having a kind of slime upon it; but if fresh, it will be stiff, and the flesh white and dry.

OF FISH.

To choose Salmon, Trout, Carp, Tench, Pike, Graylings, Barbel, Chub, Whiting, Smelt, Ruff, Eel, Shad, &c.

THE newness or staleness of these fish is known by the colour of their gills, their being hard or easy to be opened, the standing out or sinking of their eyes, their fins being stiff or limber, and by smelling to their gills. Eels taken in running water are better than those taken in ponds; of these, the silver ones are most esteemed.

Turbot.

IF this fish be plump and thick, and its belly of a cream colour, it is good; but if thin, and of a blueish white on the belly, not so.

Soals.

IF these are thick and stiff, and of a cream colour on the belly, they will spend firm; but if thin, limber, and their bellies of a blueish white, they will eat very loose.

Plaice and Flounders.

WHEN these fish are new, they are stiff, and the eyes look lively and stand out; but when stale, the contrary. The best plaice are blueish on the belly; but flounders of a cream colour.

Cod and Codling.

CHOOSE those which are thick towards the head, and their flesh, when cut, very white.

Fresh Herrings and Mackerel.

IF these are new, their gills will be of a lively shining redness, their eyes sharp and full, and the fish stiff; but if stale,
their

their gills will look dusky and faded, their eyes dull and sunk down, and their tails limber.

Pickled Salmon.

The scales of this fish, when new and good, are stiff and shining, the flesh oily to the touch, and parts in fleaks without crumbling; but the opposite, when bad.

Pickled and Red Herrings.

Take the former, and open the back to the bone; if it be white, or of a bright red, and the flesh white, oily, and fleaky, they are good. If the latter smell well, be of a good gloss, and part well from the bone, they are also good.

Dried Ling.

The best sort of dried ling is that which is thickest in the pole, and the flesh of the brightest yellow.

Pickled Sturgeon.

The veins and gristle of the fish, when good, are of a blue colour, the flesh white, the skin limber, the fat underneath of a pleasant scent, and you may cut it without its crumbling.

Lobsters.

If a lobster be new, it has a pleasant scent at that part of the tail which joins to the body, and the tail will, when opened, fall smart, like a spring; but when stale, it has a rank scent, and the tail limber and flagging. If it be spent, a white scurf will issue from the mouth and roots of the small legs. If it be full, the tail, about the middle, will be full of hard reddish skinned meat, which you may discover by thrusting a knife between the joints, on the bend of the tail. The heaviest are best, if there be no water in them. The cock is generally smaller than the hen, of a deeper red when boiled, has no spawn or seed under its tail, and the uppermost fins within its tail are stiff and hard.

Crab fish, great and small.

When they are stale, their shells will be of a dusky red colour, the joints of their claws limber; they are loose, and may be turned any way with the finger, and from under their throat will issue an ill smell; but if otherwise, they are good.

Prawns and Shrimps.

If they are hard and stiff, of a pleasant scent, and their tails turn strongly inward, they are new; but if they are limber, their

their colour faded, of a faint smell, and feel slimy, they are stale.

The seasons for eating all the above-mentioned articles may be seen in the foregoing chapter.

Of BUTTER, EGGS, and CHEESE.

To choose Butter and Eggs.

WHEN you buy butter, taste it yourself at a venture, and do not trust to the taste they give you, lest you be deceived by a well-tasted and scented piece artfully placed in the lump. Salt butter is better scented than tasted, by putting a knife into it, and putting it immediately to your nose; but, if it be a cask, it may be purposely packed, therefore trust not to the top alone, but unhoop it to the middle, thrusting your knife between the staves of the cask, and then you cannot be deceived.

When you buy eggs, put the great end to your tongue; if it feels warm, it is new; but if cold, it is stale; and according to the heat or coldness of it, the egg is newer or staler. Or take the egg, hold it up against the sun or a candle; if the white appears clear and fair, and the yolk round, it is good; but if muddy or cloudy, and the yolk broken, it is bad. Or take the egg, and put it into a pan of cold water; the fresher it is, the sooner it will sink to the bottom; but if it be rotten, or addled, it will swim on the surface of the water. The best way to keep them is in bran or meal; though some place their small ends downwards in fine wood-ashes. But for longer keeping, burying them in salt will preserve them almost in any climate.

Cheese.

CHEESE is to be chosen by its moist and smooth coat; if old cheese be rough-coated, rugged or dry at top, beware of little worms or mites; if it be over-full of holes, moist or spungy, is subject to maggots. If any soft or perished place appear on the outside, try how deep it goes, for the greater part may be hid within.

CHAP. III.

Of ROASTING, BOILING, &c.

THAT professed cooks will find fault with me for touching upon a branch of Cookery which they never thought worth their notice, is what I expect: however, this I know, it is the most necessary part of it; and few servants there are that know how to roast and boil to perfection.

I do not pretend to teach profeſſed cooks, but my deſign is to inſtruct the ignorant and unlearned (which will likewiſe be of great uſe in all private families), and in ſo plain and full a manner, that the moſt illiterate and ignorant perſon, who can but read, will know how to do every thing in Cookery well.

Rules to be observed in roasting Meat, Poultry, and Game.

I shall firſt begin with roaſt of all ſorts, and muſt deſire the cook to order her fire according to what ſhe is to dreſs; if any thing very little or thin, then a pretty little briſk fire, that it may be done quick and nice; if a very large joint, then be ſure a good fire be laid to cake. Let it be clear at the bottom: and when your meat is half done, move the dripping-pan and ſpit a little from the fire, and ſtir up a good briſk fire; for according to the goodneſs of your fire, your meat will be done ſooner or later. Take great care the ſpit be very clean; and be ſure to clean it with nothing but ſand and water. Waſh it clean, and wipe it with a dry cloth; for oil, brick-duſt, and ſuch things, will ſpoil your meat.

B E E F.

To roaſt a piece of beef about ten pounds will take an hour and a half, at a good fire. Twenty pounds weight will take three hours, if it be a thick piece; but if it be a thin piece of twenty pounds weight, two hours and a half will do it; and ſo on according to the weight of your meat, more or leſs. Obſerve, in froſty weather your beef will take half an hour longer.

Be ſure to paper the top, and baſte it well all the time it is roaſting, and throw a handful of ſalt on it. When you ſee the ſmoak draw to the fire, it is near enough; then take off the paper, baſte it well, and drudge it with a little flour to make a fine froth: take up your meat, and garniſh your diſh with nothing but horſe-radiſh.

Never ſalt your roaſt meat before you lay it to the fire, for that draws out all the gravy. If you would keep it a few days before you dreſs it, dry it very well with a clean cloth, then flour it all over, and hang it where the air will come to it; but be ſure always to mind that there is no dampneſs about it; if there is, you muſt dry it well with a cloth.

M U T T O N.

A leg of mutton of ſix pounds will take an hour at a quick fire; if froſty weather, an hour and a quarter; nine pounds, an hour and a half; a leg of twelve pounds will take two hours; if froſty, two hours and a half; a large ſaddle of mutton will take three hours, becauſe of papering it; a ſmall ſaddle will take

take an hour and a half, and so on, according to the size; a breast will take half an hour at a quick fire; a neck, if large, an hour; if very small, little better than half an hour; a shoulder much about the same time as a leg.

In roasting of mutton, the loin, the chine, or saddle, must have the skin raised and skewered on, and, when near done, take off the skin, baste and flour it to froth it up. All other sorts of mutton must be roasted with a quick, clear fire, without the skin being raised, or paper put on. You should always observe to baste your meat as soon as you lay it down to roast, sprinkle some salt on, and, when near done, dredge it with a little flour to froth it up. Garnish with horse-radish.

LAMB.

If a large fore-quarter, an hour and a half; if a small one, an hour. The outside must be papered, basted with good butter, and you must have a very quick fire. If a leg, about three quarters of an hour; a neck, a breast, or shoulder, three quarters of an hour; if very small, half an hour will do. These last-mentioned joints are not to be papered, or have the skin raised, but to be dressed like mutton, and garnished with cresses or small sallading.

VEAL.

As to veal, you must be careful to roast it of a fine brown; if a large joint, a very good fire; if a small joint, a pretty little brisk fire; if a fillet or loin, be sure to paper the fat, that you lose as little of that as possible. Lay it some distance from the fire till it is soaked, then lay it near the fire. When you lay it down, baste it well with good butter; and when it is near enough, baste it again, and dredge it with a little flour. The breast you must roast with the caul on, till it is enough; and skewer the sweetbread on the backside of the breast. When it is nigh enough, take off the caul, baste it, and dredge it with a little flour. To every pound allow a quarter of an hour's roasting.

PORK.

Pork must be well done, or it is apt to surfeit. To every pound allow a quarter of an hour: for example, a joint of twelve pounds weight, three hours, and so on; if it be a thin piece of that weight, two hours will roast it. When you roast a loin, take a sharp pen-knife and cut the skin a-cross, to make the crackling eat the better. The chine must be cut, and so must all pork that has the rind on. Roast a leg of pork thus: take a knife, as above, and score it; stuff the knuckle part with sage and onion, chopped fine with pepper and salt: or cut a hole under the twift, and put the fage, &c. there, and fkewer it up with a fkewer. Roaft it crifp, becaufe moft people like the rind crifp, which they call crackling. Make fome good apple-fauce, and fend up in a boat; then have a little drawn gravy to put in the difh. This they call a mock goofe. The fpring or hand of pork, if very young, roafted like a pig, eats very well; or take the fpring, and cut off the fhank or knuckle, and fprinkle fage and onion over it, and roll it round, and tie it with a ftring, and roaft it two hours, otherwife it is better boiled. The fparerib fhould be bafted with a little bit of butter, a very little duft of flour, and fome fage fhred fmall: but we never make any fauce to it but apple-fauce. The beft way to drefs pork grifkins is to roaft them, bafte them with a little butter and fage, and a little pepper and falt. Few eat any thing with thefe but muftard.

To kill a Pig and prepare it for roafting.

STICK your pig juft above the breaft-bone, run your knife to the heart, when it is dead put it in cold water for a few minutes, then rub it over with a little rofin beat exceeding fine, or its own blood, put your pig into a pail of fcalding water half a minute, take it out, lay it on a clean table, pull off the hair as quick as poffible, if it does not come clean off put it in again, when you have got it all clean off wafh it in warm water, then in two or three cold waters, for fear the rofin fhould tafte; take off the four feet at the firft joint, make a flit down the belly, take out all the entrails, put the liver, heart, and lights to the pettitoes, wafh it well out of cold water, dry it exceedingly well with a cloth.

To roaft a Pig.

SPIT your pig and lay it to the fire, which muft be brifker at the ends than in the middle, or hang a flat iron in the middle of the grate. Before you lay your pig down, take a little fage fhred fmall, a piece of butter as big as a walnut, and a little pepper and falt, and a cruft of bread; put them into the pig, and few it up with coarfe thread; then flour it all over very well, and keep flouring it till the eyes drop out, or you find the crackling hard. Be fure to fave all the gravy that comes out of it, which you muft do by fetting bafons or pans under the pig in the dripping-pan, as foon as you find the gravy begins to run. If juft killed, let it roaft an hour; if killed the day before, an hour and a quarter; if a very large one, an hour and a half. But the beft way to judge, is when the eyes drop out, and the fkin is grown very hard. When it is enough, ftir the fire up brifk; take a coarfe cloth, with a good lump of butter

in

in it, and rub the pig all over till the crackling is quite crisp, and then take it up. Lay it in your dish, and with a sharp knife cut off the head, and then cut the pig in two, before you draw out the spit. Cut the ears off the head and lay at each end, and cut the under jaw in two and lay on each side: melt some good butter, take the gravy you saved and put it into it, boil it, and pour it into the dish with the brains bruised fine, and the sage mixed all together, and then send it to table.

Another way to roast a Pig.

CHOP some sage and onion very fine, a few crumbs of bread, a little butter, pepper, and salt rolled up together, put it into the belly, and sew it up before you lay down the pig: rub it all over with sweet oil; when it is done, take a dry cloth and wipe it, then take it into a dish, cut it up, and send it to table with the sauce as above.

To roast the Hind-quarter of Pig lamb-fashion.

AT the time of the year when house-lamb is very dear, take the hind-quarter of a large roasting pig, take off the skin and roast it, and it will eat like lamb with mint-sauce, or with a sallad, or Seville orange. Half an hour will roast it.

To bake a Pig.

LAY it in a dish, flour it all over well, and rub it over with butter; butter the dish you lay it in, and put it into the oven. When it is enough, draw it out of the oven's mouth, and rub it over with a buttery cloth; then put it into the oven again till it is dry; take it out, and lay it in a dish: cut it up, take a little veal gravy, and take off the fat in the dish it was baked in, and there will be some good gravy at the bottom; put that to it, with a little piece of butter rolled in flour; boil it up, and put it into the dish, with the brains and sage in the belly. Some love a pig brought whole to table; then you are only to put what sauce you like into the dish.

To roast Venison.

TAKE a haunch of venison and spit it; take four sheets of paper well buttered, put two on the haunch; then make a paste with some flour, a little butter and water; roll it out half as big as your haunch, and put it over the fat part, then put the other two sheets of paper on, and tie them with some pack-thread; lay it to a brisk fire, and baste it well all the time of roasting; if a large haunch of twenty-four pounds, it will take three hours and an half, except it is a very large fire, then three hours will do; smaller in proportion. When it is near done, take off the paper and paste, dust it well with flour, and baste it with butter; when it is a light brown, dish it up with brown gravy.

To dress a Haunch of Mutton.

HANG it up for a fortnight, and dress it as directed for a haunch of venison.

To dress Mutton venison-fashion.

TAKE the largest and fattest leg of mutton you can get, cut out like a haunch of venison, as soon as it is killed, while it is warm, it will eat the tenderer; take out the bloody vein, pour over it a bottle of red wine, turn it in the wine four or five times a day, for five days, then dry it exceeding well with a clean cloth, hang it up in the air, with the thick end uppermost, for five days, dry it night and morning to keep it from growing musty. When you roast it, cover it with paper and paste as you do venison. Serve it up with venison sauce. It will take four hours roasting. A fine fat neck may be done the same way.

To keep Venison or Hares sweet; or to make them fresh when they stink.

IF your venison be very sweet, only dry it with a cloth, and hang it where the air comes. If you would keep it any time, dry it very well with clean cloths, rub it all over with ground pepper, and hang it in an airy place, and it will keep a great while. If it stinks, or is musty, take some lukewarm water, and wash it clean; then take some fresh milk and water of the same warmth, and wash it again; then dry it in clean cloths very well, and rub it all over with ground pepper, and hang it in an airy place. When you roast it, you need only wipe it with a clean cloth, and paper it as before-mentioned. Never do any thing else to venison, for all other things spoil it and take away the fine flavour, and this preserves it better than any thing you can do. A hare you may manage just the same way.

To roast a Tongue and Udder.

PARBOIL them first for two hours, then roast them, stick eight or ten cloves about them; baste them with butter, and have some gravy and galintine sauce, made thus: take a few bread crumbs, and boil in a little water, beat it up, then put in a gill of red-wine, some sugar to sweeten it; put it in a bason or boat.

To roast Geese, Turkies, &c.

WHEN you roast a goose, turkey, or fowls of any sort, take care to singe them with a piece of white paper, and baste them
with

with butter; dredge them with a little flour, and sprinkle a little salt on; and when the smoak begins to draw to the fire, and they look plump, baste them again, and dredge them with a little flour, and take them up.

As to geese and ducks, you should have sage and onion shred fine, with pepper and salt put into the belly, with gravy in the dish; or some like sage and onion and gravy mixed together. Put only pepper and salt into wild ducks, easterlings, wigeon, teal, and all other sorts of wild fowl. A middling turkey will take an hour to roast; a very large one, an hour and a quarter; a small one, three quarters of an hour. You must paper the breast till it is near done enough, then take the paper off and froth it up. Your fire must be very good. The same time does for a goose.

To roast a Fowl pheasant-fashion.

IF you should have but one pheasant, and want two in a dish, take a large full-grown fowl, keep the head on, and truss it just as you do a pheasant; lard it with bacon, but do not lard the pheasant, and nobody will know it.

To roast a Fowl.

ROAST a large fowl three quarters of an hour; a middling one, half an hour; very small chickens, twenty minutes. Your fire must be very quick and clear when you lay them down.

To roast Pigeons.

TAKE some parsley shred fine, a piece of butter as big as a nutmeg, a little pepper and salt; tie the neck end tight: tie a string round the legs and rump, and fasten the other end to the top of the chimney-piece; baste them with butter, and when they are enough, lay them in the dish, and they will swim with gravy. You may put them on a little spit, and then tie both ends close. Twenty minutes will roast them..

To roast Partridges.

LET them be nicely roasted, but not too much; baste them gently with a little butter, and dredge with flour, sprinkle a little salt on, and froth them nicely up; have good gravy in the dish, with bread-sauce in a boat, made thus: take about a handful or two of crumbs of bread, put in a pint of milk or more, a small whole onion, a little whole white pepper, a little salt, and a bit of butter, boil it all well up; then take the onion out, and beat it well with a spoon; or take poivrade-sauce in a boat, made thus: chop four shalots fine, a gill of good gravy, and a spoonful of vinegar, a little pepper and salt; boil them up one minute, then put it in a boat. Twenty minutes is enough to roast them.

To roast Larks.

PUT a small bird-spit through them, and tie them on another; all the time they are roasting keep basting them very gently with butter, and sprinkle crumbs of bread on them till they are almost done; then let them brown before you take them up.

The best way of making crumbs of bread is to take the crumb of a stale loaf, rub it through a fine cullender, and put into a little butter in a stew-pan; melt it, put in your crumbs of bread, and keep them stirring till they are of a light brown; put them on a sieve to drain a few minutes; lay your larks in a dish, and the crumbs all round, almost as high as the larks, with plain butter in a cup, and some gravy in another. Twenty minutes will roast them.

To roast Woodcocks and Snipes.

PUT them on a little bird-spit, and tie them on another, and put them down to roast; take a round of a threepenny loaf, and toast it brown and butter it; then lay it in a dish under the birds; baste them with a little butter; take the trail out before you spit them, and put into a small stew-pan, with a little gravy; simmer it gently over the fire for five or six minutes; add a little melted butter to it, put it over your toast in the dish, and when your woodcocks are roasted put them on the toast, and set it over a lamp or chafing dish for three minutes, and send them to table.

Another Way.

PLUCK them, but do not draw them, put them on a small spit, dust and baste them well with butter, toast a few slices of a penny loaf, put them on a clean plate, and set it under the birds while they are roasting; if the fire be good they will take about ten minutes roasting; when you draw them, lay them upon the toasts on the dish, pour melted butter round them, and serve them up.

To roast a Hare.

TAKE your hare when it is cased, truss it in this manner, bring the two hind-legs up to its sides, pull the fore-legs back, put your skewer first into the hind-leg, then into the fore-leg, and thrust it through the body; put the fore leg on, and then the hind-leg, and a skewer through the top of the shoulders and back part of the head, which will hold the head up. Make a pudding thus: take a quarter of a pound of beef-suet, as much crumb of bread, a handful of parsley chopped fine, some sweet herbs of all sorts, such as basil, marjoram, winter-savory, and a little thyme chopped very fine, a little nutmeg grated, some

lemon

lemon-peel cut fine, pepper and salt, chop the liver fine, and put in with an egg, mix it up, and put it into the belly, and sew or skewer it up; then spit it and lay it to the fire, which must be a good quick one. Put three half pints of good milk in your dripping-pan, baste your hare with it till reduced to half a gill, then dust and baste it well with butter; if it be a large one, it will take an hour and a half roasting, and require a little more milk.

To roast Rabbits.

BASTE them with good butter, and dredge them with a little flour. Half an hour will do them, at a very quick, clear fire; and if they are very small, twenty minutes will do them. Take the liver, with a little bunch of parsley, and boil them, and then chop them very fine together; melt some good butter, and put half the liver and parsley into the butter; pour it into the dish, and garnish the dish with the other half. Let your rabbits be done of a fine light brown; or put the sauce in a boat.

To roast a Rabbit hare-fashion.

LARD a rabbit with bacon; roast it as you do a hare, with a stuffing in the belly, and it eats very well. But then you must make gravy-sauce; but if you do not lard it, white sauce, made thus: take a little veal broth, boil it up with a little flour and butter, to thicken it, then add a gill of cream; keep it stirring one way till it is smooth, then put it in a boat or in the dish.

N. B. If your fire is not very quick and clear when you lay your poultry or game down to roast, it will not eat near so sweet, or look so beautiful to the eye.

To keep Meat hot.

THE best way to keep meat, poultry, or game hot, if it be done before your company is ready, is to set the dish over a pan of boiling water; cover the dish with a deep cover, so as not to touch the meat, and throw a cloth over all. Thus you may keep your meat hot a long time, and it is better than over-roasting and spoiling the meat. The steam of the water keeps the meat hot, and does not draw the gravy out, or draw it up; whereas if you set a dish of meat any time over a chafing-dish of coals, it will dry up all the gravy and spoil the meat.

BROILING.

General Directions concerning Broiling.

As to mutton and pork steaks, you must keep them turning quick on the gridiron, and have your dish ready over a chafing-dish of hot coals, and carry them to table covered hot, and only a few at a time. When you broil fowls or pigeons, always take care your fire is clear; and never baste any thing on the gridiron, for it only makes it smoked and burnt.

To broil Beef Steaks.

FIRST have a very clear brisk fire; let your gridiron be very clean; put it on the fire, and take a chafing-dish with a few hot coals out of the fire. Put the dish on it which is to lay your steaks on, then take fine rump steaks about half an inch thick; put a little pepper and salt on them, lay them on the gridiron, and (if you like it) take a shalot or two, or a fine onion, and cut it fine; put it into your dish. Keep turning your steaks quick till they are done, for that keeps the gravy in them. When the steaks are enough, take them carefully off into your dish, that none of the gravy be lost; then have ready a hot dish and cover, and carry them hot to table with the cover on. You may send a shalot in a plate, chopt fine.

To broil Mutton Chops.

CUT your steaks half an inch thick, when your gridiron is hot rub it with fresh suet, lay on your steaks, keep turning them as quick as possible; if you do not take great care the fat that drops from the steak will smoke them; when they are enough, put them into a hot dish, rub them well with butter, slice a shalot very thin into a spoonful of water, pour it on them with a spoonful of mushroom catchup and salt, serve them up hot, and in small quantities, fresh and fresh.

To broil Pork Steaks.

OBSERVE the same as for mutton steaks, only pork requires more broiling; when they are enough put in a little good gravy; a little sage rubbed very fine strewed over them gives them a fine taste.

To broil Chickens.

SLIT them down the back, and season them with pepper and salt; lay them on a very clear fire, and at a great distance. Let the inside lie next the fire till it is above half done; then turn them, and take great care the fleshy side do not burn, and let them be of a fine brown. Let your sauce be good gravy, with mushrooms, and garnish with lemon and the livers broiled, the gizzards cut, flashed, and broiled with pepper and salt.

Or this sauce: take a handful of sorrel dipped in boiling water, drain it, and have ready half a pint of good gravy, a shalot shred small; and some parsley boiled very green; thicken

it

it with a piece of butter rolled in flour, and add a glafs of red wine; then lay your forrel in heaps round the fowls, and pour the fauce over them. Garnifh with lemon.

Note, You may make juft what fauce you fancy.

To broil Pigeons.

TAKE young pigeons, pick and draw them, fplit them down the back, and feafon them with pepper and falt, lay them on the gridiron with the breaft upward. Take care your fire is very clear, and fet your gridiron high, that they may not burn; turn them, rub them over with butter, and keep turning them till they are enough; difh them up, and lay round them crifped parfley, and pour over them melted butter or gravy, which you pleafe, and fend them up.

FRYING.

To fry Beef Steaks.

TAKE rump fteaks, pepper and falt them, fry them in a little butter very quick and brown; take them out and put them into a difh, pour the fat out of the frying-pan, and then take half a pint of hot gravy; if no gravy, half a pint of hot water, and put into the pan, and a little butter rolled in flour, a little pepper and falt, and two or three fhalots chopped fine; boil them up in your pan for two minutes, then put it over the fteaks, and fend them to table.

A fecond Way to fry Beef-Steaks.

CUT the lean by itfelf, and beat them well with the back of a knife, fry them in juft as much butter as will moiften the pan, pour out the gravy as it runs out of the meat, turn them often, do them over a gentle fire, then fry the fat by itfelf and lay upon the meat, and put to the gravy a glafs of red wine, half an anchovy, a little nutmeg, a little beaten pepper, and a fhalot cut fmall; give it two or three little boils, feafon it with falt to your palate, pour it over the fteaks, and fend them to table.

To fry Tripe.

CUT your tripe in long pieces of about three inches wide, and all the breadth of the double; put it in fome fmall-beer batter, or yolks of eggs; have a large pan of good fat, and fry it brown, then take it out and put it to drain; difh it up with plain butter in a cup.

To fry Saufages.

CUT them in fingle links, and fry them in frefh butter, then take a flice of bread and fry it a good brown in the butter you

fried

fried the saufages in, and lay it in the bottom of your dish, put the saufages on the toaft, in four parts.

BOILING.

General Directions concerning Boiling.

To all forts of boiled meats, allow a quarter of an hour to every pound; be fure the pot is very clean, and fkim it well, for every thing will have a fcum rife, and if that boils down, it makes the meat black. All forts of frefh meat you are to put in when the water boils, but falt meat when the water is warm.

To boil a Ham.

WHEN you boil a ham, put it into your copper when the water is pretty warm, for cold water draws the colour out; when it boils, be careful it boils very flowly. A ham of twenty pounds takes four hours and a half, larger and fmaller in proportion. Keep the copper well fkimmed. A green ham wants no foaking, but an old ham muft be foaked fixteen hours in a large tub of foft water.

To boil a Tongue.

A TONGUE, if falt, foak it in foft water all night, boil it three hours; if frefh out of the pickle, two hours and an half, and put it in when the water boils; take it out and pull it, trim it, garnifh with greens and carrots.

To boil a Round of Beef.

TAKE a round of beef, falt it well with common falt, let it lay ten days, turning it over and rubbing it with the brine every other day, then wafh it in foft water, tie it up as round as you can, and put it into cold foft water, boil it very gently, if it weighs thirty pounds, it will take three hours and a half; if you ftuff it, do it thus; take half a pound of beef fuet, fome green beet, parfley, pot-marjoram, thyme, and leeks; chop all thefe very fine, put to them a handful of ftale bread crumbs, pepper and falt, mix thefe well together, make holes in your beef and put it in, tie it up in a cloth.

To boil a Brifket of Beef.

TAKE a thick piece of the brifket, falt it well with common falt, rub it with the brine every other day, and turn it over, let it lay a fortnight or three weeks, if you think it will be too falt, fteep it all night in cold water; fet it on to boil in cold water, keep it clofe covered, and ftew it gently four hours, but if it be very thick it will take more; mind to fkim your pot well

well when it begins to boil, which muſt be carefully obſerved in all kinds of boiled meats; if you take out the bones and roll it like collared meat, it will look much handſomer, particularly to eat cold.

To dreſs a Calf's Head plain.

TAKE a calf's head when freſh killed, ſplit and clean it well, take care of the brains, waſh it in ſoft water juſt aired, then put it into cold ſoft water, let it ſtand three or four hours, or all night if you have time, wrap it in a cloth and boil it in milk and ſoft water, if a large head it will take near two hours; tie the brains in a cloth with a few ſage leaves and a little parſley, an hour will boil them; take them out and chop the ſage and parſley well, and the brains a little, put them into a ſauce-pan, with a little good melted butter and a little ſalt, make them hot, then take up half the head, ſcore it and do it over with the yolk of egg, ſeaſon it with a little pepper and ſalt, ſtrew over a few ſtale bread crumbs mixed with a little chopped parſley, ſet it before the fire till brown, baſte it, but do not let it burn, then diſh it up, lay the boiled and broiled both on a diſh, and garniſh with greens, ſkin the tongue and ſplit it, lay the brains on a diſh and the tongue upon them; it is common to ſend up greens and bacon with it.

To boil a Lamb's Head.

BOIL the head and pluck tender, but do not let the liver be too much done. Take the head up, hack it croſs and croſs with a knife, grate ſome nutmeg over it, and lay it in a diſh before a good fire; then grate ſome crumbs of bread, ſome ſweet herbs rubbed, a little lemon-peel chopped fine, a very little pepper and ſalt, and baſte it with a little butter; then throw a little flour over it, and juſt before it is done do the ſame, baſte it and dredge it. Take half the liver, the lights, the heart, and tongue, chop them very ſmall, with ſix or eight ſpoonfuls of gravy or water; firſt ſhake ſome flower over the meat, and ſtir it together, then put in the gravy or water, a good piece of butter rolled in a little flour, a little pepper and ſalt, and what runs from the head in the diſh; ſimmer all together a few minutes, and add half a ſpoonful of vinegar, pour it into your diſh, lay the head in the middle of the mince-meat, have ready the other half of the liver cut thin, with ſome ſlices of bacon broiled, and lay round the head. Garniſh the diſh with lemon, and ſend it to table.

Boiled Leg of Lamb and the Loin fried round it.

LET the leg be boiled very white. An hour will do it. Cut the loin into ſteaks, dip them into a few crumbs of bread and egg, fry them nice and brown, boil a good deal of spinage, and lay in the dish; put the leg in the middle, lay the loin round it, cut an orange in four and garnish the dish, and have butter in a cup. Some love the spinage boiled, then drained, put into a sauce-pan with a good piece of butter, and stewed.

To boil a Leg of Pork.

TAKE a leg of pork that has been salted a fortnight or three weeks, about eight pounds weight, put it into cold soft water, and boil it three hours and a quarter, then take off the skin. All salt meats require gently boiling. It is common to send up pease pudding with boiled pork.

To boil Pickled Pork.

BE sure you put it in when the water boils. If a middling piece, an hour will boil it; if a very large piece, an hour and a half, or two hours. If you boil pickled pork too long, it will go to a jelly. You will know when it is done by trying it with a fork.

POULTRY.

To boil a Turkey.

TAKE a turkey, cut off the legs and head, truss it as you would a fowl for boiling; lay it in milk and water an hour or two, drain it well, put some force-meat into the craw, made of beef suet shred fine, stale bread crumbs an equal quantity, a bit of lean veal the size of an egg, beat it in a marble mortar, pick the skins out, put to it an anchovy chopped, a little beaten mace, a little nutmeg, chyan, salt, lemon-peel shred fine, and a little lemon juice, mix these all together with an egg; sew up the craw, rub the breast well with lemon juice, dredge it a little, pin it up in a clean cloth, boil it in soft water and milk; put your turkey in when it boils, boil it gently, if it is a large one it will take an hour and a quarter, if a middling size, an hour; dish it up, and garnish with lemon; you may serve it up with oyster sauce, celery, or white sauce; you may dress a full grown fowl the same way.

To boil young Chickens.

TAKE chickens, pull and pick them clean whilst warm, let them hang one night, then drain them, cut off the heads and legs, then truss them, if your chickens be fat do not break the breast-bone; lay them into milk and water two hours, rub their breasts with lemon juice, dredge them and put them into boiling milk and water; if they are fine chickens half an hour, if small twenty minutes; dish them up, and pour the sauce over them, garnish with sliced lemon and chopped parsley.

MADE PLAIN AND EASY.

To boil Fowls and House Lamb.

BOIL these in a pot by themselves, with a good deal of water, scum the pot carefully; they will be both sweeter and whiter than if boiled in a cloth. A fowl takes half an hour.

To dress GREENS, ROOTS, *&c.*

ALWAYS be very careful that your greens be nicely picked and washed. You should lay them in a clean pan, for fear of sand or dust which is apt to hang round wooden vessels. Boil all your greens in a copper or sauce-pan, by themselves, with a great quantity of water. Boil no meat with them, for that discolours them. Use no iron pans, &c. for they are not proper; but let them be copper, brass, or silver.

Most people spoil garden things by over-boiling them. All things that are green should have a little crispness, for if they are over-boiled, they neither have any sweetness or beauty.

To dress Spinage.

PICK it very clean, and wash it in five or six waters; put it in a sauce-pan that will just hold it, throw a little salt over it, and cover the pan close. Do not put any water in, but shake the pan often. You must put your sauce-pan on a clear quick fire. As soon as you find the greens are shrunk and fallen to the bottom, and that the liquor which comes out of them boils up, they are enough. Throw the spinage into a clean sieve to drain, and squeeze it well between two plates, and cut it in any form you like. Lay it in a plate, or small dish, and never put any butter on it, but put it in a cup or boat.

To dress Cabbage, &c.

CABBAGE, and all sorts of young sprouts, must be boiled in a great deal of water. When the stalks are tender, or fall to the bottom, they are enough; then take them off, before they lose their colour. Always throw salt in your water before you put your greens in. Young sprouts you send to table just as they are, but cabbage is best chopped and put into a sauce-pan with a good piece of butter, stirring it for about five or six minutes, till the butter is all melted, and then send it to table.

To dress Carrots.

LET them be scraped very clean, and when they are enough, rub them in a clean cloth, then slice them into a plate, and pour some melted butter over them. If they are young spring carrots, half an hour will boil them; if large, an hour; but old Sandwich carrots will take two hours.

To dress Turnips.

THEY eat best boiled in the pot with the meat, and, when enough, which you will know by trying them with a fork, take them out and put them in a pan, and mash them with butter, a little cream, and a little salt, and send them to table. But you may do them thus: pare your turnips and cut them into dice, as big as the top of one's finger; put them into a clean sauce-pan, and just cover them with water. When enough, throw them into a sieve to drain, and put them into a sauce-pan with a good piece of butter and a little cream; stir them over the fire for five or six minutes, and send them to table.

To dress Parsnips.

THEY should be boiled in a great deal of water, and when you find they are soft, (which you will know by running a fork into them,) take them up, and carefully scrape all the dirt off them, and then with a knife scrape them all fine, throwing away all the sticky parts, and send them up plain in a dish with melted butter.

To dress Broccoli.

STRIP all the little branches off till you come to the top one, then with a knife peel off all the hard outside skin, which is on the stalks and little branches, and throw them into water. Have a stew-pan of water with some salt in it; when it boils put in the broccoli, and when the stalks are tender it is enough, then send it to table with a piece of toasted bread soaked in the water the broccoli is boiled in under it, the same way as asparagus, with butter in a cup. The French eat oil and vinegar with it.

To dress Potatoes.

YOU must boil them in as little water as you can, without burning the sauce-pan. Cover the sauce-pan close, and when the skin begins to crack they are enough. Drain all the water out, and let them stand covered for a minute or two; then peel them, lay them in your plate, and pour some melted butter over them. The best way to do them is, when they are peeled to lay them on a gridiron till they are of a fine brown, and send them to table. Another way is to put them into a sauce-pan with some good beef dripping, cover them close, and shake the sauce-pan often for fear of burning to the bottom. When they are of a fine brown, and crisp, take them up in a plate, then put them into another for fear of the fat, and put butter in a cup.

To dress Cauliflowers.

TAKE your flowers, cut off all the green part, and then cut the flowers into four, and lay them into water for an hour;

then

then have some milk and water boiling, put in the cauliflowers, and be sure to skim the sauce-pan well. When the stalks are tender, take them carefully up, and put them into a cullender to drain; then put a spoonful of water into a clean stew-pan with a little dust of flour, about a quarter of a pound of butter, and shake it round till it is all finely melted, with a little pepper and salt; then take half the cauliflower and cut it as you would for pickling, lay it into the stew-pan, turn it, and shake the pan round. Ten minutes will do it. Lay the stewed in the middle of your plate, and the boiled round it. Pour the butter you did it in over it, and send it to table.

To boil them in the common Way.

CUT the cauliflower stalks off, leave a little green on, and boil them in spring water and salt; about fifteen minutes will do them. Take them out and drain them; send them whole in a dish, with some melted butter in a cup.

To dress French Beans.

FIRST string them, then cut them in two, and afterwards across; but if you would do them nice, cut the bean into four, and then across, which is eight pieces. Lay them into water and salt, and when your pan boils put in some salt and the beans; when they are tender they are enough; they will be soon done. Take care they do not lose their fine green. Lay them in a plate, and have butter in a cup.

To dress Artichokes.

WRING off the stalks, and put the artichokes into cold water, and wash them well, then put them in, when the water boils, with the tops downwards, that all the dust and sand may boil out. An hour and a half will do them.

To dress Asparagus.

SCRAPE all the stalks very carefully till they look white, then cut all the stalks even alike, throw them into water, and have ready a stew-pan boiling. Put in some salt, and tie the asparagus in little bundles. Let the water keep boiling, and when they are a little tender take them up. If you boil them too much you lose both colour and taste. Cut the round of a small loaf, about half an inch thick, toast it brown on both sides, dip it in the asparagus liquor, and lay it in your dish; pour a little butter over the toast, then lay your asparagus on the toast all round the dish, with the white tops outward. Do not pour butter over the asparagus, for that makes them greasy to the fingers, but have your butter in a bason, and send it to table.

To boil green Peaſe.

Shell your peaſe juſt before you want them, put them into a very ſmall quantity of boiling water, with a little ſalt and a lump of loaf ſugar, when they begin to dent in the middle they are enough, ſtrain them in a ſieve, put a good lump of butter into a mug or ſmall diſh, give your peaſe a ſhake up with the butter, put them on a diſh, and ſend them to table. Boil a ſprig of mint in another water, chop it fine, and lay it in lumps round the edge of your diſh.

To dreſs Beans and Bacon.

When you dreſs beans and bacon, boil the bacon by itſelf and the beans by themſelves, for the bacon will ſpoil the colour of the beans. Always throw ſome ſalt into the water, and ſome parſley, nicely picked. When the beans are enough, (which you will know by their being tender,) throw them into a cullender to drain. Take up the bacon and ſkin it; throw ſome raſpings of bread over the top, and if you have an iron, make it red hot and hold over it, to brown the top of the bacon; if you have not one, hold it to the fire to brown; put the bacon in the middle of the diſh, and the beans all round, cloſe up to the bacon, and ſend them to table, with parſley and butter in a baſon.

CHAP. IV.

Sauces for all the Diſhes mentioned in the foregoing Chapter.

To melt Butter.

In melting of butter you muſt be very careful; let your ſaucepan be well tinned; take a ſpoonful of cold water, a little duſt of flour, and a piece of butter ſufficient for your purpoſe, cut to pieces; be ſure to keep ſhaking your pan one way, for fear it ſhould oil; when it is all melted, let it boil, and it will be ſmooth and fine. A ſilver pan is beſt, if you have one.

To make Veal, Mutton, or Beef Gravy.

Take a raſher or two of bacon or ham, lay it at the bottom of your ſtew-pan; put your meat, cut in thin ſlices, over it; and cut ſome onions, turnips, carrots, and celery, a little thyme, and put over the meat, with a little all-ſpice; put a little water at the bottom, then ſet it on the fire, which muſt be a gentle one, and draw it till it is brown at the bottom

(which

(which you may know by the pan's hissing), then pour boiling water over it, and stew it gently for one hour and a half: if a small quantity, less time will do it. Season it with salt.

To make Gravy.

IF you live in the country, where you cannot always have gravy meat, when your meat comes from the butcher's, take a piece of beef, a piece of veal, and a piece of mutton; cut them into as small pieces as you can, and take a large deep sauce-pan with a cover, lay your beef at bottom, then your mutton, then a very little piece of bacon, a slice or two of carrot, some mace, cloves, whole pepper black and white, a large onion cut in slices, a bundle of sweet herbs, and then lay in your veal. Cover it close over a slow fire for six or seven minutes, shaking the sauce-pan now and then: then shake some flour in, and have ready some boiling water; pour it in till you cover the meat and something more. Cover it close, and let it stew till it is quite rich and good; then season it to your taste with salt, and strain it off. This will do for most things.

Different Sorts of Sauce for a Pig.

THERE are several ways of making sauce for a pig. Some do not love any sage in the pig, only a crust of bread; but then you should have a little dried sage rubbed and mixed with the gravy and butter. Some love bread-sauce in a bason, made thus: take a pint of water, put in a good piece of crumb of bread, a blade of mace, and a little whole pepper; boil it for about five or six minutes, and then pour the water off; take out the spice, and beat up the bread with a good piece of butter, and a little milk or cream. Some love a few currants boiled in it, a glass of wine, and a little sugar; but that you must do just as you like it. Others take half a pint of good beef gravy, and the gravy which comes out of the pig, with a piece of butter rolled in flour, two spoonfuls of catchup, and boil them all together; then take the brains of the pig and bruise them fine; put all these together, with the sage in the pig, and pour into your dish. It is a very good sauce. When you have not gravy enough comes out of your pig with the butter for sauce, take about half a pint of veal gravy and add to it; or stew the pettitoes, and take as much of that liquor as will do for sauce, mixed with the other.—*N. B.* Some like the sauce sent in a boat, or bason.

Different Sorts of Sauce for Venison.

YOU may take either of these sauces for venison: Currant-jelly warmed; or a pint of red wine, with a quarter of a pound of sugar, simmered over a clear fire for five or six minutes; or a

D pint

pint of vinegar, and a quarter of a pound of sugar, simmered till it is a syrup.

Sauce for a Goose.

For a goose make a little good gravy, and put it into a bason by itself, and some apple-sauce into another, made thus:

Apple-Sauce.

Pare, core, and slice your apples, put them in a sauce-pan with as much water as will keep them from burning, set them over a very slow fire, keep them close covered till they are all of a pulp, then put in a lump of butter, and sugar to your taste, beat them well, and send them to the table in a china bason. Add a piece of lemon-peel.

Sauce for a Turkey.

For a turkey, good gravy in the dish, and either bread or onion sauce in a bason, or both.

Sauce for Ducks.

For ducks, a little gravy in the dish, and onion-sauce in a cup, if liked.

Sauce for Fowls.

To fowls you should put good gravy in the dish, and either bread, parsley, or egg sauce in a bason.

Sauce for Pheasants and Partridges.

Pheasants and partridges should have gravy in the dish, and bread-sauce in a cup, and poivrade-sauce, which is made, either hot or cold, as under.

To make hot Poivrade-Sauce.

Take two anchovies, take out the bones, wash them, and chop them fine with two or three shalots, six spoonfuls of gravy, and six of vinegar; boil these two minutes; keep stirring it. You may either send it up strained, or with the ingredients.

To make cold Poivrade-Sauce.

Take two anchovies, take out the bones, chop them well, put them into a bason with two table-spoonfuls of the best sallad-oil, a tea-spoonful of made mustard; rub these well with the back of a spoon; add two large shalots shred fine, and shred parsley. Mix these well together with vinegar to your taste.

Different

Different Sorts of Sauce for a Hare.

TAKE for sauce, a pint of cream and half a pound of fresh butter; put them in a sauce-pan, and keep stirring it with a spoon till the butter is melted and the sauce is thick; then take up the hare, and pour the sauce into the dish. Another way to make sauce for a hare is, to make good gravy, thickened with a little piece of butter rolled in flour, and pour it into your dish. You may leave the butter out, if you do not like it, and have some currant-jelly warmed in a cup, or red wine and sugar boiled to a syrup, done thus: take a pint of red wine, a quarter of a pound of sugar, and set it over a slow fire to simmer for about a quarter of an hour. You may do half the quantity, and put it into your sauce-boat or bason.

To make Gravy for a Turkey, or any Sort of Fowls.

TAKE a pound of the lean part of the beef, hack it with a knife; flour it well; have ready a stew-pan with a piece of fresh butter. When the butter is melted, put in the beef, fry it till it is brown, and then pour in a little boiling water; shake it round, and then fill up with a tea-kettle of boiling water. Stir it all together, and put in two or three blades of mace, four or five cloves, some whole pepper, an onion, a bundle of sweet herbs, a little crust of bread baked brown, and a little piece of carrot. Cover it close, and let it stew till it is as good as you would have it. This will make a pint of rich gravy.

Turkies, Pheasants, &c. may be larded.

YOU may lard a turkey or pheasant, or any thing, just as you like it.

Directions concerning the Sauce for Steaks.

IF you love pickles or horse-raddish with steaks, never garnish your dish; because both the garnishing will be dry and the steaks will be cold; but lay those things on little plates, and carry to table. The great nicety is to have them hot and full of gravy.

Sauce for a boiled Turkey.

THE best sauce for a boiled turkey is good oyster and cellery sauce. Make OYSTER-SAUCE thus: Take as many oysters as you want, and set them off, strain the liquor from them, put them in cold water, and wash and beard them; put them into the liquor which came from them in a stew-pan, with a blade of mace, and some butter rolled in flour, and a little lemon; boil them up, then put in cream in proportion, and boil it all together gently; take the lemon and mace out, squeeze the juice of the lemon into the sauce, then serve it in your

boats

boats or basons. Make CELLERY-SAUCE thus: Take the white part of the cellery; cut it about one inch long; boil it in some water till it is tender, then take as much veal broth as you want, a blade of mace, and thicken it with a little flour and butter; put in as much cream as broth; boil them up gently together; put in your cellery, and boil it up; then pour it into your boats.

Sauce for a boiled Goose.

SAUCE for a boiled goose must be either onions or cabbage, first boiled, and then stewed in butter for five minutes.

Sauce for boiled Ducks or Rabbits.

OVER boiled ducks or rabbits you must pour boiled onions, which do thus: Take the onions, peel them, and boil them in a great deal of water; shift your water, then let them boil about two hours; take them up, and throw them into a cullender to drain, then with a knife chop them on a board, and rub them through a cullender; put them into a sauce-pan, just shake a little flour over them, put in a little milk or cream, with a good piece of butter, and a little salt; set them over the fire, and when the butter is melted they are enough. But if you would have onion-sauce in half an hour, take your onions, peel them, and cut them in thin slices, put them into milk and water, and when the water boils, they will be done in twenty minutes, then throw them into a cullender to drain, and chop them and put them into a sauce-pan; shake in a little flour, with a little cream if you have it, and a good piece of butter; stir all together over the fire till the butter is melted, and they will be very fine. This sauce is very good with roast mutton, and it is the best way of boiling onions.

To bake a Leg of Beef.

Do it just in the same manner as before directed in the making gravy for soups, &c.; and when it is baked, strain it through a coarse sieve. Pick out all the sinews and fat, put them into a sauce-pan with a few spoonfuls of the gravy, a little red wine, a piece of butter rolled in flour, and some mustard; shake your sauce-pan often, and when the sauce is hot and thick, dish it up, and send it to table. It is a pretty dish.

To bake an Ox's Head.

Do just in the same manner as the leg of beef is directed to be done in making the gravy for soups, &c. and it does full as well for the same uses. If it should be too strong for any thing you want it for, it is only putting some hot water to it. Cold water will spoil it.

CHAP.

CHAP. V.

MADE-DISHES.

Rules to be observed in all Made-Dishes.

FIRST, that the stew-pans, or sauce-pans, and covers, be very clean, free from sand, and well tinned; and that all the white sauces have a little tartness; put every ingredient into your white sauce, and have it of a proper thickness and well boiled before any eggs and cream are put in, for they add but little to the thickness; do not stir it with a spoon after they are in, nor set your pan on the fire, or it will gather at the bottom, and be in lumps; but hold your pan a good height from the fire, and keep shaking the pan round one way, it will keep the sauce from curdling; and be sure you do not let it boil.

And as to brown sauce, take great care no fat swims at the top, but that it be all smooth alike, and about as thick as good cream, and not to taste of one thing more than another. As to pepper and salt, season to your palate, but do not put too much of either, for that will take away the fine flavour of every thing.

When you use fried force-meat balls, put them on a sieve to drain the fat from them, and never let them boil in your sauce, it will give them a greasy look, and soften the balls; the best way is to put them in after your meat is dished up.

As to most made-dishes, you must put in what you think proper to enlarge it, or make it good; as mushrooms pickled, dried, fresh, or powdered; truffles, morels, cock's-combs stewed, ox-palates cut in small bits, artichoke-bottoms, either pickled, fresh boiled, or dried ones softened in warm water, each cut in four pieces, asparagus-tops, the yolks of hard eggs, force-meat balls, &c. The best things to give a sauce tartness are mushroom-pickle, white walnut-pickle, elder-vinegar, lemon-juice, or lemon-pickle.

To make Lemon-Pickle.

TAKE two dozen of lemons, grate off the out-rinds very thin, cut them in four quarters, but leave the bottoms whole, rub on them equally half a pound of bay salt, and spread them on a large pewter dish, put them in a cool oven, or let them dry gradually by the fire till all the juice is dried into the peels, then put them into a pitcher well glazed; with one ounce of mace, half an ounce of cloves beat fine, one ounce of nutmeg cut in thin slices, four ounces of garlic peeled, half a pint of mustard-seed bruised a little, and tied in a muslin bag; pour two quarts of boiling white wine vinegar upon them, close the pitcher well up, and let it stand five or six days by the fire; shake it well up every day, then tie it up, and let it stand for three months to take off the bitter; when you bottle it, put the pickle and lemon in a hair sieve, press them well to get out the liquor, and let it stand till another day, then pour off the fine, and bottle it; let the other stand three or four days, and it will refine itself, pour it off and bottle it, let it stand again and bottle it, till the whole is refined. It may be put in any white sauce, and will not hurt the colour. It is very good for fish-sauce and made-dishes; a tea-spoonful is enough for white, and two for brown sauce for a fowl; it is a most useful pickle, and gives a pleasant flavour. Be sure you put it in before you thicken the sauce or put any cream in, lest the sharpness make it curdle.

Browning for Made-Dishes.

BEAT small a quarter of a pound of treble-refined sugar, put it in a clean iron frying-pan, with an ounce of butter, set it over a clear fire, mix it very well together all the time; when it begins to be frothy, the sugar is melted; hold it higher over the fire; have ready a pint of red wine; when the sugar and butter is of a deep brown, pour in a little of the wine, and stir it well together, then add more wine, keep it stirring all the time, put in half an ounce of Jamaica pepper, six cloves, four quarters of chalots peeled, two or three blades of mace, three spoonfuls of mushroom catchup, a little salt, the rind of a lemon pared thin; boil them slowly for ten minutes, pour it into a bason, and when cold take off the scum and bottle the liquor.

To dress Scotch Collops.

TAKE a piece of fillet of veal, cut it in thin pieces, about as big as a crown-piece, but very thin; shake a little flour over it, then put a little butter in a frying-pan, and melt it; put in your collops, and fry them quick till they are brown, then lay them in a dish: have ready a good ragoo made thus: Take a little butter in your stew-pan, and melt it, then add a spoonful of flour, stir it about till it is smooth, then put in a sufficient quantity of good brown gravy; season it with pepper and salt, put in some veal sweet-breads, force-meat balls, truffles and morels, ox palates, and mushrooms; stew them gently for half an hour, add the juice of half a lemon to it; put it over the collops, and garnish with small rashers of bacon curled round a skewer. Some like the Scotch collops made thus: Put the collops into the ragoo, and stew them for five minutes.

To dress White Collops.

Cut the veal the same as for Scotch collops; throw them into a stew-pan; put some boiling water over them, and stir them about, then strain them off; take a little good veal broth, and thicken it; add a bundle of sweet herbs, with some mace; put sweetbread, force-meat balls, and fresh mushrooms; if no fresh to be had, use pickled ones washed in warm water; stew them about fifteen minutes; add the yolk of an egg, and some cream; beat them well together with some nutmeg grated, and keep stirring it till it boils up; add a squeeze of a lemon, then put it in your dish. Garnish with lemon.

To dress a Fillet of Veal with Collops.

For an alteration, take a small fillet of veal, cut what collops you want, then take the udder, and fill it with force-meat, roll it round, tie it with a pack-thread across, and roast it; lay your collops in the dish, and lay your udder in the middle. Garnish your dishes with lemon.

Scotch Collops à la Françoise.

Take a leg of veal, cut it very thin, lard it with bacon, then take half a pint of ale boiling, and pour over it till the blood is out, and then pour the ale into a bason; take a few sweet herbs chopped small, strew them over the veal, and fry it in butter, flour it a little till enough, then pour it into a dish, and pour the butter away, toast little thin pieces of bacon and lay round, pour the ale into the stew-pan with two anchovies, then beat up the yolks of two eggs and stir in, with a little nutmeg, some pepper, and a piece of butter; shake all together till thick, and then pour it into the dish. Garnish with lemon.

To make a Savoury Dish of Veal.

Cut large collops out of a leg of veal, spread them abroad on a dresser, hack them with the back of a knife, and dip them in the yolks of eggs; season them with cloves, mace, nutmeg, and pepper, beat fine; make force-meat with some of your veal, beef-suet, oysters chopped, sweet herbs shred fine, and the aforesaid spice; strew all these over your collops, roll and tie them up, put them on skewers, tie them to a spit, and roast them; to the rest of your force-meat add a raw egg or two, roll them in balls, and fry them; put them in your dish with your meat when roasted, and make the sauce with strong broth, an anchovy, a shalot, a little white wine, and some spice. Let it stew, and thicken it with a piece of butter rolled in

sour; pour the sauce into the dish, lay the meat in, and garnish with lemon.

Italian Collops.

PREPARE a fillet of veal, cut into thin slices, cut off the skin and fat, lard them with bacon, fry them brown, then take them out and lay them in a dish, pour out all the butter, take a quarter of a pound of butter and melt it in the pan, then strew in a large spoonful of flour; stir it till it is brown, and pour in three pints of good gravy, a bundle of sweet herbs, and an onion, which you must take out soon; let it boil a little, then put in the collops, let them stew half a quarter of an hour, put in some force-meat balls fried, and a few pickled mushrooms, truffles and morels; stir all together for a minute or two till it is thick, and then dish it up. Garnish with lemon.

To do them White.

AFTER you have cut your veal in thin slices, lard it with bacon; season it with cloves, mace, nutmeg, pepper and salt, some grated bread, and sweet herbs. Stew the knuckle in as little liquor as you can, a bunch of sweet herbs, some whole pepper, a blade of mace, and four cloves; then take a pint of the broth, stew the cutlets in it, and add to it some mushrooms, a piece of butter rolled in flour, and the yolk of an egg, and a gill of cream; stir all together till it is thick, and then dish it up. Garnish with lemon.

Beef Collops.

TAKE some rump steaks, or any tender piece, cut like Scotch collops, only larger, hack them a little with a knife, and flour them; put a little butter in a stew-pan, and melt it, then put in your collops, and fry them quick for about two minutes; put in a pint of gravy, a little butter rolled in flour; season with pepper and salt; cut four pickled cucumbers in thin slices, half a walnut, and a few capers, a little onion shred very fine; stew them five minutes, then put them into a hot dish, and send them to table. You may put half a glass of white wine into it.

To make Force-Meat Balls.

FORCE-MEAT balls are a great addition to all made-dishes, made thus: Take half a pound of veal, and half a pound of suet, cut fine, and beat in a marble mortar or wooden bowl; have a few sweet herbs and parsley shred fine, a little mace dried and beat fine, a small nutmeg grated, or half a large one, a little lemon-peel cut very fine, a little pepper and salt, and the yolks of two eggs; mix all these well together, then roll them

them in little round balls, and some in little long balls; roll them in flour, and fry them brown. If they are for any thing of white sauce, put a little water in a sauce-pan, and when the water boils put them in, and let them boil for a few minutes, but never fry them for white sauce.

A less quantity may be made, by using the ingredients in proportion.

Truffles and Morels, good in Sauces and Soups.

TAKE half an ounce of truffles and morels, let them be well washed in warm water, to get the sand and dirt out, then simmer them in two or three spoonfuls of water for a few minutes, then put them with the liquor into the sauce. They thicken both sauce and soup, and give it a fine flavour.

To stew Ox Palates.

STEW them very tender, which must be done by putting them into cold water, and letting them stew very softly over a slow fire; then take off the two skins, cut them in pieces, and put them either into your made-dish or soup; and cock's-combs and artichoke-bottoms, cut small, and put into the made-dish. Garnish your dishes with lemon, sweet breads stewed for white dishes, and fried for brown ones, and cut in little pieces.

To ragoo Ox Palates.

TAKE four ox palates, and boil them very tender, clean them well, cut some in square pieces, and some long; then make a rich cooley thus: Put a piece of butter in your stew-pan, and melt it, put a large spoonful of flour to it, stir it well till it is smooth; then put a quart of good gravy to it, chop three shalots, and put in a gill of Lisbon, cut some lean ham very fine and put in, also half a lemon; boil them twenty minutes, then strain it through a sieve, put it into your pan, and the palates, with some force-meat balls, truffles and morels, pickled or fresh mushrooms stewed in gravy; season with pepper and salt to your liking, and toss them up five or six minutes; then dish them up. Garnish with lemon or beet-root.

To fricassee Ox Palates.

AFTER boiling your palates very tender, (which you must do by setting them on in cold water, and letting them do softly,) then blanch and scrape them clean; take mace, nutmeg, cloves, and pepper beat fine, rub them all over with those, and with crumbs of bread; have ready some butter in a stew-pan, and when it is hot put in the palates; fry them brown on both sides, then pour out the fat, and put to them some mutton or beef gravy,

gravy, enough for sauce, an anchovy, a little nutmeg, a little piece of butter rolled in flour, and the juice of a lemon; let it simmer all together for a quarter of an hour; dish it up, and garnish with lemon.

To roast Ox Palates.

HAVING boiled your palates tender, blanch them, cut them into slices about two inches long, lard half with bacon, then have ready two or three pigeons, and two or three chicken-peepers, draw them, truss them, and fill them with force-meat; let half of them be nicely larded; spit them on a bird-spit in this order: a bird, a palate, a sage-leaf, and a piece of bacon; and so on; take cock's-combs and lamb-stones, parboiled and blanched, lard them with little bits of bacon, large oysters parboiled, and each one larded with one piece of bacon; put these on a skewer, with a little piece of bacon and a sage-leaf between them, tie them on a spit, and roast them, then beat up the yolks of three eggs, some nutmeg, a little salt, and crumbs of bread; baste them with these all the time they are roasting, and have ready two sweetbreads, each cut in two, some artichoke-bottoms cut into four and fried, and then rub the dish with shalots: lay the birds in the middle, piled upon one another, and lay the other things all separate by themselves round about in the dish. Have ready for sauce a pint of good gravy, a quarter of a pint of red wine, an anchovy, the oyster liquor, a piece of butter rolled in flour; boil all these together and pour into the dish, with a little juice of lemon. Garnish your dish with lemon.

To fricando Ox Palates.

WHEN you have washed and cleaned your palates, cut them in square pieces, lard them with little bits of bacon, fry them in hog's lard, a pretty brown, and put them in a sieve to drain the fat from them, then take better than half a pint of beef gravy, one spoonful of red wine, half as much of browning, a little lemon-pickle, one anchovy, a shalot, and a bit of horse-radish; give them a boil, and strain your gravy, then put in your palates, and stew them half an hour, make your sauce pretty thick, dish them up, and lay round them stewed spinage pressed and cut like little sippets, and serve them up.

To make a Brown Fricassee.

YOU must take your rabbits and chickens, and skin the rabbits, but not the chickens, then cut them into small pieces, and rub them over with yolks of eggs. Have ready some grated bread, a little beaten mace, and a little grated nutmeg mixed together, and then roll them in it; put a little butter into a
stew-

stew-pan, and when it is melted put in your meat. Fry it of a fine brown, and take care they do not stick to the bottom of the pan; then pour the butter from them, and pour in half a pint of brown gravy, a glass of white wine, a few mushrooms, or two spoonfuls of the pickle, a little salt (if wanted), and a piece of butter rolled in flour. When it is of a fine thickness, dish it up, and send it to table. You may add truffles and morels, and cock's-combs.

To make a White Fricassee.

TAKE two chickens, and cut them in small pieces; put them in warm water to draw out the blood, then put them into some good veal broth; if no veal broth, a little boiling water, and stew them gently with a bundle of sweet herbs, and a blade of mace, till they are tender; then take out the sweet herbs, add a little flour and butter, boiled together, to thicken it a little, then add a quarter of a pint of cream, and the yolk of an egg beat very fine; some pickled mushrooms: the best way is to put some fresh mushrooms in at first; if no fresh, then pickled; keep stirring it till it boils up, then add the juice of half a lemon, stir it well to keep it from curdling, then put it in your dish. Garnish with lemon.

To fricassee Rabbits, Lamb, or Veal.

OBSERVE the directions given in the preceding article.

A second Way to make a White Fricassee.

YOU must take two or three rabbits, or chickens, skin them, and lay them in warm water, and dry them with a clean cloth. Put them into a stew-pan with a blade or two of mace, a little black and white pepper, an onion, a little bundle of sweet herbs, and do but just cover them with water; stew them till they are tender, then with a fork take them out, strain the liquor, and put them into the pan again with half a pint of the liquor, and half a pint of cream, the yolks of two eggs beat well, half a nutmeg grated, a glass of white wine, a little piece of butter rolled in flour, and a gill of mushrooms; keep stirring all together, all the while one way, till it is smooth and of a fine thickness, and then dish it up. Add what you please.

A third Way of making a White Fricassee.

TAKE three chickens, skin them, cut them into small pieces, that is, every joint asunder; lay them in warm water for a quarter of an hour, take them out and dry them with a cloth, then put them into a stew-pan with milk and water, and boil them tender; take a pint of good cream, a quarter of a pound of butter, and stir it till it is thick, then let it stand till it is cool, and put to it a little beaten mace, half a nutmeg grated, a little salt, and a few mushrooms; stir all together, then take the chickens out of the stew-pan, throw away what they are boiled in, clean the pan, and put in the chickens and sauce together; keep the pan shaking round till they are quite hot, and dish them up. Garnish with lemon.

To fricassee Rabbits, Lamb, Sweetbreads, or Tripe.

Do them the same way.

Another Way to fricassee Tripe.

TAKE a piece of double tripe, and cut it in pieces of about two inches; put them into a sauce-pan of water, with an onion and a bundle of sweet herbs; boil it till it is quite tender, then have ready a bishemel made thus: Take some lean ham, cut it in thin pieces, and put it in a stew-pan, and some veal, having first cut off all the fat, put it over the ham; cut an onion in slices, some carrot and turnip, a little thyme, cloves, and mace, and some fresh mushrooms chopped; put a little milk at the bottom, and draw it gently over the fire; be careful it does not scorch; then put in a quart of milk, and half a pint of cream, stew it gently for an hour, thicken it with a little flour and milk, season it with salt and a very little Cayenne pepper, then strain it off through a tammy, put your tripe into it, toss it up, and add some force-meat balls, mushrooms, and oysters blanched; then put it into your dish, and garnish with fried oysters, or sweetbreads, or lemons.

To make a Fricassee of Calves' Feet and Chaldron, after the Italian Way.

TAKE the crumb of half a quartern loaf, one pound of suet, a large onion, two or three handfuls of parsley, mince it very small, season it with salt and pepper, three or four cloves of garlic, mix with eight or ten eggs; then stuff the chaldron; take the feet, and put them into a deep stew-pan: it must stew upon a slow fire till the bones are loose; then take two quarts of green peas, and put in the liquor; and when done, you must thicken it with the yolks of two eggs, and the juice of a lemon. It must be seasoned with pepper, salt, mace, and onion, some parsley, and garlic. You must serve it up with the abovesaid pudding in the middle of the dish, and garnish the dish with fried suckers and sliced onion.

A Fricassee of Pigeons.

TAKE eight pigeons new killed, cut them in small pieces, and put them into a stew-pan with a pint of white wine and a

pint

pint of water. Season your pigeons with salt and pepper, a blade or two of mace, an onion, a bundle of sweet herbs, a good piece of butter just rolled in a very little flour; cover it close, and let them stew till there is just enough for sauce, and then take out the onion and sweet herbs, beat up the yolks of three eggs, grate half a nutmeg in, and with your spoon push the birds all to one side of the pan, and the gravy to the other side, and stir in the eggs; keep them stirring for fear of turning to curds; and when the sauce is fine and thick, shake all together, and then put the pigeons into the dish, pour the sauce over them, and have ready some slices of bacon toasted, and fried oysters; throw the oysters all over, and lay the bacon round. Garnish with lemon.

A Fricassee of Lamb stones and Sweetbreads.

HAVE ready some lamb-stones blanched, parboiled, and sliced, and flour two or three sweetbreads; if very thick, cut them in two; the yolks of six hard eggs whole, a few pistachio-nut kernels, and a few large oysters: fry these all of a fine brown, then pour out all the butter, and add a pint of drawn gravy, the lamb-stones, some asparagus-tops about an inch long, some grated nutmeg, a little pepper and salt, two shalots shred small, and a glass of white wine. Stew all these together for ten minutes, then add the yolks of three eggs beat very fine, with a little cream, and a little beaten mace; stir all together till it is of a fine thickness, and then dish it up. Garnish with lemon.

Lamb Cutlets fricasseed.

TAKE a leg of lamb, cut it in thin cutlets across the grain, put them in a stew-pan; in the mean time make some good broth with the bones and shank, &c. enough to cover the meat, put it into the cover with a bundle of sweet herbs, an onion, a little cloves and mace tied in a muslin rag; stew them gently for ten minutes; take out the meat, skim the fat off, and take out the sweet herbs and mace, thicken it with butter rolled in flour, season it with salt and a little Cayenne pepper, put in a few mushrooms, truffles and morels clean washed, some forcemeat balls, three yolks of eggs beat up in half a pint of cream, some nutmeg grated; keep stirring it one way till it is thick and smooth; put in your cutlets, give them a toss up, take them out with a fork and lay them in a dish, pour the sauce over them. Garnish with lemon and beet-root.

To hash a Calf's Head.

BOIL the head almost enough, then take the best half, and with a sharp knife take it nicely from the bone, with the two eyes.

eyes. Lay it in a little deep dish before a good fire, and take great care no ashes fall into it, and then hack it with a knife crofs and crofs; grate some nutmeg all over, the yolks of two eggs, a very little pepper and salt, a few sweet herbs, some crumbs of bread, and a little lemon-peel chopped very fine, baste it with a little butter, then baste it again; keep the dish turning that it may be all brown alike; cut the other half and tongue into little thin bits, and set on a pint of drawn gravy in a sauce-pan, a little bundle of sweet herbs, an onion, a little pepper and salt, a glass of white wine, and two shalots; boil all these together a few minutes, then strain it through a sieve, and put it into a clean stew-pan with the hash. Flour the meat before you put it in, and put in a few mushrooms, a spoonful of pickle, two spoonfuls of catchup, and a few truffles and morels; stir all these together for a few minutes, then beat up half the brains, and stir into the stew-pan, and a little piece of butter rolled in flour. Take the other half of the brains, and beat them up with a little lemon-peel cut fine, a little nutmeg grated, a little beaten mace, a little thyme shred small, a little parsley, the yolk of an egg, and have some good dripping boiling in a stew-pan; then fry the brains in little cakes, about as big as a crown-piece. Fry about twenty oysters dipped in the yolk of an egg, toast some slices of bacon, fry a few force-meat balls, and have ready a hot dish; if pewter, over a few coals; if china, over a pan of hot water. Pour in your hash, then lay in your toasted head, throw the force-meat balls over the hash, and garnish the dish with fried oysters, the fried brains, and lemon; throw the rest over the hash, lay the bacon round the dish, and send it to table.

To hash a Calf's Head white.

TAKE a pint of white gravy, a large wine-glass of white wine, a little beaten mace, a little nutmeg, and a little salt; throw into your hash a few mushrooms, a few truffles and morels first parboiled; a few artichoke-bottoms, and asparagus-tops, (if you have them,) a good piece of butter rolled in flour, the yolks of two eggs, half a pint of cream, and one spoonful of mushroom catchup; stir it all together very carefully till it is of a fine thickness; then pour it into your dish, and lay the other half of the head, as before mentioned, in the middle, and garnish as before directed, with fried oysters, brains, lemon, and force-meat balls fried.

Calf's Head Hash another Way, less expensive and troublesome.

PARBOIL a calf's head; cut out the cheek-bones to broil, cut all the rest to pieces, season with cloves, mace, pepper, and
salt;

salt; toss it up in some good gravy till enough. You may add some ox palates, sweetbreads, mushrooms, force-meat balls, &c. Then make the gravy a proper thickness, and toss it up a second time, and it is fit for the table. Fry the brains in butter to lay round the dish; garnish with lemon.

To hash Venison.

TAKE it when cold, cut it into thin slices, lay it into a stew-pan, with a little shalot chopped fine, a little chyan, and salt; its own gravy or any other good gravy, as much red wine as you have gravy, let there be as much as will cover it, just give it a boil, lay it on a hot dish, and send up currant-jelly with it.

To hash Beef.

CUT your beef in very thin slices, take a little of your gravy that runs from it, put it into a tossing-pan with a tea-spoonful of lemon-pickle, a large one of walnut-catchup, the same of browning, slice a shalot in, and put it over the fire; when it boils, put in your beef; shake it over the fire till it is quite hot, the gravy is not to be thickened, slice in a small pickled cucumber; garnish with scraped horse-radish or pickled onions.

To make a Mutton Hash.

CUT your mutton in little bits as thin as you can, strew a little flour over it, have ready some gravy (enough for sauce) wherein sweet herbs, onions, pepper, and salt, have been boiled; strain it, put in your meat, with a little piece of butter rolled in flour, and a little salt, a shalot cut fine, a few capers and gerkins chopped fine; toss all together for a minute or two; have ready some bread toasted and cut into thin sippets, lay them round the dish, and pour in your hash. Garnish your dish with pickles and horse-radish.

N. B. Some love a glass of red wine, or walnut-pickle. You may put just what you will into a hash. If the sippets are toasted, it is better.

To hash Veal.

CUT your veal in thin round slices, the size of a half-crown; put into a sauce-pan a little gravy and lemon-peel cut very fine, a tea-spoonful of lemon-pickle, put it over the fire, thicken it with flour and butter; when it boils, put in your veal; just before you dish it, put in a spoonful of cream; lay sippets round your dish, and serve it up.

To hash a Turkey.

TAKE off the legs, cut the thighs in two pieces, cut off the pinions and breast in pretty large pieces, take off the skin, or it

will

will give the gravy a greafy tafte, put it into a ftew-pan, with a pint of gravy, a tea-fpoonful of lemon-pickle, a flice of the end of a lemon, and a little beaten mace; boil your turkey fix or feven minutes, (if you boil it any longer it will make it hard,) then put it on your difh, thicken your gravy with flour and butter, mix the yolks of two eggs with a fpoonful of thick cream, put it in your gravy, fhake it over your fire till it is quite hot, but do not let it boil, ftrain it, and pour it over your turkey; lay fippets round, ferve it up, and garnifh with lemon or parfley.

To hafh a Fowl.

CUT it up as for eating, put it in a toffing-pan, with half a pint of gravy, a tea-fpoonful of lemon-pickle, a little mufhroom catchup, a flice of lemon, thicken it with flour and butter; juft before you difh it up, put in a fpoonful of good cream; lay fippets round your difh, and ferve it up.

To hafh a Woodcock.

CUT your woodcock up as for eating, work the entrails very fine with the back of a fpoon, mix it with a fpoonful of red wine, the fame of water, half a fpoonful of vinegar, cut an onion in flices and pull it into rings, roll a little butter in flour, put them all in your toffing-pan, and fhake it over the fire till it boils, then put in your woodcock, and when it is thoroughly hot, lay it in your difh with fippets round it, ftrain the fauce over the woodcock, and lay on the onion in rings; it is a pretty corner-difh for dinner or fupper.

To hafh a Wild Duck.

CUT it up as for eating, put it in a toffing-pan, with a fpoonful of good gravy, the fame of red wine, a little of your onion-fauce, or an onion fliced exceeding thin; when it has boiled two or three minutes, lay the duck in your difh, pour the gravy over it, it muft not be thickened, you may add a tea-fpoonful of caper liquor, or a little browning.

To hafh a Hare.

CUT your hare in fmall pieces, if you have any of the pudding left, rub it fmall, put to it a large glafs of red wine, the fame quantity of water, half an anchovy chopped fmall, an onion ftuck with four cloves, a quarter of a pound of butter rolled in flour, fhake them all together over a flow fire, till your hare is thoroughly hot; it is a bad cuftom to let any kind of hafh boil longer, it makes the meat eat hard; fend your hare to the table in a deep difh, lay fippets round it, but take out the onion, and ferve it up.

To bake a Calf's Head.

TAKE the head, pick it and wash it very clean; take an earthen dish large enough to lay the head on, rub a little piece of butter all over the dish, then lay some long iron skewers across the top of the dish, and lay the head on them; skewer up the meat in the middle that it do not lie on the dish, then grate some nutmeg all over it, a few sweet herbs shred small, some crumbs of bread, a little lemon-peel cut fine, and then flour it all over; stick pieces of butter in the eyes and all over the head, and flour it again. Let it be well baked, and of a fine brown; you may throw a little pepper and salt over it, and put into the dish a piece of beef cut small, a bundle of sweet herbs, an onion, some whole pepper, a blade of mace, two cloves, a pint of water, and boil the brains with some sage. When the head is enough, lay it on a dish, and set it to the fire to keep warm, then stir all together in the dish, and boil it in a sauce-pan; strain it off, put it into the sauce-pan again, add a piece of butter rolled in flour, and the sage in the brains chopped fine, a spoonful of catchup, and two spoonfuls of red wine; boil them together; take the brains, beat them well, and mix them with the sauce; pour it into the dish, and send it to table. You must bake the tongue with the head, and do not cut it out; it will lie the handsomer in the dish.

To bake a Sheep's Head.

Do it the same way, and it eats very well.

To dress a Lamb's Head.

BOIL the head and pluck tender, but do not let the liver be too much done. Take the head up, hack it cross and cross with a knife, grate some nutmeg over it, and lay it in a dish, before a good fire; then grate some crumbs of bread, some sweet herbs rubbed, a little lemon-peel chopped fine, a very little pepper and salt, and baste it with a little butter; then throw a little flour over it, and just as it is done do the same, baste it and dredge it. Take half the liver, the lights, the heart and tongue, chop them very small, with six or eight spoonfuls of gravy or water; first shake some flour over the meat, and stir it together, then put in the gravy or water, a good piece of butter rolled in a little flour, a little pepper and salt, and what runs from the head in the dish; simmer all together a few minutes, and add half a spoonful of vinegar, pour it into your dish, lay the head in the middle of the mince-meat, have ready the other half of the liver cut thin, with some slices of bacon broiled, and lay round the head. Garnish the dish with lemon, and send it to table.

E

Calf's Head Surprize.

TAKE a calf's head with the skin on, take a sharp knife and raise off the skin with as much meat from the bone as you can possibly get, so that it may appear like a whole head when stuffed, then make a force-meat in the following manner: take half a pound of veal, a pound of beef-suet, the crumb of a small loaf, half a pound of fat bacon, beat them well in a mortar, with some sweet herbs and parsley shred fine, some cloves, mace and nutmeg beat fine, some salt and Cayenne pepper enough to season it, the yolks of four eggs beat up and mixt all together in a force-meat; stuff the head with it, and skewer it tight at each end; then put into a deep pot or pan, and put two quarts of water, half a pint of white wine, a blade or two of mace, a bundle of sweet herbs, and an anchovy, two spoonfuls of walnut and mushroom catchup, the same quantity of lemon-pickle, a little salt and pepper; lay a coarse paste over it to keep in the steam, and put it for two hours and a half in a quick oven; when you take it out, lay the head in a soup-dish, skim off the fat from the gravy and strain it through a sieve into a stew-pan, thicken it with butter rolled in flour; and when it has boiled a few minutes, put in the yolks of four eggs well beaten and minced with half a pint of cream; have ready boiled some force-meat balls, half an ounce of truffles and morels, but do not put them into the gravy; pour the gravy over the head, and garnish with force-meat balls, truffles, morels, and mushrooms.

A Calf's Head dressed after the Dutch Way.

TAKE half a pound of Spanish peas, lay them in water a night; then one pound of whole rice, mix the peas and rice together, and lay it round the head in a deep dish; then take two quarts of water seasoned with pepper and salt, and coloured with saffron; then send it to bake.

To stew a Lamb's or Calf's Head.

FIRST wash it and pick it very clean, lay it in water for an hour, take out the brains, and with a sharp penknife carefully take out the bones and the tongue, but be careful you do not break the meat; then take out the two eyes, and take two pounds of veal and two pounds of beef-suet, a very little thyme, a good piece of lemon-peel minced, a nutmeg grated, and two anchovies; chop all very well together, grate two stale rolls, and mix all together with the yolks of four eggs; save enough of this meat to make about twenty balls, take half a pint of fresh mushrooms clean peeled and washed, the yolks of six eggs chopped, half a pint of oysters clean washed, or pickled

pickled cockles; mix all these together; but first stew your oysters, put the force-meat into the head and close it, tie it tight with packthread and put it into a deep stew-pan, and put to it two quarts of gravy, with a blade or two of mace. Cover it close, and let it stew two hours; in the mean time beat up the brains with some lemon-peel cut fine, a little parsley chopped, half a nutmeg grated, and the yolk of an egg; have some dripping boiling, fry half the brains in little cakes, and fry the balls, keep them both hot by the fire; take half an ounce of truffles and morels, then strain the gravy the head was stewed in, put the truffles and morels to it with the liquor, and a few mushrooms; boil all together, then put in the rest of the brains that are not fried, stew them together for a minute or two, pour it over the head, and lay the fried brains and balls round it. Garnish with lemon. You may fry about twelve oysters and put over.

To grill a Calf's Head.

WASH your calf's head clean, and boil it almost enough, then take it up and hash one half, the other half rub over with the yolk of an egg, a little pepper and salt, strew over it bread crumbs, parsley chopped small, and a little grated lemon-peel, set it before the fire, and keep basting it all the time to make the froth rise; when it is a fine light brown, dish up your hash, and lay the grilled side upon it.

Blanch your tongue, slit it down the middle, and lay it on a soup-plate; skin the brains, boil them with a little sage and parsley; chop them fine, and mix them with some melted butter and a spoonful of cream, make them hot, and pour them over the tongue, serve them up, and they are sauce for the head.

A Breast of Veal in Hedge-podge.

TAKE a breast of veal, cut the brisket into little pieces, and every bone asunder, then flour it, and put half a pound of good butter into a stew-pan; when it is hot, throw in the veal, fry it all over of a fine light brown, and then have ready a tea-kettle of water boiling; pour it in the stew-pan, fill it up and stir it round, throw in a pint of green peas, a fine lettuce whole, clean washed, two or three blades of mace, a little whole pepper tied in a muslin rag, a little bundle of sweet herbs, a small onion stuck with a few cloves, and a little salt. Cover it close, and let it stew an hour, or till it is boiled to your palate, if you would have soup made of it; if you would only have sauce to eat with the veal, you must stew it till there is just as much as you would have for sauce, and season it with salt to your palate; take out the onion, sweet herbs, and spice, and pour it all together into your dish. It is a fine dish. If you have no peas, pare three or four cucumbers, scoop out the pulp, and cut it into little pieces, and take four or five heads of celery, clean washed, and cut the white part small; when you have no lettuces, take the little hearts of savoys, or the little young sprouts that grow on the old cabbage-stalks, about as big as the top of your thumb.

N. B. If you would make a very fine dish of it, fill the inside of your lettuce with force meat, and tie the top close with a thread; stew it till there is but just enough for sauce; set the lettuce in the middle and the veal round, and pour the sauce all over it. Garnish your dish with rasped bread made into figures with your fingers. This is the cheapest way of dressing a breast of veal to be good, and serve a number of people.

To collar a Breast of Veal.

TAKE a very sharp knife, and nicely take out all the bones, but take great care you do not cut the meat through: pick all the fat and meat off the bones, then grate some nutmeg all over the inside of the veal, a very little beaten mace, a little pepper and salt, a few sweet herbs shred small, some parsley, a little lemon-peel shred small, a few crumbs of bread, and the bits of fat picked off the bones; roll it up tight, stick one skewer in to hold it together, but do it cleverly, that it stands upright in the dish; tie a packthread across it to hold it together, spit it, then roll the caul all round it, and roast it. An hour and a quarter will do it. When it has been about an hour at the fire, take off the caul, dredge it with flour, baste it well with fresh butter, and let it be of a fine brown. For sauce take two-pennyworth of gravy-beef, cut it and hack it well, then flour it, fry it a little brown, then pour into your stew-pan some boiling water, stir it well together, then fill your pan two parts full of water; put in an onion, a bundle of sweet herbs, a little crust of bread toasted, two or three blades of mace, four cloves, some whole pepper, and the bones of the veal. Cover it close, and let it stew till it is quite rich and thick; then strain it, boil it up with some truffles and morels, a few mushrooms, a spoonful of catchup, two or three bottoms of artichokes, if you have them; add a little salt, just enough to season the gravy, take the packthread off the veal, and set it upright in the dish; cut the sweetbread into four, and broil it of a fine brown, with a few forcemeat balls fried; lay these round the dish, and pour in the sauce. Garnish the dish with lemon, and send it to table.

To collar a Breast of Mutton.

Do it the same way, and it eats very well; but you must take off the skin.

Another

Another good Way to dress a Breast of Mutton.

COLLAR as before; roast it, and baste it with half a pint of red wine, when that is all soaked in, baste it well with butter, have a little good gravy, set the mutton upright in the dish, pour in the gravy, have sweet-sauce as for venison, and send it to table. Do not garnish the dish, but be sure to take the skin off the mutton.

The inside of a surloin of beef is very good done this way. If you do not like the wine, a quart of milk and a quarter of a pound of butter put into the dripping-pan does full as well to baste it.

To ragoo a Leg of Mutton.

TAKE all the skin and fat off, cut it very thin the right way of the grain, then butter your stew-pan, and shake some flour into it; slice half a lemon and half an onion, cut them very small, a little bundle of sweet herbs, and a blade of mace. Put all together with your meat into the pan, stir it a minute or two, and then put in six spoonfuls of gravy, and have ready an anchovy minced small; mix it with some butter and flour, stir it all together for six minutes, and then dish it up.

To ragoo Hogs' Feet and Ears.

TAKE your ears out of the pickle they are soused in, or boil them till they are tender, then cut them into little thin bits, about two inches long, and about as thick as a quill; put them into your stew-pan with half a pint of good gravy, or as much as will cover them, a glass of white wine, a good deal of mustard, a good piece of butter rolled in flour, and a little pepper and salt; stir all together till it is of a fine thickness, and then dish it up. The hogs' feet must not be stewed but boiled tender, then slit them in two, and put the yolk of an egg over and crumbs of bread, and broil or fry them; put the ragoo of ears in the middle, and the feet round it.

N. B. They make a very pretty dish fried with butter and mustard, and a little good gravy, if you like it. Then only cut the feet and ears in two. You may add half an onion, cut small.

To ragoo a Neck of Veal.

CUT a neck of veal into steaks, flatten them with a rolling-pin, season them with salt, pepper, cloves, and mace, lard them with bacon, lemon-peel, and thyme, dip them in the yolks of eggs, make a sheet of strong foolscap paper up at the four corners in the form of a dripping-pan; pin up the corners, butter the paper and also the gridiron, and set it over a fire of charcoal; put in your meat, let it do leisurely, keep it basting and turning to keep in the gravy; and when it is enough have ready half a pint of strong gravy, season it high, put in mushrooms and pickles, force-meat balls dipped in the yolks of eggs, oysters stewed and fried, to lay round and at the top of your dish, and then serve it up. If for a brown ragoo, put in red wine. If for a white one, put in white wine, with the yolks of eggs beat up with two or three spoonfuls of cream.

To ragoo a Breast of Veal.

TAKE your breast of veal, put it into a large stew-pan, put in a bundle of sweet herbs, an onion, some black and white pepper, a blade or two of mace, two or three cloves, a very little piece of lemon-peel, and just cover it with water: when it is tender take it up, bone it, put in the bones, boil it up till the gravy is very good, then strain it off, and if you have a little rich beef-gravy, add a quarter of a pint, put in half an ounce of truffles and morels, a spoonful or two of catchup, two or three spoonfuls of white wine, and let them all boil together: in the mean time flour the veal, and fry it in butter till it is of a fine brown, then drain out all the butter, and pour the gravy you are boiling to the veal, with a few mushrooms; boil all together till the sauce is rich and thick, and cut the sweetbread into four. A few force-meat balls are proper in it. Lay the veal in the dish, and pour the sauce all over it. Garnish with lemon.

Or thus: Half roast a breast of veal, then cut it in square pieces; put it into a stew-pan, with half a pint of gravy, a pint of water, a bundle of sweet herbs, an onion stuck with cloves, a little mace, and stew it till it is tender; then take it out, and pull out all the bones, strain the gravy through a sieve, then put it into the stew-pan again, with a spoonful of mustard, some truffles and morels, a sweetbread cut in pieces, one artichoke-bottom, about twenty force-meat balls, some butter rolled in flour, enough to thicken it; boil it up till it is of a proper thickness; season it with pepper and salt, then put in your veal, stew it for five minutes, add the juice of half a lemon, then put your meat into the dish, the ragoo all over it. Garnish with lemon and beet-root.

Another Way to ragoo a Breast of Veal.

You may bone it nicely, flour it, and fry it of a fine brown, then pour the fat out of the pan, and the ingredients as above, with the bones; when enough, take it out, and strain the liquor, then put in your meat again, with the ingredients, as before directed.

MADE PLAIN AND EASY.

To ragoo a Fillet of Veal.

LARD your fillet and half roaſt it, then put it in a toſſing-pan, with two quarts of good gravy, cover it cloſe and let it ſtew till tender, then add one ſpoonful of white wine, one of browning, one of catchup, a tea-ſpoonful of lemon-pickle, a little caper liquor, half an ounce of morels, thicken with flour and butter, lay round it a few yolks of eggs.

To ragoo Sweetbreads.

RUB them over with the yolk of an egg, ſtrew over them bread-crumbs, parſley, thyme, and ſweet-marjoram ſhred ſmall, and pepper and ſalt, make a roll of force-meat like a ſweet-bread, and put it in a veal caul, and roaſt them in a Dutch oven; take ſome brown gravy, and put to it a little lemon-pickle, muſhroom-catchup, and the end of a lemon, boil the gravy, and when the ſweetbreads are enough, lay them in a diſh, with a force-meat in the middle, take the end of the lemon out, and pour the gravy into the diſh, and ſerve them up.

To make a Ragoo of Lamb.

TAKE a fore-quarter of lamb, cut the knuckle-bone off, lard it with little thin bits of bacon, flour it, fry it of a fine brown, and then put it into an earthen pot or ſtew-pan; put to it a quart of broth or good gravy, a bundle of herbs, a little mace, two or three cloves, and a little whole pepper; cover it cloſe, and let it ſtew pretty faſt for half an hour; pour the liquor all out, ſtrain it, keep the lamb hot in the pot till the ſauce is ready. Take half a pint of oyſters, flour them, fry them brown, drain out all the fat clean that you fried them in, ſkim all the fat off the gravy, then pour it in to the oyſters, put in an anchovy, and two ſpoonfuls of either red or white wine; boil all together till there is juſt enough for ſauce, add ſome freſh muſhrooms (if you can get them) and ſome pickled ones, with a ſpoonful of the pickle, or the juice of half a lemon. Lay your lamb in the diſh, and pour the ſauce over it. Garniſh with lemon.

To ragoo a Piece of Beef.

TAKE a large piece of the flank, which has fat at the top, cut ſquare, or any piece that has fat at the top, but no bones. The rump does well. Cut all nicely off the bone (which makes fine ſoup); then take a large ſtew-pan, and with a good piece of butter fry it a little brown all over, flouring your meat well before you put it into the pan, then pour in as much gravy as will cover it, made thus; take about a pound of coarſe beef, a little piece of veal cut ſmall, a bundle of ſweet herbs, an onion,

onion, some whole black pepper and white pepper, two or three large blades of mace, four or five cloves, a piece of carrot, a little piece of bacon steeped in vinegar a little while, a crust of bread toasted brown; put to this a quart of white wine, and let it boil till half is wasted. While this is making, pour a quart of boiling water into the stew-pan, cover it close, and let it be stewing softly; when the gravy is done, strain it, pour it into the pan where the beef is, take an ounce of truffles and morels cut small, some fresh or dried mushrooms cut small, two spoonfuls of catchup, and cover it close. Let all this stew till the sauce is rich and thick; then have ready some artichoke-bottoms cut into four, and a few pickled mushrooms, give them a boil or two, and when your meat is tender, and your sauce quite rich, lay the meat into a dish and pour the sauce over it. You may add a sweetbread cut in six pieces, a palate stewed tender cut into little pieces, some cock's-combs, and a few force-meat balls. These are a great addition, but it will be good without.

N. B. For variety, when the beef is ready, and the gravy put to it, add a large bunch of celery cut small and washed clean, two spoonfuls of catchup, and a glass of red wine. Omit all the other ingredients. When the meat and celery are tender, and the sauce rich and good, serve it up. It is also very good this way: take six large cucumbers, scoop out the seeds, pare them, cut them into slices, and do them just as you do the celery.

To force the Inside of a Sirloin of Beef.

TAKE a sharp knife, and carefully lift up the fat of the inside, take out all the meat close to the bone, chop it small, take a pound of suet and chop fine, about as many crumbs of bread, a little thyme and lemon-peel, a little pepper and salt, half a nutmeg grated, and two shalots chopped fine; mix and beat all very fine in a marble mortar, with a glass of red wine, then put it into the same place, cover it with the skin and fat, skewer it down with fine skewers, and cover it with paper. Do do not take the paper off till the meat is on the dish. Take a quarter of a pint of red wine, two shalots shred small, boil them, and pour into the dish, with the gravy which comes out of the meat; it eats well. Spit your meat before you take out the inside.

Another Way to force a Sirloin.

WHEN it is quite roasted, take it up, and lay it in the dish with the inside uppermost; with a sharp knife lift up the skin, hack and cut the inside very fine, shake a little pepper and salt over it, with two shalots, cover it with the skin, and send it to table. You may add red wine or vinegar, just as you like.

Sirloin

Sirloin of Beef en Epigram.

ROAST a firloin of beef, take it off the fpit, then raife the fkin carefully off, and cut the lean part of the beef out, but obferve not to cut near the ends or fides; hafh the meat in the following manner: cut it into pieces about as big as a crown-piece, put half a pint of gravy into a tofs-pan, an onion chopt fine, two fpoonfuls of catchup, fome pepper and falt, fix fmall pickled cucumbers cut in thin flices, and the gravy that comes from the beef, a little butter rolled in flour, put the meat in, and tofs it up for five minutes, put it on the firloin, and then put the fkin over, and fend it to table. Garnifh with horfe-radifh.

You may do the infide inftead of the outfide, if you pleafe.

To force the Infide of a Rump of Beef.

YOU may do it juft in the fame manner, only lift up the outfide fkin, take the middle of the meat, and do as before directed; put it into the fame place, and with fine fkewers put it down clofe.

To force a Round of Beef.

TAKE a good round of beef, and rub over it a quarter of an hour with two ounces of faltpetre, the fame of bay-falt, half a pound of brown fugar, and a pound of common falt, let it lie in it for ten or twelve days, turn it once every day in the brine, then wafh it well, and make holes in it with a penknife about an inch one from another, and fill one hole with fhred parfley, a fecond with fat pork cut in fmall pieces, and a third with bread-crumbs, beef-marrow, a little mace, nutmeg, pepper, and falt mixed together; then parfley, and fo on till you have filled all the holes; then wrap your beef in a cloth, and bind it with a fillet, and boil it four hours; when it is cold, bind it over again, and cut a thin flice off before you fend it to the table; garnifh with parfley and red cabbage.

A forced Leg of Lamb.

TAKE a large leg of lamb, cut a long flit on the back fide and take out the meat, but take great care you do not deface the other fide; then chop the meat fmall with marrow, half a pound of beef-fuet, fome oyfters, an anchovy wafhed, an onion, fome fweet herbs, a little lemon-peel, and fome beaten mace and nutmeg; beat all thefe together in a mortar, ftuff it up in the fhape it was before, few it up, and rub it over with the yolks of eggs beaten, fpit it, flour it all over, lay it to the fire, and bafte it with butter. An hour will roaft it. You may bake it, if you pleafe, but then you muft butter the difh, and lay the butter over it: cut the loin into fteaks, feafon them with pepper, salt, and nutmeg, lemon-peel cut fine, and a few sweet herbs; fry them in fresh butter of a fine brown, then pour out all the butter, put in a quarter of a pint of white wine, shake it about, and put in half a pint of strong gravy, wherein good spice has been boiled, a quarter of a pint of oysters and the liquor, some mushrooms, and a spoonful of the pickle, a piece of butter rolled in flour, and the yolk of an egg beat; stir all these together till thick, then lay your leg of lamb in the dish, and the loin round it; pour the sauce over it, and garnish with lemon.

To force a Leg of Lamb another Way.

WITH a sharp knife carefully take out all the meat, and leave the skin whole and the fat on it, make the lean you cut out into force-meat thus: to two pounds of meat add two pounds of beef-suet cut fine, and beat in a marble mortar till it is very fine, and take away all the skin of the meat and suet, then mix it with four spoonfuls of grated bread, eight or ten cloves, five or six large blades of mace dried and beat fine, half a large nutmeg grated, a little pepper and salt, a little lemon-peel cut fine, a very little thyme, some parsley, and four eggs; mix all together, put it into the skin again just as it was, in the same shape, sew it up, roast it, baste it with butter, cut the loin into steaks and fry it nicely, lay the leg in the dish and the loin round it, with stewed cauliflower all round upon the loin; pour a pint of good gravy into the dish, and send it to table. If you do not like the cauliflower, it may be omitted.

To force a large Fowl.

CUT the skin down the back, and carefully slit it up so as to take out all the meat, mix it with one pound of beef-suet, cut it small, and beat them together in a marble mortar; take a pint of large oysters cut small, two anchovies cut small, one shalot cut fine, a few sweet herbs, a little pepper, a little nutmeg grated, and the yolks of four eggs; mix all together and lay this on the bones, draw over the skin, and sew up the back, put the fowl into a bladder, boil it an hour and a quarter, stew some oysters in good gravy thickened with a piece of butter rolled in flour; take the fowl out of the bladder, lay it in your dish, and pour the sauce over it. Garnish with lemon.
It eats much better roasted with the same sauce.

To roast a Turkey the genteel Way.

FIRST cut it down the back, and with a sharp penknife, bone it, then make your force-meat thus: take a large fowl or a pound of veal, as much grated bread, half a pound of suet cut and beat very fine, a little beaten mace, two cloves, half a
nutmeg

nutmeg grated, about a large tea-spoonful of lemon-peel, and the yolks of two eggs; mix all together with a little pepper and salt, fill up the places where the bones came out, and fill the body, that it may look just as it did before, sew up the back, and roast it. You may have oyster-sauce, celery-sauce, or just as you please; put good gravy in the dish, and garnish with lemon is as good as any thing. Be sure to leave the pinions on.

To stew a Knuckle of Veal.

BE sure let the pot or sauce-pan be very clean, lay at the bottom four clean wooden skewers, wash and clean the knuckle very well, then lay it in the pot with two or three blades of mace, a little whole pepper, a little piece of thyme, a small onion, a crust of bread, and two quarts of water. Cover it down close, make it boil, then only let it simmer for two hours, and when it is enough take it up, lay it in a dish, and strain the broth over it.

Another Way to stew a Knuckle of Veal.

CLEAN it as before directed, and boil it till there is just enough for sauce, add one spoonful of catchup, one of red wine, and one of walnut-pickle, some truffles and morels, or some dried mushrooms cut small; boil all together. Take up the knuckle, lay it in a dish, pour the sauce over it, and send it up.

To stew a Fillet of Veal.

TAKE a fillet of a cow-calf, stuff it well under the udder, at the bone and quite through to the shank, put it in the oven, with a pint of water under it, till it is a fine brown, then put it in a stew-pan with three pints of gravy, stew it tender, put in a few morels, truffles, a tea-spoonful of lemon-pickle, a large one of browning, and one of catchup, and a little Cayenne pepper, thicken with a lump of butter rolled in flour, dish up your veal, strain your gravy over, lay round force-meat balls: garnish with pickles and lemon.

Beef Tremblant.

TAKE the fat end of a brisket of beef, and tie it up close with pack-thread; put it in a pot of water, and boil it six hours very gently; season the water with a little salt, a handful of all-spice, two onions, two turnips, and a carrot: in the mean while put a piece of butter in a stew-pan and melt it, then put in two spoonfuls of flour, and stir it till it is smooth; put in a quart of gravy, a spoonful of catchup, the same of browning, a gill of white wine, carrots and turnips, and cut the same as for harrico of mutton; stew them gently till the roots are tender, season with pepper and salt, skim all the fat clean off,

put

put the beef in the dish, and pour the sauce all over. Garnish with pickle of any sort; or make a sauce thus: chop a handful of parsley, one onion, four pickled cucumbers, one walnut and a gill of capers; put them in a pint of good gravy, and thicken it with a little butter rolled in flour, and season it with pepper and salt; boil it up for ten minutes, and then put over the beef; or you may put the beef in a dish, and put greens and carrots round it.

Beef à la Daub.

TAKE a rump and bone it, or a part of the leg-of-mutton-piece, or a piece of the buttock; cut some fat bacon as long as the beef is thick, and about a quarter of an inch square; take eight cloves, four blades of mace, a little all-spice, and half a nutmeg beat very fine; chop a good handful of parsley fine, some sweet herbs of all sorts chopped fine, and some pepper and salt; roll the bacon in these, and then take a large larding-pin, or a small bladed knife, and put the bacon through and through the beef with the larding-pin or knife; when that is done, put it in a stew-pan, with brown gravy enough to cover it. Chop three blades of garlic very fine, and put in some fresh mushrooms or champignons, two large onions, and a carrot: stew it gently for six hours; then take the meat out, strain off the gravy, and skim all the fat off. Put your meat and gravy into the pan again; put a gill of white wine into the gravy, and if it wants seasoning, season with pepper and salt; stew them gently for half an hour; add some artichoke-bottoms, truffles and morels, oysters, and a spoonful of vinegar. Put the meat in a soup-dish, and the sauce over it; or you may put turnips cut in round pieces, and carrots cut round, some small onions, and thicken the sauce; then put the meat in, and stew it gently for half an hour with a gill of white wine. Some like savoys or cabbage stewed and put into the sauce.

To make Beef Alamode.

TAKE a small buttock, or leg-of-mutton-piece of beef, or a clod, or a piece of buttock of beef, also two dozen of cloves, as much mace, and half an ounce of all spice beat fine; chop a large handful of parsley, and all sorts of sweet herbs fine (cut fat bacon as for beef à la Daub, and put it into the spice, &c. and into the beef the same); put it into a pot, and cover it with water; chop four large onions very fine, and six cloves of garlic, six bay-leaves, and a handful of champignons or fresh mushrooms; put all into the pot with a pint of porter or ale, and half a pint of red wine; put in some pepper and salt, some Cayenne pepper, a spoonful of vinegar, strew three handfuls of bread raspings, sifted fine, over all; cover the pot close, and stew

stew it for six hours, or according to the size of the piece; if a large piece, eight hours; then take the beef out and put it in a deep dish, and keep it hot over some boiling water; strain the gravy through a sieve, and pick out the champignons or mushrooms; skim all the fat off clean, put it into your pot again, and give it a boil up; if not seasoned enough, season it to your liking; then put the gravy over your beef, and send it to table hot; or you may cut it in slices if you like it best, or put it to get cold, and cut it in slices with the gravy over it; for when the gravy is cold, it will be in a strong jelly.

N. B. This makes an excellent dish, but many of the ingredients, such as the garlic, mushrooms, &c. may be left out.

Beef Alamode in Pieces.

You must take a buttock of beef, cut it into two-pound pieces, lard them with bacon, fry them brown, put them into a pot that will just hold them, put in two quarts of broth or gravy, a few sweet herbs, an onion, some mace, cloves, nutmeg, pepper and salt; when that is done, cover it close, and stew it till it is tender, skim off all the fat, lay the meat in the dish, and strain the sauce over it. You may serve it up hot or cold.

To stew Beef-Steaks.

Take rump-steaks, pepper and salt them, lay them in a stew-pan, pour in half a pint of water, a blade or two of mace, two or three cloves, a little bundle of sweet herbs, an anchovy, a piece of butter rolled in flour, a glass of white wine, and an onion; cover them close, and let them stew softly till they are tender; then take out the steaks, flour them, fry them in fresh butter, and pour away all the fat, strain the sauce they were stewed in, and pour into the pan; toss it all up together till the sauce is quite hot and thick. If you add a quarter of a pint of oysters, it will make it the better. Lay the steaks into the dish, and pour the sauce over them. Garnish with any pickle you like.

Beef-Steaks after the French Way.

Take some beaf-steaks, broil them till they are half done, while the steaks are doing, have ready in a stew-pan some red wine, a spoonful or two of gravy, season it with salt, pepper, some shalots; then take the steaks, and cut in squares, and put in the sauce; you must put some vinegar, cover it close, and let it simmer on a slow fire half an hour.

A pretty Side-dish of Beef.

Roast a tender piece of beef, lay fat bacon all over it, and roll it in paper, baste it, and when it is roasted cut about two pounds in thin slices, lay them in a stew-pan, and take six large cucumbers, peel them, and chop them small, lay over them a little pepper and salt, and stew them in butter for about ten minutes, then drain out the butter, and shake some flour over them; toss them up, pour in half a pint of gravy, let them stew till they are thick, and dish them up.

To stew a Rump of Beef.

HAVING boiled it till it is little more than half enough, take it up, and peel off the skin: take salt, pepper, beaten mace, grated nutmeg, a handful of parsley, a little thyme, winter-savory, sweet-marjoram, all chopped fine and mixed, and stuff them in great holes in the fat and lean, the rest spread over it, with the yolks of two eggs; save the gravy that runs out, put to it a pint of claret, and put the meat in a deep pan, pour the liquor in, cover it close, and let it bake two hours, then put it into the dish, strain the liquor through a sieve, and skim off the fat very clean, then pour it over the meat, and send it to table.

Another Way to stew a Rump of Beef.

YOU must cut the meat off the bone, lay it in your stew-pan, cover it with half gravy and half water, put in a spoonful of whole pepper, two onions, a bundle of sweet herbs, some salt, and a pint of red wine; cover it close, set it over a stove or slow fire for four hours, shaking it sometimes, and turning it four or five times; keep it stirring till dinner is ready: take ten or twelve turnips, cut them into slices the broad way, then cut them into four, flour them, and fry them brown in beef-dripping. Be sure to let your dripping boil before you put them in; then drain them well from the fat, lay the beef in your soup dish, toast a little bread very nice and brown, cut in three corner dice, lay them into the dish, and the turnips likewise; skim the fat off clean, strain in the gravy, and send it to table. If you have the convenience of a stove, put the dish over it for five or six minutes; it gives the liquor a fine flavour of the turnips, makes the bread eat better, and is a great addition. Season it with pepper and salt to your palate.

Portugal Beef.

TAKE a rump of beef, cut it off the bone, cut it across, flour it, fry the thin part brown in butter, the thick end stuff with suet, boiled chesnuts, an anchovy, an onion, and a little pepper. Stew it in a pan of strong broth, and when it is tender, lay both the fried and stewed together in your dish; cut the fried in two and lay on each side of the stewed, strain the gravy it was stewed in, put to it some pickled gerkins chopped, and boiled chesnuts, thicken it with a piece of butter rolled in flour, a spoonful of browning, give it two or three boils up, season it with salt to your palate, and pour it over the beef. Garnish with lemon.

To stew a Rump of Beef, or Brisket, the French Way.

TAKE a rump of beef, cut it from the bone; take half a pint of white port, and half a pint of red, a little vinegar, some cloves and mace, half a nutmeg beat fine, some parsley chopped, and all sorts of sweet herbs, a little pepper and salt; mix the herbs, spice, and wine all together; lay your beef in an earthen pan, put the mixture over it, and let it lay all night, then take the beef and put it into a deep stew-pan, with two quarts of good gravy, the wine, &c. an onion chopped fine, some carrot, and two or three bay-leaves; you may put in some thick rashers of bacon at the bottom of your pan; stew it very gently for five hours, if twelve pounds; if eight or nine, four hours, and keep the stew-pan close covered: then take the meat out and strain the liquor through a sieve, skim all the fat off, put it into your stew-pan with some truffles and morels, artichoke-bottoms blanched and cut in pieces, or some carrots and turnips cut as for harrico of mutton, or a few savoys tied up in quarters and stewed till tender; boil it up, season it with a little Cayenne pepper and salt to your palate, then put the meat in just to make it hot: dish it up. Garnish with fried sippets, or lemon and beet-root.

To stew Beef-Gobbets.

GET any piece of beef except the leg, cut it in pieces about the bigness of a pullet's egg, put them in a stew-pan, cover them with water, let them stew, skim them clean, and when they have stewed an hour, take mace, cloves, and whole pepper tied in a muslin rag loose, some celery cut small, put them into the pan with some salt, turnips and carrots pared and cut in slices, a little parsley, a bundle of sweet herbs, and a large crust of bread. You may put in an ounce of barley or rice, if you like it. Cover it close, and let it stew till it is tender; take out the herbs, spices, and bread, and have ready fried a French roll cut in four. Dish up all together, and send it to table.

Beef Royal.

TAKE a sirloin of beef, or a large rump, bone it and beat it very well, then lard it with bacon, season it all over with salt, pepper, mace, cloves, and nutmeg, all beat fine, some lemon-peel cut small, and some sweet herbs; in the mean time make a strong broth of the bones; take a piece of butter with a little flour,

flour, brown it, put in the beef; keep it turning often till it is brown, then strain the broth, put all together into a pot, put in a bay-leaf, a few truffles, and some ox-palates cut small; cover it close, and let it stew till it is tender; take out the beef, skim off all the fat, pour in a pint of claret, some fried oysters, an anchovy, and some gerkins shred small; boil all together, put in the beef to warm, thicken your sauce with a piece of butter rolled in flour or mushroom powder. Lay your meat in the dish, pour the sauce over it, and send it to table. This may be eat either hot or cold.

To make Stew of Ox-Cheek.

TAKE an ox-cheek when fresh killed, take out the teeth and loose bones, rub it with a little salt, put it into soft water just warm, let it lay three or four hours, then put it into cold water, let it stand all night, wash it clean and drain it well, season it with ground-pepper and salt, put it into a kettle well tinned, put to it five quarts of soft water; before it boils you must take care to skim it well, then put in six large onions, a small bunch of sweet herbs, stew it gently five or six hours, take out the herbs and let it stand all night, then take off all the fat, put in celery, carrots, and turnips cut in pieces, also Cayenne pepper, and salt, to your taste; stew it two hours more; send up all together in a tureen, and dry toast on a plate. Make stew of tongue roots the same way.

To make Stew of a Shank of Beef.

TAKE a shank of beef seven or eight pounds weight, break the bone well, put it into a kettle well tinned, put to it six quarts of soft water, season it with pepper and salt, skim it when it boils; stew it five or six hours, let it stand all night, then take off the fat, and put in celery, carrots, turnips, Cayenne, and salt; stew it two hours more, then send it up as the other stew.

To stew a Turkey or Fowl.

FIRST let your pot be very clean, lay four clean skewers at the bottom, lay your turkey or fowl upon them, put in a quart of gravy, take a bunch of celery, cut it small, and wash it very clean, put it into your pot, with two or three blades of mace, let it stew softly till there is just enough for sauce, then add a good piece of butter rolled in flour, two spoonfuls of red-wine, two of catchup, and just as much pepper and salt as will season it; lay your fowl or turkey in the dish, pour the sauce over it, and send it to table. If the fowl or turkey is enough before the sauce, take it up, and keep it up till the sauce is boiled enough, then put it in, and let it boil a minute or two, and dish it up.

A rolled

A rolled Rump of Beef.

CUT the meat all off the bone whole, flit the infide down from top to bottom, but not through the fkin, fpread it open; take the flefh of two fowls and beef-fuet, an equal quantity, and as much cold boiled ham (if you have it), a little pepper, an anchovy, a nutmeg grated, a little thyme, a good deal of parfley, a few mufhrooms, and chop them all together, beat them in a mortar, with a half-pint bafon full of crumbs of bread; mix all thefe together, with four yolks of eggs, lay it into the meat, cover it up, and roll it round, ftick one fkewer in, and tie it with a packthread crofs and crofs to hold it together; take a pot or large fauce-pan that will juft hold it, lay a layer of bacon and a layer of beef cut in thin flices, a piece of carrot, fome whole pepper, mace, fweet herbs, and a large onion; lay the rolled beef on it; juft water enough to cover the top of the beef; cover it clofe, and let it ftew very foftly on a flow fire for eight or ten hours, but not too faft. When you find the beef tender, which you will know by running a fkewer into the meat, then take it up, cover it up hot, boil the gravy till it is good, then ftrain it off, and add fome mufhrooms chopped, fome truffles and morels cut fmall, two fpoonfuls of red or white wine, the yolks of two eggs, and a piece of butter rolled in flour; boil it together, fet the meat before the fire, bafte it with butter, and throw crumbs of bread all over it; when the fauce is enough, lay the meat into the difh, and pour the fauce over it. Take care the eggs do not curdle; or you may omit the eggs.

To boil a Rump of Beef the French Fafhion.

TAKE a rump of beef, boil it half an hour, take it up, lay it into a large deep pewter difh or ftew-pan, cut three or four gafhes in it all along the fide, rub the gafhes with pepper and falt, and pour into the difh a pint of red wine, as much hot water, two or three large onions cut fmall, the hearts of eight or ten lettuces cut fmall, and a good piece of butter rolled in a little flour; lay the flefhy part of the meat downwards, cover it clofe, let it ftew two hours and a half over a charcoal fire, or a very flow coal fire. Obferve that the butcher chops the bone fo clofe that the meat may lie as flat as it can in the difh. When it is enough, take the beef, lay it in the difh, and pour the fauce over it.

N.B. When you do it in a pewter difh, it is beft done over a chafing-difh of hot coals, with a bit or two of charcoal to keep it alive.

Beef-Escarlot.

TAKE a brisket of beef, half a pound of coarse sugar, two ounces of bay-salt, one ounce of saltpetre, a pound of common salt; mix all together, and rub the beef; lay it in an earthen pan, and turn it every day. It may lie a fortnight in the pickle; then boil it, and serve it up either with savoys, cabbage, or greens, or peas-pudding.

N. B. It eats much finer cold, cut into slices, and sent to table.

A Fricando of Beef.

CUT a few slices of beef five or six inches long, and half an inch thick, lard it with bacon, dredge it well with flour, and set it before a brisk fire to brown, then put it in a tossing-pan, with a quart of gravy, a few morels and truffles, half a lemon, and stew them half an hour, then add one spoonful of catchup, the same of browning, and a litttle Cayenne, thicken your sauce and pour it over your fricando, lay round them force-meat balls, and the yolks of hard eggs.

Beef Olives.

TAKE a rump of beef, cut it into steaks of half an inch thick, cut them as square as you can, and about ten inches long, cut a piece of fat bacon as wide as the beef, and about three parts as long, put some yolk of an egg on the beef, put the bacon on it, and the yolk of an egg on the bacon, and some good savoury force-meat on that, some yolk of an egg on the force-meat, then roll them up and tie them round with a string in two places; put some yolk of an egg on them and some crumbs of bread, then fry them brown in a large pan of good beef-dripping; take them out and put them to drain; take some butter and put into a stew-pan, melt it, and put in a spoonful of flour, stir it well till it is smooth; then put a pint of good gravy in, and a gill of white wine, put in the olives and stew them for an hour; add some mushrooms, truffles and morels, force-meat balls and sweetbreads, cut in small square pieces, some ox-palates; season with pepper and salt, and squeeze the juice of half a lemon; toss them up. Be careful to skim all the fat off, then put them in your dish. Garnish with beet-root and lemon.

To dress a Fillet of Beef.

IT is the inside of a sirloin. You must carefully cut it all out from the bone, grate some nutmeg over it, a few crumbs of bread, a little pepper and salt, a little lemon-peel, a little thyme, some parsley shred small, and roll it up tight; tie it with a packthread, roast it, put a quart of milk and a quarter

of

of a pound of butter into the dripping-pan, and baste it; when it is enough take it up, untie it, leave a little skewer in it to hold it together, have a little good gravy in the dish, and some sweet sauce in a cup. You may baste it with red-wine and butter, if you like it better; or it will do very well with butter only.

Beef-Steaks rolled.

TAKE three or four beef-steaks, flat them with a cleaver, and make a force-meat thus: take a pound of veal beat fine in a mortar, the flesh of a large fowl cut small, half a pound of cold ham chopped small, the kidney-fat of a loin of veal chopped small, a sweetbread cut in little pieces, an ounce of truffles and morels first stewed and then cut small, some parsley, the yolks of four eggs, a nutmeg grated, a very little thyme, a little lemon-peel cut fine, a little pepper and salt, and half a pint of cream: mix all together, lay it on your steaks, roll them up firm, of a good size, and put a little skewer into them, put them into the stew-pan and fry them of a nice brown; and pour all the fat quite out, and put in a pint of good fried gravy, put one spoonful of catchup, two spoonfuls of red wine, a few mushrooms, and let them stew for half an hour. Take up the steaks, cut them in two, lay the cut side uppermost, and pour the sauce over it. Garnish with lemon.

N. B. Before you put the force-meat into the beef, you are to stir it all together over a slow fire for eight or ten minutes.

To dress the Inside of a cold Sirloin of Beef.

CUT out all the inside (free from fat) of the sirloin in pieces as thick as your finger and about two inches long, dredge it with a little flour, and fry it in nice butter of a light brown, then drain it, and toss it up in rich gravy that has been well seasoned with pepper, salt, shalot, and an anchovy; just before you send it up, add two spoonfuls of vinegar taken from pickled capers; garnish with fried oysters, or what you please.

Boullie Beef.

TAKE the thick end of a brisket of beef, put it into a kettle of water quite covered over, let it boil fast for two hours, then keep stewing it close by the fire for six hours more, and as the water wastes fill up the kettle, put in with the beef some turnips cut in little balls, carrots, and some celery cut in pieces; an hour before it is done take out as much broth as will fill your soup-dish, and boil in it for that hour turnips and carrots cut out in balls or in little square pieces, with some celery, salt and pepper to your taste, serve it up in two dishes, the beef by itself, and the soup by itself; you may put pieces of fried bread, if you like it, in your soup, boil in a few knots of greens, and if you think your soup will not be rich enough, you may add a pound or two of fried mutton chops to your broth when you take it from the beef, and let it stew for that hour in the broth, but be sure to take out the mutton when you send it to the table: the soup must be very clear.

To make Mock-Hare of a Beast's Heart.

WASH a large beast's heart clean, and cut off the deaf-ears, and stuff it with some force-meat, as you do a hare, lay a caul of veal or paper over the top, to keep in the stuffing, roast it either in a cradle-spit or hanging one, it will take an hour and a half before a good fire, baste it with red wine; when roasted, take the wine out of the dripping-pan and skim off the fat, and add a glass more of wine; when it is hot, put in some lumps of red-currant jelly, and pour it in the dish; serve it up, and send in red-currant jelly cut in slices on a saucer.

Tripe à la Kilkenny.

THIS is a favourite Irish dish, and is done thus: take a piece of double tripe cut in square pieces, have twelve large onions peeled and washed clean, cut them in two, and put them on to boil in clean water till they are tender; then put in your tripe and boil it ten minutes; pour off almost all the liquor, shake a little flour in, and put some butter in, and a little salt and mustard; shake it all over the fire till the butter is melted; then put it in your dish, and send it to table as hot as possible. Garnish with barberries or lemon.

A Tongue and Udder forced.

FIRST parboil the tongue and udder, blanch the tongue and stick it with cloves; as for the udder, you must carefully raise it, and fill it with force-meat made with veal: first wash the inside with the yolk of an egg, then put in the force-meat, tie the ends close and spit them, roast them, and baste them with butter; when enough, have good gravy in the dish, and sweet sauce in a cup.

N. B. For variety, you may lard the udder.

To fricassee Neats' Tongues brown.

TAKE neats' tongues, boil them tender, peel them, cut them into thin slices, and fry them in fresh butter; then pour out the butter, put in as much gravy as you shall want for sauce, a bundle of sweet herbs, an onion, some pepper and salt, and a blade or two of mace, a glass of white wine, simmer all together half an hour; then take out your tongue, strain the

gravy,

gravy, put it with the tongue in the stew-pan again, beat up the yolks of two eggs, a little grated nutmeg, a piece of butter as big as a walnut, rolled in flour; shake all together for four or five minutes. Dish it up and send it to table.

To force a Tongue.

BOIL it till it is tender; let it stand till it is cold, then cut a hole at the root end of it, take out some of the meat, chop it with as much beef-suet, a few pippins, some pepper and salt, a little mace beat, some nutmeg, a few sweet herbs, and the yolks of two eggs; beat all together well in a marble mortar; stuff it, cover the end with a veal caul or buttered paper, roast it, baste it with butter, and dish it up. Have for sauce good gravy, a little melted butter, the juice of an orange or lemon, and some grated nutmeg; boil it up, and pour it into the dish.

To stew Neats' Tongues whole.

TAKE two tongues, let them stew in water just to cover them for two hours, then peel them, put them in again with a pint of strong gravy, half a pint of white wine, a bundle of sweet herbs, a little pepper and salt, some mace, cloves, and whole pepper tied in a muslin rag, a spoonful of capers chopped, turnips and carrots sliced, and a piece of butter rolled in flour; let all stew together very softly over a slow fire for two hours, then take out the spice and sweet herbs, and send it to table. You may leave out the turnips and carrots, or boil them by themselves, and lay them in a dish, just as you like.

To dress a Leg of Mutton à la Royale.

HAVING taken off all the fat, skin, and shank-bone, lard it with bacon, season it with pepper and salt, and a round piece of about three or four pounds of beef or leg of veal, lard it, have ready some hog's-lard boiling, flour your meat, and give it a colour in the lard, then take the meat out and put it into a pot, with a bundle of sweet herbs, some parsley, an onion stuck with cloves, two or three blades of mace, some whole pepper, and three quarts of gravy; cover it close, and let it boil very softly for two hours, meanwhile get ready a sweet-bread split, cut into four, and broiled, a few truffles and morels stewed in a quarter of a pint of strong gravy, a glass of red wine, a few mushrooms, two spoonfuls of catchup, and some asparagus-tops; boil all these together, then lay the mutton in the middle of the dish, cut the beef or veal into slices, make a rim round your mutton with the slices, and pour the ragoo over it; when you have taken the meat out of the pot, skim all the fat off the gravy; strain it, and add as much to the other as will fill the dish. Garnish with lemon.

A Leg of Mutton à la Haut Goût.

LET it hang a fortnight in an airy place, then have ready some cloves of garlic, and stuff it all over, rub it with pepper and salt; roast it, have ready some good gravy and red wine in the dish, and send it to table.

To roast a Leg of Mutton with Oysters.

TAKE a leg about two or three days killed, stuff it all over with oysters, and roast it. Garnish with horse-radish.

A second Way to roast a Leg of Mutton with Oysters.

STUFF a leg of mutton with mutton-suet, salt, pepper, nutmeg, and the yolks of eggs; then roast it, stick it all over with cloves, and when it is about half done, cut off some of the under-side of the fleshy end in little bits, put these into a pipkin with a pint of oysters, liquor and all, a little salt and mace, and half a pint of hot water: stew them till half the liquor is wasted, then put in a piece of butter rolled in flour, shake all together, and when the mutton is enough, take it up; pour this sauce over it, and send it to table.

To roast a Leg of Mutton with Cockles.

STUFF it all over with cockles, and roast it. Garnish with horse-radish.

A Shoulder of Mutton en Epigram.

ROAST it almost enough, then very carefully take off the skin about the thickness of a crown-piece, and the shank-bone with it at the end; then season that skin and shank-bone with pepper and salt, a little lemon-peel cut small, and a few sweet herbs and crumbs of bread, then lay this on the gridiron, and let it be of a fine brown; in the mean time take the rest of the meat and cut it like a hash about the bigness of a shilling; save the gravy and put to it, with a few spoonfuls of strong gravy, half an onion cut fine, a little nutmeg, a little pepper and salt, a little bundle of sweet herbs, some gerkins cut very small, a few mushrooms, two or three truffles cut small, two spoonfuls of wine, either red or white, and throw a little flour over the meat: let all these stew together very softly for five or six minutes, but be sure it does not boil; take out the sweet herbs, and put the hash into the dish, lay the broiled upon it, and send it to table.

A Harrico of Mutton.

TAKE a neck or loin of mutton, cut it into thick chops, flour them, and fry them brown in a litttle butter; take them out, and lay them to drain on a sieve, then put them into a
stew-

stew-pan, and cover them with gravy; put in a whole onion and a turnip or two, and stew them till tender; then take out the chops, strain the liquor through a sieve, and skim off all the fat; put a little butter in the stew-pan and melt it, with a spoonful of flour, stir it well till it is smooth, then put the liquor in, and stir it well all the time you are pouring it, or it will be in lumps; put in your chops and a glass of Lisbon; have ready some carrot about three quarters of an inch long, and cut round with an apple-corer, some turnips cut with a turnip-scoop, a dozen small onions all blanched well; put them to your meat, and season with pepper and salt; stew them very gently for fifteen minutes, then take out the chops with a fork, lay them in your dish, and pour the ragoo over it. Garnish with beet-root. The wine may be omitted.

To French a Hind-Saddle of Mutton.

IT is the two chumps of the loins. Cut off the rump, and carefully lift up the skin with a knife: begin at the broad end, but be sure you do not crack it nor take it quite off; then take some slices of ham or bacon chopped fine, a few truffles, some young onions, some parsley, a little thyme, sweet-marjoram, winter-savory, a little lemon-peel, all chopped fine, a little mace and two or three cloves beat fine, half a nutmeg, and a little pepper and salt; mix all together, and throw over the meat where you took off the skin, then lay on the skin again, and fasten it with two fine skewers at each side, and roll it in well-buttered paper. It will take two hours roasting: then take off the paper, baste the meat, strew it all over with crumbs of bread, and when it is of a fine brown take it up. For sauce take six large shalots, cut them very fine, put them into a sauce-pan with two spoonfuls of vinegar and two of white wine; boil them for a minute or two, pour it into the dish, and garnish with horse-radish.

Another French Way, called St. Menehout.

TAKE the hind-part of a chine of mutton, take off the skin, lard it with bacon, season it with pepper, salt, mace, cloves beat, and nutmeg, sweet herbs, young onions, and parsley, all chopped fine; take a large oval or a large gravy-pan, lay layers of bacon, and then layers of beef all over the bottom; lay in the mutton; then lay layers of bacon on the mutton, and then a layer of beef, put in a pint of wine, and as much good gravy as will stew it, put in a bay-leaf and two or three shalots, cover it close, put fire over and under it (if you have a close-pan), and let it stand stewing for two hours; when done, take it out, strew crumbs of bread all over it, and put it into the oven to brown, strain the gravy it was stewed in, and boil it till there is just enough for sauce; lay the mutton into a dish, pour the sauce in, and serve it up. You must brown it before a fire, if you have not an oven.

Cutlets à la Maintenon. A very good Dish.

TAKE a neck of mutton, cut it into chops, in every chop must be a long bone; take the fat off the bone, and scrape it clean; have some bread-crumbs, parsley, marjoram, thyme, winter-savory, and basil, all chopped fine, grate some nutmeg on it, some pepper and salt; mix these all together, melt a little butter in a stew-pan, dip the chop in the butter, then roll them in the herbs, and put them in half sheets of buttered paper; leave the end of the bone bare, then broil them on a clear fire for twenty minutes: send them up in the paper with poivrade-sauce in a boat.

Mutton-Chops in Disguise.

TAKE as many mutton-chops as you want, rub them with pepper, salt, nutmeg, and a little parsley; roll each chop in half a sheet of white paper, well buttered on the inside, and rolled on each end close. Have some hog's-lard, or beef-dripping, boiling in a stew-pan; put in the steaks, fry them of a fine brown, lay them in your dish, and garnish with fried parsley; throw some all over, have a little good gravy in a cup; but take great care you do not break the paper, nor have any fat in the dish; but let them be well drained.

To dress a Leg of Mutton to eat like Venison.

TAKE a hind-quarter of mutton, and cut the leg in the shape of a haunch of venison, save the blood of the sheep and steep the haunch in it for five or six hours, then take it out and roll it in three or four sheets of white paper well buttered on the inside, tie it with a packthread, and roast it, basting it with good beef-dripping or butter. It will take two hours at a good fire, for your mutton must be fat and thick. About five or six minutes before you take it up, take off the paper, baste it with a piece of butter, and shake a little flour over it to make it have a fine froth, and then have a little good drawn gravy in a bason, and sweet sauce in another. Do not garnish with any thing.

To dress Mutton the Turkish Way.

FIRST cut your meat into thin slices, then wash it in vinegar, and put it into a pot or sauce-pan that has a close cover to it, put in some rice, whole pepper, and three or four whole onions; let all these stew together, skimming it frequently;

when

when it is enough, take out the onions, and season it with salt to your palate, lay the mutton in the dish, and pour the rice and liquor over it.

N. B. The neck or leg are the best joints to dress this way; put to a leg four quarts of water, and a quarter of a pound of rice; to a neck, two quarts of water, and two ounces of rice. To every pound of meat allow a quarter of an hour, being close covered. If you put in a blade or two of mace, and a bundle of sweet herbs, it will be a great addition. When it is just enough, put in a piece of butter, and take care the rice do not burn to the pot. In all these things you should lay skewers at the bottom of the pot to lay your meat on, that it may not stick.

A Hodge-podge of Mutton.

CUT a neck or loin of mutton into steaks, take off all the fat, then put the steaks into a pitcher, with lettuce, turnips, carrots, two cucumbers cut in quarters, four or five onions, and pepper and salt; you must not put any water to it, and stop the pitcher very close, then set it in a pan of boiling water, let it boil four hours, keep the pan supplied with fresh boiling water as it wastes.

A Shoulder of Mutton with a Ragoo of Turnips.

TAKE a shoulder of mutton, get the blade bone taken out as neat as possible, and in the place put a ragoo, done thus: take one or two sweetbreads, some cock's-combs, half an ounce of truffles, some mushrooms, a blade or two of mace, a little pepper and salt; stew all these in a quarter of a pint of good gravy, and thicken it with a piece of butter rolled in flour, or yolks of eggs, which you please: let it be cold before you put it in, and fill up the place where you took the bone out just in the form it was before, and sew it up tight: take a large deep stew-pan, or one of the round deep copper pans with two handles, lay at the bottom thin slices of bacon, then slices of veal, a bundle of parsley, thyme, and sweet herbs, some whole pepper, a blade or two of mace, three or four cloves, a large onion, and put in just thin gravy enough to cover the meat; cover it close, and let it stew two hours, then take eight or ten turnips, pare them, and cut them into what shape you please, put them into boiling water, and let them be just enough; throw them into a sieve to drain over the hot water that they may keep warm; then take up the mutton, drain it from the fat, lay it in a dish, and keep it hot covered; strain the gravy it was stewed in, and take off all the fat, put in a little salt, a glass of white wine, two spoonfuls of catchup, and a piece of butter rolled in flour, boil them to-

gether

gether till there is juft enough for fauce; then put in the turnips, give them a boil up, pour them over the meat, and fend it to table. You may fry the turnips of a light brown, and tofs them up with the fauce; but that is according to your palate.

Note: For a change you may leave out the turnips, and add a bunch of celery cut and wafhed clean, and ftewed in a very little water, till it is quite tender, and the water almoft boiled away. Pour the gravy, as before directed, into it, and boil it up till the fauce is good: or you may leave both thefe out, and add truffles, morels, frefh and pickled mufhrooms, and artichoke-bottoms.

N. B. A fhoulder of veal without the knuckle, half roafted, very quick and brown, and then done like the mutton, eats well. Do not garnifh your mutton, but garnifh your veal with lemon.

To ftuff a Leg or Shoulder of Mutton.

Take a little grated bread, fome beef-fuet, the yolks of three hard eggs, three anchovies, a bit of onion, fome pepper and falt, a little thyme and winter-favory, twelve oyfters, and fome nutmeg grated; mix all thefe together, fhred them very fine, work them up with raw eggs like a pafte, ftuff your mutton under the fkin in the thickeft place, or where you pleafe, and roaft it: for fauce, take fome of the oyfter-liquor, fome claret, one anchovy, a little nutmeg, a bit of onion, and a few oyfters; ftew all thefe together, then take out your onion, pour fauce under your mutton, and fend it to table. Garnifh with horfe-racifh.

Oxford John.

Keep a leg of mutton till it is ftale, cut it into thin collops, and take out all the finews and fat, feafon them with pepper and falt, a little beaten mace, and ftrew among them a little fhred parfley, thyme, and three or four fhalots; put about a quarter of a pound of butter in a ftew-pan, and make it hot, put all your collops in, keep them ftirring with a wooden fpoon till they are three parts done, and then add a pint of gravy, a little juice of lemon, and thicken it with butter rolled in flour; let it fimmer four or five minutes, and they will be enough. Take care you do not let them boil, nor have them ready before you want them, for they will grow hard; fry fome bread fippets, and throw over and round them, and fend them up hot.

Mutton-Rumps à la Braife.

Take fix mutton-rumps, and boil them for fifteen minutes in water; take them out, cut them in two, and put them into a ftew-

a stew-pan with half a pint of good gravy, a gill of white wine, an onion stuck with cloves, a little salt and Cayenne pepper, cover them close and stew them till tender; take them out and the onion, skim off all the fat, thicken the gravy with a little butter rolled in flour, a spoonful of browning, the juice of half a lemon; boil it up till it is smooth, but not too thick; put in your rumps, give them a toss or two, dish them up hot. Garnish with horse-radish and beet-root.

For variety, you may leave the rumps whole, and lard six kidneys on one side, and do them the same as the rumps, only not boil them, and put the rumps in the middle of the dish, and kidneys round them, with sauce over all. The kidneys make a pretty side-dish of themselves.

Sheeps' Rumps with Rice.

TAKE six rumps, put them into a stew-pan, with some mutton gravy enough to fill it; stew them about half an hour; take them up and let them stand to cool, then put into the liquor a quarter of a pound of rice, an onion stuck with cloves, and a blade or two of mace; let it boil till the rice is as thick as a pudding, but take care it does not stick to the bottom, which you must prevent by stirring it often; in the mean time take a clean stew-pan, put a piece of butter into it; dip your rumps in the yolks of eggs beat, and then in crumbs of bread with a little nutmeg, lemon-peel, and a very little thyme in it, fry them in the butter of a fine brown, then take them out, lay them in a dish to drain, pour out all the fat, and toss the rice into that pan; stir it all together for a minute or two, then lay the rice into the dish, and the rumps all round upon the rice; have ready four eggs boiled hard, cut them into quarters, lay them round the dish with fried parsley between them, and send it to table.

Mutton Kebobbed.

TAKE a loin of mutton and joint it between every bone; season it with pepper and salt moderately, grate a small nutmeg all over, dip the chops in the yolks of three eggs, and have ready crumbs of bread and sweet herbs, dip them in, and clap them together in their former shape again, and put it on a small spit; roast it before a quick fire, set a dish under, and baste it with a little piece of butter, and then keep basting with what comes from it, and throw some crumbs of bread and sweet herbs all over it while roasting; when it is enough take it up, lay it in the dish, and have ready half a pint of good made gravy and what comes from the mutton; take two spoonfuls of catchup, and mix a tea-spoonful of flour with it and put to the gravy, stir it together and give it a boil, and pour over the mutton.

N. B.

N. B. You must observe to take off all the fat of the inside, and the skin of the top of the meat, and some of the fat, if there be too much. When you put what comes from your meat into the gravy, observe to pour out all the fat.

A Neck of Mutton, called The Hasty Dish.

TAKE a large pewter or silver dish, made like a deep soup-dish, with an edge about an inch deep on the inside, on which the lid fixes (with an handle at top) so fast that you may lift it up full by that handle without falling. This dish is called a necromancer. Take a neck of mutton about six pounds, take off the skin, cut it into chops, not too thick, slice a French roll thin, peel and slice a very large onion, pare and slice three or four turnips, lay a row of mutton in the dish, on that a row of roll, then a row of turnips, and then onions, a little salt, then the meat, and so on; put in a little bundle of sweet herbs, and two or three blades of mace; have a tea-kettle of water boiling, fill the dish, and cover it close, hang the dish on the back of two chairs by the rim, have ready three sheets of brown paper, tear each sheet into five pieces, and draw them through your hand, light one piece and hold it under the bottom of the dish, moving the paper about, as fast as the paper burns; light another till all is burnt, and your meat will be enough. Fifteen minutes just does it. Send it to table hot in the dish.

N. B. This dish was first contrived by Mr. Rich, and is much admired by the nobility.

To bake Lamb and Rice.

TAKE a neck or loin of lamb, half roast it, take it up, cut it into steaks, then take half a pound of rice boiled in a quart of water ten minutes, put it into a quart of good gravy, with two or three blades of mace, and a little nutmeg. Do it over a stove or slow fire till the rice begins to be thick; then take it off, stir in a pound of butter, and when that is quite melted, stir in the yolks of six eggs, first beat; then take a dish and butter it all over, take the steaks and put a little pepper and salt over them, dip them in a little melted butter, lay them into the dish, pour the gravy which comes out of them over them, and then the rice; beat the yolks of three eggs and pour all over, send it to the oven, and bake it better than half an hour.

To fry a Loin of Lamb.

CUT your lamb into chops, rub it over on both sides with the yolk of an egg, and sprinkle some bread-crumbs, a little parsley, thyme, marjoram, and winter-savory chopped very fine, and a little lemon-peel chopped fine; fry it in butter of a nice
light

light brown, send it up in a dish by itself. Garnish with a good deal of fried parsley.

Another Way of frying a Neck or Loin of Lamb.

CUT it into thin steaks, beat them with a rolling-pin, fry them in half a pint of ale, season them with a little salt, and cover them close; when enough, take them out of the pan, lay them in a plate before the fire to keep hot, and pour all out of the pan into a bason; then put in half a pint of white wine, a few capers, the yolks of two eggs beat, with a little nutmeg and a little salt; add to this the liquor they were fried in, and keep stirring it one way all the time till it is thick, then put in the lamb, keep shaking the pan for a minute or two, lay the steaks into the dish, pour the sauce over them, and have some parsley in a plate before the fire to crisp. Garnish your dish with that and lemon.

Lamb-Chops larded.

CUT the best end of a neck of lamb in chops, and lard one side, season them with beaten cloves, mace and nutmeg, a little pepper and salt; put them into a stew-pan, the larded side uppermost; put in half a pint of gravy, a gill of white wine, an onion, a bundle of sweet herbs, stew them gently till tender; take the chops out, skim the fat clean off, and take out the onion and sweet herbs; thicken the gravy with a little butter rolled in flour, add a spoonful of browning, a spoonful of catchup, and one of lemon-pickle. Boil it up till it is smooth, put in the chops larded side down, stew them up gently for a minute or two; take the chops out and put the larded side uppermost in the dish, and the sauce over them. Garnish with lemon and pickles of any sort; you may add truffles and morels and pickled mushrooms in the sauce, if you please; or you may do the chops without larding.

Lamb-Chops en Caserole.

CUT a loin of lamb in chops, put yolk of egg on both sides, and strew bread crumbs over, with a little cloves and mace, pepper and salt mixed; fry them of a nice light brown, and put them round in a dish close as you can, and leave a hole in the middle to put the following sauce in: all sorts of sweet herbs and parsley chopt fine, stewed a little in some good thick gravy. Garnish with fried parsley.

To dress a Dish of Lambs' Bits.

SKIN the stones and split them, lay them on a dry cloth with the sweetbreads and liver, and dredge them well with flour,

and

and fry them in boiling lard, or butter, a light brown, then lay them on a sieve to drain, fry a good quantity of parsley, lay your bits on the dish, and the parsley in lumps over it, pour melted butter round them.

To dress Veal à la Bourgeoise.

CUT pretty thick slices of veal, lard them with bacon, and season them with pepper, salt, beaten mace, cloves, nutmeg, and chopped parsley; then take the stew-pan and cover the bottom with slices of fat bacon, lay the veal upon them, cover it, and set it over a very slow fire for eight or ten minutes, just to be hot and no more, then brisk up your fire, and brown your veal on both sides, then shake some flour over it and brown it; pour in a quart of good broth or gravy, cover it close, and let it stew gently till it is enough; when enough, take out the slices of bacon, and skim all the fat off clean, and beat up the yolks of three eggs with some of the gravy; mix all together, and keep it stirring one way till it is smooth and thick, then take it up, lay your meat in the dish, and pour the sauce over it. Garnish with lemon.

A disguised Leg of Veal and Bacon.

LARD your veal all over with slips of bacon and a little lemon-peel, and boil it with a piece of bacon; when enough, take it up, cut the bacon into slices, and have ready some dried sage and pepper rubbed fine; rub over the bacon, lay the veal in the dish and the bacon round it, strew it all over with fried parsley, and have green-sauce in cups, made thus: take two handfuls of sorrel, pound it in a mortar, and squeeze out the juice, put it into a sauce-pan with some melted butter, a little sugar, and the juice of a lemon. Or you may make it thus: beat two handfuls of sorrel in a mortar, with two pippins quartered, squeeze the juice out, with the juice of a lemon, or vinegar, and sweeten it with sugar.

Loin of Veal en Epigram.

ROAST a fine loin of veal as directed in the chapter for roasting; take it up, and carefully take the skin off the back part without breaking; take and cut out all the lean meat, but mind and leave the ends whole, that it may hold the following mince-meats: mince all the meat very fine with the kidney part, put it in a little veal gravy, enough to moisten it with the gravy that comes from the loin; put in a little pepper and salt, some lemon-peel shred fine, the yolks of three eggs, a spoonful of catchup, and thicken it with a little butter rolled in flour; give it a shake or two over the fire and put it into the loin, and

then

then pull the skin over; if the skin should not quite cover it, give it a brown with a hot iron, or put it in an oven for fifteen minutes. Send it up hot, and garnish with barberries and lemon.

To make a Porcupine of a Breast of Veal.

BONE the finest and largest breast of veal you can get, rub it over with the yolks of two eggs, spread it on a table, lay over it a little bacon cut as thin as possible, a handful of parsley shred fine, the yolks of five hard-boiled eggs chopped small, a little lemon-peel cut fine, nutmeg, pepper, and salt to your taste, and the crumb of a penny loaf steeped in cream, roll the breast close, and skewer it up, then cut fat bacon and the lean of ham that has been a little boiled, or it will turn the veal red, and pickled cucumbers about two inches long to answer the other lardings, and lard it in rows, first ham, then bacon, then cucumbers, till you have larded it all over the veal; put it in a deep earthen pot with a pint of water, and cover it and set it in a slow oven two hours; when it comes from the oven skim the fat off, and strain the gravy through a sieve into a stew-pan; put in a glass of white wine, a little lemon-pickle, and caper-liquor, a spoonful of mushroom catchup, thicken it with a little butter rolled in flour, lay your porcupine on the dish, and pour it hot upon it, cut a roll of force-meat in four slices, lay one at each end and the other at the sides; have ready your sweet-bread cut in slices and fried, lay them round it with a few mushrooms. It is a grand bottom-dish when game is not to be had.

N. B. Make the force-meat of a few chopped oysters, the crumbs of a penny loaf, half a pound of beef-suet shred fine, and the yolks of four eggs; mix them well together with nutmegs, Cayenne pepper, and salt to your taste, spread it on a veal caul, and roll it up close like a collared eel, bind it in a cloth, and boil it one hour.

A Pillaw of Veal.

TAKE a neck or breast of veal, half roast it, then cut it into six pieces, season it with pepper, salt, and nutmeg; take a pound of rice, put to it a quart of broth, some mace, and a little salt, do it over a stove or very slow fire till it is thick, but butter the bottom of the dish or pan you do it in; beat up the yolks of six eggs and stir into it; then take a little round deep dish, butter it, lay some of the rice at the bottom, then lay the veal on a round heap, and cover it all over with rice, wash it over with the yolks of eggs, and bake it an hour and a half; then open the top and pour in a pint of rich good gravy. Garnish with a Seville orange cut in quarters, and send it to table hot.

To make a Fricando of Veal.

Cut steaks half an inch thick and six inches long out of the thick part of a leg of veal, lard them with small cardoons, and dust them with flour, put them before the fire to broil a fine brown, then put them into a large tossing-pan, with a quart of good gravy, and let it stew half an hour, then put in two tea-spoonfuls of lemon-pickle, a meat-spoonful of walnut-catchup, the same of browning, a slice of lemon, a little anchovy and Cayenne, a few morels and truffles; when your fricandos are tender, take them up, and thicken your gravy with flour and butter, strain it, place your fricandos in the dish, pour your gravy on them: garnish with lemons and barberries. You may lay round them force-meat balls fried, or force-meat rolled in a veal caul, and yolks of eggs boiled hard.

Bombarded Veal.

Get a fillet of veal, cut out of it five lean pieces as thick as your hand, round them up a little, then lard them very thick on the round side with little narrow thin pieces of bacon, take five sheeps' tongues (being first boiled and blanched), lard them here and there with very little bits of lemon peel, and make a well-seasoned force-meat of veal, bacon, ham, beef-suet, and anchovy beat well; make another tender force-meat of veal, beef-suet, mushrooms, spinage, parsley, thyme, sweet-marjoram, winter-savory, and green onions. Season with pepper, salt, and mace; beat it well, make a round ball of the other force-meat and stuff in the middle of this, roll it up in a veal caul, and bake it; what is left, tie up like a Bologna sausage and boil it, but first rub the caul with the yolk of an egg; put the larded veal into a stew-pan with some good gravy, and stew it gently till it is enough; skim off the fat, put in some truffles and morels, and some mushrooms. Your force-meat being baked enough, lay it in the middle, the veal round it, and the tongues fried, and laid between; the boiled cut into slices and fried, and throw all over. Pour on them the sauce. You may add artichoke-bottoms, sweetbreads, and cock's-combs, if you please. Garnish with lemon.

Veal Rolls.

Take ten or twelve little thin slices of veal, lay on them some force-meat, according to your fancy, roll them up, and tie them just across the middle with coarse thread, put them on a bird-spit, rub them over with the yolks of eggs, flour them, and baste them with butter. Half an hour will do them. Lay them into a dish, and have ready some good gravy with a few

truffles

truffles and morels, and some mushrooms. Garnish with lemon.

Veal Olives.

CUT them out of a leg of veal, and do them the same as beef olives, with the same sauce and garnish.

Or thus: cut some slices of a leg of veal, about three inches long, and two broad, cut them thin, spread them on the table, and hack them with the back of a knife; put some yolk of egg over them, and some savoury force-meat on the egg as thick as the veal, then some yolk of egg over it; roll them up tight, and tie them with a string; rub them all over with yolk of egg, and strew bread-crumbs over them; have ready a pan of boiling fat; fry them of a gold colour, put them before the fire to drain. Have ready the following ragoo: put about two ounces of butter in your stew-pan, and melt it, put a spoonful of flour, and stir it about till it is small; put a pint of gravy, a glass of white wine, some pepper and salt, a little cloves and mace, a little ham or lean bacon cut fine, two shalots cut fine, and half a lemon, stew them gently for ten minutes, strain it through a sieve, skim off the fat, then put it into your pan again, add a sweetbread cut in pieces, artichoke-bottoms cut in pieces, some force-meat balls, a few truffles and morels, and mushrooms, a spoonful of catchup, give them a boil up; put your olives in the dish, and pour the ragoo over them. Garnish with lemon.

Olives of Veal the French Way.

TAKE two pounds of veal, some marrow, two anchovies, the yolks of two hard eggs, a few mushrooms, and some oysters, a little thyme, marjoram, parsley, spinage, lemon-peel, salt, pepper, nutmeg, and mace, finely beaten, take your veal caul, lay a layer of bacon and a layer of the ingredients, roll it in the veal caul, and either roast it or bake it. An hour will do either. When enough, cut it into slices, lay it into your dish, and pour good gravy over it. Garnish with lemon.

Veal Blanquets.

ROAST a piece of fillet of veal, cut off the skin and nervous parts, cut it into little thin bits, put some butter into a stew-pan over the fire with some chopped onions, fry them a little, then add a dust of flour, stir it together, and put in some good broth or gravy, and a bundle of sweet herbs; season it with spice, make it of a good taste, and then put in your veal, the yolks of two eggs beat up with cream and grated nutmeg, some chopped parsley, a shalot, some lemon-peel grated, and a little juice of lemon. Keep it stirring one way; when enough, dish it up.

A Shoulder of Veal à la Piedmontoise.

TAKE a shoulder of veal, cut off the skin that it may hang at one end, then lard the meat with bacon and ham, and season it with pepper, salt, mace, sweet herbs, parsley, and lemon-peel; cover it again with the skin, stew it with gravy, and when it is just tender, take it up; then take sorrel, some lettuce chopped small, and stew them in some butter with parsley, onions, and mushrooms; the herbs being tender put to them some of the liquor, some sweetbreads and some bits of ham. Let all stew together a little while; then lift up the skin, lay the stewed herbs over and under, cover it with the skin again, wet it with melted butter, strew it over with crumbs of bread, and send it to the oven to brown; serve it hot, with some good gravy in the dish: The French strew it over with Parmesan before it goes to the oven.

Sweetbreads of Veal à la Dauphiné.

TAKE the largest sweetbreads you can get, and lard them; open them in such a manner as you can stuff in force-meat, three will make a fine dish: make your force-meat with a large fowl or young cock; skin it, and pluck off all the flesh; take half a pound of fat and lean bacon, cut these very fine and beat them in a mortar; season it with an anchovy, some nutmeg, a little lemon-peel, a very little thyme, and some parsley; mix these up with the yolks of two eggs, fill your sweetbreads and fasten them with fine wooden skewers; take the stew-pan, lay layers of bacon at the bottom of the pan, season them with pepper, salt, mace, cloves, sweet herbs, and a large onion sliced; upon that lay thin slices of veal, and then lay on your sweetbreads; cover it close, let it stand eight or ten minutes over a slow fire, and then pour in a quart of boiling water or broth; cover it close, and let it stew two hours very softly; then take out the sweetbreads, keep them hot, strain the gravy, skim all the fat off, boil it up till there is about half a pint, put in the sweetbreads, and give them two or three minutes stew in the gravy, then lay them in the dish, and pour the gravy over them. Garnish with lemon.

Another Way to dress Sweetbreads.

Do not put any water or gravy into the stew-pan, but put the same veal and bacon over the sweetbreads, and season as under directed; cover them close, put fire over as well as under, and when they are enough, take out the sweetbreads, put in a ladleful of gravy, boil it, and strain it, skim off all the fat, let it boil till it jellies, then put in the sweetbreads to

glaze;

glaze; lay essence of ham in the dish, and lay the sweetbreads upon it; or make a very rich gravy with mushrooms, truffles, and morels, a glass of white wine, and two spoonfuls of catchup. Garnish with cock's-combs forced, and stewed in the gravy.

N. B. You may add to the first, truffles, morels, mushrooms, cock's-combs, palates, artichoke-bottoms, two spoonfuls of white wine, two of catchup, or just as you please.

*** There are many ways of dressing sweetbreads: you may lard them with thin slips of bacon, and roast them with what sauce you please; or you may marinate them, cut them into thin slices, flour them and fry them. Serve them up with fried parsley, and either butter or gravy. Garnish with lemon.

Sweetbreads en Cordonnier.

TAKE three sweetbreads and parboil them, take a stew-pan and lay layers of bacon or ham and veal, over that lay the sweetbreads on with the upper side downwards, put a layer of veal and bacon over them, a pint of veal broth, three or four blades of mace, stew them gently three quarters of an hour; take the sweetbreads out, strain off the gravy through a sieve, and skim off the fat; make an aumlet of yolks of eggs in the following manner: beat up four yolks of eggs, put two in a plate, and put them over a stew-pan of water boiling on the fire, put another plate over them, and they will soon be done; put a little spinage-juice into the other half and serve it the same; cut it out in sprigs or what form you please, and put it over the sweetbreads in the dish, and keep them as hot as you can; put some butter rolled in flour to thicken the gravy, two yolks of eggs beat up in a gill of cream; put it over the fire and keep stirring it one way till it is thick and smooth; put it under the sweetbreads and send them up. Garnish with lemon and beet-root.

Calf's Chitterlings, or Andouilles.

TAKE some of the largest calf's nuts, cleanse them, cut them in pieces proportionable to the length of the puddings you design to make, and tie one end to those pieces; then take some bacon, with a calf's udder and chaldron blanched and cut into dice or slices, put them into a stew-pan and season with fine spice pounded, a bay leaf, some salt, pepper, and shalot cut small, and about half a pint of cream; toss it up take off the pan and thicken your mixture with four or five yolks of eggs, add some crumbs of bread, then fill up your chitterlings with the stuffing; keep it warm, tie the other ends with packthread, blanch and boil them like hog's chitterlings, let them grow cold in their own liquor before you serve them up; broil them over a moderate fire, and serve them up pretty hot. This sort of andouilles or puddings must be made in summer, when hogs are seldom killed.

To dress Calf's Chitterlings curiously.

CUT a calf's nut in slices of its length, and the thickness of a finger, together with some ham, bacon, and the white of chickens cut after the same manner; put the whole into a stew-pan seasoned with salt, pepper, sweet herbs, and spice; then take the guts cleansed, cut and divide them in parcels, and fill them with your slices; then lay in the bottom of a kettle or pan some slices of bacon and veal, season them with some pepper, salt, a bay-leaf, and an onion, and lay some bacon and veal over them; then put in a pint of white wine, and let it stew softly, close covered, with fire over and under it, if the pot or pan will allow it; then broil the puddings on a sheet of white paper, well buttered on the inside.

To dress a Calf's Liver in a Caul.

TAKE off the under-skins, and shred the liver very small, then take an ounce of truffles and morels chopped small, with parsley; roast two or three onions, take off their outermost coats, pound six cloves and a dozen coriander-seeds, add them to the onions, and pound them together in a marble mortar; then take them out, and mix them with the liver; take a pint of cream, half a pint of milk, and seven or eight new-laid eggs; beat them together, boil them, but do not let them curdle; shred a pound of suet as small as you can, half melt it in a pan, and pour it into your egg and cream, then pour it into your liver, then mix all well together, season it with pepper, salt, nutmeg, and a little thyme, and let it stand till it is cold; spread a caul over the bottom and sides of the stew-pan, and put in your hashed liver and cream all together, fold it up in the caul in the shape of a calf's liver, then turn it upside down carefully, lay it in a dish that will bear the oven, and do it over with beaten egg, dredge it with grated bread, and bake it in an oven. Serve it up hot for a first course.

To roast a Calf's Liver.

LARD it with bacon, spit it first, and roast it: serve it up with good gravy.

Calves' Feet stewed.

CUT a calf's foot into four pieces, put it into a sauce-pan with half a pint of soft water and a middling potatoe; scrape the outside skin clean off, slice it thin, and a middling onion peeled and sliced thin, some beaten pepper and salt, cover it
close,

close, and let it stew very softly for about two hours after it boils; be sure to let it simmer as softly as you can; eat it without any other sauce: it is an excellent dish.

To make Fricandillas.

TAKE two pounds of lean veal and half a pound of kidney-suet chopped small, the crumb of a two-penny French roll soaked in hot milk; squeeze the milk out and put it to the veal; season it pretty high with pepper and salt, and grated nutmeg; make it into balls as big as a tea-cup, with the yolks of eggs over it, and fry them in butter till they are of a fine light brown; have a quart of veal broth in a stew-pan, stew them gently three quarters of an hour, thicken it with butter rolled in flour, and add the juice of half a lemon; put it in a dish with the sauce over, and garnish with notched lemon and beet root.

To make a Scotch Haggass.

TAKE the lights, heart, and chitterlings of a calf, chop them very fine, and a pound of suet chopped fine; season with pepper and salt to your palate; mix in a pound of flour or oatmeal, roll it up, and put it into a calf's bag, and boil it; an hour and a half will do it. Some add a pint of good thick cream, and put in a little beaten mace, cloves, or nutmeg; or all-spice is very good in it.

To make it sweet with Fruit.

TAKE the meat and suet as above, and flour, with beaten mace, cloves, and nutmeg to your palate, a pound of currants washed very clean, a pound of raisins stoned and chopped fine, half a pint of sack; mix all well together, and boil it in the calf's bag two hours. You must carry it to table in the bag it was boiled in.

To dress a Ham à la Braise.

CLEAR the knuckle, take off the swerd, and lay it in water to freshen; then tie it about with a string; take slices of bacon and beef, beat and season them well with spice and sweet herbs; then lay them in the bottom of a kettle, with onions, parsnips, and carrots sliced, with some cives and parsley; lay in your ham the fat side uppermost, and cover it with slices of beef, and over that with slices of bacon; then lay on some sliced roots and herbs the same as under it: cover it close, and stop it close with paste; put fire both over and under it, and let it stew with a very slow fire twelve hours; put it in a pan, dredge it well with grated bread, and brown it with a hot iron; or put it in the oven, and bake it one hour: then serve it upon a clean napkin. Garnish with raw parsley.

N. B. If you eat it hot, make a ragoo thus: take a veal sweetbread, some livers of fowls, cocks-combs, mushrooms, and truffles; toss them up in a pint of good gravy, seasoned with spice as you like it; thicken it with a piece of butter rolled in flour, and a glass of red wine; then brown your ham as above, and let it stand a quarter of an hour to drain the fat out; take the liquor it was stewed in, strain it, skim all the fat off, put it to the gravy, and boil it up with a spoonful of browning. It will do as well as the essence of ham. Sometimes you may serve it up with a ragoo of crawfish, and sometimes with carp-sauce.

To roast a Ham or Gammon.

TAKE off the swerd, or what we call the skin, or rind, and lay it in lukewarm water for two or three hours; then lay it in a pan, pour upon it a quart of canary, and let it steep in it for ten or twelve hours. When you have spitted it, put some sheets of white paper over the fat side, pour the canary in which it was soaked in the dripping-pan, and baste it all the time it is roasting; when it is roasted enough pull off the paper, and dredge it well with crumbled bread and parsley shred fine; make the fire brisk, and brown it well. If you heat it hot, garnish it with raspings of bread: if cold, serve it on a clean napkin, and garnish it with parsley for a second course.

Or thus: take off the skin of the ham or gammon, when you have half-boiled it, and dredge it with oatmeal sifted very fine, baste it with butter, then roast it gently two hours; stir up your fire, and brown it quick; when so done, dish it up, and pour brown gravy in the dish. Garnish with bread raspings, if hot; if cold, garnish with parsley.

To make Essence of Ham.

TAKE a ham, and cut off all the fat, cut the lean in thin pieces, and lay them in the bottom of your stew pan; put over them six onions sliced, two carrots, and one parsnip, two or three leeks, a few fresh mushrooms, a little parsley and sweet-herbs, four or five shalots, and some cloves and mace; put a little water at the bottom; set it on a gentle stove till it begins to stick; then put in a gallon of veal broth to a ham of fourteen pounds, (more or less broth, according to the size of the ham,) let it stew very gently for one hour; then strain it off, and put it away for use.

To stuff a Chine of Pork.

MAKE a stuffing of the fat leaf of pork, parsley, thyme, sage, eggs, crumbs of bread; season it with pepper, salt, shalot,

lot, and nutmeg, and stuff it thick; then roast it gently, and when it is about a quarter roasted, cut the skin in slips: and make your sauce with apples, lemon-peel, two or three cloves, and a blade of mace; sweeten it with sugar, put some butter in, and have mustard in a cup.

To barbecue a Leg of Pork.

LAY down your leg to a good fire, put into the dripping-pan two bottles of red wine, baste your pork with it all the time it is roasting; when it is enough, take up what is left in the pan, put to it two anchovies, the yolks of three eggs boiled hard and pounded fine, with a quarter of a pound of butter and half a lemon, a bunch of sweet herbs, a tea-spoonful of lemon-pickle, a spoonful of catchup, and one of tarragon vinegar, or a little tarragon shred small), boil them a few minutes, then draw your pork, and cut the skin down from the bottom of the shank in rows an inch broad, raise every other row, and roll it to the shank, strain your sauce, and pour it on boiling hot; lay oyster-patties all round the pork, and sprigs of green parsley.

Various Ways of dressing a Pig.

FIRST skin your pig up to the ears whole, then make a good plumb-pudding batter, with good beef fat, fruit, eggs, milk, and flour; fill the skin, and sew it up; it will look like a pig; but you must bake it, flour it very well, and rub it all over with butter, and when it is near enough, draw it to the oven's mouth, rub it dry, and put it in again for a few minutes; lay it in the dish, and let the sauce be small gravy and butter in the dish: cut the other part of the pig into four quarters, roast them as you do lamb, throw mint and parsley on it as it roasts; then lay them on water-cresses, and have mint-sauce in a bason. Any one of these quarters will make a pretty side-dish: or take one quarter and roast, cut the other in steaks, and fry them fine and brown. Have stewed spinage in the dish, and lay the roast upon it, and the fried in the middle. Garnish with hard eggs and Seville oranges cut into quarters, and have some butter in a cup: or for change, you may have good gravy in the dish, and garnish with fried parsley and lemon; or you may make a ragoo of sweetbreads, artichoke-bottoms, truffles, morels, and good gravy, and pour over them. Garnish with lemon. Either of these will do for a top-dish of a first course. You may fricassee it white for a second course at top, or a side-dish.

You may take a pig, skin him, and fill him with force-meat made thus: take two pounds of young pork, fat and all, two pounds of veal the same, some sage, thyme, parsley, a little

lemon-

lemon-peel, pepper, salt, mace, cloves, and a nutmeg: mix them and beat them fine in a mortar, then fill the pig, and sew it up. You may either roast or bake it. Have nothing but good gravy in the dish. Or you may cut it into slices, and lay the head in the middle. Save the head whole with the skin on, and roast it by itself: when it is enough, cut it in two and lay it in your dish: have ready some good gravy and dried sage rubbed in it, thicken it with a piece of butter rolled in flour, take out the brains, beat them up with the gravy, and pour them into the dish.

N. B. You may make a very good pie of it, as you may see in the directions for pies, which you may either make a bottom or side-dish.

You must observe in your white fricassee that you take off the fat. Or you may make a very good dish thus: take a quarter of a pig skinned, cut it into chops, season them with spice, and wash them with the yolks of eggs, butter the bottom of a dish, lay these steaks on the dish, and upon every steak lay some force-meat the thickness of half a crown, made thus: Take half a pound of veal, and of fat pork the same quantity, chop them very well together, and beat them in a mortar fine; add some sweet herbs and sage, a little lemon-peel, nutmeg, pepper, and salt, and a little beaten mace; upon this lay a layer of bacon or ham, and then a bay leaf; take a little fine skewer and stick it just in about two inches long to hold them together, then pour a little melted butter over them, and send them to the oven to bake: when they are enough, lay them in your dish, and pour good gravy over them, with mushrooms, and garnish with lemon.

A Pig in Jelly.

CUT it into quarters, and lay it into your stew-pan; put in one calf's foot and the pig's feet, a pint of Rhenish wine, the juice of four lemons, and one quart of water, three or four blades of mace, two or three cloves, some salt, and a very little piece of lemon-peel; stove it, or do it over a slow fire two hours; then take it up, lay the pig into the dish you intended for it, then strain the liquor, and when the jelly is cold, skim off the fat, and leave the settling at the bottom. Beat up the whites of six eggs, and boil up with the jelly about ten minutes, and put it through a bag till it is clear, then pour the jelly over the pig; then serve it up cold in the jelly.

Collared Pig.

KILL a fine young roasting pig, dress off the hair and draw it, and wash it clean, rip it open from one end to the other, and take out all the bones; rub it all over with pepper and salt, a

little

little cloves and mace beat fine, six sage leaves and sweet herbs chopped small; roll up your pig tight, and bind it with a fillet; fill the pot you intend to boil it in with soft water, a bunch of sweet herbs, some pepper-corns, some cloves and mace, a handful of salt, and a pint of vinegar; when the liquor boils, put in your pig; boil it till it is tender; take it up, and when it is almost cold bind it over again, put it into an earthen pan and pour the liquor your pig was boiled in over it, and always keep it covered; when you want it, take it out of the pan, untie the fillet as far as you want to cut it; then cut it in slices and lay it in your dish. Garnish with parsley.

To dress a Pig the French Way.

SPIT your pig, lay it down to the fire, let it roast till it is thoroughly warm, then cut it off the spit, and divide it in twenty pieces. Set them to stew in half a pint of white wine and a pint of strong broth, seasoned with grated nutmeg, pepper, two onions cut small, and some stripped thyme. Let it stew an hour, then put to it half a pint of strong gravy, a piece of butter rolled in flour, some anchovies, and a spoonful of vinegar or mushroom-pickle; when it is enough, lay it in your dish, and pour the gravy over it, then garnish with orange and lemon.

To dress a Pig au Pere Douillet.

CUT off the head, and divide it into quarters, lard them with bacon, season them well with mace, cloves, pepper, nutmeg, and salt. Lay a layer of fat bacon at the bottom of a kettle, lay the head in the middle, and the quarters round; then put in a bay-leaf, an onion sliced, lemon, carrots, parsnips, parsley, and cives; cover it again with bacon, put in a quart of broth, stew it over the fire for an hour, and then take it up; put your pig into a stew-pan or kettle, pour in a bottle of white wine, cover it close, and let it stew for an hour very softly. If you would serve it cold, let it stand till it is so; then drain it well, and wipe it, that it may look white, and lay it in a dish with the head in the middle and the quarters round, then throw some green parsley all over: or any one of the quarters is a very pretty dish, laid on water-cresses. If you would have it hot, whilst your pig is stewing in the wine, take the first gravy it was stewed in, and strain it, skim of all the fat, then take a sweetbread cut into five or six slices, some truffles, morels, and mushrooms; stew all together till they are enough, thicken it with the yolks of two eggs, or a piece of butter rolled in flour, and when your pig is enough take it out, and lay it in your dish; put the wine it was stewed in to the ragoo, then pour all over the pig, and garnish with lemon.

A Pig

A Pig Matelote.

GUT and scald your pig, cut off the head and pettitoes, then cut your pig in four quarters, put them with the head and toes into cold water; cover the bottom of a stew-pan with slices of bacon, and place over them the said quarters, with the pettitoes, and the head cut in two. Season the whole with pepper, salt, thyme, bay leaf, an onion, and a bottle of white wine; lay over more slices of bacon, put over it a quart of water, and let it boil. Take two large eels, skin and gut them, and cut them about five or six inches long; when your pig is half done, put in your eels, then boil a dozen of large crawfish, cut off the claws, and take off the shells of the tails; and when your pig and eels are enough, lay first your pig and the pettitoes round it, but do not put in the head, (it will be a pretty dish cold,) then lay your eels and crawfish over them, and take the liquor they were stewed in, skim off all the fat, then add to it half a pint of strong gravy, thickened with a little piece of butter rolled in flour, and a spoonful of browning, and pour over it, then garnish with crawfish and lemon. This will do for a first course or remove. Fry the brains and lay round, and all over the dish.

To dress a Pig like a fat Lamb.

TAKE a fat pig, cut off his head, slit and truss him up like a lamb; when he is slit through the middle and skinned, parboil him a little, then throw some parsley over him, roast it and dredge it. Let your sauce be half a pound of butter and a pint of cream, stirring all together till it is smooth; then pour it over and send it to table.

Barbecued Pig.

HAVING dressed a pig ten or twelve weeks old, as if you intended to roast it, make a force-meat in the following manner: take the liver of the pig, two anchovies, and six sage leaves chopped small; put them into a marble mortar with the crumbs of a penny-loaf, half a pint of Madeira wine, four ouces of butter, and half a tea-spoonful of Cayenne pepper, beat them all together to a paste, put it into your pig's belly, and sew it up; lay your pig down, at a good distance, before a large brisk fire; put into your dripping-pan two bottles of red wine and one of Madeira, baste it with the wine all the time it is roasting, and when it is half roasted, put two penny loaves under the pig; if there is not wine enough put in more, and when the pig is near done, take the loaves and sauce out of the pan, and put to the sauce half a lemon, a bundle of sweet herbs, an anchovy chopped

chopped small, boil it five minutes, and then draw your pig when it has roasted four hours; put into the pig's mouth an orange or lemon, and a loaf on each side; skim off the fat, and strain your sauce through a sieve, and pour over the pig boiling hot; serve it up garnished with lemon and barberries; or you may bake it, only keep it basting with wine.

To dress Pigs' Pettitoes.

PUT your pettitoes into a sauce-pan with half a pint of water, a blade of mace, a little whole pepper, a bundle of sweet herbs, and an onion. Let them boil five minutes, then take out the liver, lights, and heart, mince them very fine, grate a little nutmeg over them, and shake a little flour on them; let the feet do till they are tender, then take them out and strain the liquor, put all together with a little salt and a piece of butter as big as a walnut, shake the sauce-pan often, let it simmer five or six minutes, then cut some toasted sippets and lay round the dish, lay the mince-meat and sauce in the middle, and the pettitoes split round it. You may add the juice of half a lemon, or a very little vinegar.

To make a pretty Dish of a Breast of Venison.

TAKE half a pound of butter, flour your venison, and fry it of a fine brown on both sides; then take it up and keep it hot covered in the dish; take some flour and stir it into the butter till it is quite thick and brown (but take great care it do not burn), stir in it half a pound of lump-sugar beat fine, and pour in as much red wine as will make it of the thickness of a ragoo; squeeze in the juice of a lemon, give it a boil up, and pour it over the venison. Do not garnish the dish, but send it to table.

To boil a Haunch or Neck of Venison.

LAY it in salt for a week, then boil it in a cloth well floured; for every pound of venison allow a quarter of an hour for the boiling. For sauce you must boil some cauliflowers, pulled into little sprigs, in milk and water, some fine white cabbage, some turnips cut into dice, with some beet-root cut into long narrow pieces about an inch and a half long and half an inch thick; lay a sprig of cauliflower, and some of the turnips mashed with some cream and a little butter; let your cabbage be boiled and then beat in a sauce-pan with a piece of butter and salt, lay that next the cauliflower, then the turnips, then cabbage, and so on till the dish is full; place the beet-root here and there, just as you fancy: it looks very pretty, and is a fine dish. Have a little melted butter in a cup, if wanted.

N. B. A

N. B. A leg of mutton cut venison-fashion, and dressed the same way, is a pretty dish : or a fine neck, with the scrag cut off. This eats well boiled or hashed, with gravy and sweet sauce, next day.

CHAP. VI.

To dress POULTRY, GAME, &c.

To roast a Turkey.

THE best way to roast a turkey is to loosen the skin on the breast, and fill it with force-meat, made thus : take a quarter of a pound of beef-suet, as much of crumbs of bread, a little lemon-peel, an anchovy, some nutmeg, pepper, parsley, and a little thyme. Chop and beat them all well together, mix them with the yolk of an egg, and stuff up the breast ; when you have no suet, butter will do : or you may make your force-meat thus : spread bread and butter thin, and grate some nutmeg over it ; when you have enough roll it up, and stuff the breast of the turkey ; then roast it of a fine brown, but be sure to pin some white paper on the breast till it is near enough. You must have good gravy in the dish, and bread-sauce, made thus : take a good piece of crumb, put it into a pint of water, with a blade or two of mace, two or three cloves, and some whole pepper. Boil it up five or six times, then with a spoon take out the spice you had before put in, and then you must pour off the water (you may boil an onion in it, if you please) ; then beat up the bread with a good piece of butter and a little salt. Or onion-sauce, made thus : take some onions, peel them, and cut them into thin slices, and boil them half an hour in milk and water ; then drain the water from them, and beat them up with a good piece of butter ; shake a little flour in, and stir it all together with a little cream (if you have it), or milk will do ; put the sauce into boats, and garnish with lemon.

Another way to make sauce : take half a pint of oysters, strain the liquor, and put the oysters with the liquor into a sauce-pan, with a blade or two of mace ; let them just lump, then pour in a glass of white wine, let it boil once, and thicken it with a piece of butter rolled in flour. Serve this up in a bason by itself, with good gravy in the dish, for every body does not love oyster-sauce. This makes a pretty side-dish for supper, or a corner-dish of a table for dinner. If you chafe it in the dish, add half a pint of gravy, and boil it up together. This sauce

MADE PLAIN AND EASY. 93

fauce is good either with boiled or roasted turkies or fowls; but you may leave the gravy out, adding as much butter as will do for sauce, and garnishing with lemon.

Another bread-sauce: take some crumbs of bread, rubbed through a fine cullender, put to it a pint of milk, a little butter, and some salt, a few corns of white pepper, and an onion; boil them for fifteen minutes, take out the onion and beat it up well, then toss it up and put it in your sauce-boats.

A white Sauce for Fowls or Chickens.

TAKE a little strong veal gravy, with a little white pepper, mace, and salt boiled in it; have it clear from any skin or fat; as much cream, with a little flour mixed in the cream, a little mountain wine to your liking; boil it up gently for five minutes, then strain it over your chickens or fowls, or in boats.

To make Mock Oyster-Sauce, either for Turkies or Fowls boiled.

FORCE the turkies or fowls as above, and make your sauce thus: take a quarter of a pint of water, an anchovy, a blade or two of mace, a piece of lemon-peel, and five or six whole pepper-corns; boil these together, then strain them, add as much butter with a little flour as will do for sauce; let it boil, and lay sausages round the fowl or turkey. Garnish with lemon.

To make Mushroom-Sauce for white Fowls of all Sorts.

TAKE a quart of fresh mushrooms, well cleaned and washed, cut them in two, put them in a stew-pan, with a little butter, a blade of mace, and a little salt; stew it gently for half an hour, then add a pint of cream and the yolks of two eggs beat very well, and keep stirring it till it boils up; then squeeze half a lemon, put it over your fowls or turkies, or in basons, or in a dish, with a piece of French bread, first buttered then toasted brown, and just dip it in boiling water; put it in the dish, and the mushrooms over.

Mushroom-Sauce for white Fowls boiled.

TAKE half a pint of cream and a quarter of a pound of butter, stir them together one way till it is thick; then add a spoonful of mushroom-pickle, pickled mushrooms, or fresh, if you have them. Garnish only with lemon.

To make Celery-Sauce, either for roasted or boiled Fowls, Turkies, Partridges, or any other Game.

TAKE a large bunch of celery, wash and pare it very clean, cut it into little thin bits, and boil it softly in a little water till it is tender; then add a little beaten mace, some nutmeg, pep-

per,

per, and salt, thickened with a good piece of butter rolled in flour; then boil it up and pour in your dish.

You may make it with cream thus: boil your celery as above, and add some mace, nutmeg, a piece of butter as big as a walnut rolled in flour, and half a pint of cream; boil them all together.

To make brown Celery-Sauce.

STEW the celery as above, then add mace, nutmeg, pepper, salt, a piece of butter rolled in flour, with a glass of red wine, a spoonful of catchup, and half a pint of good gravy; boil all these together, and pour into the dish. Garnish with lemon.

To stew a Turkey or Fowl in Celery Sauce.

YOU must judge according to the largeness of your turkey or fowl what celery or sauce you want. Take a large fowl, put it into a sauce-pan or pot, and put to it one quart of good broth or gravy, a bunch of celery washed clean and cut small, with some mace, cloves, pepper, and all-spice, tied loose in a muslin rag; put in an onion and a sprig of thyme, a little salt and Cayenne pepper; let these stew softly till they are enough, then add a piece of butter rolled in flour; take up your fowl and pour the sauce over it. An hour will do a large fowl, or a small turkey; but a very large turkey will take two hours to do it softly. If it is over-done or dry, it is spoiled; but you may be a judge of that if you look at it now and then. Mind to take out the onion, thyme, and spice before you send it to table.

N. B. A neck of veal done this way is very good, and will take two hours doing.

To make Egg-Sauce proper for roasted Chickens.

MELT your butter thick and fine, chop two or three hard-boiled eggs fine, put them into a bason, pour the butter over them, and have good gravy in the dish.

Shalot-Sauce for roasted Fowls.

TAKE six shalots chopped fine, put them into a sauce-pan with a gill of gravy, a spoonful of vinegar, some pepper and salt, stew them for a minute; then pour them into your dish, or put it in sauce-boats.

Carrier-Sauce.

TAKE a Spanish onion, and cut it in thin slices, put it into a deep plate, take half a pint of boiling water, with a spoonful of vinegar, a little pepper and salt, and pour it over the onion.

Shalot-Sauce for a Scrag of Mutton boiled.

TAKE two spoonfuls of the liquor the mutton is boiled in, two spoonfuls of vinegar, two or three shalots cut fine, with a little salt; put it into a sauce-pan, with a piece of butter as big as a walnut rolled in a little flour; stir it together, and give it a boil. For those who love shalot, it is the prettiest sauce that can be made to a scrag of mutton.

To dress Livers with Mushroom-Sauce.

TAKE some pickled or fresh mushrooms cut small (both if you have them), and let the livers be bruised fine, with a good deal of parsley chopped small, a spoonful or two of catchup, a glass of white wine, and as much good gravy as will make sauce enough; thicken it with a piece of butter rolled in flour. This does either for roasted or boiled.

A pretty little Sauce.

TAKE the liver of the fowl, bruise it with a little of the liquor, cut a little lemon-peel fine, melt some good butter, and mix the liver by degrees; give it a boil, and pour it into the dish.

To make Lemon-Sauce for boiled Fowls.

TAKE a lemon and pare off the rind, cut it into slices, and take the kernels out, cut it into square bits, blanch the liver of the fowl, and chop it fine; mix the lemon and liver together in a boat, and pour some hot melted butter on it, and stir it up. Boiling of it will make it go to oil.

A German Way of dressing Fowls.

TAKE a turkey or fowl, stuff the breast with what force-meat you like, and fill the body with roasted chesnuts peeled. Roast it, and have some more roasted chesnuts peeled, put them in half a pint of good gravy, with a little piece of butter rolled in flour; boil these together with some small turnips and sausages cut in slices, and fried or boiled. Garnish with chesnuts. You may leave the turnips out.

N. B. You may dress ducks the same way.

To dress a Turkey or Fowl to Perfection.

BONE them, and make a force-meat thus: take the flesh of a fowl, cut it small, then take a pound of veal, beat it in a mortar with half a pound of beef-suet, as much crumbs of bread, some mushrooms, truffles, and morels cut small, a few sweet herbs and parsley, with some nutmeg, pepper, and salt, a little mace beaten, some lemon-peel cut fine; mix all these together

together with the yolks of two eggs, then fill your turkey and roast it. This will do for a large turkey, and so in proportion for a fowl. Let your sauce be good gravy, with mushrooms, truffles, and morels in it: then garnish with lemon, and for variety sake, you may lard your fowl or turkey.

To stew a Turkey brown.

TAKE your turkey after it is nicely picked and drawn, fill the skin of the breast with force-meat, and put an anchovy, a shalot, and a little thyme in the belly; lard the breast with bacon, then put a good piece of butter in the stew-pan, flour the turkey, and fry it just of a fine brown; then take it out, and put it into a deep stew-pan, or little pot, that will just hold it, and put in as much gravy as will barely cover it, a glass of white wine, some whole pepper, mace, two or three cloves, and a little bundle of sweet herbs; cover it close, and stew it for an hour, then take up the turkey, and keep it hot covered by the fire, and boil the sauce to about a pint, strain it off, add the yolks of two eggs and a piece of butter rolled in flour; stir it till it is thick, and then lay your turkey in the dish and pour your sauce over it. You may have ready some little French loaves about the bigness of an egg, cut off the tops, and take out the crumb; then fry them of a fine brown, fill them with stewed oysters, lay them round the dish, and garnish with lemon.

To stew a Turkey brown the nice Way.

BONE it, and fill it with a force-meat made thus: take the flesh of a fowl, half a pound of veal, and the flesh of two pigeons, with a well-picked or dry tongue, peel it, and chop it all together, then beat it in a mortar, with the marrow of a beef bone, or a pound of the fat of a loin of veal; season it with two or three blades of mace, two or three cloves, and half a nutmeg dried at a good distance from the fire, and pounded, with a little pepper and salt; mix all these well together, fill your turkey, fry it of a fine brown, and put it into a little pot that will just hold it; lay four or five skewers at the bottom of the pot to keep the turkey from sticking; put in a quart of good beef and veal gravy wherein was boiled spice and sweet herbs, cover it close, and let it stew half an hour; then put in a glass of white wine, one spoonful of catchup, a large spoonful of pickled mushrooms, and a few fresh ones (if you have them), a few truffles and morels, a piece of butter as big as a walnut rolled in flour; cover it close, and let it stew half an hour longer; get the little French rolls ready fried, take some oysters and strain the liquor from them, then put the oysters and liquor into a sauce-pan, with a blade of mace, a

little

little white wine, and a piece of butter rolled in flour; let them stew till thick, then fill the loaves, lay the turkey in the dish, and pour the sauce over it. If there is any fat on the gravy take it off, and lay the loaves on each side of the turkey. Garnish with lemon when you have no loaves, and take oysters dipped in butter and fried.

N. B. The same will do for any white fowl.

Turkies and Chickens dressed after the Dutch Way.

Boil them, season them with salt, pepper, and cloves; then to every quart of broth put a quarter of a pound of rice or vermicelli: it is eat with sugar and cinnamon. The two last may be left out.

A Turkey stuffed after the Hamburgh Way.

Take one pound of beef, three quarters of a pound of suet, mince it very small, season it with salt, pepper, cloves, mace, and sweet-marjoram; then mix two or three eggs with it, loosen the skin all round the turkey, and stuff, and roast it.

A Turkey à la daub, to be sent up hot.

Cut the turkey down the back just enough to bone it, without spoiling the look of it, then stuff it with a nice forcemeat made of oysters chopped fine, crumbs of bread, pepper, salt, shalots, a very little thyme, parsley and butter, fill it as full as you like, and sew it up with a thread, tie it up in a clean cloth and boil it very white, but not too much. You may serve it up with oyster-sauce made good, or take the bones with a piece of veal, mutton, and bacon, and make a rich gravy seasoned with pepper, salt, shalots, and a little bit of mace, strain it off through a sieve, and stew your turkey in it; (after it is half boiled,) just half an hour, dish it up in the gravy after it is well skimmed, strained, and thickened with a few mushrooms stewed white, or stewed pallets, force-meat balls, fried oysters, or sweetbreads, and pieces of lemon. Dish it up with the breast upwards; if you send it up garnished with pallets, take care to have them stewed tender first; before you add them to the turkey, you may put a few morels and truffles in your sauce, if you like it, but take care to wash them clean.

Turkey à la daub, to be sent up cold.

Bone the turkey, and season it with pepper and salt, then spread over it some slices of ham, upon that some force-meat, upon that a fowl, boned and seasoned as above, then more ham and force-meat, then sew it up with thread; cover the bottom of the stew-pan with veal and ham, then lay in the turkey the breaſt down, chop all the bones to pieces, and put them on the turkey, cover the pan and ſet it on the fire five minutes, then put in as much clear broth as will cover it, let it boil two hours, when it is more than half done, put in one ounce of iſing-glaſs and a bundle of herbs. When it is done enough, take out the turkey, and ſtrain the jelly through a hair ſieve, ſkim off all the fat, and when it is cold, lay the turkey upon it, the breaſt down, and cover it with the reſt of the jelly. Let it ſtand in ſome cold place; when you ſerve it up, turn it on the diſh it is to be ſerved in: if you pleaſe, you may ſpread butter over the turkey's breaſt, and put ſome green parſley or flowers, or what you pleaſe, and in what form you like.

A Turkey, &c. in Jelly.

Boil a turkey, or a fowl, as white as you can, let it ſtand till cold, and have ready a jelly made thus: take a fowl, ſkin it, take off all the fat, do not cut it to pieces, nor break the bones; take four pounds of a leg of veal, without any fat or ſkin, put it into a well-tinned ſauce-pan, put to it full three quarts of water, ſet it on a very clear fire till it begins to ſimmer; be ſure to ſkim it well, but take great care it does not boil. When it is well ſkimmed, ſet it ſo as it will but juſt ſeem to ſimmer; put to it two large blades of mace, half a nutmeg, and twenty corns of white pepper, a little bit of lemon-peel as big as a ſixpence. This will take ſix or ſeven hours doing. When you think it is a ſtiff jelly, which you will know by taking a little out to cool; be ſure to ſkim off all the fat, if any, and be ſure not to ſtir the meat in the ſauce-pan. A quarter of an hour before it is done, throw in a large tea-ſpoonful of ſalt, ſqueeze in the juice of half a fine Seville orange or lemon; when you think it is enough, ſtrain it off through a clean ſieve, but do not pour it off quite to the bottom, for fear of ſettlings. Lay the turkey or fowl in the diſh you intend to ſend it to the table in, beat up the whites of ſix eggs to a froth, and put the liquor to it, then boil it five or ſix minutes, and run it through a jelly-bag till it is very clear, then pour the liquor over it, let it ſtand till quite cold; colour ſome of the jelly in different colours, and when it is near cold, with a ſpoon ſprinkle it over, in what form or fancy you pleaſe, and ſend it to table; a few naſtertium flowers ſtuck here and there, look pretty, if you can get them, but theſe as well as lemon, &c. are entirely fancy. This is a very pretty diſh for a cold collation or a ſupper. All ſorts of birds or fowls may be done this way.

A Fowl à la Braiſe.

Truss your fowl, with the legs turned into the belly, ſeaſon it both inſide and out, with beaten mace, nutmeg, pepper, and

and salt, lay a layer of bacon at the bottom of a deep stew-pan, then a layer of veal, and afterwards the fowl, then put in an onion, two or three cloves stuck in a little bundle of sweet herbs, with a piece of carrot, then put at the top a layer of bacon, another of veal, and a third of beef, cover it close, and let it stand over the fire for two or three minutes, then pour in a pint of broth, or hot water; cover it close, and let it stew an hour; afterwards take up your fowl, strain the sauce, and after you have skimmed off the fat, boil it down till it is of a glaze, then put it over the fowl. You may add just what you please to the sauce. A ragoo of sweetbreads, cocks'-combs, truffles, and morels, or mushrooms, with force-meat balls, look very pretty, or any of the sauces above.

A Capon done after the French Way.

TAKE a quart of white wine, season the capon with salt, cloves, and whole pepper, and a few shalots; then put the capon in an earthen pan; you must take care it has not room to shake; it must be covered close, and done on a slow charcoal fire.

To roast a Fowl with Chesnuts.

FIRST take some chesnuts, roast them very carefully, so as not to burn them; take off the skin and peel them; take about a dozen of them cut small, and bruise them in a mortar; parboil the liver of the fowl, bruise it, cut about a quarter of a pound of ham or bacon, and pound it; then mix them all together, with a good deal of parsley chopped small, a little sweet herbs, some mace, pepper, salt, and nutmeg; mix these together and put into your fowl, and roast it. The best way of doing it is to tie the neck, and hang it up by the legs to roast with a string, and baste it with butter. For sauce, take the rest of the chesnuts peeled and skinned; put them into some good gravy, with a little white wine, and thicken it with a piece of butter rolled in flour; then take up your fowl, lay it in the dish, and pour in the sauce. Garnish with lemon.

To marinate Fowls.

TAKE a fine large fowl or turkey, raise the skin from the breast-bone with your finger; then take a veal sweetbread and cut it small, a few oysters, a few mushrooms, an anchovy, some pepper, a little nutmeg, some lemon-peel, and a little thyme; chop all together small, and mix it with the yolk of an egg, stuff it in between the skin and the flesh, but take great care you do not break the skin; and then stuff what oysters you please into the body of the fowl. You may lard the breast of the fowl with bacon, if you chuse it. Paper the breast, and roast it. Make good gravy, and garnish with lemon. You may add a few mushrooms to the sauce.

To make a Frangas Incopades.

TAKE three quarters of a pound of lean bacon or ham, two large onions sliced, four shalots, and two quarts of water, with a little beaten pepper, cloves, and mace, and a pennyworth of saffron, stew it gently till it is reduced to three pints, and strain it through a sieve; cut two fowls, as for a fricassee, and stew them in the broth till they are tender; mix two spoonfuls of flour in two spoonfuls of vinegar, and beat it up with some of the liquor till it is quite smooth; and mix the whole together, and boil it for ten minutes gently; put sippets in a soup-dish, and pour it all over them. You may add small force-meat balls, if you please, in it; or you may make it of veal in the form of veal olives; and you may send it in a tureen, if you like.

Pullets à la Sainte Menehout.

AFTER having trussed the legs in the body, slit them along the back, spread them open on a table, take out the thigh-bones, and beat them with a rolling-pin; then season them with pepper, salt, mace, nutmeg, and sweet herbs; after that take a pound and a half of veal, cut it into thin slices, and lay it in a stew-pan, of a convenient size, to stew the pullets in; cover it, and set it over a stove or slow fire; and when it begins to cleave to the pan, stir in a little flour, shake the pan about till it be a little brown; then pour in as much broth as will stew the fowls, stir it together, put in a little whole pepper, an onion, and a little piece of bacon or ham; then lay in your fowls, cover them close, and let them stew half an hour; then take them out, lay them on the gridiron to brown on the inside; then lay them before the fire to do on the outside; strew them over with the yolk of an egg, some crumbs of bread, and baste them with a little butter; let them be of a fine brown, and boil the gravy till there is about enough for sauce; strain it, put a few mushrooms in, and a little piece of butter rolled in flour; lay the pullets in the dish, and pour in the sauce. Garnish with lemon.

N. B. You may brown them in an oven, or fry them, which you please.

Chicken-Surprize.

IF a small dish, one large fowl will do; roast it, and take the lean from the bone; cut it in thin slices, about an inch long, toss it up with six or seven spoonfuls of cream, and a piece of butter rolled in flour, as big as a walnut. Boil it up and set it to cool; then cut six or seven thin slices of bacon
round,

round, place them in a patty-pan, and put some force-meat on each side; work them up in the form of a French roll, with a raw egg in your hand, leaving a hollow place in the middle; put in your fowl, and cover them with some of the same force-meat, rubbing them smooth with your hand and a raw egg; make them of the height and bigness of a French roll, and throw a little fine grated bread over them. Bake them three quarters or an hour, in a gentle oven, or under a baking cover, till they come to a fine brown, and place them on your mazarine, that they may not touch one another; but place them so that they may not fall flat in the baking; or you may form them on your table with a broad kitchen-knife, and place them on the thing you intend to bake them on. You may put the leg of a chicken into one of the loaves you intend for the middle. Let your sauce be gravy, thickened with butter and a little juice of lemon. This is a pretty side-dish for a first course, summer or winter, if you can get them.

Chickens in Savoury Jelly.

ROAST two chickens, then boil a gang of calf's-feet to a strong jelly, take out the feet, skim off the fat, beat the whites of three eggs very well, then mix them with half a pint of white wine vinegar, the juice of three lemons, a blade or two of mace, a few pepper-corns, and a little salt, put them to your jelly; when it has boiled five or six minutes, run it through a jelly-bag several times till it is very clear, then put a little in the bottom of a bowl that will hold your chickens; when they are cold, and the jelly quite set, lay them in with their breasts down, then fill up your bowl quite full with the rest of your jelly, which you must take care to keep from setting, (so that when you pour it into your bowl it will not break,) let it stand all night, the next day put your bason into warm water, pretty near the top; as soon as you find it loose in the bason, lay your dish over it, and turn it out upon it.

Chickens roasted with Force-meat and Cucumbers.

TAKE two chickens, dress them very neatly, break the breast-bone; and make force-meat thus: take the flesh of a fowl, and of two pigeons, with some slices of ham or bacon; chop them all well together, take the crumb of a penny-loaf soaked in milk and boiled, then set to cool; when it is cool, mix it all together; season it with beaten mace, nutmeg, pepper, and a little salt, a very little thyme, some parsley, and a little lemon-peel, with the yolks of two eggs; then fill your fowls, spit them, and tie them at both ends; after you have papered the breast, take four cucumbers, cut them in two, and lay them in salt and water two or three hours before; then dry them, and fill them with some of the force-meat, (which you must take care to save,) and tie them with a packthread; flour them, and fry them of a fine brown; when your chickens are enough, lay them in the dish, and untie your cucumbers; but take care the meat do not come out; then lay them round the chickens, with the flat side downwards, and the narrow end upwards. You must have some rich fried gravy, and pour into the dish; then garnish with lemon.

N. B. One large fowl done this way, with the cucumbers laid round it, looks pretty, and is a very good dish.

Chickens à la Braise.

TAKE a couple of fine chickens, lard them, and season them with pepper, salt, and mace; then lay a layer of veal in the bottom of a deep stew-pan, with a slice or two of bacon, an onion cut to pieces, a piece of carrot, and a layer of beef; then lay in the chickens with the breast downward, and a bundle of sweet herbs; after that, a layer of beef, and put in a quart of broth or water; cover it close, let it stew very softly for an hour, after it begins to simmer. In the mean time, get ready a ragoo made thus: take a good veal sweetbread or two, cut them small, set them on the fire, with a very little broth or water, a few cocks'-combs, truffles, and morels, cut small, with an ox-palate, if you have it; stew them all together till they are enough; and when your chickens are done, take them up, and keep them hot; then strain the liquor they were stewed in, skim the fat off, and pour into your ragoo; add a glass of red wine, a spoonful of catchup, and a few mushrooms; then boil all together with a few artichoke-bottoms cut in four, and asparagus-tops. If your sauce is not thick enough, take a little piece of butter rolled in flour; and when enough, lay your chickens in the dish, and pour the ragoo over them. Garnish with lemon.

Or, you may make your sauce thus: take the gravy the fowls were stewed in, strain it, skim off the fat; have ready half a pint of oysters with the liquor strained; put them to your gravy with a glass of white wine, a good piece of butter rolled in flour; then boil them all together, and pour over your fowls. Garnish with lemon.

To broil Chickens.

SLIT them down the back, and season them with pepper and salt; lay them on a very clear fire, and at a great distance. Let the inside lie next the fire till it is above half done; then turn them, and take great care the fleshy side do not burn, and let them be of a fine brown. Let your sauce be good gravy,

gravy, with mushrooms, and garnish with lemon and the livers broiled, the gizzards cut, flashed, and broiled with pepper and salt.

Or this sauce: take a handful of sorrel dipped in boiling water, drain it, and have ready half a pint of good gravy, a shalot shred small, and some parsley boiled very green, thicken it with a piece of butter rolled in flour, and add a glass of red wine; then lay your sorrel in heaps round the fowls, and pour the sauce over them. Garnish with lemon.

N. B. You may make just what sauce you fancy.

Pulled Chickens.

TAKE three chickens, boil them just fit for eating, but not too much; when they are boiled enough, flay all the skin off, and take the white flesh off the bones, pull it into pieces about the size of a large quill, and half as long as your finger. Have ready a quarter of a pint of good cream, and a piece of fresh butter about as big as an egg; stir them together till the butter is all melted, and then put in your chicken with the gravy that came from them; give them two or three tosses round on the fire, put them into a dish, and send them up hot.

N. B. The legs, pinions, and rump must be peppered and salted, done over with the yolk of an egg and bread crumbs, and broiled on a clear fire; put the white meat, with the rump, in the middle, and the legs and pinions round.

Chickens Chiringrate.

CUT off their feet, break the breast-bone flat with a rolling-pin; but take care you do not break the skin; flour them, fry them of a fine brown in butter, then drain all the fat out of the pan, but leave the chickens in. Lay a pound of gravy-beef, cut very thin, over your chickens, and a piece of veal cut very thin, a little mace, two or three cloves, some whole-pepper, an onion, a little bundle of sweet herbs, and a piece of carrot, and then pour in a quart of boiling water; cover it close, let it stew for a quarter of an hour; then take out the chickens and keep them hot: let the gravy boil till it is quite rich and good; then strain it off, and put it into your pan again, with two spoonfuls of red wine and a few mushrooms; put in your chickens to heat, then take them up, lay them into your dish, and pour your sauce over them. Garnish with lemon, and a few slices of cold ham broiled.

N. B. You may fill your chickens with force-meat, and lard them with bacon, and add truffles, morels, and sweetbreads, cut small; but then it will be a very high dish.

Chickens dressed the French Way.

QUARTER, then broil them, crumble over them a little bread and parsley; when they are half done, put them in a stew-pan, with three or four spoonfuls of gravy, and double the quantity of white wine, salt, and pepper, some fried veal-balls, and some suckers, onions, shalots, and some green gooseberries or grapes when in season; cover the pan close, and let it stew on a charcoal fire for an hour; thicken the liquor with the yolks of eggs, and the juice of lemon; garnish the dish with fried suckers, sliced lemon, and the livers.

Chickens boiled with Bacon and Celery.

BOIL two chickens very white in a pot by themselves, and a piece of ham, or good thick bacon; boil two bunches of celery tender; then cut them about two inches long, all the white part; put it into a sauce-pan, with half a pint of cream, a piece of butter rolled in flour, and some pepper and salt; set it on the fire, and shake it often: when it is thick and fine, lay your chickens in the dish, and pour your sauce in the middle, that the celery may lie between the fowls; and garnish the dish all round with slices of ham or bacon.

N. B. If you have cold ham in the house, that, cut into slices and broiled, does full as well, or better, to lay round the dish.

Chickens with Tongues. A good Dish for a great deal of Company.

TAKE six small chickens, boiled very white, six hogs tongues boiled and peeled, a cauliflower boiled very white in milk and water whole, and a good deal of spinage boiled green; then lay your cauliflower in the middle, the chickens close all round, and the tongues round them with the roots outward, and the spinage in little heaps between the tongues. Garnish with little pieces of bacon toasted, and lay a little piece on each of the tongues.

Scotch Chickens.

FIRST wash your chickens, dry them in a clean cloth, and singe them; then cut them into quarters; put them into a stew-pan or sauce-pan, and just cover them with water; put in in a blade or two of mace, and a little bundle of parsley; cover them close, and let them stew half an hour; then chop half a handful of clean washed parsley, and throw in, and have ready six eggs, whites and all, beat fine. Let your liquor boil up, and pour the eggs all over them as it boils; then send all together hot in a deep dish, but take out the bundle of parsley first.

first. You must be sure to skim them well before you put in your mace, and the broth will be fine and clear.

N. B. This is also a very pretty dish for sick people; but the Scotch gentlemen are very fond of it.

To stew Chickens the Dutch Way.

TAKE two chickens, truss them as for boiling; beat fine six cloves, and four blades of mace, a handful of parsley shred fine, some pepper and salt; mix all together, and put into the inside of your chickens; singe them and flour them; put them into a stew-pan; clarify as much butter as will cover them; stew them gently one hour; put them into a china bowl with the butter, and send them up hot.

To stew Chickens.

TAKE two chickens, cut them into quarters, wash them clean, and then put them into a sauce-pan; put to them a quarter of a pint of water, half a pint of red wine, some mace, pepper, a bundle of sweets herbs, an onion, and a few raspings; cover them close, let them stew half an hour; then take a piece of butter about as big as an egg, rolled in flour, put in, and cover it close for five or six minutes; shake the sauce-pan about, then take out the sweet herbs and onion. You may take the yolks of two eggs, beat and mixed with them, or leave them out. Garnish with lemon.

A pretty Way of stewing Chickens.

TAKE two fine chickens, half boil them, then take them up in a pewter, or silver dish; cut up your fowls, and separate all the joint-bones one from another, and then take out the breast-bones. If there is not liquor enough from the fowls, add a few spoonfuls of the water they were boiled in, put in a blade of mace, and a little salt; cover it close with another dish; set it over a stove, or chafing-dish of coals; let it stew till the chickens are enough, and then send them hot to the table in the same dish they were stewed in.

Note: This is a very pretty dish for any sick person, or for a lying-in lady. For change it is better than butter, and the sauce is very agreeable and pretty.

N. B. You may do rabbits, partridges, or moor-game this way.

Ducks Alamode.

TAKE two fine ducks, cut them into quarters, fry them in butter a little brown; then pour out all the fat, and throw a little flour over them, and half a pint of good gravy, a quarter of a pint of red wine, two shalots, an anchovy, and a bundle
of

of sweet herbs; cover them close, aud let them stew a quarter of an hour; take out the herbs, skim off the fat, and let your sauce be as thick as cream; send it to table, and garnish with lemon.

To stew Ducks with green Peas.

HALF roast your ducks, then put them into a stew-pan with a pint of good gravy, a little mint, and three or four sage leaves chopped small, cover them close and stew them half an hour, boil a pint of green peas, as for eating, and put them in after you have thickened the gravy; dish up your ducks, and pour the gravy and peas over them.

To dress a Wild Duck the best Way.

FIRST half roast it, then lay it in a dish, carve it, but leave the joints hanging together; throw a little pepper and salt, and squeeze the juice of a lemon over it; turn it on the breast, and press it hard with a plate, and add to its own gravy two or three spoonfuls of good gravy; cover it close with another dish, and set it over a stove ten minutes; then send it to table hot in the dish it was done in, and garnish with lemon. You may add a little red wine, and a shalot cut small, if you like it; but it is apt to make the duck eat hard, unless you first heat the wine, and pour it in just as it is done.

Another Way to dress a Wild Duck.

TAKE a wild duck, put some pepper and salt in the inside, and half roast it; have ready the following sauce: a gill of good gravy, and a gill of red wine; put it in a stew-pan, with three or four shalots cut fine; boil it up; then cut the duck in small pieces, and put it in with a little Cayenne pepper and salt; be careful to put in all the gravy that comes from the duck; simmer it for three minutes, and squeeze in a Seville orange or lemon; put it in the dish, and garnish with lemon.

To boil a Duck or a Rabbit with Onions.

BOIL your duck, or rabbit, in a good deal of water; be sure to skim your water; for there will always rise a scum, which, if it boils down, will discolour your fowls, &c. They will take about half an hour boiling. For sauce, your onions must be peeled, and throw them into water as you peel them; then cut them into thin slices, boil them in milk and water, and skim the liquor. Half an hour will boil them. Throw them into a clean sieve to drain; chop them and rub them through a cullender; put them into a sauce-pan, shake in a little flour; put to them two or three spoonfuls of cream, a good piece of butter; stew all together over the fire till they

are

are thick and fine; lay the duck or rabbit in the dish, and pour the sauce all over: if a rabbit, you must pluck out the jaw-bones, and stick one in each eye, the small end inwards.

Or you may make this sauce for change: take one large onion, cut it small, half a handful of parsley clean washed and picked, chop it small, a lettuce cut small, a quarter of a pint of good gravy, a good piece of butter rolled in a little flour; add a little juice of lemon, a little pepper and salt; let all stew together for half an hour; then add two spoonfuls of red wine. This sauce is most proper for a duck; lay your duck in the dish, and pour your sauce over it.

To dress a Duck with Green Peas.

PUT a deep stew-pan over the fire, with a piece of fresh butter; singe your duck and flour it, turn it in the pan two or three minutes; then pour out all the fat, but let the duck remain in the pan; put to it a pint of good gravy, a pint of peas, two lettuces cut small, a small bundle of sweet herbs, a little pepper and salt; cover them close, and let them stew for half an hour; now and then give the pan a shake; when they are just done, grate in a little nutmeg, and put in a very little beaten mace, and thicken it either with a piece of butter rolled in flour, or the yolk of an egg beat up with two or three spoonfuls of cream; shake it all together for three or four minutes, take out the sweet herbs, lay the duck in the dish, and pour the sauce over it. You may garnish with boiled mint chopped, or let it alone.

To dress a Duck with Cucumbers.

TAKE three or four cucumbers, pare them, take out the seeds, cut them into little pieces, lay them in vinegar for two or three hours before, with two large onions peeled and sliced; then do your duck as above; then take the duck out, and put in the cucumbers and onions, first drain them in a cloth, let them be a little brown; shake a little flour over them. In the mean time let your duck be stewing in the sauce-pan with a pint of gravy, for a quarter of an hour; then add to it the cucumbers and onions, with pepper and salt to your palate, a good piece of butter rolled in flour, and two or three spoonfuls of red wine; shake all together, and let it stew for eight or ten minutes; then take up your duck, and pour the sauce over it.

Or, you may roast your duck, and make this sauce, and pour over it; but then half a pint of gravy will be enough.

To dress a Duck à la Braise.

TAKE a duck, lard it with little pieces of bacon, season it inside and out with pepper and salt; lay a layer of bacon, cut
thin,

thin, in the bottom of a stew-pan, and then a layer of lean beef, cut thin; then lay your duck with some carrot, an onion, a little bundle of sweet herbs, a blade or two of mace, and a thin layer of beef over the duck; cover it close, and set it over a slow fire for eight or ten minutes; then take off the cover and shake in a little flour, give the pan a shake; pour in a pint of small broth, or boiling water; give the pan a shake or two, cover it close again, and let it stew half an hour; then take off the cover, take out the duck, and keep it hot; let the sauce boil till there is about a quarter of a pint, or a little better; then strain it, and put it into the stew-pan again, with a glass of red wine; put in your duck, shake the pan, and let it stew four or five minutes; then lay your duck in the dish, and pour the sauce over it, and garnish with lemon. If you love your duck very high, you may fill it with the following ingredients; take a veal sweetbread cut in eight or ten pieces, a few truffles, some oysters, a few sweet herbs and parsley chopped fine, a little pepper, salt, and beaten mace; fill your duck with the above ingredients, tie both ends tight, and dress as above. Or, you may fill it with force-meat made thus: take a little piece of veal, take all the skin and fat off, beat it in a mortar, with as much suet, and an equal quantity of crumbs of bread, a few sweet herbs, some parsley chopped, a little lemon-peel, pepper, salt, beaten mace, and nutmeg, and mix it up with the yolk of an egg.

You may stew an ox's palate tender, and cut it into pieces, with some artichoke-bottoms cut into four, and tossed up in the sauce. You may lard your duck, or let it alone, just as you please: for my part I think it best without.

To boil Ducks the French Way.

LET your ducks be larded, and half roasted; then take them off the spit, put them into a large earthen pipkin, with half a pint of red wine, and a pint of good gravy, some chesnuts, first roasted and peeled, half a pint of large oysters, the liquor strained, and the beards taken off, two or three little onions minced small, a very little stripped thyme, mace, pepper, and a little ginger beat fine; cover it close, and let them stew half an hour over a slow fire; add the crust of a French roll grated when you put in your gravy and wine. When they are enough, take them up, and pour the sauce over them.

To dress a Goose with Onions and Cabbage.

SALT the goose for a week, then boil it. It will take an hour. You may either make onion-sauce, as we do for ducks or cabbage boiled, chopped and stewed in butter, with a little pepper

pepper and salt; lay the goose in the dish, and pour the sauce over it. It eats very good with either.

Directions for roasting a Goose.

TAKE some sage, wash and pick it clean, and an onion; chop them very fine, with some pepper and salt, and put them into the belly; let your goose be clean picked, and wiped dry with a dry cloth, inside and out; put it down to the fire, and roast it brown: one hour will roast a large goose, three quarters of an hour, a small one. Serve it in your dish with some brown gravy, apple-sauce in a boat, and some gravy in another.

A Green Goose.

NEVER put any thing but a little pepper and salt, unless desired; put gravy in the dish, and green sauce in a boat; made thus: take half a pint of the juice of sorrel; if no sorrel, spinage-juice: have ready a cullis of veal broth, about half a pint, some sugar, the juice of an orange or lemon; boil it up for five or six minutes, then put your sorrel-juice in, and just boil it up. Be careful to keep it stirring all the time, or it will curdle; then put it in your boat.

To dress a Stubble Goose.

TAKE a goose, kill, and hang it up in the feathers, two or three nights, as it suits you; when you dress it, season it well with pepper and salt, take two middle sized onions, half a sour apple, a few sage leaves, chop these well, and put them into the inside with a lump of butter, the size of an egg, and a tea-cup full of water, tie it up close at both ends; if a large goose, it will take an hour and a half, if a small one, an hour, and so on in proportion; dish it up, pour into your dish some brown gravy, with two spoonfuls of red wine, the same of ale, serve it up with apple-sauce.

To dry a Goose.

GET a fat goose, take a handful of common salt, a quarter of an ounce of salt-petre, a quarter of a pound of coarse sugar; mix all together, and rub your goose very well; let it lie in this pickle a fortnight, turning and rubbing it every day; then roll it in bran, and hang it up in a chimney where wood-smoke is, for a week. If you have not that conveniency, send it to the baker's: the smoke of the oven will dry it: or you may hang it in your own chimney, not too near the fire, but make a fire under it, and lay horse-dung and saw-dust on it, and that will smother and smoke-dry it; when it is well dried, keep it in a dry place; you my keep it two or three months, or more; when you boil it, put in a good deal of water, and be sure to skim it well.

N. B.

N. B. You may send it up with boiled turnips, or cabbage, boiled and stewed in butter, or onion-sauce.

To dress a Goose in Ragoo.

FLAT the breast down with a cleaver, then press it down with your hand, skin it, dip it into scalding water; let it be cold, lard it with bacon, season it well with pepper, salt, and a little beaten mace; then flour it all over, take a pound of good beef-suet cut small, put it into a deep stew-pan, let it be melted, then put in your goose; let it be brown on both sides; when it is brown, put in a quart of boiling gravy, an onion or two, a bundle of sweet herbs, a bay leaf, some whole pepper, and a few cloves; cover it close, and let it stew softly till it is tender. About an hour will do it, if small; if a large one, an hour and a half. In the mean time make a ragoo: boil some turnips almost enough, some carrots and onions quite enough; cut your turnips and carrots the same as for a harrico of mutton, put them into a sauce-pan with half a pint of good beef gravy, a little pepper and salt, a piece of butter rolled in flour, and let this stew all together a quarter of an hour. Take the goose and drain it well; then lay it in the dish, and pour the ragoo over it.

Where the onion is disliked, leave it out. You may add cabbage boiled and chopped small.

A Goose Alamode.

TAKE a large fine goose, pick it clean, skin it, bone it nicely, take the fat off; then take a dried tongue, boil it, and peel it: take a fowl, and do it in the same manner as the goose; season it with pepper, salt, and beaten mace, roll it round the tongue; season the goose with the same; put the tongue and fowl in the goose, with some slices of ham or good bacon between them; put it into a little pot that will just hold it; put to it two quarts of beef gravy, a bundle of sweet herbs, and an onion; cover it close, and let it stew an hour over a good fire: when it begins to boil, let it do very softly; then take up your goose, and skim off all the fat; strain it, put in a glass of red wine, two spoonfuls of catchup, a veal sweetbread cut small, some truffles, morels and mushrooms, a piece of butter rolled in flour, and some pepper and salt, if wanted; put in the goose again, cover it close, and let it stew half an hour longer; then take it up, and pour the ragoo over. Garnish with lemon.

Note: This is a very fine dish. You must mind to save the bones of the goose and fowl, and put them into the gravy when it is first set on; and it will be better if you roll some beef-
marrow

marrow between the tongue and the fowl, and between the fowl and goose, it will make them mellow and eat fine. You may add six or seven yolks of hard eggs whole in the dish; they are a pretty addition. Take care to skim off the fat.

N. B. The best method to bone a goose or fowl of any sort, is to begin at the breast, and take all off the bones without cutting the back; for when it is sewed up, and you come to stew it, it generally bursts in the back, and spoils the shape of it.

To stew Giblets.

LET them be nicely scalded and picked, cut the pinions in two; cut the head, and the neck, and legs in two, and the gizzards in four; wash them very clean, put them into a stew-pan or soup-pot, with three pounds of scrag of veal, just cover them with water; let them boil up, take all the scum clean off; then put three onions, two turnips, one carrot, a little thyme and parsley, stew them till they are tender, strain them through a sieve, wash the giblets clean with some warm water out of the herbs, &c.; then take a piece of butter as big as a large walnut, put it in a stew-pan, melt it, and put in a large spoonful of flour, keep it stirring till it is smooth; then put in your broth and giblets, stew them for a quarter of an hour; season with salt: or, you may add a gill of Lisbon, and just before you serve them up, chop a handful of green parsley and put in; give them a boil up, and serve them in a tureen or soup dish.

N. B. Three pair will make a handsome tureen-ful.

To make Giblets à la Turtle.

LET three pair of giblets be done as before (well cleaned), put them into your stew-pan with four pounds of scrag of veal, and two pounds of lean beef, covered with water; let them boil up, and skim them very clean; then put in six cloves, four blades of mace, eight corns of all-spice, beat very fine, some basil, sweet-marjoram, winter-savoury, and a little thyme chopped very fine, three onions, two turnips, and one carrot; stew them till tender, then strain them through a sieve, and wash them clean out of the herbs in some warm water; then take a piece of butter, put it in your stew-pan, melt it, and put in as much flour as will thicken it, stir it till it is smooth, then put your liquor in, and keep stirring it all the time you pour it in, or else it will go into lumps, which, if it happens, you must strain it through a sieve; then put in a pint of Madeira wine, some pepper and salt, and some Cayenne pepper; stew it for ten minutes, then put in your giblets, add the juice of a lemon, and stew them fifteen minutes;

nutes; then serve them in a tureen. You may put in some egg-balls, made thus: boil six eggs hard, take out the yolks, put them in a mortar and beat them, throw in a spoonful of flour, and the yolk of a raw egg, beat them together till smooth; then roll them in little balls, and scald them in boiling water, and just before you serve the giblets up, put them in.

N. B. Never put your livers in at first, but boil them in a sauce-pan of water by themselves.

To roast Pigeons.

FILL them with parsley, clean washed and chopped, and some pepper and salt rolled in butter; fill the bellies, tie the neck-end close, so that nothing can run out; put a skewer through the legs, and have a little iron on purpose, with six hooks to it, and on each hook hang a pigeon; fasten one end of the string to the chimney, and the other end to the iron (this is what we call the poor man's spit); flour them, baste them with butter, and turn them gently for fear of hitting the bars. They will roast nicely, and be full of gravy. Take care how you take them off, not to lose any of the liquor. You may melt a very little butter, and put into the dish. Your pigeons ought to be quite fresh, and not too much done. This is by much the best way of doing them, for then they will swim in their own gravy, and a very little melted butter will do.

N. B. You may spit them on a long small spit, only tie both ends close; and send parsley and butter in one boat and gravy in another.

When you roast them on a spit, all the gravy runs out; or if you stuff them and broil them whole, you cannot save the gravy so well; though they will be very good with parsley and butter in the dish; or split and broiled, with pepper and salt.

To boil Pigeons.

BOIL them by themselves for fifteen minutes; then boil a handsome square piece of bacon and lay in the middle; stew some spinage to lay round; and lay the pigeons on the spinage. Garnish your dish with parsley, laid on a plate before the fire to crisp. Or, you may lay one pigeon in the middle, and the rest round, and the spinage between each pigeon, and a slice of bacon on each pigeon. Garnish with slices of bacon, and melted butter in a cup.

To à la daub Pigeons.

TAKE a large sauce-pan, lay a layer of bacon, then a layer of veal, a layer of coarse beef, and another little layer of
veal,

veal, about a pound of veal and a pound of beef cut very thin, a piece of carrot, a bundle of sweet herbs, an onion, some black and white pepper, a blade or two of mace, four or five cloves; cover the sauce-pan close, set it over a slow fire, draw it till it is brown to make the gravy of a fine light brown; then put in a quart of boiling water, and let it stew till the gravy is quite rich and good; then strain it off, and skim off all the fat. In the mean time stuff the bellies of the pigeons with force-meat, made thus: take a pound of veal, a pound of beef-suet, beat both in a mortar fine, an equal quantity of crumbs of bread, some pepper, salt, nutmeg, beaten mace, a little lemon-peel cut small, some parsley cut small, and a very little thyme stripped; mix all together with the yolks of two eggs; fill the pigeons and flat the breast down, flour them and fry them in fresh butter a little brown; then pour the fat clean out of the pan, and put the gravy to the pigeons; cover them close and let them stew a quarter of an hour, or till you think they are quite enough; then take them up, lay them in a dish, and pour in your sauce; on each pigeon lay a bay-leaf, and on the leaf a slice of bacon. You may garnish with a lemon notched, or let it alone.

N. B. You may leave out the stuffing; they will be very rich and good without it, and it is the best way of dressing them for a fine made-dish.

Pigeons au Poire.

MAKE a good force-meat as above, cut the feet quite off, stuff them in the shape of a pear, roll them in the yolk of an egg and then in crumbs of bread, stick the leg at the top, and butter a dish to lay them in; then send them to an oven to bake, but do not let them touch each other; when they are enough, lay them in a dish, and pour in good gravy thickened with the yolk of an egg, or butter rolled in flour; do not pour your gravy over the pigeons. You may garnish with lemon. It is a pretty genteel dish: or, for change, lay one pigeon in the middle, the rest round, and stewed spinage between; poached eggs on the spinage. Garnish with notched lemon and orange cut into quarters, and have melted butter in boats.

Or thus: bone your pigeons, and stuff them with force-meat; make them in the shape of a pear, with one foot stuck at the small end to appear like the stalk of a pear; rub them over with the yolk of an egg, and strew some crumbs of bread on; fry them in a pan of good dripping a nice light brown; put them in a drainer to drain all the fat off; then put them in a stew-pan with a pint of gravy, a gill of white wine, an onion stuck with cloves; cover them close and stew them for half an hour; take them out, skim off all the fat, and take out the onion; put in some butter rolled in flour, a spoonful of catchup, the same of browning, some truffles and morels, pickled mushrooms, two artichoke-bottoms cut in six pieces each, a little salt and Cayenne pepper, the juice of half a lemon; stew it five minutes, put in your pigeons and make them hot; put them in your dish and pour the sauce over them. Garnish with fried force-meat balls, or with a lemon cut in quarters.

Pigeons stoved.

TAKE a small cabbage-lettuce, just cut out the heart, and make a force-meat as before, only chop the heart of the lettuce and mix with it; then fill up the place, and tie it across with a packthread; fry it of a light brown in fresh butter, pour out all the fat, lay the pigeons round, flat them with your hand, season them a little with pepper, salt, and beaten mace, (take great care not to put too much salt,) pour in half a pint of Rhenish wine, cover it close, and let it stew about five or six minutes; then put in half a pint of good gravy, cover them close, and let them stew half an hour. Take a good piece of butter rolled in flour, shake it in; when it is fine and thick take it up, untie it, lay the lettuce in the middle, and the pigeons round; squeeze in a little lemon-juice, and pour the sauce all over them. Stew a little lettuce, and cut it into pieces for garnish, with pickled cabbage.

N. B. Or for change, you may stuff your pigeons with the same force-meat, and cut two cabbage-lettuces into quarters, and stew it as above; so lay the lettuce between each pigeon, and one in the middle with the lettuce round it, and pour the sauce all over them.

Pigeons Surtout.

FORCE your pigeons as above, then lay a slice of bacon on the breast, and a slice of veal beat with the back of a knife, and seasoned with mace, pepper, and salt; tie them on with a small packthread, or two little fine skewers are better; spit them on a fine bird-spit, roast them, and baste with a piece of butter, then with the yolk of an egg, and then baste them again with crumbs of bread, a little nutmeg and sweet herbs; when enough, lay them in your dish, have good gravy ready, with truffles, morels, and mushrooms, to pour into your dish. Garnish with lemon.

Pigeons Compote.

TAKE six young pigeons and skewer them as for boiling; make a force-meat thus: grate the crumb of a penny loaf, half a pound of fat bacon, shred some sweet herbs and parsley fine, two shalots, or a little onion, a little lemon-peel, a little grated nutmeg, season it with pepper and salt, and mix it up with the yolk of two eggs; put it into the craws and bellies, lard them down the breast, and fry them brown with a little butter; then put them in a stew-pan, with a pint of strong brown gravy, a gill of white wine; stew them three quarters of an hour, thicken it with a little butter rolled in flour, season with salt and Cayenne pepper, put the pigeons in the dish, and strain the gravy over them. Lay some hot force-meat balls round them, and send them up hot.

A French Pupton of Pigeons.

TAKE savoury force-meat rolled out like paste, put it in a butter-dish, lay a layer of very thin bacon, squab pigeons, sliced sweetbread, asparagus-tops, mushrooms, cock's-combs, a palate boiled tender and cut into pieces, and the yolks of hard eggs; make another force-meat and lay over like a pie, bake it, and when enough turn it into a dish, and pour gravy round it.

Pigeons boiled with Rice.

TAKE six pigeons, stuff their bellies with parsley, pepper, and salt rolled in a very little piece of butter; put them into a quart of mutton broth, with a little beaten mace, a bundle of sweet herbs, and an onion; cover them close, and let them boil a full quarter of an hour; then take out the onion and sweet herbs, and take a good piece of butter rolled in flour, put it in and give it a shake, season it with salt (if it wants it); then have ready half a pound of rice boiled tender in milk; when it begins to be thick (but take great care it does not burn), take the yolks of two or three eggs beat up with two or three spoonfuls of cream and a little nutmeg, stir it together till it is quite thick; then take up the pigeons and lay them in a dish; pour the gravy to the rice, stir all together and pour over the pigeons. Garnish with hard eggs cut into quarters.

Pigeons transmogrified.

TAKE your pigeons, season them with pepper and salt, take a large piece of butter, make a puff-paste, and roll each pigeon in a piece of paste; tie them in a cloth so that the paste do not break, boil them in a good deal of water; they will take an hour and a half boiling; untie them carefully that they do not break; lay them in the dish, and you may pour a little good gravy in the dish. They will eat exceeding good and nice, and will yield sauce enough of a very agreeable relish.

Pigeons transmogrified, a second Way.

PICK and clean six small young pigeons, but do not cut off their heads, cut off their pinions, and boil them ten minutes in water, then cut off the ends of six large cucumbers and scrape out the seeds, put your pigeons into the cucumbers, but let the heads be out at the ends, and stick a bunch of barberries in their bills, and then put them in a tossing-pan with a pint of veal gravy, a little anchovy, a glass of red wine, a spoonful of browning, a little slice of lemon, Cayenne and salt to your taste, stew them seven minutes, take them out, thicken your gravy with a little butter rolled in flour, boil it up and strain it over your pigeons, and serve them up.

Pigeons in Fricando.

AFTER having trussed your pigeons with their legs in their bodies, divide them in two, and lard them with bacon; then lay them in a stew-pan with the larded side downwards, and two whole leeks cut small, two ladlefuls of mutton broth or veal gravy; cover them close over a very slow fire, and when they are enough make your fire very brisk to waste away what liquor remains: when they are of a fine brown take them up and pour out all the fat that is left in the pan; then pour in some veal gravy to loosen what sticks to the pan, and a little pepper; stir it about for two or three minutes, and pour it over the pigeons. This is a pretty little side-dish.

To roast Pigeons with a Farce.

MAKE a farce with the livers minced small, as much sweet suet or marrow, grated bread, and hard eggs, an equal quantity of each; season with beaten mace, nutmeg, or a little pepper, salt, and sweet herbs; mix all these together with the yolk of an egg, then cut the skin of your pigeon between the legs and body, and very carefully with your fingers raise the skin from the flesh, but take care you do not break it; then force them with this farce between the skin and flesh, then truss the legs close to keep it in; spit them and roast them, dredge them with a little flour, and baste them with a piece of butter, save the gravy which runs from them and mix it up with a little red wine, a little of the force-meat, and some nutmeg; let it boil, then thicken it with a piece of butter rolled in flour, and the yolk of an egg beat up, and some minced lemon: when enough, lay the pigeons in the dish, and pour in the sauce. Garnish with lemon.

Pigeons in Savoury Jelly.

ROAST your pigeons with the head and feet on, put a sprig of myrtle in their bills, make a jelly for them the same way as for the chickens, pour a little into a bason, when it is set lay in the pigeons with their breasts down, fill up your bowl with jelly, and turn it out.

Pigeons à la Souffel.

TAKE four pigeons and bone them; make a force-meat as for pigeons Compote, and stuff them, put them in a stew-pan with a pint of veal gravy, stew them half an hour very gently, then take them out; in the mean time make a veal force-meat and wrap all round them, rub it over with the yolk of an egg, and fry them in good dripping of a nice brown; take the gravy they were stewed in, skim off the fat, thicken it with a little butter rolled in flour, the yolk of an egg, and a gill of cream beat up, season it with pepper and salt, mix it all together, and keep it stirring one way till it is smooth; strain it into your dish, and put the pigeons on. Garnish with plenty of fried parsley; you may leave out the egg and cream, and put in a spoonful of browning, a little lemon pickle and catch-up, if you like best.

Pigeons in Pimlico.

TAKE the livers, with some fat and lean of ham or bacon, mushrooms, truffles, parsley, and sweet herbs; season with beaten mace, pepper, and salt; beat all these together with two raw eggs, put it into the bellies, roll them all in a thin slice of veal, over that a thin slice of bacon; wrap them up in white paper, spit them on a small spit, and roast them. In the mean time make for them a ragoo of truffles and mushrooms chopped small, with parsley cut small; put to it half a pint of good veal gravy, thicken with a piece of butter rolled in flour; an hour will do your pigeons; baste them, when enough lay them in your dish, take off the paper, and pour your sauce over them. Garnish with patties, made thus: take veal and cold ham, beef-suet, an equal quantity, some mushrooms, sweet herbs, and spice; chop them small, set them on the fire, and moisten with milk or cream; then make a little puff-paste, roll it, and make little patties about an inch deep and two inches long; fill them with the above ingredients, cover them close and bake them; lay six of them round a dish. This makes a fine dish for a first course.

Pigeons in a Hole.

PICK, draw, and wash four young pigeons; stick their legs in their belly as you do boiled pigeons, season them with pepper, salt, and beaten mace; put into the belly of every pigeon a lump of butter the size of a walnut, lay your pigeons in a pie-dish, pour over them a batter made of three eggs, two spoonfuls of flour, and half a pint of good milk; bake it in a moderate oven, and serve them to table in the same dish.

To jug Pigeons.

PULL, crop, and draw pigeons, but do not wash them; save the livers and put them in scalding water, and set them on the fire for a minute or two: then take them out and mince them small, and bruise them with the back of a spoon; mix them with a little pepper, salt, grated nutmeg, and lemon-peel shred very fine, chopped parsley, and two yolks of eggs very hard; bruise them as you do the liver, and put as much suet as liver, shaved exceeding fine, and as much grated bread; work these together with raw eggs, and roll it in fresh butter; put a piece into the crops and bellies, and sew up the neck and vents; then dip your pigeons in water, and season them with pepper and salt as for a pie; put them in your jug, with a piece of celery, a bundle of sweet herbs, four cloves, and three blades of mace beat fine, stop them close and set them in a kettle of cold water; first cover them close, and lay a tile on the top of the jug, and let it boil three hours; then take them out of the jug and lay them in a dish, take out the celery and sweet herbs, put in a piece of butter rolled in flour, shake it about till it is thick, and pour it on your pigeons. Garnish with lemon.

To stew Pigeons.

SEASON your pigeons with pepper and salt, a few cloves and mace, and some sweet herbs; wrap this seasoning up in a piece of butter, and put it in their bellies; then tie up the neck and vent, and half roast them: put them in a stew-pan, with a quart of good gravy, a little white wine, a few peppercorns, three or four blades of mace, a bit of lemon, a bunch of sweet herbs, and a small onion; stew them gently till they are enough; then take the pigeons out, and strain the liquor through a sieve; skim it, and thicken it in your stew-pan; put in the pigeons, with some pickled mushrooms and oysters, stew it five minutes, and put the pigeons in a dish, and the sauce over.

To stew Pigeons another Way,—An excellent Receipt.

MAKE a pudding of bread, suet, the livers of the pigeons, lemon, thyme, parsley, and sweet marjoram, moistened with an egg and a bit of butter; put in nutmeg, pepper, and salt; stuff the pigeons and sew them up, then fry them in butter till they look brown; then put them into some good gravy with an onion stuck with cloves, stew them till they are tender; when they are so take them out, and add a little red wine and
catchup

catchup to your taste; thicken with butter and toss them together; add some morels and truffles, which must be boiled a quarter of an hour before they go in. Pickled mushrooms and artichoke-bottoms are an improvement; but they and the truffles and morels may be done without.

To fricassee Pigeons the Italian Way.

QUARTER them, and fry them in oil; take some green peas and let them fry in the oil till they are almost ready to burst, then put some boiling water to them; season it with salt, pepper, onions, garlic, parsley, and vinegar. Veal and lamb do the same way, and thicken with yolks of eggs.

To make Force-meat for Pigeons.

TAKE a little fat bacon, beat it in a marble mortar, take two anchovies, two or three of the pigeons' livers, chop them together; add a little lemon-peel shred, a little beaten mace, nutmeg, Cayenne, stale bread crumbs, and beef-suet an equal quantity, mix all together with an egg.

To boil Partridges.

PUT them in a good deal of water, let them boil quick; fifteen minutes will be sufficient. For sauce, take a quarter of a pint of cream and a piece of fresh butter as big as a walnut, stir it one way till it is melted, and pour it into the dish.

Or this sauce: take a bunch of celery clean washed, cut all the white very small, wash it again very clean, put it into a sauce-pan with a blade of mace, a little beaten pepper, and a very little salt; put to it a pint of water, let it boil till the water is just wasted away, then add a quarter of a pint of cream and a piece of butter rolled in flour; stir all together, and when it is thick and fine pour it over the birds.

Or this sauce: take the livers and bruise them fine, some parsley chopped fine, melt a little nice fresh butter, and then add the livers and parsley to it, squeeze in a little lemon, just give it a boil, and pour over the birds.

Or this sauce: take a quarter of a pint of cream, the yolk of an egg beat fine, a little grated nutmeg, a little beaten mace, a piece of butter as big as a nutmeg rolled in flour, and one spoonful of white wine; stir all together one way, when fine and thick pour it over the birds. You may add a few mushrooms.

Or this sauce: take a few mushrooms fresh peeled and wash them clean, put them in a sauce-pan with a little salt, put them over a quick fire, let them boil up, then put in a quarter of a pint of cream and a little nutmeg; shake them together with a very little piece of butter rolled in flour, give it two or three shakes over the fire, three or four minutes will do; then pour it over the birds.

Or this sauce: boil half a pound of rice very tender in beef-gravy; season it with pepper and salt, and pour over your birds. These sauces do for boiled fowls; a quart of gravy will be enough, and let it boil till it is quite thick.

To dress Partridges à la Braise.

TAKE two brace, truss the legs into the bodies, lard them, season with beaten mace, pepper, and salt; take a stew-pan, lay slices of bacon at the bottom, then slices of beef, and then slices of veal, all cut thin, a piece of carrot, an onion cut small, a bundle of sweet herbs, and some whole pepper; lay the partridges with the breast downwards, lay some thin slices of beef and veal over them, and some parsley shred fine; cover them and let them stew eight or ten minutes over a slow fire, then give your pan a shake, and pour in a pint of boiling water; cover it close and let it stew half an hour over a little quicker fire; then take out your birds, keep them hot, pour into the pan a pint of thin gravy, let them boil till there is about half a pint, then strain it off, and skim off all the fat: in the mean time have a veal sweetbread cut small, truffles and morels, cock's-combs and fowls livers, stewed in a pint of good gravy half an hour, some artichoke-bottoms and asparagus-tops, both blanched in warm water, and a few mushrooms; then add the other gravy to this, and put in your partridges to heat; if it is not thick enough, take a piece of butter rolled in flour and toss up in it; if you will be at the expence, thicken it with veal and ham cullis, but it will be full as good without.

To make Partridge Panes.

TAKE two roasted partridges and the flesh of a large fowl, a little parboiled bacon, a little marrow or sweet suet chopped very fine, a few mushrooms and morels chopped fine, truffles and artichoke-bottoms; season with beaten mace, pepper, a little nutmeg, salt, sweet herbs chopped fine, and the crumb of a two-penny loaf soaked in hot gravy; mix all well together with the yolks of two eggs, make your panes on paper of a round figure and the thickness of an egg, at a proper distance one from another, dip the point of a knife in the yolk of an egg in order to shape them, bread them neatly, and bake them a quarter of an hour in a quick oven: observe that the truffles and morels be boiled tender in the gravy you soak the bread in. Serve them up for a side-dish, or they will serve to garnish the above dish, which will be a very fine one for a first course.

N. B. When

N. B. When you have cold fowls in the house, this makes a pretty addition in an entertainment.

To stew Partridges.

TRUSS your partridges as for roasting, stuff the craws, and lard them down each side of the breast; then roll a lump of butter in pepper, salt, and beaten mace, and put it into the bellies, sew up the vents, dredge them well and fry them a light brown; then put them into a stew-pan with a quart of good gravy, a spoonful of Madeira wine, the same of mushroom catchup, a tea-spoonful of lemon-pickle, and half the quantity of mushroom powder, one anchovy, half a lemon, a sprig of sweet marjoram; cover the pan close and stew them half an hour, then take them out and thicken the gravy, boil it a little and pour it over the partridges, and lay round them artichokebottoms boiled and cut in quarters, and the yolks of four hard eggs, if agreeable.

To stew Partridges, a second Way—much more expensive.

TAKE three partridges when dressed, singe them, blanch and beat three ounces of almonds, and grate the same quantity of fine white bread, chop three anchovies, mix them with six ounces of butter, stuff the partridges, and sew them up at both ends; truss them and wrap slices of fat bacon round them, half roast them, then take one and pull the meat off the breast, and beat it in a marble mortar with the force-meat it was stuffed with; have ready a strong gravy made of ham and veal, strain it into a stew-pan, then take the bacon off the other two, wipe them clean and put them into the gravy with a good deal of shalots, let them stew till tender, then take them out, and boil the gravy till it is almost as thick as bread sauce, then add to it a glass of sweet oil, the same of Champagne, and the juice of a China orange; put your partridges in and make them hot. Garnish with slices of bacon and lemon.

To stew Partridges or Pigeons with red or white Cabbage.

SKEWER them neatly, season them with Cayenne, salt, and beaten mace, fry them in butter not too brown, put them into a stew-pan with a little brown gravy, cover them close, and stew them gently till tender, keep turning them over. Prepare the cabbage thus: take red cabbage when touched with frost, cut it round as you would to pickle, wash it, put it into a stew-pan, with three ounces of butter, a pint of spring water, a little Cayenne and salt, a halfpenny worth of cochineal beat, cover it close, stew it gently quite tender, pour out some of the liquor, and put in some of the gravy that the pigeons are stewed in,

squeeze

squeeze in juice of lemon so as to make it taste, and a spoonful of melted butter, and give it a boil, lay your pigeons or partridges on the dish, with the remainder of the gravy they were stewed in; lay the cabbage over and about them, so send them up; do white or green cabbage the same way cut into quarters, leaving out the cochineal; this may be sent up without meat, but remember to use a little gravy.

To roast Pheasants.

PICK and draw a brace of pheasants, and singe them, lard one with bacon but not the other, spit them, roast them fine, and paper them all over the breast; when they are just done, flour and baste them with a little nice butter, and let them have a fine white froth; then take them up, and pour good gravy in the dish, and bread-sauce in boats or basons.

Or you may put water-cresses, with gravy in the dish, and lay the cresses under the pheasants.

Or you may make celery-sauce, stewed tender, strained and mixed with cream, and poured into the dish.

If you have but one pheasant, take a large fowl about the bigness of a pheasant, pick it nicely with the head on, draw it, and truss it with the head turned as you do a pheasant's, lard the fowl all over the breast and legs with bacon cut in little pieces; when roasted put them both in a dish, and nobody will know it. They will take three quarters of an hour doing, and the fire must not be too brisk. Put gravy in the dish, and garnish with water-cresses.

A stewed Pheasant.

TAKE your pheasant and stew it in veal gravy, take artichoke-bottoms parboiled, some chesnuts, roasted and blanched; when your pheasant is enough (but it must stew till there is just enough for sauce, then skim it), put in the chesnuts and artichoke-bottoms, a little beaten mace, pepper and salt enough to season it, and a glass of white wine; if you do not think it thick enough, thicken it with a little piece of butter rolled in flour: squeeze in a little lemon, pour the sauce over the pheasant, and have some force-meat balls fried and put into the dish.

N. B. A good fowl will do full as well, trussed with the head on like a pheasant. You may fry sausages instead of force-meat balls.

To dress a Pheasant à la Braise.

LAY a layer of beef all over your pan, then a layer of veal, a little piece of bacon, a piece of carrot, an onion stuck with
cloves,

cloves, a blade or two of mace, a spoonful of pepper black and white, and a bundle of sweet herbs; then lay in the pheasant, lay a layer of veal and then a layer of beef to cover it, set it on the fire five or six minutes, then pour in two quarts of boiling gravy; cover it close and let it stew very softly an hour and a half, then take up your pheasant, keep it hot, and let the gravy boil till there is about a pint; then strain it off and put it in again, and put in a veal sweetbread, first being stewed with the pheasant; then put in some truffles and morels, some livers of fowls, artichoke-bottoms, and asparagus-tops (if you have them); let these simmer in the gravy about five or six minutes, then add two spoonfuls of catchup, two of red wine, and a little piece of butter rolled in flour, a spoonful of browning, shake all together, put in your pheasant, let them stew all together with a few mushrooms about five or six minutes more, then take up your pheasant and pour your ragoo all over, with a few force-meat balls. Garnish with lemon. You may lard it, if you choose.

To boil a Pheasant.

TAKE a fine pheasant, boil it in a good deal of water, keep your water boiling; half an hour will do a small one, and three quarters of an hour a large one. Let your sauce be celery stewed and thickened with cream, and a little piece of butter rolled in flour; take up the pheasant, and pour the sauce all over. Garnish with lemon. Observe to stew your celery so that the liquor will not be all wasted away before you put your cream in; if it wants salt, put in some to your palate.

To salmec a Snipe or Woodcock.

HALF roast them and cut them in quarters, put them in a stew-pan with a little gravy, two shalots chopt fine, a glass of red wine, a little salt and Cayenne pepper, the juice of half a lemon; stew them gently for ten minutes, and put them on a toast served the same as for roasting, and send them up hot. Garnish with lemon.

Snipes in a Surtout, or Woodcocks.

TAKE force-meat made with veal, as much beef-suet chopped and beat in a mortar, with an equal quantity of crumbs of bread; mix in a little beaten mace, pepper and salt, some parsley, and a little sweet herbs, mix it with the yolk of an egg: lay some of this meat round the dish, then lay in the snipes, being first drawn and half roasted. Take care of the trail; chop it and throw it all over the dish.

Take some good gravy, according to the bigness of your surtout, some truffles and morels, a few mushrooms, a sweetbread
cut

cut into pieces, and artichoke-bottoms cut small; let all stew together, shake them, and take the yolks of two or three eggs (according as you want them), beat them up with a spoonful or two of white wine; stir all together one way, when it is thick take it off, let it cool, and pour it into the surtout; have the yolks of a few hard eggs put in here and there; season with beaten mace, pepper, and salt, to your taste; cover it with the force-meat all over; rub the yolks of eggs all over to colour it, then send it to the oven. Half an hour does it, and send it hot to table.

To boil Snipes or Woodcocks.

BOIL them in good strong broth, or beef gravy made thus: take a pound of beef, cut it into little pieces, put it into two quarts of water, an onion, a bundle of sweet herbs, a blade or two of mace, six cloves, and some whole pepper; cover it close, let it boil till about half wasted, then strain it off, put the gravy into a sauce-pan with salt enough to season it; take the snipes and gut them clean (but take care of the guts), put them into the gravy and let them boil, cover them close, and ten minutes will boil them: in the mean time, chop the guts and liver small, take a little of the gravy the snipes are boiling in, and stew the guts in, with a blade of mace; take some crumbs of bread, and have them ready fried in a little fresh butter crisp, of a fine light brown; you must take about as much bread as the inside of a stale roll, and rub them small into a clean cloth; when they are done, let them stand ready in a plate before the fire.

When your snipes are ready, take about half a pint of the liquor they are boiled in, and add to the guts two spoonfuls of red wine, and a piece of butter as big as a walnut, rolled in a little flour; set them on the fire, shake your sauce-pan often (but do not stir it with a spoon) till the butter is all melted, then put in the crumbs, give your sauce-pan a shake, take up your birds, lay them in the dish, and pour this sauce over them. Garnish with lemon.

To dress Ortolans.

SPIT them sideways, with a vine-leaf between; baste them with butter, and have fried crumbs of bread round the dish. Dress quails the same way.

To dress Ruffs and Rees.

THESE birds are found in Lincolnshire and the Isle of Ely: the food proper for them is new milk boiled and put over white bread, or white bread boiled in milk, with a little fine sugar;

sugar; and be careful to keep them in separate cages: they feed very fast, and will die of their fat if not killed in time; when you kill them, slip the skin off the head and neck with the feathers on, then pluck and draw them; when you roast them, put them a good distance from the fire, if the fire be good they will take about twelve minutes; when they are roasted, slip the skin on again with the feathers on, send them up with the gravy under them made the same as for the pheasant, and bread-sauce in a boat, and crisp crumbs of bread round the edge of the dish.

To dress Larks.

PUT them on a bird-spit, tie them on another spit, and roast them twenty-five minutes with a gentle fire; put them in a dish with crumbs of bread fried brown, or you may put a toast under with gravy and butter, or gravy only.

To dress Larks Pear Fashion.

YOU must truss the larks close and cut off the legs, season them with salt, pepper, cloves, and mace; make a force-meat thus: take a veal sweetbread, as much beef-suet, a few morels and mushrooms, chop all fine together, some crumbs of bread, a few sweet herbs, and a little lemon-peel cut small, mix all together with the yolk of an egg, wrap up the larks in force-meat, and shape them like a pear, stick one leg on the top like the stalk of a pear, rub them over with the yolk of an egg and crumbs of bread, bake them in a gentle oven, serve them without sauce: or they will make a good garnish to a very fine dish.

You may use veal, if you have not a sweetbread.

To dress Plovers.

To two plovers take two artichoke-bottoms boiled, some chesnuts roasted and blanched, some skirrets boiled, cut all very small, mix it with some marrow or beef-suet, the yolks of two hard eggs, chop all together, season with pepper, salt, nutmeg, and a little sweet herbs; fill all the bodies of the plovers, lay them in a sauce-pan, put to them a pint of gravy, a glass of white wine, a blade or two of mace, some roasted chesnuts blanched, and artichoke-bottoms cut into quarters, two or three yolks of eggs, and a little juice of lemon; cover them close and let them stew very softly an hour. If you find the sauce is not thick enough, take a piece of butter rolled in flour and put into the sauce; shake it round, and when it is thick take up your plovers, and pour the sauce over them. Garnish with roasted chesnuts.

Ducks

Ducks are very good done this way.

If they are well fed they need no butter, being fat enough of themselves.

Or boil them in good celery-sauce, either white or brown, just as you like.

The same way you may dress wigeons.

N. B. The best way to dress plovers, is to roast them the same as woodcocks, with a toast under them, and gravy and butter.

Jugged Hare.

CUT it into little pieces, lard them here and there with little slips of bacon, season them with Cayenne pepper and salt, put them into an earthen jug, with a blade or two of mace, an onion stuck with cloves, and a bundle of sweet herbs; cover the jug or jar you do it in so close that nothing can get in, then set it in a pot of boiling water, and three hours will do it; then turn it out into the dish, and take out the onion and sweet herbs, and send it to table hot. If you do not like it larded, leave it out.

To jug a Hare, a second Way.—An excellent Receipt.

CUT a hare to pieces, but do not wash it; season it with an onion shred fine, thyme, parsley, savoury, marjoram, lemon-peel, pepper, salt, and half a nutmeg; strew all these over your hare, slice some fat bacon thin, then put the hare into an earthen jug, without any water, and put a layer of hare and a layer of bacon; stop it close with a cloth tied on, and cover it with a tile, put it in a pot of cold water, and let it boil three hours. When you take it up, shake in some fresh butter till it is melted; garnish with lemon.

Florendine Hare.

TAKE a full grown hare and let it hang four or five days before you case it; leave the ears on, and take out all the bones except the head, which must be left whole; lay the hare on the dresser, and put in the following force-meat; take the crumbs of a penny loaf, the liver shred fine, half a pound of fat bacon scraped, a glass of red wine, some sweet herbs chopped fine, season with pepper, salt, and nutmeg, an anchovy chopped fine, the yolks of two eggs, mix all together and put into your hare's belly, roll it up to the head, skewer it with the head and ears leaning back, and tie it with pack-thread as you would a collar of veal, wrap it in a cloth, and boil it one hour and a half in a stew-pan (covered close), with two quarts of water; as soon as the liquor is reduced to a quart, add a pint of red wine, a spoonful of lemon-pickle, one of catchup, and one of browning; then take out your hare, and stew the gravy till it is reduced to a pint, thicken it with butter rolled in flour; put the hare in the dish, and pour the sauce over it; pull the jaw-bones out, and put them in the eyes; put some force-meat balls and truffles round it; and garnish with water-cresses.

To scare a Hare.

LARD a hare, and put a pudding in the belly; put it into a pot or fish-kettle, then put to it two quarts of strong-drawn gravy, one of red wine, a whole lemon cut, a faggot of sweet herbs, nutmeg, pepper, a little salt, and six cloves; cover it close, and stew it over a slow fire till it is three parts done; then take it up, put it into a dish, and strew it over with crumbs of bread, sweet herbs chopped fine, some lemon-peel grated, and half a nutmeg; set it before the fire, and baste it till it is of a fine light brown; in the mean time, take the fat off your gravy, and thicken it with the yolk of an egg; take six eggs boiled hard and chopped small, some pickled cucumbers cut very thin: mix these with the sauce, and pour it into the dish.

A fillet of mutton or neck of venison may be done the same way.

N. B. You may do rabbits the same way, but it must be veal gravy and white wine, adding mushrooms for cucumbers.

To stew a Hare.

CUT it into pieces, and put it into a stew-pan, with a blade or two of mace, some whole pepper black and white, an onion stuck with cloves, a bundle of sweet herbs, and a nutmeg cut to pieces, and cover it with water; cover the stew-pan close, let it stew till the hare is tender, but not too much done: then take it up, and with a fork take out the hare into a clean pan, strain the sauce through a coarse sieve, empty all out of the pan, put in the hare again with the sauce, take a piece of butter as big as a walnut, rolled in flour, and put in likewise one spoonful of catchup and a gill of red wine; stew all together (with a few fresh mushrooms or pickled ones, if you have any) till it is thick and smooth; then dish it up and send it to table. You may cut a hare in two, and stew the fore-quarters thus, and roast the hind-quarters with a pudding in the belly.

To hodge-podge a Hare.

CUT the hare in pieces as you do for stewing, and put it into the pitcher, with two or three onions, some salt, and a little pepper, a bunch of sweet herbs, and a piece of butter: stop

stop the pitcher very close, that no steam may get out, set it in a kettle full of boiling water, keep the kettle filled up as the water wastes; let it stew four or five hours at least. You may, when you first put in the hare into the kettle, put in lettuce, cucumbers, celery, and turnips, if you like it better.

A Hare Civet.

BONE the hare, and take out all the sinews; cut one half in thin slices, and the other half in pieces an inch thick, flour them, and fry them in a little fresh butter as collops, quick, and have ready some gravy made good with the bones of the hare and beef, put a pint of it into the pan to the hare, some mustard, and a little alder vinegar; cover it close, and let it do softly till it is as thick as cream, then dish it up, with the head in the middle.

Portuguese Rabbits.

GET some rabbits, truss them chicken-fashion, the head must be cut off, and the rabbit turned with the back upwards, and two of the legs stripped to the claw-end, and so trussed with two skewers. Lard them, and roast them with what sauce you please. If you want chickens, and they are to appear as such, they must be dressed in this manner: send them up hot with gravy in the dish, and garnish with lemon and beet-root.

Rabbits Surprise.

ROAST two half-grown rabbits, cut off the heads close to the shoulders and the first joints; then take off all the lean meat from the back-bones, cut it small, and toss it up with six or seven spoonfuls of cream and milk, and a piece of butter as big as a walnut, rolled in flour, a little nutmeg and a little salt, shake all together till it is as thick as good cream, and set it to cool: then make a force-meat, with a pound of veal, a pound of suet, as much crumbs of bread, two anchovies, a little piece of lemon-peel cut fine, a little sprig of thyme, and a little nutmeg grated; let the veal and suet be chopped very fine and beat in a mortar, then mix it all together with the yolks of two raw eggs; place it all round the rabbits, leaving a long trough in the back-bone open that you think will hold the meat you cut out with the sauce; pour it in and cover it with the force-meat, smooth it all over with your hand as well as you can with a raw egg, make it square at both ends, throw on a little grated bread, and butter a mazarine, or pan, and take them from the dresser where you formed them, and place them on it very carefully. Bake them three quarters of an hour till they are of a fine brown colour. Let your sauce be gravy thickened with butter and the juice of a lemon; lay them into the dish, and pour in the sauce. Garnish with orange cut into quarters, and serve it up for a first course.

To dress Rabbits in Casserole.

DIVIDE the rabbits into quarters; you may lard them or not (just as you please), shake some flour over them and fry them with lard or butter, then put them into an earthen pipkin with a quart of good broth, a glass of white wine, a little pepper and salt (if wanted), a bunch of sweet herbs, and a piece of butter as big as a walnut, rolled in flour; cover them close and let them stew half an hour, then dish them up and pour the sauce over them. Garnish with Seville orange, cut into thin slices and notched; the peel that is cut out lay prettily between the slices.

To make a Curry the Indian Way.

TAKE two small chickens, skin them and cut them as for a fricassee, wash them clean, and stew them in about a quart of water for about five minutes, then strain off the liquor and put the chickens in a clean dish; take three large onions, chop them small and fry them in about two ounces of butter, then put in the chickens and fry them together till they are brown; take a quarter of an ounce of turmeric, a large spoonful of ginger and beaten pepper together, and a little salt to your palate, strew all these ingredients over the chickens whilst frying, then pour in the liquor and let it stew about half an hour, then put in a quarter of a pint of cream and the juice of two lemons, and serve it up. The ginger, pepper, and turmeric must be beat very fine.

To boil the Rice.

PUT two quarts of water to a pint of rice, let it boil till you think it is done enough, then throw in a spoonful of salt and turn it out into a cullender; then let it stand about five minutes before the fire to dry, and serve it up in a dish by itself. Dish it up and send it to table; the rice in a dish by itself.

Another Way to make a Curry; easier, and much approved.

FRY your chickens or rabbits a light brown, fry three onions and put to them, add some water, Cayenne pepper, salt, and two large spoonfuls of curry powder; cover your pan close and set it over the fire to stew all together till your gravy is thick, then put in a few pickles chopped small, and half the juice of a lemon.

You may make it of veal or mutton the same way. The chickens or rabbits are to be cut up as for a fricassee.

To boil the Rice.

Let the rice be well picked and washed, put it into a tin pan that shuts close, with water enough to cover it about an inch; let it boil with a little salt, very quick, till the water is reduced even with the rice, then set it high on the fire and keep it close covered till ready for table. Send it up in a dish by itself.

To make a Pellaw the Indian Way.

Take three pounds of rice, pick and wash it very clean, put it into a cullender and let it drain very dry; take three quarters of a pound of butter and put it into a pan over a very slow fire till it melts, then put in the rice and cover it over very close that it may keep all the steam in; add to it a little salt, some whole pepper, half a dozen blades of mace, and a few cloves; you must put in a little water to keep it from burning, then stir it up very often, and let it stew till the rice is soft. Boil two fowls, and a fine piece of bacon of about two pounds weight, as common, cut the bacon into two pieces, lay it in the dish with the fowls, cover it over with the rice, and garnish it with about half a dozen of hard eggs and a dozen of onions fried whole and very brown.

N. B. This is the true Indian way of dressing them.

Another Way to make a Pellaw.

Take a leg of veal about twelve or fourteen pounds weight, an old cock skinned, chop both to pieces, put it into a pot with five or six blades of mace, some whole white pepper, and three gallons of water, half a pound of bacon, two onions, and six cloves; cover it close, and when it boils let it do very softly till the meat is good for nothing and above two thirds wasted, then strain it; the next day put this soup into a sauce-pan with a pound of rice, set it over a very slow fire, take great care it do not burn; when the rice is very thick and dry turn it into a dish. Garnish with hard eggs cut in two, and have roasted fowls in another dish.

N. B. You are to observe, if your rice simmers too fast it will burn when it comes to be thick. It must be very thick and dry, and the rice not boiled to a mummy.

CHAP.

CHAP. VII.

Read this CHAPTER, and you will find how expensive a FRENCH COOK's Sauce is.

The French Way of dressing Partridges.

WHEN they are newly picked and drawn, singe them: you must mince their livers with a bit of butter, some scraped bacon, green truffles (if you have any), parsley, chimbol, salt, pepper, sweet herbs, and all-spice; the whole being minced together, put it into the inside of your partridges, then stop both ends of them, after which give them a fry in the stew pan; that being done, spit them, and wrap them up in slices of bacon and paper; then take a stew-pan, and having put in an onion cut into slices, a carrot cut into little bits, with a little oil, give them a few tosses over the fire; then moisten them with gravy, cullis, and a little essence of ham; put therein half a lemon cut in slices, four cloves of garlic, a little sweet basil, thyme, a bay-leaf, a little parsley, chimbol, two glasses of white wine, and four of the carcases of the partridges; let them be pounded, and put them in this sauce; when the fat of your cullis is taken away be careful to make it relishing, and after your pounded livers are put into your cullis you must strain them through a sieve; your partridges being done, take them off, as also take off the bacon and paper, and lay them in your dish with your sauce over them.

This dish I do not recommend; for I think it an odd jumble of trash: by that time the cullis, the essence of ham, and all other ingredients are reckoned, the partridges will come to a fine penny. But such receipts as this are what you have in most books of Cookery yet printed.

To make Essence of Ham.

TAKE the fat off a Westphalia ham, cut the lean in slices, beat them well and lay them in the bottom of a stew-pan, with slices of carrots, parsnips, and onions; cover your pan and set it over a gentle fire; let them stew till they begin to stick, then sprinkle on a little flour and turn them; then moisten with broth and veal gravy; season with three or four mushrooms, as many truffles, a whole leek, some basil, parsley, and half a dozen cloves; or, instead of the leek, you may put a clove of garlic; put in some crusts of bread, and let them simmer over the fire for three quarters of an hour. Strain it, and set it by for use.

A Cullis for all Sorts of Ragoo.

HAVING cut three pounds of lean veal and half a pound of ham into slices, lay it in the bottom of a stew-pan; put in carrots and parsnips, and an onion sliced; cover it and set it a-stewing over a stove; when it has a good colour, and begins to stick, put to it a little melted butter, and shake in a little flour, keep it moving a little while till the flour is fried; then moisten it with gravy and broth, of each a like quantity; then put in some parsley and basil, a whole leek, a bay-leaf, some mushrooms and truffles minced small, three or four cloves, and the crust of two French rolls; let all these simmer together for three quarters of an hour; then take out the slices of veal, strain it, and keep it for all sorts of ragoos. Now compute the expence, and see if this dish cannot be dressed full as well without this expence.

A Cullis for all Sorts of Butchers' Meat.

YOU must take meat according to your company; if ten or twelve, you cannot take less than a leg of veal and a ham, with all the fat, skin, and outside cut off. Cut the leg of veal in pieces about the bigness of your fist, place them in your stew-pan, and then the slices of ham, two carrots, an onion cut in two; cover it close, let it stew softly at first, and as it begins to be brown take off the cover and turn it, to colour it on all sides the same; but take care not to burn the meat; when it has a pretty brown colour, moisten your cullis with broth made of beef, or other meat; season your cullis with a little sweet basil, some cloves, and some garlic; pare a lemon, cut it in slices and put it into your cullis, with some mushrooms; put into a stew-pan a good lump of butter and set it over a slow fire, put into it two or three handfuls of flour, stir it with a wooden ladle, and let it take a colour; if your cullis be pretty brown, you must put in some flour; your flour being brown with your cullis, pour it very softly into your cullis, keeping it stirring with a wooden ladle; then let your cullis stew softly, and skim off all the fat, put in two glasses of Champaign, or other white wine; but take care to keep your cullis very thin, so that you may take the fat well off and clarify it. To clarify it, you must put it in a stove that draws well, cover it close, and let it boil without uncovering till it boils over; then uncover it and take off the fat that is round the stew-pan, then wipe it off the cover also, and cover it again. When your cullis is done, take out the meat and strain your cullis through a silk strainer. This cullis is for all sorts of ragoos, fowls, pies, and terrines.

Cullis

Cullis the Italian Way.

PUT into a stew-pan half a ladleful of cullis, as much essence of ham, half a ladleful of gravy, as much of broth, three or four onions cut into slices, four or five cloves of garlic, a little beaten coriander-seed, with a lemon pared and cut into slices, a little sweet basil, mushrooms and good oil; put all over the fire, let it stew a quarter of an hour, take the fat well off; let it be of a good taste, and you may use it with all sorts of meat and fish, particularly with glazed fish. This sauce will do for two chickens, six pigeons, quails, or ducklings, and all sorts of tame and wild fowl. Now this Italian or French sauce, is saucy.

Cullis of Craw-Fish.

YOU must get the middling sort of craw-fish, put them over the fire seasoned with salt, pepper, and onion cut in slices; being done, take them out, pick them, and keep the tails after they are scalded, pound the rest together in a mortar; the more they are pounded the finer your cullis will be. Take a bit of veal the bigness of your fist, with a small bit of ham, an onion cut into four, put it in to sweat gently: if it sticks but a very little to the pan, powder it a little. Moisten it with broth, put in it some cloves, sweet basil in branches, some mushrooms, with lemon pared and cut in slices: being done, skim the fat well off, let it be of a good taste; then take out your meat with a skimmer, and go on to thicken it a little with essence of ham; then put in your craw-fish, and strain it off. Being strained, keep it for a first-course of craw-fish.

A White Cullis.

TAKE a piece of veal, cut it into small bits, with some thin slices of ham, and two onions cut into four pieces; moisten it with broth seasoned with mushrooms, a bunch of parsley, green onions, three cloves, and so let it stew. Being stewed, take out all your meat and roots with a skimmer, put in a few crumbs of bread, and let it stew softly; take the white of a fowl, or two chickens, and pound it in a mortar; being well pounded, mix it in your cullis, but it must not boil, and your cullis must be very white; but if it is not white enough, you must pound two dozen of sweet almonds blanched, and put into your cullis; then boil a glass of milk, and put it into your cullis; let it be of a good taste, and strain it off; then put it in a small kettle and keep it warm. You may use it for white loaves, white crust of bread, and biscuits.

Sauce for a Brace of Partridges, Pheasants, or any thing you please.

ROAST a partridge, pound it well in a mortar with the pinions of four turkies, with a quart of strong gravy, and the livers of the partridges, and some truffles, and let it simmer till it be pretty thick; let it stand in a dish for a while, then put two glasses of Burgundy into a stew-pan, with two or three slices of onions, a clove or two of garlic, and the above sauce. Let it simmer a few minutes, then press it through a hair-bag into a stew-pan, add the essence of ham, let it boil for some time, season it with good spice and pepper, lay your partridges, &c. in the dish, and pour your sauce in.

They will use as many fine ingredients to stew a pigeon, or fowl, as will make a very fine dish, which is equal to boiling a leg of mutton in Champaign.

It would be needless to name any more, though you have much more expensive sauce than this: however, I think here is enough to shew the folly of these fine French cooks. In their own country, they will make a grand entertainment with the expence of one of these dishes; but here they want the little petty profit; and by this sort of legerdemain, some fine estates are juggled into France.

CHAP. VIII.

To make a Number of pretty little Dishes fit for a Supper or Side-dish, and little Corner-dishes for a great Table; and the rest you have in the CHAPTER for LENT.

Hogs' Ears forced.

TAKE four hogs' ears and half boil them, or take them soused; make a force-meat thus: take half a pound of beef-suet, as much crumbs of bread, an anchovy, some sage; boil and chop very fine a little parsley: mix all together with the yolk of an egg and a little pepper; slit your ears very carefully to make a place for your stuffing; fill them, flour them, and fry them in fresh butter till they are of a fine brown; then pour out all the fat clean, and put to them half a pint of gravy, a glass of white wine, three tea-spoonfuls of mustard, a piece of butter as big as a nutmeg rolled in flour, a little pepper, a small onion whole; cover them close, and let them stew softly for half an hour, shaking your pan now and then. When they are enough, lay them in your dish, and pour your sauce over them,

them, but first take out the onion. This makes a very pretty dish; but if you would make a fine large dish, take the feet, and cut all the meat in small thin pieces, and stew with the ears. Season with salt to your palate.

To force Cock's-Combs.

PARBOIL your cock's-combs, then open them with a point of a knife at the great end: take the white of a fowl, as much bacon and beef-marrow, cut these small, and beat them fine in a marble mortar; season them with salt, pepper, and grated nutmeg, and mix it with an egg; fill the cock's-combs, and stew them in a little strong gravy softly for half an hour; then slice in some fresh mushrooms and a few pickled ones; then beat up the yolk of an egg in a little gravy, stirring it. Season with salt. When they are enough, dish them up in little dishes or plates.

A forced Cabbage.

TAKE a fine white-heart cabbage about as big as a quarter of a peck, lay it in water two or three hours, then half boil it, set it in a cullender to drain, then very carefully cut out the heart, but take great care not to break off any of the outside leaves, fill it with force-meat made thus: take a pound of veal, half a pound of bacon, fat and lean together, cut them small, and beat them fine in a mortar, with four eggs boiled hard. Season it with pepper and salt, a little beaten mace, a very little lemon-peel cut fine, some parsley chopped fine, a very little thyme, and two anchovies: when they are beat fine, take the crumb of a stale roll, some mushrooms (if you have them) either pickled or fresh, and the heart of the cabbage you cut out chopped fine; mix all together with the yolk of an egg, then fill the hollow part of the cabbage, and tie it with a packthread; then lay some slices of bacon to the bottom of a stew-pan or sauce-pan, and on that a pound of coarse lean beef cut thin; put in the cabbage, cover it close and let it stew over a slow fire till the bacon begins to stick to the pan, shake in a little flour, then pour in a quart of broth, an onion stuck with cloves, two blades of mace, some whole pepper, a little bundle of sweet herbs; cover it close and let it stew very softly an hour and a half, put in a glass of red wine, give it a boil, then take it up, lay it in the dish, and strain the gravy and pour over: untie it first. This is a fine side-dish, and the next day makes a fine hash, with a veal-steak nicely broiled and laid on it.

Savoys forced and stewed.

TAKE two savoys, fill one with force-meat and the other without; stew them with gravy; season them with pepper and salt,

salt, and when they are near enough, take a piece of butter as big as a large walnut, rolled in flour, and put in; let them stew till they are enough, and the sauce thick; then lay them in your dish, and pour the sauce over them. These things are best done on a stove.

Forced Eggs.

Boil the eggs hard and peel the shells off, wrap them up in force-meat and fry them a fine brown, then cut them lengthways with the yolks, put fine brown gravy into the dish thickened a little; do not pour it over the eggs.

To force Cucumbers.

Take three large cucumbers, scoop out the pith, fill them with fried oysters seasoned with pepper and salt; put on the piece again you cut off, sew it with a coarse thread, and fry them in the butter the oysters are fried in: then pour out the butter and shake in a little flour, pour in half a pint of gravy, shake it round and put in the cucumbers; season it with a little pepper and salt; let them stew softly till they are tender, then lay them in a plate and pour the gravy over them: or you may force them with any sort of force-meat you fancy, and fry them in hog's lard, and then stew them in gravy and red wine.

To preserve Cock's-Combs.

Let them be well cleaned, then put them into a pot, with some melted bacon, and boil them a little; about half an hour after add a little bay-salt, some pepper, a little vinegar, a lemon sliced, and an onion stuck with cloves; when the bacon begins to stick to the pot, take them up, put them into the pan you would keep them in, lay a clean linen cloth over them, and pour melted butter clarified over them to keep them close from the air. These make a pretty plate at a supper.

To preserve or pickle Pig's Feet and Ears.

Take your feet and ears single and wash them well, split the feet in two, put a bay-leaf between every foot, put in almost as much water as will cover them; when they are well steamed, add to them cloves, mace, whole pepper, and ginger, coriander-seed and salt, according to your discretion; put to them a bottle or two of Rhenish wine (according to the quantity you do), half a score of bay-leaves, and a bunch of sweet herbs; let them boil softly till they are very tender, then take them out of the liquor, lay them in an earthen pot, then strain the liquor over them; when they are cold, cover them down close and keep them for use.

You should let them stand to be cold; skim off all the fat, and then put in the wine and spice.

Pig's Feet and Ears another Way.

TAKE two pig's ears foufed, cut them into long flips about three inches, and about as thick as a goofe quill; put them in a ftew-pan with a pint of good gravy and half an onion cut very fine, ftew them till they are tender; then add a little butter rolled in flour, a fpoonful of muftard, fome pepper and falt, a little alder vinegar; tofs them up and put them in a difh: have the feet cut in two, and put a bay-leaf between; tie them up, and boil them very tender in water and a little vinegar, with an onion or two, rub them over with the yolk of an egg, and fprinkle bread crumbs on them; broil or fry them, and put them round the ears.

To pickle Ox Palates.

TAKE your palates, wafh them well with falt and water, and put them in a pipkin with water and fome falt; and when they are ready to boil, fkim them well, and put to them pepper, cloves, and mace, as much as will give them a quick tafte; when they are boiled tender (which will require four or five hours), peel them and cut them into fmall pieces, and let them cool; then make the pickle of white wine and vinegar, an equal quantity; boil the pickle and put in the fpices that were boiled in the palates; when both the pickle and palates are cold, lay your palates in a jar and put to them a few bay-leaves and a little frefh fpice; pour the pickle over them, cover them clofe and keep them for ufe.

Of thefe you may at any time make a pretty little difh, either with brown fauce or white, or butter and muftard and a fpoonful of white wine; or they are ready to put in made-difhes.

To ftew Cucumbers.

TAKE fix cucumbers, pare them and cut them in two lengthways, take out the feeds; take a dozen of fmall round-headed onions peeled; put fome butter in a ftew-pan, melt it, put in your onions and fry them brown; then put a fpoonful of flour in, ftir it till it is fmooth, put in three quarters of a pint of brown gravy, and ftir it all the time; then put in your cucumbers with a glafs of Lifbon, ftew them till they are tender; feafon with pepper and falt and a little Cayenne pepper to your liking: obferve to fkim it well, becaufe the butter will rife to the top. Send them to table in a difh or under your meat.

Stewed Red Cabbage.

TAKE a red cabbage, lay it in cold water an hour, then cut it into thin flices acrofs and cut it into little pieces; put it into

a ftew-

a stew-pan with a pound of sausages, a pint of gravy, a little bit of ham or lean bacon; cover it close and let it stew half an hour; then take the pan off the fire and skim off the fat, shake in a little flour and set it on again; let it stew two or three minutes, then lay the sausages in your dish and pour the rest all over. You may, before you take it up, put in half a spoonful of vinegar.

Stewed Peas and Lettuce.

Take a quart of green peas, two large cabbage-lettuces cut small across and washed very clean, put them in a stew-pan with a quart of gravy, and stew them till tender; put in some butter rolled in flour, season with pepper and salt: when of a proper thickness dish them up.

N. B. Some like them thickened with the yolks of four eggs; others like an onion chopped very fine and stewed with them, with two or three rashers of lean ham.

Another Way to stew Peas.

Take a pint of peas, put them in a stew-pan with a handful of chopped parsley; just cover them with water, stew them till tender; then beat up the yolks of two eggs, put in some double-refined sugar to sweeten them, put in the eggs and toss them up; then put them in your dish.

Stewed Spinage and Eggs.

Pick and wash your spinage very clean, put it into a sauce-pan with a little salt, cover it close, shake the pan often; when it is just tender and whilst it is green throw it into a sieve to drain, lay it into your dish: in the mean time have a stew-pan of water boiling, break as many eggs into cups as you would poach; when the water boils put in the eggs, have an egg-slice ready to take them out with, lay them on the spinage, and garnish the dish with orange cut into quarters, with melted butter in a cup.

To stew Mushrooms.

Take large buttons, wipe them with a wet flannel, put them in a stew-pan with a little water, let them stew a quarter of an hour, then put in a little salt, work a little flour and butter to make it as thick as cream, let it boil five minutes; when you dish it up put two large spoonfuls of cream mixed with the yolk of an egg, shake it over the fire about a minute or two, but do not let it boil for fear of curdling; put sippets round the inside of the rim of the dish, but not toasted, and serve it up. It is proper for a side-dish for supper, or a corner for dinner.

Another Way to stew Mushrooms.

Put your mushrooms in salt and water, wipe them with a flannel and put them again in salt and water, then throw them into a sauce-pan by themselves and let them boil up as quick as possible, then put in a little Cayenne pepper, a little mace (if you like the flavour), let them stew in this a quarter of an hour, then add a tea-cupful of cream, with a little flour and butter the size of a walnut; let them be served up as soon as done.

To stew Chardoons.

Take the inside of your chardoons, wash them well, boil them in salt and water, put them into a tossing-pan with a little veal gravy, a tea-spoonful of lemon-pickle, a large one of mushroom catchup, pepper and salt (to your taste), thicken it with flour and butter, boil it a little, and serve it up in a soup-plate.

To dress Windsor-Beans.

Take the seed, boil them till they are tender; then blanch them, and fry them in clarified butter; melt butter, with a little vinegar, and pour over them; stew them with salt, pepper, and nutmeg.

Or you may eat them with butter, sack, sugar, and a little powder of cinnamon.

To make Jumballs.

Take a pound of fine flour and a pound of fine powder-sugar, make them into a light paste, with whites of eggs beat fine; then add half a pint of cream, half a pound of fresh butter melted, and a pound of blanched almonds well beat; knead them all together thoroughly with a little rose-water, and cut out your jumballs in what figures you fancy; and either bake them in a gentle oven or fry them in fresh butter, and they make a pretty side or corner-dish. You may melt a little butter with a spoonful of sack, throw fine sugar all over the dish. If you make them in pretty figures, they make a fine little dish.

To ragoo Cucumbers.

Take two cucumbers and two onions, slice them and fry them in a little butter, then drain them in a sieve; put them into a sauce-pan, add six spoonfuls of gravy, two of white wine, a blade of mace; let them stew five or six minutes; then take a piece of butter as big as a walnut, rolled in flour, a little salt and Cayenne pepper; shake them together, and when it is thick, dish them up.

To make a Ragoo of Onions.

TAKE a pint of little young onions, peel them, and take four large ones, peel them, and cut them very small; put a quarter of a pound of good butter into a stew-pan, when it is melted and done making a noise, throw in your onions, and fry them till they begin to look a little brown; then shake in a little flour, and shake them round till they are thick; throw in a little salt, a little beaten pepper, a quarter of a pint of good gravy, and a tea-spoonful of mustard; stir all together, and when it is well-tasted and of a good thickness pour it into your dish, and garnish it with fried crumbs of bread. They make a pretty little dish, and are very good. You may stew raspings in the room of flour, if you please.

A Ragoo of Oysters.

OPEN twenty large oysters, take them out of the liquor, save the liquor, and dip the oysters in a batter made thus: take two eggs, beat them well, a little lemon-peel grated, a little nutmeg grated, a blade of mace pounded fine, a little parsley chopped fine, beat all together with a little flour, have ready some butter or dripping in a stew-pan; when it boils, dip in your oysters one by one into the batter, and fry them of a fine brown; then with an egg-slice take them out, and lay them in a dish before the fire; pour the fat out of the pan, and shake a little flour over the bottom of the pan, then rub a little piece of butter (as big as a small walnut) all over with your knife whilst it is over the fire; then pour in three spoonfuls of the oyster-liquor strained, one spoonful of white wine, and a quarter of a pint of gravy; grate a little nutmeg, stir all together, throw in the oysters, give the pan a toss round, and when the sauce is of a good thickness, pour all into the dish, and garnish with raspings.

A Ragoo of Asparagus.

SCRAPE a hundred of grass very clean, and throw them into cold water; when you have scraped all, cut as far as is good and green about an inch long, and take two heads of endive clean washed and picked, cut it very small, a young lettuce clean washed and cut small, a large onion peeled and cut small, put a quarter of a pound of butter into a stew-pan, when it is melted throw in the above things: toss them about, and fry them ten minutes; then season them with a little pepper and salt, shake in a little flour, toss them about, then pour in half a pint of gravy; let them stew till the sauce is very thick and good; then pour all into your dish. Save a few of the little tops of the grass to garnish the dish.

N. B. You

N. B. You must not fry the asparagus: boil it in a little water and put them in your ragoo, and then they will look green.

A Ragoo of Livers.

TAKE as many livers as you would have for your dish. A turkey's liver and six fowls' livers will make a pretty dish. Pick the galls from them, and throw them into cold water; take the six livers, put them into a sauce-pan with a quarter of a pint of gravy, a spoonful of mushrooms (either pickled or fresh), a spoonful of catchup, a little piece of butter as big as a nutmeg, rolled in flour; season them with pepper and salt to your palate; let them stew softly ten minutes; in the mean while, butter one side of a piece of writing paper and wrap the turkey's liver in it, and broil it nicely, lay it in the middle, and the stewed livers round; pour the sauce all over, and garnish with lemon.

To ragoo Cauliflowers.

TAKE a large cauliflower, wash it very clean and pick it in pieces, as for pickling; make a nice brown cullis, and stew them till tender, season with pepper and salt, put them into your dish with the sauce over; boil a few sprigs of the cauliflower in water, to garnish with.

Fried Sausages.

TAKE half a pound of sausages, and six apples, slice four about as thick as a crown, cut the other two in quarters, fry them with the sausages of a fine light brown, lay the sausages in the middle of the dish, and the apples round. Garnish with the quartered apples.

Stewed cabbage and sausages fried is a good dish.

Collops and Eggs.

CUT either bacon, hung-beef, or hung-mutton into thin slices, broil them nicely, lay them in a dish before the fire, have ready a stew-pan of water boiling, break as many eggs as you have collops, break them one by one in a cup, and pour them into the stew-pan; when the whites of the eggs begin to harden, and all look of a clear white, take them up one by one in an egg-slice, lay them on the collops.

To dress cold Fowl or Pigeon.

CUT them in four quarters, beat up an egg or two (according to what you dress), grate a little nutmeg in, a little salt, some parsley chopped, a few crumbs of bread, beat them well together, dip them in this batter, and have ready some dripping hot in a stew-pan, in which fry them of a fine light brown;

have ready a little good gravy, thickened with a little flour, mixed with a spoonful of catchup; lay the fry in the dish and pour the sauce over. Garnish with lemon, and a few mushrooms, if you have any. A cold rabbit eats well done thus.

To fry cold Veal.

CUT it in pieces about as thick as half-a-crown, and as long as you please, dip them in the yolk of an egg, and then in crumbs of bread, with a few sweet herbs, and shred lemon-peel in it; grate a little nutmeg over them, and fry them in fresh butter. The butter must be hot, just enough to fry them in: in the mean time, make a little gravy of the bone of the veal; when the meat is fried take it out with a fork, and lay it in a dish before the fire, then shake a little flour into the pan and stir it round; then put in a little gravy, squeeze in a little lemon, and pour it over the veal. Garnish with lemon.

To toss up cold Veal white.

CUT the veal into little thin bits, put milk enough to it for sauce, grate in a little nutmeg, a very little salt, a little piece of butter rolled in flour: to half a pint of milk, the yolks of two eggs well beat, a spoonful of mushroom-pickle, stir all together till it is thick; then pour it into your dish, and garnish with lemon.

Cold fowl skinned, and done this way, eats well: or the best end of a cold breast of veal; first fry it, drain it from the fat, then pour this sauce to it.

To hash cold Mutton.

CUT your mutton with a very sharp knife in very little bits, as thin as possible; then boil the bones with an onion, a little sweet herbs, a blade of mace, a very little whole pepper, a little salt, a piece of crust toasted very crisp; let it boil till there is just enough for sauce, strain it and put it into a sauce-pan with a piece of butter rolled in flour; put in the meat; when it is very hot it is enough; season with pepper and salt; have ready some thin bread toasted brown, cut three-corner ways, lay them round the dish, and pour in the hash. As to walnut-pickle, and all sorts of pickles, you must put in according to your fancy. Garnish with pickles. Some love a small onion peeled and cut very small, and done in the hash. Or you may use made-gravy, if you have not time to boil the bones.

To hash Mutton like Venison.

CUT it very thin as above; boil the bones as above; strain the liquor, where there is just enough for the hash; to a quarter
of

of a pint of gravy put a large spoonful of red wine, an onion peeled and chopped fine, a very little lemon-peel shred fine, a piece of butter as big as a small walnut, rolled in flour; put it into a sauce-pan with the meat, shake it all together, and when it is thoroughly hot pour it into your dish. Hash beef the same way.

To make Collops of cold Beef.

IF you have any cold inside of a sirloin of beef, take off all the fat, cut it very thin in little bits, cut an onion very small; boil as much water or gravy as you think will do for sauce; season it with a little pepper and salt and a bundle of sweet herbs; let the water boil, then put in the meat, with a good piece of butter rolled in flour, shake it round and stir it. When the sauce is thick and the meat done, take out the sweet herbs, and pour it into your dish. They do better than fresh meat.

To mince Veal.

CUT your veal as fine as possible, but do not chop it; grate a little nutmeg over it, shred a little lemon-peel very fine, throw a very little salt on it, dredge a little flour over it. To a large plate of veal, take four or five spoonfuls of water, let it boil, then put in the veal with a piece of butter as big as an egg, stir it well together; when it is all thorough hot, it is enough. Have ready a very thin piece of bread toasted brown, cut it into three-corner sippets, lay it round the plate, and pour in the veal. Just before you pour it in, squeeze in half a lemon, or half a spoonful of vinegar. Garnish with lemon. You may put gravy in the room of water, if you love it strong; but it is better without.

To make a Florentine of Veal.

TAKE two kidneys of veal, fat and all, and mince them very fine, then chop a few herbs and put to them, and add a few currants; season with cloves, mace, nutmeg, and a little salt, four or five yolks of eggs chopped fine, and some crumbs of bread, a pippin or two chopped, some candied lemon-peel cut small, a little sack, and orange-flower water. Lay a sheet of puff-paste at the bottom of your dish and put in the ingredients, and cover it with another sheet of puff-paste. Bake it in a slack oven, scrape sugar on the top, and serve it up hot.

A Salmagundy.

TAKE two pickled herrings and bone them, a handful of parsley, four eggs boiled hard, the white of one roasted chicken or fowl; chop all very fine separately, that is, the yolks of eggs by themselves, and the whites the same; scrape some lean boiled ham very fine, hung-beef or Dutch beef scraped; turn a small

china

china bason, or deep saucer, into your dish; make some butter into the shape of a pine-apple, or any other shape you please, and set on the top of the bason or saucer; lay round your bason a ring of shred parsley, then whites of eggs, then ham, then chickens, then beef, then yolks of eggs, then herrings, till you have covered the bason and used all your ingredients. Garnish the dish with whole capers and pickles of any sort you choose, chopped fine; or you may leave out the butter and put the ingredients on, and put a flower of any sort at the top, or a sprig of myrtle.

Another Way.

MINCE veal or fowl very small, a pickled herring boned and picked small, cucumbers minced small, apples minced small, an onion peeled and minced small, some pickled red-cabbage chopped small, cold pork minced small, or cold duck or pigeons minced small, boiled parsley chopped fine, celery cut small, the yolks of hard eggs chopped small, and the whites chopped small, and either lay all the ingredients by themselves separate on saucers, or in heaps in a dish. Dish them out with what pickles you have, and sliced lemon nicely cut; and if you can get nastertium-flowers, lay them round it. This is a fine middle-dish for supper; but you may always make salmagundy of such things as you have, according to your fancy. The other sorts are in the Chapter of Lent.

To make little Pasties.

TAKE the kidney of a loin of veal cut very fine, with as much of the fat, the yolks of two hard eggs, seasoned with a little salt, and half a small nutmeg; mix them well together, then roll it well in a puff-paste crust; make three of it, and fry them nicely in hog's-lard or butter.

They make a pretty little dish for a change. You may put in some carrots, and a little sugar and spice, with the juice of an orange, and sometimes apples, first boiled and sweetened, with a little juice of lemon, or any fruit you please.

Petit Pasties for garnishing Dishes.

MAKE a short crust, roll it thick, make them about as big as the bowl of a spoon and about an inch deep; take a piece of veal, enough to fill the patty, as much bacon and beef-suet, shred them all very fine, season them with pepper and salt, and a little sweet herbs; put them into a little stew-pan, keep turning them about, with a few mushrooms chopped small, for eight or ten minutes; then fill your petty-patties and cover them with some crust; colour them with the yolk of an egg, and bake them. Sometimes fill them with oysters for fish, or

the

the melts of the fish pounded, and seasoned with pepper and salt; fill them with lobsters, or what you fancy. They make a fine garnishing, and give a dish a fine look: if for a calf's head, the brains seasoned is most proper, and some with oysters.

CHAP. IX.

Turtle, Mock-Turtle, &c.

AS all the articles contained in the Chapter formerly distinguished by the name of ADDITIONS are (in this edition) put in their proper places, a separate Chapter is allotted to the King of Fish; and if little alteration is made from the manner of dressing it and making mock-turtle, given in former editions, it is because such alterations have more affectation than use in them; the receipts here given being, in reality, the best extant.

To dress a Turtle the West India Way.

TAKE the turtle out of water the night before you dress it, and lay it on its back, in the morning cut its head off, and hang it up by its hind-fins for it to bleed till the blood is all out; then cut out the callapee (which is the belly) round, and raise it up; cut as much meat to it as you can; throw it into spring-water with a little salt, cut the fins off and scald them with the head; take off all the scales, cut all the white meat out and throw it into spring-water and salt; the guts and lungs must be cut out; wash the lungs very clean from the blood; then take the guts and maw and slit them open, wash them very clean, and put them on to boil in a large pot of water, and boil them till they are tender; then take off the inside skin, and cut them in pieces of two or three inches long. Have ready a good veal broth made as follows: take one large or two small knuckles of veal and put them on in three gallons of water; let it boil, skim it well, season with turnips, onions, carrots, and celery, and a good large bundle of sweet herbs; boil it till it is half wasted, then strain it off. Take the fins and put them in a stew-pan, cover them with veal broth, season with an onion chopped fine, all sorts of sweet herbs chopped very fine, half an ounce of cloves and mace, half a nutmeg beat very fine, stew it very gently till tender; then take the fins out, and put in a pint of Madeira wine, and stew it for fifteen minutes; beat up the whites of six eggs, with the juice of two lemons; put the liquor in and boil it up, run it through a flannel bag, make it hot, wash the fins very clean and put them in. Take a piece of butter and put at the bottom of a stew-pan, put your white meat in, and sweat it gently till it is almost tender. Take the lungs and heart and cover them with veal broth, with an onion, herbs, and spice; as for the fins, stew them till tender; take out the lungs, strain the liquor off, thicken it, and put in a bottle of Madeira wine, season with Cayenne pepper and salt pretty high; put in the lungs and white meat, stew them up gently for fifteen minutes; have some force-meat balls made out of the white part instead of veal, as for Scotch collops: if the turtle has any eggs, scald them; if not, take twelve hard yolks of eggs, made into egg-balls; have your callapash, or deep shell, done round the edges with paste, season it in the inside with Cayenne pepper and salt, and a little Madeira wine, bake it half an hour, then put in the lungs and white meat, force-meat, and eggs over, and bake it half an hour; take the bones, and three quarts of veal broth, seasoned with an onion, a bundle of sweet herbs, two blades of mace, stew it an hour, strain it through a sieve, thicken it with flour and butter, put in half a pint of Madeira wine, stew it half an hour; season with Cayenne pepper and salt to your liking: this is the soup. Take the callapee, run your knife between the meat and shell, and fill it full of force-meat; season it all over with sweet herbs chopped fine, a shalot chopped, Cayenne pepper and salt, and a little Madeira wine; put a paste round the edge, and bake it an hour and a half; take the guts and maw, put them in a stew-pan, with a little broth, a bundle of sweet herbs, two blades of mace beat fine; thicken with a little butter rolled in flour; stew them gently for half an hour, season with Cayenne pepper and salt, beat up the yolks of two eggs in half a pint of cream, put it in, and keep stirring it one way till it boils up; then dish them up as follows:

Callapee.
Fricassee. Soup. Fins.
Callapash.

The fins eat fine when cold, put by in the liquor.

Another Way to dress a Turtle.

KILL your turtle as before, then cut the belly-shell clean off, cut off the fins, take all the white meat out, and put it into spring-water; take the guts and lungs out; do the guts as before; wash the lungs well, scald the fins, head, and belly-shell; take a saw and saw the shell all round about two inches deep, scald it, and take the shell off, cut it in pieces; take the shells, fins, and head and put them in a pot, cover them with veal broth; season with two large onions chopped fine, all sorts of sweet herbs chopped fine, half an ounce of cloves and mace,

a whole

a whole nutmeg, stew them till tender; take out all the meat, and strain the liquor through a sieve, cut the fins in two or three pieces; take all the brawn from the bones, cut it in pieces of about two inches square; take the white meat, put some butter at the bottom of a stew-pan, put your meat in, and sweat it gently over a slow fire till almost done; take it out of the liquor, and cut it in pieces about the bigness of a goose's egg; take the lungs and heart and cover them with veal broth; season with an onion, sweet herbs, and a little beat spice (always observe to boil the liver by itself); stew it till tender, take the lungs out, and cut them in pieces; strain off the liquor through a sieve; take a pound of butter and put in a large stew-pan (big enough to hold all the turtle) and melt it; put half a pound of flour in, and stir it till it is smooth; put in the liquor, and keep stirring it till it is well mixed, if lumpy, strain it through a sieve; put in your meat of all sorts, a great many force-meat balls and egg-balls, and put in three pints of Madeira wine; season with pepper and salt, and Cayenne pepper, pretty high; stew it three quarters of an hour, add the juice of two lemons; have your deep shell baked, put some into the shells, and bake it or brown it with a hot iron, and serve the rest in tureens.

N. B. This is for a turtle of sixty pounds weight.

To make a Mock-Turtle.

TAKE a large calf's head with the skin on, well scalded and cleaned, boil it three quarters of an hour; take it out, and slit down the face, take all the skin and meat from the bones as clean as possible, be careful you do not break off the ears; lay it on the dresser, and fill the ears full of force-meat, tie them round with a cloth; take out the eyes, and pick all the meat from the bones, put it in a large stew-pan with the best and fattest parts of another head without the skin, boiled as long as the above, and three quarts of veal gravy; lay the skin on the meat, with the flesh side up, cover the pan close, and let it stew one hour over a moderate fire; put in three sweetbreads cut in pieces, two ounces of truffles and morels, four artichoke-bottoms boiled and cut in four pieces each, an anchovy boned and chopped small, season it pretty high with salt and Cayenne pepper, put in half a lemon, three pints of Madeira wine, two spoonfuls of catchup, one of lemon-pickle, half a pint of pickled or fresh mushrooms, a quarter of a pound of butter rolled in flour, and let it all stew half an hour longer; take the yolks of four eggs boiled hard, and the brains of both heads boiled, cut the brains in pieces of the size of a nutmeg, make a rich force-meat, and roll it up in a veal caul, and
then

then in a cloth, and boil it one hour; cut it in three parts, the middle piece the largest; put the meat into the dish and lay the head over it, the skin side uppermost; put the largest piece of force-meat between the ears, the other two slices at the narrow end opposite each other; put the brains, eggs, mushrooms, &c. over and round it, and pour the liquor hot upon it, and send it up as quick as possible, as it soon gets cold.

To make Mock-Turtle Soup.

TAKE a calf's head and scald the hair off as you would a pig, and wash it very clean; boil it in a large pot of water half an hour; then cut all the skin off by itself, take the tongue out; take the broth made of a knuckle of veal, put in the tongue and skin with three large onions, half an ounce of cloves and mace and half a nutmeg beat fine, all sorts of sweet herbs chopped fine, and three anchovies, stew it till tender, then take out the meat and cut it in pieces about two inches square, and the tongue in slices; mind to skin the tongue; strain the liquor through a sieve; take half a pound of butter and put in the stew-pan, melt it and put in a quarter of a pound of flour, keep it stirring till it is smooth; then put in the liquor, keeping it stirring till all is in, if lumpy strain it through a sieve; then put to your meat a bottle of Madeira wine, season with pepper and salt and Cayenne pepper pretty high; put in force-meat balls and egg-balls boiled, the juice of two lemons, stew it one hour gently, and then serve it up in tureens.

N. B. If it is too thick put some more broth in before you stew it the last time.

CHAP. X.
FISH.

To boil a Turbot.

LAY it in a good deal of salt and water an hour or two, and if it is not quite sweet shift your water five or six times; first put a good deal of salt in the mouth and belly.

In the mean time set on your fish-kettle with clean spring-water and salt, a little vinegar, and a piece of horse-radish; when the water boils lay the turbot on a fish-plate, put it into the kettle, let it be well boiled, but take great care it is not too much done; when enough take off the fish-kettle, set it before the fire, then carefully lift up the fish-plate and set it across the kettle to drain: in the mean time melt a good deal of fresh butter, and bruise in either the spawn of one or two lobsters, and the

the meat cut small, with a spoonful of anchovy-liquor; then give it a boil, and pour it into basons. This is the best sauce; but you may make what you please. Lay the fish in the dish. Garnish with scraped horse-radish and lemon.

To bake a Turbot.

TAKE a dish the size of your turbot, rub butter all over it thick, throw a little salt, a little beaten pepper, and half a large nutmeg, some parsley minced fine and thrown all over, pour in a pint of white wine, cut off the head and tail, lay the turbot in the dish, pour another pint of white wine all over, grate the other half of the nutmeg over it, and a little pepper, some salt, and chopped parsley; lay a piece of butter here and there all over, and throw a little flour all over, and then a good many crumbs of bread: bake it, and be sure that it is of a fine brown; then lay it in your dish, stir the sauce in your dish all together, pour it into a sauce-pan, shake in a little flour, let it boil, then stir in a piece of butter and two spoonfuls of catchup, let it boil, and pour it into basons. Garnish your dish with lemon; and you may add what you fancy to the sauce, as shrimps, anchovies, mushrooms, &c. If a small turbot half the wine will do. It eats finely thus: lay it in a dish, skim off all the fat, and pour the rest over it. Let it stand till cold and it is good with vinegar, and a fine dish to set out a cold table.

To dress a Brace of Carp.

TAKE a piece of butter and put into a stew-pan, melt it and put in a large spoonful of flour, keep it stirring till it is smooth; then put in a pint of gravy and a pint of red port or claret, a little horse-radish scraped, eight cloves, four blades of mace, and a dozen corns of all-spice, tie them in a little linen rag, a bundle of sweet herbs, half a lemon, three anchovies, a little onion chopped very fine; season with pepper, salt, and Cayenne pepper, to your liking; stew it for half an hour, then strain it through a sieve into the pan you intend to put the fish in; let your carp be well cleaned and scaled, then put the fish in with the sauce and stew them very gently for half an hour, then turn them and stew them fifteen minutes longer; put in along with your fish some truffles and morels scalded, some pickled mushrooms, an artichoke-bottom, and about a dozen large oysters, squeeze the juice of half a lemon in, stew it five minutes; then put your carp in your dish and pour all the sauce over. Garnish with fried sippits and the roe of the fish done thus: beat the roe up well with the yolks of two eggs, a little flour, a little lemon-peel chopped fine, some pepper, salt, and a little anchovy liquor; have ready a pan of beef-dripping boiling, drop the roe in to be about as big as a crown-piece, fry it of a light brown and put it round the dish, with some oysters fried in batter and some scraped horse-radish.

N. B. Stick your fried sippits in the fish.

You may fry the carp first if you please, but the above is the most modern way.

Or if you are in a great hurry, while the sauce is making you may boil the fish with spring-water, half a pint of vinegar, a little horse-radish, and bay-leaf; put your fish in the dish, and pour the sauce over.

To dress Carp au Beu.

TAKE a brace of carp alive and gut them, but do not wash or scale them; tie them to a fish-drainer, and put them into a fish-kettle, and pour boiling vinegar over till they are blue, or you may hold them down in a fish-kettle with two forks, and another person pour the vinegar over them; put in a quart of boiling water, a handful of salt, some horse-radish cut in slices; boil them gently twenty minutes: put a fish-plate in the dish, a napkin over that, and send them up hot. Garnish with horse-radish. Boil half a pint of cream and sweeten it with some sugar, for sauce, in a boat or bason.

To stew a Brace of Carp.

SCRAPE them very clean, then gut them, wash them and the roes in a pint of good stale beer to preserve all the blood, and boil the carp with a little salt in the water.

In the mean time strain the beer and put it into a sauce-pan with a pint of red wine, two or three blades of mace, some whole pepper black and white, an onion stuck with cloves, half a nutmeg bruised, a bundle of sweet herbs, a piece of lemon-peel as big as a sixpence, an anchovy, a little piece of horse-radish; let these boil together softly for a quarter of an hour, covered close; then strain it and add to it half the hard roe beat to pieces, two or three spoonfuls of catchup, a quarter of a pound of fresh butter, and a spoonful of mushroom-pickle, let it boil and keep stirring it till the sauce is thick and enough; if it wants any salt you must put some in; then take the rest of the roe and beat it up with the yolk of an egg, some nutmeg, and a little lemon-peel cut small; fry them in fresh butter in little cakes, and some pieces of bread cut three-cornerways and fried brown. When the carp are enough take them up, pour your sauce over them, lay the cakes round the dish, with horse-radish scraped fine, and fried parsley; the rest lay on the carp, and stick the bread about them and lay round them, then sliced lemon notched and lay round the dish, and two or three pieces on the carp. Send them to table hot.

If you would have your sauce white, put in good fish-broth instead of beer, and white wine in the room of red wine. Make your broth with any sort of fresh fish you have, and season it as you do gravy.

To fry Carp.

First scale and gut them, wash them clean, lay them in a cloth to dry, then flour them and fry them of a fine light brown; fry some toast cut three-cornerways and the roes; when your fish is done lay them on a coarse cloth to drain: let your sauce be butter and anchovy, with the juice of lemon. Lay your carp in the dish, the roes on each side, and garnish with the fried toast and lemon.

To bake Carp.

Scale, wash, and clean a brace of carp very well; take an earthen pan deep enough to lie closely in, butter the pan a little, lay in your carp; season with mace, clove, nutmeg, and black and white pepper, a bundle of sweet herbs, an onion, and anchovy; pour in a bottle of white wine, cover it close and let them bake an hour in a hot oven, if large; if small, a less time will do them; when they are enough, carefully take them up and lay them in a dish; set it over hot water to keep it hot, and cover it close, then pour all the liquor they were baked in into a sauce-pan; let it boil a minute or two, then strain it and add half a pound of butter rolled in flour; let it boil, keep stirring it, squeeze in the juice of half a lemon and put in what salt you want; pour the sauce over the fish, lay the roes round, and garnish with lemon. Observe to skim all the fat off the liquor.

To stew Carp or Tench.

Gut and scale your fish, wash and dry them well with a clean cloth, dredge them well with flour, fry them in dripping or sweet rendered suet until they are a light brown, and then put them in a stew-pan with a quart of water and one quart of red wine, a meat-spoonful of walnut or mum catchup, a little mushroom-powder, and Cayenne to your taste, a large onion stuck with cloves, and a stick of horse-radish, cover your pan close to keep in the steam, let them stew gently over a stove fire till your gravy is reduced to just enough to cover your fish in the dish; then take the fish out and put them on the dish you intend for table, set the gravy on the fire and thicken it with flour and a large lump of butter, boil it a little and strain it over your fish. Garnish them with pickled mushrooms and scraped horse-radish, put a bunch of pickled barberries or a sprig of myrtle in their mouths, and send them to the table.

It is a top dish for a grand entertainment.

To fry Tench.

SLIME your tenches, flit the skin along the backs, and with the point of your knife raise it up from the bone, then cut the skin across at the head and tail, then strip it off and take out the bone; then take another tench or carp and mince the flesh small with mushrooms, cives, and parsley; season them with salt, pepper, beaten mace, nutmeg, and a few savoury herbs minced small; mingle all these well together, then pound them in a mortar, with crumbs of bread as much as two eggs soaked in cream, the yolks of three or four eggs, and a piece of butter; when these have been well pounded, stuff the tenches with this sauce: take clarified butter and put it in a pan set over the fire, when it is hot flour your tenches, and put them into the pan one by one and fry them brown; then take them up, lay them in a coarse cloth before the fire to keep hot; in the mean time pour all the grease and fat out of the pan, put in a quarter of a pound of butter, shake some flour all over the pan, keep stirring with a spoon till the butter is a little brown; then pour in half a pint of white wine, stir it together, pour in half a pint of boiling water, an onion stuck with cloves, a bundle of sweet herbs, and two blades of mace; cover them close and let them stew as softly as you can for a quarter of an hour; then strain off the liquor, put it into the pan again, add two spoonfuls of catchup, have ready an ounce of truffles or morels boiled in half a pint of water tender, pour in truffles, water, and all into the pan, a few mushrooms, and either half a pint of oysters clean washed in their own liquor and the liquor and all put into the pan, or some craw-fish; but then you must put in the tails, and after clean picking them boil them in half a pint of water, then strain the liquor and put into the sauce; or take some fish-melts and toss up in your sauce. All this is as you fancy.

When you find your sauce is very good put your tench into the pan, make them quite hot, then lay them into your dish and pour the sauce over them. Garnish with lemon.

Or you may, for change, put in half a pint of stale beer instead of water. You may dress tench just as you do carp.

To roast a Cod's Head.

WASH it very clean and score it with a knife, strew a little salt on it, and lay it in a stew-pan before the fire, with something behind it that the fire may roast it; all the water that comes from it the first half hour throw away, then throw on it a little nutmeg, cloves, mace beat fine, and salt; flour it and baste it with butter; when this has lain some time, turn and season it, and baste the other side the same; turn it often, then baste it

with

with butter and crumbs of bread: if it is a large head it will take four or five hours roasting; have ready some melted butter with an anchovy, some of the liver of the fish boiled and bruised fine; mix it well with the butter and two yolks of eggs beat fine and mixed with the butter, then strain them through a sieve and put them into the sauce-pan again with a few shrimps or pickled cockles, two spoonfuls of red wine and the juice of a lemon; pour it into the pan the head was roasted in and stir it all together, pour it into the sauce-pan, keep it stirring, and let it boil; pour it into a bason. Garnish the head with fried fish, lemon, and scraped horse-radish. If you have a large tin oven it will do better.

To boil a Cod's Head.

SET a fish-kettle on the fire with water enough to boil it, a good handful of salt, a pint of vinegar, a bundle of sweet herbs, and a piece of horse-radish; let it boil a quarter of an hour, then put in the head, and when you are sure it is enough lift up the fish-plate with the fish on it, set it across the kettle to drain, then lay it in your dish and lay the liver on one side. Garnish with lemon and horse-radish scraped; melt some butter with a little of the fish-liquor, an anchovy, oysters or shrimps, or just what you fancy.

To stew Cod.

CUT your cod into slices an inch thick, lay them in the bottom of a large stew-pan; season them with nutmeg, beaten pepper and salt, a bundle of sweet herbs and an onion, half a pint of white wine, and a quarter of a pint of water, cover it close and let it simmer softly for five or six minutes, then squeeze in the juice of a lemon, put in a few oysters and the liquor strained, a piece of butter as big as an egg, rolled in flour, and a blade or two of mace; cover it close and let it stew softly, shaking the pan often; when it is enough take out the sweet herbs and onion and dish it up, pour the sauce over it and garnish with lemon.

To fricassee Cod.

GET the sounds, blanch them, then make them very clean and cut them into little pieces; if they be dry sounds you must first boil them tender; get some of the roes, blanch them and wash them clean, cut them into round pieces about an inch thick, with some of the livers, an equal quantity of each to make a handsome dish, and a piece of cod (about one pound) in the middle; put them into a stew-pan, season them with a little beaten mace, grated nutmeg, and salt, a little bundle of sweet herbs, an onion, and a quarter of a pint of fish-broth or boiling water;

water; cover them close and let them stew a few minutes, then put in half a pint of red wine, a few oysters with the liquor strained, a piece of butter rolled in flour; shake the pan round and let them stew softly till they are enough, take out the sweet herbs and onion and dish it up. Garnish with lemon. Or you may do them white thus: instead of red wine add white, and a quarter of a pint of cream.

To bake a Cod's Head.

BUTTER the pan you intend to bake it in, make your head very clean, lay it in the pan, put in a bundle of sweet herbs, an onion stuck with cloves, three or four blades of mace, half a large spoonful of black and white pepper, a nutmeg bruised, a quart of water, a little piece of lemon-peel, and a little piece of horse-radish; flour your head, grate a little nutmeg over it, stick pieces of butter all over it, and throw raspings all over that; send it to the oven to bake; when it is enough take it out of that dish and lay it carefully into the dish you intend to serve it up in; set the dish over boiling water and cover it up to keep it hot; in the mean time be quick, pour all the liquor out of the dish it was baked in into a sauce-pan, set it on the fire to boil three or four minutes, then strain it and put to it a gill of red wine, two spoonfuls of catchup, a pint of shrimps, half a pint of oysters or muscles, liquor and all, but first strain it; a spoonful of mushroom-pickle, a quarter of a pound of butter rolled in flour, stir it all together till it is thick and boils; then pour it into the dish, have ready some toast cut three-corner-ways and fried crisp; stick pieces about the head and mouth and lay the rest round the head. Garnish with lemon notched, scraped horse-radish, and parsley crisped in a plate before the fire. Lay one slice of lemon on the head and serve it up hot.

To crimp Cod the Dutch Way.

TAKE a gallon of pump-water and a pound of salt, mix them well together; take your cod whilst alive and cut it in slices of one inch and a half thick, throw it into the salt and water for half an hour; then take it out and dry it well with a clean cloth, flour it and broil it; or have a stew-pan with some pump-water and salt boiling, put in your fish and boil it quick for five minutes; send oyster-sauce, anchovy-sauce, shrimp-sauce, or what sauce you please. Garnish with horse-radish and green parsley.

To broil Cod-Sounds.

YOU must first lay them in hot water a few minutes; take them out and rub them well with salt to take off the skin and black dirt, then they will look white, then put them in water

and

MADE PLAIN AND EASY. 155

and give them a boil. Take them out and flour them well, pepper and salt them and broil them; when they are enough lay them in your dish and pour melted butter and mustard into the dish. Broil them whole.

Cod-Sounds broiled with Gravy.

SCALD them in hot water and rub them with salt well, blanch them, that is, take off the black dirty skin, then set them on in cold water, and let them simmer till they begin to be tender; take them out and flour them and broil them on a gridiron; in the mean time take a little good gravy, a little mustard, a little bit of butter rolled in flour, give it a boil, season it with pepper and salt; lay the sounds in your dish and pour your sauce over them.

To fricassee Cod-Sounds.

CLEAN them very well as above, then cut them into little pretty pieces, boil them tender in milk and water, then throw them into a cullender to drain, pour them into a clean saucepan, season them with a little beaten mace and grated nutmeg, and a very little salt; pour to them just cream enough for sauce and a good piece of butter rolled in flour, keep shaking your sauce-pan round all the time till it is thick enough; then dish it up and garnish with lemon.

To broil Crimp-Cod, Salmon, Whiting, or Haddock.

FLOUR it, have a quick clear fire and set your gridiron high, broil it of a fine brown, lay it in your dish, and for sauce have good melted butter; take a lobster, bruise the spawn in the butter, cut the meat small, put all together into the melted butter, make it hot and pour it into your dish or into basons. Garnish with horse-radish and lemon.

To dress little Fish.

As to all sorts of little fish, such as smelts, roach, &c. they should be fried dry and of a fine brown, and nothing but plain butter. Garnish with lemon.

And with all boiled fish you should put a good deal of salt and horse-radish in the water, except mackarel, with which put salt, parsley, and fennel, which you must chop to put into the butter; and some love scalded gooseberries with them; and be sure to boil your fish well, but take great care they do not break.

To broil Mackarel.

CLEAN them, split them down the back, season them with pepper and salt, some parsley and fennel chopped very fine, and

flour

flour them; broil them of a fine light brown, put them on a dish and strainer. Garnish with parsley; let your sauce be fennel and butter in a boat.

To broil Mackarel whole.

CUT off their heads, gut them, wash them clean, pull out the roe at the neck-end, boil it in a little water, then bruise it with a spoon, beat up the yolk of an egg, with a little nutmeg, a little lemon-peel cut fine, a little thyme, some parsley boiled and chopped fine, a little pepper and salt, a few crumbs of bread: mix all well together and fill the mackarel; flour it well, and broil it nicely: let your sauce be plain butter, with a little catchup or walnut-pickle.

Mackarel à la Maitre d'Hotel.

TAKE three mackarel, and wipe them very dry with a clean cloth, cut them down the back from head to tail, but not open them; flour them and broil them nicely; chop a handful of parsley and a handful of green onions very fine, mix them up with butter, and pepper and salt; put your mackarel in the dish, and put the parsley, &c. into the cut in the back, and put them before the fire till the butter is melted. Squeeze the juice of two lemons over them, and send them up hot.

To boil Mackarel.

GUT your mackarel and dry them carefully with a clean cloth, then rub them slightly over with a little vinegar, and lay them straight on your fish-plate (for turning them round often breaks them); put a little salt in the water when it boils; put them into your fish-pan and boil them gently fifteen minutes, then take them up and drain them well, and put the water that runs from them into a sauce-pan, with two tea-spoonfuls of lemon-pickle, one meat-spoonful of walnut-catchup, the same of browning, a blade or two of mace, one anchovy, a slice of lemon; boil them all together a quarter of an hour, then strain it through a hair-sieve, and thicken it with flour and butter; send it in a sauce-boat, and parsley-sauce in another; dish up your fish with the tails in the middle; garnish it with scraped horse-radish and barberries. Or, instead of all this sauce, a little melted butter and fennel and parsley.

To broil Weavers.

GUT them and wash them clean, dry them in a clean cloth, flour, then broil them, and have melted butter in a cup: they are fine fish, and cut as firm as a sole; but you must take care not to hurt yourself with the two sharp bones in the head.

To dress a Jowl of Pickled Salmon.

LAY it in fresh water all night, then lay it in a fish-plate, put it into a large stew-pan, season it with a little whole pepper, a blade or two of mace tied in a coarse muslin-rag, a whole onion, a nutmeg bruised, a bundle of sweet herbs and parsley, a little lemon-peel, put to it three large spoonfuls of vinegar, a pint of white wine, and a quarter of a pound of fresh butter rolled in flour; cover it close and let it simmer over a slow fire for a quarter of an hour, then carefully take up your salmon and lay it in your dish; set it over hot water and cover it; in the mean time let your sauce boil till it is thick and good; take out the spice, onion, and sweet herbs, and pour it over the fish. Garnish with lemon.

To broil Salmon.

CUT fresh salmon into thick pieces, flour them and broil them, lay them in your dish, and have plain melted butter in a cup; or anchovy and butter.

Baked Salmon.

TAKE a little piece cut into slices about an inch thick, butter the dish that you would serve it to table on, lay the slices in the dish, take off the skin, and make a force-meat thus: take the flesh of an eel, the flesh of a salmon, an equal quantity, beat in a mortar, season it with beaten pepper, salt, nutmeg, two or three cloves, some parsley, a few mushrooms, a piece of butter, and ten or a dozen coriander-seeds beat fine; beat all together, boil the crumb of a halfpenny-roll in milk, beat up four eggs, stir it together till it is thick, let it cool and mix it well together with the rest; then mix all together with four raw eggs; on every slice lay this force-meat all over, pour a very little melted butter over them, and a few crumbs of bread, lay a crust round the edge of the dish, and stick oysters round upon it; bake it in an oven, and when it is of a very fine brown serve it up; pour a little plain butter (with a little red wine in it) into the dish, and the juice of a lemon: or you may bake it in any dish, and when it is enough lay the slices into another dish; pour the butter and wine into the dish it was baked in; give it a boil, and pour it into the dish. Garnish with lemon. This is a fine dish: squeeze the juice of a lemon in.

To dress Salmon au Court Bouillon.

AFTER having washed and made your salmon very clean, score the side pretty deep that it may take the seasoning; take a quarter of an ounce of mace, a quarter of an ounce of cloves, a nutmeg, a nutmeg, dry them and beat them fine, a quarter of an ounce of black pepper beat fine, and an ounce of salt; lay the salmon in a napkin, season it well with this spice, cut some lemon-peel fine, and parsley, throw all over, and in the notches put about a pound of fresh butter rolled in flour, roll it up tight in the napkin, and bind it about with packthread; put it in a fish-kettle just big enough to hold it; pour in a quart of white wine, a quart of vinegar, and as much water as will just boil it; set it over a quick fire, cover it close; when it is enough (which you must judge by the bigness of your salmon), set it over a stove to stew till you are ready; then have a clean napkin folded in the dish it is to lay in, turn it out of the napkin it was boiled in, on the other napkin. Garnish the dish with a good deal of parsley crisped before the fire.

For sauce have nothing but plain butter in a cup, or horse-radish and vinegar. Serve it up for a first course.

To dress Salmon à la Braise.

TAKE a fine large piece of salmon, or a large salmon-trout; make a pudding thus; take a large eel, make it clean, slit it open, take out the bone, and take all the meat clean from the bone, chop it fine, with two anchovies, a little lemon-peel cut fine, a little pepper, and a grated nutmeg with parsley chopped, and a very little bit of thyme, a few crumbs of bread, the yolk of an hard egg chopped fine; roll it up in a piece of butter, and put it into the belly of the fish, sew it up, lay it in an oval stew-pan, or little kettle that will just hold it, take half a pound of fresh butter, put it into a sauce-pan, when it is melted shake in a handful of flour, stir it till it is a little brown, then pour to it a pint of fish-broth, stir it together, pour it to the fish, with a bottle of white wine; season it with salt to your palate; put some mace, cloves, and whole pepper into a coarse muslin rag, tie it, put to the fish an onion and a little bundle of sweet herbs; cover it close, and let it stew very softly over a slow fire, put in some fresh mushrooms, or pickled ones cut small, an ounce of truffles and morels cut small. let them all stew together; when it is enough, take up your salmon carefully, lay it in your dish, and pour the sauce all over. Garnish with scraped horse-radish and lemon notched, serve it up hot: this is a fine dish for a first course.

Salmon in Cases.

CUT your salmon into little pieces, such as will lay rolled in half sheets of paper; season it with pepper, salt, and nutmeg; butter the inside of the paper well, fold the paper so as nothing can come out, then lay them in a tin-plate to be baked, pour a

little

little melted butter over the papers, and then crumbs of bread all over them. Do not let your oven be too hot, for fear of burning the paper: a tin oven before the fire does beſt; when you think they are enough, ſerve them up juſt as they are: there will be ſauce enough in the papers; or put the ſalmon in buttered papers only, and broil them.

To boil Salmon-Crimp.

SCALE your ſalmon, take out the blood, waſh it well and lay it on a fiſh-plate, put your water in a fiſh-pan with a little ſalt; when it boils put in your fiſh for half a minute, then take it out for a minute or two; when you have done it four times, boil it until it be enough; when you take it out of the fiſh-pan, ſet it over the water to drain; cover it well with a clean cloth dipped in hot water; fry ſome ſmall fiſhes, or a few ſlices of ſalmon, and lay round it; garniſh with ſcraped horſe-radiſh and fennel.

To broil Herrings.

SCALE them, gut them, cut off their heads, waſh them clean, dry them in a cloth, flour them and broil them; lay the fiſh in the diſh, in a boat plain melted butter and muſtard: ſend them up hot and hot.

To fry Herrings.

CLEAN them as above, fry them in butter; have ready a good many onions peeled and cut thin; fry them of a light brown with the herrings; lay the herrings in your diſh, and the onions round, butter and muſtard in a cup. You muſt do them with a quick fire.

To bake Herrings.

WHEN you have cleaned your herrings as above, lay them on a board, take a little black and Jamaica pepper, a few cloves, mace, and a good deal of ſalt, mix them together, then rub it all over the fiſh, lay them ſtraight in a pot, cover them with vinegar, tie ſtrong paper over the pot, and bake them in a ſoaking oven; add a few bay-leaves, when cold, ſkim off the fat and fill them up with vinegar: you may eat them either hot or cold. If the vinegar be good they will keep three or four months.

To make Water-Sokey.

TAKE ſome of the ſmalleſt plaice or flounders you can get, waſh them clean, cut the fins cloſe, put them into a ſtew-pan with juſt water enough to boil them, a little ſalt, and a bunch of parſley; when they are enough ſend them to table in a ſoup-diſh, with the liquor to keep them hot; have parſley and butter in a cup.

To dress Flat Fish.

In dressing all sorts of flat fish, take great care in the boiling of them; be sure to have them enough, but do not let them be broke; mind to put a good deal of salt and horse-radish in the water, let your fish be well drained, and mind to cut the fins off: when you fry them let them be well drained in a cloth, and floured, and fry them of a fine light brown either in oil or butter; if there be any water in your dish with the boiled fish, take it out with a spunge: as to your fried fish, a coarse cloth is the best thing to drain it on.

To dress Salt Fish.

Old ling (which is the best sort of salt fish) lay in water twelve hours, then lay it twelve hours on a board, and then twelve more in water; when you boil it, put it into the water cold; if it is good, it will take about fifteen minutes boiling softly: boil parsnips very tender, scrape them, and put them into a sauce-pan, put to them some milk, stir them till thick, then stir in a good piece of butter and a little salt; when they are enough lay them in a plate, the fish by itself dry, and butter and hard eggs chopped in a bason.

Water-cod need only be boiled and well skimmed.

Scotch haddocks you must lay in water all night. You may boil or broil them: if you broil, you must split them in two.

You may garnish your dishes with hard eggs, parsnips, and potatoes.

The Manner of dressing various Sorts of Dried Fish, as Stock-Fish, Cod, Salmon, Whitings, &c.

The General Rule for steeping of Dried Fish, the Stock-Fish excepted.

All the kinds, except stock-fish, are salted, or either dried in the sun, as the most common way, or in prepared kilns, or by the smoke of wood-fires in chimney-corners; and, in either case, require the being softened and freshened in proportion to their bulk, their nature, or dryness; the very dry sort, as bacalao, cod-fish, or whiting, and such like, should be steeped in lukewarm milk and water: the steeping kept as near as possible to an equal degree of heat. The larger fish should be steeped twelve hours; the small, as whiting, &c. about two; the cod are therefore laid to steep in the evening, the whitings, &c. in the morning before they are to be dressed; after the time of steeping, they are to be taken out, and hung up by the tails until they are dressed; the reason of hanging them up is, that they soften equally as in the steeping, without extracting

too

too much of the relish, which would make them insipid; when thus prepared, the small fish, as whiting, tusk, and such like, are floured and laid on the gridiron, and when a little hardened on the one side, must be turned and basted with oil upon a feather; and when basted on both sides, and well hot through, taken up, always observing that as sweet oil supples and supplies the fish with a kind of artificial juices, so the fire draws out those juices, and hardens them; therefore be careful not to let them broil too long; no time can be prescribed, because of the difference of fires, and various bigness of the fish. A clear charcoal-fire is much the best, and the fish kept at a good distance to broil gradually: the best way to know when they are enough is, they will swell a little in the basting, and you must not let them fall again.

The sauces are the same as usual to salt fish; and garnish with oysters fried in batter.

But for a supper, for those that like sweet oil, the best sauce is oil, vinegar, and mustard, beat up to a consistence, and served up in saucers.

If boiled, as the great fish usually are, it should be in milk and water, but not so properly boiled as kept just simmering over an equal fire; in which way, half an hour will do the largest fish, and five minutes the smallest. Some people broil both sorts after simmering, and some pick them to pieces, and then toss them up in a pan with fried onions and apples.

They are either way very good, and the choice depends on the weak or strong stomachs of the eaters.

Dried Salmon must be differently managed:

For though a large fish they do not require more steeping than a whiting; and when laid on the gridiron, should be moderately peppered.

The Dried Herring;

Instead of milk and water, should be steeped the like time as the whiting in small-beer; and to which, as to all kinds of broiled salt fish, sweet oil will always be found the best basting, and no ways affect even the delicacy of those who do not love oil.

Stock-Fish;

Are very different from those before mentioned; they being dried in the frost without salt, are in their kind very insipid, and are only eatable by the ingredients that make them so, and the art of Cookery: they should be first beat with a sledge-hammer on an iron anvil, or on a very solid smooth oaken block; and when reduced almost to atoms, the skin and bones taken away, and the remainder of the fish steeped in milk and warm water until very soft; then strained out, and put into a soup-dish with new milk, powdered cinnamon, mace, and nutmeg, the chief part cinnamon; a paste round the edge of the dish, and put in a temperate oven to simmer for about an hour, and then served up in the place of pudding.

N. B. The Italians eat the skin boiled, either hot or cold, and most usually with oil and vinegar, preferring the skin to the body of the fish.

To stew Eels.

Skin, gut, and wash them very clean in six or eight waters, to wash away all the sand; then cut them in pieces, about as long as your finger, put just water enough for sauce, put in a small onion stuck with cloves, a little bundle of sweet herbs, a blade or two of mace, and some whole pepper in a thin muslin-rag: cover it close, and let them stew very softly.

Look at them now and then, put in a little piece of butter rolled in flour, and a little chopped parsley: when you find they are quite tender and well done, take out the onion, spice, and sweet herbs: put in salt enough to season it; then dish them up with the sauce.

To stew Eels with Broth.

Cleanse your eels as above; put them into a sauce-pan with a blade or two of mace and a crust of bread; put just water enough to cover them close, and let them stew very softly: when they are enough, dish them up with the broth, and have a little plain melted butter and parsley in a cup to eat the eels with. The broth will be very good, and it is fit for weakly and consumptive constitutions.

To stew Eels excellently.

Skin and clean the eel, cut it to pieces, stew it in just as much water as will cover it, an onion stuck with cloves, a bundle of sweet herbs, whole pepper, a blade of mace, and a little salt; cover it close, and when it begins to simmer put in red wine to your taste and let it stew till tender, then strain it; add a piece of butter the size of a walnut, rolled in flour, giving it a quick boil; pour out the sauce to the quantity you want, with wine. Garnish with lemon.

To dress Lampreys.

The best of this sort of fish is taken in the river Severn; and, when they are in season, the fishmongers and others in London have them from Gloucester: but if you are where they are to be had fresh, you may dress them as you please.

To fry Lampreys.

BLEED them and save the blood, then wash them in hot water to take off the slime, and cut them to pieces; fry them in a little fresh butter not quite enough, pour out the fat, put in a little white wine, give the pan a shake round, season it with whole pepper, nutmeg, salt, sweet herbs, and a bay-leaf, put in a few capers, a good piece of butter rolled up in flour, and the blood; give the pan a shake round often, and cover them close; when you think they are enough take them out, strain the sauce, then give them a boil quick, squeeze in a little lemon and pour over the fish. Garnish with lemon; and dress them just what way you fancy.

To pitchcock Eels.

TAKE a large eel and scour it well with salt to clean off all the slime; then slit it down the back, take out the bone, and cut it in three or four pieces; take the yolk of an egg and put over the inside, sprinkle crumbs of bread, with some sweet herbs and parsley chopped very fine, a little nutmeg grated, and some pepper and salt, mixed all together; then put it on a gridiron over a clear fire, broil it of a fine light brown, dish it up, and garnish with raw parsley and horse-radish; or put a boiled eel in the middle and the pitchcocked round. Garnish as above with anchovy-sauce, and parsley and butter in a boat.

To fry Eels.

MAKE them very clean, cut them into pieces, season them with pepper and salt, flour them and fry them in butter; let your sauce be plain melted butter, with the juice of lemon. Be sure they be well drained from the fat before you lay them in the dish.

To broil Eels.

TAKE a large eel, skin it and make it clean; open the belly, cut it into four pieces; take the tail end and strip off the flesh, beat it in a mortar, season it with a little beaten mace, a little grated nutmeg, pepper and salt, a little parsley and thyme, a little lemon-peel, an equal quantity of crumbs of bread, roll it in a little piece of butter; then mix it again with the yolk of an egg, roll it up again, and fill the three pieces of belly with it; cut the skin of the eel, wrap the pieces in, and sew up the skin; broil them well, have butter and an anchovy for sauce, with the juice of a lemon. Or you may turn them round, and run a skewer through them, and broil them whole.

To farce Eels with White Sauce.

SKIN and clean your eels well, pick off all the flesh clean from the bone, which you must leave whole to the head; take the flesh, cut it small and beat it in a mortar; then take half the quantity of crumbs of bread, beat it with the fish, season it with nutmeg and beaten pepper, an anchovy, a good deal of parsley chopped fine, a few truffles boiled tender in a very little water, chop them fine, put them into the mortar with the liquor and a few mushrooms: beat it well together, mix in a little cream, then take it out and mix it well together in your hand, lay it round the bone in the shape of the eel, lay it on a buttered pan, dredge it well with fine crumbs of bread, and bake it: when it is done, lay it carefully in your dish; have ready half a pint of cream, a quarter of a pound of fresh butter, stir it one way till it is thick, pour it over your eels, and garnish with lemon.

To dress Eels with Brown Sauce.

SKIN and clean a large eel very well, cut it in pieces, put it into a sauce-pan or stew-pan, put to it a quarter of a pint of water, a bundle of sweet herbs, an onion, some whole pepper, a blade of mace, and a little salt: cover it close, and when it begins to simmer, put in a gill of red wine, a spoonful of mushroom-pickle, a piece of butter as big as a walnut, rolled in flour; cover it close, and let it stew till it is enough, which you will know by the eel being very tender: take up your eel, lay it in a dish: you must make sauce according to the largeness of your eel, more or less. Garnish with lemon.

To dress a Pike.

SCALE and gut your pike, and wash it very clean, then make a stuffing in the following manner: take the crumb of a penny loaf soaked in cream, a quarter of a pound of butter, an anchovy chopped fine, a handful of parsley, and a little sweet herbs chopped fine; the liver or roe of the fish bruised, a little lemon-peel chopped fine, a little grated nutmeg, some pepper and salt, the yolks of two eggs; mix all together, and put it in the belly of your fish; sew it up, and then make it in the form of an S; rub the yolk of an egg over, grate some nutmeg on it, and strew some crumbs of bread on it; put some butter here and there on it; put it on an iron plate, and bake it, or roast it before the fire in a tin-oven; for sauce, good anchovies and butter, and plain melted butter. Garnish with horse-radish and barberries, or you may boil it without the stuffing.

To broil Haddocks, when they are in high Season.

SCALE them, gut and wash them clean; do not rip open their bellies, but take the guts out with the gills; dry them in a clean cloth very well: if there be any roe or liver take it out, but put it in again; flour them well, and have a clear good fire: let your gridiron be hot and clean, lay them on, turn them quick two or three times for fear of sticking; then let one side be enough, and turn the other side: when that is done, lay them in a dish, and have plain butter in a cup, or anchovy and butter.

They eat finely salted a day or two before you dress them, and hung up to dry, or boiled with egg-sauce. Newcastle is a famous place for salted haddocks: they come in barrels, and keep a great while. Or you may make a stuffing the same as for the pike, and broil them.

To dress Haddocks after the Spanish Way.

TAKE a haddock, washed very clean and dried, and boil it nicely; then take a quarter of a pint of oil in a stew-pan, season it with mace, cloves, and nutmeg, pepper and salt, two cloves of garlic (some love apples when in season), a little vinegar; put in the fish, cover it close, and let it stew half an hour over a slow fire.

Flounders done the same way are very good.

To dress Haddocks the Jews Way.

TAKE two large fine haddocks, wash them very clean, cut them in slices about three inches thick, and dry them in a cloth; take a gill either of oil or butter in a stew-pan, a middling onion cut small, a handful of parsley washed and cut small; let it just boil up in either butter or oil, then put in the fish; season it with beaten mace, pepper, and salt, half a pint of soft water; let it stew softly till it is thoroughly done; then take the yolks of two eggs, beat up with the juice of a lemon, and just as it is done enough, throw it over, and send it to table.

To roast a Piece of fresh Sturgeon.

GET a piece of fresh sturgeon of about eight or ten pounds, let it lay in water and salt six or eight hours, with its scales on; then fasten it on the spit, and baste it well with butter for a quarter of an hour, then with a little flour, grate a nutmeg all over it, a little mace and pepper beaten fine, and salt thrown over it, and a few sweet herbs dried and powdered fine, and then crumbs of bread; then keep basting a little, and dredging with crumbs of bread and with what falls from it, till it is enough:

enough: in the mean time prepare this sauce; take a pint of water, an anchovy, a little piece of lemon-peel, an onion, a bundle of sweet herbs, mace, cloves, whole pepper black and white, a little piece of horse-radish; cover it close, let it boil a quarter of an hour, then strain it, put it into the sauce-pan again, pour in a pint of white wine, about a dozen of oysters and the liquor, two spoonfuls of catchup, two of walnut-pickle, the inside of a crab bruised fine, or lobster, shrimps, or prawns, a good piece of butter rolled in flour, a spoonful of mushroom-pickle, or juice of lemon; boil all together; when your fish is enough, lay it in your dish, and pour the sauce over it. Garnish with fried toasts and lemon.

To roast a Fillet or Collar of Sturgeon.

TAKE a piece of fresh sturgeon, scale it, gut it, take out the bones, and cut it in lengths about seven or eight inches; then provide some shrimps and oysters chopped small, an equal quantity of crumbs of bread, and a little lemon-peel grated, some nutmeg, a little beaten mace, a little pepper and chopped parsley, a few sweet herbs, an anchovy, mix them together; when this is done, butter one side of your fish, and strew some of your mixture upon it; then begin to roll it up as close as possible, and when the first piece is rolled up, roll upon that another, prepared in the same manner, and bind it round with a narrow fillet, leaving as much of the fish apparent as may be; but you must mind that the roll is not above four inches and a half thick, or else one part will be done before the inside is warm; therefore we often parboil the inside roll before we roll it: when it is enough, lay it in your dish, and prepare sauce as above. Garnish with lemon.

To boil Sturgeon.

CLEAN your sturgeon, and prepare as much liquor as will just boil it: to two quarts of water, a pint of vinegar, a stick of horse-radish, two or three bits of lemon-peel, some whole pepper, a bay-leaf, add a small handful of salt; boil your fish in this, and serve it with the following sauce: melt a pound of butter, dissolve an anchovy in it, put in a blade or two of mace, bruise the body of a crab in the butter, a few shrimps or craw-fish, a little catchup, a little lemon-juice; give it a boil, drain your fish well, and lay it in your dish. Garnish with fried oysters, sliced lemon, and scraped horse-radish; pour your sauce into boats or basons. So you may fry it, ragoo it, or bake it.

To Crimp Skate.

CUT it into long slips cross-ways, about an inch broad, and put it into spring-water and salt, as above; then have spring-water and salt boiling, put it in, and boil it fifteen minutes. Shrimp-sauce, or what sauce you like.

To fricassee Skate or Thornback white.

CUT the meat clean from the bone, fins, &c. and make it very clean; cut it into little pieces, about an inch broad and two inches long, lay it in your stew-pan: to a pound of the fish put a quarter of a pint of water, a little beaten mace, and grated nutmeg, a little bundle of sweet herbs, and a little salt; cover it, and let it boil fifteen minutes: take out the sweet herbs, put in a quarter of a pint of good cream, a piece of butter as big as a walnut, rolled in flour, a glass of white wine, keep shaking the pan all the while one way, till it is thick and smooth; then dish it up, and garnish with lemon.

To fricassee it brown.

TAKE your fish as above, flour it, and fry it of a fine brown in fresh butter; then take it up, lay it before the fire to keep warm, pour the fat out of the pan, shake in a little flour, and with a spoon stir in a piece of butter as big as an egg; stir it round till it is well mixed in the pan, then pour in a quarter of a pint of water, stir it round, shake in a very little beaten pepper, a little beaten mace; put in an onion, and a little bundle of sweet herbs, an anchovy, shake it round and let it boil; then pour in a quarter of a pint of red wine, a spoonful of catchup, a little juice of lemon, stir it all together, and let it boil: when it is enough, take out the sweet herbs and onion, and put in the fish to heat. Then dish it up, and garnish with lemon.

To fricassee Soals white.

SKIN, wash, and gut your soals very clean, cut off their heads, dry them in a cloth, then with your knife very carefully cut the flesh from the bones and fins on both sides; cut the flesh longways and then across, so that each soal will be in eight pieces: take the heads and bones and put them into a sauce-pan with a pint of water, a bundle of sweet herbs, an onion, a little whole pepper, two or three blades of mace, a little salt, a very little piece of lemon-peel and a little crust of bread: cover it close, let it boil till half is wasted, then strain it through a fine sieve, put it into a stew-pan, put in the soals and half a pint of white wine, a little parsley chopped fine, a few mushrooms cut small, a piece of butter as big as a hen's egg, rolled in flour, grate in a little nutmeg, set all together on the fire, but keep shaking the pan all the while till the fish is enough. Then dish it up and garnish with lemon.

To fricaſſee Soals brown.

CLEANSE and cut your ſoals, boil the water as in the foregoing receipt, flour your fiſh and fry them in freſh butter of a fine light brown. Take the fleſh of a ſmall ſoal, beat it in a mortar, with a piece of bread as big a hen's egg, ſoaked in cream, the yolks of two hard eggs and a little melted butter, a little bit of thyme, a little parſley, an anchovy, ſeaſon it with nutmeg, mix all together with the yolk of a raw egg, and with a little flour, roll it up into little balls and fry them, but not too much; then lay your fiſh and balls before the fire, pour all the fat out of the pan, pour in the liquor which is boiled with the ſpice and herbs, ſtir it round the pan, then put in half a pint of red wine, a few truffles and morels, a few muſhrooms, a ſpoonful of catchup, and the juice of half a ſmall lemon: ſtir in all together and let it boil, then ſtir in a piece of butter rolled in flour; ſtir it round, when your ſauce is of a fine thickneſs put in your fiſh and balls, and when it is hot diſh it up, put in the balls, and pour your ſauce over it. Garniſh with lemon. In the ſame manner dreſs a ſmall turbot, or any flat fiſh.

To boil Soals.

TAKE a pair of ſoals, make them clean, lay them in vinegar, ſalt, and water two hours; then dry them in a cloth, put them into a ſtew-pan, put to them a pint of white wine, a bundle of ſweet herbs, an onion ſtuck with ſix cloves, ſome whole pepper and a little ſalt; cover them and let them boil: when they are enough, take them up, lay them in your diſh, ſtrain the liquor, and thicken it with butter and flour; pour the ſauce over, and garniſh with ſcraped horſe-radiſh and lemon. In this manner dreſs a little turbot: it is a genteel diſh for ſupper. You may add prawns, or ſhrimps, or muſcles to the ſauce.

Another Way to boil Soals.

TAKE three quarts of ſpring-water and a handful of ſalt, let it boil; then put in your ſoals, boil them gently for ten minutes; then diſh them up in a clean napkin, with anchovy-ſauce or ſhrimp-ſauce in boats.

To make a Collar of Fiſh in Ragoo, to look like a Breaſt of Veal collared.

TAKE a large eel, ſkin it, waſh it clean, and parboil it, pick off the fleſh, and beat it in a mortar; ſeaſon it with beaten mace, nutmeg, pepper, ſalt, a few ſweet herbs, parſley, and a little lemon-peel chopped ſmall; beat all well together with an equal quantity of crumbs of bread; mix it well together, then

take

take a turbot, soals, skate, or thornback, or any flat fish that will roll cleverly: lay the flat fish on the dresser, take away all the bones and fins, and cover your fish with the farce; then roll it up as tight as you can, and open the skin of your eel, and bind the collar with it nicely, so that it may be flat top and bottom, to stand well in the dish; then butter an earthen dish and set it in upright; flour it all over, and stick a piece of butter on the top and round the edges, so that it may run down on the fish; and let it be well baked, but take great care it is not broke: let there be a quarter of a pint of water in the dish.

In the mean time take the water the eel was boiled in, and all the bones of the fish, set them on to boil, season them with mace, cloves, black and white pepper, sweet herbs, an onion; cover it close, and let it boil till there is about a quarter of a pint; then strain it, add to it a few truffles and morels, a few mushrooms, two spoonfuls of catchup, a gill of red wine, a piece of butter as big a large walnut, rolled in flour: stir all together, season with salt to your palate: save some of the farce you make of the eel, and mix with the yolk of an egg, and roll them up in little balls with flour, and fry them of a light brown: when your fish is enough, lay it in your dish, skim all the fat off the pan, and pour the gravy to your sauce; let it all boil together till it is thick, then pour it it over the roll, and put in your balls. Garnish with lemon.

This does best in a tin oven before the fire, because then you can baste it as you please. It is a fine bottom-dish.

To butter Crabs or Lobsters.

TAKE two crabs or lobsters, being boiled, and cold, take all the meat out of the shells and bodies, mince it small, and put it all together into a sauce-pan; add to it a glass of white wine, two spoonfuls of vinegar, a nutmeg grated, then let it boil up till it is thoroughly hot: then have ready half a pound of fresh butter, melted with an anchovy, and the yolks of two eggs beat up and mixed with the butter; then mix crabs and butter all together, shaking the sauce-pan constantly round till it is quite hot; then have ready the great shell either of a crab or lobster; lay it in the middle of your dish, pour some into the shell, and the rest in little saucers round the shell, sticking three-corner toasts between the saucers and round the shell. This is a fine side-dish at a second course.

To butter Lobsters another Way.

PARBOIL your lobsters, then break the shells, pick out all the meat, cut it small, take the meat out of the body, mix it

fine

fine with a spoon in a little white wine; for example, a small lobster, one spoonful of wine, put it into a sauce-pan with the meat of the lobster, four spoonfuls of white wine, a blade of mace, a little beaten pepper and salt; let it stew all together a few minutes, then stir in a piece of butter, shake your sauce-pan round till your butter is melted, put in a spoonful of vinegar, and strew in as many crumbs of bread as will make it thick enough: when it is hot, pour it into your plate, and garnish with the chine of a lobster cut in four, peppered, salted, and broiled. This makes a pretty plate, or a fine dish, with two or three lobsters. You may add one tea-spoonful of fine sugar to your sauce.

To roast Lobsters.

Boil your lobsters, then lay them before the fire, and baste them with butter till they have a fine froth: dish them up with plain melted butter in a cup. This is as good a way to the full as roasting them alive, and not half the trouble, not to mention the cruelty.

To make a fine Dish of Lobsters.

Take three lobsters, boil the largest as above, and froth it before the fire; take the other two boiled, and butter them as in the foregoing receipt; take the two body-shells, heat them hot, and fill them with the buttered meat; lay the large lobster in the middle, and the two shells on each side, and the two great claws of the middle lobster at each end; and the four pieces of chines of the two lobsters broiled and laid on each end. This, if nicely done, makes a pretty dish.

To dress a Crab.

Having taken out the meat of a fine large crab, and cleansed it from the skin, put it into a stew-pan, with half a pint of white wine, a little nutmeg, pepper, and salt over a slow fire; throw in a few crumbs of bread, beat up one yolk of an egg with one spoonful of vinegar, throw it in, then shake the sauce-pan round a minute, and serve it up on a plate.

To stew Prawns, Shrimps, or Craw-fish.

Pick out the tails about the quantity of two quarts; take the bodies, give them a bruise and put them into a pint of white wine, with a blade of mace; let them stew a quarter of an hour, stir them together, and strain them; then wash out the sauce-pan, put to it the strained liquor and tails: grate a small nutmeg in, add a little salt, and a quarter of a pound of butter rolled in flour; shake it all together, cut a pretty thin toast round a quartern loaf, toast it brown on both sides, cut it into six pieces, lay it close together in the bottom of your dish, and
pour

MADE PLAIN AND EASY.   171

pour your fish and sauce over it; send it to table hot. If it be craw-fish or prawns, garnish your dish with some of the biggest claws laid thick round. Water will do in the room of wine, only add a spoonful of vinegar.

Scolloped Oysters.

PUT them on a gridiron over a good clear fire, let them remain till you think they are enough, then have ready some crumbs of bread rubbed in a clean napkin, fill your shells and set them before a good fire and baste them with butter; let them be of a fine brown, keeping them turning to be brown all over alike; but a tin does them best before the fire. They eat much the best done this way, though most people stew the oysters first in a sauce-pan, with a blade of mace thickened with a bit of butter, and fill the shells, then cover them with crumbs, and brown them with a hot iron; but the bread has not the fine taste of the former.

To ragoo Oysters.

TAKE a quart of the largest oysters you can get, open them, save the liquor and strain it through a fine sieve; wash your oysters in warm water; make a batter thus: take two yolks of eggs, beat them well, grate in half a nutmeg, cut a little lemon-peel small, a good deal of parsley, a spoonful of the juice of spinage, two spoonfuls of cream or milk, beat it up with flour to a thick batter; have ready some butter in a stew-pan, dip your oysters one by one into the batter, and have ready crumbs of bread, then roll them in it and fry them quick and brown; some with the crumbs of bread and some without; take them out of the pan and set them before the fire, then have ready a quart of chesnuts shelled and skinned, fry them in the butter; when they are enough take them up, pour the fat out of the pan, shake a little flour all over the pan, and rub a piece of butter as big as a hen's egg all over the pan with your spoon till it is melted and thick; then put in the oyster liquor, three or four blades of mace, stir it round, put in a few pistachio nuts shelled, let them boil, then put in the chesnuts and half a pint of white wine; have ready the yolks of two eggs beat up with four spoonfuls of cream; stir all well together; when it is thick and fine lay the oysters in the dish and pour the ragoo over them. Garnish with chesnuts and lemon.

You may ragoo muscles the same way. You may leave out the pistachio nuts if you do not like them, but they give the sauce a fine flavour.

To fry Oysters.

TAKE a quarter of an hundred of large oysters, beat the yolk of two eggs, add a little nutmeg and a blade of mace
pounded,

pounded, a spoonful of flour and a little salt, dip in your oysters and fry them in hog's-lard a light brown; if you choose you may add a little parsley shred fine.

N. B. They are a proper garnish for cod's head, calf's head, or most made-dishes.

To stew Oysters and all sorts of Shell Fish.

WHEN you have opened your oysters put their liquor into a tossing-pan with a little beaten mace, thicken it with flour and butter, boil it three or four minutes, toast a slice of white bread and cut it into three-cornered pieces, lay them round your dish, put in a spoonful of good cream, put in your oysters and shake them round in your pan; you must not let them boil, for if they do it will make them hard and look small; serve them up in a little soup dish or plate.

N. B. You may stew cockles, muscles, or any shell fish the same way.

To make Oyster Loaves.

TAKE all the crumbs out of three French rolls, by cutting a piece of the top crust off, in such a manner as it may fit again in the same place; fry the rolls out of which the crumb has been taken brown in fresh butter; take half a pint of oysters, stew them in their own liquor, then take out the oysters with a fork, strain the liquor to them, put them into a sauce-pan again with a glass of white wine, a little beaten mace, a little grated nutmeg, a quarter of a pound of butter rolled in flour; shake them well together, then put them into the rolls; and these make a pretty side-dish for a first course. You may rub in the crumbs of two of the rolls and toss up with the oysters.

To stew Muscles.

WASH them very clean from the sand in two or three waters, put them into a stew-pan, cover them close and let them stew till all the shells are opened; then take them out one by one, pick them out of the shells, and look under the tongue to see if there be a crab; if there is, you must throw away the muscle; some will only pick out the crab and eat the muscle, but this is dangerous; when you have picked them all clean put them into a sauce-pan; to a quart of muscles put half a pint of the liquor strained through a sieve, put in a blade or two of mace, a piece of butter as big as a large walnut, rolled in flour; let them stew; toast some bread brown and lay them round the dish cut three-corner-ways; pour in the muscles and send them to table hot.

Another Way to stew Muscles.

CLEAN and stew your muscles as in the foregoing receipt, only to a quart of muscles put in a pint of liquor, and a quarter

ter of a pound of butter rolled in a very little flour; when they are enough have some crumbs of bread ready, and cover the bottom of your dish thick, grate half a nutmeg over them, and pour the muscles and sauce all over the crumbs and send them to table.

A third Way to dress Muscles.

STEW them as above and lay them in your dish; strew your crumbs of bread thick all over them, then set them before a good fire, turning the dish round and round that they may be brown all alike; keep basting them with butter that the crumbs may be crisp, and it will make a pretty side-dish. You may do cockles the same way.

To stew Scollops.

BOIL them very well in salt and water, take them out and stew them in a little of the liquor, a little white wine, a little vinegar, two or three blades of mace, two or three cloves, a piece of butter rolled in flour, and the juice of a Seville orange; stew them well and dish them up.

To grill Shrimps.

SEASON them well with salt and pepper, shred parsley, butter in scollop-shells; add some grated bread, and let them stew for half an hour; brown them with a hot iron and serve them up.

Buttered Shrimps.

STEW two quarts of shrimps in a pint of white wine with nutmeg; beat up eight eggs with a little white wine and half a pound of butter, shaking the sauce-pan one way all the time over the fire till they are thick enough; lay toasted sippets round a dish and pour them over it; so serve them up.

To fry Smelts.

LET your smelts be fresh caught, wipe them very dry with a cloth, beat up yolks of eggs and rub over them, strew crumbs of bread on; have some clear dripping boiling in a frying-pan, and fry them quick of a fine gold colour; put them on a plate to drain, and then lay them in your dish. Garnish with fried parsley, with plain butter in a cup.

To dress White-bait.

TAKE your white-bait fresh caught and put them in a cloth with a handful of flour, and shake them about till they are

separated

separated and quite dry; have some hog's lard boiling quick, fry them two minutes, drain them and dish up with plain butter and soy.

CHAP. XI.

SAUCES for FISH.

To make Quins Fish-Sauce.

TAKE a quart of walnut-pickle, put to it six anchovies with mace, cloves, and whole pepper, six bay-leaves, six shalots, boil them all together till the anchovies are dissolved, when cold put in half a pint of red wine and bottle it up; when you use it give it a shake, two spoonfuls of this to a little rich melted butter makes good sauce.

Quins Sauce another Way.

TAKE half a pint of mushroom catchup, a quarter of a pint of pickled walnut-liquor, three anchovies, two cloves of garlic pounded, a quarter of a tea-spoonful of Cayenne pepper, put all into a bottle and shake it well.

Lobster-Sauce.

TAKE a fine hen lobster, take out all the spawn and bruise it on a mortar very fine with a little butter; take all the meat out of the claws and tail and cut it in small square pieces; put the spawn and meat in a stew-pan with a spoonful of anchovy-liquor, and one spoonful of catchup, a blade of mace, a piece of a stick of horse-radish, half a lemon, a gill of gravy, a little butter rolled in flour, just enough to thicken it; put in a sufficient quantity of butter nicely melted, boil it gently up for six or seven minutes; take out the horse-radish, mace, and lemon, and squeeze the juice of the lemon into the sauce; just simmer it up and then put it in your boats.

Shrimp-Sauce.

TAKE half a pint of shrimps, wash them very clean, put them in a stew-pan with a spoonful of fish-lear or anchovy-liquor, butter melted thick, boil it up for five minutes, and squeeze in half a lemon; toss it up and then put it in your cups or boats.

To make Oyster-Sauce for Fish.

Take a pint of large oysters, scald them and then strain them through a sieve, wash the oysters very clean in cold water and take the beards off; put them in a stew-pan, pour the liquor over them, but be careful to pour the liquor gently out of the vessel you have strained it into and you will leave all the sediment at the bottom, which you must be careful not to put into your stew-pan; then add a large spoonful of anchovy-liquor, two blades of mace, half a lemon, some butter rolled in flour enough to thicken it; then put in half a pound of butter, boil it up till the butter is melted; then take out the mace and lemon, squeeze the lemon-juice into the sauce, give it a boil up, stir it all the time, and then put it into your boats or basons.

N. B. You may put in a spoonful of catchup or a spoonful of mountain wine.

To make Anchovy-Sauce.

Take a pint of gravy, put in an anchovy, take a piece of butter rolled in a little flour, and stir all together till it boils; you may add a little juice of a lemon, catchup, red wine, and walnut-liquor, just as you please.

Plain butter melted thick with a spoonful of walnut-pickle or catchup is good sauce, or anchovy; in short you may put as many things as you fancy into sauce.

To make Dutch Sauce.

Take a quarter of a pound of butter, four spoonfuls of water, dredge in a little flour, chop three anchovies and put in with three spoonfuls of good vinegar, a little scraped horse-radish, boil all together and send sent it up immediately, or else it will oil. This sauce is proper to all fresh-water fish.

To make Sauce for a Cod's Head.

Take a lobster, if it be alive stick a skewer in the vent of the tail to keep the water out, and throw a handful of salt in the water, when it boils put in the lobster and boil it half an hour; if it has spawn on, pick them off and pound them exceeding fine in a marble mortar, and put them into half a pound of good melted butter, then take the meat out of your lobster, pull it in bits and put it in your butter with a meat spoonful of lemon-pickle and the same of walnut-catchup, a slice of an end of a lemon, one or two slices of horse-radish, as much beaten mace as will lie on a sixpence, salt and Cayenne to your taste, boil them one minute, then take out the horse-radish and lemon, and serve it up in your sauce-boat.

N. B. If

N. B. If you can get no lobster you may make shrimp, cockle, or muscle sauce the same way; if there can be no kind of shell fish got, you then may add two anchovies cut small, a spoonful of walnut-liquor, a large onion stuck with cloves, strain it and put it in the sauce-boat.

To make a very nice Sauce for most Sorts of Fish.

TAKE a little gravy made of either veal or mutton, put to it a little of the water that drains from your fish, when it is boiled enough, put it in a sauce-pan, and put in a whole onion, one anchovy, a spoonful of catchup, and a glass of white wine, thicken it with a good lump of butter rolled in flour and a spoonful of cream; if you have oysters, cockles, or shrimps put them in after you take it off the fire (but it is very good without), you may use red wine instead of white by leaving out the cream.

To make White Fish-Sauce.

WASH two anchovies, put them into a sauce-pan with one glass of white wine and two of water, half a nutmeg grated, and a little lemon-peel; when it has boiled five or six minutes strain it through a sieve, add to it a spoonful of white wine vinegar, thicken it a little, then put in a pound of butter rolled in flour, boil it well and pour it hot upon your fish.

CHAP. XII.

SOUPS and BROTHS.

(Not included in the Lent Chapter on account of their being made with meat; but what Soups are not in this Chapter may be found there.)

Rules to be observed in making Soups and Broths.

FIRST take great care the pots or sauce-pans and covers be very clean and free from all grease and sand, and that they be well tinned, for fear of giving the broths or soups any brassy taste. If you have time to stew as softly as possible, it will both have a finer flavour and the meat will be tenderer; but then observe, when you make soups or broths for present use, if it is to be done softly, do not put much more water than you intend to have soup or broth; and if you have the convenience of an earthen pan or pipkin, set it on wood embers till it boils, then skim it, and put in your seasoning; cover it close and set it on embers,

so

so that it may do very softly for some time, and both the meat and broths will be delicious. You must observe in all broths and soups that one thing does not taste more than another, but that the taste be equal, and that it has a fine agreeable relish, according to what you design it for; and you must be sure that all the greens and herbs you put in be cleaned, washed, and picked.

To make strong Broth for Soup or Gravy.

TAKE a shin of beef, a knuckle of veal, and a scrag of mutton, put them in five gallons of water, then let it boil up, skim it clean, and season it with six large onions, four good leeks, four heads of celery, two carrots, two turnips, a bundle of sweet herbs, six cloves, a dozen corns of all-spice and some salt; skim it very clean and let it stew gently for six hours; then strain it off, and put it by for use.

When you want very strong gravy, take a slice of bacon and lay it in a stew-pan; take a pound of beef, cut it thin, lay it on the bacon, slice a good piece of carrot in, an onion sliced, a good crust of bread, a few sweet herbs, a little mace, cloves, nutmeg, whole pepper, and an anchovy; cover it and set it on a slow fire for five or six minutes, and pour in a quart of the above gravy; cover it close, and let it boil softly till half is wasted: this will be a rich, high brown sauce for fish, fowl, or ragoo.

Gravy for White Sauce.

TAKE a pound of any part of the veal, cut it into small pieces, boil it in a quart of water, with an onion, a blade of mace, two cloves, and a few whole pepper-corns; boil it till it is as rich as you would have it.

Gravy for Turkey, Fowl, or Ragoo.

TAKE a pound of lean beef, cut and hack it well, then flour it well, put a piece of butter as big as an hen's egg in a stew-pan; when it is melted, put in your beef, fry it on all sides a little brown, then pour in three pints of boiling water and a bundle of sweet herbs, two or three blades of mace, three or four cloves, twelve whole pepper-corns, a little bit of carrot, a little piece of crust of bread toasted brown; cover it close, and let it boil till there is about a pint or less; then season it with salt, and strain it off.

Gravy for a Fowl, when you have no Meat nor Gravy ready.

TAKE the neck, liver and gizzard, boil them in half a pint of water, with a little piece of bread toasted brown, a little pepper and salt, and a little bit of thyme; let them boil till there is about a quarter of a pint; then pour in half a glass of red wine, boil it and strain it, then bruise the liver well in and strain it again, thicken it with a little piece of butter rolled in flour, and it will be very good.

An ox's kidney makes good gravy, cut all to pieces and boiled with spice, &c. as in the foregoing receipts.

You have a receipt in the beginning of the book, in the preface for Gravies.

Vermicelli Soup.

TAKE three quarts of the broth and one of the gravy mixed together, a quarter of a pound of vermicelli blanched in two quarts of water; put it into the soup, boil it up for ten minutes and season with salt, if it wants any; put it in your tureen, with a crust of a French roll baked.

Macaroni Soup.

TAKE three quarts of the strong broth and one of the gravy mixed together; take half a pound of small pipe macaroni and boil it in three quarts of water, with a little butter in it, till it is tender; then strain it through a sieve, cut it in pieces of about two inches long, put it in your soup, and boil it up for ten minutes, and then send it to table in a tureen, with the crust of a French roll toasted.

Soup Cressu.

TAKE a pound of lean ham and cut it into small bits, and put at the bottom of a stew-pan, then cut a French roll and put over the ham; take two dozen heads of celery cut small, six onions, two turnips, one carrot, cut and washed very clean, six cloves, four blades of mace, two handfuls of water-cresses; put them all into the stew-pan with a pint of good broth; cover them close, and sweat it gently for twenty minutes, then fill it up with veal broth, and stew it four hours; rub it through a fine sieve or cloth, put it in your pan again, season it with salt and a little Cayenne pepper; give it a simmer up and send it to table hot with some French roll toasted hard in it: boil a handful of cresses till tender in water, and put in over the bread.

To make Mutton or Veal Gravy.

CUT and hack your meat well; set it on the fire with water, sweet herbs, mace, and pepper: let it boil till it is as good as you would have it, then strain it off. Your fine cooks always (if they can) chop a partridge or two and put into gravies.

To make a strong Fish Gravy.

TAKE two or three eels, or any fish you have, skin or scale them, gut them and wash them from grit, cut them into little pieces,

pieces, put them into a sauce-pan, cover them with water, a little crust of bread toasted brown, a blade or two of mace and some whole pepper, a few sweet herbs, and a very little bit of lemon-peel: let it boil till it is rich and good, then have ready a piece of butter, according to your gravy, if a pint, as big as a walnut; melt it in the sauce-pan, then shake in a little flour, and toss it about till it is brown, and then strain in the gravy to it; let it boil a few minutes, and it will be good.

To make Plumb-Porridge for Christmas.

TAKE a leg and shin of beef, put them into eight gallons of water, and boil them till they are very tender, and when the broth is strong strain it out; wipe the pot and put in the broth again; then slice six penny-loaves thin, cut off the top and bottom, put some of the liquor to it, cover it up and let it stand a quarter of an hour, boil it and strain it, and then put it into your pot; let it boil a quarter of an hour, then put in five pounds of currants, clean washed and picked; let them boil a little, and put in five pounds of raisins of the sun stoned, and two pounds of prunes, and let them boil till they swell; then put in three quarters of an ounce of mace, half an ounce of cloves, two nutmegs, all of them beat fine, and mix it with a little liquor cold, and put them in a very little while, and take off the pot, then put in three pounds of sugar, a little salt, a quart of sack, a quart of claret, and the juice of two or three lemons. You may thicken with sago instead of bread (if you please); pour them into earthen pans, and keep them for use.

To make a strong Broth to keep for Use.

TAKE part of a leg of beef and the scrag-end of a neck of mutton, break the bones in pieces, and put to it as much water as will cover it, and a little salt; and when it boils, skim it clean, and put into it a whole onion stuck with cloves, a bunch of sweet herbs, some whole pepper, and a nutmeg quartered: let these boil till the meat is boiled in pieces, and the strength boiled out of it; strain it out, and keep it for use.

A Craw-fish Soup.

TAKE a gallon of water and set it a-boiling; put in it a bunch of sweet herbs, three or four blades of mace, an onion stuck with cloves, pepper and salt; then have about two hundred craw-fish, save about twenty, then pick the rest from the shells, save the tails whole; beat the body and shells in a mortar with a pint of peas (green or dry), first boiled tender in fair water; put your boiling water to it and strain it boiling hot through a cloth till you have all the goodness out of it; set it over a slow fire or stew-hole, have ready a French roll cut very thin, and let it be very dry, put it to your soup, let it stew till half is wasted, then put a piece of butter as big as an egg into a sauce-pan, let it simmer till it is done making a noise, shake in two tea-spoonfuls of flour, stirring it about, and an onion; put in the tails of the fish, give them a shake round, put to them a pint of good gravy, let it boil four or five minutes softly, take out the onion, and put to it a pint of the soup, stir it well together, bruise the live spawn of a hen lobster and put it all together, and let it simmer very softly a quarter of an hour; fry a French roll very nice and brown, and the twenty craw-fish; pour your soup into the dish, and lay the roll in the middle and the craw-fish round the dish.

Fine cooks boil a brace of carp and tench, and perhaps a lobster or two, and many more rich things, to make a craw-fish soup; but the above is full as good, and wants no addition.

To make Soup-Santea, or Gravy-Soup.

TAKE six good rashers of lean ham, put it in the bottom of a stew-pan; then put over it three pounds of lean beef, and over the beef three pounds of lean veal, six onions cut in slices, two carrots, and two turnips sliced, two heads of celery, and a bundle of sweet herbs, six cloves, and two blades of mace; put a little water at the bottom, draw it very gently till it sticks, then put in a gallon of boiling water; let it stew for two hours, season with salt, and strain it off; then have ready a carrot cut in small slices of two inches long and about as thick as a goose-quill, a turnip, two heads of leeks, two heads of celery, two heads of endive cut across, two cabbage-lettuces cut across, a very little sorrel and chervil; put them in a stew-pan and sweat them for fifteen minutes gently, then put them in your soup, boil it up gently for ten minutes; put it in your tureen with the crust of a French roll.

N. B. You may boil the herbs in two quarts of water for ten minutes (if you like them best so); your soup will be the clearer; or you may take one quart of the broth, page 177, and one of the fowling gravy, and boil the herbs that are cut fine in it for a quarter of an hour.

A Green Peas Soup.

TAKE a knuckle of veal and one pound of lean ham, cut them in thin slices, lay the ham at the bottom of a soup-pot, the veal upon the ham; then cut six onions in slices and put on, two or three turnips, two carrots, three heads of celery cut small, a little thyme, four cloves, and four blades of mace;

put

put a little water at the bottom, cover the pot close, and draw it gently but do not let it stick; then put in six quarts of boiling water, let it stew gently for four hours, and skim it well; take two quarts of green peas and stew them in some of the broth till tender; then strain them off, and put them in a marble mortar, and beat them fine, put the liquor in, and mix them up (if you have no mortar, you must bruise them in the best manner you can): take a tammy or a fine cloth and rub them through till you have rubbed all the pulp out, and then put your soup in a clean pot, with half a pint of spinage-juice, and boil it up for fifteen minutes; season with salt and a little pepper: if your soup is not thick enough, take the crumb of a French roll and boil it in a little of the soup, beat it in the mortar and rub it through your tammy cloth, then put it in your soup and boil it up; then put it in your tureen, with dice of bread toasted very hard.

Another Way to make Green Peas Soup.

TAKE a gallon of water, make it boil, then put in six onions, four turnips, two carrots, and two heads of celery cut in slices, four cloves, four blades of mace, four cabbage-lettuces cut small; stew them for an hour; then strain it off, and put in two quarts of old green peas and boil them in the liquor till tender; then beat or bruise them and mix them up with the broth, and rub them through a tammy or cloth, and put it in a clean pot, with half a pint of spinage-juice, and boil it up fifteen minutes, season with pepper and salt to your liking; then put your soup in your tureen, with small dice of bread toasted very hard.

A Peas-Soup for Winter.

TAKE about four pounds of lean beef, cut it in small pieces, about a pound of lean bacon, or pickled pork, set it on the fire with two gallons of water, let it boil, and skim it well; then put in six onions, two turnips, one carrot, and four heads of celery cut small, and put in a quart of split peas, boil it gently for three hours, then strain them through a sieve, and rub the peas well through; then put your soup in a clean pot, and put in some dried mint rubbed very fine to powder, cut the white of four heads of celery, and two turnips in dice, and boil them in a quart of water for fifteen minutes; then strain them off, and put them in your soup; take about a dozen of small rashers of bacon fried, and put them into your soup, season with pepper and salt to your liking, boil it up for fifteen minutes; then put it in your tureen, with dice of bread fried very crisp.

Another Way to make it.

When you boil a leg of pork, or a good piece of beef, save the liquor; when it is cold take off the fat; the next day boil a leg of mutton, save the liquor, and when it is cold take off the fat, set it on the fire, with two quarts of peas; let them boil till they are tender, then put in the pork or beef liquor, with the ingredients as above, and let it boil till it is as thick as you would have it, allowing for the boiling again; then strain it off, and add the ingredients as above. You may make your soup of veal or mutton gravy (if you please), that is according to your fancy.

A Chesnut Soup.

Take half a hundred of chesnuts, pick them, put them in an earthen pan, and set them in the oven half an hour, or roast them gently over a slow fire, but take care they do not burn; then peel them, and set them to stew in a quart of good beef, veal, or mutton broth, till they are quite tender; in the mean time, take a piece or slice of ham, or bacon, a pound of veal, a pigeon beat to pieces, a bundle of sweet herbs, an onion, a little pepper and mace, and a piece of carrot; lay the bacon at the bottom of a stew-pan, and lay the meat and ingredients at top; set it over a slow fire till it begins to stick to the pan, then put in a crust of bread, and pour in two quarts of broth; let it boil softly till one third is wasted, then strain it off, and add to it the chesnuts; season it with salt, and let it boil till it is well tasted, stew two pigeons in it, and fry a French roll crisp; lay the roll in the middle of the dish, and the pigeons on each side; pour in the soup, and send it away hot.

Hare Soup.

Take and cut a large hare into pieces, and put it into an earthen mug, with three blades of mace, two large onions, a little salt, a red herring, half a dozen large morels, a pint of red wine, and three quarts of water; bake it three hours in a quick oven, and then strain it into a stew-pan; have ready boiled four ounces of French barley, and put in; just scald the liver and rub it through a sieve with a wooden spoon; put it into the soup, set it over the fire, and keep it stirring, but it must not boil: send it up with crisp bread in it.

Soup à la Reine.

Take a pound of lean ham and cut it small, and put it at the bottom of a soup-pot; cut a knuckle of veal into pieces and put in, and an old fowl cut in pieces; put three blades of mace, four onions, six heads of celery, two turnips, one carrot, a

bundle

bundle of sweet herbs washed clean; put in half a pint of water, and cover it close, and sweat it gently for half an hour, but be careful it does not burn, for that will spoil it; then pour in boiling water enough to cover it, and let it stew till all the goodness is out, then strain it into a clean pan, and let it stand half an hour to settle, then skim it well, and pour it off the settlings into a clean pan; boil half a pint of cream and pour upon the crumb of a halfpenny roll, and let it soak well; take half a pound of almonds, blanch them and beat them in a mortar as fine as you can, putting now and then a little cream to keep them from oiling; take the yolks of six hard eggs and the roll and cream, and put to the almonds, and beat them up together in your broth; rub it through a fine hair sieve or cloth till all the goodness is rubbed through, and put it into a stew-pan; keep stirring it till it boils, and skim off the froth as it rises; season with salt, and then pour it into your tureen, with three slices of French roll crisped before the fire.

To make Mutton-Broth.

TAKE a neck of mutton about six pounds, cut it in two, boil the scrag in a gallon of water, skim it well, then put in a little bundle of sweet herbs, an onion, and a good crust of bread: let it boil an hour, then put in the other part of the mutton, take a turnip or two, some dried marigolds, a few cives chopped fine, a little parsley chopped small, put these in about a quarter of an hour before your broth is enough; season it with salt; or you may put in a quarter of a pound of barley or rice at first. Some love it thickened with oatmeal and some with bread, and some love it seasoned with mace, instead of sweet herbs and onion; all this is fancy and different palates. If you boil turnips for sauce, do not boil all in the pot, it makes the broth too strong of them, but boil them in a sauce-pan.

Beef-Broth.

TAKE a leg of beef, crack the bone in two or three parts, wash it clean, put it into a pot with a gallon of water, skim it well, then put in two or three blades of mace, a little bundle of parsley, and a good crust of bread; let it boil till the beef is quite tender, and the sinews; toast some bread and cut it in dice, and put it in your tureen; lay in the meat, and pour the soup in.

To make Scotch Barley-Broth.

TAKE a leg of beef, chop it all to pieces, boil it in three gallons of water with a piece of carrot and a crust of bread, till it is half boiled away; then strain it off, and put it into the pot again with half a pound of barley, four or five heads of celery washed clean and cut small, a large onion, a bundle of sweet herbs, a little parsley chopped small, and a few marigolds; let this boil an hour: take a cock or a large fowl clean picked and washed, and put into the pot, boil it till the broth is quite good, then season with salt, and send it to table with the fowl in the middle. This broth is very good without the fowl. Take out the onion and sweet herbs before you send it to table.

Some make this broth with a sheep's head instead of a leg of beef, and it is very good; but you must chop the head all to pieces. The thick flank (about six pounds to six quarts of water) makes good broth; then put the barley in with the meat, first skim it well, boil it an hour very softly, then put in the above ingredients with turnips and carrots clean scraped and pared and cut into little pieces; boil all together softly till the broth is very good; then season it with salt, and send it to table with the beef in the middle, turnips and carrots round, and pour the broth over all.

To make Hodge-Podge.

TAKE a piece of beef, fat and lean together, about a pound of veal, a pound of scrag of mutton, cut all into little pieces, set it on the fire, with two quarts of water, an ounce of barley, an onion, a little bundle of sweet herbs, three or four heads of celery washed clean and cut small, a little mace, two or three cloves, some whole pepper, tied all in a muslin rag, and put to the meat three turnips pared and cut in two, a large carrot scraped clean and cut in six pieces, a little lettuce cut small, put it all in the pot and cover it close: let it stew very softly over a slow fire five or six hours; take out the spice, sweet herbs, and onion, and pour all into a soup dish, and send it to table; first season it with salt. Half a pint of green peas, when it is the season for them, is very good. If you let this boil fast, it will waste too much; therefore you cannot do it too slow, if it does but simmer.

Hodge-Podge of Mutton.

TAKE a neck of mutton of about six pounds, cut about two pounds of the best end whole, cut the rest into chops, put them into a stew-pan or little pot; put in two large onions whole, two heads of celery, four turnips whole, a carrot cut in pieces, a small savoy or cabbage, all washed clean; stew it gently till you have drawn all the gravy out, but be sure it don't burn; put in about three quarts of boiling water, and let it stew gently for three hours; put in a spoonful of browning, and season it with salt; skim off all the fat clean. Put your meat in a soup-dish,

and

and put the herbs over, and pour the soup over all. Garnish with toasted sippets. You put only the best end in the dish, and leave out the chops.

Partridge Soup.

TAKE two large old partridges, skin them and cut them into pieces, with three or four slices of ham, a little celery, and three large onions cut in slices; fry them in butter till they are brown; be sure not to burn them; then put them to three quarts of boiling water, with a few pepper-corns, and a little salt; stew it very gently for two hours, then strain it, and put some stewed celery and fried bread. Serve it up hot in a tureen.

To make Portable Soup.

TAKE two legs of beef, of about fifty pounds weight, take off all the skin and fat as well as you can, then take all the meat and sinews clean from the bones, which meat put into a large pot, and put to it eight or nine gallons of soft water; first make it boil, then put in twelve anchovies, an ounce of mace, a quarter of an ounce of cloves, an ounce of whole pepper black and white together, six large onions peeled and cut in two, a little bundle of thyme, sweet marjoram, and winter-savory, the dry hard crust of a two-penny loaf, stir it all together and cover it close, lay a weight on the cover to keep it close down, and let it boil softly for eight or nine hours, then uncover it and stir it together; cover it close again and let it boil till it is a very rich good jelly, which you will know by taking a little out now and then, and letting it cool: when you think it is a thick jelly, take it off, strain it through a coarse hair bag, and press it hard; then strain it through a hair sieve into a large earthen pan; when it is quite cold, take off the scum and fat, and take the fine jelly clear from the settlings at bottom, and then put the jelly into a large deep well-tinned stew-pan; set it over a stove with a slow fire, keep stirring it often, and take great care it neither sticks to the pan or burns: when you find the jelly very stiff and thick, as it will be in lumps about the pan, take it out, and put it into large deep china cups, or well glazed earthen-ware. Fill the pan two-thirds full of water, and when the water boils set it in your cups. Be sure no water gets into the cups, and keep the water boiling softly all the time till you find the jelly is like a stiff glue; take out the cups, and when they are cool, turn out the glue into a coarse new flannel; let it lay eight or nine hours, and then put it into the sun till it is quite hard and dry. Put it into tin boxes, with a piece of writing paper between each piece, and keep them in a dry place.

When you use it, pour boiling water on it, and stir it all the time till it is melted; season with salt to your palate. A

piece

piece as big as a large walnut will make a pint of water very rich; but as to that you are to make it as good as you please; if for soup, fry a French roll and lay it in the middle of the dish, and when the glue is diſſolved in the water, give it a boil and pour it into a diſh. If you chooſe it for change, you may boil either rice or barley, vermicelli, celery cut ſmall, or truffles or morels; but let them be very tenderly boiled in the water before you ſtir in the glue, and then give it a boil all together. You may, when you would have it very fine, add force-meat balls, cock's-combs, or a palate boiled very tender, and cut into little bits; but it will be very rich and good without any of theſe ingredients.

If for gravy, pour the boiling water on to what quantity you think proper; and when it is diſſolved, add what ingredients you pleaſe, as in other ſauces. This is only in the room of a rich good gravy. You may make your ſauce either weak or ſtrong, by adding more or leſs; or you may make it of veal, or of mutton the ſame way.

To make an Ox Cheek Soup.

First break the bones of an ox cheek, and waſh it in many waters, then lay it in warm water, throw in a little ſalt to fetch out the ſlime, waſh it out very well, then take a large ſtew-pan, put two ounces of butter at the bottom of the pan, and lay the fleſh ſide of the cheek down, add to it half a pound of a ſhank of ham cut in ſlices, and four heads of celery, pull off the leaves, waſh the heads clean, and cut them in with three large onions, two carrots and one parſnip ſliced, a few beets cut ſmall, and three blades of mace, ſet it over a moderate fire a quarter of an hour; this draws the virtue from the roots, which gives a pleaſant ſtrength to the gravy.

A good gravy may be made by this method, with roots and butter, only adding a little browning to give it a pretty colour; when the head has ſimmered a quarter of an hour, put to it ſix quarts of water, and let it ſtew till it is reduced to two quarts: if you would have it eat like ſoup, ſtrain and take out the meat and other ingredients, and put in the white part of a head of celery cut in ſmall pieces, with a little browning to make it a fine colour, take two ounces of vermicelli, give it a ſcald in the ſoup, and put the top of a French roll in the middle of a tureen, and ſerve it up.

To make Almond Soup.

Take a neck of veal, and the ſcrag-end of a neck of mutton, chop them in ſmall pieces, put them in a large toſſing-pan, cut in a turnip, with a blade or two of mace, and five quarts of water, ſet it over the fire, and let it boil gently till it is reduced to two quarts, strain it through a hair sieve into a clear pot, then put in six ounces of almonds blanched and beat fine, half a pint of thick cream, and Cayenne pepper to your taste, have ready three small French rolls, made for that purpose, the size of a small tea-cup; if they are larger they will not look well, and drink up too much of the soup; blanch a few Jordan almonds, and cut them lengthways, stick them round the edge of the rolls slantways, then stick them all over the top of the rolls, and put them in the tureen; when dished up pour the soup upon the rolls: these rolls look like a hedge-hog: some French cooks give this soup the name of hedge-hog soup.

To make a Transparent Soup.

TAKE a leg of veal and cut off the meat as thin as you can; when you have cut off all the meat clean from the bone, break the bone in small pieces, put the meat in a large jug, and the bones at top, with a bunch of sweet herbs, a quarter of an ounce of mace, half a pound of Jordan almonds blanched and beat fine, pour on it four quarts of boiling water, let it stand all night by the fire covered close, the next day put it into a well-tinned sauce-pan, and let it boil slowly till it is reduced to two quarts; be sure you take the scum and fat off as it rises, all the time it is boiling; strain it into a punch bowl, let it settle for two hours, pour it into a clean sauce-pan clear from the sediments, if any at the bottom; have ready three ounces of rice boiled in water; if you like vermicelli better, boil two ounces; when enough, put it in and serve it up.

To make Brown Pottage.

TAKE a piece of lean gravy-beef, and cut it into thin collops, and hack them with the back of a cleaver; have a stew-pan over the fire with a piece of butter, a little bacon cut thin; let them be brown over the fire, and put in your beef, let it stew till it be very brown; put in a little flour, and then have your broth ready, and fill up the stew-pan; put in two onions, a bunch of sweet herbs, cloves, mace, and pepper; let all stew together an hour covered, then have your bread ready toasted hard to put in your dish, and strain some of the broth to it through a fine sieve; put a fowl of some sort in the middle, with a little boiled spinage minced in it: garnish your dish with boiled lettuces, spinage, and lemon.

To make White Barley Pottage, with a large Chicken in the Middle.

FIRST make your stock with an old hen, a knuckle of veal, a scrag-end of mutton, some spice, sweet herbs, and onions; boil all together till it be strong enough, then have your barley ready boiled very tender and white, and strain some of it

through

through a cullender; have your bread ready toasted in your dish, with some fine green herbs, minced chervil, spinage, sorrel; and put into your dish some of the broth to your bread, herbs, and chicken, then barley strained and re-strained; stew all together in the dish a little while: garnish your dish with boiled lettuces, spinage, and lemon.

CHAP. XIII.

PUDDINGS, PIES, &c.

(The Lent Chapter contains all the Puddings, &c. which are not in this; those which are here are either entirely of meat, or have suet or some other ingredient in them, which prevents their being included in the Lent Chapter.)

Rules to be observed in making Puddings, &c.

IN boiled puddings, take great care the bag or cloth be very clean, not soapy, but dipped in hot water, and well floured. If a bread-pudding, tie it loose; if a batter pudding, tie it close; and be sure the water boils when you put the pudding in, and you should move the puddings in the pot now and then, for fear they stick. When you make a batter-pudding, first mix the flour well with a little milk, then put in the ingredients by degrees, and it will be smooth and not have lumps; but for a plain batter-pudding, the best way is to strain it through a coarse hair sieve, that it may neither have lumps nor the treadles of the eggs: and for all other puddings strain the eggs when they are beat. If you boil them in wooden bowls, or China dishes, butter the inside before you put in your batter; and for all baked puddings, butter the pan or dish before the pudding is put in.

An Oat-Pudding to bake.

OF oats decorticated take two pounds, and new milk enough to drown it, eight ounces of raisins of the sun stoned, an equal quantity of currants neatly picked, a pound of sweet suet finely shred, six new laid eggs well beat; season with nutmeg, beaten ginger, and salt; mix it all well together: it will make a better pudding than rice.

To make a Calf's-Foot Pudding.

TAKE of calves feet one pound minced very fine, the fat and the brown to be taken out, a pound and an half of suet,

pick

pick off all the skin and shred it small, six eggs, but half the whites, beat them well, the crumb of a halfpenny-roll grated, a pound of currants clean picked and washed, and rubbed in a cloth; milk, as much as will moisten it with the eggs, a handful of flour, a little salt, nutmeg, and sugar, to season it to your taste; boil it nine hours with your meat; when it is done, lay it in your dish, and pour melted butter over it. It is very good with white wine and sugar in the butter.

To make a Pith-Pudding.

TAKE a quantity of the pith of an ox, and let it lie all night in water to soak out the blood; the next morning strip it out of the skin and beat it with the back of a spoon in orange-water till it is as fine as pap; then take three pints of thick cream and boil in it two or three blades of mace, a nutmeg quartered, a stick of cinnamon; then take half a pound of the best Jordan almonds blanched in cold water, then beat them with a little of the cream, and as it dries put in more cream; and when they are all beaten, strain the cream from them to the pith; then take the yolks of ten eggs, the white of but two, beat them very well and put them to the ingredients; take a spoonful of grated bread or Naples biscuit, mingle all these together, with half a pound of fine sugar, and the marrow of four large bones, and a little salt; fill them in a small ox or hog's guts, or bake in a dish, with a puff-paste under it, and round the edges.

To make a Marrow Pudding.

TAKE a quart of cream or milk, and a quarter of a pound of Naples biscuit, put them on the fire in a stew-pan, and boil them up; then take the yolks of eight eggs, the whites of four beat up very fine, a little moist sugar, some marrow chopped; mix all well together, and put them on the fire, keep it stirring till it is thick, then take it off the fire and keep stirring it till it is cold; when it is almost cold, put in a small glass of brandy, one of sack, and a spoonful of orange-flower water; then have ready your dish rimmed with puff-paste, put your stuff in, sprinkle some currants that have been well washed in cold water and rubbed clean in a cloth, some marrow cut in slices, and some candied lemon, orange, and citron, cut in shreds, and send it to the oven; three quarters of an hour will bake it; send it up hot.

A boiled Suet-Pudding.

TAKE a quart of milk, four spoonfuls of flour, a pound of suet shred small, four eggs, one spoonful of beaten ginger, a tea-spoonful of salt; mix the eggs and flour with a pint of the milk very thick, and with the seasoning mix in the rest of the

milk

milk and suet. Let your batter be pretty thick, and boil it two hours.

A boiled Plumb-Pudding.

TAKE a pound of suet cut in little pieces, not too fine, a pound of currants, and a pound of raisins stoned, eight eggs, half the whites, half a nutmeg grated, and a tea-spoonful of beaten ginger, a pound of flour, a pint of milk; beat the eggs first, then half the milk, beat them together, and by degrees stir in the flour, then the suet, spice, and fruit, and as much milk as will mix it well together very thick. Boil it five hours.

A Hunting-Pudding.

TAKE ten eggs, the whites of six, and all the yolks, beat them up well with half a pint of cream, six spoonfuls of flour, one pound of beef suet chopped small, a pound of currants well washed and picked, a pound of jar raisins stoned and chopped small, two ounces of candied citron, orange, and lemon shred fine, put two ounces of fine sugar, a spoonful of rose-water, a glass of brandy, and half a nutmeg grated; mix all well together, tie it up in a cloth, and boil it four hours; be sure to put it in when the water boils, and keep it boiling all the time; turn it out into a dish, and garnish with powder sugar.

A Yorkshire Pudding.

TAKE a quart of milk and five eggs, beat them up well together, and mix them with flour till it is of a good pancake batter, and very smooth; put in a little salt, some grated nutmeg and ginger; butter a dripping or frying pan and put it under a piece of beef, mutton, or a loin of veal that is roasting, and then put in your batter, and when the top side is brown, cut it in square pieces, and turn it, and then let the under side be brown; then put it in a hot dish as clean of fat as you can, and send it to table hot.

Vermicelli Pudding.

TAKE a quarter of a pound of vermicelli, and boil it in a pint of milk till it is tender, with a stick of cinnamon, then take out the cinnamon, and put in half a pint of cream, a quarter of a pound of butter melted, a quarter of a pound of sugar, with the yolks of four eggs well beat; put it in a dish with or without paste round the rim, and bake it three quarters of an hour; or if you like it, for variety, you may add half a pound of currants clean washed and picked, or a handful of marrow chopped fine, or both.

A Steak

A Steak Pudding.

MAKE a good cruſt with ſuet ſhred fine with flour, and mix it up with cold water; ſeaſon it with a little ſalt, and make it pretty ſtiff; about two pounds of ſuet to a quarter of a peck of flour: let your ſteaks be either beef or mutton, well ſeaſoned with pepper and ſalt, make it up as you do an apple-pudding, tie it in a cloth, and put it into the water boiling. If it be a large pudding, it will take five hours; if a ſmall one, three hours. This is the beſt cruſt for an apple-pudding. Pigeons eat well this way.

Suet Dumplings.

TAKE a pint of milk, four eggs, a pound of ſuet, and a pound of currants, two tea-ſpoonfuls of ſalt, three of ginger; firſt take half the milk, and mix it like a thick batter, then put the eggs and the ſalt and ginger, then the reſt of the milk by degrees, with the ſuet and currants and flour, to make it like a light paſte: when the water boils, make them in rolls as big as a large turkey's egg, with a little flour; then flat them, and throw them into boiling water; move them ſoftly, that they do not ſtick together; keep the water boiling all the time, and half an hour will boil them.

An Oxford Pudding.

A QUARTER of a pound of biſcuit grated, a quarter of a pound of currants clean waſhed and picked, a quarter of a pound of ſuet ſhred ſmall, half a large ſpoonful of powder ſugar, a very little ſalt, and ſome grated nutmeg; mix all well together, then take two yolks of eggs, and make it up in balls as big as a turkey's egg: fry them in freſh butter of a fine light brown; for ſauce, have melted butter and ſugar, with a little ſack or white wine. You muſt mind to keep the pan ſhaking about, that they may be all of a fine light brown.

Obſervations on PIES.

RAISED pies ſhould have a quick oven, and well cloſed up, or your pie will fall in the ſides; it ſhould have no water put in till the minute it goes to the oven, it makes the cruſt ſad, and is a great hazard of the pie running.

To make a very fine ſweet Lamb or Veal Pie.

SEASON your lamb with ſalt, pepper, cloves, mace, and nutmeg, all beat fine, to your palate: cut your lamb or veal into little pieces; make a good puff-paſte cruſt, lay it into your diſh,

then

then lay in your meat, strew on it some stoned raisins and currants clean washed, and some sugar; then lay on it some forcemeat balls made sweet, and in the summer some artichoke-bottoms boiled, and scalded grapes in the winter; boil Spanish potatoes cut in pieces, candied citron, candied orange and lemon-peel, and three or four blades of mace; put butter on the top, close up your pie, and bake it; have ready against it comes out of the oven a caudle made thus: take a pint of white wine and mix in the yolks of three eggs, stir it well together over the fire, one way all the time, till it is thick; then take it off, stir in sugar enough to sweeten it, and squeeze in the juice of a lemon; pour it hot into your pie, and close it up again; send it hot to table.

A savoury Veal Pie.

TAKE a breast of veal, cut it into pieces, season it with pepper and salt, lay it all into your crust, boil six or eight eggs hard, take only the yolks, put them into the pie here and there, fill your dish almost full of water, put on the lid, and bake it well, or you may put some force meat balls in.

To make a savoury Lamb or Veal Pie.

MAKE a good puff-paste crust, cut your meat into pieces, season it to your palate with pepper, salt, mace, cloves, and nutmeg finely beat; lay it into your crust with a few lamb-stones and sweetbreads seasoned as your meat, also some oysters and force-meat balls, hard yolks of eggs, and tops of asparagus two inches long, first boiled green; put butter all over the pie, put on the lid, and set it in a quick oven an hour and a half, and then have ready the liquor, made thus: take a pint of gravy, the oyster-liquor, a gill of red wine, and a little grated nutmeg; mix all together with the yolks of two or three eggs beat, and keep it stirring one way all the time; when it boils, pour it into your pie, put on the lid again; send it hot to table: you must make liquor according to your pie.

To make a Calf's-Foot Pie.

FIRST set your calf's-feet on in a sauce-pan, in three quarts of water, with three or four blades of mace; let them boil softly till there is about a pint and a half, then take out your feet, strain the liquor, and make a good crust; cover your dish, then pick off the flesh from the bones, lay half in the dish, strew half a pound of currants clean washed and picked over, and half a pound of raisins stoned; lay on the rest of the meat, then skim the liquor, sweeten it to the palate, and put in half a pint of white wine; pour it into the dish, put on your lid, and bake it an hour and a half.

To make an Olive Pie.

MAKE your cruſt ready, then take the thin collops of the beſt end of a leg of veal, as many as you think will fill your pie, hack them with the back of a knife, and ſeaſon them with ſalt, pepper, cloves, and mace: waſh over your collops with a bunch of feathers dipped in eggs, and have in readineſs a good handful of ſweet herbs ſhred ſmall; the herbs muſt be thyme, parſley, and ſpinage, the yolks of eight hard eggs minced, and a few oyſters parboiled and chopped, ſome beef ſuet ſhred very fine; mix theſe together, and ſtrew them over your collops, then ſprinkle a little orange-flower water over them, roll the collops up very cloſe, and lay them in your pie, ſtrewing the ſeaſoning over what is left, put butter on the top, and cloſe your pie; when it comes out of the oven, have ready ſome gravy hot, with one anchovy diſſolved in the gravy; pour it in boiling hot. You may put in artichoke-bottoms and cheſnuts (if you pleaſe). You may leave out the orange-flower water (if you do not like it).

To ſeaſon an Egg-Pie.

BOIL twelve eggs hard, and ſhred them with one pound of beef ſuet or marrow ſhred fine; ſeaſon them with a little cinnamon and nutmeg beat fine, one pound of currants clean waſhed and picked, two or three ſpoonfuls of cream, and a little ſack and roſe-water mixed all together; and fill the pie; when it is baked, ſtir in half a pound of freſh butter, and the juice of a lemon.

To make a Mutton-Pie.

TAKE a loin of mutton, take off the ſkin and fat of the inſide; cut it into ſteaks, ſeaſon it well with pepper and ſalt to your palate; lay it into your cruſt, fill it, pour in as much water as will almoſt fill the diſh; then put on the cruſt, and bake it well.

A Beef-Steak Pie.

TAKE fine rump-ſteaks, beat them with a rolling-pin, then ſeaſon them with pepper and ſalt, according to your palate; make a good cruſt, lay in your ſteaks, fill your diſh, then pour in as much water as will half fill the diſh; put on the cruſt, and bake it well.

A Ham-Pie.

TAKE ſome cold boiled ham and ſlice it about half an inch thick, make a good cruſt, and thick, over the diſh, and lay a layer of ham, ſhake a little pepper over it, then taſte a large young fowl clean picked, gutted, waſhed, and ſinged; put a little pepper and ſalt in the belly, and rub a very little ſalt on the outſide; lay the fowl on the ham, boil ſome eggs hard, put in the yolks, and cover all with ham, then shake some pepper on the ham, and put on the top-crust; bake it well, have ready when it comes out of the oven some very rich beef gravy, enough to fill the pie; lay on the crust again, and send it to table hot: if you put two large fowls in, they will make a fine pie; but that is according to your company, more or less; the larger the pie the finer the meat eats; the crust must be the same you make for a venison-pasty; you should pour a little strong gravy into the pie when you make it, just to bake the meat, and then fill it up when it comes out of the oven; boil some truffles and morels and put into your pie, which is a great addition, and some fresh mushrooms or dried ones.

To make a Pigeon-Pie.

MAKE a puff-paste crust, cover your dish, let your pigeons be very nicely picked and cleaned, season them with pepper and salt, and put a good piece of fine fresh butter, with pepper and salt in their bellies; lay them in your pans, the necks, gizzards, livers, pinions, and hearts, lay between, with the yolk of a hard egg and beef-steak in the middle; put as much water as will almost fill the dish, lay on the top-crust and bake it well; this is the best way to make a pigeon-pie; but the French fill the pigeons with a very high force meat, and lay force-meat balls round the inside, with asparagus-tops, artichoke-bottoms, mushrooms, truffles and morels, and season high; but that is according to different palates.

To make a Giblet-Pie.

TAKE two pair of giblets nicely cleaned, put all but the livers into a sauce-pan; with two quarts of water, twenty corns of whole pepper, three blades of mace, a bundle of sweet herbs, and a large onion; cover them close, and let them stew very softly till they are quite tender, then have a good crust ready, cover your dish, lay a fine rump steak at the bottom, seasoned with pepper and salt; then lay in your giblets with the livers, and strain the liquor they were stewed in; season it with salt, and pour into your pie; put on the lid, and bake it an hour and a half.

To make a Duck-Pie.

MAKE a puff-paste crust, take two ducks, scald them and make them very clean, cut off the feet, the pinions, the neck and head, all clean picked and scalded, with the gizzards, livers and hearts; pick out all the fat of the inside, lay a crust all over the dish, season the ducks with pepper and salt, inside and out, lay them in your dish, and the giblets at each end seasoned; put in as much water as will almost fill the pie, lay on the crust, and bake it, but not too much.

To

To make a Chicken-Pie.

MAKE a puff-paste crust, take two chickens, cut them to pieces, season them with pepper and salt, a little beaten mace, lay a force-meat made thus round the side of the dish: take half a pound of veal, half a pound of suet, beat them quite fine in a marble mortar, with as many crumbs of bread; season it with a very little pepper and salt, an anchovy with the liquor, cut the anchovy to pieces, a little lemon-peel cut very fine and shred small, a very little thyme, mix all together with the yolk of an egg; make some into round balls, about twelve, the rest lay round the dish; lay in one chicken over the bottom of the dish, take two sweetbreads, cut them into five or six pieces, lay them all over, season them with pepper and salt, strew over them half an ounce of truffles and morels, two or three artichoke-bottoms cut to pieces, a few cock's-combs, (if you have them,) a palate boiled tender and cut to pieces; then lay on the other part of the chicken, put half a pint of water in, and cover the pie; bake it well, and when it comes out of the oven, fill it with good gravy, lay it on the crust, and send it to table.

To make a Cheshire Pork-Pie.

TAKE a loin of pork, skin it, cut it into steaks, season it with salt, nutmeg, and pepper; make a good crust, lay a layer of pork, then a large layer of pippins pared and cored, a little sugar, enough to sweeten the pie, then another layer of pork; put in half a pint of white wine, lay some butter on the top, and close your pie: if your pie be large, it will take a pint of white wine.

To make a Devonshire Squab-Pie.

MAKE a good crust, cover the dish all over, put at the bottom a layer of sliced pippins, then a layer of mutton-steaks cut from the loin, well seasoned with pepper and salt, then another layer of pippins; peel some onions and slice them thin, lay a layer all over the apples, then a layer of mutton, then pippins and onions, pour in a pint of water; so close your pie and bake it.

To make an Ox-Cheek-Pie.

FIRST bake your ox-cheek as at other times, but not too much, put it in the oven over night, and then it will be ready the next day; make a fine puff-paste crust, and let your side and top crust be thick; let your dish be deep to hold a good deal of gravy, cover your dish with crust, then cut off all the flesh, kernels, and fat of the head, with the palate cut in pieces, cut the meat into little pieces as you do for a hash, lay in the meat, take an ounce of truffles and morels and throw them over the meat, the yolks of six eggs boiled hard, a gill of pickled mushrooms, or fresh ones are better (if you have them); put in a good many force-meat balls, a few artichoke-bottoms and asparagus-tops (if you have any); season your pie with pepper and salt to your palate, and fill the pie with the gravy it was baked in: if the head be rightly seasoned when it comes out of the oven, it will want very little more; put on the lid, and bake it. When the crust is done your pie will be enough.

To make a Shropshire Pie.

FIRST make a good puff-paste crust, then cut two rabbits to pieces, with two pounds of fat pork cut into little pieces; season both with pepper and salt to your liking, then cover your dish with crust and lay in your rabbits; mix the pork with them, take the livers of the rabbits, parboil them and beat them in a mortar, with as much fat bacon, a little sweet herbs, and some oysters (if you have them); season with pepper, salt, and nutmeg; mix it up with the yolk of an egg, and make it into balls; lay them here and there in your pie, some artichoke-bottoms cut in dice, and cock's-combs (if you have them); grate a small nutmeg over the meat, then pour in half a pint of red wine, and half a pint of water; close your pie, and bake it an hour and a half in a quick, but not too fierce, oven.

To make a Yorkshire Christmas-Pie.

FIRST make a good standing crust, let the wall and bottom be very thick; bone a turkey, a goose, a fowl, a partridge, and a pigeon; season them all very well, take half an ounce of mace, half an ounce of nutmegs, a quarter of an ounce of cloves, and half an ounce of black pepper, all beat fine together, two large spoonfuls of salt, and then mix them together; open the fowls all down the back, and bone them; first the pigeon, then the partridge; cover them; then the fowl, then the goose, and then the turkey, which must be large; season them all well first, and lay them in the crust, so as it will look only like a whole turkey; then have a hare ready cased and wiped with a clean cloth; cut it to pieces, that is, joint it; season it, and lay it as close as you can on one side; on the other side woodcocks, moor game, and what sort of wild fowl you can get; season them well, and lay them close; put at least four pounds of butter into the pie, then lay on your lid, which must be a very thick one, and let it be well baked; it must have a very hot oven, and will take at least four hours.

This crust will take a bushel of flour. In this chapter you will see how to make it. These pies are often sent to London in a box, as presents; therefore the walls must be well built.

To make a Goose-Pie.

HALF a peck of flour will make the walls of a goose-pie, made as in the receipts for crust: raise your crust just big enough to hold a large goose; first have a pickled dried tongue boiled tender enough to peel, cut off the root, bone a goose and a large fowl; take a quarter of an ounce of mace beat fine, a large tea-spoonful of beaten pepper, three tea-spoonfuls of salt; mix all together, season your fowl and goose with it, then lay the fowl in the goose, and tongue in the fowl, and the goose in the same form as if whole; put half a pound of butter on the top, and lay on the lid. This pie is delicious, either hot or cold, and will keep a great while: a slice of this pie cut down across makes a pretty little side-dish for supper.

To make a Venison-Pasty.

TAKE a neck and breast of venison, bone it, season it with pepper and salt according to your palate; cut the breast in two or three pieces, but do not cut the fat off the neck if you can help it; lay in the breast and neck-end first, and the best end of the neck on the top, that the fat may be whole; make a good rich puff-paste crust, and rim your dish, then lay in your venison, put in half a pound of butter, about a quarter of a pint of water, then put a very thick paste over, and ornament it in any form you please with leaves, &c. cut in paste, and let it be baked three hours in a very quick oven; put a sheet of buttered paper over it to keep it from scorching. In the mean time set on the bones of the venison in two quarts of water, with two or three blades of mace, an onion, a little piece of crust baked crisp and brown, a little whole pepper; cover it close, and let it boil softly over a slow fire till above half is wasted, then strain it off; when the pasty comes out of the oven, lift up the lid and pour in the gravy.

When your venison is not fat enough, take the fat of a loin of mutton, steeped in a little rape-vinegar and red wine twenty-four hours, then lay it on the top of the venison, and close your pasty. It is a wrong notion of some people to think venison cannot be baked enough, and will first bake it in a false crust, and then bake it in the pasty; by this time the fine flavour of the venison is gone: no; if you want it to be very tender, wash it in warm milk and water, dry it in clean cloths till it is very dry, then rub it all over with vinegar, and hang it in the air; keep it as long as you think proper, it will keep thus a fortnight good; but be sure there be no moistness about it, if there is, you must dry it well and throw ginger over it, and it will keep a long time; when you use it, just dip it in lukewarm water, and dry it; bake it in a quick oven: if it is a large pasty, it will take three hours; then your venison will be tender, and have all the fine flavour: the shoulder makes a pretty pasty, boned and made as above with the mutton fat.

A loin of mutton makes a fine pasty: take a large fat loin of mutton, let it hang four or five days, then bone it, leaving the meat as whole as you can; lay the meat twenty-four hours in half a pint of red wine and half a pint of rape-vinegar; then take it out of the pickle, and order it as you do a pasty, and boil the bones in the same manner, to fill the pasty, when it comes out of the oven.

To make a Calf's-Head Pie.

CLEANSE your head very well, and boil it till it is tender; then carefully take off the flesh as whole as you can, take out the eyes, and slice the tongue; make a good puff-paste crust, cover the dish, lay on your meat, throw over it the tongue, lay the eyes cut in two at each corner; season it with a very little pepper and salt, pour in half a pint of the liquor it was boiled in, lay a thin top-crust on and bake it an hour in a quick oven; in the mean time boil the bones of the head in two quarts of liquor, with two or three blades of mace, half a quarter of an ounce of whole pepper, a large onion, and a bundle of sweet herbs; let it boil till there is about a pint, then strain it off, and add two spoonfuls of catchup, three of red wine, a piece of butter as big as a walnut, rolled in flour, half an ounce of truffles and morels; season with salt to your palate; boil it, and have half the brains boiled with some sage; beat them, and twelve leaves of sage chopped fine, stir all together, and give it a boil; take the other part of the brains, and beat them with some of the sage chopped fine, a little lemon-peel minced fine, and half a small nutmeg grated; beat it up with an egg, and fry it in little cakes of a fine light brown; boil six eggs hard, take only the yolks; when your pie comes out of the oven take off the lid, lay the eggs and cakes over it, and pour the sauce all over; send it to table hot without the lid. This is a fine dish; you may put in it as many fine things as you please, but it wants no addition.

To make a Tort.

FIRST make a fine puff-paste, cover your dish with the crust, make a good force-meat thus: take a pound of veal and a pound of beef-suet, cut them small, and beat them fine in a mortar; season it with a small nutmeg grated, a little lemon-peel shred fine, a few sweet herbs, not too much, a little pepper and salt, just enough to season it, the crumb of a penny-loaf rubbed fine; mix it up with the yolk of an egg, make one third into balls, and the rest lay round the sides of the dish;

get

get two fine large veal sweetbreads, cut each into four pieces; two pair of lamb's-stones, each cut in two; twelve cock's-combs, half an ounce of truffles and morels, four artichoke-bottoms, cut each into four pieces, a few asparagus tops, some fresh mushrooms and some pickled, put all together in your dish: lay first your sweetbreads, then the artichoke-bottoms, then the cock's-combs, then the truffles and morels, then the asparagus, then the mushrooms, and then the force-meat balls; season the sweetbreads with pepper and salt; fill your pie with water and put on the crust; bake it two hours.

To make Mince Pies the best Way.

TAKE three pounds of suet shred very fine, and chopped as small as possible; two pounds of raisins stoned and chopped as fine as possible; two pounds of currants nicely picked, washed, rubbed, and dried at the fire; half a hundred of fine pippins, pared, cored, and chopped small; half a pound of fine sugar pounded fine; a quarter of an ounce of mace, a quarter of an ounce of cloves, two large nutmegs, all beat fine; put all together into a great pan, and mix it well together with half a pint of brandy, and half a pint of sack; put it down close in a stone pot, and it will keep good four months. When you make your pies take a little dish, something bigger than a soup-plate, lay a very thin crust all over it, lay a thin layer of meat, and then a thin layer of citron cut very thin, then a layer of mince-meat, and a layer of orange-peel cut thin, over that a little meat, squeeze half the juice of a fine Seville orange or lemon, lay on your crust and bake it nicely. These pies eat finely cold. If you make them in little patties, mix your meat and sweetmeats accordingly: if you choose meat in your pies, parboil a neat's-tongue, peel it, and chop the meat as fine as possible, and mix with the rest; or two pounds of the inside of a sirloin of beef boiled: but you must double the quantity of fruit when you use meat.

Mince Pies excellent.

TAKE about a pound of very tender beef, two pounds of suet, and about two pounds of currants; cloves and mace to your taste; lemon-peel and the juice of two good lemons, white wine and red sufficient to moisten the meat; add some chopped nonpareils, and sweetmeats (if you please); beat the spice with a little salt, and sweeten with moist sugar to your taste.

Tort de Moy.

MAKE puff-paste and lay round your dish, then a layer of biscuit and a layer of butter and marrow, and then a layer of all sorts of sweetmeats (or as many as you have), and so do till your dish is full; then boil a quart of cream and thicken it with four eggs, and a spoonful of orange-flower water; sweeten it with sugar to your palate, and pour over the rest: half an hour will bake it.

To make Orange or Lemon Tarts.

TAKE six large lemons and rub them very well with salt, and put them for two days in water, with a handful of salt in it; then change them into fresh water every day (without salt), for a fortnight, then boil them for two or three hours till they are tender, then cut them into half-quarters, and then cut them three-corner ways, as thin as you can; take six pippins pared, cored and quartered, and a pint of fair water: let them boil till the pippins break; put the liquor to your orange or lemon, and half the pulp of the pippins well broken and a pound of sugar; boil these together a quarter of an hour, then put it in a gallipot, and squeeze an orange in it; if it be a lemon tart, squeeze a lemon; two spoonfuls is enough for a tart. Your patty-pans must be small and shallow: put fine puff-paste, and very thin; a little while will bake it. Just as your tarts are going into the oven, with a feather or brush do them over with melted butter, and then sift double refined sugar over them; and this is a pretty iceing on them.

To make different Sorts of Tarts.

If you bake in tin patties butter them, and you must put a little crust all over, because of the taking them out; if in China or glass, no crust but the top one; lay fine sugar at the bottom, then your plums, cherries, or any other sort of fruit, and sugar at top; then put on your lid, and bake them in a slack oven. Mince-pies must be baked in tin patties, because of taking them out, and puff-paste is best for them; for sweet tarts the beaten crust is best; but as you fancy. Apple, pear, apricot, &c. make thus: apples and pears, pare them, cut them into quarters, and core them; cut the quarters across again, set them on in a sauce-pan with just as much water as will barely cover them, let them simmer on a slow fire just till the fruit is tender; put a good piece of lemon-peel in the water with the fruit, then have your patties ready; lay fine sugar at bottom, then your fruit, and a little sugar at top; that you must put in at your discretion; pour over each tart a tea-spoonful of lemon-juice, and three tea-spoonfuls of the liquor they were boiled in; put on your lid, and bake them in a slack oven. Apricots do the same way, only do not use lemon.

As to preserved tarts, only lay in your preserved fruit, and put a very thin crust at top, and let them be baked as little as possible; but if you would make them very nice, have a large patty the size you would have your tart; make your sugar crust, roll it as thick as a halfpenny, then butter your patties and cover it; shape your upper crust on a hollow thing on purpose, the size of your patty, and mark it with a marking-iron for that purpose, in what shape you please, to be hollow and open to see the fruit through; then bake your crust in a very slack oven, not to discolour it, but to have it crisp; when the crust is cold, very carefully take it out, and fill it with what fruit you please, lay on the lid, and it is done; therefore if the tart is not eat, your sweetmeat is not the worse, and it looks genteel.

Paste for Tarts.

ONE pound of flour, three quarters of a pound of butter; mix up together, and beat well with a rolling-pin.

Another Paste for Tarts.

HALF a pound of butter, half a pound of flour, and half a pound of sugar; mix it well together, and beat it with a rolling-pin well, then roll it out thin.

Puff-Paste.

TAKE a quarter of a peck of flour, rub in a pound of butter very fine, make it up in a light paste with cold water, just stiff enough to work it up; then roll it up about as thick as a crown-piece, put a layer of butter all over; sprinkle on a little flour, double it up, and roll it out again; double it, and roll it three times; then it is fit for all sorts of pies and tarts that require a puff-paste.

A good Crust for great Pies.

TO a peck of flour add the yolks of three eggs, then boil some water, and put in half a pound of fried suet, and a pound and a half of butter; skim off the butter and suet, and as much of the liquor as will make a light good crust; work it up well, and roll it out.

A standing Crust for great Pies.

TAKE a peck of flour, and six pounds of butter boiled in a gallon of water; skim it off into the flour, and as little of the liquor as you can; work it up well into a paste, then pull it into pieces till it is cold; then make it up into what form you will have it; this is fit for the walls of a goose-pie.

A cold

A cold Crust.

To three pounds of flour, rub in a pound and half of butter, break in two eggs, and make it up with cold water.

A dripping Crust.

TAKE a pound and a half of beef-dripping, boil it in water, strain it, then let it stand to be cold, and take off the hard fat; scrape it, boil it so four or five times; then work it well up into three pounds of flour as fine as you can, and make it up up into paste with cold water. It makes a very fine crust.

A Crust for Custards.

TAKE half a pound of flour, six ounces of butter, the yolks of two eggs, three spoonfuls of cream; mix them together, and let them stand a quarter of an hour, then work it up and down and roll it very thin.

Paste for Crackling Crust.

BLANCH four handfuls of almonds, and throw them into water, then dry them in a cloth, and pound them in a mortar very fine, with a little orange-flour water and the white of an egg; when they are well pounded, pass them through a coarse hair-sieve, to clear them from all the lumps or clods; then spread it on a dish till it is very pliable; let it stand for a while, then roll out a piece of the under crust, and dry it in the oven on the pie-pan, while other pastry-works are making; as knots, cyphers, &c. for garnishing your pies.

An Hottentot Pie.

BOIL and bone two calf's feet, clean very well a calf's chitterling, boil it and chop it small, take two chickens and cut them up as for eating, put them in a stew-pan with two sweetbreads, a quart of veal or mutton gravy, half an ounce of morels, Cayenne pepper and salt to your palate, stew them all together an hour over a gentle fire, then put in six force-meat balls that have been boiled, and the yolks of four hard eggs, and put them in a good raised crust that has been baked for it, strew over the top of your pie a few green peas boiled as for eating; or peel and cut some young green brocoli stalks about the size of peas, give them a gentle boil, and strew them over the top of your pie, and send it up hot without a lid, the same way as the French pie.

A Bride's Pie.

BOIL two calf's feet, pick the meat from the bones, and chop it very fine, shred small one pound of beef suet, and
a pound

a pound of apples, wash and pick one pound of currants very small, dry them before the fire, stone and chop a quarter of a pound of jar raisins, a quarter of an ounce of cinnamon, the same of mace and nutmeg, two ounces of candied citron, two ounces of candied lemon cut thin, a glass of brandy and one of champagne, put them in a China dish with a rich puff paste over it, roll another lid and cut it in leaves, flowers, figures, and put a glass ring in it.

A Thatched House Pie.

TAKE an earthen dish that is pretty deep, rub the inside with two ounces of butter, then spread over it two ounces of vermicelli, make a good puff-paste, and roll it pretty thick, and lay it on the dish; take three or four pigeons, season them very well with pepper and salt, and put a good lump of butter in them, and lay them in the dish with the breast down, and put a thick lid over them, and bake it in a moderate oven; when enough, take the dish you intend for it and turn the pie on to it, and the vermicelli will appear like thatch, which gives it the name of thatched house pie. It is a pretty side or corner dish for a large dinner, or a bottom for a supper.

To make a French Pie.

TO two pounds of flour put three quarters of a pound of butter, make it into a paste, and raise the walls of the pie, then roll out some paste thin as for a lid, cut it into vine leaves, or the figures of any moulds you have, if you have no moulds, you may make use of a crocran, and pick out pretty shapes, beat the yolks of two eggs and rub the outside of the walls of the pie with it, and lay the vine leaves or shapes round the walls, and rub them over with the eggs, fill the pie with the bones of the meat to keep the steam in, that the crust may be well soaked; it is to go to table without a lid.

Take a calf's head, wash and clean it well, boil it half an hour, when it is cold cut it in thin slices and put it in a tossing-pan, with three pints of veal gravy and three sweet-breads cut thin, and let it stew one hour, with half an ounce of morels, and half an ounce of truffles, then have ready two calves feet boiled and boned, cut them in small pieces and put them into your tossing-pan, with a spoonful of lemon pickle and one of browning, Cayenne pepper, and a little salt; when the meat is tender thicken the gravy a little with flour and butter, strain it and put in a few pickled mushrooms, but fresh ones if you can get them; put the meat into the pie you took the bones out, and lay the nicest part at the top, have ready a quarter of an hundred of asparagus-heads, strew them over the top of the pie and serve it up.

A savoury

A savoury Chicken Pie.

LET your chickens be small, season them with mace, pepper, and salt; put a lump of butter into every one of them, lay them in the dish with the breasts up, and lay a thin slice of bacon over them, it will give them a pleasant flavour, then put in a pint of strong gravy, and make a good puff-paste, lid it and bake it in a moderate oven: French cooks generally put morels and yolks of eggs chopped small.

Egg and Bacon Pie to eat cold.

STEEP a few thin slices of bacon all night in water to take out the salt, lay your bacon in the dish, beat eight eggs, with a pint of thick cream, put in a little pepper and salt, and pour it on the bacon, lay over it a good cold paste, bake it a day before you want it in a moderate oven.

To make a Pork Pie.

TAKE from a loin, neck, or any nice part, an equal quantity of fat and lean pork, cut it into pieces the size of a crown piece; shred some onion and apple not very small, season the meat with Cayenne, white pepper, salt, and dried sage, lay in your dish a layer of seasoning, and one of meat, alternately till filled, then add some lumps of butter, and put on the lid: you may make a raised pie.

To make savoury Patties.

TAKE one pound of the inside of a cold loin of veal, or the same quantity of cold fowl, that have been either boiled or roasted, a quarter of a pound of beef-suet, chop them as small as possible, with six or eight sprigs of parsley, season them well with half a nutmeg grated fine, pepper and salt, put them in a tossing-pan with half a pint of veal gravy, thicken the gravy with a little flour and butter, and two spoonfuls of cream, and shake them over the fire two minutes, and fill your patties. You must make your patties thus: raise them of an oval form, and bake them as for custards, cut some long narrow bits of paste and bake them on a dusting box, but not to go round, they are for handles; fill your patties when quite hot with the meat, then set your handles a-cross the patties; they will look like baskets if you have nicely pinched the walls of the patties, when you raised them; five will be a dish: you may make them with sugar and currants instead of parsley.

Common Patties.

TAKE the kidney part of a very fat loin of veal, chop the kidney, veal, and fat very small all together, season it with mace,

mace, pepper, and salt to your taste, raise little patties the size of a tea-cup, fill them with your meat, put thin lids on them, bake them very crisp; five is enough for a side dish.

To make fine Patties.

SLICE either turkey, house-lamb, or chicken, with an equal quantity of the fat of lamb, loin of veal, or the inside of a sirloin of beef, a little parsley, thyme, and lemon-peel shred, put it all in a marble mortar and pound it very fine, season it with white pepper and salt, then make a fine puff-paste, roll it out in thin square sheets, put the force-meat in the middle, cover it over, close them all round, and cut the paste even: just before they go into the oven wash them over with the yolk of an egg, and bake them twenty minutes in a quick oven; have ready a little white gravy seasoned with pepper, salt, and a little shalot, thickened up with a little cream or butter; as soon as the patties come out of the oven, make a hole in the top and pour in some gravy; you must take care not to put too much gravy in, for fear of its running out at the sides, and spoiling the patties.

CHAP. XIV.

For LENT, *or a* FAST DINNER.

A Number of good Dishes which may be made use of at any other Time.

(Though Lent is not kept so strictly as it was in former times, the receipts in this chapter are kept together, for the convenience of those persons who may, by being near the sea-coast, or in the country at a distance from market towns, find it easier to get fish and vegetables than meat whenever they want it: at the same time, all the dishes in the chapter are useful and elegant, fit for any table, and good without being too expensive.)

A Peas Soup.

BOIL a quart of split-peas in a gallon of water; when they are quite soft put in half a red herring, or two anchovies, a good deal of whole pepper, black and white, two or three blades of mace, four or five cloves, a bundle of sweet herbs, a large onion, and the green tops of a bunch of celery, a good bundle of dried mint, cover them close, and let them boil softly till there is about two quarts; then strain it off, and have ready the white part of the celery washed clean and cut small, and

stewed

stewed tender in a quart of water, some spinage picked and washed clean put to the celery; let them stew till the water is quite wasted, and put it to your soup.

Take a French roll, take out the crumb, fry the crust brown in a little fresh butter; take some spinage, stew it in a little butter after it is boiled, and fill the roll; take the crumb, cut it in pieces, beat it in a mortar with a raw egg, a little spinage, and a little sorrel, a little beaten mace, a little nutmeg, and an anchovy; then mix it up with your hand, and roll them into balls with a little flour, and cut some bread into dice, and fry them crisp; pour your soup into your dish, put in the balls and bread, and the roll in the middle. Garnish your dish with spinage. If it wants salt, you must season it to your palate: rub in some dried mint.

A Green Peas Soup.

TAKE a quart of old green peas, and boil them till they are quite tender as pap, in a quart of water; then strain them through a sieve, and boil a quart of young peas in that water. In the mean time put the old peas into a sieve, pour half a pound of melted butter over them, and strain them through the sieve with the back of a spoon, till you have got all the pulp: when the young peas are boiled enough, add the pulp and butter to the young peas and liquor; stir them together till they are smooth, and season with pepper and salt: you may fry a French roll, and let it swim in the dish. If you like it, boil a bundle of mint in the peas.

Another Green Peas Soup.

TAKE a quart of green peas, boil them in a gallon of water, with a bundle of mint, and a few sweet herbs, mace, cloves, and whole pepper, till they are tender; then strain them, liquor and all, through a coarse sieve, till the pulp is strained; put this liquor into a sauce-pan, put to it four heads of celery clean washed and cut small, a handful of spinage clean washed and cut small, a lettuce cut small, a fine leek cut small, a quart of green peas, a little salt; cover them and let them boil very softly till there is about two quarts, and that the celery is tender; then send it to table.

Just before you send up your soup, put in half a pint of spinage juice into it; but do not let it boil after.

Soup Meagre.

TAKE half a pound of butter, put it into a deep stew-pan, shake it about, and let it stand till it has done making a noise; then have ready six middling onions peeled and cut small, throw them in and shake them about; take a bunch of celery clean

washed

washed and picked, cut it in pieces half as long as your finger, a large handful of spinage clean washed and picked, a good lettuce clean washed, if you have it, and cut small, a little bundle of parsley chopped fine; shake all this well together in the pan for a quarter of an hour, then shake in a little flour, stir all together, and pour into the stew-pan two quarts of boiling water: take a handful of dry hard crust, throw in a tea-spoonful of beaten pepper, three blades of mace beat fine, stir all together, and let it boil softly for half an hour; then take it off the fire, and beat up the yolks of two eggs and stir in, and one spoonful of vinegar; pour it into the soup-dish and send it to table. If you have any green peas, boil half a pint in the soup for change.

To make an Onion-Soup.

TAKE half a pound of butter, put it in a stew-pan on the fire, let it all melt, and boil it till it has done making any noise; then have ready ten or a dozen middling onions peeled and cut small, throw them into the butter and let them fry a quarter of an hour; then shake in a little flour, and stir them round; shake your pan, and let them do a few minutes longer; then pour in a quart or three pints of boiling water, stir them round; take a piece of upper crust, the stalest bread you have, about as big as the top of a penny-loaf cut small, and throw it in; season with salt to your palate; let it boil ten minutes, stirring it often: then take it off the fire, and have ready the yolks of two eggs beat fine, with half a spoonful of vinegar; mix some of the soup with them, then stir it into your soup and mix it well, and pour it into your dish. This is a delicious dish.

To make an Eel Soup.

TAKE eels, according to the quantity of soup you would make, (a pound will make a pint of good soup,) so, to every pound of eels put a quart of water, a crust of bread, two or three blades of mace, a little whole pepper, an onion, and a bundle of sweet herbs; cover them close and let them boil till half the liquor is wasted, then strain it, and toast some bread, cut it small, lay the bread into the dish, and pour in your soup: if you have a stew-hole, set the dish over it for a minute, and send it to table. If you find your soup not rich enough, you must let it boil till it is as strong as you would have it. You may make this soup as rich and good as if it was meat. You may add a piece of carrot to brown it.

To make a Craw-Fish Soup.

TAKE a carp, a large eel, half a thornback, cleanse and wash them clean, put them into a sauce-pan, or little pot, put to
them

them a gallon of water, the cruft of a penny-loaf; fkim them well, feafon it with mace, cloves, whole pepper, black and white, an onion, a bundle of fweet herbs, fome parfley, a piece of ginger, let them boil by themfelves clofe covered; then take the tails of half a hundred craw-fifh, pick out the bag, and all the woolly parts that are about them, put them into a fauce-pan with two quarts of water, a little falt, a bundle of fweet herbs; let them ftew foftly, and when they are ready to boil, take out the tails, and beat all the other part of the craw-fifh with the fhells, and boil in the liquor the tails you took out, with a blade of mace, till it comes to about a pint, ftrain it through a clean fieve, and add it to the fifh boiling; let all boil foftly till there is about three quarts; then ftrain it off through a coarfe fieve, put it into your pot again, and if it wants falt you muft put fome in, and the tails of the craw-fifh; beat the live fpawn of a hen lobfter very fine, and put in to give it a colour: take a French roll, and fry it crifp, and add to it; let them ftew all together for a quarter of an hour: you may ftew a carp with them; pour your foup into your difh, the roll fwimming in the middle.

When you have a carp, there fhould be a roll on each fide. Garnifh your difh with craw-fifh. If your craw-fifh will not lie on the fides of your difh, make a little pafte, and lay round the rim, and lay the fifh on that all round the difh.

Take care that your foup be well feafoned, but not too high.

To make a Muffel-Soup.

GET a hundred of muffels, wafh them very clean, put them into a ftew-pan, cover them clofe; let them ftew till they open, then pick them out of the fhells, ftrain the liquor through a fine lawn fieve to your muffels, and pick the beard or crab out, if any.

Take a dozen craw-fifh, beat them to mafh, with a dozen of almonds blanched and beat fine, then take a fmall parfnip and a carrot fcraped and cut in thin flices, fry them brown with a little butter: then take two pounds of any frefh fifh, and boil in a gallon of water, with a bundle of fweet herbs, a large onion ftuck with cloves, whole pepper, black and white, a little parfley, a little piece of horfe-radifh, and falt the muffel-liquor, the craw-fifh, and almonds; let them boil till half is wafted, then ftrain them through a fieve, put the foup into a fauce-pan; put in twenty of the muffels, a few mufhrooms, and truffles cut fmall, and a leek wafhed and cut very fmall; take two French rolls, take out the crumb, fry it brown, cut it into little pieces, put it into the foup; let it boil all together for a quarter of an hour, with the fried carrot and parfnip; in the mean while take the cruft of the rolls fried crifp; take half a hundred of the

muffels,

mussels, a quarter of a pound of butter, a spoonful of water, shake in a little flour, set them on the fire, keeping the sauce-pan shaking all the time till the butter is melted; season it with pepper and salt, beat the yolks of three eggs, put them in, stir them all the time for fear of curdling, grate a little nutmeg; when it is thick and fine, fill the rolls, pour your soup into the dish, put in the rolls, and lay the rest of the mussels round the rim of the dish.

To make a Scate or Thornback Soup.

TAKE two pounds of scate or thornback, skin it and boil it in six quarts of water; when it is enough, take it up, pick off the flesh and lay it by; put in the bones again and about two pounds of any fresh fish, a very little piece of lemon-peel, a bundle of sweet herbs, whole pepper, two or three blades of mace, a little piece of horse-radish, the crust of a penny-loaf, a little parsley; cover it close, and let it boil till there is about two quarts, then strain it off, and add an ounce of vermicelli, set it on the fire and let it boil softly; in the meantime take a French roll, cut a little hole in the top, take out the crumb, fry the crust brown in butter, take the flesh of the fish you laid by and cut it into little pieces, put it into a sauce-pan with two or three spoonfuls of the soup; shake in a little flour, put in a piece of butter, a little pepper and salt, shake them together in the sauce-pan over the fire till it is quite thick, then fill the roll with it; pour your soup into your dish, let the roll swim in the middle, and send it to table.

To make an Oyster-Soup.

YOUR stock must be made of any sort of fish the place affords; let there be about two quarts, take a pint of oysters, beard them, put them into a sauce-pan, strain the liquor, let them stew two or three minutes in their own liquor, then take the hard parts of the oysters and beat them in a mortar with the yolks of four hard eggs, mix them with some of the soup, put them with the other parts of the oysters and liquor into a sauce-pan, a little nutmeg, pepper, and salt, stir them well together, and let it boil a quarter of an hour: dish it up and send it to table.

To make an Almond-Soup.

TAKE a quart of almonds, blanch them, and beat them in a marble mortar, with the yolks of twelve hard eggs, till they are a fine paste; mix them by degrees with two quarts of new milk, a quart of cream, a quarter of a pound of double-refined sugar beat fine; stir all well together: when it is well mixed, set it over a slow fire, and keep it stirring quick all the while till you find it is thick enough, then pour it into your dish, and send it to table. If you be not very careful, it will curdle.

To make a Rice-Soup.

TAKE two quarts of water, a pound of rice, a little cinnamon; cover it close, and let it simmer very softly till the rice is quite tender; take out the cinnamon, then sweeten it to your palate, grate half a nutmeg, and let it stand till it is cold; then beat up the yolks of three eggs with half a pint of white wine, mix them very well, then stir them into the rice, set them on a slow fire, and keep stirring all the time for fear of curdling: when it is of a good thickness, and boils, take it up; keep stirring it till you put it into your dish.

To make a Barley-Soup.

TAKE a gallon of water, half a pound of barley, a blade or two of mace, a large crust of bread, a little lemon-peel; let it boil till it comes to two quarts; then add half a pint of white wine, and sweeten to your palate.

To make a Turnip-Soup.

TAKE a gallon of water, and a bunch of turnips, pare them, save three or four out, put the rest into the water, with half an ounce of whole pepper, an onion stuck with cloves, a blade of mace, half a nutmeg bruised, a little bundle of sweet herbs, and a large crust of bread; let these boil an hour pretty fast, then strain it through a sieve, squeezing the turnips through; wash and cut a bunch of celery very small, set it in the liquor on the fire, cover it close and let it stew; in the mean time cut the turnips you saved into dice, and two or three small carrots clean scraped, and cut in little pieces; put half these turnips and carrots into the pot with the celery, and the other half fry brown in fresh butter; you must flour them first, and two or three onions peeled, cut in thin slices, and fried brown; then put them all into the soup, with an ounce of vermicelli: let your soup boil softly till the celery is quite tender, and your soup good: season it with salt to your palate.

To make an Egg-Soup.

BEAT the yolks of two eggs in your dish with a piece of butter as big as a hen's egg; take a tea-kettle of boiling water in one hand, and a spoon in the other, pour in about a quart by degrees, keep stirring it all the time well till the eggs are well mixed and the butter melted; then pour it into a sauce-pan, and keep stirring it all the time till it begins to simmer; take it off the fire and pour it between two vessels, out of one into another, till it is quite smooth, and has a great froth; set it on the fire again, keep stirring it till it is quite hot; then put it into the soup-dish, and send it to table hot.

To make Peas-Porridge.

TAKE a quart of green peas, put to them a quart of water, a bundle of dried mint, and a little salt; let them boil till the peas are quite tender; then put in some beaten pepper, a piece of butter as big as a walnut, rolled in flour, stir it all together, and let it boil a few minutes; then add two quarts of milk, let it boil a quarter of an hour, take out the mint, and serve it up.

A Spanish Peas-Soup.

TAKE one pound of Spanish peas, and lay them in water the night before you use them; then take a gallon of water, one quart of fine sweet oil, a head of garlic; cover the pot close, and let it boil till the peas are soft; then season with pepper and salt; then beat the yolk of an egg, and vinegar to your palate; poach some eggs, lay on the dish on sippets, and pour the soup on them: send them to table.

To make Onion-Soup the Spanish Way.

TAKE two large Spanish onions, peel and slice them; let them boil very softly in half a pint of sweet oil till the onions are very soft, then pour on them three pints of boiling water; season with beaten pepper, salt, a little beaten clove and mace, two spoonfuls of vinegar, a handful of parsley washed clean and chopped fine; let it boil fast a quarter of an hour; in the meantime, get some sippets to cover the bottom of the dish, fried quick, not hard; lay them in the dish, and cover each sippet with a poached egg; beat up the yolks of two eggs and throw over them; pour in your soup, and send it to table.

Garlic and sorrel, done the same way, eats well.

Milk-Soup the Dutch Way.

TAKE a quart of milk, boil it with cinnamon and moist sugar; put sippets in the dish, pour the milk over it, and set it over a charcoal fire to simmer till the bread is soft; take the yolks of two eggs, beat them up, and mix it with a little of the milk, and throw it in; mix it all together, and send it up to table.

To make a White-Pot.

TAKE two quarts of new milk, eight eggs, and half the whites, beat up with a little rose-water, a nutmeg, a quarter of a pound of sugar; cut a penny-loaf in very thin slices, and pour milk and eggs over; put a little bit of sweet butter at the top. Bake it in a slow oven half an hour.

To make a Rice White-Pot.

BOIL a pound of rice in two quarts of new milk till it is tender and thick; beat it in a mortar with a quarter of a pound of sweet almonds blanched; then boil two quarts of cream, with a few crumbs of white bread, and two or three blades of mace; mix it all with eight eggs, a little rose-water, and sweeten to your taste; cut some candied orange and citron peels thin, and lay it in. It must be put into a slow oven.

To make Rice-Milk.

TAKE half a pound of rice, boil it in a quart of water, with a little cinnamon; let it boil till the water is all wasted; take great care it does not burn; then add three pints of milk, and the yolk of an egg beat up; keep it stirring, and when it boils take it up; sweeten to your palate.

To make an Orange-Fool.

TAKE the juice of six oranges, and six eggs well beaten, a pint of cream, a quarter of a pound of sugar, a little cinnamon and nutmeg. Mix all together, and keep stirring over a slow fire till it is thick; then put in a little piece of butter, and keep stirring till cold, and dish it up.

To make a Westminster Fool.

TAKE a penny-loaf, cut it into thin slices, wet them with sack, lay them in the bottom of a dish; take a quart of cream, beat up six eggs, two spoonfuls of rose-water, a blade of mace, and some grated nutmeg; sweeten to your taste; put all this into a sauce-pan, and keep stirring all the time over a slow fire for fear of curdling: when it begins to be thick, pour it into the dish over the bread; let it stand till it is cold, and serve it up.

To make a Gooseberry-Fool.

TAKE two quarts of gooseberries, set them on the fire in about a quart of water; when they begin to simmer, turn yellow, and begin to plump, throw them into a cullender to drain the water out, then with the back of a spoon carefully squeeze the pulp, throw the sieve into a dish, make them pretty sweet, and let them stand till they are cold: in the meantime take two quarts of new milk, and the yolks of four eggs beat up with a little grated nutmeg; stir it softly over a slow fire; when it begins to simmer take it off, and by degrees stir it into

the

the gooseberries; let it stand till it is cold, and serve it up: if you make it with cream, you need not put any eggs in; and if it is not thick enough, it is only boiling more gooseberries: but that you must do as you think proper.

To make Furmity.

TAKE a quart of ready-boiled wheat, two quarts of milk, a quarter of a pound of currants clean picked and washed; stir these together and boil them; beat up the yolks of three or four eggs, a little nutmeg, with two or three spoonfuls of milk, and add to the wheat; stir them together for a few minutes; then sweeten to your palate, and send it to table.

To make Plumb-Porridge, or Barley-Gruel.

TAKE a gallon of water, half a pound of barley, a quarter of a pound of raisins clean washed, a quarter of a pound of currants clean washed and picked: boil these till above half the water is wasted, with two or three blades of mace; then sweeten it to your palate, and add half a pint of white wine.

To make Buttered Wheat.

PUT your wheat into a sauce-pan; when it is hot, stir in a good piece of butter, a little grated nutmeg, and sweeten it to your palate.

To make Plumb-Gruel.

TAKE two quarts of water, two large spoonfuls of oatmeal, stir it together, a blade or two of mace, a little piece of lemon-peel; boil it for five or six minutes (take care it do not boil over), then strain it off, and put it into the sauce-pan again, with half a pound of currants clean washed and picked; let them boil about ten minutes, add a glass of white wine, a little grated nutmeg, and sweeten to your palate.

To make a Flour Hasty-Pudding.

TAKE a quart of milk and four bay-leaves, set it on the fire to boil, beat up the yolks of two eggs, and stir in a little salt; take two or three spoonfuls of milk, and beat up with your eggs, and stir in your milk; then, with a wooden spoon in one hand and the flour in the other, stir it in till it is of a good thickness, but not too thick; let it boil, and keep it stirring, then pour it into a dish, and stick pieces of butter here and there: you may omit the egg if you do not like it; but it is a great addition to the pudding; and a little piece of butter stirred in the milk makes it eat short and fine; take out the bay-leaves before you put in the flour.

To make an Oatmeal Hasty-Pudding.

TAKE a quart of water, set it on to boil, put in a piece of butter and some salt; when it boils, stir in the oatmeal as you do the flour, till it is of a good thickness; let it boil a few minutes, pour it in your dish, and stick pieces of butter in it; or eat with wine and sugar, or ale and sugar, or cream, or new milk. This is best made with Scotch oatmeal.

To make a fine Hasty-Pudding.

BREAK an egg into fine flour, and with your hand work up as much as you can into as stiff paste as is possible; then mince it as small as herbs to the pot, as small as if it were to be sifted; then set a quart of milk a-boiling, and put it in the paste so cut: put in a little salt, a little beaten cinnamon and sugar, a piece of butter as big as a walnut, and keep stirring all one way; when it is as thick as you would have it, stir in such another piece of butter, then pour it into your dish, and stick pieces of butter here and there: send it to table hot.

To make an excellent Sack-Posset.

BEAT fifteen eggs, whites and yolks very well, and strain them; then put three quarters of a pound of white sugar into a pint of canary, and mix it with your eggs in a bason; set it over a chafing-dish of coals, and keep continually stirring it till it is scalding hot; in the meantime grate some nutmeg in a quart of milk and boil it; then pour it into your eggs and wine, they being scalding hot: hold your hand very high as you pour it, and somebody stirring it all the time you are pouring in the milk; then take it off the chafing-dish, set it before the fire half an hour, and serve it up.

To make another Sack-Posset.

TAKE a quart of new milk, four Naples biscuits, crumble them, and when the milk boils throw them in; just give it one boil, take it off, grate in some nutmeg, and sweeten to your palate; then pour in half a pint of sack, stirring it all the time, and serve it up. You may crumble white bread instead of biscuit.

Or make it thus:

BOIL a quart of cream or new milk, with the yolks of two eggs; first take a French roll and cut it as thin as possibly you can in little pieces; lay it in the dish you intend for the posset; when the milk boils (which you must keep stirring all the time), pour it over the bread, and stir it together; cover it close, then take a pint of canary, a quarter of a pound of sugar,
and

and grate in some nutmeg; when it boils, pour it into the milk, stirring it all the time, and serve it up.

To make Hasty Fritters.

TAKE a stew-pan, put in some butter, and let it be hot. In the mean time take half a pint of all ale not bitter, and stir in some flour by degrees in a little of the ale; put in a few currants, or chopped apples, beat them up quick, and drop a large spoonful at a time all over the pan: take care they do not stick together, turn them with an egg-slice, and when they are of a fine brown, lay them in a dish, and throw some sugar over them. Garnish them with orange cut into quarters.

To make fine Fritters.

DRY some of the finest flour well before the fire; mix it with a quart of new milk, not too thick, six or eight eggs, a little nutmeg, a little mace, a little salt, and a quarter of a pint of sack or ale, or a glass of brandy: beat them well together, then make them pretty thick with pippins, and fry them dry.

To make Apple-Fritters.

BEAT the yolks of eight eggs, the whites of four, well together, and strain them into a pan; then take a quart of cream, make it as hot as you can bear your finger in it; then put to it a quarter of a pint of sack, three quarters of a pint of ale, and make a posset of it: when it is cool, put it to your eggs, beating it well together; then put in nutmeg, ginger, salt, and flour to your liking: your batter should be pretty thick; then put in pippins sliced or scraped, and fry them in a good deal of butter quick.

To make Curd-Fritters.

HAVING a handful of curds and a handful of flour, and ten eggs well beaten and strained, some sugar, cloves, mace, and nutmeg beat, a little saffron; stir all well together, and fry them quick, and of a fine light brown.

To make Fritters-Royal.

TAKE a quart of new milk, put it into a skillet or saucepan, and, as the milk boils up, pour in a pint of sack; let it boil up, then take it off, and let it stand five or six minutes; then skim off all the curd and put it into a bason; beat it up well with six eggs, season it with nutmeg; then beat it with a whisk, add flour to make it as thick as batter usually is, put in some fine sugar, and fry them quick.

To make Skirret-Fritters.

TAKE a pint of pulp of skirrets, and a spoonful of flour, the yolks of four eggs, sugar and spice, make into a thick batter, and fry them quick.

To make White Fritters.

HAVING some rice, wash it in five or six several waters and dry it very well before the fire; then beat it in a mortar very fine, and sift it through a lawn sieve that it may be very fine; you must have at least an ounce of it, then put it into a sauce-pan, just wet it with milk, and when it is well incorporated with it, add to it another pint of milk; set the whole over a stove or a very slow fire, and take care to keep it always moving; put in a little sugar, and some candied lemon-peel grated, keep it over the fire till it is almost come to the thickness of a fine paste, flour a peel, pour it on it and spread it abroad with a rolling-pin: when it is quite cold, cut it into little morsels, taking care they stick not one to the other; flour your hands and roll up your fritters handsomely, and fry them. When you serve them up, pour a little orange-flower water over them, and sugar. These make a pretty side-dish; or are very pretty to garnish a fine dish with.

To make Syringed Fritters.

TAKE about a pint of water, and a bit of butter the size of an egg, with some lemon-peel (green if you can get it), rasped preserved lemon-peel, and crisped orange-flowers; put all together in a stew-pan over the fire, and when boiling throw in some fine flour; keep it stirring; put in by degrees more flour till your butter be thick enough, take it off the fire; then take an ounce of sweet almonds, four bitter ones, pound them in a mortar, stir in two Naples biscuits crumbled, two eggs beat; stir all together, and more eggs till your batter be thin enough to be syringed: fill your syringe, the batter being hot, syringe your fritters in it to make it of a true lover's knot, and, being well coloured, serve them up for a side-dish.

At another time, you may rub a sheet of paper with butter, over which you may syringe your fritters, and make them in what shape you please. Your butter being hot, turn the paper upside down over it, and your fritters will easily drop off: when fried, stew them with sugar and glaze them.

To make Vine-Leaf Fritters.

TAKE some of the smallest vine-leaves you can get, and having cut off the great stalks, put them in a dish with some

French

French brandy, green lemon rasped, and some sugar; take a good handful of fine flour, mixed with white wine or ale; let your butter be hot, and with a spoon drop in your batter; take great care they do not stick one to the other; on each fritter lay a leaf; fry them quick, and strew sugar over them, and glaze them with a red-hot shovel or salamander.

With all fritters made with milk and eggs you should have beaten cinnamon and sugar in a saucer, and either squeeze an orange over it, or pour a glass of white wine, and so throw sugar all over the dish, and they should be fried in a good deal of fat; therefore they are best fried in beef-dripping, or hog's-lard, when it can be done.

To make Clary-Fritters.

TAKE your clary-leaves, cut off the stalks, dip them one by one in a batter made with milk and flour, your butter being hot, fry them quick. This is a pretty heartening dish for a sick or weak person; and comfrey-leaves do the same way.

To make Spanish Fritters.

TAKE the inside of a roll, and slice it in three; then soak it in milk; then pass it through a batter of eggs, fry them in oil; when almost done, repass them in another batter; then let them fry till they are done, draw them off the oil, and lay them in a dish; over every pair of fritters you must throw cinnamon, small coloured sugar-plumbs, and clarified sugar.

To make Plumb-Fritters with Rice.

GRATE the crumbs of a penny-loaf, pour over it a pint of boiling cream, or good milk, let it stand four or five hours, then beat it exceeding fine, put to it the yolks of five eggs, four ounces of sugar, and a nutmeg grated; beat them well together, and fry them in hog's-lard; drain them on a sieve, and serve them up with white wine sauce under them.

N. B. You may put currants in if you please.

To make Apple Frazes.

CUT your apples in thick slices, and fry them of a fine light brown; take them up, and lay them to drain, keep them as whole as you can, and either pare them or let it alone; then make a batter as follows: take five eggs, leaving out two whites, beat them up with cream and flour, and a little sack, make it the thickness of a pancake-batter, pour in a little melted butter, nutmeg, and a little sugar: let your batter be hot, and drop in your fritters, and on every one lay a slice of apple, and then more batter on them: fry them of a fine light brown;

brown; take them up, and strew some double-refined sugar all over them.

To make an Almond Fraze.

GET a pound of Jordan almonds, blanched, steep them in a pint of sweet cream, ten yolks of eggs, and four whites; take out the almonds and pound them in a mortar fine; then mix them again in the cream and eggs, put in sugar and grated white bread, stir them all together, put some fresh butter into the pan, let it be hot and pour it in, stirring it in the pan till they are of a good thickness; and when it is enough, turn it into a dish, throw sugar over it, and serve it up.

To make German Puffs.

PUT half a pint of good milk into a tossing-pan, and dredge it in flour till it is as thick as hasty-pudding, keep stirring it over a slow fire till it is all of a lump, then put it in a marble mortar; when it is cold put to it the yolks of eight eggs, four ounces of sugar, a spoonful of rose-water, grate a little nutmeg and the rind of half a lemon, beat them together an hour or more, when it looks light and bright, drop them into a pan of boiling lard with a tea-spoon, the size of a large nutmeg, they will rise and look like a large yellow plumb if they are well beat; as you fry them lay them on a sieve to drain, grate sugar round your dish, and serve them up with sack for sauce. It is a proper corner dish for dinner or supper.

To make Pancakes.

TAKE a quart of milk, beat in six or eight eggs, leaving half the whites out, mix it well till your batter is of a fine thickness; you must observe to mix your flour first with a little milk, then add the rest by degrees; put in two spoonfuls of beaten ginger, a glass of brandy, a little salt; stir all together, make your stew-pan very clean, put in a piece of butter as big as a walnut, then pour in a ladleful of batter, which will make a pancake, moving the pan round that the batter be all over the pan, shake the pan, and when you think that side is enough, toss it; if you cannot, turn it cleverly; and when both sides are done, lay it in a dish before the fire, and so do the rest; you must take care they are dry: when you send them to table strew a little sugar over them.

The brandy may be left out.

To make fine Pancakes.

TAKE half a pint of cream, half a pint of sack, the yolks of eighteen eggs beat fine, a little salt, half a pound of fine sugar, a little beaten cinnamon, mace, and nutmeg; then put in as much

much flour as will run thin over the pan, and fry them in fresh butter. This sort of pancake will not be crisp, but very good.

A second sort of fine Pancakes.

TAKE a pint of cream, and eight eggs well beat, a nutmeg grated, a little salt, half a pound of good dish butter melted; mix all together, with as much flour as will make them into a thin batter, fry them nice, and turn them on the back of a plate.

A third Sort.

TAKE six new-laid eggs well beat, mix them with a pint of cream, a quarter of a pound of sugar, some grated nutmeg, and as much flour as will make the batter of a proper thickness; fry these fine pancakes in small pans, and let your pans be hot: you must not put above the bigness of a nutmeg of butter at a time into the pan.

A fourth Sort, called a Quire of Paper.

TAKE a pint of cream, six eggs, three spoonfuls of fine flour, three of sack, one of orange flower water, a little sugar, and half a nutmeg grated, half a pound of melted butter almost cold; mingle all well together, and butter the pan for the first pancake; let them run as thin as possible; when they are just coloured they are enough; and so do with all the fine pancakes.

To make Rice Pancakes.

TAKE a quart of cream, and three spoonfuls of flour of rice; set it on a slow fire, and keep it stirring till it is thick as pap; stir in half a pound of butter, a nutmeg grated; then pour it out into an earthen pan, and when it is cold, stir in three or four spoonfuls of flour, a little salt, some sugar, nine eggs well beaten; mix all well together, and fry them nicely. When you have no cream, use new milk, and one spoonful or more of the flour of rice.

To make Wafer Pancakes.

BEAT four eggs well with two spoonfuls of fine flour, and two of cream, one ounce of loaf-sugar, beat and sifted, half a nutmeg grated, put a little cold butter in a clean cloth, and rub your pan well with it, pour in your batter and make it as thin as a wafer, fry it only on one side, put them on a dish, and grate sugar betwixt every pancake, and send them hot to the table.

To make Tansey Pancakes.

BEAT four eggs, and put to them half a pint of cream, four spoonfuls of flour, and two of fine sugar, beat them a quarter of an hour, then put in one spoonful of the juice of tansey, and two of the juice of spinage, with a little grated nutmeg, beat all well together, and fry them in fresh butter: garnish them with quarters of Seville oranges, grate double-refined sugar over them, and send them up hot.

To make a pink-coloured Pancake.

Boil a large beet-root tender, and beat it fine in a marble mortar, then add the yolks of four eggs, two spoonfuls of flour, and three spoonfuls of good cream, sweeten it to your taste, and grate in half a nutmeg, and put in a glass of brandy; beat them all together half an hour, fry them in butter, and garnish them with green sweet-meats, preserved apricots, or green sprigs of myrtle. It is a pretty corner-dish for either dinner or supper.

To make a Pupton of Apples.

Pare some apples, take out the cores and put them into a skillet: to a quart mugful heaped put in a quarter of a pound of sugar, and two spoonfuls of water; do them over a slow fire, keep them stirring, add a little cinnamon; when it is quite thick and like a marmalade, let it stand till cool; beat up the yolks of four or five eggs, and stir in a handful of grated bread and a quarter of a pound of fresh butter; then form it into what shape you please, and bake it in a slow oven, and then turn it upside down on a plate, for a second course.

To make Black-Caps.

Cut twelve large apples in halves, and take out the cores, place them on a thin patty-pan, or mazarine, as close together as they can lie, with the flat side downwards; squeeze a lemon in two spoonfuls of orange-flower water and pour over them; shred some lemon-peel fine and throw over them, and grate fine sugar all over; set them in a quick oven, and half an hour will do them. When you send them to table throw fine sugar all over the dish.

To bake Apples whole.

Put your apples into an earthen pan with a few cloves, a little lemon-peel, some coarse sugar, a glass of red wine; put them in a quick oven, and they will take an hour baking.

To make a Dish of roasted Apples.

Take small apples, roast them in a slow oven till they are soft, mind they do not fall; have ready some rice, cree it stiff with a little lemon-peel in it and a stick of cinnamon, when the rice is enough take out the seasoning, put to it a spoonful of rose-water and one of almond-water, sweeten it to your taste;

when

when cold lay apples into the dish, lay the rice neatly over them; with a knife stick them with bits of candied orange, and garnish with any thing green.

To stew Pippins whole.

TAKE twelve golden pippins, pare them, put the parings into a sauce-pan with water enough to cover them, a blade of mace, two or three cloves, a piece of lemon-peel; let them simmer till there is just enough to do the pippins in, then strain it and put it into the sauce-pan again, with sugar enough to make it like syrup; then put them in a preserving-pan, or clean stew-pan, or large sauce-pan, and pour the syrup over them; let there be enough to stew them in: when they are enough, which you will know by the pippins being soft, take them up, lay them in a hot dish with the syrup: when cold, serve them up; or hot, if you choose it.

To stew Pears.

PARE six large winter pears, and either quarter them or do them whole: they make a pretty dish with one whole, the rest cut in quarters, and the cores taken out; lay them in a deep earthen pot, with a few cloves, a piece of lemon-peel, a gill of red wine, and a quarter of a pound of fine sugar; if the pears are very large, they will take half a pound of sugar, and half a pint of red wine; cover them close with brown paper, and bake them till they are enough.

Serve them hot or cold (just as you like them), and they will be very good with water in the place of wine.

To stew Pears in a Sauce-pan.

PUT them into a sauce-pan with the ingredients as before; cover them and do them over a slow fire; when they are enough take them off, add a pennyworth of cochineal, bruised very fine.

To stew Pears purple.

PARE four pears, cut them into quarters, core them, put them into a stew-pan, with a quarter of a pint of water, a quarter of a pound of sugar; cover them with a pewter-plate then cover the pan with the lid, and do them over a slow fire; look at them often for fear of melting the plate; when they are enough, and the liquor looks of a fine purple, take them off and lay them in your dish with the liquor; when cold, serve them up for a side-dish at a second course, or just as you please.

A pretty Made-Dish.

TAKE half a pound of almonds blanched and beat fine, with a little rose or orange-flower water; then take a quart of
sweet

sweet thick cream and boil it with a piece of cinnamon and mace; sweeten it with sugar to your palate, and mix it with your almonds; stir it well together, and strain it through a sieve; let your cream cool and thicken it with the yolks of six eggs; then garnish a deep dish and lay paste at the bottom, then put in shred artichoke-bottoms (being first boiled), upon that a little melted butter, shred citron, and candied orange; so do till your dish is near full, then pour in your cream, and bake it without a lid; when it is baked, scrape sugar over it, and serve it up hot: half an hour will bake it.

To make Kickshaws.

MAKE puff paste, roll it thin, and if you have any moulds work it upon them; make them up with preserved pippins: you may fill some with gooseberries, some with raspberries, or what you please; then close them up, and either bake or fry them; throw grated sugar over them, and serve them up.

Pain Perdu, or Cream Toasts.

HAVING two French rolls, cut them into slices as thick as your finger, crumb and crust together; lay them on a dish, put to them a pint of cream and half a pint of milk; strew them over with beaten cinnamon and sugar; turn them frequently till they are tender, but take care not to break them; then take them from the cream with the slice, break four or five eggs, turn your slices of bread in the eggs, and fry them in clarified butter: make them of a good brown colour, but not black; scrape a little sugar over them. They may be served for a second-course dish, but are fittest for supper.

Salmagundy for a Middle-Dish at Supper.

IN the top plate in the middle, which should stand higher than the rest, take a fine pickled-herring, bone it, take off the head and mince the rest fine; in the other plates round put the following things: in one pare a cucumber and cut it very thin; in another, apples pared and cut small; in another, an onion peeled and cut small; in another, two hard eggs chopped small, the whites in one and the yolks in another; pickled girkins cut small; in another celery cut small; in another pickled red cabbage chopped fine; take some water-cresses clean washed and picked, stick them all about and between every plate or saucer, and throw nastertium-flowers about the cresses. You must have oil and vinegar, and lemon, to eat with it. If it is neatly set out, it will make a pretty figure in the middle of the table, or you may lay them in heaps in a dish: if you have not all these ingredients set out your plates or saucers

with

with just what you fancy, and in the room of a pickled herring you may mince anchovies.

To make a Tansey.

TAKE ten eggs, break them into a pan, put to them a little salt, beat them very well; then put to them eight ounces of loaf-sugar beat fine, and a pint of the juice of spinage and a little juice of tansey; mix them well together, and strain it into a quart of cream; then grate in eight ounces of Naples biscuit or white bread, a nutmeg grated, a quarter of a pound of Jordan almonds, beat in a mortar with a little juice of tansey to your taste: mix these all together, put it into a stew-pan with a piece of butter as large as a pippin; set it over a flow charcoal fire, keep it stirring till it is hardened very well; then butter a dish very well, put in your tansey, bake it, and when it is enough turn it out on a pie-plate; squeeze the juice of an orange over it, and throw sugar all over. Garnish with orange cut into quarters, and sweetmeats cut into long bits, and lay all over its side.

Another Way.

TAKE a pint of cream, and half a pint of blanched almonds beat fine, with rose and orange flower water, stir them together over a flow fire; when it boils take it off, and let it stand till cold; then beat in ten eggs, grate in a small nutmeg, four Naples biscuits, a little grated bread; sweeten to your taste; and if you think it is too thick, put in some more cream, the juice of spinage to make it green; stir it well together, and either fry it or bake it: if you fry it, do one side first, and then with a dish turn the other.

To make a Bean Tansey.

TAKE two quarts of beans, blanch and beat them very fine in a mortar; season with pepper, salt, and mace; then put in the yolks of six eggs, and a quarter of a pound of butter, a pint of cream, half a pint of sack, and sweeten to your palate; soak four Naples biscuits in half a pint of milk, mix them with the other ingredients, half a pint of the juice of spinage, with two or three sprigs of tansey beat with it; butter a pan and bake it, then turn it on a dish and stick citron and orange-peel candied, cut small, and stuck about it. Garnish with Seville orange.

To make a Water Tansey.

TAKE twelve eggs, beat them very well, half a manchet grated, and sifted through a cullender, or half a penny roll, half a pint of fair water; colour it with the juice of spinage and one small sprig of tansey beat together; season it with sugar to your palate, a little salt, a small nutmeg grated, two or three

three spoonfuls of rose-water, put it into a skillet, stir it all one way and let it thicken like a hasty-pudding, then bake it; or you may butter a stew-pan and put it into; butter a dish and lay over it; when one side is enough, turn it with the dish, and slip the other side into the pan. When that is done, set it into a massereen, throw sugar all over, and garnish with orange.

To make a Hedge-Hog.

TAKE two pounds of sweet almonds blanched, beat them well in a mortar, with a little canary and orange-flower water, to keep them from oiling; make them into a stiff paste, then beat in the yolks of twelve eggs, leave out five of the whites, put to it a pint of cream, sweeten it with sugar, put in half a pound of sweet butter melted, set it on a furnace or slow fire, and keep continually stirring till it is stiff enough to be made into the form of a hedge-hog, then stick it full of blanched almonds slit, and stuck up like the bristles of a hedge-hog, then put it into a dish. Take a pint of cream and the yolks of four eggs beat up, and mix with the cream; sweeten to your palate, and keep them stirring over a slow fire all the time till it is hot, then pour it into your dish round the hedge-hog; let it stand till it is cold, and serve it it up.

Or you may make a fine harshorn-jelly, and pour into the dish, which will look very pretty. You may eat wine and sugar with it, or eat it without.

Or cold cream sweetened with a glass of white wine in it, and the juice of a Seville orange, and pour it into the dish. It will be pretty for change.

This is a pretty side-dish at a second course, or in the middle for supper, or in a grand desert; plump two currants for the eyes.

Or make it thus for Change:

TAKE two pounds of sweet almonds blanched, twelve bitter ones, beat them in a marble mortar well together, with canary and orange-flower water, two spoonfuls of the tincture of saffron, two spoonfuls of the juice of sorrel, beat them into a fine paste, put in half a pound of melted butter, mix it up well, a little nutmeg and beaten mace, an ounce of citron, an ounce of orange-peel, both cut fine, mix them in the yolks of twelve eggs, and half the whites beat up and mixed in half a pint of cream, half a pint of double-refined sugar, and work it up all together; if it is not stiff enough to make up into the form you would have it, you must have a mould for it; butter it well, then put in your ingredients, and bake it. The mould must be made in such a manner as to have the head peeping out; when it comes out of the oven have ready some almonds

blanched

blanched and flit, and boiled up in sugar till brown; stick it all over with the almonds; and, for sauce, have red wine and sugar made hot, and the juice of an orange: send it hot to table for a first course.

You may leave out the saffron and sorrel, and make it up like chickens, or any other shape you please, or alter the sauce to your fancy. Butter, sugar, and white wine is a pretty sauce for either baked or boiled, and you may make the sauce of what colour you please; or put it into a mould, with half a pound of currants added to it, and boil it for a pudding. You may use cochineal in the room of saffron.

The following liquor you may make to mix with your sauces: beat an ounce of cochineal very fine, put in a pint of water in a skillet, and a quarter of an ounce of roche-alum; boil it till the goodness is out, strain it into a phial, with an ounce of fine sugar, and it will keep six months.

To ragoo Endive.

TAKE some fine white endive, three heads, lay them in salt and water two or three hours; take a hundred of asparagus, cut off the green heads, chop the rest small, as far as is tender; lay it in salt and water; take a bunch of celery, wash it and scrape it clean, cut it in pieces about three inches long, put it into a sauce-pan, with a pint of water, three or four blades of mace, some whole pepper tied in a rag, let it stew till it is quite tender; then put in the asparagus, shake the sauce-pan, let it simmer till the grass is enough; take the endive out of the water, drain it, leave one large head whole, the other leaf by leaf, put it into a stew-pan, put to it a pint of white wine; cover the pan close, let it boil till the endive is just enough, then put in a quarter of a pound of butter rolled in flour, cover it close, shaking the pan; when the endive is enough, take it up, lay the whole head in the middle, and with a spoon take out the celery and grass and lay round, the other part of the endive over that; then pour the liquor out of the sauce-pan into the stew-pan, stir it together, season it with salt, and have ready the yolks of two eggs, beat up with a quarter of a pint of cream, and half a nutmeg grated in; mix this with the sauce, keep it stirring all one way till it is thick; then pour it over your ragoo, and send it to table hot.

To ragoo French Beans.

TAKE a few beans, boil them tender; then take your stew-pan, put in a piece of butter, when it is melted shake in some flour, and peel a large onion, slice it and fry it brown in that butter; then put in the beans, shake in a little pepper and a

little

little salt, grate a little nutmeg in, have ready the yolk of an egg and some cream; stir them all together for a minute or two, and dish them up.

Another Way to ragoo French Beans.

TAKE a quarter of a peck of French beans, string them, do not split them, cut them in three across, lay them in salt and water, then take them out and dry them in a coarse cloth; fry them brown, then pour out all the fat, put in a quarter of a pint of hot water, stir it into the pan by degrees, let it boil; then take a quarter of a pound of fresh butter rolled in a very little flour, two spoonfuls of catchup, one spoonful of mushroom-pickle, and four of white wine, an onion stuck with six cloves, two or three blades of mace beat, half a nutmeg grated, a little pepper and salt; stir it all together for a few minutes, then throw in the beans; shake the pan for a minute or two, take out the onion, and pour them into your dish. This is a pretty side-dish; and you may garnish with what you fancy, either pickled French beans, mushrooms, samphire, or any thing else.

A Ragoo of Beans, with a Force.

RAGOO them as above; take two large carrots, scrape and boil them tender, then mash them in a pan, season with pepper and salt, mix them with a little piece of butter and the yolks of two raw eggs; make it into what shape you please, and baking it a quarter of an hour in a quick oven will do, but a tin oven is the best; lay it in the middle of the dish, and the ragoo round; serve it up hot for a first course.

Or this Way, Beans ragooed with Cabbage.

TAKE a nice little cabbage, about as big as a pint bason; when the outside leaves, top, and stalks are cut off, half boil it, cut a hole in the middle pretty big, take what you cut out and chop it very fine, with a few of the beans boiled, a carrot boiled and mashed, and a turnip boiled; mash all together, put them into a sauce-pan, season them with pepper, salt, and nutmeg, a good piece of butter, stew them a few minutes over the fire, stirring the pan often; in the meantime put the cabbage into a saucepan, but take great care it does not fall to pieces; put to it four spoonfuls of water, two of wine, and one of catchup; have a spoonful of mushroom-pickle, a piece of butter rolled in a little flour, a very little pepper; cover it close, and let it stew softly till it is tender; then take it up carefully and lay it in the middle of the dish, pour your mashed roots in the middle to fill it up high, and your ragoo round it: you may add the liquor the cabbage was stewed in, and send it to table hot.

hot. This will do for a top, bottom, middle, or side dish. When beans are not to be had, you may cut carrots and turnips into little slices and fry them; the carrots in little round slices, the turnips in pieces about two inches long, and as thick as one's finger, and toss them up in the ragoo.

Beans ragooed with Parsnips.

TAKE two large parsnips, scrape them clean, and boil them in water; when tender take them up. scrape all the soft into a sauce-pan, add to them four spoonfuls of cream, a piece of butter as big as an hen's egg, chop them in a sauce-pan well; and when they are quite thick, heap them up in the middle of the dish, and the ragoo round.

Beans ragooed with Potatoes.

BOIL two pounds of potatoes soft, then peel them, put them into a sauce-pan, put to them half a pint of milk, stir them about, and a little salt; then stir in a quarter of a pound of butter, keep stirring all the time till it is so thick that you cannot stir the spoon in it hardly for stiffness, then put it into a halfpenny Welsh dish, first buttering the dish; heap them as high as they will lie, flour them, pour a little melted butter over it, and then a few crumbs of bread; set it into a tin oven before the fire; and when brown, lay it in the middle of the dish (take great care you do not mash it,) pour your ragoo round it, and send it to table hot.

To dress Beans in Ragoo.

YOU must boil your beans so that the skin will slip off; take about a quart, season them with pepper, salt, and nutmeg, then flour them; have ready some butter in a stew-pan, throw in your beans, fry them of a fine brown, then drain them from the fat, and lay them in your dish; have ready a quarter of a pound of butter melted, and half a pint of blanched beans boiled, and beat in a mortar, with a very little pepper, salt, and nutmeg; then by degrees mix them in the butter, and pour over the other beans: garnish with boiled and fried beans, and so on till you fill the rim of your dish. They are very good without frying, and only plain melted butter over them.

An Amlet of Beans.

BLANCH your beans, and fry them in sweet butter, with a little parsley, pour out the butter, and pour in some cream; let it simmer, shaking your pan; season with pepper, salt, and nutmeg, thicken with three or four yolks of eggs; have ready a pint of cream, thickened with the yolks of four eggs, season

with

with a little salt, pour it in your dish, and lay your beans on the amlet, and serve it up hot.

The same way you may dress mushrooms, truffles, green peas, asparagus, and artichoke-bottoms, spinage, sorrel, &c. all being first cut into small pieces, or shred fine.

Carrots and French Beans dressed the Dutch Way.

SLICE the carrots very thin, and just cover them with water, season them with pepper and salt, cut a good many onions and parsley small, a piece of butter; let them simmer over a slow fire till done. Do French beans the same way.

Beans dressed the German Way.

TAKE a large bunch of onions, peel and slice them, a great quantity of parsley washed and cut small, throw them into a stew-pan, with a pound of butter; season them well with pepper and salt, put in two quarts of beans; cover them close, and let them do till the beans are brown, shaking the pan often. Do peas the same way.

To ragoo Celery.

WASH and make a bunch of celery very clean, cut it in pieces about too inches long, put it into a stew-pan with just as much water as will cover it, tie three or four blades of mace, two or three cloves, about twenty corns of whole pepper in a muslin rag loose, put it into a stew-pan, a little onion, a little bundle of sweet herbs; cover it close, and let it stew softly till tender; then take out the spice, onion, and sweet herbs, put in half an ounce of truffles and morels, two spoonfuls of catchup, a gill of red wine, a piece of butter as big as an egg, rolled in flour, six farthing French rolls, season with salt to your palate, stir it all together, cover it close, and let it stew till the sauce is thick and good; take care that the rolls do not break, shake your pan often; when it is enough dish it up, and garnish with lemon. The yolks of six hard eggs, or more, put in with the rolls, will make it a fine dish. This for a first course.

If you would have it white, put in white wine instead of red, and some cream for a second course.

To ragoo Mushrooms.

PEEL and scrape the flaps, put a quart into a sauce-pan, a very little salt, set them on a quick fire, let them boil up, then take them off, put to them a gill of red wine, a quarter of a pound of butter rolled in a little flour, a little nutmeg, a little beaten mace, set it on the fire, stir it now and then; when it is thick and fine, have ready the yolks of six eggs hot, and

boiled

boiled in a bladder hard, lay it in the middle of your dish, and pour the ragoo over it: garnish with broiled mushrooms.

To make good Brown Gravy.

TAKE half a pint of small beer, or ale that is not bitter, and half a pint of water, an onion cut small, a little bit of lemon-peel cut small, three cloves, a blade of mace, some whole pepper, a spoonful of mushroom-pickle, a spoonful of walnut-pickle, a spoonful of catchup, and an anchovy; first put a piece of butter into a sauce-pan, as big as a hen's egg, when it is melted shake in a little flour, and let it be a little brown; then by degrees stir in the above ingredients, and let it boil a quarter of an hour, then strain it, and it is fit for fish or roots.

To fricassee Skirrets.

WASH the roots very well, and boil them till they are tender; then the skin of the roots must be taken off, cut in slices, and have ready a little cream, a piece of butter rolled in flour, the yolk of an egg beat, a little nutmeg grated, two or three spoonfuls of white wine, a very little salt, and stir all together: your roots being in the dish, pour the sauce over them. It is a pretty side-dish. So likewise you may dress root of salsify and scorzonera.

A Fricassee of Artichoke-Bottoms.

TAKE them either dried or pickled; if dried, you must lay them in warm water for three or four hours, shifting the water two or three times; then have ready a little cream, and a piece of fresh butter, stirred together one way over the fire till it is melted; then put in the artichokes, and when they are hot, dish them up.

A White Fricassee of Mushrooms.

TAKE a quart of fresh mushrooms, make them very clean, cut the largest ones in two, put them in a stew-pan with four spoonfuls of water, a blade of mace, a piece of lemon-peel; cover your pan close, and stew them gently for half an hour; beat up the yolks of two eggs with half a pint of cream, and a little nutmeg grated in it, take out the mace and lemon-peel, put in the eggs and cream, keep it stirring one way all the time till it is thick, season with salt to your palate; squeeze a little lemon-juice in, butter the crust of a French roll and toast it brown; put it in your dish, and the mushrooms over.

N. B. Be careful not to squeeze the lemon-juice in till they are finished and ready to put in your dish, then squeeze it in, and stir them about for a minute, then put them in your dish.

Chardoons fried and buttered.

You must cut them about six inches long, and string them; then boil them till tender; take them out, have some butter melted in your stew-pan, flour them and fry them brown; send them in a dish, with melted butter in a cup: or you may tie them up in bundles, and boil them like asparagus; put a toast under them, and pour a little melted butter over them; or cut them into dice, and boil them like peas: toss them up in butter, and send them up hot.

Chardoons à la Fromage.

After they are stringed, cut them an inch long, stew them in a little red wine till they are tender; season with pepper and salt, and thicken it with a piece of butter rolled in flour; then pour them into your dish, squeeze the juice of orange over it, then scrape Parmesan or Cheshire cheese all over them; then brown it with a cheese-iron, and serve it up quick and hot.

To make a Scotch Rabbit.

Toast a piece of bread very nicely on both sides, butter it, cut a slice of cheese about as big as the bread, toast it on both sides and lay it on the bread.

To make a Welsh Rabbit.

Toast the bread on both sides, then toast the cheese on one side, lay it on the toast, and with a hot iron brown the other side. You may rub it over with mustard.

To make an English Rabbit.

Toast a slice of bread brown on both sides, then lay it in a plate before the fire, pour a glass of red wine over it, and let it soak the wine up; then cut some cheese very thin, and lay it very thick over the bread, and put it in a tin oven before the fire, and it will be toasted and browned presently. Serve it away hot.

Or do it thus.

Toast the bread and soak it in the wine; set it before the fire, cut your cheese in very thin slices, rub butter over the bottom of a plate, lay the cheese on, pour in two or three spoonfuls of white wine, cover it with another plate, set it over a chafing-dish of hot coals for two or three minutes; then stir it till it is done and well mixed: you may stir in a little mustard; when it is enough, lay it on the bread, just brown it with a hot shovel. Serve it away hot.

To fry Artichokes.

FIRST blanch them in water, then flour them, fry them in fresh butter, lay them in your dish and pour melted butter over them: or you may put a little red wine into the butter, and season with nutmeg, pepper, and salt.

Artichoke-Suckers dressed the Spanish Way.

CLEAN and wash them and cut them in halves; then boil them in water, drain them from the water and put them into a stew-pan, with a little oil, a little water, and a little vinegar; season them with pepper and salt; stew them a little while, and then thicken them with yolks of eggs.

They make a pretty garnish done thus: clean them, and half boil them; then dry them, flour them, and dip them in yolks of eggs, and fry them brown.

Broccoli as a Salad.

BROCCOLI is a pretty dish by way of salad in the middle of a table; boil it like asparagus (in the beginning of the book you have an account how to clean it); lay it in your dish, beat up with oil and vinegar and a little salt. Garnish with nastertium-buds.

Or boil it, and have plain butter in a cup: or farce French rolls with it and buttered eggs together, for change: or farce your rolls with muscles, done the same way as oysters, only no wine.

To make Potatoe Cakes.

TAKE potatoes, boil them, peel them, beat them in a mortar, mix them with the yolks of eggs, a little sack, sugar, a little beaten mace, a little nutmeg, a little cream, or melted butter, work it up into a paste; then make it into cakes, or just what shape you please with moulds, fry them brown in fresh butter, lay them in plates or dishes, melt butter with sack and sugar, and pour over them.

A Pudding, made thus:

MIX it as before; make it up in the shape of a pudding, and bake it; pour butter, sack, and sugar over it.

To make Potatoes like a Collar of Veal or Mutton.

MAKE the ingredients as before; make it up in the shape of a collar of veal, and with some of it make round balls; bake it with the balls, set the collar in the middle, lay the balls round; let your sauce be half a pint of red wine, sugar enough to sweeten it, the yolks of two eggs, beat up a little nutmeg, stir all these together for fear of curdling; when it is thick enough,

enough, pour it over the collar. This is a pretty dish for a first or a second course.

To broil Potatoes.

FIRST boil them, peel them, cut them in two, broil them till they are brown on both sides; then lay them in the plate or dish, pour melted butter over them.

To fry Potatoes.

CUT them into thin slices as big as a crown-piece, fry them brown, lay them in the plate or dish, pour melted butter and sack and sugar over them. These are a pretty corner-plate.

Mashed Potatoes.

BOIL your potatoes, peel them, and put them into a sauce-pan, mash them well: to two pounds of potatoes put a pint of milk, a little salt; stir them well together, take care they do not stick to the bottom; then take a quarter of a pound of butter, stir it in, and serve it up.

To dress Spinage.

PICK and wash your spinage well, put it into a sauce-pan with a little salt; cover it close, and let it stew till it is just tender, and throw it into a sieve; drain all the liquor out, and chop it small (as much as the quantity of a French roll), add half a pint of cream to it, season with salt, pepper, and grated nutmeg, put in a quarter of a pound of butter, and set it a-stewing over the fire a quarter of an hour, stirring it often; cut a French roll into long pieces about as thick as your finger, fry them, poach six eggs, lay them round on the spinage, stick the pieces of roll in and about the eggs. Serve it up either for supper, or a side-dish at a second course.

To boil Spinage, when you have not Room on the Fire to do it by itself.

HAVE a tin-box, or any other thing that shuts very close, put in your spinage, cover it so close as no water can get in, and put into water, or a pot of liquor, or any thing you are boiling; It will take about an hour, if the pot or copper boils. In the same manner you may boil peas without water.

Asparagus forced in French Rolls.

TAKE three French rolls, take out all the crumb, by first cutting a piece of the top-crust off; but be careful that the crust fits again the same place; fry the rolls brown in fresh butter; then take a pint of cream, the yolks of six eggs beat fine,

fine, a little salt and nutmeg, stir them well together over a slow fire till it begins to be thick; have ready a hundred of small grass boiled; then save tops enough to stick the rolls with, the rest cut small and put into the cream, fill the loaves with them: before you fry the rolls make holes thick in the top-crust and stick the grass in; then lay on the piece of crust and stick the grass in, that it may look as if it were growing. It makes a pretty side-dish at a second course.

Asparagus dressed the Italian Way.

TAKE the asparagus, break them in pieces, then boil them soft and drain the water from them; take a little oil, water, and vinegar, let it boil, season it with pepper and salt, throw in the asparagus and thicken with yolks of eggs.

Endive done this way is good; the Spaniards add sugar, but that spoils them. Green peas done as above are very good; only add a lettuce cut small, and two or three onions, and leave out the eggs.

To stew Parsnips.

BOIL them tender, scrape them from the dust, cut them into slices, put them into a sauce-pan with cream enough; for sauce, a piece of butter rolled in flour, a little salt, and shake the sauce-pan often; when the cream boils, pour them into a plate for a corner-dish, or a side-dish at supper.

To mash Parsnips.

BOIL them tender, scrape them clean, then scrape all the soft into a sauce-pan, put as much milk or cream as will stew them; keep them stirring, and when quite thick, stir in a good piece of butter, and send them to table.

Sorrel with Eggs.

FIRST your sorrel must be quite boiled and well strained, then poach three eggs soft, and three hard, butter your sorrel well; fry some three-cornered toasts brown, lay the sorrel in the dish, lay the soft eggs on it, and the hard between; stick the toast in and about it. Garnish with quartered orange.

Broccoli and Eggs.

BOIL your broccoli tender, saving a large bunch for the middle, and six or eight little thick sprigs to stick round; take a toast half an inch thick, toast it brown, as big as you would have it for your dish or butter-plate; butter some eggs thus: take six eggs (more or less as you have occasion), beat them well, put them into a sauce-pan with a good piece of butter, a little salt, keep beating them with a spoon till they are thick enough,

enough, then pour them on the toast; set the highest bunch of broccoli in the middle, and the other little pieces round about; and garnish the dish with little sprigs of broccoli: this is a pretty side-dish or corner-plate.

Asparagus and Eggs.

TOAST a bit of bread as big as you want, butter it and lay it on your dish; butter some eggs as above, and lay over it; in the meantime boil some grass tender, cut it small and lay it over the eggs. This makes a pretty side-dish for a second course, or a corner-plate.

A pretty Dish of Eggs.

BOIL six eggs hard, peel them, and cut them into thin slices, put a quarter of a pound of butter into the stew-pan, then put in your eggs and fry them quick: half a quarter of an hour will do them. You must be very careful not to break them; throw over them pepper, salt, and nutmeg, lay them in your dish before the fire, pour out all the fat, shake in a little flour, and have ready two shalots cut small; throw them into the pan, pour in a quarter of a pint of white wine, a little juice of lemon, and a little piece of butter rolled in flour; stir all together till it is thick; if you have not sauce enough, put in a little more wine, toast some thin slices of bread cut three-corner ways, and lay round your dish, pour the sauce all over, and send it to table hot. You may put sweet oil on the toast, if it be agreeable.

Eggs à la Tripe.

BOIL your eggs hard, take off the shells, and cut them long-ways in four quarters, put a little butter into a stew-pan, let it melt, shake in a little flour, stir it with a spoon, then put in your eggs, throw a little grated nutmeg all over, a little salt, a good deal of shred parsley; shake your pan round, pour in a little cream, toss the pan round carefully, so that you do not break the eggs; when your sauce is thick and fine, take up your eggs, pour the sauce all over them; and garnish with lemon.

A Fricassee of Eggs.

BOIL eight eggs hard, take off the shells, cut them into quarters, have ready half a pint of cream, and a quarter of a pound of fresh butter; stir it together over the fire till it is thick and smooth, lay the eggs in the dish and pour the sauce all over. Garnish with the hard yolks of three eggs cut in two, and lay round the edge of the dish.

A Ragoo

A Ragoo of Eggs.

Boil twelve eggs hard, take off the shells, and with a little knife very carefully cut the white acrofs longways, fo that the white may be in two halves, and the yolks whole; be careful neither to break the whites nor yolks, take a quarter of a pint of pickled mushrooms chopped very fine, half an ounce of truffles and morels boiled in three or four spoonfuls of water, fave the water, and chop the truffles and morels very small, boil a little parfley, chop it fine, mix them together with the truffle-water you faved, grate a little nutmeg in, a little beaten mace, put it into a fauce-pan with three fpoonfuls of water, a gill of red wine, one fpoonful of catchup; a piece of butter as big as a large walnut, rolled in flour, ftir all together and let it boil; in the meantime get ready your eggs, lay the yolks and whites in order in your difh, the hollow parts of the whites uppermoft, that they may be filled; take fome crumbs of bread and fry them brown and crifp, as you do for larks, with which fill up the whites of the eggs as high as they will lie, then pour in your fauce all over, and garnifh with fried crumbs of bread. This is a very genteel pretty difh, if it be well done.

To broil Eggs.

Cut a toaft round a quartern loaf, brown it, lay it on your difh, butter it, and very carefully break fix or eight eggs on the toaft, and take a red-hot fhovel and hold over them; when they are done, fqueeze a Seville orange over them, grate a little nutmeg over it, and ferve it up for a fide-plate. Or you may poach your eggs, and lay them on a toaft: or toaft your bread crifp, and pour a little boiling water over it; feafon with a little falt, and then lay your poached eggs on it.

To drefs Eggs with Bread.

Take a penny-loaf, foak it in a quart of hot milk two hours, or till the bread is foft, then ftrain it through a coarfe fieve, put to it two fpoonfuls of orange-flower water, or rofe-water; fweeten it, grate in a little nutmeg, take a little difh, butter the bottom of it, break in as many eggs as will cover the bottom of the difh, pour in the bread and milk, fet it in a tin oven before the fire, and half an hour will bake it; it will do on a chafing-difh of coals; cover it clofe before the fire, or bake it in a flow oven.

To farce Eggs.

Get two cabbage-lettuces, fcald them, with a few mufh-rooms, parfley, forrel, and chervil; then chop them very fmall

with

with the yolks of hard eggs, seasoned with salt and nutmeg; then stew them in butter, and when they are enough, put in a little cream, then pour them into the bottom of a dish; take the whites and chop them very fine with parsley, nutmeg, and salt; lay this round the brim of the dish; and run a red-hot fire-shovel over it, to brown it.

Eggs with Lettuce.

SCALD some cabbage-lettuce in fair water, squeeze them well, then slice them and toss them up in a sauce-pan with a piece of butter; season them with pepper, salt, and a little nutmeg; let them stew half an hour, chop them well together; when they are enough, lay them in your dish, fry some eggs nicely in butter and lay on them. Garnish with Seville orange.

To fry Eggs as round as Balls.

HAVING a deep frying-pan and three pints of clarified butter, heat as hot as for fritters, and stir it with a stick till it runs round like a whirlpool; then break an egg into the middle, and turn it round with your stick till it be as hard as a poached egg; the whirling round of the butter will make it as round as a ball, then take it up with a slice, and put it in a dish before the fire: they will keep hot half an hour and yet be soft; so you may do as many as you please. You may serve these with what you please, nothing better than stewed spinage, and garnish with orange.

To make an Egg as big as Twenty.

PART the yolks from the whites, strain them both separate through a sieve, tie the yolks up in a bladder in the form of a ball; boil them hard, then put this ball into another bladder and the whites round it; tie it up oval-fashion, and boil it: these are used for grand salads. This is very pretty for a ragoo; boil five or six yolks together and lay in the middle of the ragoo of eggs; and so you may make them of any size you please.

To make a grand Dish of Eggs.

YOU must break as many eggs as the yolks will fill a pint bason, the whites by themselves, tie the yolks by themselves in a bladder round, boil them hard; then have a wooden bowl that will hold a quart, made like two butter-dishes, but in the shape of an egg, with a hole through one at the top. You are to observe when you boil the yolks, to run a packthread through, and leave a quarter of a yard hanging out. When the yolk is boiled hard, put it into the bowl-dish, but be careful to hang it so as to be in the middle; the string being drawn
through

through the hole, then clap the two bowls together, and tie them tight, and with a funnel pour in the whites through the hole, then stop the hole close and boil it hard; it will take an hour: when it is boiled enough, carefully open it, and cut the string close; in the meantime take twenty eggs, beat them well, the yolks by themselves and the whites by themselves; divide the whites into two, and boil them in bladders the shape of an egg; when they are boiled hard, cut one in two longways, and one crossways, and with a fine sharp knife cut out some of the white in the middle; lay the great egg in the middle, the two long halves on each side with the hollow part uppermost, and the two round flat between; take an ounce of truffles and morels, cut them very small, boil them in half a pint of water till they are tender, then take a pint of fresh mushrooms clean picked, washed, and chopped small, and put into the truffles and morels; let them boil, add a little salt, a little beaten nutmeg, a little beaten mace, a gill of pickled mushrooms chopped fine; boil sixteen of the yolks hard in a bladder, then chop them and mix them with the other ingredients; thicken it with a lump of butter rolled in flour, shaking your sauce-pan round till hot and thick, then fill the round with this, turn them down again, and fill the two long ones; what remains save to put into the sauce-pan; take a pint of cream, a quarter of a pound of butter, the other four yolks beat fine, a gill of white wine, a gill of pickled mushrooms, a little beaten mace, and a little nutmeg; put all into the sauce-pan to the other ingredients, and stir all well together one way till it is thick and fine; pour it over all, and garnish with notched lemon.

This is a grand dish at a second course. Or you may mix it up with red wine and butter, and it will do for a first course.

To make a pretty Dish of Whites of Eggs.

TAKE the whites of twelve eggs, beat them up with four spoonfuls of rose-water, a little grated lemon-peel, a little nutmeg, and sweeten with sugar; mix them well, boil them in four bladders, tie them in the shape of an egg, and boil them hard; they will take half an hour; lay them in your dish; when cold, mix half a pint of thick cream, a gill of sack, and half the juice of a Seville orange; mix all together, sweeten with fine sugar, and pour over the eggs. Serve it up for a side-dish at supper, or when you please.

To stew Cucumbers.

PARE twelve cucumbers and slice them as thick as a half-crown, lay them in a coarse cloth to drain, and when they are dry,

dry, flour them and fry them brown in fresh butter; then take them out with an egg-slice, lay them in a plate before the fire, and have ready one cucumber whole, cut a long piece out of the side, and scoop out all the pulp; have ready fried onions peeled and sliced, and fried brown with the sliced cucumbers; fill the whole cucumber with the fried onion, season with pepper and salt; put on the piece you cut out and tie it round with a packthread; fry it brown, first flouring it, then take it out of the pan and keep it hot; keep the pan on the fire, and with one hand put in a little flour, while with the other you stir it; when it is thick, put in two or three spoonfuls of water, and half a pint of white or red wine, two spoonfuls of catchup, stir it together, put in three blades of mace, four cloves, half a nutmeg, a little pepper and salt, all beat fine together; stir it into the sauce-pan, then throw in your cucumbers, give them a toss or two, then lay the whole cucumbers in the middle, the rest round, pour the sauce all over, untie the cucumbers before you lay it into the dish. Garnish the dish with fried onions, and send it to table hot. This is a pretty side-dish at a first course.

To farce Cucumbers.

TAKE six large cucumbers, cut a piece off the top, and scoop out all the pulp; take a large white cabbage boiled tender, take only the heart, chop it fine, cut a large onion fine, shred some parsley and pickled mushrooms small, two hard eggs chopped very fine, season it with pepper, salt, and nutmeg; stuff your cucumbers full, and put on the pieces, tie them with a packthread, and fry them in butter of a light brown; have the following sauce ready: take a quarter of a pint of red wine, a quarter of a pint of boiling water, a small onion chopped fine, a little pepper and salt, a piece of butter as big as a walnut, rolled in flour; when the cucumbers are enough, lay them in your dish, pour the fat out of the pan, and pour in this sauce; let it boil, and have ready the yolks of two eggs beat fine, mixed with two or three spoonfuls of the sauce, then turn them into the pan, let them boil, keeping it stirring all the time, untie the strings, and pour the sauce over. Serve it up for a side-dish. Garnish with the tops.

To stew Cucumbers.

TAKE six large cucumbers, slice them; take six large onions, peel and cut them in thin slices, fry them both brown, then drain them and pour out the fat, put them into the pan again, with three spoonfuls of hot water, a quarter of a pound of butter rolled in flour, and a tea-spoonful of mustard; season with pepper and salt, and let them stew a quarter of an hour

softly,

softly, shaking the pan often; when they are enough dish them up.

Fried Celery.

TAKE six or eight heads of celery, cut off the green tops, and take off the outside stalks, wash them clean and pare the roots clean; then have ready half a pint of white wine, the yolks of three eggs beat fine, and a little salt and nutmeg; mix all well together with flour into a batter, dip every head into the batter and fry them in butter; when enough, lay them in your dish, and pour melted butter over them.

Celery with Cream.

WASH and clean six or eight heads of celery, cut them about three inches long, boil them tender, pour away all the water, and take the yolks of four eggs beat fine, half a pint of cream, a little salt and nutmeg, pour it over, keeping the pan shaking all the while: when it begins to be thick, dish it up.

Peas Françoise.

TAKE a quart of shelled peas, cut a large Spanish onion, or two middling ones small, and two cabbage or Silesia lettuces cut small, put them into a sauce-pan with half a pint of water, season them with a little salt, a little beaten pepper, and a little beaten mace and nutmeg; cover them close and let them stew a quarter of an hour, then put in a quarter of a pound of fresh butter rolled in a little flour, a spoonful of catchup, a little piece of burnt butter as big as a nutmeg; cover them close and let it simmer softly an hour, often shaking the pan. When it is enough, serve it up for a side-dish.

For an alteration, you may stew the ingredients as above; then take a small cabbage-lettuce and half boil it; then drain it, cut the stalks flat at the bottom, so that it will stand firm in the dish, and with a knife very carefully cut out the middle, leaving the outside leaves whole; put what you cut out into a sauce-pan, chop it, and put a piece of butter, a little pepper, salt, and nutmeg, the yolk of a hard egg chopped, a few crumbs of bread, mix all together, and when it is hot fill your cabbage; put some butter into a stew-pan, tie your cabbage and fry it till you think it is enough; then take it up, untie it, and first pour the ingredients of peas into your dish, set the forced cabbage in the middle, and have ready four artichoke-bottoms fried and cut in two, and laid round the dish. This will do for a top-dish.

Green

Green Peas with Cream.

TAKE a quart of fine green peas, put them into a stew-pan with a piece of butter as big as an egg, rolled in a little flour, season them with a little salt and nutmeg, a bit of sugar as big as a nutmeg, a little bundle of sweet herbs, some parsley chopped fine, a quarter of a pint of boiling water; cover them close, and let them stew very softly half an hour, then pour in a quarter of a pint of good cream: give it one boil, and serve it up for a side-plate.

A Farce-meagre Cabbage.

TAKE a white-heart cabbage, as big as the bottom of a plate, let it boil five minutes in water, then drain it, cut the stalk flat to stand in the dish, then carefully open the leaves and take out the inside, leaving the outside leaves whole; chop what you take out very fine, take the flesh of two or three flounders or plaice clean from the bone; chop it with the cabbage, the yolks and whites of four hard eggs, a handful of picked parsley, beat all together in a mortar, with a quarter of a pound of melted butter; mix it up with the yolk of an egg and a few crumbs of bread, fill the cabbage and tie it together, put it into a deep stew-pan or sauce-pan, put to it half a pint of water, a quarter of a pound of butter rolled in a little flour, the yolks of four hard eggs, an onion stuck with six cloves, whole pepper and mace tied in a muslin rag, half an ounce of truffles and morels, a spoonful of catchup, a few pickled mushrooms; cover it close and let it simmer an hour: if you find it is not enough, you must do it longer. When it is done, lay it in your dish, untie it, and pour the sauce over it.

Red Cabbage dressed after the Dutch Way, good for a Cold in the Breast.

TAKE the cabbage, cut it small and boil it soft, then drain it, and put it in a stew-pan with a sufficient quantity of oil and butter, a little water and vinegar, and an onion cut small; season it with pepper and salt, and let it simmer on a slow fire till all the liquor is wasted.

Cauliflowers dressed the Spanish Way.

BOIL them, but not too much; then drain them and put them into a stew-pan: to a large cauliflower put a quarter of a pint of sweet oil, and two or three cloves of garlic; let them fry till brown; then season them with pepper and salt, two or three spoonfuls of vinegar; cover the pan very close, and let them simmer over a very slow fire an hour.

Cauliflowers

Cauliflowers fried.

TAKE two fine cauliflowers, boil them in milk and water, then leave one whole, and pull the other to pieces; take half a pound of butter, with two spoonfuls of water, a little dust of flour, and melt the butter in a stew-pan; then put in the whole cauliflower cut in two, and the other pulled to pieces, and fry it till it is of a very light brown; season it with pepper and salt: when it is enough, lay the two halves in the middle, and pour the rest all over.

To make an Oatmeal Pudding.

TAKE a pint of fine oatmeal, boil it in three pints of new milk, stirring it till it is as thick as a hasty-pudding; take it off, and stir in half a pound of fresh butter, a little beaten mace and nutmeg, and a gill of sack; then beat up eight eggs, half the whites, stir all well together, lay puff-paste all over the dish, pour in the pudding and bake it half an hour: or you may boil it with a few currants.

To make a Potatoe Pudding.

TAKE a quart of potatoes, boil them soft, peel them, and mash them with the back of a spoon, and rub them through a sieve, to have them fine and smooth; take half a pound of fresh butter melted, half a pound of fine sugar, beat them well together till they are very smooth, beat six eggs, whites and all, stir them in, and a glass of sack or brandy; you may add half a pound of currants, boil it half an hour, melt butter with a glass of white wine, sweeten with sugar, and pour over it: you may bake it in a dish, with puff-paste all round the dish at the bottom.

To make a second Potatoe Pudding.

BOIL two pounds of potatoes, and beat them in a mortar fine, beat in half a pound of melted butter, boil it half an hour, pour melted butter over it, with a glass of white wine, or the juice of a Seville orange, and throw sugar all over the pudding and dish.

To make a third Sort of Potatoe Pudding.

TAKE two pounds of white potatoes, boil them soft, peel and beat them in a mortar, or strain them through a sieve till they are quite fine; then mix in half a pound of fresh butter melted, then beat up the yolks of eight eggs and three whites, stir them in, and half a pound of white sugar finely pounded, half a pint of sack, stir it well together, grate in half a large nutmeg, and stir in half a pint of cream, make a puff-paste and lay all over the dish and round the edges; pour it in the pudding, and bake it of a fine light brown.

For change, put in half a pound of currants; or you may strew over the top half an ounce of citron and orange peel cut thin, before you put it into the oven.

To make Buttered Loaves.

BEAT up the yolks of twelve eggs, with half the whites, and a quarter of a pint of yeast, strain them into a dish; season with salt and beaten ginger, then make it into a high paste with flour, lay it in a warm cloth for a quarter of an hour; then make it up into little loaves, and bake them or boil them with butter, and put in a glass of white wine; sweeten well with sugar, lay the loaves in the dish, pour the sauce over them, and throw sugar over the dish.

To make an Orange Pudding.

TAKE the yolks of sixteen eggs, beat them well with half a pound of melted butter, grate in the rind of two fine Seville oranges, beat in half a pound of fine sugar, two spoonfuls of orange-flower water, two of rose-water, a gill of sack, half a pint of cream, two Naples biscuits, or the crumb of a halfpenny roll soaked in the cream, and mix all well together; make a thin puff-paste and lay all over the dish and round the rim, pour in the pudding and bake it: it will take about as long baking as a custard.

To make a second Sort of Orange Pudding.

YOU must take sixteen yolks of eggs, beat them fine, mix them with half a pound of fresh butter melted, and half a pound of white sugar, half a pint of cream, a little rose-water, and a little nutmeg; cut the peel of a fine large Seville orange so thin as none of the white appears, beat it fine in a mortar till it is like a paste, and by degrees mix in the above ingredients all together; then lay a puff-paste all over the dish, pour in the ingredients and bake it.

To make a third Orange Pudding.

TAKE two large Seville oranges and grate off the rind as far as they are yellow; then put your oranges in fair water, and let them boil till they are tender; shift the water three or four times to take out the bitterness; when they are tender, cut them open and take away the seeds and strings, and beat the other part in a mortar, with half a pound of sugar, till it is a paste; then put to it the yolks of six eggs, three or four spoonfuls of thick cream, half a Naples biscuit grated; mix
these

these together, and melt a pound of fresh butter very thick, and stir it well in; when it is cold, put a little thin puff-paste about the bottom and rim of your dish; pour in the ingredients, and bake it about three quarters of an hour.

To make a fourth Orange Pudding.

TAKE the outside rind of three Seville oranges, boil them in several waters till they are tender, then pound them in a mortar, with three quarters of a pound of sugar; then blanch half a pound of sweet almonds, beat them very fine with rose-water to keep them from oiling, then beat sixteen eggs, but six whites, a pound of fresh butter, and beat all these together till it is light and hollow; then lay a thin puff-paste all over a dish, and put in the ingredients. Bake it with your tarts.

To make a Lemon Pudding.

TAKE three lemons, and cut the rind off very thin, boil them in three separate waters till very tender, then pound them very fine in a mortar; have ready a quarter of a pound of Naples biscuit, boiled up in a quart of milk or cream, mix them and the lemon rind with it; beat up twelve yolks and six whites of eggs very fine, melt a quarter of a pound of fresh butter, half a pound of fine sugar, a little orange-flower water; mix all well together, put it over the stove, and keep it stirring till it is thick, squeeze the juice of half a lemon in; put puff-paste round the rim of your dish, put the pudding stuff in, cut some candied sweetmeats and put over: bake it three quarters of an hour, and send it up hot.

Another Way to make a Lemon Pudding.

TAKE three lemons and grate the rinds off, beat up twelve yolks and six whites of eggs, put in half a pint of cream, half a pound of fine sugar, a little orange-flower water, a quarter of a pound of butter melted; mix all well together, squeeze in the juice of two lemons, put it over the stove, and keep stirring it till it is thick; put a puff-paste round the rim of the dish, put in your pudding stuff with some candied sweetmeats cut small over it, and bake it three quarters of an hour.

To bake an Almond Pudding.

BLANCH half a pound of sweet almonds, and four bitter ones, in warm water, take them and pound them in a marble mortar, with two spoonfuls of orange-flower water, and two of rose-water, a gill of sack; mix in four grated Naples biscuits, three quarters of a pound of melted butter; beat eight eggs, and mix them with a quart of cream boiled, grate in half a nutmeg

meg and a quarter of a pound of sugar; mix all well together, make a thin puff-paste, and lay all over the dish; pour in the ingredients, and bake it.

To boil an Almond Pudding.

BEAT a pound of sweet almonds as small as possible, with three spoonfuls of rose-water, and a gill of sack or white wine, and mix in half a pound of fresh butter melted, with five yolks of eggs and two whites, a quart of cream, a quarter of a pound of sugar, half a nutmeg grated, one spoonful of flour, and three spoonfuls of crumbs of white bread; mix all well together, and boil it: it will take half an hour boiling.

To make a Sago Pudding.

LET half a pound of sago be washed well in three or four hot waters, then put to it a quart of new milk, and let it boil together till it is thick; stir it carefully (for it is apt to burn), put in a stick of cinnamon when you set it on the fire; when it is boiled take it out; before you pour it out, stir in half a pound of fresh butter, then pour it into a pan, and beat up nine eggs, with five of the whites, and four spoonfuls of sack; stir all together, and sweeten to your taste; put in a quarter of a pound of currants clean washed and rubbed, and just plumped in two spoonfuls of sack and two of rose-water; mix all well together, stir it well over a slow fire till it is thick, lay a puff-paste over a dish; pour in the ingredients, and bake it.

To make a Millet Pudding.

YOU must get half a pound of millet seed, and after it is washed and picked clean, put to it half a pound of sugar, a whole nutmeg grated, and three quarts of milk; when you have mixed all well together, break in half a pound of fresh butter, and butter your dish; pour it in, and bake it.

To make a Carrot Pudding.

YOU must take a raw carrot, scrape it very clean, and grate it; take half a pound of the grated carrot, and a pound of grated bread, beat up eight eggs, leave out half the whites, and mix the eggs with half a pint of cream; then stir in the bread and carrot, half a pound of fresh butter melted, half a pint of sack, and three spoonfuls of orange-flower water, a nutmeg grated; sweeten to your palate; mix all well together, and if it is not thin enough, stir in a little new milk or cream; let it be of a moderate thickness, lay a puff-paste all over the dish, and pour in the ingredients; bake it; it will take an hour's baking:

baking: or you may boil it; but then you must melt butter, and put in white wine and sugar.

A second Carrot Pudding.

GET two penny loaves, pare off the crust, soak them in a quart of boiling milk, let it stand till it is cold, then grate in two or three large carrots, then put in eight eggs well beat, and three quarters of a pound of fresh butter melted, grate in a little nutmeg, and sweeten to your taste; cover your dish with puff-paste, pour in the ingredients, and bake it an hour.

To make a Cowslip Pudding.

HAVING got the flowers of a peck of cowslips, cut them and pound them small, with half a pound of Naples biscuits grated, and three pints of cream; boil them a little, then take them off the fire, and beat up sixteen eggs with a little cream and rose-water; sweeten to your palate; mix it all well together, butter a dish and pour it in; bake it, and when it is enough, throw fine sugar over and serve it up: or you may make half the quantity.

N. B. New milk will do in all those puddings, when you have no cream.

To make a Quince, Apricot, or White-Pear Plum Pudding.

SCALD your quinces very tender, pare them very thin, scrape off the soft, mix it with sugar very sweet, put in a little ginger and a little cinnamon; to a pint of cream you must put three or four yolks of eggs, and stir it into your quinces till they are of a good thickness: it must be pretty thick.

So you may do apricots or white-pear plums. Butter your dish, pour it in and bake it.

To make a Pearl-Barley Pudding.

GET a pound of pearl-barley, wash it clean, put to it three quarts of new milk, and half a pound of double-refined sugar, a nutmeg grated; then put it into a deep pan and bake it with brown bread: take it out of the oven, beat up six eggs, mix all well together, butter a dish, pour it in, bake it again an hour, and it will be excellent.

To make a French Barley Pudding.

PUT to a quart of cream six eggs well beaten, half the whites, sweeten to your palate, a little orange-flower water, or rose-water, and a pound of melted butter; then put in six handfuls of French barley that has been boiled tender in milk; butter a dish and put it in: it will take as long baking as a venison-pasty.

To make an Apple Pudding.

TAKE twelve large pippins, pare them, and take out the cores, put them into a sauce-pan with four or five spoonfuls of water, boil them till they are soft and thick; then beat them well, stir in a pound of loaf-sugar, the juice of three lemons, the peel of two lemons cut thin and beat fine in a mortar, the yolks of eight eggs beat; mix all well together, bake it in a slack oven; when it is near done, throw over a little fine sugar. You may bake it in a puff-paste, as you do the other puddings.

To make an Apple Pudding.

MAKE a good puff-paste, roll it out half an inch thick, pare your apples, and core them, enough to fill the crust, and close it up, tie it in a cloth and boil it; if a small pudding, two hours; if a large one, three or four hours; when it is enough, turn it into your dish, cut a piece of the crust out of the top, butter and sugar it to your palate, lay on the crust again, and send it to table hot. A pear pudding make the same way. And thus you may make a damson pudding, or any sort of plums, apricots, cherries, or mulberries; and are very fine.

A baked Apple Pudding.—Excellent.

TAKE eight large apples, pare and core them, put them into a sauce-pan with just water enough to cover them till soft, then pour it away and beat them very fine, stir in while hot a quarter of a pound of butter, loaf-sugar to your taste, a quarter of a pound of biscuits finely grated, half a nutmeg, three large spoonfuls of brandy, two of rose-water, the peel of a lemon grated; when cold, put in a quarter of a pint of cream, the yolks of six eggs well beat; put paste at the bottom of the dish.

To make an Italian Pudding.

TAKE a pint of cream, and slice in some French rolls, as much as you think will make it thick enough, beat ten eggs fine, grate a nutmeg, butter the bottom of the dish, slice twelve pippins into it, throw some orange-peel and sugar over, and half a pint of red wine, then pour your cream, bread, and eggs over it; first lay a puff-paste at the bottom of the dish and round the edges, and bake it half an hour.

To make a Rice Pudding.

TAKE a quarter of a pound of rice, put it into a sauce-pan, with a quart of new milk, a stick of cinnamon, stir it often to keep it from sticking to the sauce-pan; when it has boiled thick, pour it into a pan, stir in a quarter of a pound of fresh butter,

butter, and sugar to your palate; grate in half a nutmeg, add three or four spoonfuls of rose-water, and stir it all well together; when it is cold, beat up eight eggs, with half the whites, beat it all well together, butter a dish, pour it in and bake it. You may lay a puff-paste first all over the dish. For change, put in a few currants and sweetmeats, if you choose it.

A second Rice Pudding.

GET half a pound of rice, put to it three quarts of milk, stir in half a pound of sugar, grate a small nutmeg in, and break in half a pound of fresh butter; butter a dish and pour it in and bake it; you may add a quarter of a pound of currants, for change. If you boil the rice and milk, and then stir in the sugar, you may bake it before the fire, or in a tin oven. You may add eggs, but it will be good without.

A third Rice Pudding.

TAKE six ounces of the flour of rice, put it into a quart of milk and let it boil till it is pretty thick, stirring it all the while; then pour it into a pan, stir in half a pound of fresh butter and a quarter of a pound of sugar; when it is cold, grate in a nutmeg, beat six eggs with a spoonful or two of sack, beat and stir all well together, lay a thin puff-paste on the bottom of your dish, pour it in and bake it.

A Carolina Rice Pudding.

TAKE half a pound of rice, wash it clean, put it into a sauce-pan with a quart of milk, keep stirring it till it is very thick; take great care it does not burn; then turn it into a pan and grate some nutmeg into it, and two tea-spoonfuls of beaten cinnamon, a little lemon-peel shred fine, six apples pared and chopped small; mix all together with the yolks of three eggs, and sweeten to your palate; then tie it up close in a cloth, put it into boiling water, and be sure to keep it boiling all the time; an hour and a quarter will boil it; melt butter and pour over it, and throw some fine sugar all over it: a little wine in the sauce will be a great addition to it.

To boil a Custard Pudding.

TAKE a pint of cream, out of which take two or three spoonfuls and mix with a spoonful of fine flour, set the rest to boil; when it is boiled, take it off, and stir in the cold cream, and flour very well; when it is cool, beat up five yolks and two whites of eggs, and stir in a little salt and some nutmeg, and two or three spoonfuls of sack; sweeten to your palate; butter a wooden bowl, and pour it in, tie a cloth over it, and boil it half an hour; when it is enough, untie the cloth, turn the pudding out into your dish, and pour melted butter over it.

To make a Flour Pudding.

TAKE a quart of milk, beat up eight eggs, but four of the whites, mix them with a quarter of a pint of milk, and stir into that four large spoonfuls of flour, beat it well together, boil six bitter almonds in two spoonfuls of water, pour the water into the eggs, blanch the almonds and beat them fine in a mortar; then mix them in with half a large nutmeg and a tea-spoonful of salt; then mix in the rest of the milk, flour your cloth well, and boil it an hour; pour melted butter over it, and sugar (if you like it) thrown all over. Observe always in boiling puddings, that the water boils before you put them into the pot; and have ready, when they are boiled, a pan of clean cold water, just give your pudding one dip in, then untie the cloth, and it will turn out without sticking to the cloth.

To make a Batter Pudding.

TAKE a quart of milk, beat up six eggs, half the whites, mix as above, six spoonfuls of flour, a tea-spoonful of salt, and one of beaten ginger; then mix all together, boil it an hour and a quarter, and pour melted butter over it: you may put in eight eggs (if you have plenty) for change, and half a pound of prunes or currants.

To make a Batter Pudding without Eggs.

TAKE a quart of milk, mix six spoonfuls of flour with a little of the milk first, a tea-spoonful of salt, two tea-spoonfuls of beaten ginger, and two of the tincture of saffron; then mix all together, and boil it an hour. You may add fruit as you think proper.

To make a grateful Pudding.

TAKE a pound of fine flour, and a pound of white bread grated, take eight eggs, but half the whites, beat them up, and mix with them a pint of new milk, then stir in the bread and flour, a pound of raisins stoned, a pound of currants, half a pound of sugar, a little beaten ginger; mix all well together, and either bake or boil it: It will take three quarters of an hour baking: put cream instead of milk, if you have it; it will be an addition to the pudding.

To make a Bread Pudding.

CUT off all the crust of a penny white loaf, and slice it thin into a quart of milk, set it over a chafing-dish of coals till the bread has soaked up all the milk, then put in a piece of sweet butter,

butter, ſtir it round, let it ſtand till cool; or you may boil your milk and pour over your bread, and cover it up cloſe, does full as well; then take the yolks of ſix eggs, the whites of three, and beat them up with a little roſe-water and nutmeg, a little ſalt and ſugar, if you chooſe it; mix all well together, and boil it one hour.

To make a fine Bread Pudding.

TAKE all the crumb of a ſtale penny-loaf, cut it thin, a quart of cream, ſet it over a ſlow fire till it is ſcalding hot, then let it ſtand till it is cold, beat up the bread and cream well together, grate in ſome nutmeg, take twelve bitter almonds, boil them in two ſpoonfuls of water, pour the water to the cream and ſtir it in with a little ſalt, ſweeten it to your palate, blanch the almonds and beat them in a mortar with two ſpoonfuls of roſe or orange-flower water till they are a fine paſte; then mix them by degrees with the cream till they are well mixed in the cream, then take the yolks of eight eggs, the whites of four, beat them well and mix them with your cream, then mix all well together: a wooden diſh is beſt to boil it in; but if you boil it in a cloth, be ſure to dip it in the hot water, and flour it well, tie it looſe and boil it an hour; be ſure the water boils when you put it in, and keeps boiling all the time; when it is enough, turn it into your diſh, melt butter and put in two or three ſpoonfuls of white wine or ſack, give it a boil and pour it over your pudding; then ſtrew a good deal of fine ſugar all over the pudding and diſh, and ſend it to table hot. New milk will do when you cannot get cream. You may, for change, put in a few currants.

To make an ordinary Bread Pudding.

TAKE two halfpenny rolls, ſlice them thin, cruſt and all, pour over them a pint of new milk boiling hot, cover them cloſe, let it ſtand ſome hours to ſoak; then beat it well with a little melted butter, and beat up the yolks and whites of two eggs, beat all together well with a little ſalt; boil it half an hour; when it is done, turn it into your diſh, pour melted butter and ſugar over it. Some love a little vinegar in the butter. If your rolls are ſtale and grated, they will do better; add a little ginger. You may bake it with a few currants.

To make a baked Bread Pudding.

TAKE the crumb of a penny-loaf, as much flour, the yolks of four eggs, and two whites, a tea-ſpoonful of ginger, half a pound of raiſins ſtoned, half a pound of currants clean waſhed and picked, a little ſalt; mix firſt the bread and flour, ginger, ſalt, and ſugar to your palate, then the eggs, and as much milk

milk as will make it like a good batter, then the fruit, butter the dish, pour it in, and bake it.

To make a boiled Loaf.

TAKE a penny-loaf, pour over it half a pint of milk boiling hot, cover it close, let it stand till it has soaked up the milk, then tie it up in a cloth and boil it half an hour; when it is done, lay it in your dish, pour melted butter over it, and throw sugar all over; a spoonful of wine or rose-water does as well in the butter, or juice of Seville orange. A French manchet does best; but there are little loaves made on purpose for the use. A French roll or oat-cake does very well boiled thus.

To make a Chesnut Pudding.

PUT a dozen and a half of chesnuts into a skillet or saucepan of water, boil them a quarter of an hour, then blanch and peel them, and beat them in a marble mortar, with a little orange-flower or rose-water and sack, till they are a fine thin paste; then beat up twelve eggs with half the whites, and mix them well, grate half a nutmeg, a little salt, mix them with three pints of cream and half a pound of melted butter; sweeten to your palate, and mix all together; put it over the fire, and keep stirring it till it is thick; lay a puff-paste all over the dish, pour in the mixture, and bake it: when you cannot get cream, take three pints of milk, beat up the yolks of four eggs and stir into the milk, set it over the fire, stirring it all the time till it is scalding hot, then mix it in the room of the cream.

To make a fine plain baked Pudding.

YOU must take a quart of milk and put three bay-leaves into it; when it has boiled a little with fine flour, make it into a hasty-pudding, with a little salt, pretty thick; take it off the fire, and stir in half a pound of butter, a quarter of a pound of sugar, beat up twelve eggs, and half the whites, stir all well together, lay a puff-paste all over the dish, and pour in your stuff: half an hour will bake it.

To make pretty little Cheese-Curd Puddings.

YOU must take a gallon of milk and turn it with rennet, then drain all the curd from the whey, put the curd into a mortar and beat it with half a pound of fresh butter till the butter and curd is well mixed; then beat six eggs, half the whites, and strain them to the curd, two Naples biscuits, or half a penny roll grated; mix all these together, and sweeten to your palate; butter your patty-pans, and fill them with the ingredients; bake them, but do not let your oven be too hot; when

they

they are done, turn them out into a dish, cut citron and candied orange-peel into little narrow bits, about an inch long, and blanched almonds cut in long slips, stick them here and there on the tops of the puddings, just as you fancy; pour melted butter with a little sack in it into the dish, and throw fine sugar all over the puddings and dish. They make a pretty side-dish.

To make an Apricot Pudding.

CODDLE six large apricots very tender, break them very small, sweeten them to your taste; when they are cold, add six eggs, only two whites, well beat; mix them all well together with a pint of good cream, lay a puff-paste all over your dish, and pour in your ingredients: bake it half an hour, do not let the oven be too hot; when it is enough, throw a little fine sugar all over it, and send it to table hot.

To make an Ipswich Almond Pudding.

STEEP somewhat above three ounces of the crumb of white bread sliced in a pint and a half of cream, or grate the bread; then beat half a pint of blanched almonds very fine till they are like a paste, with a little orange-flower water, beat up the yolks of eight eggs, and the whites of four: mix all well together, put in a quarter of a pound of white sugar, and stir in a little melted butter, about a quarter of pound; put it over the fire, and keep stirring it till it is thick; lay a sheet of puff-paste at the bottom of your dish, and pour in the ingredients: half an hour will bake it.

Transparent Pudding.

TAKE eight eggs and beat them well; put them in a pan with half a pound of fresh butter, half a pound of fine powdered sugar, and half a nutmeg grated; set it on the fire, and keep stirring it till it is of the thickness of buttered eggs, then put it away to cool; put a thin puff-paste round the edge of your dish; pour in the ingredients, bake it half an hour in a moderate oven, and send it up hot.

Puddings for little Dishes.

YOU must take a pint of cream and boil it, and slit a halfpenny loaf and pour the cream hot over it, and cover it close till it is cold; then beat it fine and grate in half a large nutmeg, a quarter of a pound of sugar, the yolks of four eggs, but two whites, well beat, beat it all well together: with the half of this fill four little wooden dishes; colour one yellow with saffron, one red with cochineal, green with the juice of spinage, and blue with the syrup of violets; the rest mix with

an

an ounce of sweet almonds blanched and beat fine, and fill a dish: your dishes must be small, and tie your covers over very close with packthread; when your pot boils put them in; an hour will boil them; when enough turn them out in a dish, the white one in the middle and the four coloured ones round; when they are enough, melt some fresh butter with a glass of sack and pour over, and throw sugar over the dish. The white pudding dish must be of a larger size than the rest; and be sure to butter your dishes well before you put them in, and do not fill them too full.

To make a Sweetmeat Pudding.

PUT a thin puff-paste all over your dish; then have candied orange, lemon-peel, and citron, of each an ounce, slice them thin, and lay them all over the bottom of your dish; then beat eight yolks of eggs and two whites, near half a pound of sugar, and half a pound of melted butter; beat all well together; when the oven is ready, pour it on your sweetmeats: an hour or less will bake it; the oven must not be too hot.

To make a fine plain Pudding.

GET a quart of milk, put into it six laurel-leaves, boil it, then take out your leaves, and stir in as much flour as will make it a hasty pudding pretty thick, take it off, and then stir in half a pound of butter, then a quarter of a pound of sugar, a small nutmeg grated, and twelve yolks and six whites of eggs well beaten; mix all well together, butter a dish and put in your stuff: a little more than half an hour will bake it.

To make a Ratifia Pudding.

GET a quart of cream, boil it with four or five laurel-leaves, then take them out, and break in half a pound of Naples biscuits, half a pound of butter, some sack, nutmeg, and a little salt; take it off the fire, cover it up; when it is almost cold, put in two ounces of blanched almonds beat fine, and the yolks of five eggs; mix all well together, and bake it in a moderate oven half an hour; scrape sugar on it as it goes into the oven.

To make a Bread and Butter Pudding.

GET a penny-loaf and cut it into thin slices of bread and butter as you do for tea; butter your dish as you cut them, lay slices all over the dish, then strew a few currants clean washed and picked, then a row of bread and butter, then a few currants, and so on till all your bread and butter is in; then take a pint of milk, beat up four eggs, a little salt, half a nutmeg grated; mix all together with sugar to your taste; pour this over the bread,

bread, and bake it half an hour: a puff-paste under does best. You may put in two spoonfuls of rose-water.

To make a boiled Rice-Pudding.

HAVING got a quarter of a pound of the flour of rice, put it over the fire with a pint of milk, and keep it stirring constantly that it may not clod nor burn; when it is of a good thickness take it off, and pour it into an earthen pan; stir in half a pound of butter very smooth, and half a pint of cream or new milk, sweeten to your palate, grate in half a nutmeg and the outward rind of a lemon; beat up the yolks of six eggs and two whites, beat all well together, boil it either in small china basons or wooden bowls: when boiled turn them into a dish, pour melted butter over them, with a little sack, and throw sugar all over.

To make a cheap Rice-Pudding.

GET a quarter of a pound of rice, and half a pound of raisins stoned, and tie them in a cloth; give the rice a great deal of room to swell; boil it two hours; when it is enough, turn it into your dish, and pour melted butter and sugar over it, with a little nutmeg.

To make a cheap plain Rice-Pudding.

GET a quarter of a pound of rice, tie it in a cloth, but give room for swelling; boil it an hour, then take it up, untie it, and with a spoon stir in a quarter of a pound of butter, grate some nutmeg, and sweeten to your taste; then tie it up close and boil it another hour; then take it up, turn it into your dish and pour your melted butter over it.

To make a cheap baked Rice-Pudding.

YOU must take a quarter of a pound of rice, boil it in a quart of new milk, stir it that it does not burn; when it begins to be thick, take it off, let it stand till it is a little cool, then stir in well a quarter of a pound of butter, and sugar to your palate; grate a small nutmeg, butter your dish, pour it in, and bake it.

To make a Hanover Cake or Pudding.

TAKE half a pound of almonds blanched and beat fine with a little rose-water, half a pound of fine sugar pounded and sifted, fifteen eggs, leaving out half the whites, and the rind of a lemon grated very fine; put a few almonds in the mortar at a time, and put in by degrees about a tea-cupful of rose-water; keep throwing in the sugar; when you have done the almonds and sugar together a little at a time till they are all used up,

then

then put it into your pan with the eggs; beat them very well together: half an hour will bake it; it must be a light brown.

To make a Yam Pudding.

TAKE a middling white yam and either boil or roast it, then pare off the skin and pound it very fine, with three quarters of a pound of butter, half a pound of sugar, a little mace, cinnamon, and twelve eggs, leaving out half the whites, beat them with a little rose-water: you may put in a little citron cut small (if you like it), and bake it nicely.

A Vermicelli Pudding.

BOIL four ounces of vermicelli in a pint of new milk till it is soft, with a stick or two of cinnamon, then put in half a pint of thick cream, a quarter of a pound of butter, a quarter of a pound of sugar, and the yolks of four beaten eggs: bake it in an earthen dish without a paste.

A red Sago Pudding.

TAKE two ounces of sago, boil it in water with a stick of cinnamon till it be quite soft and thick, let it stand till quite cold; in the meantime grate the crumb of a halfpenny-loaf, and pour over it a large glass of red wine, chop four ounces of marrow, and half a pound of sugar, and the yolks of four beaten eggs, beat them all together for a quarter of an hour, lay a puff-paste round your dish, and send it to the oven; when it comes back, stick it over with blanched almonds cut the long way, and bits of citron cut the same; send it to table.

To make a Spinage Pudding.

TAKE a quarter of a peck of spinage picked and washed clean, put it into a sauce-pan with a little salt, cover it close, and when it is boiled just tender, throw it into a sieve to drain; then chop it with a knife, beat up six eggs, mix well with it half a pint of cream and a stale roll grated fine, a little nutmeg, and a quarter of a pound of melted butter; stir all well together, put it into the sauce-pan you boiled the spinage, and keep stirring it all the time till it begins to thicken; then wet and flour your cloth very well, tie it up, and boil it an hour: when it is enough, turn it into your dish, pour melted butter over it, and the juice of a Seville orange (if you like it); as to sugar, you may add or let it alone, just to your taste: you may bake it; but then you should put in a quarter of a pound of sugar. You may add biscuit in the room of bread (if you like it better).

To make a Quaking Pudding.

TAKE a pint of good cream, six eggs, but half the whites, beat them well, and mix with the cream; grate a little nutmeg in, add a little salt, and a little rose-water (if it be agreeable); grate in the crumb of a halfpenny-roll, or a spoonful of flour, first mixed with a little of the cream, or a spoonful of the flour of rice (which you please); butter a cloth well, and flour it, then put in your mixture, tie it not too close, and boil it half an hour fast: be sure the water boils before you put it in.

To make a Cream Pudding.

TAKE a quart of cream, boil it with a blade of mace and half a nutmeg grated, let it cool; beat up eight eggs and three whites, strain them well, mix a spoonful of flour with them, a quarter of a pound of almonds blanched and beat very fine, with a spoonful of orange-flower or rose-water, mix with the eggs, then by degrees mix in the cream, beat all well together, take a thick cloth, wet it and flour it well, pour in your stuff, tie it close, and boil it half an hour: let the water boil all the time fast; when it is done, turn it into your dish, pour melted butter over, with a little sack, and throw fine sugar all over it.

To make a Prune Pudding.

TAKE a quart of milk, beat six eggs, half the whites, with half a pint of the milk, and four spoonfuls of flour, a little salt, and two spoonfuls of beaten ginger; then by degrees mix in all the milk and a pound of prunes, tie it in a cloth, boil it an hour, melt butter and pour over it. Damsons eat well done this way in the room of prunes.

To make a Spoonful Pudding.

TAKE a spoonful of flour, a spoonful of cream or milk, an egg, a little nutmeg, ginger, and salt; mix all together, and boil it in a little wooden dish half an hour. You may add a few currants.

To make a Lemon Tower or Pudding.

GRATE the outward rind of three lemons; take three quarters of a pound of sugar, and the same of butter, the yolks of eight eggs, beat them in a marble mortar at least an hour, then lay a thin rich crust in the bottom of the dish you bake it in, as you may something also over it: three quarters of an hour will bake it. Make an orange pudding the same way, but pare the rinds, and boil them first in several waters till the bitterness is boiled out.

To make Yeast Dumplings.

First make a light dough as for bread, with flour, water, salt, and yeast, cover with a cloth, and set it before the fire for half an hour; then have a sauce-pan of water on the fire, and when it boils take the dough and make it into little round balls, as big as a large hen's egg; then flat them with your hand, and put them into the boiling water; a few minutes boils them; take great care they do not fall to the bottom of the pot or sauce-pan, for then they will be heavy; and be sure to keep the water boiling all the time: when they are enough take them up (which they will be in ten minutes or less), lay them in your dish, and have melted butter in a cup. As good a way as any to save trouble, is to send to the baker's for half a quartern of dough (which will make a great many), and then you have only the trouble of boiling it.

To make Norfolk Dumplings.

Mix a good thick batter, as for pancakes; take half a pint of milk, two eggs, a little salt, and make it into a batter with flour; have ready a clean sauce-pan of water boiling, into which drop this batter; be sure the water boils fast, and two or three minutes will boil them; then throw them into a sieve to drain the water away; then turn them into a dish, and stir a lump of fresh butter into them; eat them hot, and they are very good.

To make Hard Dumplings.

Mix flour and water with a little salt, like a paste, roll them in balls as big as a turkey's egg, roll them in a little flour, have the water boiling, throw them in the water, and half an hour will boil them: they are best boiled with a good piece of beef. You may add for change a few currants; have melted butter in a cup.

Another Way to make Hard Dumplings.

Rub into your flour first a good piece of butter, then make it like a crust for a pie; make them up, and boil them as above.

To make Apple Dumplings.

Make a good puff-paste, pare some large apples, cut them in quarters, and take out the cores very nicely; take a piece of crust, and roll it round enough for one apple; if they are big, they will not look pretty; so roll the crust round each apple, and make them round like a ball, with a little flour in your hand; have a pot of water boiling, take a clean cloth, dip it in the water and shake flour over it; tie each dumpling

by

by itself, and put them in the water boiling, which keep boiling all the time; and if your crust is light and good, and the apples not too large, half an hour will boil them; but if the apples be large, they will take an hour's boiling; when they are enough, take them up and lay them in a dish; throw fine sugar all over them, and send them to table; have good fresh butter melted in a cup, and fine beaten sugar in a saucer.

Another Way to make Apple Dumplings.

MAKE a good puff-paste crust, roll it out a little thicker than a crown-piece, pare some large apples and core them with an apple-scoop; fill the hole with beaten cinnamon, coarse or fine sugar, and lemon-peel shred fine, and roll every apple in a piece of this paste, tie them close in a cloth separate, boil them an hour, cut a little piece of the top off, pour in some melted butter, and lay on your piece of crust again; lay them in a dish, and throw fine sugar all over.

To make Raspberry Dumplings.

MAKE a good cold paste, roll it a quarter of an inch thick, and spread over it raspberry-jam to your own liking, roll it up and boil it in a cloth one hour at least; take it up and cut it in five slices, and lay one in the middle and the other four round it; pour a little good melted butter in the dish, and grate fine sugar round the edge of the dish. It is proper for a corner or side for dinner.

Citron Puddings.

TAKE half a pint of cream, mix in it a spoonful of fine flour, two ounces of sugar, a little grated nutmeg, and the yolks of three eggs beat well, put it in tea-cups, and stick two ounces of citron cut very thin in it; bake them in a quick oven, and turn them out on a dish.

To make a Cheese-Curd Florendine.

TAKE two pounds of cheese-curd, break it all to pieces with your hand, a pound of blanched almonds finely pounded, with a little rose-water, half a pound of currants clean washed and picked, a little sugar to your palate, some stewed spinage cut small; mix all well together, lay a puff-paste in a dish, put in your ingredients, cover it with a thin crust rolled and laid across, and bake it in a moderate oven half an hour: as to the top-crust lay it in what shape you please, either rolled or marked with an iron on purpose.

A Florendine of Oranges or Apples.

GET half a dozen of Seville oranges, save the juice, take out the pulp, lay them in water twenty-four hours, shift them three

three or four times, then boil them in three or four waters, then drain them from the water, put them in a pound of sugar, and their juice, boil them to a syrup, take great care they do not stick to the pan you do them in, and set them by for use; when you use them lay a puff-paste all over the dish, boil ten pippins, pared, quartered, and cored, in a little water and sugar, and slice two of the oranges and mix with the pippins in the dish; bake it in a slow oven with a crust as above: or just bake the crust, and lay in the ingredients.

To make an Artichoke Pie.

BOIL twelve artichokes, take off all the leaves and chokes, take the bottoms clear from the stalk, make a good puff-paste crust, and lay a quarter of a pound of good fresh butter all over the bottom of your pie; then lay a row of artichokes, strew a little pepper, salt, and beaten mace over them; then another row, and strew the rest of your spice over them; put in a quarter of a pound more of butter in little bits, take half an ounce of truffles and morels, boil them in a quarter of a pint of water, pour the water into the pie, cut the truffles and morels very small, throw all over the pie; then have ready twelve eggs boiled hard, take only the hard yolks, lay them all over the pie, pour in a gill of white wine, cover your pie, and bake it: when the crust is done, the pie is enough: four large blades of mace and twelve pepper-corns well beat will do, with a tea-spoonful of salt.

To make a sweet Egg Pie.

MAKE a good crust, cover your dish with it, then have ready twelve eggs boiled hard, cut them in slices and lay them in your pie, throw half a pound of currants clean washed and picked all over the eggs, then beat up four eggs well mixed with half a pint of white wine, grate in a small nutmeg, and make it pretty sweet with sugar. You are to mind to lay a quarter of a pound of butter between the eggs, then pour in your wine and eggs and cover your pie; bake it half an hour, or till the crust is done.

To make a Potatoe Pie.

BOIL three pounds of potatoes, peel them, make a good crust and lay in your dish; lay at the bottom half a pound of butter, then lay in your potatoes, throw all over them first three tea-spoonfuls of salt and a small nutmeg grated, next six eggs boiled hard and chopped fine, then a tea-spoonful of pepper and half a pint of white wine; cover your pie, and bake it half an hour, or till the crust is enough.

To make an Onion Pie.

WASH and pare some potatoes and cut them in slices, peel some onions, cut them in slices, pare some apples and slice them, make a good crust, cover your dish, lay a quarter of a pound of butter all over, take a quarter of an ounce of mace beat fine, a nutmeg grated, a tea-spoonful of beaten pepper, three tea-spoonfuls of salt; mix all together, strew some over the butter, lay a layer of potatoes, a layer of onions, a layer of apples, and a layer of eggs, and so on till you have filled your pie, strewing a little of the seasoning between each layer, and a quarter of a pound of butter in bits, and six spoonfuls of water; close your pie, and bake it an hour and a half. A pound of potatoes, a pound of onions, a pound of apples, and twelve eggs will do.

To make an Orangeado Pie.

MAKE a good crust, lay it over your dish, take two oranges, boil them with two lemons till tender, in four or five quarts of water; in the last water (of which there must be about a pint), add a pound of loaf sugar, boil it, take them out and slice them into your pie; then pare twelve pippins, core them, and give them one boil in the syrup; lay them all over the orange and lemon, pour in the syrup, and pour on them some orangeado syrup; cover your pie, and bake it in a slow oven half an hour.

To make a Vegetable Pie.

TAKE cauliflowers broken into neat pieces, white cabbage cut into small quantities, a few heads of celery neatly cut, a few small onions and potatoes peeled, and some endive (if white and not bitter); boil these separately in milk and water, drain and keep them hot; raise the walls of your pie; fill it with something to support it, and lay on the lid, bake it sufficiently to stand, but not quite enough; take off the lid, lay in the vegetables neatly in rows thus—a row of cauliflower, a row of onions, &c. add Cayenne, salt, and beaten mace as you go on, then put on your lid again; bake your pie half an hour more, take care not to burn it; have ready good fricassee-sauce, take off the lid, pour over it the sauce, and serve it up without the lid.

To make a Skirret Pie.

TAKE your skirrets and boil them tender, peel them, slice them, fill your pie, and take to half a pint of cream the yolk of an egg, beat fine with a little nutmeg, a little beaten mace, and a little salt; beat all together well, with a quarter of a pound of fresh butter melted, then pour in as much as your dish will hold,

hold, put on the top-cruft and bake it half an hour. You may put in fome hard yolks of eggs; if you cannot get cream, put in milk, but cream is beft: about two pounds of the root will do.

To make an Apple Pie.

MAKE a good puff-pafte cruft, lay fome round the fides of the difh, pare and quarter your apples and take out the cores, lay a row of apples thick, throw in half the fugar you defign for your pie, mince a little lemon-peel fine, throw over, and fqueeze a little lemon over them, then a few cloves, here and there one, then the reft of your apples and the reft of your fugar; you muft fweeten to your palate, and fqueeze a little more lemon; boil the peeling of the apples and the cores in fome fair water with a blade of mace, till it is very good; ftrain it, and boil the fyrup with a little fugar till there is but very little and good, pour it into your pie, put on your upper cruft and bake it. You may put in a little quince or marmalade (if you pleafe).

Thus make a pear pie, but do not put in any quince. You may butter them when they come out of the oven: or beat up the yolks of two eggs and half a pint of cream with a little nutmeg, fweetened with fugar; put it over a flow fire and keep ftirring it till it juft boils up, take off the lid and pour in the cream; cut the cruft in little three-corner pieces, ftick about the pie, and fend it to table cold.

Green Codling Pie.

TAKE fome green codlings and put them in a clean pan with fpring-water; lay vine or cabbage leaves over them, and wrap a cloth over and round the pan to keep in the fteam; as foon as you think they are foft take the fkins off, put them in the fame water with the leaves over them, hang them a good diftance from the fire to green; and as foon as you fee them of a fine green, take them out of the water and put them in a deep difh, and fweeten them with fugar, and ftrew a little lemon-peel fhred fine over, put a lid of puff-pafte over them and bake it; when it is baked, cut the lid off, and cut it into three-corner pieces and put them round your pie, with one corner uppermoft; let it ftand till it is cold, and then make the following cream: boil a pint of cream or milk, beat up the yolks of four eggs, fweeten it with fine fugar, mix all well together and put it over the fire till it is thick and fmooth; but be fure you do not let it boil, for that will curdle it, and put it over your codlings; or you may put clouted cream (if you like it beft) and fend it to table cold.

To make a Cherry Pie.

MAKE a good cruſt, lay a little round the ſides of your diſh, throw ſugar at the bottom, and lay in your fruit and ſugar at top. A few red currants do well with them; put on your lid, and bake in a ſlack oven.

Make a plum pie the ſame way, and a gooſeberry pie. If you would have it red, let it ſtand a good while in the oven after the bread is drawn. A cuſtard is very good with the gooſeberry pie.

To make a Salt Fiſh Pie.

GET a ſide of ſalt fiſh, lay it in water all night, next morning put it over the fire in a pan of water till it is tender, drain it and lay it on the dreſſer, take off all the ſkin, and pick the meat clean from the bones, mince it ſmall, then take the crumb of two French rolls cut in ſlices, and boil it up with a quart of new milk, break your bread very fine with a ſpoon, put to it your minced ſalt fiſh, a pound of melted butter, two ſpoonfuls of minced parſley, half a nutmeg grated, a little beaten pepper, and three tea-ſpoonfuls of muſtard; mix all well together, make a good cruſt and lay all over your diſh, and cover it up: bake it an hour.

To make a Carp Pie.

TAKE a large carp, ſcale, waſh, and gut it clean; take an eel, boil it juſt a little tender, pick off all the meat, and mince it fine with an equal quantity of crumbs of bread, a few ſweet herbs, a lemon-peel cut fine, a little pepper, ſalt, and grated nutmeg, an anchovy, half a pint of oyſters parboiled and chopped fine, the yolks of three hard eggs cut ſmall, roll it up with a quarter of a pound of butter, and fill the belly of the carp; make a good cruſt, cover the diſh, and lay in your carp; ſave the liquor you boil your eel in, put in the eel bones, boil them with a little mace, whole pepper, an onion, ſome ſweet herbs, and an anchovy; boil it till there is about half a pint, ſtrain it, add to it a quarter of a pint of white wine, and a lump of butter as big as a hen's egg, mixed in a very little flour; boil it up, and pour into your pie; put on the lid, and bake it an hour in a quick oven. If there be any force-meat left after filling the belly, make balls of it, and put into the pie; if you have not liquor enough, boil a few ſmall eels to make enough to fill your diſh.

To make a Seal Pie.

MAKE a good cruſt, cover your diſh, boil two pounds of eels tender, pick all the fleſh clean from the bones; throw the bones into the liquor you boil the eels in, with a little mace and salt, till it is very good, and about a quarter of a pint, then strain it; in the meantime cut the shell of your eel fine, with a little lemon-peel shred fine, a little salt, pepper, and nutmeg, a few crumbs of bread, chopped parsley, and an anchovy; melt a quarter of a pound of butter and mix with it, then lay it in the dish, cut the flesh off a pair of large soals, or three pair of very small ones, clean from the bones and fins, lay it on the force-meat, and pour in the broth of the eels you boiled; put the lid of the pie on, and bake it. You should boil the bones of the soals with the eel bones, to make it good; if you boil the soal bones with one or two little eels, without the force-meat, your pie will be very good. And thus you may do a turbot.

To make an Eel Pie.

MAKE a good crust; clean, gut, and wash your eels very well, then cut them in pieces half as long as your finger; season them with pepper, salt, and a little beaten mace to your palate, either high or low; fill your dish with eels, and put as much water as the dish will hold; put on your cover, and bake them well.

To make a Flounder Pie.

GUT some flounders, wash them clean, dry them in a cloth, just boil them, cut off the meat clean from the bones, lay a good crust over the dish, and lay a little fresh butter at the bottom, and on that the fish; season with pepper and salt to your mind; boil the bones in the water your fish was boiled in, with a little bit of horse-radish, a little parsley, a very little bit of lemon-peel, and a crust of bread; boil it till there is just enough of liquor for the pie, then strain it, and put it into your pie; put on the top-crust, and bake it.

To make a Herring Pie.

SCALE, gut, and wash them very clean, cut off the heads, fins, and tails; make a good crust, cover your dish, then season your herrings with beaten mace, pepper, and salt; put a little butter in the bottom of your dish, then a row of herrings, pare some apples and cut them in thin slices all over, then peel some onions and cut them in slices all over thick, lay a little butter on the top, put in a little water, lay on the lid, and bake it well.

To make a Salmon Pie.

MAKE a good crust, cleanse a piece of salmon well, season it with salt, mace, and nutmeg, lay a piece of butter at the
bottom

bottom of the dish, and lay your salmon in; melt butter according to your pie; take a lobster, boil it, pick out all the flesh, chop it small, bruise the body, mix it well with the butter, which must be very good; pour it over your salmon, put on the lid, and bake it well.

To make a Lobster Pie.

TAKE two or three lobsters and boil them; take the meat out of the tails whole, cut them in four pieces, longways; take out the spawn and the meat of the claws, beat it well in a mortar; season it with pepper, salt, two spoonfuls of vinegar, and a little anchovy liquor; melt half a pound of fresh butter, stir all together with the crumbs of a halfpenny roll rubbed through a fine cullender, and the yolks of two eggs; put a fine puff-paste over your dish, lay in your tails, and the rest of the meat over them; put on your cover, and bake it in a slow oven.

To make a Muscle Pie.

MAKE a good crust, lay it all over the dish, wash your muscles clean in several waters, then put them in a deep stew-pan, cover them and let them stew till they are open, pick them out, and see there be no crabs under the tongue; put them in a sauce-pan with two or three blades of mace, strain liquor just enough to cover them, a good piece of butter, and a few crumbs of bread; stew them a few minutes, fill your pie, put on the lid, and bake it half an hour. So you make an oyster pie; always let your fish be cold before you put on the lid, or it will spoil the crust.

To make Lent Mince-Pies.

SIX eggs boiled hard and chopped fine, twelve pippins pared and chopped small, a pound of raisins of the sun stoned and chopped fine, a pound of currants washed, picked, and rubbed clean, a large spoonful of sugar beat fine, an ounce of citron, an ounce of candied orange, both cut fine, a quarter of an ounce of mace and cloves and a little nutmeg beat fine; mix all together with a gill of brandy and a gill of sack; make your crust good, and bake it in a slack oven: when you make your pie, squeeze in the juice of a Seville orange.

Fish Pasties the Italian Way.

TAKE some flour and knead it with oil; take a slice of salmon, season it with pepper and salt, and dip into sweet oil; chop an onion and parsley fine and strew over it; lay it in the paste, and double it up in the shape of a slice of salmon; take a piece of white paper, oil it and lay under the pasty, and bake it: it is best cold, and will keep a month.

Mackarel done the same way, head and tail together folded in a pasty, eats fine.

To roast a Pound of Butter.

LAY it in salt and water two or three hours, then spit it and rub it all over with crumbs of bread, with a little grated nutmeg, lay it to the fire, and, as it roasts, baste it with the yolks of two eggs and then with crumbs of bread all the time it is roasting; but have ready a pint of oysters stewed in their own liquor, and lay in the dish under the butter; when the bread has soaked up all the butter, brown the outside, and lay it on your oysters. Your fire must be very slow.

CHAP. XV.

DIRECTIONS FOR THE SICK.

[I do not pretend to meddle here in the Physical Way; but a few Directions for the Cook, or Nurse, I presume, will not be improper, to make such a Diet, &c, as the Doctor shall order.]

To make Mutton Broth.

TAKE a pound of loin of mutton, take off the fat, put to it one quart of water, let it boil and skim it well; then put in a good piece of upper-crust of bread, and one large blade of mace; cover it close and let it boil slowly an hour; do not stir it, but pour the broth clear off; season it with a little salt, and the mutton will be fit to eat. If you boil turnips, do not boil them in the broth, but by themselves in another sauce-pan.

To boil a Scrag of Veal.

SET on the scrag in a clean sauce-pan; to each pound of veal put a quart of water, skim it very clean, then put in a good piece of upper-crust, a blade of mace to each pound, and a little parsley tied with a thread; cover it close; then let it boil very softly two hours, and both broth and meat will be fit to eat.

To make Beef or Mutton Broth for very weak People, who take but little Nourishment.

TAKE a pound of beef or mutton, or both together; to a pound put two quarts of water, first skin the meat and take off the fat; then cut it into little pieces, and boil it till it comes to a quarter of a pint; season it with a very little corn of salt, skim off all the fat, and give a spoonful of this broth at a time; to very weak people half a spoonful is enough; to some a tea-spoonful at a time; and to others a tea-cupful: there is greater nourishment from this than any thing else.

To make Beef-Drink, which is ordered for weak People.

TAKE a pound of lean beef, then take off all the fat and skin, cut it into pieces, put it into a gallon of water with the under-crust of a penny loaf, and a very little salt; let it boil till it comes to two quarts, then strain it off; and it is a very hearty drink.

To make Beef Tea.

TAKE a pound of lean beef and cut it very fine, pour a pint of boiling water over it and put it on the fire to raise the scum; skim it clean, strain it off and let it settle; pour it clear from the settling, and then it is fit for use.

To make Pork Broth.

TAKE two pounds of young pork, then take off the skin and fat, boil it in a gallon of water with a turnip, and a very little corn of salt; let it boil till it comes to two quarts, strain it off and let it stand till cold; take off the fat, then leave the settling at the bottom of the pan, and drink half a pint in the morning fasting, an hour before breakfast; and noon, if the stomach will bear it.

To boil a Chicken.

LET your sauce-pan be very clean and nice; when the water boils put in your chicken, which must be very nicely picked and clean, and laid in cold water a quarter of an hour before it is boiled; then take it out of the water boiling, and lay it in a pewter dish; save all the liquor that runs from it in the dish; cut up your chicken all in joints in the dish; then bruise the liver very fine, add a little boiled parsley chopped fine, a very little salt, and a little grated nutmeg; mix it all well together with two spoonfuls of the liquor of the fowl, and pour it into the dish with the rest of the liquor in the dish; if there is not liquor enough, take two or three spoonfuls of the liquor it was boiled in, clap another dish over it; then set it over a chafing-dish of hot coals five or six minutes, and carry it to table hot with the cover on. This is better than butter, and lighter for the stomach, though some choose it only with the liquor, and no parsley nor liver, and that is according to different palates: if it is for a very weak person, take off the skin of the chicken

before

before you set it on the chafing-dish. If you roast it, make nothing but bread-sauce, and that is lighter than any sauce you can make for a weak stomach.

Thus you may dress a rabbit, only bruise but a little piece of the liver.

To boil Pigeons.

LET your pigeons be cleaned, washed, drawn, and skinned; boil them in milk and water ten minutes, and pour over them sauce made thus: take the livers parboiled and bruise them fine, with as much parsley boiled and chopped fine; melt some butter, mix a little with the liver and parsley first, then mix all together, and pour over the pigeons.

To boil a Partridge, or any other Wild Fowl.

WHEN your water boils put in your partridge, let it boil ten minutes; then take it up into a pewter plate, and cut it in two, laying the insides next the plate, and have ready some bread-sauce made thus: take the crumb of a halfpenny roll, or thereabouts, and boil it in half a pint of water, with a blade of mace; let it boil two or three minutes, pour away most of the water; then beat it up with a little piece of nice butter, a little salt, and pour it over your partridge; clap a cover over it, then set it over a chafing-dish of coals four or five minutes, and send it away hot, covered close.

Thus you may dress any sort of wild fowl, only boiling it more or less according to the bigness. Ducks, take off the skins before you pour the bread-sauce over them; and if you roast them, lay bread-sauce under them: it is lighter than gravy for weak stomachs.

To boil a Plaice or Flounder.

LET your water boil, throw some salt in; then put in your fish; boil it till you think it is enough, and take it out of the water in a slice to drain; take two spoonfuls of the liquor, with a little salt, a little grated nutmeg; then beat up the yolk of an egg very well with the liquor, and stir in the egg; beat it well together, with a knife carefully slice away all the little bones round the fish, pour the sauce over it; then set it over a chafing-dish of coals for a minute, and send it hot away: or in the room of this sauce, add melted butter in a cup.

To mince Veal or Chicken for the Sick, or weak People.

MINCE a chicken, or some veal, very fine, take off the skin; just boil as much water as will moisten it, and no more, with a very little salt, grate a very little nutmeg; then throw a little flour over it, and when the water boils put in the meat; keep

shaking

MADE PLAIN AND EASY.

shaking it about over the fire a minute; then have ready two or three very thin sippets, toasted nice and brown, laid in the plate, and pour the mince-meat over it.

To pull a Chicken for the Sick.

You must take as much cold chicken as you think proper, take off the skin, and pull the meat into little bits as thick as a quill; then take the bones, boil them with a little salt till they are good, strain it, then take a spoonful of the liquor, a spoonful of milk, a little bit of butter as big as a large nutmeg rolled in flour, a little chopped parsley as much as will lie on a sixpence, and a little salt, if wanted, (this will be enough for half a small chicken,) put all together into the sauce-pan, then keep shaking it till it is thick, and pour it into a hot plate.

To make Chicken Broth.

You must take an old cock, or large fowl, flay it, then pick off all the fat, and break it all to pieces with a rolling-pin; put it into two quarts of water with a good crust of bread and a blade of mace, let it boil softly till it is as good as you would have it; if you do it as it should be done, it will take five or six hours doing; pour it off, then put a quart more of boiling water, cover it close, let it boil softly till it is good, and strain it off; season with a very little salt. When you boil a chicken, save the liquor; and when the meat is eat, take the bones, then break them, and put to the liquor you boiled the chicked in, with a blade of mace, and a crust of bread, let it boil till it is good, and strain it off.

To make Chicken Water.

Take a cock or large fowl, flay it, then bruise it with a hammer and put it into a gallon of water with a crust of bread, let it boil half away, and strain it off.

To make White Caudle.

You must take two quarts of water, mix in four spoonfuls of oatmeal, a blade or two of mace, a piece of lemon-peel, let it boil, and keep stirring it often: let it boil about a quarter of an hour, and take care it does not boil over; then strain it through a coarse sieve: when you use it, sweeten it to your palate, grate in a little nutmeg, and what wine is proper; and if it is not for a sick person, squeeze in the juice of a lemon.

To make Brown Caudle.

Boil the gruel as above, with six spoonfuls of oatmeal, and strain it; then add a quart of good ale, not bitter; boil it, then

sweeten

sweeten it to your palate, and add half a pint of white wine: when you do not put in white wine, let it be half ale.

To make Water-Gruel.

You must take a pint of water and a large spoonful of oatmeal; then stir it together and let it boil up three or four times, stirring it often; do not let it boil over; then strain it through a sieve, salt it to your palate, put in a good piece of fresh butter, brew it with a spoon till the butter is all melted, then it will be fine and smooth, and very good: some love a little pepper in it.

To make Panado.

You must take a quart of water in a nice clean sauce-pan, a blade of mace, a large piece of crumb of bread; let it boil two minutes; then take out the bread and bruise it in a bason very fine; mix as much water as will make it as thick as you would have it; the rest pour away, and sweeten it to your palate; put in a piece of butter as big as a walnut; do not put in any wine, it spoils it: you may grate in a little nutmeg. This is hearty and good diet for sick people.

To boil Sago.

Put a large spoonful of sago into three quarters of a pint of water, stir it, and boil it softly till it is as thick as you would have it; then put in wine and sugar, with a little nutmeg to your palate.

To boil Salop.

It is a hard stone ground to powder, and generally sold for one shilling an ounce: take a large tea-spoonful of the powder and put it into a pint of boiling water, keep stirring it till it is like a fine jelly; then put in wine and sugar to your palate, and lemon, if it will agree.

To make Isinglass Jelly.

Take a quart of water, one ounce of isinglass, half an ounce of cloves; boil them to a pint, then strain it upon a pound of loaf-sugar, and when cold sweeten your tea with it: you may make the jelly as above, and leave out the cloves; sweeten to your palate, and add a little wine. All other jellies you have in another Chapter.

To make the Pectoral Drink.

Take a gallon of water and half a pound of pearl-barley, boil it with a quarter of a pound of figs split, a pennyworth of liquorice sliced to pieces, a quarter of a pound of raisins of the

sun

sun stoned; boil all together till half is wasted, then strain it off. This is ordered in the measles, and several other disorders, for a drink.

To make Buttered Water, or what the Germans call Egg-Soup, who are very fond of it for Supper. You have it in the Chapter for Lent.

TAKE a pint of water, beat up the yolk of an egg with the water, put in a piece of butter as big as a small walnut, two or three knobs of sugar, and keep stirring it all the time it is on the fire; when it begins to boil, bruise it between the saucepan and a mug till it is smooth and has a great froth; then it is fit to drink. This is ordered in a cold, or where eggs will agree with the stomach.

To make Seed-Water.

TAKE a spoonful of coriander-seed, half a spoonful of caraway-seed, bruised and boiled in a pint of water; then strain it, and bruise it with the yolk of an egg: mix it with sack and double-refined sugar, according to your palate.

To make Bread-Soup for the Sick.

TAKE a quart of water, set it on the fire in a clean saucepan, and as much dry crust of bread cut to pieces as the top of a penny loaf (the drier the better) a bit of butter as big as a walnut; let it boil, then beat it with a spoon, and keep boiling it till the bread and water is well mixed; then season it with a very little salt, and it is a pretty thing for a weak stomach.

To make artificial Asses Milk.

TAKE two ounces of pearl-barley, two large spoonfuls of hartshorn-shavings, one ounce of eringo-root, one ounce of China-root, one ounce of preserved ginger, eighteen snails bruised with the shells, to be boiled in three quarts of water till it comes to three pints, then boil a pint of new milk, mix it with the rest, and put in two ounces of balsam of Tolu. Take half a pint in the morning, and half a pint at night.

Cows Milk, next to Asses Milk, done thus.

TAKE a quart of milk, set it in a pan over night, the next morning take off all the cream, then boil it and set it in the pan again till night; then skim it again, boil it, set it in the pan again, and the next morning skim it, warm it blood warm, and drink it as you do asses milk: it is very near as good, and with some consumptive people it is better.

To make a good Drink.

BOIL a quart of milk and a quart of water, with the top-cruſt of a penny loaf, and one blade of mace, a quarter of an hour very ſoftly, then pour it off, and when you drink it let it be warm.

To make Barley-Water.

PUT a quarter of a pound of pearl-barley into two quarts of water, let it boil, ſkim it very clean, boil half away, and ſtrain it off; ſweeten to your palate, but not too ſweet, and put in two ſpoonfuls of white wine; drink it lukewarm.

To make Sage-Tea.

TAKE a little ſage, a little baum, put it into a pan, ſlice a lemon, peel and all, a few knobs of ſugar, one glaſs of white wine, pour on theſe two or three quarts of boiling water, cover it, and drink when thirſty; when you think it ſtrong enough of the herbs, take them out, otherwiſe it will make it bitter.

To make it for a Child.

A LITTLE ſage, baum, rue, mint, and penny-royal, pour boiling water on, and ſweeten to your palate. Syrup of cloves, &c. and black cherry-water, you have in the Chapter of Preſerves.

Liquor for a Child that has the Thruſh.

TAKE half a pint of ſpring-water, a knob of double-refined ſugar, a very little bit of alum, beat it well together with the yolk of an egg, then beat it in a large ſpoonful of the juice of ſage; tie a rag to the end of a ſtick, dip it in this liquor, and often clean the mouth. Give the child over night one drop of laudanum, and the next day proper phyſic, waſhing the mouth often with the liquor.

To boil Comfrey-Roots.

TAKE a pound of comfrey-roots, ſcrape them clean, cut them into little pieces, and put them into three pints of water, let them boil till there is about a pint, then ſtrain it, and when it is cold put it into a ſauce-pan; if there is any ſettling at the bottom, throw it away; mix it with ſugar to your palate, add half a pint of mountain wine and the juice of a lemon, let it boil, then pour it into a clean earthen pot, and ſet it by for uſe. Some boil it with milk, and it is very good where it will agree, and is reckoned a very great ſtrengthener.

To make the Knuckle Broth.

TAKE twelve ſhank-ends of a leg of mutton, break them well and ſoak them in cold ſpring-water for an hour, then take a ſmall a small brush and scour them clean with warm water and salt, then put them into two quarts of spring-water and let them simmer till reduced to one quart; when they have been on one hour, put in one ounce of hartshorn-shavings and the bottom of a halfpenny-roll; be careful to take the scum off as it rises; when done, strain it off, and if any fat remains, take it off with a knife when cold; drink a quarter of a pint warm when you go to bed, and one hour before you rise: it is a certain restorative at the beginning of a decline, or when any weakness is the complaint.

N. B. If it is made right, it is the colour of calf's foot jelly, and is strong enough to bear a spoon upright. [From the College of Physicians, London.]

A Medicine for a Disorder in the Bowels.

TAKE an ounce of beef-suet, half a pint of milk, and half a pint of water, mix together with a table-spoonful of wheat-flour, put it over the fire ten minutes, and keep it stirring all the time; and take a coffee-cupful two or three times a-day.

CHAP. XVI.
For CAPTAINS of SHIPS.

(Many of the Receipts in this Chapter are very useful in Families.)

To make Catchup to keep twenty Years.

TAKE a gallon of strong stale beer, one pound of anchovies washed from the pickle, a pound of shalots peeled, half an ounce of mace, half an ounce of cloves, a quarter of an ounce of whole pepper, three or four large races of ginger, two quarts of the large mushroom-flaps rubbed to pieces; cover all this close, and let it simmer till it is half wasted, then strain it through a flannel bag; let it stand till it is quite cold, then bottle it. You may carry it to the Indies. A spoonful of this to a pound of fresh butter melted makes a fine fish-sauce, or in the room of gravy sauce. The stronger and staler the beer is, the better the catchup will be.

To make Fish-Sauce to keep the whole Year.

YOU must take twenty-four anchovies, chop them, bones and all, put to them ten shalots cut small, a handful of scraped horse-radish, a quarter of an ounce of mace, a quart of white wine, a pint of water, one lemon cut into slices, half a pint of anchovy liquor, a pint of red wine, twelve cloves, twelve pepper-corns; boil them together till it comes to a quart; strain it off, cover it close, and keep it in a cold dry place. Two spoonfuls will be sufficient for a pound of butter.

It is a pretty sauce either for boiled fowl, veal, &c. or in the room of gravy, lowering it with hot water, and thickening it with a piece of butter rolled in flour.

To put Dripping to fry Fish, Meat, Fritters, &c.

TAKE six pounds of good beef-dripping, boil it in soft water, strain it into a pan, let it stand till cold; then take off the hard fat, and scrape off the gravy which sticks to the inside; thus do eight times; when it is cold and hard, take it off clean from the water, put it into a large sauce-pan with six bay-leaves, twelve cloves, half a pound of salt, and a quarter of a pound of whole pepper; let the fat be all melted and just hot, let it stand till it is hot enough to strain through a sieve into the pot, and stand till it is quite cold, then cover it up: thus you may do what quantity you please. The best way to keep any sort of dripping is to turn the pot upside down, and then no rats can get at it. If it will keep on ship-board, it will make as fine puff-paste crust as any butter can do, or crust for puddings, &c.

To pickle Mushrooms for the Sea.

WASH them clean with a piece of flannel in salt and water, put them into a sauce-pan and throw a little salt over them; let them boil up three times in their own liquor, then throw them into a sieve to drain, and spread them on a clean cloth; let them lie till cold, then put them in wide-mouthed bottles, put in with them a good deal of whole mace, a little nutmeg sliced, and a few cloves: boil the sugar-vinegar of your own making with a good deal of whole pepper, some races of ginger, and two or three bay-leaves; let it boil a few minutes, then strain it, when it is cold pour it on and fill the bottle with mutton-fat fried; cork them, tie a bladder, then a leather over them, keep it down close, and in as cool a place as possible. As to all other pickles, you have them in the Chapter of Pickles.

To make Mushroom Powder.

TAKE half a peck of fine large thick mushrooms, wash them clean from grit and dirt with a flannel rag, scrape out the inside, cut out all the worms, put them into a kettle over the fire without any water, two large onions stuck with cloves, a large handful of salt, a quarter of an ounce of mace, two tea-spoonfuls of beaten pepper, let them simmer till the liquor is boiled away; take great care they do not burn; then lay them
on

on sieves to dry in the sun, or in tin plates, and set them in a slack oven all night to dry, till they will beat to powder: press the powder down hard in a pot, and keep it for use. You may put what quantity you please for the sauce.

To keep Mushrooms without Pickle.

TAKE large mushrooms, peel them, scrape out the inside, put them into a sauce-pan, throw a little salt over them, and let them boil in their own liquor, then throw them into a sieve to drain, then lay them on tin plates and set them in a cool oven; repeat it often till they are perfectly dry, put them into a clean stone jar, tie them down tight, and keep them in a dry place. They eat deliciously, and look as well as truffles.

To keep Artichoke-Bottoms dry.

BOIL them just so as you can pull off the leaves and the choke, cut them from the stalks, lay them on tin plates, set them in a very cool oven, and repeat it till they are quite dry; then put them in a paper bag, tie them up close, and hang them up, and always keep them in a dry place; and when you use them lay them in warm water till they are tender; shift the water two or three times. They are fine in almost all sauces cut in little pieces, and put in just before your sauce is enough.

To fry Artichoke-Bottoms.

LAY them in water as above, then have ready some butter hot in a pan, flour the bottoms and fry them; lay them in your dish and pour melted butter over them.

To ragoo Artichoke-Bottoms.

TAKE twelve bottoms, soften them in warm water, as in the foregoing receipts; take half a pint of water, a piece of the strong soup, as big as a small walnut, half a spoonful of the catchup, five or six of the dried mushrooms, a tea-spoonful of the mushroom powder, set it on the fire, shake all together and let it boil softly two or three minutes; let the last water you put to the bottoms boil; take them out hot, lay them in your dish, pour the sauce over them, and send them to table hot.

To dress Fish.

As to frying fish, first wash it very clean, then dry it well and flour it; take some of the beef-dripping, make it boil in the stew-pan, then throw in your fish, and fry it of a fine light brown; lay it on the bottom of a sieve, or coarse cloth, to drain, and make sauce according to your fancy.

T

To bake Fish.

BUTTER the pan, lay in the fish, throw a little salt over it and flour; put a very little water in the dish, an onion, and a bundle of sweet herbs, stick some little bits of butter, or the fine dripping, on the fish; let it be baked of a fine light brown; when enough, lay it on a dish before the fire, and skim off all the fat in the pan; strain the liquor and mix it up either with the fish-sauce or strong soup, or the catchup.

To make a Gravy-Soup.

ONLY boil soft water, and put as much of the strong soup to it as will make it to your palate; let it boil, and if it wants salt, you must season it. The receipts for the soup you have in the Chapter for Soups.

To make Peas-Soup.

GET a quart of peas, boil them in two gallons of water till they are tender, then have ready a piece of salt pork, or beef, which has been laid in water the night before, put it into the pot, with two large onions pealed, a bundle of sweet herbs, celery (if you have it), half a quarter of an ounce of whole pepper; let it boil till the meat is enough, then take it up, and if the soup is not enough, let it boil till the soup is good; then strain it, set it on again to boil, and rub in a good deal of dry mint; keep the meat hot; when the soup is ready, put in the meat again for a few minutes and let it boil, then serve it away: if you add a piece of the portable soup, it will be very good. The onion-soup you have in the Lent Chapter.

To make a Pudding of Pork, Beef, &c.

MAKE a good crust with the dripping, or mutton-suet (if you have it) shred fine; make a thick crust, take a piece of salt pork or beef which has been twenty-four hours in soft water, season it with a little pepper, put it into this crust, roll it up close, tie it in cloth, and boil it; if of about four or five pounds, boil it five hours.

And when you kill mutton, make a pudding the same way, only cut the steaks thin; season them with pepper and salt, and boil it three hours, if large; or two hours, if small; and so according to the size.

Apple-pudding make with the same crust, only pare the apples, core them, and fill your pudding; if large, it will take five hours boiling; when it is enough, lay it in the dish, cut a hole in the top and stir in butter and sugar; lay the piece on again, and send it to table.

A prune-

A prune-pudding eats fine made the same way, only when the crust is ready fill it with prunes, and sweeten it according to your fancy, close it up, and boil it two hours.

To make a Rice-Pudding.

TAKE what rice you think proper, tie it loose in a cloth, and boil it an hour; then take it up and untie it, grate a good deal of nutmeg in, stir in a good piece of butter, and sweeten to your palate; tie it up close, boil it an hour more, then take it up and turn it into your dish; melt butter, with a little sugar, and a little white wine for sauce.

To make a Suet-Pudding.

GET a pound of suet shred fine, a pound of flour, a pound of currants picked clean, half a pound of raisins stoned, two tea-spoonfuls of beaten ginger, and a spoonful of tincture of saffron; mix all together with salt water very thick; then either boil or bake it.

A Liver-Pudding boiled.

GET the liver of the sheep, when you kill one, and cut it as thin as you can, and chop it; mix it with as much suet shred fine, half as many crumbs of bread or biscuit grated, season it with some sweet herbs shred fine, a little nutmeg grated, a little beaten pepper, and an anchovy shred fine; mix all together with a little salt, or the anchovy liquor, with a piece of butter, fill the crust and close it; boil it three hours.

To make an Oatmeal-Pudding.

GET a pint of oatmeal once cut, a pound of suet shred fine, a pound of currants, and half a pound of raisins stoned; mix all together well with a little salt, tie it in a cloth, leaving room for the swelling.

To bake an Oatmeal-Pudding.

BOIL a quart of water, season it with a little salt; when the water boils, stir in the oatmeal till it is so thick you cannot easily stir your spoon: then take it off the fire, stir in two spoonfuls of brandy, or a gill of mountain, and sweeten it to your palate; grate in a little nutmeg, and stir in half a pound of currants, clean washed and picked; then butter a pan, pour it in, and bake it half an hour.

A Rice Pudding baked.

BOIL a pound of rice just till it is tender, then drain all the water from it as dry as you can, but do not squeeze it; then stir in a good piece of butter, and sweeten to your palate;

grate a small nutmeg in, stir it all well together, butter a pan, and pour it in and bake it: you may add a few currants for change.

To make a Peas-Pudding.

BOIL it till it is quite tender, then take it up, untie it, stir in a good piece of butter, a little salt, and a good deal of beaten pepper, then tie it up tight again, boil it an hour longer, and it will eat fine. All other puddings you have in the Chapter of Puddings.

To make a Harrico of French Beans.

TAKE a pint of the seeds of French beans which are ready dried for sowing, wash them clean and put them into a two-quart sauce-pan, fill it with water, and let them boil two hours; if the water wastes away too much, you must put in more boiling water to keep them boiling; in the meantime take almost half a pound of nice fresh butter, put it into a clean stew-pan, and when it is all melted, and done making any noise, have ready a pint bason heaped up with onions peeled and sliced thin, throw them into the pan and fry them of a fine brown, stirring them about that they may be all alike, then pour off the clear water from the beans into a bason, and throw the beans all into the stew-pan; stir all together, and throw in a large tea-spoonful of beaten pepper, two heaped full of salt, and stir it all together for two or three minutes. You may make this dish of what thickness you think proper (either to eat with a spoon or otherwise) with the liquor you poured off the beans. For change you may make it thin enough for soup. When it is of the proper thickness you like it, take it off the fire, and stir in a large spoonful of vinegar and the yolk of two eggs beat. The eggs may be left out if disliked. Dish it up and send it to table.

To make a Fowl Pie.

FIRST make rich thick crust, cover the dish with the paste, then take some very fine bacon, or cold boiled ham, slice it, and lay a layer all over; season with a little pepper, then put in the fowl, after it is picked and cleaned, and singed; shake a very little pepper and salt into the belly, put in a little water, cover it with ham seasoned with a little beaten pepper, put on the lid and bake it two hours: when it comes out of the oven, take half a pint of water, boil it, and add to it as much of the strong soup as will make the gravy quite rich, pour it boiling hot into the pie, and lay on the lid again; send it to table hot. Or lay a piece of beef or pork in soft water twenty-four hours, slice it in the room of the ham, and it will eat fine.

To make a Cheshire Pork Pie for Sea.

TAKE some salt pork that has been boiled, cut it into thin slices, an equal quantity of potatoes pared and sliced thin, make a good crust, cover the dish, lay a layer of meat seasoned with a little pepper, and a layer of potatoes, then a layer of meat, a layer of potatoes, and so on till your pie is full; season it with pepper when it is full, lay some butter on the top, and fill your dish above half full of soft water; close your pie up, and bake it in a gentle oven.

To make Sea Venison.

WHEN you kill a sheep, keep stirring the blood all the time till it is cold, or at least as cold as it will be, that it may not congeal; then cut up the sheep, take one side, cut the leg like a haunch, cut off the shoulder and loin, the neck and breast in two, steep them all in the blood as long as the weather will permit you, then take out the haunch and hang it out of the sun as long as you can to be sweet, and roast it as you do a haunch of venison; it will eat very fine, especially if the heat will give you leave to keep it long. Take off all the suet before you lay it in the blood, take the other joints and lay them in a large pan, pour over them a quart of red wine and a quart of rape vinegar; lay the fat side of the meat downwards in the pan, (on a hollow tray is best,) and pour the wine and vinegar over it; let it lie twelve hours, then take the neck, breast, and loin out of the pickle; let the shoulder lie a week, if the heat will let you, rub it with bay-salt, saltpetre, and coarse sugar, of each a quarter of an ounce, one handful of common salt, and let it lie a week or ten days: bone the neck, breast, and loin; season them with pepper and salt to your palate, and make a pasty as you do for venison: boil the bones for gravy to fill the pie when it comes out of the oven; and the shoulder boil fresh out of the pickle with a peas-pudding.

And when you cut up the sheep, take the heart, liver, and lights, boil them a quarter of an hour, then cut them small, and chop them very fine, season them with four large blades of mace, twelve cloves, and a large nutmeg, all beat to powder; chop a pound of suet fine, half a pound of sugar, two pounds of currants clean washed, half a pint of red wine; mix all well together and make a pie; bake it an hour: it is very rich.

To make Dumplings when you have White Bread.

TAKE the crumb of a two-penny loaf grated fine, as much beef-suet shred as fine as possible, a little salt, half a small nutmeg grated, a large spoonful of sugar, beat two eggs with two spoonfuls of sack; mix all well together, and roll them up as big as a turkey's egg; let the water boil and throw them in: half an hour will boil them. For sauce, melt butter with a little salt, lay the dumplings in a dish, pour the sauce over them, and strew sugar all over the dish.

These are very pretty either at land or sea. You must observe to rub your hands with flour when you make them up.

The portable soup to carry abroad, you have in the Twelfth Chapter.

To make Chouder, a Sea Dish.

TAKE a belly-piece of pickled pork, slice off the fatter parts, and lay them at the bottom of the kettle, strew over it onions and such sweet herbs as you can procure; take a middling large cod, bone and slice it as for crimping, pepper, salt, allspice, and flour it a little; make a layer with part of the slices, upon that a slight layer of pork again, and on that a layer of biscuit, and so on, pursuing the like rule until the kettle is filled to about four inches; cover it with nice paste, pour in about a pint of water, lute down the cover of the kettle, and let the top be supplied with live wood embers: keep it over a slow fire about four hours. When you take it up lay it in the dish, pour in a glass of hot Maderia wine, and a very little India pepper; if you have oysters, or truffles or morels, it is still better; thicken it with butter. Observe, before you put this sauce in, to skim the stew, and then lay on the crust, and send it to table reverse as in the kettle; cover it close with the paste, which should be brown.

CHAP. XVII.

Of HOGS'-PUDDINGS, SAUSAGES, &c.

To make Almond Hogs'-Puddings.

TAKE two pounds of beef-suet or marrow shred very small, a pound and a half of almonds blanched and beat very fine with rose-water, one pound of grated bread, a pound and a quarter of fine sugar, a little salt, half an ounce of mace, nutmeg, and cinnamon together, twelve yolks of eggs, four whites, a pint of sack, a pint and a half of thick cream, some rose or orange-flower water; boil the cream, tie the saffron in a bag and dip in the cream to colour it; first beat your eggs very well, then stir in your almonds, then the spice, the salt, and suet, and mix all your ingredients together; fill he guts but half full, put some bits of citron in the guts as you fill them, tie them up, and boil them a quarter of an hour.

Another Way.

TAKE a pound of beef-marrow chopped fine, half a pound of sweet almonds blanched and beat fine with a little orange-flower or rose water, half a pound of white bread grated fine, half a pound of currants clean washed and picked, a quarter of a pound of fine sugar, a quarter of an ounce of mace, nutmeg, and cinnamon together, of each an equal quantity, and half a pint of sack; mix all well together with half a pint of good cream, and the yolks of four eggs; fill the guts half full, tie them up, and boil them a quarter of an hour, and prick them as they boil to keep the guts from breaking. You may leave out the currants for change, but then you must add a quarter of a pound more of sugar.

A third Way.

HALF a pint of cream, a quarter of a pound of sugar, a quarter of a pound of currants, the crumb of a halfpenny roll grated fine, six large pippins pared and chopped fine, a gill of sack, or two spoonfuls of rose-water, six bitter almonds blanched and beat fine, the yolks of two eggs, and one white beat fine; mix all together, fill the guts better than half full, and boil them a quarter of an hour.

To make Hogs'-Puddings with Currants.

TAKE three pounds of grated bread to four pounds of beef-suet finely shred, two pounds of currants clean picked and washed, cloves, mace, and cinnamon, of each a quarter of an ounce finely beaten, a little salt, a pound and a half of sugar, a pint of sack, a quart of cream, a little rose-water, twenty eggs well beaten, but half the whites; mix all these well together, fill the guts half full, boil them a little, and prick them as they boil to keep them from breaking the guts; take them up upon clean cloths, then lay them on your dish; or when you use them, boil them a few minutes, or eat them cold.

To make Black Puddings.

FIRST, before you kill your hog, get a peck of grits, boil them half an hour in water, then drain them, and put them into a clean tub or large pan; then kill your hog, and save two quarts of the blood of the hog, and keep stirring it till the blood is quite cold, then mix it with your grits, and stir them well together; season with a large spoonful of salt, a quarter of an ounce of cloves, mace, and nutmeg together, an equal quantity of each; dry it, beat it well, and mix in; take a little winter-savoury, sweet-marjoram, and thyme, penny-royal stripped of the stalks, and chopped very fine; just enough to season them and to give them a flavour, but no more. The next day take the leaf of the hog and cut into dice, scrape and wash the guts very clean, then tie one end, and begin to fill them; mix in the fat as you fill them, be sure put in a good deal of fat, fill the skins three parts full, tie the other end, and make your puddings what length you please; prick them with a pin, and put them in a kettle of boiling water; boil them very softly an hour, then take them out and lay them on clean straw.

In Scotland they make a pudding with the blood of a goose: chop off the head and save the blood, stir it till it is cold, then mix it with grits, spice, salt, and sweet herbs, according to their fancy, and some beef-suet chopped; take the skin off the neck, then pull out the windpipe and fat, fill the skin, tie it at both ends, so make a pie of the giblets, and lay the pudding in the middle: or you may leave the grits out (if you please).

Savoloys.

TAKE six pounds of young pork, free it from bone and skin, and salt it with one ounce of salt-petre, and a pound of common salt, for two days; chop it very fine, put in three tea-spoonfuls of pepper, twelve sage leaves chopped fine, and a pound of grated bread; mix it well, and fill the guts, and bake them half an hour in a slack oven, and eat either hot or cold.

To make fine Sausages.

YOU must take six pounds of good pork free from skin, gristles, and fat, cut it very small, and beat it in a mortar till it is very fine; then shred six pounds of beef-suet very fine and free from all skin; shred it as fine as possible: take a good deal of sage, wash it very clean, pick off the leaves, and shred it very fine; spread your meat on a clean dresser or table, then shake the sage all over, about three large spoonfuls; shred the thin rind of a middling lemon very fine and throw over, with as many sweet herbs (when shred fine) as will fill a large spoon; grate two nutmegs over, throw over two tea-spoonfuls of pepper, a large spoonful of salt, then throw over the suet and mix it all well together; put it down close in a pot; when you use them, roll them up with as much egg as will make them roll smooth; make them the size of a sausage, and fry them in butter, or good dripping; be sure it be hot before you put them in, and keep rolling them about: when they are thorough hot and of a fine light brown, they are enough. You may chop this meat very fine, if you do not like it beat. Veal eats well done thus, or veal and pork together: you may clean some guts and fill them.

To make common Sausages.

TAKE three pounds of nice pork, fat and lean together, without skin or gristles, chop it as fine as possible, season it with a tea-spoonful of beaten pepper and two of salt, some sage shred fine, about three tea-spoonfuls; mix it well together, have the guts very nicely cleaned and fill them, or put them down in a pot, so roll them of what size you please, and fry them. Beef makes very good sausages.

Oxford Sausages.

TAKE a pound of lean veal, a pound of young pork, fat and lean, free from skin and gristle, a pound of beef suet, chopped all fine together; put in half a pound of grated bread, half the peel of a lemon shred fine, a nutmeg grated, six sage leaves washed and chopped very fine, a tea-spoonful of pepper and two of salt, some thyme, savoury, and marjoram shred fine; mix it all well together, and put it close down in a pan: when you use it, roll it out the size of a common sausage, and fry them in fresh butter of a fine brown, or broil them over a clear fire, and send them to table as hot as possible.

To make Bologna Sausages.

TAKE a pound of bacon, fat and lean together, a pound of beef, a pound of veal, and a pound of pork, a pound of beef-suet, cut them small and chop them fine, take a small handful of sage, pick off the leaves, chop it fine with a few sweet herbs; season pretty high with pepper and salt. You must have a large gut, and fill it, then set on a sauce-pan of water, when it boils put it in, and prick the gut for fear of bursting: boil it softly an hour, then lay it on clean straw to dry.

To make Hamburgh Sausages.

TAKE a pound of beef, mince it very small, with half a pound of the best suet; then mix three quarters of a pound of suet cut in large pieces; then season it with pepper, cloves, nutmeg, a great quantity of garlic cut small, some white wine vinegar, some bay-salt and common salt, a glass of red wine, and one of rum; mix all these very well together, then take the largest gut you can find, stuff it very tight; then hang it up in a chimney, and smoke it with saw-dust for a week or ten days; hang them in the air till they are dry, and they will keep a year. They are very good boiled in peas-pottage, and roasted with toasted bread under it, or in an amlet.

Sausages

Sausages after the German Way.

TAKE the crumb of a two-penny loaf, one pound of suet, half a lamb's lights, a handful of parsley, some thyme, marjoram, and onion, mince all very small, then season it with salt and pepper: these must be stuffed in a sheep's gut; they are fried in oil or melted suet, and are only fit for immediate use.

CHAP. XVIII.

To POT AND MAKE HAMS, &c. &c.

Observations on preserving Salt Meat, so as to keep it mellow and fine for three or four Months; and to preserve Potted Butter.

TAKE care when you salt your meat in the summer that it be quite cool after it comes from the butcher's; the way is, to lay it on cold bricks for a few hours, and when you salt it, lay it upon an inclining board to drain off the blood; then salt it afresh, add to every pound of salt half a pound of Lisbon sugar, and turn it in the pickle every day; at the month's end it will be fine. The salt which is commonly used hardens and spoils all the meat; the right sort is that called Lowndes's salt, it comes from Nantwich in Cheshire; there is a very fine sort that comes from Malden in Essex, and from Suffolk, which is the reason of that butter being finer than any other; and if every body would make use of that salt in potting butter, we should not have so much bad come to market; observing all the general rules of a dairy. If you keep your meat long in salt, half the quantity of sugar will do; and then bestow loaf sugar, it will eat much finer. This pickle cannot be called extravagant, because it will keep a great while; at three or four months end, boil it up; if you have no meat in the pickle, skim it, and when cold, only add a little more salt and sugar to the next meat you put in, and it will be good a twelvemonth longer.

Take a leg-of-mutton-piece, veiny or thick flank-piece without any bone, pickled as above, only add to every pound of salt an ounce of salt-petre; after being a month or two in the pickle, take it out and lay it in soft water a few hours, then roast it; it eats fine. A leg of mutton or shoulder of veal does the same. It is a very good thing where a market is at a

great

great distance, and a large family obliged to provide a great deal of meat.

As to the pickling of hams and tongues, you have the receipt in the foregoing Chapters; but use either of these fine salts, and they will be equal to any Bayonne hams, provided your porkling is fine and well fed.

To pot Pigeons or Fowls.

CUT off their legs, draw them and wipe them with a cloth, but do not wash them; season them pretty well with pepper and salt, put them into a pot with as much butter as you think will cover them, when melted, and baked very tender; then drain them very dry from the gravy; lay them on a cloth, and that will suck up all the gravy; season them again with salt, mace, cloves, and pepper beaten fine, and put them down close into a pot; take the butter, when cold, clear from the gravy, set it before the fire to melt, and pour over the birds; if you have not enough, clarify some more, and let the butter be near an inch thick above the birds. Thus you may do all sorts of fowl; only wild fowl should be boned (but that you may do as you please).

To pot a cold Tongue, Beef, or Venison.

CUT it small, beat it well in a marble mortar with melted butter, season it with mace, cloves, and nutmeg, beat very fine, and some pepper and salt, till the meat is mellow and fine; then put it down close in your pots, and cover it with clarified butter. Thus you may do cold wild fowl; or you may pot any sort of cold fowl whole; seasoning them with what spice you please.

To pot Venison.

TAKE a piece of venison, fat and lean together, lay it in a dish, and stick pieces of butter all over; tie brown paper over it, and bake it; when it comes out of the oven take it out of the liquor hot, drain it, and lay it in a dish; when cold, take off all the skin, and beat it in a marble mortar, fat and lean together, season it with mace, cloves, nutmeg, black pepper, and salt to your mind; when the butter is cold that it was baked in, take a little of it and beat in with it to moisten it; then put it down close, and cover it with clarified butter. You must be sure to beat it till it is like a paste.

To pot a Hare.

TAKE a hare that has hung four or five days, case it, and cut it in quarters; put it in a pot, season it with pepper, salt, and mace, and a pound of butter over it, and bake it four

hours;

hours; when it comes out, pick it from the bones, and pound it in a mortar with the butter that comes off your gravy, and a little beaten cloves and mace, till it is fine and smooth, then put it close down in potting pots, and put clarified butter over it; tie it over with white paper.

To pot Tongues.

TAKE a neat's tongue, rub it with a pound of white salt, an ounce of salt-petre, half a pound of coarse sugar, rub it well, turn it every day in this pickle for a fortnight: this pickle will do several tongues, only adding a little more white salt; or we generally do them after our hams. Take the tongues out of the pickle, cut off the root, and boil it well till it will peel; then take your tongues and season them with salt, pepper, cloves, mace, and nutmeg, all beat fine; rub it well with your hands whilst it is hot; then put it in a pot, and melt as much butter as will cover it all over; bake it an hour in the oven, then take it out, let it stand to cool, rub a little fresh spice on it; and when it is quite cold, lay it in your pickling-pot; when the butter is cold you baked it in, take it off clean from the gravy, set it in an earthen pan before the fire, and when it is melted, pour it over the tongue. You may lay pigeons or chickens on each side; be sure to let the butter be about an inch above the tongue.

A fine Way to pot a Tongue.

TAKE a dried tongue, boil it till it is tender, then peel it; take a large fowl, bone it; a goose, and bone it; take a quarter of an ounce of mace, a quarter of an ounce of cloves, a large nutmeg, a quarter of an ounce of black pepper, beat all well together; a spoonful of salt; rub the inside of the fowl well, and the tongue; put the tongue into the fowl; then season the goose, and fill the goose with the fowl and tongue, and the goose will look as if it was whole; lay it in a pan that will just hold it, melt fresh butter enough to cover it, send it to the oven, and bake it an hour and a half; then uncover the pot and take out the meat; carefully drain it from the butter, lay it on a coarse cloth till it is cold, and when the butter is cold, take off the hard fat from the gravy, and lay it before the fire to melt, put your meat into the pot again, and pour the butter over; if there is not enough, clarify more, and let the butter be an inch above the meat; and this will keep a great while, eats fine, and looks beautiful: when you cut it, it must be cut crossways down through, and looks very pretty: it makes a pretty corner-dish at table, or side-dish for supper: if you cut a slice down the middle quite through, lay it in a plate, and

garnish

garnish with green parsley and nastertium-flowers. If you will be at the expence, bone a turkey, and put over the goose. Observe, when you pot it, to save a little of the spice to throw over it, before the last butter is put on, or the meat will not be seasoned enough.

To pot Beef like Venison.

CUT the lean of a buttock of beef into pound pieces; for eight pounds of beef take four ounces of salt-petre, four ounces of petre-salt, a pint of white salt, and an ounce of sal-prunella; beat the salts all very fine, mix them well together, rub the salts into the beef; then let it lie four days, turning it twice a day, then put it into a pan, cover it with pump-water and a little of its own brine: then bake it in an oven with household bread till it is as tender as a chicken, then drain it from the gravy, and bruise it abroad, and take out all the skin and sinews; then pound it in a marble mortar, then lay it in a broad dish, mix in it an ounce of cloves and mace, three quarters of an ounce of pepper, and one nutmeg, all beat very fine; mix it all very well with the meat, then clarify a little fresh butter and mix with the meat to make it a little moist; mix it very well together, press it down into pots very hard, set it at the oven's mouth just to settle, and cover it two inches thick with clarified butter: when cold, cover it with white paper.

To pot Cheshire Cheese.

TAKE three pounds of Cheshire cheese, and put it into a mortar with half a pound of the best fresh butter you can get, pound them together, and in the beating add a gill of rich Canary wine, and half an ounce of mace finely beat, then sifted like a fine powder; when all is extremely well mixed, press it hard down into a gallipot, cover it with clarified butter, and keep it cool. A slice of this excels all the cream cheese that can be made.

To pot Ham with Chickens.

TAKE as much lean of a boiled ham as you please, and half the quantity of fat, cut it as thin as possible, beat it very fine in a mortar, with a little oiled butter, beaten mace, pepper, and salt, put part of it into a China pot, then beat the white part of a fowl with a very little seasoning; it is to qualify the ham; put a lay of chicken, then one of ham, then chicken at the top, press it hard down, and when it is cold, pour clarified butter over it; when you send it to the table, cut out a thin slice in the form of half a diamond, and lay it round the edge of your pot.

To pot Woodcocks.

PLUCK six woodcocks, draw out the train, skewer their bills through their thighs, and put the legs through each other, and their feet upon their breasts; season them with three or four blades of mace, and a little pepper and salt; then put them into a deep pot with a pound of butter over them, tie a strong paper over them, and bake them in a moderate oven; when they are enough, lay them on a dish to drain the gravy from them, then put them into potting pots, and take all the clear butter from your gravy and put it upon them, and fill up your pots with clarified butter, and keep them in a dry place.

To pot red and black Moor-Game.

PLUCK and draw them, and season them with pepper, cloves, mace, ginger, and nutmeg, well beaten and sifted, with a quantity of salt not to overcome the spices, roll a lump of butter in the seasoning, and put it into the body of the fowls, rub the outside with seasoning, and then put them into pots with the breast downwards and cover them with butter, lay a paper and then a paste over them, and bake them till they are tender; then take them out and lay them to drain, then put them into potting pots with the breast upwards, and take all the butter they were baked in clean from the gravy and pour upon them; fill up the pots with clarified butter, and keep them in a dry place.

To pot all Kinds of small Birds.

PICK and gut your birds, dry them well with a cloth, season them with mace, pepper, and salt, then put them into a pot with butter, tie your pot down with paper, and bake them in a moderate oven; when they come out, drain the gravy from them, and put them into potting pots, and cover them with clarified butter.

To save potted Birds that begin to be bad.

I HAVE seen potted birds, which have come a great way, often smell so bad that no body could bear the smell for the rankness of the butter, and by managing them in the following manner have made them as good as ever was eat:

Set a large sauce-pan of clean water on the fire, when it boils, take off the butter at the top, then take the fowls out one by one, throw them into that sauce-pan of water half a minute, whip it out and dry it in a clean cloth inside and out; so do all till they are quite done; scald the pot clean; when the birds are quite cold, season them with mace, pepper, and salt to your mind, pot them down close in a pot, and pour clarified butter over them.

To pot Charrs.

AFTER having cleanſed them, cut off the fins, tails, and heads, then lay them in rows in a long baking-pan; cover them with butter, and order them as above.

To pot a Pike.

YOU muſt ſcale it, cut off the head, ſplit it, and take out the chine-bone, then ſtrew all over the inſide ſome bay-ſalt and pepper, roll it up round, and lay it in a pot; cover it, and bake it an hour; then take it out and lay it on a coarſe cloth to drain; when it is cold, put it into your pot and cover it with clarified butter.

To pot Salmon.

TAKE a piece of freſh ſalmon, ſcale it, and wipe it clean, (let your piece or pieces be as big as will lie cleverly on your pot,) ſeaſon it with Jamaica pepper, black pepper, mace, and cloves, beat fine, mixed with ſalt, a little ſal-prunella beat fine, and rub the bone with; ſeaſon with a little of the ſpice, pour clarified butter over it, and bake it well; then take it out carefully, and lay it to drain; when cold, ſeaſon it well, lay it in your pot cloſe, and cover it with clarified butter as above.

Thus you may do carp, tench, trout, and ſeveral ſorts of fiſh.

Another Way to pot Salmon.

SCALE and clean your ſalmon, cut it down the back, dry it well, and cut it as near the ſhape of your pot as you can; take two nutmegs, an ounce of mace and cloves beaten, half an ounce of white pepper, and an ounce of ſalt; then take out all the bones, cut off the jowl below the fins, and cut off the tail; ſeaſon the ſcaly ſide firſt, lay that at the bottom of the pot; then rub the ſeaſoning on the other ſide, cover it with a diſh, and let it ſtand all night: it muſt be put double, and the ſcaly ſide top and bottom; put butter bottom and top, and cover the pot with ſome ſtiff coarſe paſte: three hours will bake it, if a large fiſh; if a ſmall one, two hours; and when it comes out of the oven, let it ſtand half an hour; then uncover it, and raiſe it up at one end that the gravy may run out, then put a trencher and a weight on it to preſs out the gravy: when the butter is cold, take it out clear from the gravy, add ſome more to it, and put it in a pan before the fire; when it is melted, pour it over the ſalmon; and when it is cold, paper it up. As to the ſeaſoning of theſe things, it muſt be according to your palate, more or leſs.

N. B. Always take great care that no gravy or whey of the butter is left in the potting; if there is, it will not keep.

To pot a Lobster.

Take a live lobster, boil it in salt and water, and peg it that no water gets in; when it is cold, pick out all the flesh and body, take out the gut, beat it fine in a mortar, and season it with beaten mace, grated nutmeg, pepper, and salt; mix all together; melt a piece of butter as big as a large walnut, and mix it with the lobster as you are beating it; when it is beat to a paste, put it into your potting pot, and put it down as close and hard as you can; then set some fresh butter in a deep broad pan before the fire, and when it is all melted, take off the scum at the top (if any), and pour the clear butter over the meat as thick as a crown piece; the whey and churn-milk will settle at the bottom of the pan, but take care none of that goes in, and always let your butter be very good, or you will spoil all; or only put the meat whole, with the body mixed among it, laying them as close together as you can, and pour the butter over them. You must be sure to let the lobster be well boiled. A middling one will take half an hour boiling.

To pot Eels.

Take a large eel, skin it, cleanse it, and wash it very clean, dry it in a cloth, and cut it into pieces as long as your finger; season them with a little beaten mace and nutmeg, pepper, salt, and a little sal-prunella beat fine; lay them in a pan, then pour as much good butter over them as will cover them, and clarified as above: they must be baked half an hour in a quick oven; if a slow oven, longer, till they are enough, but that you must judge by the largeness of the eels: with a fork take them out, and lay them on a coarse cloth to drain; when they are quite cold, season them again with the same seasoning, lay them in the pot close; then take off the butter they were baked in clear from the gravy of the fish, and set it in a dish before the fire; when it is melted, pour the clear butter over the eels, and let them be covered with the butter.

In the same manner you may pot what you please. You may bone your eels, if you choose it; but then do not put in any sal-prunella.

To pot Lampreys.

Skin them, cleanse them with salt, then wipe them dry; beat some black pepper, mace, and cloves, mix them with salt, and season them; lay them in a pan, and cover them with clarified butter; bake them an hour; order them as the eels, only let them be seasoned, and one will be enough for a pot: you must season them well; let your butter be good, and they will keep a long time.

To collar a Breaſt of Veal.

TAKE a breaſt of veal and bone it, beat it with a rolling-pin, rub it over with the yolk of an egg, beat a little mace, cloves, nutmeg, and pepper very fine, with a little ſalt, a handful of parſley, and ſome ſweet herbs, and lemon-peel ſhred fine, a few crumbs of bread; mix all together and ſtrew over; roll it up very tight, bind it with a filler, and wrap it in a cloth, then boil it two hours and a half in water made pretty ſalt, then hang it up by one end till cold: make a pickle: to a pint of ſalt and water put half a pint of vinegar, and lay it in a pan, and let the pickle cover it; and when you uſe it, cut it in ſlices, and garniſh with parſley and pickles.

To make Marble Veal.

TAKE a neat's tongue and boil it till tender; peel it and cut it in ſlices, and beat it in a mortar with a pound of butter, with a little beaten mace and pepper, till it is like a paſte; have ſome veal ſtewed and beat in the ſame manner; put ſome veal in a potting-pot, then ſome tongue in lumps over the veal, then ſome veal over that, tongue over that, and then veal again; preſs it down hard, pour ſome clarified butter over it, keep it in a cold dry place, and when you uſe it, cut it in ſlices, and garniſh with parſley.

To collar Beef.

TAKE a piece of thin flank of beef and bone it, cut the ſkin off, then ſalt it with two ounces of ſalt-petre, two ounces of ſal-prunella, two ounces of bay-ſalt, half a pound of coarſe ſugar, and two pounds of white ſalt, beat the hard ſalts fine, and mix all together; turn it every day, and rub it with the brine well, for eight days; then take it out of the pickle, waſh it and wipe it dry; then take a quarter of an ounce of cloves, and a quarter of an ounce of mace, twelve corns of all-ſpice, and a nutmeg beat very fine, with a ſpoonful of beaten pepper, a large quantity of chopped parſley, with ſome ſweet herbs chopped fine; ſprinkle it on the beef, and roll it up very tight, put a coarſe cloth round, and tie it very tight with beggar's tape; boil it in a large copper of water; if a large collar, ſix hours, a ſmall one, five hours; take it out and put it in a preſs till cold; if you have never a preſs, put it between two boards, and a large weight upon it till it is cold; then take it out of the cloth and cut it into ſlices: Garniſh with raw parſley.

To collar a Pig.

KILL your pig, dreſs off the hair, draw out the entrails, and waſh it clean, take a ſharp knife, rip it open and take out all the bones, then rub it all over with pepper and salt beaten fine, a few sage leaves and sweet herbs chopped small, then roll up your pig tight, and bind it with a fillet, then fill your boiler with soft water, one pint of vinegar, and a handful of salt, eight or ten cloves, a blade or two of mace, a few pepper-corns, and a bunch of sweet herbs; when it boils put in your pig, and boil it till it is tender, then take it up, and when it is almost cold, bind it over again, and put it into an earthen pot, and pour the liquor your pig was boiled in upon it, keep it covered, and it is fit for use.

To callar Swine's Face.

CHOP the face in many places, and wash it in several waters, then boil it till the meat will leave the bones, take out the bones, cut open the ears, and take out the ear-roots, cut the meat in pieces, and season it with pepper and salt; while it is hot put it into an earthen pot, but put the ears round the outside of the meat, put a board on that will go on the inside of the pot, and set a heavy weight upon it, and let it stand all night, the next day turn it out, cut it round-ways, and it will look close and bright.

To collar Salmon.

TAKE a side of salmon, cut off a handful of the tail, wash your large piece very well, dry it with a clean cloth, wash it over with the yolks of eggs, and then make force-meat with what you cut off the tail; but take off the skin, and put to it a handful of parboiled oysters, a tail or two of lobsters, the yolks of three or four eggs, boiled hard, six anchovies, a handful of sweet herbs chopped small, a little salt, cloves, mace, nutmeg, pepper beat fine, and grated bread; work all these together into a body, with the yolks of eggs, lay it all over the fleshy part, and a little more pepper and salt over the salmon; so roll it up into a collar, and bind it with broad tape, then boil it in water, salt, and vinegar, but let the liquor boil first; then put in your collars, a bunch of sweet herbs, sliced ginger, and nutmeg; let it boil, but not too fast: it will take near two hours boiling: when it is enough, take it up into your sousing-pan, and when the pickle is cold, put it to your salmon, and let it stand in it till used, or otherwise you may pot it. Fill it up with clarified butter, as you pot fowls: that way will keep longest.

To collar Eels.

TAKE your eel and scour it well with salt, wipe it clean; then cut it down the back, take out the bone, cut the head and tail off; put the yolk of an egg over it, and then take four

cloves,

cloves, two blades of mace, half a nutmeg beat fine, a little pepper and salt, some chopped parsley, and sweet herbs chopped very fine; mix them all together and sprinkle over it, roll the eel up very tight, and tie it in a cloth; put on water enough to boil it, and put in an onion, some cloves and mace, four bay-leaves; boil it up with the bones, head, and tail for half an hour, with a little vinegar and salt; then take out the bones, &c. and put in your eels, boil them if large two hours, lesser in proportion; when done, put them away to cool; then take them out of the liquor and cloth, and cut them in slices, or send them whole, with raw parsley under and over.

N. B. You must take them out of the cloth, and put them in the liquor, and tie them close down to keep.

To collar Mackerel.

GUT and slit your mackerel down the belly, cut off the head, take out the bones, take care you do not cut it in holes, then lay it flat upon its back, season it with mace, nutmeg, pepper, and salt, and a handful of parsley shred fine, strew it over them, roll them tight, and tie them well separately in cloths, boil them gently twenty minutes in vinegar, salt, and water, then take them out, put them into a pot, pour the liquor on them, or the cloth will stick to the fish, the next day take the cloth off your fish, put a little more vinegar to the pickle, keep them for use; when you send them to the table, garnish with fennel and parsley, and put some of the liquor under them.

To make Dutch Beef.

TAKE the lean of a buttock of beef raw, rub it well with brown sugar all over, and let it lie in a pan or tray two or three hours, turning it two or three times, then salt it well with common salt and salt-petre, and let it lie a fortnight, turning it every day; then roll it very strait in a coarse cloth, put it in a cheese-press a day and a night, and hang it to dry in a chimney: when you boil it, you must put it in a cloth; when it is cold, it will cut in slivers as Dutch beef.

To make Sham Brawn.

TAKE the belly piece and head of a young porker, rub it well with salt-petre, let it lie three or four days, wash it clean; boil the head, and take off all the meat and cut it in pieces, have four neat's feet boiled tender, take out the bones, cut it in thin slices, mix it with the head, lay it in the belly-piece, roll it up tight, bind it round with sheeting, and boil it four hours; take it up and set it on one end, put a trencher on it within the tin, and a large weight upon that, and let it stand all night; in the morning take it out and bind it with a fillet; put it in spring-water and salt, and it will be fit for use: when you use it, cut it in slices like brawn. Garnish with parsley. Observe to change the pickle every four or five days, and it will keep a long time.

To souce a Turkey in imitation of Sturgeon.

You must take a fine large turkey, dress it very clean, dry and bone it, then tie it up as you do sturgeon, put into the pot you boil it in one quart of white wine, one quart of water, one quart of good vinegar, a very large handful of salt; let it boil, skim it well, and then put in the turkey; when it is enough, take it out and tie it tighter; let the liquor boil a little longer; and if you think the pickle wants more vinegar or salt, add it when it is cold, and pour it upon the turkey; it will keep some months, covering it close from the air, and keeping it in a dry cool place. Eat it with oil, vinegar, and sugar (just as you like it); some admire it more than sturgeon; it looks pretty covered with fennel for a side-dish.

To pickle Pork.

Bone your pork, cut it into pieces of a size fit to lie in the tub or pan you design it to lie in, rub your pieces well with salt-petre, then take two parts of common salt, and two of bay-salt, and rub every piece well; lay a layer of common salt in the bottom of your vessel, cover every piece over with common salt, lay them one upon another as close as you can, filling the hollow places on the sides with salt; as your salt melts on the top strew on more, lay a coarse cloth over the vessel, a board over that, and a weight on the board to keep it down; keep it close covered; it will, thus ordered, keep the whole year; put a pound of salt-petre and two pounds of bay-salt to a hog.

A Pickle for Pork which is to be eat soon.

You must take two gallons of pump-water, one pound of bay-salt, one pound of coarse sugar, six ounces of salt-petre; boil it all together, and skim it when cold; cut the pork in what pieces you please, lay it down close, and pour the liquor over it; lay a weight on it to keep it close, and cover it close from the air, and it will be fit to use in a week: if you find the pickle begins to spoil, boil it again and skim it; when it is cold, pour it on your pork again.

The Jews' Way to pickle Beef, which will go good to the West Indies, and keep a Year good in the Pickle, and with Care will go to the East Indies.

Take any piece of beef without bones, or take the bones out, if you intend to keep it above a month; take mace, cloves, nutmeg,

nutmeg, and pepper, and juniper-berries beat fine, and rub the beef well, mix salt and Jamaica pepper and bay-leaves; let it be well seasoned, let it lie in this seasoning a week or ten days, throw in a good deal of garlic and shalot; boil some of the best white wine vinegar, lay your meat in a pan or good vessel for the purpose with the pickle; and when the vinegar is quite cold, pour it over, cover it close; if it is for a voyage, cover it with oil, and let the cooper hoop up the barrel very well. This is a good way in a hot country where meat will not keep; then it must be put into the vinegar directly with the seasoning, then you may either roast it or stew it, but it is best stewed; and add a good deal of onion and parsley chopped fine, some white wine, a little catch-up, truffles and morels, a little good gravy, a piece of butter rolled in flour, or a little oil, in which the shalot and onions ought to stew a quarter of an hour before the other ingredients are put in; then put all in, and stir it together, and let it stew till you think it is enough. This is a good pickle in a hot country to keep beef or veal, that is dressed to eat cold.

Pickled Beef for present Use.

TAKE the rib of beef, stick it with garlic and cloves, season it with salt, Jamaica pepper, mace, and some garlic pounded; cover the meat with white wine vinegar and Spanish thyme; you must take care to turn the meat every day, and add more vinegar, (if required,) for a fortnight; then put it in a stew-pan, and cover it close, and let it simmer on a slow fire for six hours, adding vinegar and white wine; (if you choose) you may stew a good quantity of onions, it will be more palatable.

To preserve Tripe to go to the East Indies.

GET a fine belly of tripe, quite fresh, take a four gallon cask well hooped, lay in your tripe, and have your pickle ready, made thus: take seven quarts of spring-water, and put as much salt into it as will make an egg swim, that the little end of the egg may be about an inch above the water (you must take care to have the fine clear salt, for the common salt will spoil it); add a quart of the best white wine vinegar, two sprigs of rosemary, an ounce of all-spice, pour it on your tripe; let the cooper fasten the cask down directly; when it comes to the Indies it must not be opened till it is just going to be dressed, for it will not keep after the cask is opened; the way to dress it is, lay it in water half an hour, then fry it or boil as we do here.

The Jews Way of preserving Salmon, and all Sorts of Fish.

TAKE either salmon, cod, or any large fish, cut off the head, wash it clean, and cut it in slices as crimped cod is, dry it very well in a cloth, then flour it, and dip it in yolks of eggs, and fry it in a great deal of oil till it is of a fine brown and well done; take it out, and lay it to drain till it is very dry and cold. Whitings, mackarel, and flat-fish are done whole: when they are quite dry and cold lay them in your pan or vessel, throw in between them a good deal of mace, cloves, and sliced nutmeg, a few bay-leaves; have your pickle ready, made of the best white wine vinegar, in which you must boil a great many cloves of garlic and shalot, black and white pepper, Jamaica and long pepper, juniper-berries, and salt; when the garlic begins to be tender the pickle is enough; when it is quite cold pour it on your fish, and a little oil on the top: they will keep good a twelvemonth, and are to be eat cold with oil and vinegar: they will go good to the East Indies. All sorts of fish fried well in oil, eat very fine cold with shalot, or oil and vinegar. Observe in the pickling of your fish, to have the pickling ready; first put a little pickle in, then a layer of fish, then pickle, then a little fish, and so lay them down very close to be well covered; put a little saffron in the pickle. Frying fish in common oil is not so expensive with care; for present use a little does, and if the cook is careful not to burn the oil, or black it, it will fry them two or three times.

To pickle Oysters, Cockles, and Muscles.

TAKE two hundred oysters, the newest and best you can get, be careful to save the liquor in some pan as you open them, cut off the black verge, saving the rest, put them into their own liquor; then put all the liquor and oysters into a kettle, boil them about half an hour on a very gentle fire, do them very slowly, skimming them as the scum rises, then take them off the fire, take out the oysters, strain the liquor through a fine cloth, then put in the oysters again, then take out a pint of the liquor whilst it is hot, put thereto three quarters of an ounce of mace, and half an ounce of cloves; just give it one boil, then put it to the oysters, and stir up the spices well among them; then put in about a spoonful of salt, three quarters of a pint of the best white wine vinegar, and a quarter of an ounce of whole pepper; then let them stand till they are cold; then put the oysters, as many as you well can into the barrel; put in as much liquor as the barrel will hold, letting them settle a while, and they will soon be fit to eat. Or you may put them in stone-jars, cover them close with a bladder and leather, and be sure they be quite cold before you cover them up. Thus do cockles and muscles; only this, cockles are small, and to this spice you must have at least two quarts; there is nothing to pick off them: muscles you must have two quarts; take great care to pick the crab out under the tongue,

and

and a little fus which grows at the root of the tongue: the two latter, cockles and muscles, must be washed in several waters, to clean them from the grit; put them in a stew-pan by themselves, cover them close; and when they are open, pick them out of the shells, and strain the liquor.

To pickle Mackerel, called Caveach.

CUT your mackerel into round pieces, and divide one into five or six pieces: to six large mackerel you may take one ounce of beaten pepper, three large nutmegs, a little mace, and a handful of salt; mix your salt and beaten spice together, then make two or three holes in each piece, and thrust the seasoning into the holes with your finger, rub the piece all over with the seasoning, fry them brown in oil, and let them stand till they are cold; then put them into vinegar, and cover them with oil: they will keep well covered a great while, and are delicious.

To make Veal Hams.

CUT the leg of veal like a ham, then take a pint of bay-salt, two ounces of salt-petre, and a pound of common salt, mix them together with an ounce of juniper berries beat; rub the ham well, and lay it on a hollow tray, with the skinny side downwards; baste it every day with the pickle for a fortnight, and then hang it in wood-smoke for a fortnight: you may boil it, or parboil it and roast it. In this pickle you may do two or three tongues, or a piece of pork.

To make Beef Hams.

YOU must take the leg of a fat, but small beef, the fat Scotch or Welch cattle is best, and cut it ham-fashion; take an ounce of bay-salt, an ounce of salt-petre, a pound of common salt, and a pound of coarse sugar (this quantity for about fourteen or fifteen pounds weight, and so accordingly, if you pickle the whole quarter), rub it with the above ingredients, turn it every day, and baste it well with the pickle for a month; take it out and roll it in bran or saw-dust, then hang it in wood-smoke, where there is but little fire, and a constant smoke, for a month; then take it down and hang it in a dry place, not hot, and keep it for use; you may cut a piece off as you have occasion, and either boil it or cut it in rashers, and broil it with poached eggs, or boil a piece, and it eats fine cold, and will sliver like Dutch beef. After this beef is done you may do a thick brisket of beef in the same pickle: let it lie a month, rubbing it every day with the pickle, then boil it till it is tender, hang it in a dry place, and it eats finely cold, cut in slices on a plate. It is a pretty thing for a side-dish, or for supper. A shoulder of mutton laid in this pickle for a week, hung in wood-smoke two or three days, and then boiled with cabbage, is very good.

To make Mutton Hams.

You must take a hind-quarter of mutton, cut it like a ham, take an ounce of salt-petre, a pound of coarse sugar, a pound of common salt; mix them and rub your ham, lay it in a hollow tray with the skin downwards, baste it every day for a fortnight, then roll it in saw-dust and hang it in the wood-smoke a fortnight; then boil it and hang it in a dry place, and cut it out in rashers, and broil it as you want.

To make Pork Hams.

You must take a fat hind-quarter of pork, and cut off a fine ham; take two ounces of salt-petre, a pound of coarse sugar, a pound of common salt, and two ounces of sal-prunella, mix all together, and rub it well; let it lie a month in this pickle, turning and basting it every day, then hang it in wood-smoke as you do beef, in a dry place, so as no heat comes to it; and if you keep them long, hang them a month or two in a damp place, and it will make them cut fine and short. Never lay these hams in water till you boil them, and then boil them in a copper, (if you have one,) or the biggest pot you have; put them in the cold water, and let them be four or five hours before they boil; skim the pot well and often till it boils: if it is a very large one, three hours will boil it; if a small one, two hours will do, provided it be a great while before the water boils; take it up half an hour before dinner, pull off the skin, and throw raspings finely sifted all over; hold a red-hot fire-shovel over it, and when dinner is ready, take a few raspings in a sieve and sift all over the dish; then lay in your ham, and with your finger make fine figures round the edge of the dish; be sure to boil your ham in as much water as you can, and to keep it skimming all the time till it boils: it must be at least four hours before it boils. This pickle does finely for tongues, afterwards to lie in it a fortnight, and then hang in the wood-smoke a fortnight; or to boil them out of the pickle.

Yorkshire is famous for hams; and the reason is this: their salt is much finer than ours in London; it is a large clear salt, and gives the meat a fine flavour. I used to have it from Malden in Essex, and that salt will make any ham as fine as you can desire; it is by much the best salt for salting of meat; a deep hollow wooden tray is better than a pan, because the pickle swells about it. When you broil any of these hams in slices, or bacon, have some boiling water ready, and let the slices lie a minute or two in the water, then broil them; it takes out the salt and makes them eat finer.

To make Bacon.

TAKE a fide of pork, then take off all the infide fat, lay it on a long board or dreffer, that the blood may run away, rub it well with good falt on both fides, let it lie thus a day; then take a pint of bay falt, a quarter of a pound of falt-petre, beat them fine, two pounds of coarfe fugar, and a quarter of a peck of common falt; lay your pork in fomething that will hold the pickle, and rub it well with the above ingredients; lay the fkinny fide downwards, and bafte it every day with the pickle for a fortnight; then hang it in wood-fmoke as you do the beef, and afterwards hang it in a dry place, but not hot. You are to obferve, that all hams and bacon fhould hang clear from every thing, and not againft a wall. Obferve to wipe off all the old falt before you put it into this pickle, and never keep bacon or hams in a hot kitchen, or in a room where the fun comes; it makes them rufty.

CHAP. XIX.

Of PICKLING.

Rules to be obferved in Pickling.

ALWAYS ufe ftone jars for all forts of pickles that require hot pickle to them: the firft charge is the leaft; for thefe not only laft longer, but keep the pickle better; for vinegar and falt will penetrate through all earthen veffels; ftone and glafs are the only things to keep pickles in. Be fure never to put your hands in to take pickles out, it will foon fpoil it; the beft method is, to every pot tie a wooden fpoon, full of little holes, to take the pickles out with.

To pickle Walnuts green.

TAKE the largeft and cleareft you can get, pare them as thin as you can, have a tub of fpring-water ftand by you, and throw them in as you do them; put into the water a pound of bay-falt, let them lie in the water twenty-four hours, take them out, then put them into a ftone-jar, and between every layer of walnuts lay a layer of vine-leaves at the bottom and top, and fill it up with cold vinegar; let them ftand all night, then pour that vinegar from them into a copper, with a pound of bay-falt; fet it on the fire, let it boil, then pour it hot on your nuts, tie them over with a woollen cloth, and let them ftand a week,

then

then pour that pickle away, rub your nuts clean with a piece of flannel, then put them again in your jar with vine-leaves, as above, and boil fresh vinegar; put into your pot to every gallon of vinegar a nutmeg sliced, cut four large races of ginger, a quarter of an ounce of mace, the same of cloves, a quarter of an ounce of whole black pepper, the like of Ordingal pepper; then pour your vinegar boiling-hot on your walnuts, and cover them with a woollen cloth; let it stand three or four days, so do two or three times; when cold, put in half a pint of mustard-seed, a large stick of horse-radish sliced, tie them down close with a bladder, and then with a leather; they will be fit to eat in a fortnight; take a large onion, stick the cloves in, and lay in the middle of the pot; if you do them for keeping, do not boil your vinegar, but then they will not be fit to eat under six months; and the next year you may boil the pickle this way: they will keep two or three years good and firm.

To pickle Walnuts white.

TAKE the largest nuts you can get, just before the shell begins to turn, pare them very thin till the white appears, and throw them into spring-water, with a handful of salt as you do them; let them stand in that water six hours, lay on them a thin board to keep them under the water, then set a stew-pan on a charcoal fire, with clean spring-water; take your nuts out of the other water, and put them into the stew-pan; let them simmer four of five minutes, but not boil; then have ready by you a pan of spring-water, with a handful of white salt in it, stir it with your hand till the salt is melted, then take your nuts out of the stew-pan with a wooden ladle, and put them into the cold water and salt; let them stand a quarter of an hour, lay the board on them as before; if they are not kept under the liquor they will turn black, then lay them on a cloth, and cover them with another to dry; then carefully wipe them with a soft cloth, put them into your jar or glass, with some blades of mace and nutmeg sliced thin; mix your spice between your nuts, and pour distilled vinegar over them; first let your glass be full of nuts, pour mutton fat over them, and tie a bladder, and then a leather.

To pickle Walnuts black.

YOU must take large full-grown nuts at their full growth, before they are hard, lay them in salt and water; let them lie two days, then shift them into fresh water; let them lie two days longer, then shift them again, and let them lie three in your pickling jar; when the jar is half full, put in a large onion stuck with cloves. To a hundred of walnuts put in half a pint of mustard-seed, a quarter of an ounce of mace, half an ounce of
black

black pepper, half an ounce of all-spice, six bay-leaves, and a stick of horse-radish; then fill your jar, and pour boiling vinegar over them; cover them with a plate, and when they are cold, tie them down with a bladder and leather, and they will be fit to eat in two or three months: the next year, if any remains, boil up your vinegar again, and skim it; when cold, pour it over your walnuts. This is by much the best pickle for use; therefore you may add more vinegar to it, what quantity you please: if you pickle a great many walnuts and eat them fast, make your pickle for a hundred or two, the rest keep in a strong brine of salt and water, boiled till it will bear an egg, and as your pot empties fill them up with those in the salt and water: take care they are covered with pickle.

In the same manner you may do a smaller quantity; but if you can get rape-vinegar, use that instead of salt and water; do them thus: put your nuts into the jar you intend to pickle them in, throw in a good handful of salt and fill the pot with rape vinegar; cover it close, and let them stand a fortnight, then pour them out of the pot, wipe it clean, and just rub the nuts with a coarse cloth, and then put them in the jar with the pickle, as above: if you have the best sugar-vinegar of your own making, you need not boil it the first year, but pour it on cold; and the next year, (if any remains,) boil it up again, skim it, put fresh spice to it, and it will do again.

To pickle Gerkins.

TAKE five hundred gerkins, and have ready a large earthen pan of spring-water and salt, to every gallon of water two pounds of salt; mix it well together and throw in your gerkins, wash them out in two hours, and put them to drain, let them be drained very dry, and put them in a jar; in the meantime get a bell-metal pot, with a gallon of the best white wine vinegar, half an ounce of cloves and mace, one ounce of all-spice, one ounce of mustard-seed, a stick of horse-radish cut in slices, six bay-leaves, a little dill, two or three races of ginger cut in pieces, a nutmeg cut in pieces, and a handful of salt; boil it up in the pot all together, and put it over the gerkins; cover them close down, and let them stand twenty-four hours; then put them in your pot, and simmer them over the stove till they are green; be careful not to let them boil, if you do, you will spoil them; then put them in your jar, and cover them close down till cold; then tie them over with a bladder and a leather over that; put them in a cold dry place: mind always to keep your pickles tied down close, and take them out with a wooden spoon, or a spoon kept on purpose.

To pickle Gerkins another Way.

WIPE your small gerkins with a dry cloth, then make a pickle of vinegar, salt, whole pepper, cloves, and mace, boil it, and pour it on hot; set the jar in an oven almost cold for three or four different days till the cucumbers are green; when cold cover them close.

N. B. You must cover the gerkins with a linen cloth and a plate while they are doing to keep in the steam.

To pickle large Cucumbers in Slices.

TAKE the large cucumbers before they are too ripe, slice them the thickness of crown-pieces in a pewter dish; to every dozen of cucumbers slice two large onions thin, and so on till you have filled your dish, with a handful of salt between every row; then cover them with another pewter dish, and let them stand twenty-four hours, then put them into a cullendar, and let them drain very well; put them in a jar, cover them over with white-wine vinegar, and them stand four hours; pour the vinegar from them into a copper sauce-pan, and boil it with a little salt: put to the cucumbers a little mace, a little whole pepper, a large race of ginger sliced, and then pour the boiling vinegar on; cover them close, and when they are cold tie them down. They will be fit to eat in two or three days.

To pickle Asparagus.

TAKE the largest asparagus you can get, cut off the white ends, and wash the green ends in spring-water, then put them in another clean water, and let them lie two or three hours in it; then have a large broad stew-pan full of spring-water, with a good large handful of salt; set it on the fire, and when it boils put in the grass, not tied up, but loose, and not too many at a time, for fear you break the heads; just scald them, and no more, take them out with a broad skimmer, and lay them on a cloth to cool; then for your pickle take a gallon, or more according to your quantity of asparagus, of white wine vinegar, and one ounce of bay-salt, boil it, and put your asparagus in your jar; to a gallon of pickle, two nutmegs, a quarter of an ounce of mace, the same of whole white pepper, and pour the pickle hot over them; cover them with a linen cloth, three or four times double, let them stand a week, and boil the pickle; let them stand a week longer, boil the pickle again, and pour it on hot as before; when they are cold, cover them close with a bladder and leather.

To pickle Peaches.

TAKE your peaches when they are at their full growth, just before they turn to be ripe; be sure they are not bruised; then take

take spring-water, as much as you think will eover them, make it salt enough to bear an egg, with bay and common salt an equal quantity each; then put in your peaches, and lay a thin board over them to keep them under the water; let them stand three days, and then take them out and wipe them very carefully with a fine soft cloth, and lay them in your glass or jar, then take as much white-wine vinegar as will fill your glass or jar: to every gallon put one pint of the best well made mustard, two or three heads of garlick, a good deal of ginger sliced, half an ounce of cloves, mace, and nutmeg; mix your pickle well together, and pour over your peaches; tie them close with a bladder and leather; they will be fit to eat in two months; you may with a fine pen-knife cut them across; take out the stone, fill them with made mustard and garlick, and horse-radish and ginger; tie them together. You may pickle nectarines and apricots the same way.

To pickle Radish-Pods.

MAKE a strong pickle, with cold spring-water and bay-salt, strong enough to bear an egg, then put your pods in, and lay a thin board on them, to keep them under water; let them stand ten days, then drain them in a sieve, and lay them on a cloth to dry; then take white-wine vinegar, as much as you think will cover them, boil it, and put your pods in a jar, with ginger, mace, cloves, and Jamaica pepper. Pour your vinegar boiling hot on, cover them with a coarse cloth, three or four times double, that the steam may come through a little, and let them stand two days; repeat this two or three times; when it is cold, put in a pint of mustard-seed, and some horse-radish; cover it close.

To pickle French Beans.

PICKLE your beans as you do the gerkins.

To pickle Cauliflowers.

TAKE the largest and closest you can get; pull them in sprigs; put them in an earthen dish, and sprinkle salt over them; let them stand twenty-four hours to draw out all the water, then put them in a jar, and pour salt and water boiling over them; cover them close, and let them stand till the next day; then take them out, and lay them on a coarse cloth to drain; put them into glass jars, and put in a nutmeg sliced, two or three blades of mace in each jar; cover them with distilled vinegar, and tie them down with a bladder, and over that a leather. They will be fit for use in a month.

To pickle Beet-Root.

SET a pot of spring-water on the fire, when it boils put in your beets, and let them boil till they are tender; take them out, and with a knife take off all the outside, cut them in pieces according to your fancy; put them in a jar, and cover them with cold vinegar, and tie them down close; when you use the beet take it out of the pickle, and cut it into what shapes you like; put it in a little dish with some of the pickle over it. You may use it for sallads, or garnish.

To pickle White Plums.

TAKE the large white plums: and if they have stalks, let them remain on, and do them as you do your peaches.

To pickle Onions.

TAKE your onions when they are dry enough to lay up for winter, the smaller they are the better they look; put them into a pot, and cover them with spring-water, with a handful of white salt, let them boil up; then strain them off, and take three coats off; put them on a cloth, and let two people take hold of it, one at each end, and rub them backward and forward till they are very dry; then put them in your bottles, with some blades of mace and cloves, a nutmeg cut in pieces; have some double-distilled white-wine vinegar; boil it up with a little salt; let it be cold, and put it over the onions; cork them close, and tie a bladder and leather over it.

To pickle Onions another Way.

TAKE small onions, lay them in water and salt two or three days, shift them once, then dry them in a cloth; boil the best vinegar with spice to your taste, and when cold put them in it, covered with a bladder.

To pickle Lemons.

TAKE twelve lemons, scrape them with a piece of broken glass; then cut them cross in two, four parts downright, but not quite through, but that they will hang together; put in as much salt as they will hold, rub them well, and strew them over with salt; let them lie in an earthen dish three days, and turn them every day; slit an ounce of ginger very thin, and salted for three days, twelve cloves of garlick, parboiled and salted three days, a small handful of mustard-seeds bruised and searced through a hair-sieve, and some red India pepper; take your lemons out of the salt, squeeze them very gently, put them into a jar with the spice and ingredients, and cover them with the best white-wine vinegar. Stop them up very close, and in a month's time they will be fit to eat.

To pickle Mushrooms White.

TAKE small buttons, cut the stalk, and rub off the skin with flannel dipped in salt, and throw them into milk and water; drain them out, and put them into a stew-pan, with a handful of salt over them; cover them close, and put them over a gentle stove for five minutes, to draw out all the water; then put them on a coarse cloth to drain till cold.

To make Pickle for Mushrooms.

TAKE a gallon of the best vinegar, put it into a cold still; to every gallon of vinegar put half a pound of bay-salt, a quarter of a pound of mace, a quarter of an ounce of cloves, a nutmeg cut in quarters; keep the top of the still covered with a wet cloth; as the cloth dries, put on a wet one; do not let the fire be too large, lest you burn the bottom of the still; draw it as long as you taste the acid, and no longer. When you fill your bottles, put in your mushrooms, here and there put in a few blades of mace, and a slice of nutmeg; then fill the bottle with pickle, and melt some mutton fat, strain it, and pour over it; it will keep them better than oil. You must put your nutmeg over the fire in a little vinegar, and give it a boil; while it is hot you may slice it as you please; when it is cold, it will not cut, for it will crack to pieces.

N. B. In the 24th Chapter, at the end of the receipt for making vinegar, you will see the best way of pickling mushrooms, only they will not be so white.

To pickle Codlings.

GATHER your codlings when they are the size of a large double walnut; take a pan, and put vine-leaves thick at the bottom. Put in your codlings, and cover them well with vine-leaves and spring water; put them over a slow fire till you can peel the skin off; take them carefully up in a hair-sieve, peel them very carefully with a pen-knife; put them into the same water again, with the vine-leaves as before. Cover them close, and set them at a distance from the fire, till they are of a fine green; drain them in a cullender till cold; put them in jars, with some mace and a clove or two of garlick; cover them with distilled vinegar; pour some mutton-fat over, and tie them with a bladder and leather down very tight.

To pickle Fennel.

SET spring-water on the fire, with a handful of salt; when it boils, tie your fennel in bunches, and put them into the water, just give them a scald, lay them on a cloth to dry; when cold, put it in a glass, with a little mace and nutmeg, fill it with cold vinegar, lay a bit of green fennel on the top, and over that a bladder and leather.

To pickle Grapes.

GET grapes at the full growth, but not ripe; cut them in small bunches fit for garnishing, put them in a stone jar, with vine-leaves between every layer of grapes; then take as much spring-water as you think will cover them, put in a pound of bay-salt, and as much white-salt as will make it bear an egg: Dry your bay-salt and pound it, it will melt the sooner; put it into a bell-metal, or copper-pot, boil it and skim it very well; as it boils, take all the black scum off, but not the white scum; when it has boiled a quarter of an hour, let it stand to cool and settle; when it is almost cold, pour the clear liquor on the grapes, lay vine leaves on the top, tie them down close with a linen cloth, and cover them with a dish; let them stand twenty-four hours; then take them out, and lay them on a cloth, cover them over with another, let them be dried between the cloths; then take two quarts of vinegar, one quart of spring-water, and one pound of coarse sugar. Let it boil a little while, skim it as it boils very clean, let it stand till it is quite cold, dry your jar with a cloth, put fresh vine-leaves at the bottom, and between every bunch of grapes, and on the top; then pour the clear off the pickle on the grapes, fill your jar that the pickle may be above the grapes, tie a thin bit of board in a piece of flannel, lay it on the top of the jar, to keep the grapes under the pickle; tie them down with a bladder, and then a leather; take them out with a wooden spoon. Be sure to make pickle enough to cover them.

To pickle Barberries.

TAKE white-wine vinegar; to every quart of vinegar put in half a pound of sixpenny sugar, then pick the worst of your barberries, and put into this liquor, and the best into glasses; then boil your pickle with the worst of your barberries, and skim it very clean; boil it till it looks of a fine colour, then let it stand to be cold before you strain; then strain it through a cloth, wringing it to get all the colour you can from the barberries; let it stand to cool and settle, then pour it clear into the glasses in a little of the pickle; boil a little fennel; when cold, put a little bit at the top of the pot or glass, and cover it close with a bladder and leather. To every half pound of sugar put a quarter of a pound of white salt. Red currants are done the same way. Or you may do barberries thus: pick them clean from leaves and spotted ones; put them into jars; mix spring-water and salt pretty strong, and put over them; and when you see the scum rise, change the salt and water, and they will keep a long time.

To pickle Red Cabbage.

SLICE the cabbage very fine cross-ways; put it on an earthen dish, and sprinkle a handful of salt over it, cover it with another dish, and let it stand twenty-four hours; then put it in a cullender to drain, and lay it in your jar; take white wine vinegar enough to cover it, a little cloves, mace, and all-spice, put them in whole, with one pennyworth of cochineal bruised fine; boil it up, and put it over hot or cold (which you like best), and cover it close with a cloth till cold; then tie it over with leather.

To pickle Golden Pippins.

TAKE the finest pippins you can get, free from spots and bruises, put them into a preserving-pan of cold spring-water, and set them on a charcoal fire; keep them turning with a wooden spoon till they will peel; do not let them boil. When they are enough, peel them, and put them into the water again, with a quarter of a pint of the best vinegar, and a quarter of an ounce of alum, cover them very close with a pewter dish, and set them on the charcoal fire again, a slow fire, not to boil. Let them stand, turning them now and then, till they look green; then take them out, and lay them on a cloth to cool; when cold, make your pickle as for the peaches, only instead of made mustard, this must be mustard-seed whole. Cover them close, and keep them for use.

To pickle Nastertium Berries and Limes; you pick them off the Lime-Trees in the Summer.

TAKE nastertium berries gathered as soon as the blossom is off, or the limes, and put them in cold spring-water and salt; change the water for three days successively. Make a pickle of white wine vinegar, mace, nutmeg, slice six shalots, six blades of garlic, some pepper-corns, salt, and horse-radish cut in slices. Make your pickle very strong; drain your berries very dry, and put them in bottles. Mix your pickle well up together, but you must not boil it; put it over the berries or limes, and tie them down close.

To pickle young Suckers, or young Artichokes, before the Leaves are hard.

TAKE young suckers, pare them very nicely, all the hard ends of the leaves and stalks, just scald them in salt and water, and when they are cold, put them into little glass bottles, with two or three large blades of mace, and a nutmeg sliced thin; fill them either with distilled vinegar, or the sugar-vinegar of your own making, with half spring-water.

To pickle Artichoke-Bottoms.

BOIL artichokes till you can pull the leaves off, then take off the chokes, and cut them from the stalk; take great care you do not let the knife touch the top, throw them into salt and water for an hour, then take them out, and lay them on a cloth to drain; then put them into large wide-mouthed glasses; put a little mace and sliced nutmeg between, fill them either with distilled vinegar, or sugar-vinegar and spring-water; cover them with mutton-fat fried, and tie them down with a bladder and leather.

To pickle Samphire.

TAKE the samphire that is green, lay it in a clean pan, throw two or three handfuls of salt over, then cover it with spring-water; let it lie twenty-four hours, then put it into a clean brass sauce-pan, throw in a handful of salt, and cover it with good vinegar; cover the pan close, and set it over a very slow fire; let it stand till it is just green and crisp; then take it off in a moment, for if it stands to be soft it is spoiled; put it in your pickling-pot, and cover it close; when it is cold, tie it down with a bladder and leather, and keep it for use; or you may keep it all the year in a very strong brine of salt and water, and throw it into vinegar just before you use it.

To pickle Mock Ginger.

TAKE the largest cauliflowers you can get, cut off all the flower from the stalks, and peel them, throw them into strong spring water and salt for three days, then drain them in a sieve pretty dry; put them in a jar, boil white wine vinegar with cloves, mace, long pepper, and all-spice, each half an ounce, forty blades of garlic, a stick of horse-radish cut in slices, a quarter of an ounce of Cayenne pepper, and a quarter of a pound of yellow turmerick, two ounces of bay-salt; pour it boiling over the stalks; cover it down close till the next day, then boil it again, and repeat it twice more; and when cold, tie it down close.

To pickle Melon Mangoes.

TAKE as many green melons as you want, and slit them two thirds up the middle, and with a spoon take all the seeds out; put them in strong spring-water and salt for twenty-four hours, then drain them in a sieve; mix half a pound of white mustard, two ounces of long-pepper, the same of all-spice, half an ounce of cloves and mace, a good quantity of garlic, and horse-radish cut in slices, and a quarter of an ounce of Cayenne pepper; fill the seed-holes full of this mixture; put a small skewer through the end, and tie it round with packthread close to the skewer, put them in a jar, and boil up vinegar with some of the mixture in it, and pour over the melons; cover them close, and let them stand till next day, then green them the same as you do gerkins. You may do large cucumbers the same way; tie them down close when cold, and keep them for use.

Elder-Shoots, in imitation of Bamboo.

TAKE the largest and youngest shoots of elder, which put out in the middle of May, the middle stalks are most tender and biggest; the small ones are not worth doing. Peel off the outward peel or skin, and lay them in a strong brine of salt and water for one night, then dry them in a cloth, piece by piece. In the mean time, make your pickle of half white wine and half beer vinegar: to each quart of pickle you must put an ounce of white or red pepper, an ounce of ginger sliced, a little mace, and a few corns of Jamaica pepper; when the spice has boiled in the pickle, pour it hot upon the shoots, stop them close immediately, and set the jar two hours before the fire, turning it often. It is as good a way of greening pickles as often boiling; or you may boil the pickle two or three times, and pour it on boiling hot, just as you please: if you make the pickle of the sugar-vinegar, you must let one half be spring-water.

To make Paco-lilla, or Indian Pickle, the same the Mangoes come over in.

TAKE a pound of race-ginger, and lay it in water one night; then scrape it, and cut it in thin slices, and put to it some salt, and let it stand in the sun to dry; take long-pepper two ounces, and do it as the ginger. Take a pound of garlic, and cut it in thin slices, and salt it, and let it stand three days; then wash it well, and let it be salted again, and stand three days more; then wash it well, and drain it, and put it in the sun to dry; take a quarter of a pound of mustard-seeds bruised, and half a quarter of ounce of turmerick, put these ingredients, when prepared, into a large stone or glass jar, with a gallon of very good white wine vinegar, and stir it very often for a fortnight, and tie it up close. In this pickle you may put white cabbage, cut in quarters and put in a brine of salt and water for three days, and then boil fresh salt and water, and just put in the cabbage to scald, and press out the water, and put it in the sun to dry, in the same manner as you do cauliflowers, cucumbers, melons, apples, French beans, plums, or any sort of fruit. Take care they are well dried before you put them into the pickle: you need never empty the jar, but as the things come in season, put them in, and supply it with vinegar as often as there is occasion. If you would have your pickle look green, leave out the turmerick, and green them as usual, and put them into this pickle cold. In the above, you may do walnuts in a jar by themselves; put the walnuts in without any preparation, tied close down, and kept some time.

To pickle the fine Purple Cabbage, so much admired at the great Tables.

TAKE two cauliflowers, two red cabbages, half a peck of kidney-beans, six sticks, with six cloves of garlic on each stick; wash all well, give them one boil up, then drain them on a sieve, and lay them, leaf by leaf, upon a large table, and salt them with bay-salt; then lay them a-drying in the sun, or in a slow oven, until as dry as cork.

To make the Pickle.

TAKE a gallon of the best vinegar, with one quart of water, and a handful of salt, and an ounce of pepper; boil them, let it stand till it is cold, then take a quarter of a pound of ginger, cut in pieces, salt it, let it stand a week; take half a pound of mustard-seed, wash it, and lay it to dry; when very dry, bruise half of it; when half is ready for the jar, lay a row of cabbage, a row of cauliflowers and beans, and throw betwixt every row your mustard-seed, some black pepper, some Jamaica pepper, some ginger, mix an ounce of the root of turmerick powdered; put it in the pickle, which must go over all. It is best when it hath been made two years, though it may be used the first year.

To make India Pickle.

To a gallon of vinegar, one pound of garlic, three quarters of a pound of long-pepper, a pint of mustard-seed, one pound of ginger, and two ounces of turmerick; the garlic must be laid in salt three days, then wiped clean and dried in the sun; the long-pepper broke, and the mustard-seed bruised: mix all together in the vinegar; then take two large hard cabbages, and two cauliflowers, cut them in quarters, and salt them well; let them lie three days, and dry them well in the sun.

N. B.—The ginger must lie twenty-four hours in salt and water, then cut small, and laid in salt three days.

CHAP.

CHAP. XX.

OF MAKING CAKES, &c.

To make a rich Cake.

TAKE four pounds of flour dried and sifted, seven pounds of currants washed and rubbed, six pounds of the best fresh butter, two pounds of Jordan almonds blanched, and beaten with orange-flower water and sack till fine; then take four pounds of eggs, put half the whites away, three pounds of double-refined sugar beaten and sifted, a quarter of an ounce of mace, the same of cloves and cinnamon, three large nutmegs, all beaten fine, a little ginger, half a pint of sack, half a pint of right French brandy, sweet-meats to your liking, they must be orange, lemon, and citron; work your butter to a cream with your hands before any of your ingredients are in; then put in your sugar, and mix all well together; let your eggs be well beat and strained through a sieve, work in your almonds first, then put in your eggs, beat them together till they look white and thick; then put in your sack, brandy, and spices, shake your flour in by degrees, and when your oven is ready, put in your currants and sweet-meats as you put it in your hoop: it will take four hours baking in a quick oven: you must keep it beating with your hand all the while you are mixing of it, and when your currants are well washed and cleaned, let them be kept before the fire, so that they may go warm into your cake. This quantity will bake best in two hoops.

To ice a great Cake.

TAKE the whites of twenty-four eggs, and a pound of double-refined sugar beat and sifted fine; mix both together in a deep earthen pan, and with a whisk whisk it well for two or three hours, till it looks white and thick; then with a thin broad board, or bunch of feathers, spread it all over the top and sides of the cake; set it at a proper distance before a good clear fire, and keep turning it continually for fear of its changing colour; but a cool oven is best, and an hour will harden it: you may perfume the icing with what perfume you please.

To make a Pound Cake.

TAKE a pound of butter, beat it in an earthen pan with your hand one way till it is like a fine thick cream; then have ready twelve eggs, but half the whites, beat them well, and beat them up with the butter, a pound of flour beat in it, a pound of sugar, and a few carraways; beat all well together for an hour with your hand, or a great wooden spoon, butter a pan and put it in, and then bake it an hour in a quick oven.

For change, you may put in a pound of currants, clean washed and picked.

To make a cheap Seed Cake.

You must take half a peck of flour, a pound and a half of butter, put it in a sauce-pan with a pint of new milk, set it on the fire; take a pound of sugar, half an ounce of all-spice beat fine, and mix them with the flour; when the butter is melted, pour the milk and butter in the middle of the flour, and work it up like paste; pour in with the milk half a pint of good ale-yeast, set it before the fire to rise, just before it goes to the oven: either put in some currants or carraway-feeds, and bake it in a quick oven; make it into two cakes: they will take an hour and a half baking.

To make a Butter Cake.

You must take a dish of butter, and beat it like cream with your hands, two pounds of fine sugar well beat, three pounds of flour well dried, and mix them in with the butter, twenty-four eggs, leave out half the whites, and then beat all together for an hour: just as you are going to put it into the oven, put in a quarter of an ounce of mace, a nutmeg beat, a little sack or brandy, and feeds or currants, just as you please.

To make Gingerbread Cakes.

Take three pounds of flour, one pound of sugar, one pound of butter rubbed in very fine, two ounces of ginger beat fine, a large nutmeg grated; then take a pound of treacle, a quarter of a pint of cream, make them warm together, and make up the bread stiff; roll it out, and make it up into thin cakes, cut them out with a tea-cup, or small glass; or roll them round like nuts, and bake them on tin plates in a slack oven.

To make a fine Seed or Saffron Cake.

You must take a quarter of a peck of fine flour, a pound and a half of butter, three ounces of carraway-feeds, six eggs beat well, a quarter of an ounce of cloves and mace beat together very fine, a pennyworth of cinnamon beat, a pound of sugar, a pennyworth of rose-water, a pennyworth of saffron, a pint and a half of yeast, and a quart of milk; mix it all together lightly with your hands thus: first boil your milk and butter, then skim off the butter, and mix with your flour, and a little of the milk; stir the yeast into the rest and strain it, mix it with the flour, put in your seed and spice, rose-water, tincture of saffron, sugar, and eggs; beat it all up well with your hands lightly, and bake it in a hoop or pan, but be sure to butter the pan well: it will take an hour and a half in a quick oven. You may leave out the seed if you choose it, and I think it rather better without it; but that you may do as you like.

To make a rich Seed Cake called the Nun's Cake.

You must take four pounds of the finest flour, and three pounds of double-refined sugar beaten and sifted; mix them together, and dry them by the fire till you prepare the other materials; take four pounds of butter, beat it with your hand till it is soft like cream; then beat thirty-five eggs, leave out sixteen whites, strain off your eggs from the treads, and beat them and the butter together till all appears like butter; put in four or five spoonfuls of rose or orange-flower water, and beat again; then take your flour and sugar, with six ounces of carraway-seeds, and strew them in by degrees, beating it up all the time for two hours together; you may put in as much tincture of cinnamon or ambergris as you please; butter your hoop, and let it stand three hours in a moderate oven. You must observe always, in beating of butter, to do it with a cool hand, and beat it always one way in a deep earthen dish.

To make Pepper Cakes.

Take half a gill of sack, half a quarter of an ounce of whole white pepper, put it in, and boil it together a quarter of an hour; then take the pepper out, and put in as much double-refined sugar as will make it like a paste; then drop it in what shape you please on plates, and let it dry itself.

To make Portugal Cakes.

Mix into a pound of fine flour a pound of loaf-sugar beat and sifted, then rub it into a pound of pure sweet butter till it is thick like grated white bread, then put to it two spoonfuls of rose-water, two of sack, ten eggs, whip them very well with a whisk, then mix it into eight ounces of currants, mixed all well together; butter the tin pans, fill them but half full, and bake them; if made without currants they will keep half a year; add a pound of almonds blanched, and beat with rose-water as above, and leave out the flour: these are another sort, and better.

To make a pretty Cake.

Take five pounds of flour well dried, one pound of sugar, half an ounce of mace, as much nutmeg; beat your spice very fine, mix the sugar and spice in the flour, take twenty-two eggs,

eggs, leave out six whites, beat them, put a pint of ale-yeast and the eggs in the flour, take two pounds and a half of fresh butter, a pint and a half of cream; set the cream and butter over the fire till the butter is melted; let it stand till it is blood-warm: before you put it into the flour, set it an hour by the fire to rise; then put in seven pounds of currants, which must be plumped in half a pint of brandy, and three quarters of a pound of candied peels: it must be an hour and a quarter in the oven: you must put two pounds of chopped raisins in the flour, and a quarter of a pint of sack: when you put the currants in, bake it in a hoop.

To make Gingerbread.

TAKE three quarts of fine flour, two ounces of beaten ginger, a quarter of an ounce of nutmeg, cloves, and mace beat fine, but most of the last; mix all together, three quarters of a pound of fine sugar, two pounds of treacle, set it over the fire, but do not let it boil; three quarters of a pound of butter melted in the treacle, and some candied lemon and orange peel cut fine; mix all these together well: an hour will bake it in a quick oven.

To make little fine Cakes.

ONE pound of butter beaten to cream, a pound and a quarter of flour, a pound of fine sugar beat fine, a pound of currants clean washed and picked, six eggs, two whites left out, beat them fine; mix the flour, sugar, and eggs by degrees into the batter, beat it all well with both hands; either make into little cakes, or bake it in one.

Another Sort of little Cakes.

A POUND of flour, and half a pound of sugar; beat half a pound of butter with your hand, and mix them well together: bake it in little cakes.

To make Drop-Biscuits.

TAKE eight eggs, and one pound of double-refined sugar beaten fine, twelve ounces of fine flour well dried, beat your eggs very well, then put in your sugar and beat it, and then your flour by degrees, beat it all very well together without ceasing; your oven must be as hot as for halfpenny bread; then flour some sheets of tin, and drop your biscuits of what bigness you please, put them in the oven as fast as you can, and when you see them rise, watch them; if they begin to colour, take them out, and put in more; and if the first is not enough, put them in again: if they are right done, they will have a white ice on them: you may, if you choose, put in a few carraways;

caraways; when they are all baked, put them in the oven again to dry, then keep them in a very dry place.

To make common Biscuits.

BEAT up six eggs, with a spoonful of rose-water and a spoonful of sack; then add a pound of fine powdered sugar, and a pound of flour; mix them into the eggs by degrees, and an ounce of coriander-seeds; mix all well together, shape them on white thin paper, or tin moulds, in any form you please: beat the white of an egg, with a feather rub them over, and dust fine sugar over them; set them in an oven moderately heated, till they rise and come to a good colour, take them out; and when you have done with the oven, if you have no stove to dry them in, put them in the oven again, and let them stand all night to dry.

To make French Biscuits.

HAVING a pair of clean scales ready, in one scale put three new-laid eggs, in the other scale put as much dried flour, an equal weight with the eggs, take out the flour, and put in as much fine powdered sugar; first beat the whites of the eggs up well with a whisk till they are of a fine froth; then whip in half an ounce of candied lemon-peel cut very thin and fine, and beat well: then by degrees whip in the flour and sugar, then slip in the yolks, and with a spoon temper it well together; then shape your biscuits on fine white paper with your spoon, and throw powdered sugar over them: bake them in a moderate oven, not too hot, giving them a fine colour on the top: when they are baked, with a fine knife cut them off from the paper, and lay them in boxes for use.

To make Mackeroons.

TAKE a pound of almonds, let them be scalded, blanched, and thrown into cold water, then dry them in a cloth, and pound them in a mortar, moisten them with orange-flower water, or the white of an egg, lest they turn to oil; afterwards take an equal quantity of fine powder sugar, with three or four whites of eggs, and a little musk, beat all well together, and shape them on a wafer-paper, with a spoon round: bake them in a gentle oven on tin plates.

To make Shrewsbury Cakes.

TAKE two pounds of flour, a pound of sugar finely searced, mix them together (take out a quarter of a pound to roll them in); take four eggs beat, four spoonfuls of cream, and two spoonfuls of rose-water; beat them well together, and mix them

them with the flour into a paste, roll them into thin cakes, and bake them in a quick oven.

To make Madling Cakes.

To a quarter of a peck of flour, well dried at the fire, add two pounds of mutton-suet tried and strained clear off; when it is a little cool, mix it well with the flour, some salt, and a very little all-spice beat fine; take half a pint of good yeast, and put in half a pint of water, stir it well together, strain it, and mix up your flour into a paste of moderate stiffness: you must add as much cold water as will make the paste of a right order; make it into cakes about the thickness and bigness of an oat-cake: have ready some currants clean washed and picked, strew some just in the middle of your cakes between your dough, so that none can be seen till the cake is broke. You may leave the currants out, if you do not choose them.

Wiggs.

TAKE three pounds of well dried flour, one nutmeg, a little mace and salt, and almost half a pound of carraway-comfits; mix these well together, and melt half a pound of butter in a pint of sweet thick cream, six spoonfuls of good sack, four yolks and three whites of eggs, and near a pint of good light yeast; work these well together, cover it, and set it down to the fire to rise; then let them rest, and lay the remainder, the half pound of carraways on the top of the wiggs, and put them upon papers well floured and dried, and let them have as quick an oven as for tarts.

To make light Wiggs.

TAKE a pound and a half of flour, and half a pint of milk made warm, mix these together, cover it up, and let it lie by the fire half an hour; then take half a pound of sugar, and half a pound of butter, then work these into a paste, and make it into wiggs, with as little flour as possible; let the oven be pretty quick, and they will rise very much: mind to mix a quarter of a pint of good ale-yeast in the milk.

To make very good Wiggs.

TAKE a quarter of a peck of the finest flour, rub it into three quarters of a pound of fresh butter till it is like grated bread, something more than half a pound of sugar, half a nutmeg, half a race of ginger grated, three eggs (yolks and whites) beat very well, and put to them half a pint of thick ale-yeast, three or four spoonfuls of sack, make a hole in the flour, and pour in your yeast and eggs, as much milk, just warm, as will

make

make it into a light paste; let it stand before the fire to rise half an hour, then make it into a dozen and a half of wiggs, wash them over with egg just as they go into the oven: in a quick oven half an hour will bake them.

To make Buns.

TAKE two pounds of fine flour, a pint of good ale-yeast, put a little sack in the yeast, and three eggs beaten, knead all these together with a little warm milk, a little nutmeg, and a little salt; and lay it before the fire till it rises very light, then knead in a pound of fresh butter, a pound of rough carraway-comfits, and bake them in a quick oven, in what shape you please, on floured paper.

A Cake the Spanish Way.

TAKE twelve eggs, three quarters of a pound of the best moist sugar, mill them in a chocolate-mill till they are all of a lather; then mix in one pound of flour, half a pound of pounded almonds, two ounces of candied orange-peel, two ounces of citron, four large spoonfuls of orange-water, half an ounce of cinnamon, and a glass of sack: it is better when baked in a slow oven.

Another Way.

TAKE one pound of flour, one pound of butter, eight eggs, one pint of boiling milk, two or three spoonfuls of ale-yeast, or a glass of French brandy; beat all well together; then set it before the fire in a pan, where there is room for it to rise; cover it close with a cloth and flannel, that no air comes to it; when you think it is raised sufficiently, mix half a pound of the best moist sugar, an ounce of cinnamon beat fine, four spoonfuls of orange-flower water, one ounce of candied orange-peel, one ounce of citron; mix all well together, and bake it.

How to make Uxbridge Cakes.

TAKE a pound of wheat-flour, seven pounds of currants, half a nutmeg, four pounds of butter, rub your butter cold very well amongst the meal; dress your currants very well in the flour, butter, and seasoning; and knead it with so much good new yeast as will make it into a pretty high paste, (usually two pennyworth of yeast to that quantity); after it is kneaded well together let it stand an hour to rise: you may put half a pound of paste in a cake.

To make Biscuit Bread.

TAKE half a pound of very fine wheat-flour, and as much sugar finely searced, and dry them very well before the fire, dry the flour more than the sugar; then take four new-laid eggs,

eggs, take out the strains, then swing them very well, then put the sugar in, and swing it well with the eggs, then put the flour in it, and beat all together half an hour at the least; put in some anise-seeds, or carraway-seeds, and rub the plates with butter, and set them into the oven.

To make Carraway Cakes.

TAKE two pounds of white flour, and two pounds of coarse loaf-sugar well dried and fine sifted; after the flour and sugar are sifted and weighed, mingle them together, sift the flour and sugar together, through a hair sieve, into the bowl you use it in; to them you must have two pounds of good butter, eighteen eggs, leaving out eight of the whites; to these you must add four ounces of candied orange, five or six ounces of carraway-comfits; you must first work the butter with rose-water till you can see none of the water, and your butter must be very soft; then put in flour and sugar, a little at a time, and likewise your eggs; but you must beat your eggs very well, with ten spoonfuls of sack, so you must put in each as you think fit, keeping it constantly beating with your hand till you have put it into the hoop for the oven; do not put in your sweet-meats and seeds till you are ready to put it into your hoops; you must have three or four doubles of cap-paper under the cakes, and butter the paper and hoop: you must sift some fine sugar upon your cake when it goes into the oven.

To make a Bride Cake.

TAKE four pounds of fine flour well dried, four pounds of fresh butter, two pounds of loaf-sugar, pound and sift fine a quarter of an ounce of mace, the same of nutmegs, to every pound of flour put eight eggs, wash four pounds of currants, pick them well, and dry them before the fire, blanch a pound of sweet almonds, and cut them lengthways very thin, a pound of citron, one pound of candied orange, the same of candied lemon, half a pint of brandy; first work the butter with your hand to a cream, then beat in your sugar a quarter of an hour, beat the whites of your eggs to a very strong froth, mix them with your sugar and butter, beat your yolks half an hour at least, and mix them with your cake, then put in your flour, mace, and nutmeg, keep beating it well till your oven is ready, put in your brandy, and beat your currants and almonds lightly in, tie three sheets of paper round the bottom of your hoop to keep it from running out, rub it well with butter, put in your cake, and lay your sweet-meats in three lays, with cake betwixt every lay; after it is risen and coloured, cover it with paper before your oven is stopped up; it will take three hours baking.

To make Bath Cakes.

RUB half a pound of butter into a pound of flour, and one spoonful of good barm, warm some cream, and make it into a light paste, set it to the fire to rise; when you make them up, take four ounces of carraway-comfits, work part of them in, and strew the rest on the top, make them into a round cake, the size of a French roll, bake them on sheet-tins, and send them in hot for breakfast.

To make Queen Cakes.

TAKE a pound of loaf-sugar, beat and sift it, a pound of flour well dried, a pound of butter, eight eggs, half a pound of currants washed and picked, grate a nutmeg, the same quantity of mace and cinnamon, work your butter to a cream, then put in your sugar, beat the whites of your eggs near half an hour, mix them with your sugar and butter, then beat your yolks near half an hour, and put them to your butter, beat them exceedingly well together, then put in your flour, spices, and the currants; when it is ready for the oven, bake them in tins, and dust a little sugar over them.

To make Ratafia Cakes.

TAKE half a pound of sweet almonds, the same quantity of bitter, blanch and beat them fine in orange, rose, or clear water, to keep them from oiling, pound and sift a pound of fine sugar, mix it with your almonds; have ready, very well beat, the whites of four eggs, mix them lightly with the almonds and sugar, put it in a preserving-pan, and set it over a moderate fire, keep stirring it quick one way until it is pretty hot; when it is a little cool, roll it in small rolls, and cut it in thin cakes, dip your hands in flour and shake them on it, give them each a light tap with your finger, put them on sugar papers, and sift a little fine sugar over them just as you are putting them into a slow oven.

To make little Plum Cakes.

TAKE two pounds of flour dried in the oven, or at a great fire, and half a pound of sugar finely powdered, four yolks of eggs, two whites, half a pound of butter washed with rose-water, six spoonfuls of cream warmed, a pound and a half of currants unwashed, but picked and rubbed very clean in a cloth; mix all well together, then make them up in cakes, bake them in an oven almost as hot as for a manchet, and let them stand half an hour till they are coloured on both sides, then take down the oven-lid, and let them stand to soak: you must rub the butter into the flour very well, then the egg and cream, and then the currants.

CHAP.

CHAP. XXI.

Of CHEESECAKES, CREAMS, JELLIES, WHIP-SYLLABUBS, &c.

To make fine Cheesecakes.

TAKE a pint of cream, warm it, and put to it five quarts of milk warm from the cow, then put runnet to it, and give it a stir about; and when it is come, put the curd in a linen bag or cloth, let it drain well away from the whey, but do not squeeze it much; then put it in a mortar, and break the curd as fine as butter; put to your curd half a pound of sweet almonds blanched and beat exceeding fine, and half a pound of mackeroons beat very fine: if you have no mackeroons, get Naples biscuits; then add to it the yolks of nine eggs beaten, a whole nutmeg grated, two perfumed plums, dissolved in rose or orange flower water, half a pound of fine sugar; mix all well together, then melt a pound and a quarter of butter and stir it well in it, and half a pound of currants plumped, to let stand to cool till you use it; then make your puff-paste thus: take a pound of fine flour, wet it with cold water, roll it out, put into it by degrees a pound of fresh butter, and shake a little flour on each coat as you roll it: make it just as you use it.

You may leave out the currants, for change; nor need you put in the perfumed plums, if you dislike them; and for variety, when you make them of mackeroons, put in as much tincture of saffron as will give them a high colour, but no currants: this we call saffron cheesecakes; the other without currants, almond cheesecakes: with currants, fine cheesecakes; with mackeroons, mackeroon cheesecakes.

To make Lemon Cheesecakes.

TAKE the peel of two large lemons, boil it very tender, then pound it well in a mortar, with a quarter of a pound or more of loaf-sugar, the yolks of six eggs, and half a pound of fresh butter, and a little curd beat fine; pound and mix all together, lay a puff-paste in your patty-pans, fill them half full and bake them. Orange cheesecakes are done the same way, only you boil the peel in two or three waters, to take out the bitterness.

A second Sort of Lemon Cheesecakes.

TAKE two large lemons, grate off the peel of both, and squeeze out the juice of one, and add to it half a pound of double-refined sugar, twelve yolks of eggs, eight whites well beaten, then melt half a pound of butter in four or five spoonfuls

fuls of cream, then stir it all together and set it over the fire, stirring it till it begins to be pretty thick; then take it off, and when it is cold fill your patty-pans little more than half full; put a paste very thin at the bottom of your patty-pans; half an hour, with a quick oven, will bake them.

To make Almond Cheesecakes.

TAKE half a pound of Jordan almonds and lay them in cold water all night, the next morning blanch them into cold water, then take them out and dry them in a clean cloth, beat them very fine in a little orange-flower water, then take six eggs, leave out four whites, beat them and strain them, then half a pound of white sugar with a little beaten mace; beat them well together in a marble mortar, take ten ounces of good fresh butter, melt it, a little grated lemon-peel, and put them in the mortar with the other ingredients; mix all well together, and fill your patty-pans.

Cheesecakes without Currants.

TAKE two quarts of new milk, set it as it comes from the cow, with as little runnet as you can; when it is come, break it as gently as you can, and whey it well; then pass it through a hair-sieve, put it into a marble mortar, and beat into it a pound of new butter washed in rose-water; when that is well mingled in the curd, take the yolks of six eggs, and the whites of three, beat them very well with a little thick cream and salt; and after you have made the coffins, just as you put them into the crust (which must not be till you are ready to set them into the oven), then put in your eggs and sugar and a whole nutmeg finely grated; stir them all well together, and so fill your crusts; and if you put a little fine sugar searced into the crust, it will roll the thinner and cleaner; three spoonfuls of thick sweet cream will be enough to beat up your eggs with.

To make Citron Cheesecakes.

BOIL a quart of cream, beat the yolks of four eggs, mix them with your cream when it is cold, then set it on the fire, let it boil till it curds, blanch some almonds, beat them with orange-flower water, put them into the cream with a few Naples biscuits, and green citron shred fine, sweeten it to your taste, and bake them in tea-cups.

To make Lemon Custards.

TAKE a pint of white wine, half a pound of double-refined sugar, the juice of two lemons, the out-rind of one pared very thin, the inner-rind of one boiled tender and rubbed through a sieve,

a sieve; let them boil a good while, then take out the peel and a little of the liquor, set it to cool, pour the rest into the dish you intend for it; beat four yolks and two whites of eggs, mix them with your cool liquor, strain them into your dish, stir them well up together, set them on a slow fire, or boiling water to bake as a custard; when it is enough, grate the rind of a lemon all over the top; you may brown it over with a hot salamander. It may be eat either hot or cold.

To make Orange Custards.

Boil the rind of half a Seville orange very tender, beat it in a marble mortar till it is very fine, put to it one spoonful of the best brandy, the juice of a Seville orange, four ounces of loaf-sugar, and the yolks of four eggs, beat them all together ten minutes, then pour in by degrees a pint of boiling cream; keep beating them till they are cold, put them in custard-cups; and set them in an earthen dish of hot water; let them stand till they are set, then take them out and stick preserved orange on the top, and serve them up either hot or cold. It is a pretty corner-dish for dinner, or a side-dish for supper.

To make a Beest Custard.

Take a pint of beest, set it over the fire, with a little cinnamon, or three bay-leaves, let it be boiling hot, then take it off, and have ready mixed one spoonful of flour and a spoonful of thick cream; pour your hot beest upon it by degrees, mix it exceeding well together, and sweeten it to your taste: you may either put it in crusts or cups, or bake it.

To make Almond Custards.

Take a pint of cream, blanch and beat a quarter of a pound of almonds fine, with two spoonfuls of rose-water; sweeten it to your palate, beat up the yolks of four eggs, stir all together one way over the fire till it is thick, then pour it out into cups: or you may bake it in little china cups.

To make baked Custards.

One pint of cream boiled with mace and cinnamon; when cold take four eggs, two whites left out, a little rose and orange-flower water and sack, nutmeg and sugar to your palate; mix them well together, and bake them in china cups.

To make plain Custards.

Take a quart of new milk, sweeten it to your taste, grate in a little nutmeg, beat up eight eggs, leave out half the whites, beat them up well, stir them into the milk, and bake it in china

china basons, or put them in a deep china dish; have a kettle of water boiling, set the cup in, let the water come above half way, but do not let it boil too fast for fear of its getting into the cups, and take a hot iron and colour them at the top: you may add a little rose-water.

To make Orange Butter.

TAKE the yolks of ten eggs beat very well, half a pint of Rhenish, six ounces of sugar, and the juice of three sweet oranges; set them over a gentle fire, stirring them one way till it is thick: when you take it off, stir in a piece of butter as big as a large walnut.

To make Fairy Butter.

TAKE the yolks of two hard eggs, and beat them in a marble mortar, with a large spoonful of orange-flower water, and two tea-spoonfuls of fine sugar beat to powder; beat this all together till it is a fine paste, then mix it up with about as much fresh butter out of the churn, and force it through a fine strainer full of little holes into a plate. This is a pretty thing to set off a table at supper.

Almond Butter.

TAKE a quart of cream, put in some mace whole, and a quartered nutmeg, the yolks of eight eggs well beaten, and three quarters of a pound of almonds well blanched, and beaten extremely small, with a little rose-water and sugar; and put all these together, set them on the fire, and stir them till they begin to boil; then take it off, and you will find it a little cracked; so lay a strainer in a cullender and pour it into it, and let it drain a day or two, till you see it is firm like butter; then run it through a cullender, and it will be like little comfits, and so serve it up.

To make Steeple Cream.

TAKE five ounces of hartshorn, and two ounces of ivory, and put them in a stone-bottle, fill it up with fair water to the neck, put in a small quantity of gum-arabic, and gum-dragon; then tie up the bottle very close, and set it into a pot of water, with hay at the bottom; let it stand six hours, then take it out and let it stand an hour before you open it, lest it fly in your face; then strain it, and it will be a strong jelly; then take a pound of blanched almonds, beat them very fine, mix it with a pint of thick cream, and let it stand a little; then strain it out, and mix it with a pound of jelly, set it over the fire till it is scalding hot, sweeten it to your taste with double-refined sugar, then take it off, put in a little amber, and pour it into small high gallipots, like a sugar-loaf at top; when it is cold, turn them, and lay cold whipt-cream about them in heaps: be sure it does not boil when the cream is in.

Lemon Cream.

TAKE five large lemons, pare them as thin as possible, steep them all night in twenty spoonfuls of spring-water, with the juice of the lemons, then strain it through a jelly-bag into a silver sauce-pan (if you have one), the whites of six eggs beat well, ten ounces of double-refined sugar, set it over a very slow charcoal fire, stir all the time one way, skim it, and when it is as hot as you can bear your fingers in, pour it into glasses.

A second Lemon Cream.

TAKE the juice of four large lemons, half a pint of water, a pound of double-refined sugar beaten fine, the whites of seven eggs, and the yolk of one beaten very well, mix all together, strain it, and set it on a gentle fire, stirring it all the while, and skim it clean, put into it the peel of one lemon; when it is very hot, but does not boil, take out the lemon-peel, and pour it into china dishes. You must observe to keep it stirring one way all the time it is over the fire.

Jelly of Cream.

TAKE four ounces of hartshorn, put it on in three pints of water, let it boil till it is a stiff jelly, which you will know by taking a little in a spoon to cool; then strain it off, and add to it half a pint of cream, two spoonfuls of rose-water, two spoonfuls of sack, and sweeten it to your taste; then give it a gentle boil, but keep stirring it all the time or it will curdle; then take it off and stir it till it is cold; then put it into broad bottomed cups, let them stand all night, and turn them out into a dish; take half a pint of cream, two spoonfuls of rose-water, and as much sack, sweeten it to your palate, and pour over them.

To make Orange Cream.

TAKE and pare the rind of a Seville orange very fine, and squeeze the juice of four oranges; put them into a stew-pan, with half a pint of water, and half a pound of fine sugar, beat the whites of five eggs and mix into it, and set them on a slow fire; stir it one way till it grows thick and white, strain it through a gauze, and stir it till cold; then beat the yolks of five eggs very fine, and put into your pan with the cream; stir it over a gentle fire till it is ready to boil; then put it in a bason and stir it till it is cold, and put it in your glasses.

To

MADE PLAIN AND EASY.

To make Gooseberry Cream.

TAKE two quarts of gooseberries, put to them as much water as will cover them, scald them, and then run them through a sieve with a spoon; to a quart of the pulp you must have six eggs well beaten; and when the pulp is hot, put in an ounce of fresh butter, sweeten it to your taste, put in your eggs, and stir them over a gentle fire till they grow thick, then set it by; and when it is almost cold, put into it two spoonfuls of juice of spinage, and a spoonful of orange-flower water or sack; stir it well together, and put it into your bason: when it is cold, serve it to table.

To make Barley Cream.

TAKE a small quantity of pearl-barley, boil it in milk and water till it is tender, then strain the liquor from it, put your barley into a quart of cream and let it boil a little, then take the whites of five eggs and the yolk of one, beaten with a spoonful of fine flour, and two spoonfuls of orange-flower water; then take the cream off the fire, and mix in the eggs by degrees, and set it over the fire again to thicken; sweeten to your taste, pour it into basons, and, when it is cold, serve it up.

Another Way.

TAKE a quart of French barley, boil it in three or four waters till it be pretty tender; then set a quart of cream on the fire with some mace and nutmeg; when the water begins to boil, drain out the barley from it, put in the cream, and let it boil till it be pretty thick and tender; then season it with sugar and salt: when it is cold serve it up.

To make Ice Cream.

PARE and stone twelve apricots, and scald them, beat them fine in a mortar, add to them six ounces of double-refined sugar, and a pint of scalding cream, and work it through a sieve; put it in a tin with a close cover, and set it in a tub of ice broken small, with four handfuls of salt mixed among the ice; when you see your cream grows thick round the edges of your tin, stir it well, and put it in again till it is quite thick; when the cream is all froze up, take it out of the tin, and put it into the mould you intend to turn it out of; put on the lid, and have another tub of salt and ice ready as before; put the mould in the middle, and lay the ice under and over it; let it stand four hours, and never turn it out till the moment you want it, then dip the mould in cold spring-water, and turn it into a plate. You may do any sort of fruit the same way.

To make Pistachio Cream.

Take half a pound of pistachio-nuts, break them, and take out the kernels; beat them in a mortar with a spoonful of brandy, put them in a stew-pan with a pint of good cream, and the yolks of two eggs beat very fine; stir it gently over a slow fire till it is thick, but be sure it does not boil, then put it into a soup-plate; when it is cold, stick some kernels cut longways all over it, and send it to table.

Hartshorn Cream.

Take four ounces of hartshorn shavings, and boil it in three pints of water till it is reduced to half a pint, and run it through a jelly-bag; put to it a pint of cream and four ounces of fine sugar, and just boil it up; put it into cups or glasses, and let it stand till quite cold; dip your cups or glasses in scalding water and turn them out into your dish; stick sliced almonds on them: it is generally eat with white wine and sugar.

To make Almond Cream.

Take a quart of cream, boil it with a nutmeg grated, a blade or two of mace, a bit of lemon-peel, and sweeten to your taste; then blanch a quarter of a pound of almonds, beat them very fine, with a spoonful of rose or orange flower water; take the whites of nine eggs well beat and strain them to your almonds, beat them together, rub them very well through a coarse hair sieve; mix all together with your cream, set it on the fire, stir it all one way all the time till it almost boils; pour it into a bowl, and stir it till cold, and then put it in cups or glasses, and send it to table.

To make a fine Cream.

Take a quart of cream, sweeten it to your palate, grate a little nutmeg, put in a spoonful of orange-flower water and rose-water, and two spoonfuls of sack, beat up four eggs, but two whites; stir it all together one way over the fire till it is thick; have cups ready, and pour it in.

To make Ratafia Cream.

Take six large laurel-leaves, boil them in a quart of thick cream; when it is boiled, throw away the leaves; beat the yolks of five eggs with a little cold cream, and sugar to your taste, then thicken the cream with your eggs, set it over the fire again, but do not let it boil; keep it stirring all the while one way, and pour it into china dishes: when it is cold it is fit for use.

To make whipt Cream.

TAKE a quart of thick cream and the whites of eight eggs beat well, with half a pint of sack; mix it together, and sweeten it to your taste with double-refined sugar. You may perfume it (if you please) with a little musk or ambergris tied in a rag, and steeped a little in the cream; whip it up with a whisk, and some lemon-peel tied in the middle of the whisk; take the froth up with a spoon, and lay it in your glasses or basons. This does well over a fine tart.

How to make the clear Lemon Cream.

TAKE a gill of clear water, infuse in it the rind of a lemon till it tastes of it; then take the whites of six eggs, the juice of four lemons; beat all well together, and run them through a hair sieve, sweeten them with double-refined sugar, and set them on the fire, not too hot, keep stirring; and when it is thick enough, take it off.

Sack Cream like Butter.

TAKE a quart of cream, boil it with mace, put to it six egg yolks well beaten, so let it boil up; then take it off the fire, and put in a little sack, and turn it; then put it in a cloth, and let the whey run from it; then take it out of the cloth and season it with rose-water and sugar, being very well broken with a spoon; serve it up in the dish, and pink it as you would do a dish of butter, and send it in with cream and sugar.

Clouted Cream.

TAKE four quarts of new milk from the cow, and put it in a broad earthen pan and let it stand till the next day, then put it over a very slow fire for half an hour; make it nearly hot to set the cream, then put it away till it is cold, and take the cream off, and beat it smooth with a spoon. It is accounted in the west of England very fine for tea or coffee, or to put over fruit tarts or pies.

Quince Cream.

TAKE your quinces and put them in boiling water unpared, boil them apace uncovered lest they discolour when they are boiled, pare them, beat them very tender with sugar, then take cream and mix it till it be pretty thick; if you boil your cream with a little cinnamon it will be better, but let it be cold before you put it to your quince.

Citron Cream.

TAKE a quart of cream and boil it with three pennyworth of good clear isinglass, which must be tied up in a piece of thin tiffany; put in a blade or two of mace strongly boiled in your cream

cream and isinglass till the cream be pretty thick; sweeten it to your taste with perfumed hard sugar; when it is taken off the fire, put in a little rose-water to your taste; then take a piece of your green freshest citron and cut it in little bits, the breadth of point-dales, and about half as long; and the cream being first put into dishes, when it is half cold put in your citron, so as it may sink from the top that it may not be seen, and may lie before it be at the bottom; if you wash your citron before in rose-water, it will make the colour better and fresher; so let it stand till the next day, where it may get no water, and where it may not be shaken.

Cream of Apples, Quinces, Gooseberries, Prunes, or Raspberries.

TAKE to every quart of cream four eggs, being first well beat and strained, and mix them with a little cold cream, and put it to your cream, being first boiled with whole mace; keep it stirring till you find it begins to thicken at the bottom and sides; your apples, quinces, and berries must be tenderly boiled, so as they will crush in the pulp; then season it with rose-water and sugar to your taste, putting it into dishes; and when they are cold, if there be any rose-water and sugar which lies waterish at the top, let it be drained out with a spoon: this pulp must be made ready before you boil the cream, and when it is boiled, cover over your pulp a pretty thickness with your egg-cream, which must have a little rose-water and sugar put to it.

Sugar Loaf Cream.

TAKE a quarter of a pound of hartshorn, and put to it a pottle of water, and set it on the fire in a pipkin covered till it be ready to seeth; then pour off the water and put a pottle of water more to it, and let it stand simmering on the fire till it be consumed to a pint, and with it two ounces of isinglass washed in rose-water, which must be put in with the second water; then strain it and let it cool; then take three pints of cream and boil it very well with a bag of nutmeg, cloves, cinnamon, and mace; then take a quarter of a pound of Jordan almonds, and lay them one night in cold water to blanch, and when they are blanched, let them lie two hours in cold water, then take them out, and dry them in a clean linen cloth, and beat them in a marble mortar, with fair water or rose-water; beat them to a very fine pulp, then take some of the aforesaid cream well warmed, and put the pulp by degrees into it, straining it through a cloth with the back of a spoon, till all the goodness of the almonds be strained out into the cream; then season the cream with rose-water and sugar; then take the aforesaid jelly, warm it till it dissolves, and season it with rose-water and sugar, and a

grain

grain of ambergris or musk (if you please); then mix your cream and jelly together very well, and put it into glasses well warmed (like sugar-loaves), and let it stand all night; then put them out upon a plate or two, or a white china dish, and stick the cream with piony kernels, or serve them in glasses, one on every trencher.

To make Whipt Syllabubs.

TAKE a quart of thick cream, and half a pint of sack, the juice of two Seville oranges or lemons, grate in the peel of two lemons, half a pound of double-refined sugar, pour it into a broad earthen pan, and whisk it well; but first sweeten some red wine or sack, and fill your glasses as full as you choose, then as the froth rises take it off with a spoon, and lay it on a sieve to drain; then lay it carefully into your glasses till they are as full as they will hold: do not make these long before you use them. Many use cyder sweetened, or any wine you please, or lemon, or orange whey made thus: squeeze the juice of a lemon, or orange into a quarter of a pint of milk; when the curd is hard, pour the whey clear off, and sweeten it to your palate; you may colour some with the juice of spinage, some with saffron, and some with cochineal (just as you fancy).

To make Everlasting Syllabub.

TAKE five half pints of thick cream, half a pint of Rhenish, half a pint of sack, and the juice of two large Seville oranges; grate in just the yellow rind of three lemons, and a pound of double-refined sugar well beat and sifted; mix all together with a spoonful of orange-flower water; beat it well together with a whisk half an hour, then with a spoon take it off, and lay it on a sieve to drain, then fill your glasses: these will keep above a week, and are better made the day before. The best way to whip syllabub is, have a fine large chocolate-mill, which you must keep on purpose, and a large deep bowl to mill them in: it is both quicker done, and the froth stronger; for the thin that is left at the bottom, have ready some calf's-foot jelly boiled and clarified, there must be nothing but the calf's-foot boiled to a hard jelly; when cold take off the fat, clear it with the whites of eggs, run it through a flannel bag, and mix it with the clear which you saved of the syllabubs; sweeten it to your palate, and give it a boil, then pour it into basons, or what you please: when cold, turn it out, and it is a fine flummery.

To make Solid Syllabubs.

To a quart of rich cream put a pint of white-wine, the juice of two lemons, the rind of one grated, sweeten it to your taste;

mill it with a chocolate-mill till it is all of a thickness; then put it in glasses, or a bowl, and set it in a cool place till next day.

To make a Syllabub from the Cow.

MAKE your syllabub of either cyder or wine, sweeten it pretty sweet, and grate nutmeg in; then milk the milk into the liquor: when this is done, pour over the top half a pint or a pint of cream, according to the quantity of syllabub you make. You may make this syllabub at home, only have new milk; make it as hot as milk from the cow, and out of a tea-pot, or any such thing, pour it in, holding your hand very high, and strew over some currants well washed and picked, and plumped before the fire.

To make a Trifle.

COVER the bottom of your dish or bowl with Naples biscuits broke in pieces, mackeroons broke in halves, and ratafia cakes; just wet them all through with sack, then make a good boiled custard, not too thick, and when cold pour it over it, then put a syllabub over that. You may garnish it with ratafia cakes, currant jelly, and flowers, and strew different coloured nonpareils over it.

N. B.—These are bought at the confectioners.

To make Hartshorn Jelly.

BOIL half a pound of hartshorn in three quarts of water over a gentle fire, till it becomes a jelly. If you take out a little to cool, and it hangs on the spoon, it is enough. Strain it while it is hot, put it in a well-tinned sauce-pan, put to it a pint of Rhenish wine, and a quarter of a pound of loaf-sugar; beat the whites of four eggs or more to a froth; stir it all together that the whites mix well with the jelly, and pour it in, as if you were cooling it. Let it boil two or three minutes; then put in the juice of three or four lemons; let it boil a minute or two longer; when it is finely curdled, and a pure white colour, have ready a swan-skin jelly-bag over a china bason, pour in your jelly, and pour it back again till it is as clear as rock water; then set a very clean china bason under, have your glasses as clean as possible, and with a clean spoon fill your glasses. Have ready some thin rind of the lemons, and when you have filled half your glasses, throw your peel into the bason; and when the jelly is all run out of the bag, with a clean spoon, fill the rest of the glasses, and they will look of a fine amber colour. Now in putting in the ingredients there is no certain rule. You must put in lemon and sugar to your palate; most people love them sweet; and indeed they are good for nothing unless they are.

To make Orange Jelly.

TAKE half a pound of hartshorn shavings, or four ounces of isinglass, and boil it in spring-water till it is of a strong jelly; take the juice of three Seville oranges, three lemons, and six China oranges, and the rind of one Seville orange, and one lemon pared very thin; put them to your jelly, sweeten it with loaf-sugar to your palate; beat up the whites of eight eggs to a froth, and mix well in, then boil it for ten minutes, then run it through a jelly-bag till it is very clear, and put it in moulds till cold, then dip your mould in warm water, and turn it out into a china dish, or a flat glass, and garnish with flowers.

To make Ribband Jelly.

TAKE out the great bones of four calves feet, put the feet into a pot with ten quarts of water, three ounces of hartshorn, three ounces of isinglass, a nutmeg quartered, and four blades of mace; then boil this till it comes to two quarts, strain it through a flannel bag, let it stand twenty-four hours, then scrape off all the fat from the top very clean, then slice it, put to it the whites of six eggs beaten to a froth, boil it a little, and strain it through a flannel bag, then run the jelly into little high glasses, run every colour as thick as your finger, one colour must be thorough cold before you put another on, and that you put on must be but blood-warm, for fear it mix together. You must colour red with cochineal, green with spinage, yellow with saffron, blue with syrup of violets, white with thick cream, and sometimes the jelly by itself. You may add orange-flower water, or wine and sugar, and lemon if you please; but this is all fancy.

To make Calves Feet Jelly.

BOIL two calves feet in a gallon of water till it comes to a quart, then strain it, let it stand till cold, skim off all the fat clean, and take the jelly up clean. If there is any settling in the bottom, leave it; put the jelly into a sauce-pan, with a pint of mountain wine, half a pound of loaf-sugar, the juice of four large lemons; beat up six or eight whites of eggs with a whisk, then put them into a sauce-pan, and stir all together well till it boils; let it boil a few minutes; have ready a large flannel bag, pour it in, it will run through quick; pour it in again till it runs clear, then have ready a large china bason, with the lemon-peels cut as thin as possible, let the jelly run into that bason; and the peels both give it a fine amber colour, and also a flavour; with a clean silver spoon fill your glasses.

To make Currant Jelly.

STRIP the currants from the stalks, put them in a stone jar, stop it close, set it in a kettle of boiling water half way the jar, let it boil half an hour, take it out and strain the juice through a coarse hair sieve; to a pint of juice put a pound of sugar, set it over a fine quick clear fire in your preserving-pan or bell-metal skillet; keep stirring it all the time till the sugar is melted, then skim the scum off as fast as it rises. When your jelly is very clear and fine, pour it into gallipots; when cold, cut white paper, just the bigness of the top of the pot, and lay on the jelly, dip those papers in brandy; then cover them close with white paper, and prick it full of holes; set it in a dry place, put some into glasses and paper them.

To make Pippin Jelly.

PARE and core your pippins; just cover them with spring-water, set them on to boil quick till it is a kind of jelly, then put them in a jelly-bag, and let them drop; put in one small lump of sugar to preserve the colour.

To make China Orange Jelly.

TO two ounces of isinglass, boiled down very strong by itself, put one quart of orange-juice, with a little cinnamon, mace, as much sugar as you find requisite, the whites of eight eggs, boil all together about ten minutes pretty fast, run it through a bag; and after it is cleared, take some of the skin of the orange, cut small like straws, and put into it.

N. B.—It is a great improvement to add the juice of two Seville oranges.

To make Raspberry Jam.

TAKE a pint of this currant jelly and a quart of raspberries, bruise them well together, set them over a slow fire, keeping them stirring all the time till it boils. Let it boil gently half an hour, and stir it round very often to keep it from sticking, and rub it through a cullender; pour it into your gallipots, paper as you do the currant jelly, and keep it for use. They will keep for two or three years, and have the full flavour of the raspberry.

To make a Hedge-Hog.

TAKE two pounds of blanched almonds, beat them well in a mortar, with a little canary and orange-flower water, to keep them from oiling. Make them into stiff paste, then beat in the yolks of twelve eggs, leave out five of the whites, put to it a pint of cream sweetened with sugar, put in half a pound of

sweet

sweet butter melted, set it on a furnace or slow fire, and keep it constantly stirring, till it is stiff enough to be made in the form of a hedge-hog; then stick it full of blanched almonds, slit and stuck up like the bristles of a hedge-hog, then put it into a dish; take a pint of cream, and the yolks of four eggs beat up, sweetened with sugar to your palate; stir them together over a slow fire till it is quite hot; then pour it round the hedge-hog in a dish, and let it stand till it is cold, and serve it up; or a rich calf's foot jelly, made clear and good, poured into the dish round the hedge-hog; when it is cold, it looks pretty, and makes a neat dish; or it looks pretty in the middle of a table for supper.

To make Moon-Shine.

FIRST have a piece of tin made in the shape of a half-moon, as deep as a half-pint bason, and one in the shape of a large star, and two or three lesser ones; boil two calves feet in a gallon of water till it comes to a quart, then strain it off, and when cold skim off the fat, take half the jelly and sweeten it with sugar to your palate, beat up the whites of four eggs, stir all together over a slow fire till it boils; then run it through a flannel bag till clear, put it in a clean sauce-pan, and take an ounce of sweet almonds blanched and beat very fine in a marble mortar, with two spoonfuls of rose-water, and two of orange-flower water; then strain it through a coarse cloth, mix it with the jelly; stir in four large spoonfuls of thick cream, stir it all together till it boils; then have ready the dish you intend it for, lay the tin in the shape of a half-moon in the middle, and the stars round it; lay little weights on the tin to keep them in the places you would have them lie; then pour in the above blanc-mange into the dish, and when it is quite cold take out the tin things, and mix the other half of the jelly with half a pint of good white wine, and the juice of two or three lemons, with loaf-sugar enough to make it sweet, and the whites of eight eggs beat fine; stir it all together over a slow fire till it boils, then run it through a flannel bag till it is quite clear into a china bason, and very carefully fill up the places where you took the tin out; let it stand till cold, and send it to table.

N. B.—You may for change fill the dish with a fine thick almond custard; and when it is cold, fill up the half-moon and stars with a clear jelly.

The Floating-Island, a pretty Dish for the Middle of a Table at a Second Course, or for Supper.

YOU may take a soup-dish, according to the size and quantity you would make, but a pretty deep glass is best, and set it is on a china dish; first take a quart of the thickest cream you can get, make it pretty sweet with fine sugar, pour in a gill of sack, grate the yellow rind of a lemon in, and mill the cream till it is all of a thick froth; then carefully pour the thin from the froth into a dish; take a French roll (or as many as you want), cut it as thin as you can, lay a layer of that as light as possible on the cream, then a layer of currant jelly, then a very thin layer of roll, and then hartshorn jelly, then French roll, and over that whip your froth which you saved off the cream very well milled up, and lay at top as high as you can heap it; and as for the rim of the dish, set it round with fruit or sweet-meats, according to your fancy. This looks very pretty in the middle of a table with candles round it; and you may make it of as many different colours as you fancy, and according to what jellies and jams, or sweet-meats you have; or at the bottom of your dish you may put the thickest cream you can get; but that is as you fancy.

To make a Fish-Pond.

FILL four large fish-moulds with flummery, and six small ones, take a china bowl, and put in a half a pint of stiff clear calf's foot jelly, let it stand till cold, then lay two of the small fishes on the jelly, the right side down, put in half a pint more jelly, let it stand till cold, then lay in the four small fishes across one another, that when you turn the bowl upside down the heads and tails may be seen, then almost fill your bowl with jelly, and let it stand till cold, then lay in the jelly four large fishes, and fill the bason quite full with jelly, and let it stand till the next day; when you want to use it, set your bowl to the brim in hot water for one minute, take care that you do not let the water go into the bason, lay your plate on the top of the bason, and turn it upside down; if you want it for the middle, turn it out upon a salver; be sure you make your jelly very stiff and clear.

To make a Hen's Nest.

TAKE three or five of the smallest pullet eggs you can get, fill them with flummery; and when they are stiff and cold, peel off the shells, pare off the rinds of two lemons very thin, and boil them in sugar and water to take off the bitterness, when they are cold, cut them in long shreds to imitate straws, then fill a bason one-third full of stiff calf's foot jelly, and let it stand till cold, then lay in the shred of the lemons in a ring about two inches high in the middle of your bason, strew a few corns of sago to look like barley, fill the bason to the height of the peel and let it stand till cold, then lay your eggs of flummery in the middle of the ring that the straw may be seen round,

round, fill the bason quite full of jelly, and let it stand, and turn it out the same way as the fish-pond.

To make a Mouse Trap.

TAKE a pint of cream and eggs, prepared as if for custards to put into cups, fill your dish, and have ready some fine jar raisins stoned, or dried cherries, stick these into the custard, have ready some clear barley-sugar (as none else will do), set it by the fire till it dissolves, so draw it out into lengths and cross it, draw some of it as small as a thread, let the custard be cold in the dish before this is put on: garnish as you please.

To make the Moon and Stars in Jelly.

TAKE the dish you intend for the table, have ready some white jelly, the same as for flummery; likewise a mould the shape of half a moon and two or three the shape of stars, fix them on your dish before you put in your white jelly, which is to represent the sky; have ready some clear jelly such as is for glasses, when your white jelly is cold on the dish, take out the moulds of the moon and stars carefully, and fill up the places with the clear jelly, but not hot, least it dissolves the white: it is a pretty dish by candle-light.

Hen and Chickens in Jelly.

MAKE some flummery with a deal of sweet almonds in it, colour a little of it brown with chocolate, and put it in a mould the shape of a hen; then colour some more flummery with the yolk of a hard egg beat as fine as possible, leave part of your flummery white, then fill the moulds of seven chickens, three with white flummery, and three with yellow, and one the colour of the hen; when cold, turn them into a deep dish; put under and round them lemon-peel boiled tender and cut like straw; then put a little clear calf's-foot jelly under them to keep them in their places, and let it stand till it is stiff, then fill up your dish with more jelly. They are a pretty decoration for a grand table.

To make a Desert Island.

TAKE a lump of paste and form it into a rock three inches broad at the top, colour it, and set it in the middle of a deep china dish, and set a cast figure on it, with a crow on its head, and a knot of rock-candy at the feet; then make a roll of paste an inch thick, and stick it on the inner edge of the dish, two parts round, and cut eight pieces of eringo roots, about three inches long, and fix them upright to the roll of paste on the edge; make gravel-walks of shot-comfits, from the middle of the end of the dish, and set small figures in them, roll out some paste, and cut it open like Chinese rails; bake it, and fix it on either side of one of the gravel-walks with gum, have ready a web of spun sugar, and set it on the pillars of eringo root, and cut part of the webb off, to form an entrance where the Chinese rails are. It is a pretty middle dish for a second course at a grand table, or a wedding supper, only set two crowned figures on the mount instead of one.

Gilded Fish in Jelly.

MAKE a little clear blanc-mange, then fill two large fish-moulds with it, and when it is cold turn it out, and gild them with gold leaf, or strew them over with gold and silver bran mixed, then lay them on a soup dish, and fill it with clear thin calf's-foot jelly, it must be so thin as they will swim in it: if you have no jelly, Lisbon wine or any kind of pale made wines will do.

To make Hartshorn Flummery.

BOIL half a pound of the shavings of hartshorn in three pints of water till it comes to a pint, then strain it through a sieve into a bason, and set it by to cool; then set it over the fire, let it just melt, and put to it half a pint of thick cream scalded and grown cold again, a quarter of a pint of white wine, and two spoonfuls of orange-flower water; sweeten it with sugar, and beat it for an hour and a half, or it will not mix well nor look well; dip your cups in water before you put in the flummery, or else it will not turn out well: it is best when it stands a day or two before you turn it out. When you serve it up, turn it out of the cups, and stick blanched almonds cut into long narrow bits on the top. You may eat them with wine or cream.

A second Way to make Hartshorn Flummery.

TAKE three ounces of hartshorn, and put to it two quarts of spring-water, let it simmer over the fire six or seven hours till half the water is consumed, or else put it into a jug, and set it in the oven with household-bread, then strain it through a sieve, and beat half a pound of almonds very fine, with some orange-flower water in the beating; when they are beat, mix a little of your jelly with it, and some fine sugar; strain it out and mix it with your other jelly, stir it together till it is little more than blood-warm; then pour it into half pint basons or dishes for the purpose, and fill them up half full: when you use them, turn them out of the dish as you do flummery; if it does not come out clean, set your bason a minute or two in warm water. You may stick almonds in or not, just as you please. Eat it with wine and sugar. Or make your jelly this way:

put

put six ounces of hartshorn in a glazed jug with a long neck, and put to it three pints of soft water, cover the top of the jug close, and put a weight on it to keep it steady; set it in a pot or kettle of water twenty-four hours, let it not boil, but be scalding hot; then strain it out, and make your jelly.

To make Oatmeal Flummery.

GET some oatmeal, put it into a broad deep pan, then cover it with water, stir it together and let it stand twelve hours, then pour off that water clear, and put on a good deal of fresh water, shift it again in twelve hours, and so on in twelve more; then pour off the water clear, and strain the oatmeal through a coarse hair sieve, and pour it into a sauce-pan, keeping it stirring all the time with a stick till it boils and is very thick; then pour it into dishes; when cold, turn it into plates, and eat it with what you please, either wine and sugar, or beer and sugar, or milk. It eats very pretty with cyder and sugar. You must observe to put a great deal of water to the oatmeal, and when you pour off the last water, pour on just enough fresh as to strain the oatmeal well. Some let it stand forty-eight hours, some three days, shifting the water every twelve hours; but that is as you love it for sweetness or tartness. Grits once cut does better than oatmeal. Mind to stir it together when you put in fresh water.

Blanc-mange.

TAKE a quart of cream, and half an ounce of isinglass, beat it fine, and stir it into the cream; let it boil softly over a slow fire a quarter of an hour, keep it stirring all the time; then take it off, sweeten it to your palate, and put in a spoonful of rose-water, and a spoonful of orange-flower water; strain it, and pour it into a glass or bason, or what you please, and when it is cold turn it out. It makes a fine side-dish. You may eat it with cream, wine, or what you please. Lay round it baked pears. It both looks very pretty, and eats fine.

Dutch Blanc-mange.—Excellent.

To an ounce of isinglass put half a pint of boiling water; boil it till dissolved, if much wasted, add more water to make it half a pint, boil a piece of lemon-peel in it, then take half a pint of white wine, yolks of three eggs well beat, and mix with the wine, then put it to the isinglass, add the juice of lemon and sugar to your taste, mix it well and boil it a little, strain it through a lawn sieve, stir it till near cold, then put it in your shapes.

A buttered Tort.

TAKE eight or ten large codlings and scald them, when cold skin them, take the pulp and beat it as fine as you can with a silver spoon; then mix in the yolks of six eggs and the whites of four, beat all well together; squeeze in the juice of a Seville orange, and shred the rind as fine as possible, with some grated nutmeg and sugar to your taste; melt some fine fresh butter, and beat up with it according as it wants, till it is all like a fine thick cream, and then make a fine puff-paste, have a large tin patty that will just hold it, cover the patty with the paste, and pour in the ingredients; do not put any cover on, bake it a quarter of an hour, then slip it out of the patty on a dish, and throw fine sugar well beat all over it. It is a very pretty side dish for a second course. You may make this of any large apples you please.

To make Fruit Wafers, of Codlings, Plumbs, &c.

TAKE the pulp of any fruit rubbed through a hair sieve, and to every three ounces of fruit take six ounces of sugar finely sifted; dry the sugar very well till it be very hot; heat the pulp also till it be very hot; then mix it, and set over a slow charcoal fire till it be almost a-boiling, then pour it into glasses or trenchers, and set it on the stove till you see it will leave the glasses; but before it begins to candy, take them off, and turn them upon papers in what form you please: you may colour them red with clove-gilliflowers steeped in the juice of lemon.

To make White Wafers.

BEAT the yolk of an egg, and mix it with a quarter of a pint of fair water; then mix half a pound of best flour, and thin it with damask-rose-water till you think it of a proper thickness to bake; sweeten it to your palate with fine sugar finely sifted.

To make Brown Wafers.

TAKE a quart of ordinary cream, then take the yolks of three or four eggs, and as much fine flour as will make it into a thin batter; sweeten it with three quarters of a pound of fine sugar finely searced, and as much pounded cinnamon as will make it taste; do not mix them till the cream be cold; butter your pans, and make them very hot before you bake them.

How to make Gooseberry Wafers.

TAKE gooseberries before they are ready for preserving, cut off the black heads, and boil them with as much water as will cover them all, to mash; then pass the liquor and all, as it will

run,

run, through a hair sieve, and put some pulp through with a spoon, but not too near: it is to be pulped neither too thick nor too thin; measure it, and to a gill of it take half a pound of double-refined sugar, dry it, put it to your pulp, and let it scald on a slow fire, not to boil at all; stir it very well, and then will rise a frothy white scum, which take clear off as it rises; you must scald and skim it till no scum rises and it comes clean from the pan-side, then take it off, and let it cool a little; have ready sheets of glass very smooth, about the thickness of parchment, which is not very thick; you must spread it on the glasses with a knife, very thin, even, and smooth, then set it in the stove with a slow fire; if you do it in the morning, at night you must cut it into long pieces with a broad case-knife, and put your knife clear under it, and fold it two or three times over, and lay them in a stove, turning them sometimes till they are pretty dry; but do not keep them too long, for they will lose their colour: if they do not come clean off your glasses at night, keep them till next morning.

How to make Orange Wafers.

TAKE the best oranges and boil them in three or four waters till they be tender, then take out the kernels and the juice, and beat them to pulp in a clean marble mortar, and rub them through a hair sieve; to a pound of this pulp take a pound and a half of double-refined sugar, beaten and searced; take half of your sugar and put it into your oranges, and boil it till it ropes; then take it from the fire, and when it is cold make it up in paste with the other half of your sugar; make but a little at a time, for it will dry too fast; then with a little rolling-pin roll them out as thin as tiffany upon papers; cut them round with a little drinking glass, and let them dry, and they will look very clear.

How to make Orange Cakes.

TAKE the peels of four oranges, being first pared, and the meat taken out, boil them tender, and beat them small in a marble mortar; then take the meat of them, and two more oranges, your seeds and skins being picked out, and mix it with the peelings that are beaten; set them on the fire with a spoonful or two of orange-flower water, keeping it stirring till that moisture be pretty well dried up; then have ready to every pound of that pulp, four pounds and a quarter of double-refined sugar, finely searced; make your sugar very hot, and dry it upon the fire, then mix it and the pulp together, and set it on the fire again till the sugar be very well melted, but be sure it does not boil: you may put in a little peel, small, shred, or grated, and when it is cold, draw it up in double papers; dry them before the fire, and when you turn them, put two together; or you may keep them in deep glasses or pots, and dry them as you have occasion.

To make Orange Loaves.

TAKE your orange and cut a round hole in the top, take out all the meat, and as much of the white as you can, without breaking the skin; then boil them in water till tender, shifting the water till it is not bitter, then take them up and wipe them dry; then take a pound of fine sugar, a quart of water (or in proportion to the oranges), boil it, and take off the scum as it rises; then put in your oranges, and let them boil a little, and let them lie a day or two in the syrup; then take the yolks of two eggs, a quarter of a pint of cream (or more), beat them well together, then grate in two Naples biscuits, or white bread, a quarter of a pound of butter, and four spoonfuls of sack; mix it all together till your butter is melted, then fill the oranges with it, and bake them in a slow oven as long as you would a custard, then stick in some cut citron, and fill them up with sack, butter, and sugar grated over.

How to make Orange Biscuits.

PARE your oranges, not very thick, put them into water, but first weigh your peels, let it stand over the fire, and let it boil till it be very tender; then beat it in a marble mortar, till it be very fine smooth paste; to every ounce of peels put two ounces and a half of double-refined sugar well searced, mix them well together with a spoon in the mortar, then spread it with a knife upon pie-plates, and set it in an oven a little warm, or before the fire; when it feels dry upon the top, cut it into what fashion you please, and turn them into another plate, and set them in a stove till they are dry; where the edges look rough, when it is dry, they must be cut with a pair of scissars.

To make White Cakes like China Dishes.

TAKE the yolks of two eggs, and two spoonfuls of sack, and as much rose-water, some carraway-seeds, and as much flour as will make it a paste stiff enough to roll very thin: if you would have them like dishes, you must bake them upon dishes buttered: cut them out into what work you please to candy them; take a pound of fine searced sugar perfumed, and the white of an egg, and three or four spoonfuls of rose-water, stir it till it looks white; and when that paste is cold, do it with a feather on one side: this candied, let it dry, and do the other side so, and dry it also.

To make a Lemon Honeycomb.

TAKE the juice of one lemon, and sweeten it with fine sugar to your palate; then take a pint of cream, and the white of an egg, and put in some sugar, and beat it up; and as the froth rises, take it off and put it on the juice of the lemon, till you have taken all the cream off upon the lemon: make it the day before you want it, in a dish that is proper.

To make Sugar of Pearl.

TAKE damask rose-water half a pint, one pound of fine sugar, half an ounce of prepared pearl beat to powder, eight leaves of beaten gold; boil them together according to art; add the pearl and gold leaves when just done; then cast them on a marble.

Almond Rice.

BLANCH the almonds, and pound them in a marble or wooden mortar, and mix them in a little boiling water; press them as long as there is any milk in the almonds, adding fresh water every time; to every quart of almond juice, a quarter of a pound of rice, and two or three spoonfuls of orange-flower water; mix them all together, and simmer it over a very slow charcoal fire, keep stirring it often; when done, sweeten it to your palate; put it into plates, and throw beaten cinnamon over it.

Almond Knots.

TAKE two pounds of almonds and blanch them in hot water, beat them in a mortar to a very fine paste, with rose-water; do what you can to keep them from oiling; take a pound of double-refined sugar, sifted through a lawn sieve, leave out some to make up your knots, put the rest into a pan upon the fire till it is scalding hot, and at the same time have your almonds scalding hot in another pan; then mix them together with the whites of three eggs beaten to froth, and let it stand till it is cold, then roll it with some of the sugar you left out, and lay them in platters of paper: they will not roll into any shape, but lay them as well as you can, and bake them in a cool oven; it must not be hot, neither must they be coloured.

How to make fine Almond Cakes.

TAKE a pound of Jordan almonds, blanch them, beat them very fine with a little orange-flower water to keep them from oiling; then take a pound and a quarter of fine sugar, boil it to a candy height; then put in your almonds; then take two fresh lemons, grate off the rind very thin, and put as much juice as to make it of a quick taste; then put it into your glasses, and set it into your stove, stirring them often that they do not candy: so when it is a little dry, put it into little cakes upon sheets of glass.

Sugar Cakes.

TAKE a pound and a half of very fine flour, one pound of cold butter, half a pound of sugar, work all these well together into a paste, then roll it with the palms of your hands into balls, and cut them with a glass into cakes; lay them in a sheet of paper, with some flour under them: to bake them you may make tumblets, only blanch in almonds, and beat them small; lay them in the midst of a long piece of paste, and roll it round with your fingers, and cast them into knots in what fashion you please: prick them and bake them.

Sugar Cakes another Way.

TAKE half a pound of fine sugar searced, and as much flour, two eggs beaten with a little rose-water, a piece of butter about the bigness of an egg, work them well together till they be a smooth paste; then make them into cakes, working every one with the palms of your hands; then lay them in plates, rubbed over with a little butter; so bake them in an oven little more than warm. You may make knots of the same the cakes are made of; but in the mingling you must put in a few carraway-seeds; when they are wrought to a paste, roll them with the ends of your fingers into small rolls, and make it into knots; lay them upon pie-plates rubbed with butter, and bake them.

Cracknels.

TAKE half a pound of the whitest flour, and a pound of sugar beaten small, two ounces of butter cold, one spoonful of carraway-seeds steeped all night in vinegar; then put in three yolks of eggs, and a little rose-water, work your paste all together; and after that beat it with a rolling-pin till it be light; then roll it out thin, and cut it with a glass, lay it thin on plates buttered, and prick them with a pin; then take the yolks of two eggs, beaten with rose-water, and rub them over with it; then set them into a pretty quick oven, and when they are brown, take them out and lay them in a dry place.

To make German Puffs.

TAKE two spoonfuls of fine flour, two eggs beat well, half a pint of cream or milk, two ounces of melted butter, stir all well together, and add a little salt and nutmeg; put them in tea-cups, or little deep tin moulds, half full, and bake them a quarter of an hour in a quick oven; but let it be hot enough to colour them at top and bottom: turn them into a dish, and strew powder-sugar over them.

To make Carolina Snow Balls.

TAKE half a pound of rice, wash it clean, divide it into six parts; take six apples, pare them and scoop out the cores, in which place put a little lemon-peel shred very fine; then have ready some thin cloths to tie the balls in; put the rice in the cloth, and lay the apple on it; tie them up close, put them into cold water, and when the water boils they will take an hour and a quarter boiling: be very careful how you turn them into the dish that you do not break the rice, and they will look as white as snow, and make a very pretty dish. The sauce is, to this quantity, a quarter of a pound of fresh butter melted thick, a glass of white wine, a little nutmeg, and beaten cinnamon, made very sweet with sugar; boil all up together, and pour it into a bason, and send it to table.

Ginger Tablet.

MELT a pound of loaf-sugar with a little bit of butter over the fire, and put in an ounce of pounded ginger; keep it stirring till it begins to rise into a froth, then pour it into pewter plates, and let it stand to cool: the platter must be rubbed with a little oil, and then put them in a china dish, and send them to table. Garnish with flowers of any kind.

How to make the thin Apricot Chips.

TAKE your apricots or peaches, pare them and cut them very thin into chips, and take three quarters of their weight in sugar, it being finely searced; then put the sugar and the apricots into a pewter dish, and set them upon coals; and when the sugar is all dissolved, turn them upon the edge of the dish out of the syrup, and so set them by: keep them turning till they have drank up the syrup; be sure they never boil. They must be warmed in the syrup once every day, and so laid out upon the edge of the dish till the syrup be drank.

Sham Chocolate.

TAKE a pint of milk, boil it over a slow fire, with some whole cinnamon, and sweeten it with Lisbon sugar; beat up the yolks of three eggs, throw all together into a chocolate-pot, and mill it one way, or it will turn: serve it up in chocolate-cups.

To make Chocolate.

SIX pounds of cocoa-nuts, one of anise-seeds, four ounces of long pepper, one of cinnamon, a quarter of a pound of almonds,

monds, one ounce of piſtachios, as much achiote as will make it the colour of brick, three grains of muſk, and as much ambergris, ſix pounds of loaf-ſugar, one ounce of nutmegs, dry and beat them, and ſearce them through a fine ſieve; your almonds muſt be beat to a paſte and mixed with the other ingredients; then dip your ſugar in orange-flower or roſe water, and put it in a ſkillet on a very gentle charcoal fire; then put in the ſpice and ſtew it well together, then the muſk and ambergris, then put in the cocoa-nuts laſt of all, then achiote, wetting it with the water the ſugar was dipt in; ſtew all theſe very well together over a hotter fire than before; then take it up and put it into boxes, or what form you like, and ſet it to dry in a warm place: the piſtachios and almonds muſt be a little beat in a mortar, then ground upon a ſtone.

Another Way to make Chocolate.

TAKE ſix pounds of the beſt Spaniſh nuts, when parched and cleaned from the hulls, take three pounds of ſugar, two ounces of the beſt cinnamon, beaten and ſifted very fine; to every two pounds of nuts put in three good vanillas, or more or leſs as you pleaſe; to every pound of nuts half a drachm of cardamum-ſeeds, very finely beaten and ſearced.

CHAP. XXII.

OF MADE-WINES; BREWING; BAKING FRENCH BREAD AND MUFFINS; CHEESE, &c.

To make Raiſin Wine.

TAKE two hundred of raiſins (ſtalks and all), and put them into a large hogſhead, fill it with water, let them ſteep a fortnight, ſtirring them every day; then pour off all the liquor and preſs the raiſins; put both liquors together in a nice clean veſſel that will juſt hold it, for it muſt be full; let it ſtand till it has done hiſſing, or making the leaſt noiſe, then ſtop it cloſe and let it ſtand ſix months; peg it, and if you find it quite clear, rack it off in another veſſel; ſtop it cloſe and let it ſtand three months longer; then bottle it, and when you uſe it, rack it off into a decanter.

The beſt Way to make Raiſin Wine.

TAKE a clean wine or brandy hogſhead, take great care it is very ſweet and clean, put in two hundred of raiſins (ſtalks and

and all), and then fill the vessel with fine clear spring-water; let it stand till you think it has done hissing, then throw in two quarts of fine French brandy; put in the bung slightly, and, in about three weeks or a month (if you are sure it has done fretting), stop it down close; let it stand six months, peg it near the top, and if you find it very fine and good, fit for drinking, bottle it off, or else stop it up again, and let it stand six months longer: it should stand six months in the bottle. This is by much the best way of making it, as I have seen by experience, as the wine will be much stronger, but less of it: the different sorts of raisins make quite a different wine; and after you have drawn off all the wine, throw on ten gallons of spring-water; take off the head of the barrel and stir it well twice a day, pressing the raisins as well as you can; let it stand a fortnight or three weeks, then draw it off into a proper vessel to hold it, and squeeze the raisins well; add two quarts of brandy, and two quarts of syrup of alder-berries, stop it close when it has done working, and in about three months it will be fit for drinking. If you do not choose to make this second wine, fill your hogshead with spring-water, and set it in the sun for three or four months, and it will make excellent vinegar.

How to make Blackberry Wine.

TAKE your berries when full ripe, put them into a large vessel of wood or stone, with a spicket in it, and pour upon them as much boiling water as will just appear at the top of them; as soon as you can endure your hand in them, bruise them very well, till all the berries be broke: then let them stand close covered till the berries be well wrought up to the top, which usually is three or four days, then draw off the clear juice into another vessel; and add to every ten quarts of this liquor one pound of sugar, stir it well in, and let it stand to work in another vessel like the first, a week or ten days; then draw it off at the spicket through a jelly-bag into a large vessel; take four ounces of isinglass, lay it in steep twelve hours in a pint of white wine; the next morning boil it till it be all dissolved upon a slow fire; then take a gallon of your blackberry-juice, put in the dissolved isinglass, give it a boil together, and put it in hot.

To make Alder Wine.

PICK the alder-berries when full ripe, put them into a stone-jar and set them in the oven, or a kettle of boiling water till the jar is hot through; then take them out and strain them through a coarse cloth, wringing the berries, and put the juice into a clean kettle: to every quart of juice put a pound of fine Lisbon sugar, let it boil, and skim it well; when it is clear and fine, pour it into a jar; when cold, cover it clofe, and keep it till you make raifin wine; then when you tun your wine, to every gallon of wine put half a pint of the elder-fyrup.

To make Orange Wine.

TAKE twelve pounds of the beft powder fugar, with the whites of eight or ten eggs well beaten, into fix gallons of fpring-water, and boil three quarters of an hour; when cold, put into it fix fpoonfuls of yeaft, and the juice of twelve lemons, which, being pared, muft ftand with two pounds of white fugar in a tankard, and in the morning fkim off the top, and then put it into the water; then add the juice and rinds of fifty oranges, but not the white parts of the rinds, and fo let it work all together two days and two nights; then add two quarts of Rhenifh or white wine, and put it into your veffel.

To make Orange Wine with Raifins.

TAKE thirty pounds of new Malaga raifins picked clean, chop them fmall, take twenty large Seville oranges, ten of them you muft pare as thin as for preferving; boil about eight gallons of foft water till a third be confumed, let it cool a little; then put five gallons of it hot upon your raifins and orange-peel, ftill it well together, cover it up, and when it is cold let it ftand five days, ftirring it once or twice a day; then pafs it through a hair fieve, and with a fpoon prefs it as dry as you can, put it in a runlet fit for it, and put to it the rind of the other ten oranges, cut as thin as the firft; then make a fyrup of the juice of twenty oranges, with a pound of white fugar. It muft be made the day before you tun it up; ftir it well together, and ftop it clofe; let it ftand two months to clear, then bottle it up. It will keep three years, and is better for keeping.

To make Alder-Flower Wine, very like Frontiniac.

TAKE fix gallons of fpring-water, twelve pounds of white fugar, fix pounds of raifins of the fun chopped; boil thefe together one hour, then take the flowers of alder, when they are falling, and rub them off to the quantity of half a peck; when the liquor is cold, put them in; the next day put in the juice of three lemons, and four fpoonfuls of good ale yeaft; let it ftand covered up two days, then ftrain it off and put it in a veffel fit for it. To every gallon of wine put a quart of Rhenifh, and put your bung lightly on a fortnight, then ftop it down clofe: let it ftand fix months; and if you find it is fine, bottle it off.

To make Gooseberry Wine.

GATHER your gooseberries in dry weather, when they are half ripe, pick them, and bruise a peck in a tub, with a wooden mallet; then take a horse-hair cloth and press them as much as possible, without breaking the seeds; when you have pressed out all the juice, to every gallon of gooseberries put three pounds of fine dry powder sugar, stir it all together till the sugar is dissolved, then put it in a vessel or cask, which must be quite full: if ten or twelve gallons, let it stand a fortnight; if a twenty gallon cask, five weeks. Set it in a cool place, then draw it off from the lees, clear the vessel of the lees, and pour in the clear liquor again: if it be a ten gallon cask, let it stand three months; if a twenty gallon, four months; then bottle it off.

To make Currant Wine.

GATHER your currants on a fine dry day, when the fruit is full ripe; strip them, put them in a large pan, and bruise them with a wooden pestle. Let them stand in a pan or tub twenty-four hours to ferment; then run it through a hair sieve, and do not let your hand touch the liquor. To every gallon of this liquor put two pounds and a half of white sugar, stir it well together, and put it into your vessel. To every six gallons put in a quart of brandy, and let it stand six weeks. If it is fine, bottle it; if it is not, draw it off as clear as you can into another vessel or large bottles; and in a fortnight, bottle it in small bottles.

White Currant Wine.

SQUEEZE your currants through a cullender, then wring them through a cloth; to each gallon of juice, three gallons of water, three pounds and a half of sugar; boil the sugar and water together, take off the scum clear, put it to cool, put the juice to it, then put it in a barrel; let it stand a month or six weeks, then draw it off and put it in the same barrel again, with a quart of brandy; if you choose, you may add a handful of clary.

To make Cherry Wine.

PULL your cherries when full ripe off the stalks, and press them through a hair sieve; to every gallon of liquor put two pounds of lump sugar beat fine, stir it together, and put it into a vessel; it must be full: when it has done working and making any noise, stop it close for three months, and bottle it off.

To make Birch Wine.

THE season for procuring the liquor from the birch-trees is the beginning of March, while the sap is rising, and before the leaves shoot out; for when the sap is come forward, and the leaves appear, the juice, by being long digested in the bark, grows thick and coloured, which before was thin and clear. The method of procuring the juice is, by boring holes in the body of the tree, and putting in fossets, which are commonly made of the branches of elder, the pith being taken out. You may without hurting the tree, if large, tap it in several places, four or five at a time, and by that means save from a good many trees several gallons every day; if you have not enough in one day, the bottles in which it drops must be corked close, and rosined or waxed; however, make use of it as soon as you can. Take the sap and boil it as long as any scum rises, skimming it all the time: to every gallon of liquor put four pounds of good sugar, the thin peel of a lemon, boil it afterwards half an hour, skimming it very well, pour it into a clean tub, and when it is almost cold, set it to work with yeast spread upon a toast, let it stand five or six days, stirring it often; then take such a cask as will hold the liquor, fire a large match dipped in brimstone, and throw it into the cask, stop it close till the match is extinguished, tun your wine, lay the bung on light till you find it has done working; stop it close and keep it three months, then bottle it off.

To make Quince Wine.

GATHER the quinces when dry and full ripe; take twenty large quinces, wipe them clean with a coarse cloth, and grate them with a large grate or rasp as near the core as you can, but none of the core; boil a gallon of spring-water, throw in your quinces, let it boil softly about a quarter of an hour; then strain them well into an earthen pan on two pounds of double-refined sugar, pare the peel of two large lemons, throw in and squeeze the juice through a sieve, stir it about till it is very cool, then toast a little bit of bread very thin and brown, rub a little yeast on it, let it stand close covered twenty-four hours, then take out the toast and lemon, put it up in a keg, keep it three months, and then bottle it. If you make a twenty gallon cask, let it stand six months before you bottle it; when you strain your quinces, you are to wring them hard in a coarse cloth.

To make Cowslip or Clary Wine.

TAKE six gallons of water, twelve pounds of sugar, the juice of six lemons, the whites of four eggs beat very well, put all
together

together in a kettle, let it boil half an hour, skim it very well; take a peck of cowslips (if dry ones, half a peck), put them into a tub, with the thin peeling of six lemons, then pour on the boiling liquor, and stir them about; when almost cold, put in a thin toast baked dry and rubbed with yeast: let it stand two or three days to work. If you put in (before you tun it) six ounces of syrup of citron or lemons, with a quart of Rhenish wine, it will be a great addition; the third day strain it off, and squeeze the cowslips through a coarse cloth; then strain it through a flannel bag, and tun it up; lay the bung loose for two or three days to see if it works, and if it does not, bung it down tight; let it stand three months, then bottle it.

To make Turnip Wine.

TAKE a good many turnips, pare, slice, and put them in a cyder-press, and press out all the juice very well; to every gallon of juice have three pounds of lump-sugar, have a vessel ready just big enough to hold the juice, put your sugar into a vessel, and also to every gallon of juice half a pint of brandy; pour in the juice, and lay something over the bung for a week, to see if it works; if it does, you must not bung it down till it has done working: then stop it close for three months, and draw it off in another vessel. When it is fine, bottle it off.

To make Raspberry Wine.

TAKE some fine raspberries, bruise them with the back of a spoon, then strain them through a flannel bag into a stone jar; to each quart of juice put a pound of double-refined sugar, stir it well together, and cover it close; let it stand three days, then pour it off clear. To a quart of juice put two quarts of white wine, bottle it off; it will be fit to drink in a week. Brandy made thus is a very fine dram, and a much better way than steeping the raspberries.

How to make Mead.

TAKE ten gallons of water, and two gallons of honey, a handful of raced ginger; then take two lemons, cut them in pieces, and put them into it, boil it very well, keep it skimming; let it stand all night in the same vessel you boil it in, the next morning barrel it up, with two or three spoonfuls of good yeast. About three weeks or a month after, you may bottle it.

To make White Mead.

TAKE five gallons of water, add to that one gallon of the best honey; then set it on the fire, boil it together well, and skim it very clean; then take it off the fire, and set it by; then

take

take two or three races of ginger, the like quantity of cinnamon and nutmegs, bruise all these grosly, and put them in a little Holland bag in the hot liquor, and so let it stand close covered till it be cold; then put as much ale-yeast to it as will make it work. Keep it in a warm place, as they do ale; and when it hath wrought well, tun it up; at two months you may drink it, having been bottled a month. If you keep it four months, it will be the better.

RULES for BREWING.

CARE must be taken, in the first place, to have the malt clean; and after it is ground, it ought to stand four or five days.

For strong October, five quarters of malt to three hogsheads, and twenty-four pounds of hops. This will afterwards make two hogsheads of good keeping small beer, allowing five pounds of hops to it.

For middling beer, a quarter of malt makes a hogshead of ale, and one of small beer; or it will make three hogsheads of good small beer, allowing eight pounds of hops. This will keep all the year. Or it will make twenty gallons of strong ale, and two hogsheads of small beer that will keep all the year.

If you intend your ale to keep a great while, allow a pound of hops to every bushel; if to keep six months, five pounds to a hogshead; if for present drinking, three pounds to a hogshead, and the softest and clearest water you can get.

Observe the day before to have all your vessels very clean, and never use your tubs for any other use except to make wines.

Let your cask be very clean the day before with boiling water; and if your bung is big enough, scrub them well with a little birch-broom or brush; but if they be very bad, take out the heads, and let them be scrubbed clean with a hand-brush, sand, and fullers-earth. Put on the head again, and scald them well, throw into the barrel a piece of unslacked lime, and stop the bung close.

The first copper of water, when it boils, pour into your mash-tub, and let it be cool enough to see your face in; then put in your malt, and let it be well mashed; have a copper of water boiling in the mean time, and when your malt is well mashed, fill your mashing-tub, stir it well again, and cover it over with the sacks. Let it stand three hours, set a broad shallow tub under the cock, let it run very softly; and if it is thick, throw it up again till it runs fine, then throw a handful of hops in the under tub, let the mash run into it, and fill your
tub,

tubs till all is run off. Have water boiling in the copper, and lay as much more as you have occasion for, allowing one third for boiling and waste. Let that stand an hour, boiling more water to fill the mash-tub for small beer; let the fire down a little, and put it into tubs enough to fill your mash. Let the second mash be run off, and fill your copper with the first wort; put in part of your hops, and make it boil quick. About an hour is long enough; when it has half boiled, throw in a handful of salt. Have a clean white wand, and dip it into the copper; and if the wort feels clammy, it is boiled enough; then slacken your fire, and take off your wort. Have ready a large tub, put two sticks across, and set your straining basket over the tub on the sticks, and strain your wort through it. Put other wort on to boil with the rest of the hops; let your mash be covered again with water, and thin your wort that is cooled in as many things as you can; for the thinner it lies, and the quicker it cools, the better. When quite cool, put it into the tunning-tub. Throw a handful of salt into every boil. When the mash has stood an hour, draw it off; then fill your mash with cold water, take off the wort in the copper, and order it as before. When cool, add to it the first in the tub; so soon as you empty one copper, fill the other, so boil your small beer well. Let the last mash run off, and when both are boiled with fresh hops, order them as the two first boilings; when cool, empty the mash-tub, and put the small beer to work there. When cool enough, work it; set a wooden bowl of yeast in the beer, and it will work over with a little of the beer in the boil. Stir your tun up every twelve hours, let it stand two days, then tun it, taking off the yeast. Fill your vessels full, and save some to fill your barrels; let it stand till it has done working; then lay your bung lightly for a fortnight, after that stop it as close as you can. Mind you have a vent-peg at the top of the vessel; in warm weather open it; and if your drink hisses, as it often will, loosen it till it has done, then stop it close again. If you can boil your ale in one boiling it is best, if your copper will allow of it; if not, boil it as conveniency serves.

When you come to draw your beer, and find it is not fine, draw off a gallon, and set it on the fire, with two ounces of isinglass cut small and beat; dissolve it in the beer over the fire: when it is all melted, let it stand till it is cold, and pour it in at the bung, which must lay loose on till it has done fermenting, then stop it close for a month. Take great care your casks are not musty, or have any ill taste; if they have, it is a hard thing to sweeten them. You are to wash your casks with cold water before you scald them, and they should

lie

lie a day or two soaking, and clean them well, then scald them.

The best Thing for Rope.

MIX two handfuls of bean flour and one handful of salt, throw this into a kilderkin of beer, do not stop it close till it has done fermenting, then let it stand a month, and draw it off; but sometimes nothing will do with it.

When a Barrel of Beer has turned Sour.

To a kilderkin of beer throw in at the bung a quart of oatmeal, lay the bung on loose two or three days, then stop it down close, and let it stand a month. Some throw in a piece of chalk as big as a turkey's egg, and when it has done working, stop it close for a month, then tap it.

How to make Cyder.

AFTER all your apples are bruised, take half of your quantity and squeeze them; and the juice you press from them, pour upon the others half bruised, but not squeezed, in a tub for the purpose, having a tap at the bottom; let the juice remain upon the apples three or four days; then pull out your tap, and let your juice run into some other vessel set under the tub to receive it; and if it runs thick, as at the first it will, pour it upon the apples again, till you see it run clear; and as you have a quantity, put it into your vessel, but do not force the cyder, but let it drop as long as it will of its own accord; having done this, after you perceive that the sides begin to work, take a quantity of isinglass (an ounce will serve forty gallons), infuse this in some of the cyder till it be dissolved; put to an ounce of isinglass a quart of cyder, and when it is so dissolved, pour it into the vessel, and stop it close for two days, or something more; then draw off the cyder into another vessel: this do so often till you perceive your cyder to be free from all manner of sediment that may make it ferment and fret itself: after Christmas you may boil it. You may, by pouring water on the apples and pressing them, make a pretty small cyder: if it be thick and muddy, by using isinglass, you may make it as clear as the rest; you must dissolve the isinglass over the fire till it be jelly.

For fining Cyder.

TAKE two quarts of skim-milk, four ounces of isinglass, cut the isinglass in pieces, and work it lukewarm in the milk over the fire; and when it is dissolved, then put it cold into the hogshead of cyder, and take a long stick and stir it well from top to bottom for half a quarter of an hour.

After

After it has fined.

TAKE ten pounds of raisins of the sun, two ounces of turmerick, half an ounce of ginger beaten; then take a quantity of raisins, and grind them as you do mustard-seed in a bowl, with a little cyder, and so the rest of the raisins; then sprinkle the turmerick and ginger amongst it; then put all into a fine canvass bag, and hang it in the middle of the hogshead close, and let it lie. After the cyder has stood thus a fortnight or a month, then you may bottle it at your pleasure.

BAKING.

To make White Bread, after the London Way.

TAKE a bushel of the finest flour well dressed, put it in the kneading-trough at one end, take a gallon of water (which we call liquor) and some yeast; stir it into the liquor till it looks of a good brown colour and begins to curdle, strain and mix it with your flour till it is about the thickness of a seed-cake; then cover it with the lid of the trough, and let it stand three hours; and as soon as you see it begin to fall, take a gallon more of liquor; weigh three quarters of a pound of salt, and with your hand mix it well with the water: strain it, and with this liquor make your dough of a moderate thickness, fit to make up into loaves; then cover it again with the lid, and let it stand three hours more. In the mean time, put the wood into the oven and heat it. It will take two hours heating. When your spunge has stood its proper time, clear the oven, and begin to make your bread. Set it in the oven, and close it up, and three hours will bake it. When once it is in, you must not open the oven till the bread is baked; and observe in summer that your water be milk-warm, and in winter as hot as you can bear your finger in it.

N. B. As to the quantity of liquor your dough will take, experience will teach you in two or three times making; for all flour does not want the same quantity of liquor; and if you make any quantity, it will raise up the lid and run over.

To make French Bread.

TAKE three quarts of water, and one of milk; in winter scalding hot, in summer a little more than milk warm; season it well with salt, then take a pint and a half of good ale yeast not bitter, lay it in a gallon of water the night before, pour it off the water, stir in your yeast into the milk and water, then with your hand break in a little more than a quarter of a pound of butter, work it well till it is dissolved, then beat up two eggs in a bason, and stir them in; have about a peck and a half of flour, mix it with your liquor; in winter make your dough pretty stiff, in summer more slack: so that you may use a little more or less flour, according to the stiffness of your dough: mix it well, but the less you work the better: make it into rolls, and have a very quick oven. When they have lain about a quarter of an hour, turn them on the other side, let them lie about a quarter longer, and then take them out and chip all your French bread with a knife, which is better than rasping it, and make it look spungy and of a fine yellow, whereas the rasping takes off all that fine colour, and makes it look too smooth. You must stir your liquor into the flour as you do for the pie-crust. After your dough is made, cover it with a cloth, and let it lie to rise while the oven is heating.

To make Muffins and Oat-Cakes.

To a bushel of Hertfordshire white flour, take a pint and a half of good ale yeast, from pale malt, if you can get it, because it is whitest; let the yeast lie in water all night, the next day pour off the water clear, make two gallons of water just milk-warm, not to scald your yeast, and two ounces of salt; mix your water, yeast, and salt well together for about a quarter of an hour; then strain it and mix up your dough as light as possible, and let it lie in your trough an hour to rise; then with your hand roll it, and pull it into little pieces about as big as a large walnut, roll them with your hand like a ball, lay them on your table, and as fast as you do them, lay a piece of flannel over them, and be sure to keep your dough covered with flannel; when you have rolled out all your dough, begin to bake the first, and by that time they will be spread out in the right form; lay them on your iron; as one side begins to change colour, turn the other; take great care, they do not burn, or be too much discoloured, but that you will be a judge of in two or three makings. Take care the middle of the iron is not too hot, as it will be; but then you may put a brick-bat or two in the middle of the fire to slacken the heat. The thing you bake on must be made thus:

Build a place as if you were going to set a copper; and, in the stead of a copper, a piece of iron all over the top, fixed in form just the same as the bottom of an iron pot, and make your fire underneath with coal, as in a copper. Observe, muffins are made the same way; only this, when you pull them to pieces, roll them in a good deal of flour, and with a rolling-pin roll them thin, cover them with a piece of flannel, and they will rise

rise to a proper thickness; and if you find them too big or too little, you must roll dough accordingly. These must not be the least discoloured. When you eat them, toast them crisp on both sides, then with your hand pull them open, and they will be like a honeycomb; lay in as much butter as you intend to use, then clap them together again, and set it by the fire. When you think the butter is melted, turn them, that both sides may be buttered alike, but do not touch them with a knife, either to spread, or cut them open; if you do, they will be as heavy as lead, only when they are buttered and done, you may cut them across with a knife.

N. B. Some flour will soak up a quart or three pints more water than other flour; then you must add more water, or shake in more flour in making up, for the dough must be as light as possible.

A Receipt for making Bread without Barm by the Help of a Leaven.

TAKE a lump of dough, about two pounds of your last making, which has been raised by barm, keep it by you in a wooden vessel, and cover it well with flour; (this is your leaven); then the night before you intend to bake, put the said leaven to a peck of flour, and work them well together with warm water; let it lie in a dry wooden vessel, well covered with a linen cloth and a blanket, and keep it in a warm place: this dough kept warm will rise again next morning, and will be sufficient to mix with two or three bushels of flour, being worked up with warm water and a little salt; when it is well worked up, and thoroughly mixed with all the flour, let it be well covered with the linen and blanket until you find it rise; then knead it well, and work it up into bricks or loaves, making the loaves broad, and not so thick and high as is frequently done, by which means the bread will be better baked; then bake your bread.

Always keep by you two or more pounds of the dough of your last baking, well covered with flour, to make leaven to serve from one baking-day to another; the more leaven is put to the flour, the lighter and spungier the bread will be: the fresher the leaven, the bread will be the less sour.

[From the Dublin Society.]

A Method to preserve a large Stock of Yeast, which will keep and be of Use for several Months, either to make Bread or Cakes.

WHEN you have yeast in plenty, take a quantity of it, stir and work it well with a whisk until it becomes liquid and thin, then get a large wooden platter, cooler, or tub, clean and dry, and with a soft brush lay a thin layer of the yeast on the tub, and turn the mouth downwards that no dust may fall upon it, but so that the air may get under to dry it; when that coat is very dry, then lay on another till you have a sufficient quantity, even two or three inches thick, to serve for several months, always taking care the yeast in the tub be very dry before you lay more on: when you have occasion to use this yeast, cut a piece off and lay it in warm water; stir it together, and it will be fit for use. If it is for brewing, take a large handful of birch tied together, and dip it into the yeast and hang it up to dry; take great care no dust comes to it, and so you may do as many as you please. When your beer is fit to set to work, throw in one of these, and it will make it work as well as if you had fresh yeast.

You must whip it about in the wort, and then let it lie; when the vat works well, take out the broom and dry it again, and it will do for the next brewing.

N. B. In the building of your oven for baking, observe that you make it round, low roofed, and a little mouth; then it will take less fire, and keep in the heat better than a long oven and high roofed, and will bake the bread better.

CHEESE.

To make Slip-coat Cheese.

TAKE six quarts of new milk hot from the cow, the stroakings, and put to it two spoonfuls of rennet; and when it is hard coming, lay it into the fat with a spoon, not breaking it all; then press it with a four-pound weight, turning of it with a dry cloth once an hour, and every day shifting it into fresh grass. It will be ready to cut, if the weather be hot, in fourteen days.

To make a Brick-Bat Cheese. It must be made in September.

TAKE two gallons of new milk, and a quart of good cream, heat the cream, put in two spoonfuls of rennet, and when it is come, break it a little, then put it into a wooden mould, in the shape of a brick. It must be half a year old before you eat it: you must press it a little, and so dry it.

To make Cream Cheese.

PUT one large spoonful of steep to five quarts of afterings, break it down light, put it upon a cloth in a sieve bottom, and let it run till dry, break it, cut and turn it in a clean cloth, then put it into the sieve again, and put on it a two-pound weight, sprinkle a little salt on it and let it stand all night, then lay it on a board to dry; when dry, lay a few strawberry leaves on it, and

ripen

ripen it between two pewter diſhes in a warm place, turn it, and put on freſh leaves every day.

To make Bullace Cheeſe.

TAKE your bullace when they are full ripe, put them into a pot, and to every quart of bullace put a quarter of a pound of loaf-ſugar beat ſmall; bake them in a moderate oven till they are ſoft, then rub them through a hair ſieve; to every pound of pulp add half a pound of loaf-ſugar beat fine, then boil it an hour and a half over a ſlow fire, and keep ſtirring it all the time, then pour it into potting pots, and tie brandy papers over them, and keep them in a dry place; when it has ſtood a few months, it will cut out very bright and fine.

N. B. You may make ſloe cheeſe the ſame way.

To make Stilton Cheeſe.

TAKE the night's cream and put it to the morning's new milk with the rennet, when the curd is come, it is not to be broken, as is done with other cheeſes, but take it out with a ſoil-diſh all together, and place it on a ſieve to drain gradually, and as it drains, keep gradually preſſing it till it becomes firm and dry, then place it in a wooden hoop; afterwards to be kept dry on boards, turned frequently, with cloth binders round it, which are to be tightened as occaſion requires. In ſome dairies the cheeſes, after being taken out of the wooden hoop, are bound tight round with a cloth, which is changed every day till the cheeſe is firm enough to ſupport itſelf; after the cloth is taken off they are rubbed all over daily with a bruſh for two or three months, and if the weather is damp, twice a day; and even before the cloth is taken off, the top and bottom are well rubbed every day.

N. B. The dairy-maid muſt not be diſheartened if ſhe does not perfectly ſucceed the firſt time.

CHAP. XXIII.

JARRING CHERRIES, PRESERVES, &c.

To jar Cherries, Lady North's Way.

TAKE twelve pounds of cherries, ſtone them, put them in your preſerving-pan, with three pounds of double-refined ſugar and a quart of water; then ſet them on the fire till they are ſcalding hot, take them off a little while, and ſet on the fire again; boil them till they are tender, then sprinkle them with half a pound of double-refined sugar pounded, and skim them clean; put them all together in a china bowl, let them stand in the syrup three days; drain them through a sieve, take them out one by one, with the holes downwards on a wicker sieve, then set them in a stove to dry, and as they dry turn them upon clean sieves: when they are dry enough, put a clean white sheet of paper in a preserving-pan, then put all the cherries in, with another clean white sheet of paper on the top of them; cover them close with a cloth, and set them over a cool fire till they sweat: take them off the fire, then let them stand till they are cold, and put them in boxes or jars to keep.

To dry Cherries.

To four pounds of cherries put one pound of sugar, and just put as much water to the sugar as will wet it; when it is melted, make it boil; stone your cherries, put them in, and make them boil; skim them two or three times, take them off, and let them stand in the syrup two or three days, then boil your syrup and put to them again, but do not boil your cherries any more; let them stand three or four days longer, then take them out, lay them in sieves to dry, and lay them in the sun, or in a flow oven to dry; when dry, lay them in rows in papers, and so a row of cherries, and a row of white paper in boxes.

Another Way.

TAKE eight pounds of cherries, one pound of the best powdered sugar, stone the cherries over a great deep bason or glass, and lay them one by one in rows, and strew a little sugar; thus do till your bason is full to the top, and let them stand till the next day; then pour them out into a great posnip, set them on the fire, let them boil very fast a quarter of an hour, or more; then pour them again into your bason, and let them stand two or three days; then take them out, and lay them one by one on hair sieves, and set them in the sun, or an oven, till they are dry, turning them every day upon dry sieves: if in the oven, it must be as little warm as you can just feel it, when you hold your hand in it.

To preserve Cherries with the Leaves and Stalks green.

FIRST dip the stalks and leaves in the best vinegar boiling hot, stick the sprig upright in a sieve till they are dry; in the meantime boil some double-refined sugar to syrup, and dip the cherries, stalks, and leaves in the syrup, and just let them scald; lay them on a sieve, and boil them to a candy height, then dip the cherries, stalks, leaves, and all; then stick the

branches

branches in sieves, and dry them as you do other sweet-meats. They look very pretty at candle-light in a desert.

To preserve Cherries in Brandy.

CUT the stalks half off, put them in a jar, and fill them up with brandy sweetened to your taste with sugar-candy, pour in a little currant jelly, dissolved, at the top, and tie them down for use.

To preserve Cherries.

TAKE two pounds of cherries, one pound and an half of sugar, half a pint of fair water, melt your sugar in it; when it is melted, put in your other sugar and your cherries, then boil them softly till all the sugar be melted; then boil them fast, and skim them; take them off two or three times and shake them, and put them on again, and let them boil fast; and when they are of a good colour, and the syrup will stand, they are enough.

Another Way.

TAKE their weight in sugar before you stone them; when stoned, make your syrup, then put in your cherries, let them boil slowly at the first till they be thorougly warmed, then boil them as fast as you can; when they are boiled clear, put in the jelly, with almost the weight in sugar, strew the sugar on the cherries; for the colouring you must be ruled by your eye; to a pound of sugar put a jack of water, strew the sugar on them before they boil, and put in the juice of currants soon after they boil.

To barrel Morello Cherries.

To one pound of full ripe cherries, picked from the stems, and wiped with a cloth, take half a pound of double refined sugar, and boil it to a candy height, but not a high one; put the cherries into a small barrel, then put in the sugar by a spoonful at a time till it is all in, and roll them about every day till they have done fermenting; then bung it up close, and they will be fit for use in a month: it must be an iron-hooped barrel.

To make Orange Marmalade.

TAKE the clearest Seville oranges and cut them in two; take out all the pulp and juice into a pan, and pick all the skins and seeds out; boil the rinds in hard water till they are very tender, and change the water three times while they are boiling, and then pound them in a mortar, and put in the juice and pulp; put them in a preserving-pan, with double their weight of loaf-sugar, set it over a slow fire, boil it gently forty minutes, put it into pots; cover it with brandy-paper, and tie it down close.

Marmalade of Eggs the Jews Way.

TAKE the yolks of twenty-four eggs, beat them for an hour; clarify one pound of the best moist sugar, four spoonfuls of orange-flower water, one ounce of blanched and pounded almonds; stir all together over a very slow charcoal fire, keeping stirring it all the while one way till it comes to a consistence; then put it into coffee-cups, and throw a little beaten cinnamon on the top of the cups.

This marmalade, mixed with pounded almonds, with orange-peel, and citron, are made in cakes of all shapes, such as birds, fish, and fruit.

Marmalade of Cherries.

TAKE five pounds of cherries, stoned, and two pounds of hard sugar; shred your cherries, wet your sugar with the juice that runneth from them; then put the cherries into the sugar, and boil them pretty fast till it be a marmalade; when it is cold, put it up in glasses for use.

To make white Marmalade of Quinces.

PARE and core the quinces as fast as you can, then take to a pound of quinces (being cut in pieces, less than half quarters,) three quarters of a pound of double-refined sugar beat small, then throw half the sugar on the raw quinces, set it on a slow fire till the sugar is melted and the quinces tender; then put in the rest of the sugar, and boil it up as fast as you can; when it is almost enough, put in some jelly and boil it apace; then put it up, and when it is quite cold, cover it with white paper.

Marmalade of Quince White. Another way.

TAKE the quinces, pare them and core them, put them into water as you pare them, to be kept from blacking; then boil them so tender that a quarter of straw will go through them; then take their weight of sugar, and beat them, break the quinces with the back of a spoon; and then put in the sugar, and let them boil fast uncovered, till they slide from the bottom of the pan: you may make paste of the same, only dry it in a stove, drawing it out into what form you please.

To make Red Marmalade.

TAKE full ripe quinces, pare and cut them in quarters, and core them; put them in a sauce-pan, cover them with the parings, fill the sauce-pan nearly full of spring-water, cover it

close,

close, and stew them gently till they are quite soft, and a deep pink colour; then pick out the quince from the parings, and beat them to a pulp in a mortar; take their weight in loaf-sugar, put in as much of the water they were boiled in as will dissolve it, and boil and skim it well; put in your quinces, and boil them gently three quarters of an hour; keep stirring them, all the time, or it will stick to the pan and burn; put it into flat pots, and when cold tie it down close.

To preserve Oranges whole.

TAKE the best Bermudas or Seville oranges you can get, and pare them with a pen-knife very thin, and lay your oranges in water three or four days, shifting them every day; then put them in a kettle with fair water, and put a board on them to keep them down in the water, and have a skillet on the fire with water that may be ready to supply the kettle with boiling water; as it wastes, it must be filled up three or four times while the oranges are doing, for they will take seven or eight hours boiling; they must be boiled till a white straw will run through them, then take them out and scoop the seeds out of them very carefully, by making a little hole in the top, and weigh them: to every pound of oranges put a pound and three quarters of double-refined sugar, beat well and sifted through a clean lawn sieve, fill your oranges with sugar, and strew some on them; let them lie a little while, and make your jelly thus:

Take two dozen of pippins or John apples and slice them into water, and when they are boiled tender strain the liquor from the pulp, and to every pound of oranges you must have a pint and a half of this liquor, and put to it three quarters of the sugar you left in filling the oranges, set it on the fire, and let it boil, skim it well, and put it in a clean earthen pan till it is cold, then put it in your skillet; put in your oranges; with a small bodkin job your oranges as they are boiling to let the syrup into them, strew on the rest of your sugar whilst they are boiling, and when they look clear take them up and put them in your glasses, put one in a glass just fit for them, and boil the syrup till it is almost a jelly, then fill up your glasses: when they are cold, paper them up, and keep them in a dry place.

Or thus: Cut a hole out of the stalk end of your orange as big as a sixpence, scoop out all the pulp very clean, tie them singly in muslin, and lay them two days in spring water; change the water twice a day, and boil them in the muslin till tender; be careful you keep them covered with water, weigh the oranges before you scoop them; to every pound add two pounds of double-refined sugar and a pint of water; boil the sugar and water with the orange juice to a syrup, skim it well, let it stand till it is cold, take the oranges out of the muslin, and put them in and boil them till they are quite clear, and put them by till cold; then pare and core some green pippins, and boil them in water till it is very strong of the pippin; do not stir them, put them down gently with the back of a spoon, and strain the liquor through a jelly-bag till it is clear; put to every pint of liquor a pound of double-refined sugar, and the juice of a lemon strained as clear as you can; boil it to a strong jelly; drain the oranges out of your syrup, and put them in glass or white stone jars of the size of the orange, and pour the jelly on them; cover them with brandy-papers, and tie them over with a bladder. You may do lemons in the same manner.

Quinces whole.

TAKE your quinces and pare them; cut them in quarters, or leave them whole, which you please; put them into a sauce-pan and cover them with hard water; lay your parings over them to keep them under water; cover your sauce-pan close, that no steam can come out; set them over a slow fire till they are soft, and a fine pink colour; then let them stand till cold: make a syrup of double-refined sugar, with as much water as will wet it; boil and skim it well; put in your quinces, let them boil ten minutes; take them off, and let them stand three hours; then boil them till the syrup is thick and the quinces clear; then put them in deep jars, and when cold put brandy-paper over them, and tie them down close.

How to preserve White Quinces whole.

TAKE the weight of your quinces in sugar, and put a pint of water to a pound of sugar, make it into a syrup, and clarify it; then core your quince and pare it, put it into your syrup and let it boil till it be all clear, then put in three spoonfuls of jelly, which must be made thus: over night, lay your quince-kernels in water, then strain them and put them into your quinces, and let them have but one boil afterwards.

To make Quince Cakes.

YOU must let a pint of the syrup of quinces, with a quart or two of raspberries, be boiled and clarified over a clear gentle fire, taking care that it be well skimmed from time to time; then add a pound and a half of sugar, cause as much more to be brought to a candy height, and poured in hot: let the whole be continually stirred about till it is almost cold, then spread it on plates, and cut it out into cakes.

To preserve Apricots.

TAKE your apricots, stone and pare them thin, and take their weight in double-refined sugar, beaten and sifted; put your apricots in a silver cup or tankard, cover them over with sugar, and let them stand so all night; the next day put them in a preserving-pan, set them on a gentle fire, and let them simmer a little while, then let them boil till tender and clear, taking them off sometimes to turn and skim: keep them under the liquor as they are doing, and with a small clean bodkin, or great needle, job them, that the syrup may penetrate into them; when they are enough, take them up, and put them in glasses: boil and skim your syrup; and when it is cold, put it on your apricots: put brandy-paper over, and tie them close.

Another Way.

TAKE your apricots and pare them, then stone what you can whole, then give them a light boil in a pint of water, or to your quantity of fruit; then take the weight of your fruit in sugar, and take the liquor in which you boil them and your sugar, and boil it till it comes to a syrup, and give them a light boil, taking off the scum as it rises; when the syrup jellies it is enough; then take up the apricots and cover them with the jelly, and cut paper over them, and lay them down when cold.

To preserve Damsons whole.

YOU must take some damsons and cut them in pieces, put them in a skillet over the fire, with as much water as will cover them; when they are boiled, and the liquor pretty strong, strain it out; add for every pound of the damsons (wiped clean) a pound of single-refined sugar, put the third part of your sugar into the liquor, set it over the fire, and when it simmers, put in the damsons; let them have one good boil, and take them off for half an hour, covered up close; then set them on again, and let them simmer over the fire after turning them; then take them out and put them in a bason, strew all the sugar that was left on them, and pour the hot liquor over them; cover them up and let them stand till next day, then boil them up again till they are enough: take them up, and put them in pots; boil the liquor till it jellies, and pour it on them when it is almost cold; so paper them up.

To preserve Gooseberries whole without stoning.

TAKE the largest preserving gooseberries, and pick off the black eye, but not the stalk; then set them over the fire in a pot of water to scald, cover them very close, but not boil or break, and when they are tender take them up into cold water; then take a pound and a half of double-refined sugar to a pound of gooseberries, and clarify the sugar with water, a pint to a pound of sugar, and when your syrup is cold, put the gooseberries single in your preserving-pan, put the syrup to them, and set them on a gentle fire; let them boil, but not too fast, lest they break; and when they have boiled, and you perceive that the sugar has entered them, take them off, cover them with white paper, and set them by till the next day; then take them out of the syrup, and boil the syrup till it begins to be ropy; skim it and put it to them again, then set them on a gentle fire, and let them simmer gently till you perceive the syrup will rope; then take them off, set them by till they are cold, cover them with paper, then boil some gooseberries in fair water, and when the liquor is strong enough, strain it out; let it stand to settle, and to every pint take a pound of double-refined sugar, then make a jelly of it, put the gooseberries in glasses when they are cold; cover them with the jelly the next day, paper them wet, and then half dry the paper that goes in the inside, it closes down the better, and then white paper over the glass: set in your stove, or a dry place.

To preserve White Walnuts.

FIRST pare your walnuts till the white appears, and nothing else; you must be very careful in the doing of them that they do not turn black, and as fast as you do them throw them into salt and water, and let them lie till your sugar is ready; take three pounds of good loaf-sugar, put it into your preserving-pan, set it over a charcoal fire, and put as much water as will just wet the sugar; let it boil, then have ready ten or a dozen whites of eggs strained and beat up to froth; cover your sugar with a froth as it boils, and skim it; then boil it, and skim it till it is as clear as crystal, then throw in your walnuts; just give them a boil till they are tender, then take them out and lay them in a dish to cool; when cool, put them in your preserving-pan, and when the sugar is as warm as milk, pour it over them; when quite cold, paper them down.

Thus clear your sugar for all preserves, apricots, peaches, gooseberries, currants, &c.

To preserve Walnuts green.

WIPE them very clean, and lay them in strong salt and water twenty-four hours; then take them out and wipe them very clean, have ready a skillet of water boiling, throw them in, let them boil a minute and take them out; lay them on a coarse cloth, and boil your sugar as above; then just give your walnuts a scald in the sugar, take them up and lay them to cool; put them in your preserving-pot, and pour on your syrup as above.

To preserve the large Green Plums.

FIRST dip the stalks and leaves in boiling vinegar; when they are dry, have your syrup ready, and first give them a scald, and very carefully with a pin take off the skin; boil your sugar to a candy height, and dip in your plums, hang them by the stalk to dry, and they will look finely transparent, and by hanging that way to dry will have a clear drop at the top: you must take great care to clear your sugar nicely.

To preserve Peaches.

TAKE the largest peaches you can get, not over ripe, rub off the lint with a cloth, and run them down the seam with a pin, skin deep; cover them with French brandy, tie a bladder over them, and let them stand a week; make a strong syrup, and boil and skim it well; take the peaches out of the brandy, and put them in and boil them till they look clear; then take them out, put them in glasses, mix the syrup with the brandy, and when cold pour it over your peaches: tie them close down with a bladder, and leather over it.

To preserve Golden Pippins.

TAKE the rind of an orange and boil it very tender, lay it in cold water for three days; take two dozen of golden pippins, pare, core, quarter them, and boil them to a strong jelly, and run it through a jelly-bag till it is clear; take the same quantity of pippins, pare them, and take out the cores, put three pounds of loaf-sugar in a preserving-pan, with three half pints of spring-water; when it boils, skim it well, and put in your pippins, with the orange-rind cut in long thin slips, let them boil fast till the sugar is thick, and will almost candy, then put in three half-pints of pippin jelly, and boil it fast till the jelly is clear; then squeeze in the juice of a lemon, give it a boil, and put them in pots or glasses, with the orange-peel: you may use lemon-peel instead of orange, but then you must only boil it, not soak it.

To preserve Grapes.

GET some fine grapes, not over ripe, either red or white, but very close, and pick all the specked ones; put them in a jar, with a quarter of a pound of sugar-candy, and fill the jar with common brandy; tie them down close, and keep them in a dry cold place. You may do morello cherries the same way.

To preserve Green Codlings.

GATHER your codlings when they are the size of a walnut, with the stalks, and a leaf or two on; put a handful of vine-
leaves

leaves into a preserving-pan, then a layer of codlings, then vine-leaves, and then codlings, till it is full, and vine-leaves pretty thick at top, and fill it with spring-water, cover it close to keep in the steam, and set it on a slow fire till they grow soft; then take them out, and take off the skins with a pen-knife, and put them in the same water again with the vine-leaves, which must be quite cold, or it will make them crack; put in a little roche-allum, and set them over a slow fire till they are green, then take them out and lay them on a sieve to drain: make a good syrup, and give them a gentle boil for three days, then put them in small jars, with brandy-paper over them, and tie them down tight.

To preserve Apricots or Plums green.

TAKE your plums before they have stones in them, which you may know by putting a pin through them; then coddle them in many waters till they are as green as grass; peel them and coddle them again; you must take the weight of them in sugar, and make a syrup; put to your sugar a jack of water, then put them in, set them on the fire to boil slowly till they be clear, skimming them often, and they will be very green: put them up in glasses, and keep them for use.

To preserve Barberries.

TAKE the ripest and best barberries you can find; take the weight of them in sugar; then pick out the seeds and tops, wet your sugar with the juice of them, and make a syrup; then put in your barberries, and when they boil take them off and shake them, then set them on again and let them boil, and repeat the same till they are clean enough to put into glasses.

White Pear Plums.

TAKE the finest and clearest from specks you can get; to a pound of plum take a pound and a quarter of sugar, the finest you can get, a pint and a quarter of water; slit the plums and stone them, and prick them full of holes, saving some sugar beat fine, laid in a bason; as you do them, lay them in, and strew sugar over them; when you have thus done, have half a pound of sugar, and your water, ready made into a thin syrup, and a little cold; put in your plums with the slit side downwards, set them on the fire, keep them continually boiling, neither too slow nor too fast; take them often off, shake them round, and skim them well, keep them down into the syrup continually for fear they lose their colour; when they are thoroughly scalded, strew on the rest of your sugar, and keep doing so till they are enough, which you may know by their glasing; towards the latter end, boil them them up quickly.

MADE PLAIN AND EASY.

To preserve Currants.

TAKE the weight of the currants in sugar, pick out the seeds; take to a pound of sugar half a jack or water, let it melt, then put in your berries, and let them do very slowly, skim them and take them up, let the syrup boil; then put them on again, and when they are clear, and the syrup thick enough, take them off, and when they are cold put them up in glasses.

To preserve Raspberries.

TAKE of the raspberries that are not too ripe, and take the weight of them in sugar, wet your sugar with a little water, and put in your berries, and let them boil softly, take heed of breaking them; when they are clear, take them up, and boil the syrup till it be thick enough, then put them in again, and when they are cold, put them in glasses.

Pippins in Slices.

WHEN your pippins are prepared, but not cored, cut them in slices, and take the weight of them in sugar, put to your sugar a pretty quantity of water, let it melt, and skim it, let it boil again very high, then put them into the syrup when they are clear; lay them in shallow glasses, in which you mean to serve them up; then put into the syrup a candied orange-peel cut in little slices very thin, and lay about the pippin; cover them with syrup, and keep them about the pippin.

To preserve Cucumbers equal with any Italian Sweet meats.

TAKE fine young gerkins, of two or three different sizes, put them into a stone jar, cover them well with vine-leaves, fill the jar with spring-water, cover it close; let it stand near the fire, so as to be quite warm, for ten days or a fortnight; then take them out and throw them into spring-water; they will look quite yellow, and stink, but you must not mind that; have ready your preserving-pan, take them out of that water and put them into the pan, cover them well with vine-leaves, fill it with spring-water, set it over a charcoal fire, cover them close, and let them simmer very slow; look at them often, and when you see them turned quite of a fine green, take off the leaves, and throw them into a large sieve; then into a coarse cloth, four or five times doubled; when they are cold, put them into the jar, and have ready your syrup made of double-refined sugar, in which boil a great deal of lemon-peel and whole ginger, pour it hot over them, and cover them down close; do it three times; pare your lemon-peel very thin, and cut them in long thin bits, about two inches long: the ginger must

must be well boiled in water before it is put in the syrup. Take long cucumbers, cut them in halfs, scoop out the inside; do them the same way: they eat very fine in minced pies or puddings; or boil the syrup to a candy, and dry them on sieves.

To make Conserve of red Roses, or any other Flowers.

TAKE rose-buds, or any other flowers, and pick them; cut off the white part from the red, and sift the red part of the flowers through a sieve to take out the seeds; then weigh them, and to every pound of flowers take two pounds and a half of loaf-sugar; beat the flowers pretty fine in a stone mortar, then by degrees put the sugar to them, and beat it very well, till it is well incorporated together; then put it into gallipots, tie it over with paper, over that a leather, and it will keep seven years.

To make Conserve of Hips.

GATHER hips before they grow soft, cut off the heads and stalks, slit them in halves, take out all the seeds and white that is in them very clean, then put them into an earthen pan, and stir them every day, or they will grow mouldy: let them stand till they are soft enough to rub them through a coarse hair sieve; as the pulp comes, take it off the sieve: they are a dry berry, and will require pains to rub them through; then add its weight in sugar, mix them well together without boiling, and keep it in deep gallipots for use.

Conserve of Roses boiled.

TAKE red roses, take off all the whites at the bottom, or elsewhere, take three times the weight of them in sugar, put to a pint of roses a pint of water, skim it well, shred your roses a little before you put them into water, cover them, and boil the leaves tender in the water, and when they are tender put in your sugar; keep them stirring, lest they burn when they are tender, and the syrup be consumed: put them up, and so keep them for your use.

To make Syrup of Roses.

INFUSE three pounds of damask rose-leaves in a gallon of warm water, in a well-glazed earthen pot, with a narrow mouth, for eight hours, which stop so close that none of the virtue may exhale; when they have infused so long, heat the water again, squeeze them out, and put in three pounds more of rose-leaves, to infuse for eight hours more; then press them out very hard; then to every quart of this infusion add four pounds of fine sugar, and boil it up to a syrup.

To make Syrup of Citron.

PARE and slice your citrons thin, lay them in a bason, with layers of fine sugar; the next day pour off the liquor into a glass, skim it, and clarify it over a gentle fire.

To make Syrup of Clove-Gilliflowers.

CLIP your gilliflowers, sprinkle them with fair water, put them into an earthen pot, stop it up very close, set it in a kettle of water, and let it boil for two hours; then strain out the juice, put a pound and a half of sugar to a pint of juice, put it into a skillet, set it on the fire, keep it stirring till the sugar is all melted, do not let it boil; then set it by to cool, and put it into bottles.

To make Syrup of Peach-Blossoms.

INFUSE peach-blossoms in hot water, as much as will handsomely cover them; let them stand in balneo, or in sand, for twenty-four hours covered close; then strain out the flowers from the liquor, and put in fresh flowers; let them stand to infuse as before, then strain them out, and to the liquor put fresh peach-blossoms the third time, and (if you please) a fourth time; then to every pound of your infusion add two pounds of double-refined sugar; and, setting it in sand, or balneo, make a syrup, which keep for use.

To make Syrup of Quinces.

GRATE quinces, pass their pulp through a cloth to extract the juice, set their juices in the sun to settle, or before the fire, and by that means clarify it; for every four ounces of this juice take a pound of sugar boiled brown: if the putting in the juice of the quinces should check the boiling of the sugar too much, give the syrup some boiling till it becomes pearled; then take it off the fire, and when cold, put it into the bottles.

To candy any Sort of Flowers.

TAKE the best treble-refined sugar, break it into lumps, and dip it piece by piece into water, put them into a vessel of silver, and melt them over the fire; when it just boils, strain it and set it on the fire again, and let it boil till it draws in hairs, which you may perceive by holding up your spoon; then put in the flowers, and set them in cups or glasses; when it is of a hard candy, break it in lumps, and lay it as high as you please: dry it in a stove, or in the sun, and it will look like sugar-candy.

To make Citron.

QUARTER your melon, and take out all the infide, then put into the fyrup as much as will cover the coat; let it boil in the fyrup till the coat is as tender as the inward part, then put them in the pot with as much fyrup as will cover them; let them ftand for two or three days that the fyrup may penetrate through them, and boil your fyrup to a candy height, with as much mountain wine as will wet your fyrup, clarify it, and then boil it to a candy height; then dip in the quarters, and lay them on a fieve to dry, and fet them before a flow fire, or put them in a flow oven till dry. Obferve that your melon is but half ripe, and when they are dry, put them in deal boxes in paper.

To candy Cherries or Green Gages.

DIP the ftalks and leaves in white wine vinegar boiling, then fcald them in fyrup; take them out and boil the fyrup to a candy height; dip in the cherries, and hang them to dry with the cherries downwards; dry them before the fire, or in the fun; then take the plums, after boiling them in a thin fyrup, peel off the fkin and candy them, and fo hang them up to dry.

To candy Angelica.

TAKE it in April, boil it in water till it be tender; then take it up and drain it from the water very well, then fcrape the outfide of it, and dry it in a clean cloth, and lay it in the fyrup, and let it lie in three or four days, and cover it clofe; the fyrup muft be ftrong of fugar, and keep it hot a good while, and let it not boil; after it is heated a good while, lay it upon a pie-plate, and fo let it dry; keep it near the fire left it diffolve.

To candy Caffia.

TAKE as much of the powder of brown caffia as will lie upon two broad fhillings, with what mufk and ambergris you think fitting; the caffia and perfume muft be powdered together, then take a quarter of a pound of fugar, and boil it to a candy height; then put in your powder, and mix it well together, and pour it in pewter faucers or plates, which muft be buttered very thin, and when it is cold it will flip out. The caffia is to be bought at London; fometimes it is in powder, and fometimes in a hard lump.

To dry Pears without Sugar.

TAKE the Norwich pears, pare them with a knife, and put them in an earthen pot, and bake them, not too foft; put them into a white plate pan, and put dry straw under them, and lay them in an oven after bread is drawn, and every day warm the oven to the degree of heat as when bread is newly drawn. Within one week they must be dry.

To dry Plums.

TAKE pear-plums, fair and clear coloured, weigh them, and slit them up the sides; put them into a broad pan, and fill it full of water, set them over a very slow fire; take care that the skin does not come off; when they are tender take them up, and to every pound of plums put a pound of sugar, strew a little on the bottom of a large silver bason; then lay your plums in, one by one, and strew the remainder of your sugar over them; set them into your stove all night, with a good warm fire the next day; heat them and set them into your stove again, and let them stand two days more, turning them every day; then take them out of the syrup, and lay them on glass plates to dry.

How to dry Peaches.

TAKE the fairest and ripest peaches, pare them into fair water; take their weight in double-refined sugar; of one half make a very thin syrup, then put in your peaches, boiling them till they look clear, then split and stone them; boil them till they are very tender, lay them a-draining; take the other half of the sugar and boil it almost to a candy; then put in your peaches, and let them lie all night; then lay them on a glass, and set them in a stove till they are dry. If they are sugared too much, wipe them with a wet cloth a little; let the first syrup be very thin, a quart of water to a pound of sugar.

To dry Damsins.

TAKE four pounds of damsins; take one pound of fine sugar, make a syrup of it, with about a pint of fair water; then put in your damsins, stir it into your hot syrup, so let them stand on a little fire to keep them warm for half an hour; then put all into a bason and cover them, let them stand till the next day; then put the syrup from them, and set it on the fire; and when it is very hot, put it on your damsins: this do twice a day for three days together; then draw the syrup from the damsins, and lay them in an earthen dish, and set them in an oven after bread is drawn; when the oven is cold, take them and turn them, and lay them upon clean dishes; set them in the sun, or in another oven, till they are dry.

To dry Pear-Plums.

TAKE two pounds of pear-plums to one pound of sugar; stone them, and fill them every one with sugar; lay them in an earthen pot, put to them as much water as will prevent burning them; then set them in an oven after bread is drawn, let them stand till they be tender, then put them into a sieve to drain well from the syrup, then set them in an oven again until they be a little dry; then smooth the skins as well as you can, and so fill them; then set them in the oven again to harden; then wash them in water scalding hot, and dry them very well; then put them in the oven again very cool, to blue them; put them between two pewter dishes, and set them in the oven.

The Filling for the aforesaid Plums.

TAKE the plums, wipe them, prick them in the seams, put them in a pitcher, and set them in a little boiling water, let them boil very tender, then pour most of the liquor from them, then take off the skins and the stones; to a pint of the pulp put a pound of sugar well dried in the oven; then let it boil till the scum rises, which take off very clean, and put into earthen plates, and dry it in an oven, and so fill the plums.

To clarify Sugar after the Spanish Way.

TAKE one pound of the best Lisbon sugar, nineteen pounds of water, mix the white and shell of an egg, then beat it up to a lather; then let it boil, and strain it off: you must let it simmer over a charcoal fire till it diminish to half a pint; then put in a large spoonful of orange-flower water.

CHAP. XXIV.

To make Anchovies, Vermicelli, Catchup, Vinegar; and to keep Artichokes, French Beans, &c.

To make Anchovies.

TO a peck of sprats, two pounds of common salt, a quarter of a pound of bay-salt, four pounds of salt-petre, two ounces of sal-prunella, two pennyworth of cochineal; pound all in a mortar, put them into a stone pot, a row of sprats, a layer of your compound, and so on to the top alternately. Press them hard down, cover them close, let them stand six months, and they will be fit for use. Observe that your sprats be very fresh, and do not wash or wipe them, but just take them as they come out of the water.

To pickle Smelts, where you have Plenty.

TAKE a quarter of a peck of smelts, half an ounce of pepper, half an ounce of nutmeg, a quarter of an ounce of mace, half an ounce of salt-petre, a quarter of a pound of common salt, beat all very fine, wash and clean the smelts, gut them, then lay them in rows in a jar, and between every layer of smelts strew the seasoning with four or five bay-leaves, then boil red wine, and pour over enough to cover them. Cover them with a plate, and when cold tie them down close. They exceed anchovies.

To make Vermicelli.

MIX yolks of eggs and flour together in a pretty stiff paste, so as you can work it up cleverly, and roll it as thin as it is possible to roll the paste. Let it dry in the sun; when it is quite dry, with a very sharp knife cut it as thin as possible, and keep it in a dry place. It will run up like little worms, as vermicelli does; though the best way is to run it through a coarse sieve whilst the paste is soft. If you want some to be made in haste, dry it by the fire, and cut it small. It will dry by the fire in a quarter of an hour. This far exceeds what comes from abroad, being fresher.

To make Catchup.

TAKE the large flaps of mushrooms gathered dry, and bruise them; put some at the bottom of an earthen pan; strew some salt over, then mushrooms, then salt, till you have done. Put in half an ounce of cloves and mace, and the like of all-spice. Let them stand six days, stir them up every day, then send them to the oven, and bake them gently for four hours. Take them out, and strain the liquor through a cloth or fine sieve. To every gallon of liquor add a quart of red wine. If not salt enough, add a little more, a race or two of ginger cut small; boil it till one quart is wasted; strain it into a pan, and let it be cold. Pour it from the settlings; bottle it, and cork it tight.

Another Way to make Catchup.

TAKE the large flaps and salt them as above; boil the liquor, strain it through a thick flannel bag; to a quart of that liquor put a quart of stale beer, a large stick of horse-radish cut in little slips, five or six bay-leaves, an onion stuck with twenty or thirty cloves, a quarter of an ounce of mace, a quarter of an ounce of nutmegs beat, a quarter of an ounce of black and white pepper, a quarter of an ounce of all-spice, and four or five races of ginger. Cover it close, and let it simmer very softly till about one-third is wasted; then strain it through a flannel bag: when it is cold, bottle it in pint bottles, cork it close, and it will keep a great while. The other receipt you have in the Chapter for the Sea.

Artichokes to keep all the Year.

BOIL as many artichokes as you intend to keep; boil them so as just the leaves will come out; then pull off all the leaves and choke, cut them from the strings, lay them on a tin plate, and put them in an oven where tarts are drawn; let them stand till the oven is heated again, take them out before the wood is put in, and set them in again after the tarts are drawn; so do till they are as dry as a board, then put them in a paper bag, and hang them in a dry place. You should lay them in warm water three or four hours before you use them, shifting the water often. Let the last water be boiling hot. They will be very tender, and eat as fine as fresh ones. You need not dry all your bottoms at once, as the leaves are good to eat; so boil a dozen at a time, and save the bottoms for this use.

Artichokes preserved the Spanish Way.

TAKE the largest you can get, cut the tops of the leaves off, wash them well and drain them; to every artichoke, pour in a large spoonful of oil; season with pepper and salt. Send them to the oven, and bake them, they will keep a year.

N. B. The Italians, French, Portuguese, and Spaniards have variety of ways of dressing fish, which we have not, *viz.* As making fish-soups, ragoos, pies, &c. For their soups they use no gravy, nor in their sauces, thinking it improper to mix flesh and fish together; but make their fish-soups with fish, viz. either of craw-fish, lobsters, &c. taking only the juice of them. For example: take your craw-fish, tie them up in a muslin rag, and boil them; then press out their juice for the above-said use.

To keep French Beans all the Year.

TAKE fine young beans, gather them on a very fine day, have a large stone jar ready, clean and dry, lay a layer of salt at the bottom, and then a layer of beans, then salt, and then beans, and so on till the jar is full; cover them with salt, tie a coarse cloth over them, and a board on that, and then a weight to keep it close from all air; set them in a dry cellar; and when you use them, cover them close again; wash them you took out very clean, and let them lie in soft water twenty-four hours, shifting the water often; when you boil them, do not put any salt in the water. The best way of dressing them is, boil them with just the white heart of a small cabbage, then drain them, chop the cabbage, and put both into a sauce-pan with a piece of butter as big as an egg, rolled in flour; shake a little

pepper,

pepper, put in a quarter of a pint of good gravy, let them stew ten minutes, and then dish them up for a side-dish. A pint of beans to the cabbage. You may do more or less, just as you please.

To keep Green Peas till Christmas.

TAKE fine young peas, shell them, throw them into boiling water with some salt in, let them boil five or six minutes, throw them into a cullender to drain; then lay a cloth four or five times double on a table, and spread them on; dry them very well, and have your bottles ready, fill them and cover them with mutton-fat tried; when it is a little cool, fill the necks almost to the top, cork them, tie a bladder and a lath over them, and set them in a cool dry place. When you use them, boil your water, put in a little salt, some sugar, and a piece of butter; when they are boiled enough, throw them into a sieve to drain; then put them into a sauce-pan with a good piece of butter, keep shaking it round all the time till the butter is melted, then turn them into a dish, and send them to table.

Another Way to preserve Green Peas.

GATHER your peas on a very dry day, when they are neither old, nor too young, shell them, and have ready some well dried quart bottles with little mouths; fill the bottles and cork them well, have ready a pipkin of rosin melted, into which dip the necks of the bottles, and set them in a very dry place that is cool.

To keep Green Peas, Beans, &c. and Fruit, fresh and good till Christmas.

OBSERVE to gather all your things on a fine clear day, in the increase or full moon; take well-glazed earthen or stone pots quite new, that have not been laid in water, wipe them clean, lay in your fruit very carefully, and take great care none is bruised or damaged in the least, nor too ripe, but just in their prime; stop down the jar close, and pitch it, and tie a leather over. Do kidney-beans the same; bury two feet deep in the earth, and keep them there till you have occasion for them. Do peas and beans the same way, only keep them in the pods, and do not let your peas be either too young or too old; the one will run to water, and the other the worm will eat; as to the two latter, lay a layer of fine writing-sand, and a layer of pods, and so on till full; the rest as above. Flowers you may keep the same way.

To keep Green Gooseberries till Christmas.

PICK your large green gooseberries on a dry day, have ready your bottles clean and dry, fill the bottles, and cork them, set them in a kettle of water up to the neck, let the water boil very softly till you find the gooseberries are coddled, take them out, and put in the rest of the bottles till all are done; then have ready some rosin melted in a pipkin, dip the necks of the bottles in, and that will keep all air from coming at the cork, keep them in a cold dry place where no damp is, and they will bake as red as a cherry. You may keep them without scalding, but then the skins will not be so tender, nor bake so fine.

To keep Red Gooseberries.

PICK them when full ripe; to each quart of gooseberries put a quarter of a pound of Lisbon sugar, and to each quarter of a pound of sugar put a quarter of a pint of water; let it boil, then put in your gooseberries, and let them boil softly two or three minutes, then pour them into little stone jars; when cold, cover them up, and keep them for use; they make fine pies with little trouble. You may press them through a cullender; to a quart of pulp put half a pound of fine Lisbon sugar, keep stirring over the fire till both be well mixed and boiled, and pour it into a stone jar; when cold, cover it with white paper, and it makes very pretty tarts or puffs.

To keep Walnuts all the Year.

TAKE a large jar, a layer of sea-sand at the bottom, then a layer of walnuts, then sand, then the nuts, and so on till the jar is full; and be sure they do not touch each other in any of the layers. When you would use them, lay them in warm water for an hour, shift the water as it cools; then rub them dry, and they will peel well and eat sweet. Lemons will keep thus covered better than any other way.

Another Way to keep Lemons.

TAKE the fine large fruit that are quite sound and good, and take a fine packthread about a quarter of a yard long, run it through the hard nib at the end of the lemon; then tie the string together, and hang it on a little hook in an airy dry place; so do as many as you please; but be sure they do not touch one another, nor any thing else, but hang as high as you can. Thus you may keep pears, &c. only tying the string to the stalk.

To keep White Bullice, Pear Plums, or Damsins, &c. for Tarts or Pies.

GATHER them when full grown, and just as they begin to turn. Pick all the largest out, save about two-thirds of the fruit, the other third put as much water to as you think will cover the rest. Let them boil, and skim them; when the fruit is boiled very soft, then strain it through a coarse hair sieve; and to every quart of this liquor put a pound and a half of sugar, boil it, and skim it very well; then throw in your fruit, just give them a scald; take them off the fire, and when cold, put them into bottles with wide mouths; pour your syrup over them, lay a piece of white paper over them, and cover them with oil. Be sure to take the oil well off when you use them, and do not put them in larger bottles than you think you shall make use of at a time, because all these sorts of fruits spoil with the air.

To make Sour Crout.

TAKE your fine hard white cabbage, cut them very small, have a tub on purpose with the head out, according to the quantity you intend to make; put them in the tub; to every four or five cabbages throw in a large handful of salt; when you have done as many as you intend, lay a very heavy weight on them to press them down as flat as possible, throw a cloth on them, and lay on the cover; let them stand a month, then you may begin to use it. It will keep twelve months; but be sure to keep it always close covered, and the weight on it; if you throw a few carraway-seeds pounded fine amongst it, they give it a fine flavour. The way to dress it is with a fine fat piece of beef stewed together. It is a dish much made use of amongst the Germans, and in the North Countries, where the frost kills all the cabbages; therefore they preserve them in this manner before the frost takes them. Cabbage-stalks, caulliflower-stalks, and artichoke-stalks, peeled, and cut fine down in the same manner, are very good.

To raise Mushrooms.

COVER an old hot-bed three or four inches thick with fine garden mould, and cover that three or four inches thick with mouldy long muck, of a horse muck-hill, or old rotten stubble; when the bed has lain some time thus prepared, boil any mushrooms that are not fit for use, in water, and throw the water on your prepared bed; in a day or two after, you will have the best small button mushrooms.

To make Vinegar.

To every gallon of water put a pound of coarse Lisbon sugar, let it boil, and keep skimming it as long as the scum rises; then pour it into tubs, and when it is as cold as beer to work, toast a good toast, and rub it over with yeast. Let it work twenty-four hours; then have ready a vessel iron-hooped, and well painted, fixed in a place where the sun has full power, and fix it so as not to have any occasion to move it. When you draw it off, then fill your vessels, lay a tile on the bung to keep the dust out. Make it in March, and it will be fit to use in June

June or July. Draw it off into little stone bottles the latter end of June or beginning of July, let it stand till you want to use it, and it will never foul any more; but when you go to draw it off, and you find it is not four enough, let it stand a month longer before you draw it off. For pickles to go abroad use this vinegar alone; but in England you will be obliged, when you pickle, to put one half cold spring-water to it, and then it will be full four with this vinegar. You need not boil it, unless you please, for almost any sort of pickles; it will keep them quite good. It will keep walnuts very fine without boiling, even to go to the Indies; but then do not put water to it. For green pickles, you may pour it scalding hot on two or three times. All other sort of pickles you need not boil it. Mushrooms only wash them clean, dry them, put them into little bottles, with a nutmeg just scalded in vinegar, and sliced (whilst it is hot) very thin, and a few blades of mace; then fill up the bottle with the cold vinegar and spring-water, pour the mutton fat tried over it, and tie a bladder and leather over the top. These mushrooms will not be so white, but as finely tasted as if they were just gathered; and a spoonful of this pickle will give sauce a very fine flavour. White walnuts, suckers, and onions, and all white pickles, do in the same manner, after they are ready for the pickle.

CHAP. XXV.

DISTILLING.

To distil Walnut-Water.

TAKE a peck of fine green walnuts, bruise them well in a large mortar, put them in a pan, with a handful of baum bruised, put two quarts of good French brandy to them, cover them close, and let them lie three days; the next day distil them in cold still; from this quantity draw three quarts, which you may do in a day.

To distil Red Rose Buds.

WET your roses in fair water; four gallons of roses will take near two gallons of water; then still them in a cold still; take the same stilled water, and put into it as many fresh roses as it will wet, then still them again.

Mint, baum, parsley, and penny-royal water, distil the same way.

How to use this Ordinary Still.

You must lay the plate, then wood ashes thick at the bottom, then the iron pan, which you are to fill with your walnuts and liquor; then put on the head of the still; make a pretty brisk fire till the still begins to drop, then slacken it so as just to have enough to keep the still at work. Mind to keep a wet cloth all over the head of the still all the time it is at work, and always observe not to let the still work longer than the liquor is good, and take great care you do not burn the still; and thus you may distil what you please. If you draw the still too far it will burn, and give your liquor a bad taste.

To make Treacle-Water.

TAKE the juice of green walnuts, four pounds of rue, carduus, marigold, and baum, of each three pounds, roots of butter-bur half a pound, roots of burdock one pound, angelica and master-wort, of each half a pound, leaves of scordium six handfuls, Venice treacle and mithridate, of each half a pound, old Canary wine two pounds, white wine vinegar six pounds, juice of lemon six pounds; and distil this in an alembic.

To distil Treacle-Water Lady Monmouth's Way.

TAKE three ounces of hartshorn, shaved and boiled in borage-water, or succory, wood-sorrel or respice-water, or three pints of any of these waters boiled to a jelly; and put the jelly and hartshorn both into the still, and add a pint more of these waters when you put it into the still; take the roots of elecampane, gentian, cypress tuninsil, of each an ounce; blessed thistle, called carduus, and angelica, of each an ounce; sorrel-roots two ounces; baum, sweet-marjoram, and burnet, of each half a handful; lily-comvally flowers, borage, bugloss, rosemary, and marigold-flowers, of each two ounces; citron-rinds, carduus-seeds, and citron-seeds, alkermes berries, and cochineal, each of these an ounce.

Prepare all these Simples thus:

GATHER the flowers as they come in season, and put them in glasses with a large mouth, and put with them as much good sack as will cover them, and tie up the glasses close with bladders wet in the sack, with a cork and leather tied upon it close, adding more flowers and sack as occasion is; and when one glass is full, take another, till you have your quantity of flowers to distil; put cochineal into a pint bottle, with half a pint of sack, and tie it up close with a bladder under the cork, and another on the top, wet with sack, tied up close with brown thread;

and

and then cover it up close with leather, and bury it standing upright in a bed of hot horse-dung for nine or ten days; look at it, and if dissolved, take it out of the dung, but do not open it till you distil; slice all the roses, beat the seeds and the alkermes berries, and put them into another glass; amongst all, put no more sack than needs; and when you intend to distil, take a pound of the best Venice treacle and dissolve it in six pints of the best white wine, and three of red rose-water; and put all the ingredients into a bason, and stir them all together, and distil them in a glass still, balneum Mariæ; open not the ingredients till the same day you distil.

To make Black Cherry Water.

TAKE six pounds of black cherries and bruise them small; then put to them the tops of rosemary, sweet marjoram, spearmint, angelica, baum, marigold flowers, of each a handful, dried violets one ounce, anise-seeds and sweet fennel-seeds, of each half an ounce bruised; cut the herbs small, mix all together, and distil them off in a cold still.

To make Hysterical Water.

TAKE betony, roots of lovage, seeds of wild parsnips, of each two ounces; roots of single-piony four ounces, of misletoe of the oak three ounces, myrrh a quarter of an ounce, castor half an ounce; beat all these together, and add to them a quarter of a pound of dried millepedes: pour on these, three quarts of mugwort-water, and two quarts of brandy; let them stand in a close vessel eight days, then distil it in a cold still pasted up. You may draw nine pints of water, and sweeten it to your taste. Mix all together, and bottle it up.

To make Plague-Water.

Roots.	Flowers.	Seeds.
Angelica,	Wormwood,	Hart's tongue,
Dragon,	Succory,	Horehound,
Maywort,	Hysop,	Fennel,
Mint,	Agrimony,	Melilot,
Rue,	Fennel,	St. John's wort,
Carduus,	Cowslips,	Comfrey,
Origany,	Poppies,	Feverfew,
Winter-savoury,	Plaintain,	Red rose leaves,
Broad thyme,	Setfoyl,	Wood-sorrel,
Rosemary,	Vocvain,	Pellitory of the wall,
Pimpernell,	Maidenhair,	Heart's ease,
Sage,	Motherwort,	Centaury,
Fumitory,	Cowage,	Sea-drink, a good handful of
Coltsfoot,	Golden-rod,	each of the aforesaid things.
Scabeous,		

Roots.	Flowers.	Seeds.
Scabeous,	Gromwell,	Gentian-root,
Borrage,	Dill.	Dock-root,
Saxafrage,		Butterbur-root,
Betony,		Piony-root,
Liverwort,		Bay-berries,
Germander.		Juniper-berries, of each of these a pound.

One ounce of nutmegs, one ounce of cloves, and half an ounce of mace; pick the herbs and flowers, and shred them a little. Cut the roots, bruise the berries, and pound the spices fine; take a peck of green walnuts and chop them small; mix all these together, and lay them to steep in sack lees, or any white wine lees, if not in good spirits; but wine lees are best. Let them lie a week, or better; be sure to stir them once a day with a stick, and keep them close covered, then still them in an alembic with a slow fire, and take care your still does not burn. The first, second, and third running is good, and some of the fourth. Let them stand till cold, and then put them together.

To make Surfeit-Water.

You must take scurvy-grass, brook-lime, water-cresses, Roman wormwood, rue, mint, baum, sage, clivers, of each one handful; green merery two handfuls; poppies, if fresh half a peck, if dry a quarter of a peck; cochineal, six pennyworth, saffron, six pennyworth; anise-seeds, carraway-seeds, coriander-seeds, cardamom-seeds, of each an ounce; liquorice two ounces scraped, figs split a pound, raisins of the sun stoned a pound, juniper-berries an ounce bruised, nutmeg an ounce beat, mace an ounce bruised, sweet fennel-seeds an ounce bruised, a few flowers of rosemary, marigold and sage-flowers; put all these into a large stone-jar, and put to them three gallons of French brandy; cover it close, and let it stand near the fire for three weeks. Stir it three times a week, and be sure to keep it close stopped, and then strain it off; bottle your liquor, and pour on the ingredients a gallon more of French brandy. Let it stand a week, stirring it once a day, then distil it in a cold still, and this will make a fine white surfeit-water. You may make this water at any time of the year, if you live at London, because the ingredients are always to be had either green or dry; but it is the best made in summer.

To make Milk-Water.

Take two good handfuls of wormwood, as much carduus, as much rue, four handfuls of mint, as much baum, half as much

much angelica; cut these a little, put them into a cold still, and put to them three quarts of milk. Let your fire be quick till your still drops, and then slacken your fire. You may draw off two quarts. The first quart will keep all the year.

Another Way.

TAKE the herbs agrimony, endive, fumitory, baum, elder-flowers, white-nettles, water-cresses, bank-cresses, sage, each three handfuls; eye-bright, brook-lime, and celandine, each two handfuls; the roses of yellow dock, red madder, fennel, horse-radish, and liquorice, each three ounces; raisins stoned, one pound; nutmegs sliced, Winter's bark, turmerick, galangal, each two drachms; carraway and fennel seeds three ounces, one gallon of milk. Distil all with a gentle fire in one day. You may add a handful of May wormwood.

The Stag's Hart Water.

TAKE baum four handfuls, sweet-marjoram one handful, rosemary flowers, clove giliflowers dried, dried rose-buds, borage flowers, of each an ounce; marigold flowers half an ounce, lemon-peel two ounces, mace and cardamum, of each thirty grains; of cinnamon sixty grains, or yellow and white sanders, of each a quarter of an ounce, shavings of hartshorn, an ounce; take nine oranges, and put in the peel, then cut them in small pieces; pour upon these two quarts of the best Rhenish, or the best white wine; let it infuse three or four days, being very close stopped in a cellar or cool place: if it infuse nine or ten days, it is the better. Take a stag's heart and cut off all the fat, and cut it very small, and pour in so much Rhenish or white wine as will cover it; let it stand all night close covered in a cool place; the next day add the aforesaid things to it, mixing it very well together; adding to it a pint of the best rose-water, and a pint of the juice of celandine: if you please, you may put in ten grains of saffron, and so put it in a glass still, distilling in water, raising it well to keep in the steam, both of the still and receiver.

To make Angelica Water.

TAKE eight handfuls of the leaves, wash and cut them, and lay them on a table to dry; when they are dry, put them into an earthen pot, and put to them four quarts of strong wine lees; let it stay for twenty-four hours, but stir it twice in the time; then put it into a warm still or an alembic, and draw it off; cover your bottles with a paper, and prick holes in it; let it stand two or three days, then mingle it all together, and sweeten it; and when it is settled, bottle it up and stop it close.

To make Cordial Poppy Water.

TAKE two gallons of very good brandy, and a peck of poppies, and put them together in a wide-mouthed glass, and let them stand forty-eight hours, and then strain the poppies out; take a pound of raisins of the sun, stone them, and an ounce of coriander-seeds, an ounce of sweet-fennel seeds, and an ounce of liquorice sliced, bruise them all together, and put them into the brandy, with a pound of good powder-sugar, and let them stand four or eight weeks, shaking it every day; and then strain it off, and bottle it close up for use.

[How to distil Vinegar is in the Chapter of Pickles.]

CHAP. XXVI.

Necessary Directions whereby the Reader may easily attain the polite and useful ART of CARVING.

To cut up a Turkey.

RAISE the leg, open the joint, but be sure not to take off the leg; lace down both sides of the breast, and open the pinion of the breast, but do not take it off; raise the merry-thought between the breast-bone and the top; raise the brawn, and turn it outward on both sides, but be careful not to cut it off, nor break it; divide the wing pinions from the joint next the body, and stick each pinion where the brawn was turned out; cut off the sharp end of the pinion, and the middle-piece will fit the place exactly. A bustard, capon, or pheasant, is cut up in the same manner.

To rear a Goose.

CUT off both legs in the manner of shoulders of lamb; take off the belly-piece close to the extremity of the breast; lace the goose down both sides of the breast, about half an inch from the sharp bone: divide the pinions and the flesh first laced with your knife, which must be raised from the bone, and taken off with the pinion from the body; then cut off the merry-thought, and cut another slice from the breast-bone, quite through; lastly, turn up the carcase, cutting it asunder, the back above the loin-bones.

To unbrace a Mullard or Duck.

FIRST, raise the pinions and legs, but cut them not off; then raise the merry-thought from the breast, and lace it down both sides with your knife.

To unlace a Coney.

THE back muſt be turned downward, and the apron divided from the belly; this done, ſlip in your knife between the kidneys, looſening the fleſh on each ſide; then turn the belly, cut the back croſs-ways between the wings, draw your knife down both ſides of the back-bone, dividing the ſides and leg from the back. Obſerve not to pull the leg too violently from the bone when you open the ſide, but with great exactneſs lay open the ſides from the ſcut to the ſhoulder; and then put the legs together.

To wing a Partridge or Quail.

AFTER having raiſed the legs and wings, uſe ſalt and powdered ginger for ſauce.

To allay a Pheaſant or Teal.

THIS differs in nothing from the foregoing, but that you muſt uſe ſalt only for ſauce.

To diſmember a Hern.

CUT off the legs, lace the breaſt down each ſide, and open the breaſt-pinion, without cutting it off; raiſe the merry-thought between the breaſt-bone and the top of it; then raiſe the brawn, turning it outward on both ſides; but break it not, nor cut it off; ſever the wing-pinion from the joint neareſt the body; ſticking the pinions in the place where the brawn was; remember to cut off the ſharp end of the pinion, and ſupply the place with the middle-piece.

In this manner ſome people cut up a capon or pheaſant, and likewiſe a bittern, uſing no ſauce but ſalt.

To thigh a Woodcock.

THE legs and wings muſt be raiſed in the manner of a fowl, only open the head for the brains. And ſo you thigh curlews, plover, or ſnipe, uſing no ſauce but ſalt.

To diſplay a Crane.

AFTER his legs are unfolded, cut off the wings; take them up, and ſauce them with powdered ginger, vinegar, ſalt, and muſtard.

To lift a Swan.

SLIT it fairly down the middle of the breaſt, clean through the back, from the neck to the rump; divide it in two parts, neither breaking nor tearing the fleſh; then lay the halves in a charger, the ſlit ſides downwards; throw ſalt upon it, and ſet it again on the table. The ſauce muſt be chaldron ſerved up in ſaucers.

CHAP.

CHAP. XXVII.

MISCELLANEOUS.

Containing many useful MEDICAL and other FAMILY RECEIPTS.

A certain Cure for the Bite of a Mad Dog.

LET the patient be blooded at the arm nine or ten ounces. Take of the herb called in Latin *lichen cinereus terrestris*, in English, ash-coloured, ground liverwort, cleaned, dried, and powdered, half an ounce. Of black pepper, powdered, two drachms. Mix these well together, and divide the powder into four doses, one of which must be taken every morning fasting, for four mornings successively, in half a pint of cow's milk warm. After these four doses are taken, the patient must go into the cold bath, or a cold spring or river every morning fasting for a month. He must be dipped all over, but not to stay in (with his head above water) longer than half a minute, if the water be very cold. After this he must go in three times a week for a fortnight longer.

N. B.—The lichen is a very common herb, and grows generally in sandy and barren soils all over England. The right time to gather it is in the months of October and November. [*D. Mead.*]

Another Cure for the Bite of a Mad Dog.

FOR the bite of a mad dog, for either man or beast, take six ounces of rue clean picked and bruised, four ounces of garlic peeled and bruised, four ounces of Venice treacle, and four ounces of filed pewter, or scraped tin. Boil these in two quarts of the best ale, in a pan covered close, over a gentle fire, for the space of an hour; then strain the ingredients from the liquor. Give eight or nine spoonfuls of it warm to a man, or a woman, three mornings fasting. Eight or nine spoonfuls is sufficient for the strongest; a lesser quantity to those younger, or of a weaker constitution, as you may judge of their strength. Ten or twelve spoonfuls for a horse or a bullock; three, four, or five to a sheep, hog, or dog. This must be given within nine days after the bite: it seldom fails in man or beast. If you bind some of the ingredients on the wound, it will be so much the better.

Receipt against the Plague.

TAKE of rue, sage, mint, rosemary, wormwood, and lavender, a handful of each; infuse them together in a gallon of white wine vinegar, put the whole into a stone pot, closely covered up, upon warm wood-ashes for four days, after which

draw

draw off (or strain through fine flannel) the liquid, and put it into bottles well corked; and into every quart bottle put a quarter of an ounce of camphor: with this preparation wash your mouth, and rub your loins and your temples every day; snuff a little up your nostrils when you go into the air, and carry about you a bit of spunge dipped in the same, in order to smell to upon all occasions, especially when you are near any place or person that is infected. They write, that four malefactors, (who had robbed the infected houses, and murdered the people during the course of the plague,) owned, when they came to the gallows, that they had preserved themselves from the contagion by using the above medicine only: and that they went the whole time from house to house without any fear of the distemper.

To make a fine Bitter.

TAKE an ounce of the finest Jesuit powder, half a quarter of an ounce of snake-root powder, half a quarter of an ounce of salt of wormwood, half a quarter of saffron, half a quarter of cochineal; put it into a quart of the best brandy, and let it stand twenty-four hours; every now and then shaking the bottle.

For a Consumption; an approved Receipt, by a Lady at Paddington.

TAKE the yolk of a new laid egg, beat it up well with three large spoonfuls of rose water; mix it well in half a pint of new milk from the cow, sweeten it well with sirup de capillaire, and grate some nutmeg in it. Drink it every morning fasting for a month, and refrain from spirituous liquors of any kind.

N. B. Mr. Powel, who kept the Crown, a public house in Swallow-street, St. James's, was in so deep a decline as to be scarce able to walk; when he coughed, the phlegm he brought from his stomach was green and yellow; and he was given over by his physician, who, as the last resource, advised him to go into the country to try what the air would do. He happily went to lodge at Paddington: the woman of the house understanding his condition, recollected that an old lady, who had lodged in the same house, had left a book with a collection of receipts in it for various disorders, instantly fetched it, and found the foregoing, which he having strictly followed, found himself much better in a fortnight; and, by continuing the same, in less than a month he began to have an appetite, and with the blessing of God, in a short time, by degrees he recovered his health, to the astonishment and surprise of all who knew him, and declared to me he was as well and hearty as ever he was in his life, and did not scruple to tell every person the means and method of his recovery.

N. B. This receipt I had from his own mouth.

To stop a violent Purging, or the Flux.

TAKE a third part of a gill of the very best double distilled anise-seeds; grate a third part of a large nutmeg into it. To be taken the same quantity an hour after breakfast, one hour after dinner, and, if occasion, an hour before going to bed. *Probatum est.*

For Obstructions in Females.

SUCCOTORINE aloes, one ounce; cardamum-seed, a quarter of an ounce; snake-root, a quarter of an ounce; gum-myrrh, a quarter of an ounce; saffron, a quarter of an ounce; cochineal, two scruples; zedoary, two scruples; rhubarb, two scruples: let these drugs be well beaten in a mortar, and put them into a large bottle; add thereto a pint and a half of mountain wine; place it near the fire for the space of three days and nights, shaking it often. Let the patient take a small tea-cupfull twice a week in the morning, an hour before rising.

Another for Obstructions.

THREE pennyworth of alkermes, two pennyworth of Venice treacle, and a quarter of an ounce of spermaceti; to be made into four boluses, one to be taken every evening going to bed.

Half a pint of pennyroyal-water, a quarter of a pint of hysteric-water, and a quarter of a pint of pepper-mint-water; to be taken every morning and evening, a tea-cup full.

For a Hoarseness.

Two ounces of pennyroyal-water, the yolk of a new laid egg beaten, thirty drops of cochineal, twenty drops of oil of anise-seed, mixed well and sweetened with white sugar candy. A large spoonful to be taken night and morning.

Lozenges for the Heart-burn.

TAKE one pound of chalk, beat it to a powder in a mortar, with one pound and a half of white loaf-sugar, and one ounce of bole-ammoniac; mix them well together, and put in something to moisten them, to make it of a proper consistency or paste; make them into small lozenges, and let them lie in a band-box on the top of an oven a week or more to dry, shaking the box sometimes.

Lozenges for a Cold.

TAKE two pounds of common white loaf-sugar, beat it well in a mortar, dissolve six ounces of Spanish liquorice in a little warm water; one ounce of gum-arabic dissolved likewise; add thereto a little oil of anise-seed; mix them well to a proper consistency, and cut them into small lozenges; let them lie in a band box on the top of an oven a considerable time to dry, shaking the box sometimes.

The genuine Receipt to make Turlington's Balsam.

BALSAM of Peru, one ounce; best storax, two ounces; benjamin, impregnated with sweet almonds, three ounces; aloes Succotorine, myrrh elect, purest frankincense, roots of angelica, flowers of St. John's wort, of each of these half an ounce; beat the drugs well in a mortar, and put them into a large glass bottle; add thereto a pint, or rather more, of the best spirits of wine, and let the bottle stand by the kitchen fire, or in the chimney-corner, two days and two nights; then decant it off in small bottles for use, and let them be well corked and sealed.

N. B. The same quantity of spirits of wine poured on the ingredients, letting them stand by the fire, or in some warm place for the space of six days and nights, will serve for common use; pour off the same in small bottles, and let them be well corked and sealed.

How to keep clear from Bugs.

FIRST take out of your room all silver and gold lace, then set the chairs about the room, shut up your windows and doors, tack a blanket over each window, and before the chimney, and over the doors of the room, set open all closets and cupboard doors, all your drawers and boxes, hang the rest of your bedding on the chair-backs, lay the feather-bed on a table, then set a large broad earthen pan in the middle of the room, and in that set a chafing-dish that stands on feet, full of charcoal well lighted; if your room is very bad, a pound of rolled brimstone; if only a few, half a pound; lay it on the charcoal, and get out of the room as quick as possibly you can, or it will take away your breath: shut your door close, with the blanket over it, and be sure to set it so as nothing can catch fire: if you have any India pepper, throw it in with the brimstone. You must take great care to have the door open whilst you lay in the brimstone, that you may get out as soon as possible. Do not open the door under six hours, and then you must be very careful how you go in to open the windows: then brush and sweep your room very clean; wash it well with boiling lee, or boiling water with a little unslacked lime in it; get a pint of spirits of wine, a pint of spirits of turpentine, and an ounce of camphire, shake all well together, and with a bunch of feathers wash your bedstead very well, and sprinkle the rest over the feather-bed and about the room.

If

If you find great swarms about the room, and some not dead, do this over again, and you will be quite clear. Every spring and fall wash your bedstead with half a pint, and you will never have a bug; but if you find any come in with new goods or boxes, &c. only wash your bedstead, and sprinkle all over your bedding and bed, and you will be clear; but be sure to do it as soon as you find one. If your room is very bad, it will be well to paint the room after the brimstone is burnt in it.

This never fails, if rightly done.

An effectual Way to clear your Bedstead of Bugs.

TAKE quicksilver and mix it well in a mortar with the white of an egg till the quicksilver is all well mixed, and there are no bubbles; then beat up some white of an egg very fine, and mix with the quicksilver till it is like a fine ointment, then with a feather anoint the bedstead all over in every creek and corner, and about the lacing and binding, where you think there is any. Do this two or three times: it is a certain cure, and will not spoil any thing.

DIRECTIONS *to the* HOUSEMAID.

ALWAYS when you sweep a room, throw a little wet sand all over it, and that will gather up all the flew and dust, prevent it from rising, clean the boards, and save the bedding, pictures, and all other furniture from dust or dirt.

How to make Yellow Varnish.

TAKE a quart of spirit of wine, and put to it eight ounces of sandarach, shake it half an hour; next day it will be fit for use, but strain it first: take lamp-black, and put in your varnish about the thickness of a pancake; mix it well, but stir it not too fast; then do it eight times over, and let it stand still the next day; then take some burnt ivory, and oil of turpentine as fine as butter; then mix it with some of your varnish, till you have varnished it fit for polishing; then polish it with tripoly in fine flour; then lay it on the wood smooth, with one of the brushes, then let it dry, and do it so eight times at the least; when it is very dry, lay on your varnish that is mixed, and when it is dry, polish it with a wet cloth dipped in tripoly, and rub it as hard as you would do platters.

How to make a pretty Varnish to colour little Baskets, Bowls, or any Board where nothing hot is set on.

TAKE either red, black, or white wax, which colour you want to make; to every two ounces of sealing-wax one ounce of spirit of wine, pound the wax fine, then sift it through a fine lawn sieve till you have made it extremely fine; put it into a large phial with the spirits of wine, shake it, let it stand within the air of the fire forty-eight hours, shaking it often; then with a little brush rub your baskets all over with it; let it dry, and do it over a second time, and it makes them look very pretty.

How to clean Gold and Silver Lace.

TAKE alabaster finely beaten and searced, and put it into an earthen pipkin, and set it upon a chafing-dish of coals, and let it boil for some time, stirring it often with a stick first; when it begins to boil, it will be very heavy; when it is enough, you will find it in the stirring very light; then take it off the fire, lay your lace upon a piece of flannel, and strew your powder upon it; knock it well in with a hard cloth brush; when you think it is enough, brush the powder out with a clean brush.

To clean White Sattins, Flowered Silks with Gold and Silver in them.

TAKE stale bread crumbled very fine, mixed with powder-blue, rub it very well over the silk or sattin; then shake it well, and with clean soft cloths dust it well: if any gold or silver flowers, afterwards take a piece of crimson in grain velvet, and rub the flowers with it.

To keep Arms, Iron, or Steel, from rusting.

TAKE the filings of lead, or dust of lead, finely beaten in an iron mortar, putting to it oil of spike, which will make the iron smell well; and if you oil your arms, or any thing that is made of iron or steel, you may keep them in moist airs from rusting.

To take Iron-molds out of Linen.

TAKE sorrel, bruise it well in a mortar, squeeze it through a cloth, bottle it, and keep it for use: take a little of the above juice, in a silver or tin sauce-pan, boil it over a lamp; as it boils dip in the iron-mold, do not rub it, but only squeeze it; as soon as the iron-mold is out, throw it into cold water.

To take Iron-molds out of Linen, and Grease out of Woollen or Silk.—One Shilling a Bottle.

TAKE four ounces of spirits of turpentine, and one ounce of essence of lemon; mix them well together, and put it into bottles for use.

To prevent the Infection among Horned Cattle.

MAKE an issue in the dewlap, put in a peg of black hellebore, and rub all the vents both behind and before with tar.

RECEIPTS

FOR

PERFUMERY, &c.

ADVERTISEMENT.

THE following Collection of approved Receipts in Perfumery has been added to this Edition of the Art of Cookery, in order to render the Work of more extensive Utility than the former; and which, it is presumed, will be considered by the Reader as a valuable Acquisition.

RECEIPTS

FOR

PERFUMERY, &c.

To make Red, Light, or Purple Wash-Balls.

GET some white soap, beat it in a mortar; then put it into a pan, and cover it down close; let the same be put into a copper, so that the water does not come to the top of the pan; then cover your copper as close as you can, to stop the steam; make the water boil some time; take the pan out, and beat it well with a wooden stirrer till it is all melted with the heat of the water; then pour it out into drops, and cut them into square pieces as small as a walnut; let it lie three days on an oven in a band-box; afterwards put them into a pan, and damp them with rose-water, mash it well with your hands, and mould them according to your fancy, viz. squeeze them as hard and as close as you possibly can; make them very round, and put them into a band-box or a sieve two or three days; then scrape them a little with a wash-ball scraper (which are made for that purpose), and let them lie eight or nine days; afterwards scrape them very smooth and to your mind.

N. B. If you would have them red, when you first mash them, put in a little vermilion; if light, some hair-powder; and if purple, some rose-pink.

To make Blue, Red, or Purple Wash-Balls, or to marble Ditto.

GET some white soap and cut it into square pieces about the bigness of dice; let it lie in a band-box or a sieve on the top of an oven to dry; beat it in a mortar to a powder, and put it into a pan; damp it with rose-water, mix it well with your hands, put in some hair-powder to make it stiff; then scent it with oil of thyme, and oil of carraways.

If you would have them blue, put in some powder-blue; if red, some vermilion; if purple, some rose-pink; mix them well together with your hands, and squeeze them as close as possible; make them very round, of a size agreeable to your mind; put them into a sieve two or three days; then scrape them a little with a wash-ball scraper, and let them lie in the sieve eight or nine days; afterwards scrape them very smooth, and agreeable to your mind.

If you would have them marbled, after being scented with oil of thyme and oil of carraways (as in the first process), cut them into pieces, about as much as will make a ball each, make it into a flat square piece, then take a very thin knife, and dip it into the powder-blue, vermilion, or rose pink, (according to the colour you would fancy,) and chop it in according to your mind; double it up, make it into a hard and round ball, and use the same process as beforementioned.

White Almond Wash Balls.

TAKE some white soap and slice it thin, put it into a bandbox on the top of an oven to dry, three weeks or more; when it is dry, beat it in a mortar till it is a powder; to every four ounces of soap add one ounce of hair-powder, half an ounce of white-lead; put them into a pan, and damp them with rosewater to make it of a proper consistency; make them into balls as hard and close as possible, scrape them with a ball-scraper, and use the same process as beforementioned, letting them lie three weeks in a sieve to dry; then finish them with a ball-scraper to your mind.

Brown Almond Wash-Balls.

TAKE some common brown hard soap, slice it thin, and put it into a band-box on the top of an oven to dry, for the space of three weeks, or more; when quite dry, beat it in a mortar to a powder; to every three ounces of soap add one ounce of brown almond-powder; put it in a mortar, and damp it with rose-water, to make it of a proper consistency; beat it very well, then make them into balls according to a process before-mentioned, letting them lie three weeks in a sieve to dry; then finish them with a ball-scraper, agreeable to your mind.

Windsor Soap.—Two shillings per Pound.

GET some of the whitest soap, shave it into thin slices; melt it in a stew-pan over a slow fire, and scent it very strong with oil of carraways; pour it into a drawer made for that purpose; let it stand three days or more, and cut it into square pieces to your fancy.

To make Lip Salve.

TAKE half a pound of hog's lard, put it into a pan, with one ounce and a half of virgin-wax; let it stand on a slow fire till it is melted; then take a small tin-pot, and fill it with water, and put therein some alkanet-root; let it boil till it is of a fine red

red colour; then strain some of it, and mix it with the ingredients according to your fancy, and scent it with essence of lemon; pour it into small boxes, and smooth the top with your finger.

N. B.—You may pour a little out first, to see if it is of a proper colour to your fancy.

To make White Lip Salve, and for chopped Hands and Face.—Six Shillings and Threepence per Pot.

MELT some spermaceti in sweet oil; add thereto a small bit of white wax; when it is melted, put in a small quantity of white sugar-candy, and stir it well therein; then pour it into pots for use.

French Rouge.—Five Shillings per Pot.

TAKE some carmine, and mix it with hair-powder to make it as pale as you please, according to your fancy.

Opiate for the Teeth.—Two Shillings and Sixpence per Pot.

TAKE one pound of honey, let it be very well boiled and skimmed, a quarter of a pound of bole-ammoniac, one ounce of dragon's-blood, one ounce of oil of sweet almonds, half an ounce of oil of cloves, eight drops of essence of bergamot, one gill of honey-water; mix all well together, and pour it into pots for use.

Delescot's Opiate.

HALF an ounce of bole-ammoniac, one ounce of powder of myrrh, one ounce of dragon's-blood, half an ounce of orrice-root, half an ounce of roch-alum, half an ounce of ground ginger, two ounces of honey; mix all well together, and put it in pots for use.

Tooth-Powder.—One Shilling per Bottle.

BURN some roch-alum, and beat it in a mortar, sift it fine; then take some rose-pink, and mix them well together to make it of a pale red colour; add thereto a little powder of myrrh, and put it into bottles for use.

To make Shaving-Oil.—One Shilling per Bottle.

DISSOLVE a quantity of oil-soap, cut it into thin slices, in spirits of wine; let it stand a week, then put in as much soft-soap till the liquor becomes of a clammy substance: scent as you please, and bottle it for use.

To make Shaving-Powder.

TAKE some white-soap, and shave it in very thin slices; let it be well dried on the top of an oven in a band box; beat it in a mortar a mortar till it is very fine, sift it through a fine sieve, and scent it as you please.

Soap to fill Shaving-Boxes.

TAKE some of the whitest soap, beat it in a mortar, and scent it with oil of carraways, make it flat; then chop in some vermilion, or powder blue, to marble it, with a very thin knife dipt in the same; double it up, and squeeze it hard into the boxes; then scrape it smooth with a knife.

Wash for the Face.

TAKE one quart of milk, a quarter of a pound of salt-petre beaten to a powder; put in two pennyworth of oil of anise-seed, one pennyworth of oil of cloves, about four thimbles full of the best white wine vinegar; put it into a bottle, and let it stand in sand half-way up, in the sun, or in some warm place for a fortnight without the cork; afterwards cork and seal it up.

How to make Almond Milk for a Wash.

TAKE five ounces of bitter almonds, blanch them and beat them in a marble mortar very fine; you may put in a spoonful of sack when you beat them; then take the whites of three new-laid eggs, three pints of spring-water, and one pint of sack. Mix them all very well together; then strain it through a fine cloth, and put it into a bottle, and keep it for use. You may put in lemon, or powder of pearl, when you make use of it.

An approved Method practised by Mrs. Dukely, the Queen's Tire-Woman, to preserve Hair, and make it grow thick.

TAKE one quart of white wine, put in one handful of rosemary flowers, half a pound of honey, distil them together; then add a quarter of a pint of oil of sweet almonds, shake it very well together, put a little of it into a cup, warm it blood-warm, rub it well on your head, and comb it dry.

A Stick to take Hair out.

TAKE two ounces and a half of rosin, and one ounce of bees-wax; melt them together, and make them into sticks for use.

Liquid for the Hair.—Two Shillings a Quarter of a Pint.

To three quarts of sweet-oil, put a quarter of a pound of alkanet-root, cut in small pieces; let it be boiled some time over a steam; add thereto three ounces of oil of jessamine, and one ounce of oil of lavender; strain it through a coarse cloth, but do not squeeze it.

To make White Almond-Paste.

TAKE one pound of bitter-almonds, blanch and beat them very fine in a mortar; put in the whites of four eggs, one ounce of French white of Trois; add some rose-water and spirits of wine, a little at a time, until it is of a consistency for paste.

To make Brown Almond-Paste.

TAKE one pound of bitter-almonds; beat them well in a mortar; add to them one pound of raisins of the sun stoned; beat and mix them very well together, and put in a little brandy.

Sweet-scented Bags to lay with Linen.—At one Shilling and Sixpence, Two Shillings and Sixpence, &c. &c. &c. each Bag.

EIGHT ounces of coriander-seeds, eight ounces of sweet orrice root, eight ounces of damask-rose leaves, eight ounces of calamus-aromaticus, one ounce of mace, one ounce of cinnamon, half an ounce of cloves, four drachms of musk powder, two drachms of white loaf-sugar, three ounces of lavender-flowers, and some Roduam wood, beat them well together, and sew them up in small silk bags.

Orange-Butter.

MELT a small quantity of spermaceti in sweet-oil, and put in a little fine Dutch pink to colour it; then add a little oil of orange to scent it; and lastly, while it is very hot, put in some spirits of wine to curdle it.

Lemon-Butter.

Is made the same as orange butter, only put in no Dutch pink, and scent it with essence of lemons, instead of oil of orange.

Marechalle Powder. Sixteen Shillings per Pound.

ONE ounce of cloves, one ounce of mace, one ounce of cinnamon, beat them very well to a fine powder, add to them four pounds of hair-powder, and half a pound of Spanish burnt amber beaten very fine, a quarter of an ounce of oil of lavender, half an ounce of oil of thyme, a quarter of an ounce of essence of amber, five drops of oil of laurel, a quarter of an ounce of oil of sassafras; mix them all well together.

Virgin's Milk.—Two Shillings per Bottle.

PUT one ounce of tincture of benjamin into a pint of cold water: mix it well, and let it stand one day; then run it through a flannel-bag with some tow in it; put it in bottles for use.

Honey-Water.—One Shilling per Bottle.

ONE quart of rectified spirits of wine, two drachms of tincture of ambergrease, two drachms of tincture of musk, half a pint of water; filter it according to your fancy, and put it into small bottles.

Pearl-Water.

MIX pearl-powder with honey and lavender-water; and then the pearl-powder will never be discoloured.

Milk Flude Water.

ONE quart of spirits of wine, half an ounce of oil of cloves, one drachm of essence of lemons, fifteen drops of oil of Rhodium, a little cochineal in powder, to colour it of a fine pink; let it stand one day, then filter it, but with no water.

Beautifying-Water.

Is *balsamum cosmeticum* put into a small quantity of elder-flower water.

Miss in her Teens.

ONE quart of spirits of wine; essence of bergamot, one ounce; oil of Rhodium, two drachms; tincture of musk, half a drachm, and half a pint of water; mix them well together, and put them into bottles for use.

Lady Lilley's Ball.

TAKE twelve ounces of oil-soap shaved very fine, spermaceti three ounces, melt them together; two ounces of bizmuth dissolved in rose-water for the space of three hours, one ounce of oil of thyme, one ounce of the oil of carraways, one ounce of essence of lemons; mix all well together.

Nun's Cream.

One ounce of pearl-powder, twenty drops of oil of Rhodium, and two ounces of fine pomatum; mix all well together.

Cold Cream.

TAKE one pint of trotter-oil, a quarter of a pound of hog's-lard, one ounce of spermaceti, a bit of virgin-wax; warm them together with a little rose-water, and beat it up with a whisk.

The Ambrosia Nosegay.

TAKE one pint of spirits of wine, one drachm of oil of cloves, one ounce of oil of nutmegs; mix them, and filter it as you please.

Eau de Bouquet.

TAKE one quart of spirits of wine, half an ounce of musk, two drachms of tincture of saffron, mix them well together, and let them stand one day; then filter it with any water.

Eau de Luce.

Two ounces of the best rectified spirits of wine, one drachm of oil of amber, two drachms of salt of tartar, prepared powder of amber two drachms, twenty drops of oil of nutmegs; put them all into a bottle, and shake it well; let it stand five hours, then filter it, and always keep it by you, and when you would make *eau de luce*, put it into the strongest spirits of sal-ammoniac.

Eau sans Pareil.

ONE quart of spirits of wine, one ounce of essence of bergamot, two drachms of tincture of musk, add to them half a pint of water, and bottle them for use.

Hard Pomatum.

TAKE three pounds of mutton-suet, boil and skim it well till it is quite clear, pour it off from the dross which remains at the bottom; then add thereto eight ounces of virgin-wax, melt them together, and scent it with essence of lemon; make it into rolls according to fancy.

Soft Pomatum.

TAKE a quantity of hog's lard, boil and skim it very well, put in a small quantity of hair-powder, when it is cool, to make it agreeable to your mind; and scent it with essence of lemons.

N. B.—You may take a small quantity out first, and let it cool; if it is too soft, add a little hair-powder to make it stiffer.

To make Sirop de Capillaire.

PUT seven pounds of common lump-sugar into a pan, and thereto add seven pints of water; boil it well, and keep skimming it; then take the white of an egg, put it in some water, and beat it up well with a whisk; take the froth off and scatter it therein, and keep it skimming until it is quite clear; then add thereto half a pint of orange-flower-water; mix it well together, let it stand till cold, and put it into a stone bottle, or in bottles for use, let them be quite clean and dry before it is put into them, otherwise it will make it mothery and spoil it.

N. B.—If you chuse to have it of a high colour, burn a little sugar in a pan, of a brown colour; afterwards put a little capillaire thereto, stir it about with a wooden spoon, and mix it well with the capillaire according to your fancy.

To make Dragon-Roots.

TAKE some mallow-roots, skin them, and pick one end with a pin or needle till you have made it like a brush; then take some powder of brasil, and some cochineal, boil them together, and put in the roots till you think they are thoroughly dyed; then take them out, and lay them by the fire to dry.

INDEX.

INDEX.

A.

ALMOND-soup, 186. 209. Fraze, 218. Pudding, 243. Ditto boiled, 244. Ipswich ditto, 251. Almond hogs' puddings, three ways, 278. Cheesecakes, 319. Custards, 320. Butter, 321. Cream, 324. Rice, 339. Knots, ib. Fine almond cakes, ib.

Amlet, of beans, 227.

Anchovy-sauce, 175. Anchovies, 370.

Andouilles, or calf's chitterlings, to dress, 83.

Angelica, to candy, 368. Water, 380.

Apple-sauce, to make, 34. Fritters, 215. Frazes, 217. Pupton of, 220. To bake whole, ib. Black caps of, ib. A dish of roasted, ib. Pudding, two ways, 246. Baked ditto, ib. Apple dumplings, two ways, 256, 257. Florentine, 257. Pie, 260. Green coddling pie, ib. Ditto to preserve, 363.

Apricot-pudding, 245. 251. Chips thin, 341. To preserve, two ways, 361. To preserve green, 364.

April, meat, &c. in season, 3.

Arms, of iron or steel, to keep from rusting, 388.

Artichokes, to dress, 31. Bottoms to fricassee, 229. To fry artichokes, 231. Suckers, Spanish way, ib. Pie, 258. To keep artichoke bottoms dry, 273. To fry, ib. To ragoo, ib. To pickle young artichokes, 305. Ditto Artichoke bottoms, 306. To keep all the year, 372. Preserved the Spanish way, ib.

Asparagus, to dress, 31. To ragoo, 140. Forced in French rolls, 232. Italian way, 233. With eggs, 234. To pickle, 300.

August, meat, &c. in season, 4.

B.

Bacon, to choose, 9. Bacon and egg pie, 204. To make, 297. See BEANS.

Bake a pig, 19. Leg of beef, 36. Ox's head, ib. Calf's head, 49. Sheep's head, ib. Lamb and rice, 76. Turbot, 149. Carp, 151. Cod's head, 154. Salmon, 157. Herrings, 159. Apples whole, 220. Almond pudding, 243. Apple pudding, 246. Bread pudding, 248. Fish, 274. An oatmeal pudding, 275. A rice ditto, ib. Custards, 320.

Balm,

Balm, how to distil, 376.
Bamboo, an imitation of, how to pickle, 307.
Barbicue a leg of pork, 87. Pig, 90.
Barbel, a fish, to choose, 13.
Barberries, to pickle, 304. To preserve, 364.
Barley-soup, 210. Pearl barley pudding, 245. French barley pudding, ib. Water, 270. Cream, two ways, 323.
Barm, to make bread without, 353.
Bath-cakes, 317.
Batter pudding, 248. Without eggs, ib.
Beans and *Bacon*, how to dress, 32. Bean tansey, 223. Beans, French, to ragoo, two ways, 225. A ragoo of beans with a force, 226. Beans ragooed with a cabbage, ib. With parsnips, 227. With potatoes, ib. To dress beans in ragoo, ib. Amlet of beans, ib. Beans, Dutch way, 228. German way, ib. Harrico, 276. French, to keep all the year, 372. To keep till Christmas, 373.
Bedstead, to clear of Bugs, 387.
Beef, to choose, 8. To roast, 16. Why not to be salted before it is laid to the fire, ib. How to be kept before it is dressed, ib. Its proper garnish, ib. Steaks, to broil, 24. To fry, 25. Round, to boil, 27. Brisket, ib. Gravy, to make, 32. To bake a leg of beef, 36. Collops, 40. To hash, 47. To ragoo, 55. To force the inside of a sirloin, 56. To force sirloin, ib. Sirloin en epigram, ib. To force a rump, 57. To force a round, ib. Tremblant, 59. A la daub, 60. Alamode, ib. Ditto in pieces, 61. Stew beef steaks, ib. Pretty side dish of, ib. To stew a rump, two ways, 62. Portugal, ib. To stew a rump or brisket French way, 63. To stew gobbets, ib. Royal, ib. Shank of, to stew, 64. Rolled rump of, 65. To boil a rump French fashion, ib. Escarlot, 66. Fricando, ib. Olives, ib. Fillet, ib. Steaks rolled, 67. To dress inside of a cold sirloin, ib. Boullie, ib. Cold collops of, 143. Broth, 183. Ditto for weak people, 264. Beef drink, 265. Tea, ib. Pudding, 274. To pot, 283. To pot like venison, 285. To collar, 289. Dutch, 291. To pickle the Jews' way, 292. For present use, 293. Beef hams, 295.
Beer, directions for brewing, 348. The best thing for rope, 350. To cure sour beer, ib.
Beest custards, 320.
Beet-root, to pickle, 302.
Birch wine, to make, 346.
Birds, small, to pot, 286. Potted, to save them when they begin to be bad, ib.
Biscuits, drop biscuits, 312. Common, 313. French, ib. Biscuit bread, 315. Orange, 338.
Bitter, to make fine, 384.
Blackbirds, to choose, 12.
Blackcaps, to make, 220.
Blackberry wine, 343.
Black puddings, 279.
Blancmange, to make, 335. Dutch, ib.
Boil, Directions for boiling, 26. To boil a ham, ib. To boil a tongue, ib. Round of beef, ib. Brisket of beef, ib. Calf's head, 27. Lamb's head, ib. Leg of lamb, and loin fried round it, ib. Leg of pork, 28. Pickled pork, ib. Turkey, ib. Young chickens, ib. Fowls and house lamb, 29. Green

INDEX.

Green peas, 32. Duck or rabbit with onions, 106. Ducks, the French way, 108. Pigeons, 112. Ditto with rice, 115. Partridges, 119. Pheasant, 123. Snipes or Woodcocks, 124. Turbot, 148. Cod's head, 153. Crimp-cod, salmon, whiting, or haddock, 155. Mackarel, 156. Salmon crimp, 159. Sturgeon, ib. Soals, 168. Spinage, 232. Almond pudding, 244. Loaf, 250. Scrag of veal, 264. Chicken, 265. Pigeons, 266. Partridge, or any wild fowl, ib. Plaice or flounder, ib. Sago, 268. Salop, ib. A liver pudding, 275.

Bologna sausages, 281.

Bombarded veal, 80.

Bowels, medicine for a disorder in, 271.

Brawn, to choose, 9. Sham, 291.

Bread pudding, 248. Ditto fine, 249. Ordinary ditto, ib. Baked ditto, ib. A bread and butter pudding, 252. Soup for the sick, 269. White bread after the London way, 351. French, ib. Without barm, by the help of leaven, 353.

Brewing, rules for, 348.

Brick-bat cheese, to make, 354.

Bride cake, 316.

Brocoli, how to dress, 30. In sallad, 231. And eggs, 233.

Broil, general directions for broiling, 23. To broil beef steaks, 24. Mutton chops, ib. Pork steaks, ib. Chickens, ib. 102. Pigeons, 25. Cod's sounds, 154. Ditto with gravy, 155. Crimp-cod, salmon, whiting, or haddock, ib. Mackarel, ib. Ditto whole, 156. Weavers, ib. Herrings, 159. Eels, 163. Haddocks in high season, 165. Potatoes, 232. Eggs, 235.

Broth, rules to be observed in making, 176. Strong, to make for soups or gravy, 177. Strong, to keep for use, 179. Mutton, 183. Beef, ib. Scotch barley, ib. Mutton, 183. Ditto for the sick, 264. Beef or mutton broth for weak people, ib. Pork, 265. Chicken, 267. Knuckle, 270.

Browning, for made-dishes, 38.

Bugs, to keep clear from, 386. To clear a bedstead of, 387.

Bullace cheese, 355. White, to keep for tarts or pies, 374.

Bullock, the several parts of one, 6.

Buns, to make, 315.

Bustard, to choose, 11.

Butter, to choose, 15. To melt, 132. Buttered wheat, 213. Buttered loaves, 242. To roast a pound, 264. Butter cake, 310. Fairy butter, 321. Orange, ib. Almond, ib. Buttered tort, 336.

C.

Cabbages, to dress, 29. Forced, 135. Stewed red cabbage, 137. Farce meagre, 240. To dress red cabbage the Dutch way, good for a cold in the breast, ib. To pickle red cabbage, 305. To pickle fine purple cabbage, 308. Sour crout, 375.

Cake, potatoe cakes, 231. To make a rich cake, 309. To ice a great cake, ib. Pound cake, ib. Cheap seed-cake, 310. Butter, ib. Gingerbread, ib. Fine seed or saffron, ib. A rich seed cake, called the nun's cake, 311. Pepper, ib. Portugal, ib. A pretty cake, ib. Little fine cakes, 312.

D d Another

INDEX.

Another sort of little cakes, 312. Shrewsbury, 313. Madling, 314. A cake the Spanish way, 315. Uxbridge cakes, ib. Carraway, 316. Bride cake, ib. Bath, 317. Queen, ib. Ratafia, ib. Little plum, ib. Orange, 337. White, like china dishes, 338. Almond, 339. Sugar, two ways, 340. Quince, 360.

Calf, The several parts of one, 7. Head to boil, 27. Feet and chauldron to fricasee Italian way, 44. Head to hash, 45. Ditto, white, 46. To bake, 49. Surprise, 50. Dutch way, ib. To stew, ib. To grill, 51. Chitterlings or Andouilles, 83. Ditto, curiously, 84. Liver in a caul, ib. Liver to roast, ib. Feet stewed, ib. Calf's feet pudding, 188. Pie, 192. Calf's head pie, 198. Calf's feet jelly, 329.

Candy, any sort of flowers, 367. Cherries, or green gages, 368. Angelica, ib. Cassia, ib.

Capons, how to choose, 10. Done after the French way, 99.

Captains of ships, directions for, 271.

Carolina rice pudding, 247. Snow ball, 341.

Carp, to choose, 13. To dress a brace of, 149. Au bleu, 150. To stew a brace, ib. To fry, 151. To bake, ib. To stew carp or tench, ib. Pie, 261.

Carraway cakes, to make 316.

Carrots, to dress, 29. Carrots and French beans the Dutch way, 228. Pudding, two ways, 244.

Carving, directions for, 381.

Cassia, to candy, 368.

Catchup, to make, to keep twenty years, 271. To make, two ways, 371.

Cattle, horned, how to prevent the infection among them, 388.

Caudle, white, 267. Brown, ib.

Cauliflowers, to dress, two ways, 30, 31. To ragoo, 141. Spanish way, 240. To fry cauliflowers, 241. To pickle, 301.

Caveach, to make, 295.

Celery sauce, 36, 93, 94. To ragoo, 228. Fried, 239. With cream, ib.

Chardoons, to stew, 139. Fried and buttered, 230. A la fromage, ib.

Charrs, to pot, 287.

Cheese, how to choose, 15. To pot Cheshire cheese, 285. To make slip coat cheese, 354. Brick-bat, ib. Cream, ib. Bullace, 355. Stilton, ib.

Cheesecakes, to make fine cheesecakes, 318. Lemon, two sorts, ib. Almond, 319. Without currants, ib. Citron, ib.

Cheese-curd puddings, to make, 250. Florentine, 257.

Cherry, pie, 261. Wine, 345. To jar, 355. To dry, two ways, 356. To preserve with the leaves and stalks green, ib. Ditto, in brandy, 357. To preserve, two ways, ib. To barrel Morello cherries, ib. Marmalade, 358. To candy, 368. Black cherry water, 378.

Cheshire pork pie, 195. To make it for sea, 277. To pot Cheshire cheese, 285.

Chesnuts, to roast a fowl with, 99. Soup, 182. Pudding, 250.

Chickens, to know if they are new or stale, 11. To broil, 24. To boil, 28. To fricasee, 42, 43. To dress Dutch way, 97. Surprise, 100. In savoury jelly, 101. Roasted with force-

INDEX.

force-meat and cucumbers, 101. Chickens à la braise, 102. To broil, ib. Pulled, 103. Chiringrate, ib. French way, 104. Boiled with bacon and celery, ib. With tongues, a good dish for a great deal of company, ib. Scotch chickens, ib. To stew, the Dutch way, 105. To stew, ib. Ditto, a pretty way, ib. To make a currey of chickens the Indian way, 129. Pie, 195. To boil, 265. To mince for the sick, 266. Broth, 267. To pull, ib. Chicken water, ibid.

Child, sage tea for, 270. Liquor for one that has the thrush, ib.

Chocolate, to make sham chocolate, 341. To make chocolate, two ways, 341, 342.

Chouder, a sea-dish, 278.

Chub, a fish, how to choose, 13.

Citron, pudding, 257. Cheesecakes, 319. Cream, 325. Syrup of, 367. To make, 368.

Clary fritters, 217. Wine, 346.

Clouted cream, 325.

Clove gilliflowers, syrup of, 367.

Cock, how to choose, 10.

Cock's-combs, to force, 135. To preserve, 136.

Cockles, to pickle, 294.

Cod and *Codlings*, how to choose, 13. To roast a cod's head, 152. To boil a cod's head, 153. How to stew cod, ib. To fricassee, ib. To bake a cod's head, 154. To crimp, the Dutch way, ib. To broil founds, ib. Ditto, with gravy, 155. To fricassee ditto, ib. To broil crimp-cod, ib. Cod's head, sauce for, 175.

Codling, green, pie, 260. To pickle, 303. To preserve, 363.

Collar, a breast of veal, 52, 289. A breast of mutton, 52. Pig, 88. Fish in ragoo to look like a breast of veal collared, 168. To make potatoes like a collar of veal or mutton, 231. Beef, 289. Pig, ib. Swine's face, 290. Salmon, ib. Eels, ib. Mackarel, 291.

Collops, Italian, 40. White, ib. Beef, ib. Collops and eggs, 141. Cold beef, 143. See *Scotch* collops.

Comfrey roots, to boil, 270.

Conserve of red roses, or any other flowers, 365. Hips, ib. roses boiled, ib.

Consumption, an approved receipt for, 384.

Cowslip pudding, 245. Wine, 346.

Crabs, to choose, 14. To butter, 169. To dress, 170.

Cracknels, to make, 340.

Crane, to display, 382.

Craw-fish, cullis, 133. To stew 170. Soup, 179, 207.

Cream, toasts, 222. Pudding, 255. Steeple cream, 321. Lemon, two ways, 322. Jelly of cream, ib. Orange cream, ib. Gooseberry, 323. Barley, two ways, ib. Ice, ib. Pistachio, 324. Hartshorn, ib. Almond, ib. A fine cream, ib. Ratafia, ib. Whipt cream, 325. Clear lemon cream, ib. Sack cream, like butter, ib. Clouted, ib. Quince, ib. Citron, ib. Cream of apples, quince, gooseberries, prunes, or rasp-berries, 326. Sugar loaf, ib. Cheese, 354.

Crout, sour, to make, 375.

Crust, for great pies, 201. Standing ditto, ib. A cold crust, 202. A dripping crust, ib. For custards, ib. A paste for crackling crust, ib.

Cucumbers, to force, 136. To stew, 137, 237, 238. To ragoo, 139. To farce, 238. To pickle large cucumbers in slites,

slices, 300. To preserve equal with any India sweetmeat, 365.
Cullis for all sorts of ragoo, 132. For butchers meat, ib. The Italian way, 133. Of crawfish, ib. White, ib.
Curd fritters, 215.
Currant jelly, 330. Wine 345. White ditto, ib. To preserve, 365.
Curry, two ways, 129.
Custard pudding, 247. Lemon custard to make, 319. Orange, 320. Beest, ib. Almond, ib. Baked, ib. Plain, ib.
Cutlets, à la Maintenon, a very good dish, 72.
Cyder, to make, 350. To fine, ib. After it has fined, 351.

D.

Damsons, to preserve whole, 361. To dry, 369. To keep for tarts, 374.
December, meat in season, 6.
Desart island, 333.
Devonshire squab pie, 195.
Disguised mutton chops, 72. Leg of veal and bacon, 74.
Distilling, 376.
Dog, two cures for the bite of a mad dog, 383.
Dotters, how to choose, 11.
Doves, how to choose, 12. See *Pigeons*.
Drink, beef, 265. Pectoral, 268. To make a good drink, 270.
Dripping, to pot, 272.
Ducks, wild and tame, to choose, 11. To roast, 21. Sauce for, 34. 36. Wild, to hash, 48. Alamode, 105. To stew with green peas, 106. Wild duck, to dress the best way, ib. Another, ib. To boil a duck with onions, ib. To dress with green peas, 107. With cucumbers, ib. A la braise, 107. To boil, the French way, 108. Pie, 194. To unbrace, 381.
Dumplings, yeast, 256. Norfolk, ib. Hard, two ways, ib. Apple, two ways, 256, 257. Raspberry, 257. When you have white bread, 277.
Dutch, sauce for fish, 175. Beef 291. Blanc-mange, 335.

E.

Eel, to choose, 13. To stew, 162. Ditto with broth, ib. To pitchcock eels, 163. To fry, ib. To broil, ib. To farce with white sauce, 164. To dress with brown sauce, ib. Soup, 207. Pie, 262. To pot, 288. To collar, 290.
Eggs, to choose, 15. Sauce, to make, 94. Forced, 136. To season an egg pie, 193. Egg and bacon pie, 204. Soup, 210. Sorrel with eggs, 233. Brocoli and eggs, ib. Asparagus and eggs, 234. Pretty dish of eggs, ib. A la tripe, ib. Fricassee, ib. Ragoo, 235. To broil, ib. Eggs with bread, ib. To farce, ib. Eggs with lettuce, 236. To fry eggs as round as balls, ib. To make an egg as big as twenty, ib. A grand dish, ib. A pretty dish of whites, 237. Sweet egg pie, 258. Marmalade the Jews way, 358.
Elder shoots to pickle in imitation of bamboo, 307. Wine, 343. Elder flower wine, very like Frontiniac, 344.
Endive, to ragoo, 225.
Everlasting syllabubs, 327.

Fairy

INDEX.

F.

Fairy butter, to make, 321.
Farce, eels, with white sauce, 164. Eggs, 235. Cucumbers, 238. Farce-meagre cabbage, 240.
February, meat, &c. in season, 2.
Fennel, to pickle, 303.
Fieldfare, how to choose, 12.
Fire, how to be prepared for roasting or boiling, 16.
Fish, to choose, 13. To dress, 148. To dress little fish, 155. Flat fish, 160. Salt fish, ib. Manner of dressing various sorts of dried fish, ib. The general rule for steeping dried fish, ib. To collar in ragoo, to look like breast of veal, 168. Shell fish, to stew, 172. Sauces for, 174. Gravy, 178. Salt fish pie, 261. Sauce to keep a whole year, 271. To dress for sea, 273. To bake, 274. To preserve, the Jews way, 293.
Fish pond, to make, 332.
Floating-island, to make, 331.
Florendine hare, 126. Of veal, 143. Cheese curd, 257. Oranges or apples, ib.
Flour, hasty pudding, 213. Pudding, 248.
Flounder, to choose, 13. Pie, 262. To boil, 266.
Flowers, to make conserve of any sort, 366. To candy any sort, 367
Flummery, hartshorn flummery, 334. Another way, ib. Oatmeal flummery, 335.
Flux, to stop, 385.
Fool, orange, 212. Westminster, ib. Gooseberry, ib.
Force-meat balls, 40. The inside of a sirloin of beef, 56. Sirloin, ib. Inside of rump of beef, 57. Round of beef, ib. Leg of lamb, ib. Another way, 58. A large fowl, 58. Tongue and udder, 68. Neat's tongue, 69. Forcemeat for pigeons, to make, 119. Hog's ears, 134. Cock's-combs, 135. Cabbage, ib. Savoys, ib. Eggs, 136. Cucumbers, ib. Asparagus in French rolls, 232.
Fowls, to choose, 10. To roast, pheasant fashion, 21. To roast, ib. To boil, 29. Sauce for, 34, 93, 95. To hash, 48. To force a large, 58. To stew in celery sauce, 94. German way, 95. To dress to perfection, ib. To stew nice way, 97. In jelly, 98. A la braise, ib. To roast with chesnuts, 99. To marinate, ib. To dress cold, 141, Gravy for, 177. Pie, 276. To pot, 283.
Frangas incopades, to make, 100.
Fraze, apple, 217. Almond, 218.
French beans, to dress, 31. To ragoo, 202, 225. French barley pudding, 245. Harrico of French beans, 276. To pickle French beans, 301. French biscuits, 313. Bread, 351. To keep French beans all the year, 372.
Fricandillas, to make, 85.
Fricassee ox palates, 41. Brown, 42. White, three ways, 43. Rabbits, lamb, or veal, ib. 44. Sweetbreads or tripe, 44. Calf's feet and chauldron, Italian way, ib. Pigeons, ib. Lamb's stones and sweetbreads, 45. Lamb's cutlets, ib. Neat's tongues brown, 68. Pigeons the Italian way, 119. Sausages, 141. Cold veal, 142. Cod, 153. Cod sounds, 155. Skate, white, 167. Ditto, brown, ib. Soals, white, ib. Ditto, brown, 168. Skirrets, 229. Artichoke-bottoms, ib.

Mushrooms, white, 229. Eggs, 234.
Fritters, hasty, 215. Fine, ib. Apple, ib. Curd, ib. Royal, ib. Skirret, 216. White, ib. Syringed, ib. Vine leaf, ib. Clary, 217. Spanish, ib. Plum, with rice, ib.
Fruit, wafers, 336. To keep till Christmas, 373.
Fry, beef steaks, two ways, 25. Tripe, ib. Sausages, ib. Loin of lamb, 76, 77. Carp, 151. Tench, 152. Herrings, 159. Lampreys, 163. Eels, ib. Smelts, 173. Artichokes, 231. Potatoes, 232. Celery, 239. Cauliflowers, 241. Artichoke-bottoms, 273.

G.

Garden, directions concerning garden things, 29.
Gerkins, to pickle, two ways, 299, 300.
German puffs, 218, 340. Sausages, 282.
Giblets, to stew, 110. A la turtle, ib. Pie, 194.
Gilded fish in jelly, 334.
Ginger, mock, to pickle, 306. Tablet, 341.
Gingerbread cakes, to make, 310. Gingerbread, 312.
Gold lace, how to clean, 388.
Golden pippins, see *Pippins*.
Goodwits, how to choose, 11.
Goose, to choose, 11. A mock goose, how prepared, 17. To roast, 20, 109. Sauce for, 34, 36. To dress with onions or cabbage, 108. To dress a green goose, 109. To dress a stubble goose, ib. To dry a goose, ib. To dress in ragoo, 110. Alamode, ib. Pie, 197. To make a pudding with the blood, 279. To rear, 381.
Gooseberry fool, 212. Cream, 323. Wafers, 334. Wine, 345.

To preserve whole without stoning, 361. To keep green till Christmas, 373. To keep red, 374. Wafers, 336.
Grailing, a fish, to choose, 13.
Grapes, to pickle, 304. To preserve, 363.
Grateful pudding, 248.
Gravy, how to make good and cheap gravy, Pref. iii. To make beef, or mutton, or veal gravy, 32. To make, 33. Turkey, or fowl, 35. For white sauce, 177. For Turkey, fowl, or ragoo, ib. For fowl when no meat or gravy ready, ib. To make a rich mutton or veal, 178. To make a strong fish, ib. Brown for Lent, 229. Soup, 274.
Greens, directions for dressing, 29.
Green gages, how to candy, 368.
Grill, calf's head, 51. Shrimps, 173.
Gruel, to make water-gruel, 268.
Gull, how to choose, 11.

H.

Haddocks, how to broil, 155. To broil when they are in high season, 165. To dress Spanish way, ib. Jews way, ib.
Haggass, Scotch, to make, 85. To make it sweet with fruit, ib.
Ham, the absurdity of making the essence of ham, a sauce to one dish, Pref. ii. To choose, 10. To boil, 26. A la braise, 85. To roast a ham or gammon, 86. To make essence of, 86, 131. Pie, 193. To pot with chicken, 285. Veal hams, 295. Beef hams, ib. Mutton hams, 296. Pork hams, ib.
Hamburgh, a turkey stuffed after the Hamburgh way, 97. Sausages, 281.

Hanover

INDEX.

Hanover cakes or puddings, 253.
Hard dumplings, two ways, 256.
Hair, to preserve and make it grow thick, 394.
Hare, to choose, 12. To keep hares sweet, or make them fresh when they stink, 20. To roast, 22. Different sorts of sauce for, 35. To hash, 48. To make a mock hare of a beast's heart, 68. To jug, two ways, 126. Florendine, ib. To scare, 127. To stew, ib. To hodge-podge, ib. Civet, 128. Soup, 182. To pot, 283.
Harrico of mutton, 70. French beans, 276.
Hartshorn cream, 324. Jelly, 328. Flummery, two ways, 334.
Hash, a calf's head, 45. White, 46. Venison, 47. Beef, ib. Mutton, ib. Veal, ib. Turkey, ib. Fowl, 48. Woodcock, ib. Wild duck, ib. Hare, ib. Cold mutton, 142. Mutton like venison, ib.
Hasty pudding, flour, 213. Oatmeal ditto, 214. Fine ditto, ib. Fritters, 215.
Heart-burn, lozenges for, 385.
Heath poults, to choose, 12. To choose heathcock and hen, ib.
Hedge-hog, to make, three ways, 224, 330.
Hen and chickens in jelly, 333.
Hen's nest, to make, 332.
Herrings, fresh, to choose, 13. Pickled and red, to choose, 14. To broil, 159. To fry, ib. To bake, ib. Dried, to dress, 161. Pie, 262.
Hips, conserve of, 366.
Hoarseness, receipt for, 385.
Hodge-podge, breast of veal, 51. Of mutton, 73. A hare, 127. To make, 184. Of mutton, ibid.
Hog, the several parts of one, 7. Of a bacon hog, ib. Feet and ears, to ragoo, 53. Hogs' ears forced, 134. Almond hogs puddings, three ways, 278. Ditto with currants, 279.
Honeycomb, lemon, 339.
Horned cattle, to prevent infection amongst, 388.
Housemaid, directions to, 387.
Hunting pudding, 190.
Hysterical water, to make, 378.

I.

Jam, raspberry, 330.
January, meat, fruit, vegetables, &c. then in season, 1.
Ice, to ice a great cake, 309. Cream, 323.
Jelly, isinglass, 268. Of cream, 322. Hartshorn, 328. Orange, 329. Ribband, ib. Calves feet, ib. Currant, 330. Pippin, ib. China orange, ib. Fish pond, 332. Hen's nest, ib. Moon and stars, 333. Hen and chickens, ib. Gilded fish, 334.
India pickle, to make, 308.
Ipswich, almond pudding, 251.
Iron, to keep from rusting, 388.
Iron-molds, to take out of linen, 388.
Isinglass jelly, 268.
Island, floating, to make, 331. Desart, 333.
Italian collops, 40. Pudding, 246.
Jug a hare, two ways, 126.
July, meat, &c. in season, 4.
Jumballs, to make, 139.
June, meat, &c. in season, 3.

K.

Kebobbed, mutton, 75.
Kickshaws, 222.
Kidney beans. See *Beans*.
Knots, a bird, how to choose, 11.
Knuckle broth, 270.

L.

Lace, gold or silver, to clean, 388.
Lamb, the several parts of one, 7. How to choose, 8. To roast, 17. Head to boil, 27. To boil a leg, &c. ib. To boil, 29. To fricassee, 434. To fricassee lamb-stones and sweetbreads, 45. Cutlets, to fricassee, ib. Head to bake, 49. Ditto, to dress, ib. To stew, 50. To ragoo, 55. To force a leg, 57, 58. And rice to bake, 76. To fry a loin, 76. Another way of frying a neck or loin, 77. Chops larded, ib. Chops en Casarole, ib. To dress a dish of lambs' bits, ib. A pig like fat lamb, 90. To make a very fine sweet lamb pie, 191. Savoury ditto, 192.
Lampreys, to dress, 162. To fry, 163. To pot, 288.
Larks, to choose, 12. To roast, 22, 125. Sauce for, 22. To dress pear fashion, 125.
Lemon pickle, to make, 37. Sauce for boiled fowl, 95. Tarts, 209. Pudding, two ways, 243. Tower or pudding, 255. To pickle, 302. Cheesecakes, two ways, 318. Custards, 319. Cream, two ways, 322. Ditto clear, 325. Honeycomb, 339. To keep, 374.
Leveret, to choose, 13.
Limes, to pickle, 305.
Ling, how to choose, 14.
Linen, how to take iron-molds out of, 388.
Livers, to dress with mushroom sauce, 95. A ragoo of, 141. Pudding boiled, 275.
Loaf, buttered loaves, 242. boiled, 250. Orange loaves, 338.
Lobsters, to choose, 14. To butter, two ways, 169. To roast, 170. To make a fine dish of, ib. Sauce, 174. Pie, 263. To pot, 288.
Lozenges for the heart-burn, 385. For a cold, ib.

M.

Macaroni soup, 178.
Mackarel, to choose, 13. To broil, 155. Whole, 156. To boil, ib. A la maitre d'hotel, ib. To collar, 291. To pickle mackarel, called caveach, 295.
Mackeroons, to make, 313.
Mad dog, two cures for the bite of, 383.
Made-dishes, rules to be observed in, 37. A pretty made-dish, 221.
Madling cakes, to make, 314.
Maid, directions to the house-maid, 387.
March, meat, &c. in season, 2.
Marle, a bird, how to choose, 11.
Marmalade of oranges, to make, 357. Eggs the Jews way, 358. Cherries, ib. White marmalades of quinces, two ways, ib. Red ditto, ib.
Marrow pudding, 189.
May, meat, &c. in season, 3.
Mead, to make, 347. White mead, ib.
Meat, to keep hot, 23. To preserve salt meat, 282.
Melon mangoes, to pickle, 306.
Milk soup the Dutch way, 211. Rice milk, 212. Artificial asses, 269. Cow's milk next to asses, ib.
Milk-water, two ways, 379, 380.
Millet pudding, 244.
Mince pies, two ways, 199. For Lent, 263.
Mint, how to distil, 376.
Moon and Stars in jelly, 333.

Moonshine,

INDEX.

Moonshine, to make, 331.
Moor-game, red and black, to pot, 286.
Morello cherries, to barrel, 357.
Mouse trap, to make, 333.
Muffins, to make, 352.
Mushrooms, to make sauce for white fowls of all sorts, 93. For white fowls boiled, ib. To stew, two ways, 138. To ragoo, 228. White fricassee of, 229. To pickle for the sea, 272. Powder, ib. To keep without pickle, 273. To pickle white, 303. To make pickle for, ib. To raise, 375.
Muscle, to stew or dress, three ways, 172, 173. Soup, 208. Pie, 263. To pickle, 294.
Mutton, to choose, 8. To roast, 16. The time required for roasting the several pieces of mutton, ib. To roast mutton venison fashion, 20. Chops to broil, 24. To draw gravy, 32. To hash, 47, 142. To collar a breast, 52. Another way to dress a breast, 53. To ragoo a leg, ib. Leg of, à la royale, 69. A la haut goût, 70. To roast with oysters, two ways, ib. With cockles, ib. Shoulder en epigram, ib. Harrico, ib. To French a hind saddle, 71. Another way, called St. Menehout, ib. Cutlets à la Maintenon, 72. Chops in disguise, ib. To dress mutton to eat like venison, ib. Turkish way, ib. Hodge-podge of, 73. Shoulder with ragoo of turnips, ib. To stuff a shoulder or leg, 74. Rumps à la braise, ib. Rumps with rice, 75. Kebobbed, ib. Neck of, called the hasty dish, 76. To hash like venison, 142. Gravy, 178. Broth, 183. Hodge podge, 184. Pie, 193. Pasty, 198. Broth for the sick, 264. Ditto for very weak people, 264. Mutton hams, 296.

N.

Nastertium berries, to pickle, 305.
Norfolk dumplings, 256.
North, Lady, her way of jarring cherries, 355.
November, meat, &c. in season, 5.
Nuns-cake, to make, 311.

O.

Oat pudding, how to bake, 188, 252. Oatmeal hasty pudding, 214. Oatmeal pudding, ib 275. Flummery, 335. Oat-cakes, 352.
Obstructions, two receipts for, 385.
October, meat, &c. in season, 5.
Olive pie, 193.
Onions, sauce, 92. Ragoo of, 140. Soup, 207. Soup the Spanish way, 211. Pie, 259. To pickle, two ways, 302.
Orange tarts, 200, 212. Orange puddings, four ways, 241. Florendine, 257. Orangeado pie, 259. Custards, 320. Butter, 321. Cream, 322. Jelly, 329, 330. Wafers, 337. Cakes, ib. Loaves, 338. Biscuits, ib. Wine, 344. Ditto with raisins, ib. Marmalade, 357. To preserve whole, 359.
Ortolans, to dress, 124.
Oven for baking, how to be built, 354.
Ox, how to bake an ox head, 36. Palates, to stew, 41. To ragoo, ib. To fricassee, ib. To roast, 42. To fricando, ib. To pickle, 137.
Ox cheek, soup, 186. Ditto pie, 195.

Oxford,

Oxford, John, 74. Pudding, 191. Sausages, 281.
Oyster sauce, 35, 92, 175. To make mock oyster sauce, 93. To ragoo, 140, 171. Scolloped, 171. To fry, ib. To stew, 172. To make loaves, ib. Soup, 209. To pickle, 294.

P.

Paco-lilla, or Indian pickle, to make, 307.
Pain perdu, to make, 222.
Panada, to make, 268.
Pancakes, 218. Fine pancakes, four ways, ib. Rice, 219. Wafer, ib. Tansey, ib. Pink-coloured, 220.
Parsley, how to distil, 326.
Parsnips, to dress, 30. How to stew, 233. To mash, ib.
Partridge, to choose, 12. To roast, 21. Sauce for, ib. 34, 134. To boil, 119. To dress, à la braise, 120. Partridge panes, ib. To stew, two ways, 121. Ditto with red or white cabbages, ib. To dress, French way, 131. Soup, 185. To boil for the sick, 266. To wing, 382.
Paste for tarts, two ways, 201. Puff-paste, ib. For crackling crust, 202.
Pasty, to make little pasties, 144. Petit pasties, for garnishing of dishes, ib. Venison pasty, 197. Loin of mutton, 198. Fish, the Italian way, 263.
Patties, savoury, 204. Common, ib. Fine, 205.
Peaches, to pickle, 300. To preserve, 363. Blossoms, syrup of, 367. To dry, 369.
Pearl, sugar of, 339.
Pears, to stew, 221. Ditto in a sauce-pan, ib. Purple, ib. To dry without sugar, 368.

Peas, green, to boil, 32. To stew peas and lettuce, 138. Peas, ib. Green peas soup, two ways, 180. A peas soup for winter, two ways, 181, 182. Peas soup for a fast dinner, 205. Green peas soup for ditto, two ways, ib. 206. Porridge, 211. Soup, Spanish, ib. Francoise, 239. With cream, 240. Soup, 274. Pudding, 276. To keep green peas till Christmas, 373. Another way to preserve green peas, ib. Another way to dress peas, 356.
Pellow of veal, 79. To make the Indian way, 130. Another way, ib.
Penny royal, how to distil, 376.
Pepper cakes, to make, 311.
Perfumery, receipts for, 391. To make red, light, or purple wash-balls, ib. Blue, red, purple, or marbled wash-balls, ib. White almond wash-balls, 392. Brown ditto, ib. Windsor soap, 392. Lip salve, ib. White ditto, 393. French rouge, ib. Opiate for the teeth, ib. Delescot's, ib. Tooth powder, ib. Shaving oil, ib. Shaving powder, ib. Soap to fill shaving boxes, 394. Wash for the face, ib. Almond milk for a wash, ib. Mrs. Dukely's method to preserve hair, ib. Stick to take hair out, ib. Liquid for the hair, ib. White almond paste, 395. Brown ditto, ib. Sweet scented bags, ib. Orange butter, ib. Lemon ditto, ib. Mareschalle powder, ib. Virgin's milk, ib. Honey water, 396. Pearl water, ib. Milk flude water, ib. Beautifying water, ib. Miss in her teens, ib. Lady Lilley's ball, ib. Nun's cream, ib. Cold cream, ib. Ambrosia nosegay, ib. Eau de

de bouquet, 397. Eau de luce, ib. Eau fans pareil, ib. Hard pomatum, ib. Soft ditto, ib. Sirop de capillaire, ib. Dragon roots, 398.

Pheafants, cock or hen, to choofe, 11. Poults, 12. Sauce for, 34, 134. May be larded, 35. To roaft, 122. To ftew, ib. To drefs à la braife, ib. To boil, 123. To allay, 382.

Pickle ox palates, 137. Mufhrooms for fea, 272. Pork, 292. A pickle for pork which is to be eat foon, ib. The Jewifh way to pickle beef, ib. Beef for prefent ufe, 293. Oyfters, cockles, and mufcles, 294. Mackarel, called caveach, 295. Rules to be obferved in pickling, 297. To pickle walnuts green, ib. Walnuts white, 298. Walnuts black, ib. Gerkins, two ways, 299, 300. Large cucumbers in flices, 300. Afparagus, ib. Peaches, ib. Radifh pods, 301. French beans, ib. Cauliflowers, ib. Beetroot, 302. White plums, ib. Onions, two ways, ib. Lemons, ib. Mufhrooms white, 303. To make pickle for mufhrooms, ib. Codlings, ib. Fennel, ib. Grapes, 304. Barberries, ib. Red cabbage, 305. Golden pippins, ib. Naftertium berries and limes, ib. Young fuckers or young artichokes, ib. Artichokebottoms, 306. Samphire, ib. Mock ginger, ib. Melon mangoes, ib. Elder fhoots in imitation of bamboo, 307. Paco-lilla, or Indian pickle, ib. To pickle fine purple cabbage, 308. To make the pickle, ib. Indian pickle, ib. Smelts, 371.

Pig, to kill and prepare for roafting, 18. To roaft, ib. 19. To roaft the hind quarter, lamb fafhion, 19. To bake, ib. Different forts of fauce for, 33. Various ways for dreffing, 87. A pig in jelly, 88. Collared, ib. The French way, 89. Au peredouillet, ib. Matelote, 90. Like a fat lamb, ib. Barbecued, ib. Pettitoes, 91. Feet and ears, to preferve, two ways, 136. To collar, 289.

Pigeons, to choofe, 12. To roaft, 21, 112. To broil, 25. To boil, 112. To à la daube, ib. Au poir, 113. Pigeons ftoved, 114. Surtout, ib. Compote, ib. French pupton of, 115. Boiled with rice, ib. Tranfmogrified, two ways, ib. In fricando, 116. To roaft with a farce, ib. In favoury jelly, ib. A la Souffel, 117. In Pimlico, ib. In a hole, ib. To jug, 118. To ftew, two ways, ib. To fricaffee, the Italian way, 119. To make force-meat for, ib. To ftew with white or red cabbage, 121. To drefs a cold, 141. Pie, 194. To boil for the fick, 266. To pot, 283.

Pies, obfervations on, 191. To make a very fine fweet lamb or veal pie, ib. A favoury veal pie, 192. Ditto lamb or veal, ib. Calf's foot, ib. Olive, 193. To feafon an egg pie, ib. Mutton pie, ib. Beef fteak, ib. Ham, ib. Pigeon, 194. Giblet, ib. Duck, ib. Chicken, 195. Chefhire pork pie, ib. A Devonfhire fquab, ib. Ox cheek, ib. Shropfhire, 196. Yorkfhire Chriftmas pie, ib. Goofe pie, 197. Calf's head, 198. Mince pies, two ways, 199. Crufts for great pies, 201. Hottentot, 202. Bride's, ib. Thatched houfe, 203. French, ib. Savoury chicken, 204. Egg and bacon, ib.

Pork,

INDEX.

Pork, 204. Artichoke, 258. Sweet egg, ib. Potatoe, ib. Onion, 259. Orangeado, ib. Vegetable, ib. Skirret, ib. Apple, 260. Green codling, ib. Cherry, 261. Salt fish, ib. Carp, ib. Soal, ib. Eel, 262. Flounder, ib. Herring, ib. Salmon, ib. Lobster, 263. Muscle, ib. Lent mince pies, ib. Fowl, 276. Cheshire pork pie for sea, 277. To make fish pies the Spanish way, 357.

Pike, to choose, 13. To dress, 164. To pot, 287.

Pippins whole, to stew, 221. To pickle, 305. Jelly, 330. To preserve, 363. To preserve in slices, 365.

Pistachio, cream, 324.

Pith pudding, 189.

Plague water, 378. A receipt against, 383.

Plaise, to choose, 13. To boil, 266.

Plovers, to choose, 12. To dress several ways, 125.

Plum porridge for Christmas, 179. A boiled plum pudding, 190. Plum porridge, 213. Gruel, ib. Fritters with rice, 217. White pear plum pudding, 245. To pickle white plums, 302. Little plum cakes, 317. To preserve the large green plums, 363. To preserve white pear plums, 364. To dry, 369. To dry pear plums, ib. Filling for the aforesaid plums, 370. To keep pear plums for tarts, 374.

Poppy-water cordial, to make, 381.

Pork, how to choose, 9. To roast the different pieces of, 17. Gravy or sauces for pork, 18. Steaks, to broil, 24. To boil a leg, 28. Pickled, to boil, ib. To stuff a chine, 86. To barbecue a leg, 87. Cheshire pork pie, 195, 277. Pork pie, 204. Broth, 265. Pudding, 274. To pickle, 292. A pickle for pork which is to be eat soon, ib. Pork hams, 296.

Porridge, plum, for Christmas, 179. Peas, 211. Plum, or barley gruel, 213.

Portable soup, to make, 185.

Portugal beef, 62. Cakes, 311.

Posset, sack, three ways, 214.

Potatoes, several ways of dressing, 30. Cakes, 231. Potatoe pudding, several ways, 231, 241. Potatoes like a collar of veal or mutton, 231. To broil, 232. To fry, ib. Mashed, ib. Pie, 259.

Potting, to pot dripping, 272. Observations on the subject in general, 282. Pigeons or fowls, 283. Cold tongue, beef, or venison, ib. Venison, ib. Hare, ib. Tongues, two ways, 284. Beef like venison, 285. Cheshire cheese, ib. Ham with chickens, ib. Woodcocks, 286. Red and black moor-game, ib. All kinds of small birds, ib. To save potted birds, ib. Charrs, 287. Pike, ib. Salmon, two ways, ib. Lobster, 288. Eels, ib. Lampreys, ib.

Pottage, brown, 187. To make white barley pottage with a chicken in the middle, ib.

Poultry, to choose, 10. Directions concerning roasting, 23. To boil, 28. To dress, 92.

Pound cake, to make, 309.

Powder, mushroom, to make, 272.

Prawns, to choose, 14. To stew, 170.

Preserve, cock's-combs, 136. Tripe to go to the East Indies, 293. Salmon, and all sorts of fish the Jews way, ib. Yeast for several months, 353. Cherries

INDEX.

ries with the leaves and stalks green, 356. Cherries in brandy, 357. Cherries, two ways, ib. Oranges whole, 359. Quinces whole, 360. White quinces whole, ib. Apricots, two ways, 361. Damsons whole, ib. Gooseberries whole, ib. White walnuts, 362. Green walnuts, ib. Large green plums, 363. Peaches, ib. Pippins, ib. Grapes, ib. Green codlings, ib. Apricots or plums green, 364. Barberries, ib. White pear plums, ib. Currants, 365. Raspberries, ib. Pippins in slices, ib. Cucumbers equal to Italian sweetmeats, ib. Artichokes all the year, 372. Ditto the Spanish way, ib. French beans all the year, ib. Green peas till Christmas, 373. Green peas, beans, &c. and fruit, till Christmas, ib. Green gooseberries till Christmas, ib. Red ditto, 374. Walnuts all the year, ib. Lemons, ib. White bullace, &c. for tarts or pies, ib.

Prune pudding, 255. Cream, 326.

Puddings, rules to be observed in making, 188. To bake an oat pudding, ib. Calf's foot, ib. Pith, 189. Marrow, ib. Boiled suet, ib. Boiled plum, 190. Hunting ib. Yorkshire, ib. Vermicelli, ib. Steak, 191. Oxford, ib. Flour hasty pudding, 213. Oatmeal ditto, 214. Fine ditto, ib. Potatoe, 231, 241. Oatmeal pudding, 241. Orange, four ways, 242. Lemon, two ways, 243. Almond, ib. To boil ditto, 244. Sago, ib. Millet, ib. Carrot, two ways, ib. Cowslip, 245. Quince, apricot, or white pear plum, ib. Pearl barley, 245. French barley, ib. Apple, two ways, 246. Ditto baked, ib. An Italian pudding, ib. Rice, three ways, ib. Carolina rice, 247. To boil a custard pudding, ib. Flour, 248. Batter, ib. Ditto without eggs, ib. Grateful, ib. Bread, ib. Fine ditto, 249. Ordinary ditto, ib. Baked ditto, ib. Chesnut, 250. A fine plain baked pudding, ib. Pretty little cheese-curd puddings, ib. Apricot, 251. Ipswich almond pudding, ib. Transparent, ib. Puddings for little dishes, ib. Sweetmeat, 252. A fine plain pudding, ib. Ratafia, ib. Bread and butter, ib. A boiled rice, 253. Cheap rice, ib. Cheap plain rice, ib. Cheap baked rice, ib. Hanover, ib. Yam, 254. Vermicelli, ib. Red sago, ib. Spinage, ib. Quaking, 255. Cream, ib. Prune, ib. Spoonful, ib. Lemon tower or pudding, ib. Citron, 257. Pork, beef, &c. 274. Rice, ib. Suet, ib. Liver pudding boiled, ib. Oatmeal, ib. Baked ditto, ib. Rice, baked, ib. Peas, 276. Almond hogs puddings, three ways, 278. Hogs puddings with currants, 279. Black puddings, ib. A pudding with the blood of a goose, ib.

Puff-paste, 201. German puffs, 218, 340.

Pullets à la Sainte Menehout, 100.

Pupton of apples, 220.

Q.

Quaking pudding, 255.
Queen's cakes, 317.

Quince

Quince pudding, 245. Cream, 325. Wine, 346. White marmalade of, two ways, 358. Red ditto, ib. To preserve whole, 360. White ditto whole, ib. Cakes, to make, ib. Syrup of, 367.
Quins sauce, two ways, 174.
Quire of paper pancakes, 219.

R.

Rabbits, to choose, 13. To roast, 23. Sauce for, ib. To roast hare fashion, ib. To fricassee, 43, 44. To boil with onions, 106. Portuguese, 128. Surprise, ib. In casserole, 129. Scotch, 230. Welch, ib. English, two ways, ib. To boil, 266. To unlace, 582.
Radish pods, to pickle, 301.
Ragoo, ox palates, 41. Leg of mutton, 53. Hog's feet and ears, ib. Neck of veal, ib. Breast of veal several ways, 54. Fillet of veal, 55. Sweetbreads, ib. Lamb, ib. Piece of beef, ib. A goose, 110. Cucumbers, 139. Onions, 140. Oysters, ib. 171. Asparagus, ib. Livers, 141. Cauliflowers, ib. Gravy for, 177. Endive, 225. French beans, two ways, ib. Beans with a farce, 226. With cabbage, ib. With parsnips, 227. With potatoes, ib. Celery, 228. Mushrooms, ib. Eggs, 235. Artichoke-bottoms, 273.
Raisin wine, two ways, 342.
Raspberry dumplings, 257. Cream, 326. Jam, 330. Wine, 347. To preserve, 365.
Ratafia pudding, 252. Cakes, 317. Cream, 324.
Ribband jelly, to make, 329.

Rice soup, 210. White pot, 212. Milk, ib. Pancakes, 219. Pudding, four ways, 246, 275. Boiled ditto, 253. Cheap ditto, ib. Cheap plain ditto, ib. Cheap baked ditto, ib. Baked, 275. Almond rice, 339.
Rich, Mr. a dish of mutton contrived by him, 76.
Roasting, directions for, 15. To roast beef, 161. Mutton and lamb, 16. House lamb, 17. Veal, ib. Pork, ib. A pig, 18, 19. The hind quarter of a pig, lamb fashion, 19. Venison, ib. Mutton, venison fashion, 20. Tongue and udder, ib. Geese and turkies, ib. Fowl, pheasant fashion, 21. Fowls, ib. Pigeons, ib. 112. Partridges, 21. Larks, 22. Woodcocks and Snipes, ib. Hares, ib. Rabbits, 23. Rabbits, hare fashion, ib. A turkey the genteel way, 58. Calf's liver, 84. A ham or gammon, 86. Directions for roasting a goose, 109. Pigeons with a farce, 116. Pheasants, 122. A cod's head, 152. A piece of fresh sturgeon, 165. A fillet or collar of ditto, 166. Lobsters, 170. Pound of butter, 264.
Roses, to make conserve of red roses, 366. Ditto boiled, ib. Syrup of, ib. To distil red rose-buds, 376.
Royal fritters, 215.
Ruffs and *Rees*, Lincolnshire birds, to choose, 11. To dress, 124.
Ruffs, a fish, to choose, 13.

S.

Sack posset, three ways, 214. Cream like butter, 325.

Saffron

INDEX.

Saffron cake, how to make, 282.
Sage tea, 270. Ditto for a child, ib.
Sago pudding, 244. Ditto red, 254. To boil, 268.
Salmagundy, two ways, 143. For a middle dish at supper, 222.
Sallad, how to dress broccoli in, 231.
Salmon, to choose, 12. Pickled ditto, 14. To broil, 155. To dress a jowl of pickled, 157. To bake, ib. Au court Bouillon, ib. A la braise, 158. In cases, ib. To boil salmon crimp, 159. Dried, to dress, 161. Pie, 262. To pot, 287. To collar, 290. To preserve, the Jews way, 293.
Salop, to boil, 268.
Samphire, to pickle, 305.
Salt, what kind best for preserving meat or butter, 282.
Sattins, white or flowered silks with gold and silver in them, to clean, 388.
Sauce, how to make a rich and cheap sauce, Pref. iv. Sauce for a tongue and udder, 20. Poivrade, for partridges, 21, 34. For broiled chickens, 24, 93. Different sorts for a pig, 33. For venison, ib. For a goose, 34, 36. Apple, ib. For a turkey, 34, 36, 92, 93. Ducks, 34, 36. Fowls, ib. 93, 95. Pheasants and partridges, 34, 93. Different sorts for a hare, 35. Directions concerning sauce for steaks, ib. Oyster, ib. 92. Celery, 36, 93, 94. Onion, 92. Mock oyster, 93. White, ib. Mushroom, ib. Egg, 94. Shalot, ib, Carrier, ib. A pretty little sauce, 95. Lemon, ib. Quins, for fish, two ways, 174. Lobster, ib. Shrimp, ib. Oyster, 175. Anchovy, ib. Dutch, ib. For cod's head, 175. Nice sauce for most sorts of fish, 176. White fish sauce, ib. Fish sauce to keep a whole year, 271.
Sausages, to fry, 25, 141. To make fine sausages, 280. Common, 281. Oxford, ib. Bologna, ib. Hamburgh, ib. German way, 282.
Savoloys, 280.
Savoys forced and stewed, 135.
Scare a hare, 127.
Scate, to crimp, 166. To fricassee white, 167. To fricassee brown, ib. Soup, 209.
Scallops, to make, of oysters, 171. How to stew, 173.
Scotch collops, to dress, 38. Fillet of veal with ditto, 39. White ditto, ib. Ditto à la Francoise, ib. Haggass, 85. To make it sweet with fruit, ib. Chickens, 104. Barley broth, 183. Rabbit, 230.
Seed cake, to make, 310, 311.
Selery, see *Celery*.
September, meat, &c. in season, 5.
Shad, how to choose, 13.
Shalot sauce, 94. For a scrag of mutton boiled, 95.
Sheep, the different parts of one, 7. To bake a sheep's head, 49. Sheep's rumps with rice, 75.
Shrewsbury cakes, to make, 313.
Shrimps, to choose, 14. To stew, 170. To grill, 173. Buttered, ib.
Shropshire pie, 196.
Shuffler, a bird, how to choose, 11.
Sick, directions for, 264.
Silks, how to clean, 388. To take grease out of, ib.
Silver lace, to clean, 388.
Sirloin of beef, to force, two ways, 56. En epigram, 57. To dress inside cold, 67.

Skir-

Skirret fritters, 216. To fricassee, 229. Pie, 259.

Slip-coat cheese, to make, 354.

Smelts, to choose, 13. To fry, 173. To pickle, 371.

Snipes, to choose, 12. To roast, 22. To salmec, 123. To dress in a surtout, ib. To boil, 124.

Snow balls, Carolina, 341.

Soals, to choose, 13. To fricassee white, 167. Ditto brown, 167, 168. To boil, ib. Pie, 261.

Sorrel, to dress with eggs, 233.

Soups, rules to be observed in making, 176. Strong broth for, 177. Vermicelli, 178. Macaroni, ib. Cressu, ib. Craw-fish, 179. Santé, 180. Green peas, two ways, ib. Peas soup for winter, 181. Another way, 182. Chesnut, ib. Hare, ib. A la reine, ib. Partridge, 185. Portable, ib. Ox cheek, 186. Almond, ib. Transparent, 187. Peas soup for Lent, 205. Green ditto, two ways, 206. Soup meagre, ib. Onion, 207. Eel, ib. Craw-fish, ib. Muscle, 208. Scate or thornback, 209. Oyster, ib. Almond, ib. Rice, 210. Barley, ib. Turnip, ib. Egg, ib. Spanish peas, 211. Onion, the Spanish way, ib. Milk, the Dutch way, ib. Bread, for the sick, 269. Gravy, 274. Peas, for sea, ib.

Sour crout, to make, 375.

Spanish fritters, 217.

Spinage, to dress, 29, 232. Stewed spinage and eggs, 138. To boil, when you have not room on the fire to do it by itself, 232. Pudding, 254.

Spoonful pudding, 255.

Stag's heart water, to make, 380.

Steaks, beef, to broil, 24. Pork, ib. Beef, to fry, 25. Directions concerning sauce for, 35. To stew, 61. After the French way, ib. Rolled, 67. Pudding, 191. Pie, 193.

Steel, how to keep from rusting, 388.

Steeple cream, to make, 321.

Stertion (*Nastertium*) buds to pickle, 305.

Stew, ox palates, 41. Lamb or calf's head, 50. Knuckle of veal, two ways, 59. Fillet, ib. Beef steaks, 61. Rump of beef, two ways, 62. Rump or brisket of beef, French way, 63. Beef gobbets, ib. Ox cheek, 64. Shank of beef, ib. Neats tongues whole, 69. Calf's feet, 84. Turkey, brown, 96. Ditto, nice way, ib. Chickens, Dutch way, 105. Chickens, ib. Ditto, pretty way, ib. Ducks with green peas, 106. Pigeons, two ways, 118. Partridges, two ways, 121. Ditto or pigeons with white or red cabbage, ib. Pheasants, 122. A hare, 127. Cucumbers, 137, 237, 238. Red cabbage, ib. Peas and lettuce, 138. Peas, ib. Spinage and eggs, ib. Mushrooms, two ways, ib. Chardoons, 139. Carp, 150. Carp or tench, 151. Cod, 153. Eels, two ways, 162. Ditto with broth, ib. Prawns, shrimps, or craw-fish, 170. Oysters, and all sorts of shell-fish, 172. Muscles, two ways, ib. Scollops, 173. Pears, 221. Ditto in a sauce-pan, ib. Ditto purple, ib. Parsnips, 233.

Still, how to use the ordinary still, 377.

Stilton cheese, 355.

Stock fish, to dress, 161.

Sturgeon, to choose, 14. To roast a piece of fresh, 165.

To roaſt a fillet or collar, 166. To boil, ib.
Suckers, to pickle, 305.
Suet pudding boiled, 189. Dumplings, 191. Pudding, 275.
Sugar, loaf cream, 326. Of Pearl, 339. Cakes, 340. To clarify, Spaniſh way, 370.
Surfeit water, to make, 379.
Swan, to lift, 382.
Sweetbreads, to fricaſſee, 44. To ragoo, 55. A la Dauphine, 82. Another way to dreſs, ib. En cordonnier, 83.
Sweetmeat pudding, 252.
Syllabubs, whipt, 327. Everlaſting, ib. Solid ſyllabub, ib. from the cow, 328.
Syringed fritters, 216.
Syrup of roſes, to make, 366. Of citron, 367. Clove gilliflowers, ib. Peach bloſſoms, ib. Quinces, ib.

T.

Tablet ginger, 341.
Tanſey pancakes, 219. To make, two ways, 233. Bean tanſey, ib. Water tanſey, ib.
Tarts, orange and lemon, 200. To make different ſorts, ib. Paſte for tarts, two ways, 201.
Teal, to chooſe, 12. To allay, 382.
Tench, to chooſe, 13. To ſtew, 151. To fry, 152.
Thornback, ſee *Scate*.
Thruſh, how to chooſe, 12.
Thruſh, how to make a liquor for a child that has the thruſh, 270.
Tongue and udder, to roaſt, 20. To boil, 26. Tongue and udder forced, 68. To fricaſſee neat's tongues, ib. To force a tongue, 69. To ſtew neat's tongues whole, ib. To pot cold, 283. To pot, two ways, 284.

Tort, to make, 198. Tort de moy, 199. Buttered, 336.
Tranſparent ſoup, 187. Pudding, 251.
Treacle water, how to make, 377. Lady Monmouth's way, ib.
Trifle, to make, 328.
Tripe, to fry, 25. Tripe à la Kilkenny, 68. To preſerve to go to the Eaſt Indies, 293.
Trout, how to chooſe, 13.
Truffles and *Morels*, good in ſauces and ſoups, 40. How to uſe them, ib.
Turbot, to chooſe, 13. To boil, 148. To bake, 149.
Turkey, to chooſe a cock, hen, or poult, 10. To roaſt, 20. To boil, 28. Sauce for a boiled, 28, 35, 92, 93. Sauce for roaſt, 34, 92. To haſh, 47. To ſtew in celery ſauce, 94. To dreſs to perfection, 95. To ſtew brown, 96. Ditto, nice way, ib. Dutch way, 97. Hamburgh way, ib. A la daub hot, ib. Ditto cold, ib. In jelly, 98. Gravy for, 177. To ſouſe in imitation of ſturgeon, 292. To cut up, 381.
Turlington's balſam, 386.
Turnips, to dreſs, 30. Soup, 210. Wine, 347.
Turtle, to dreſs, the Weſt India way, 145. Another way, 146. To make a mock turtle, 147. Mock turtle ſoup, 148.

V. U.

Varniſh, yellow, to make, 387. A pretty varniſh, to colour little baſkets, &c. ib.
Udder, to roaſt, 20.
Veal, to chooſe, 9. To roaſt, 17. To draw gravy, 32. To dreſs a fillet of veal with collops, 39.

E e   Savoury

INDEX.

Savoury dish of, 39. To fricassee, 43, 44. To hash, 47. Breast in hodge-podge, 51. To collar a breast of, 52, 289. To ragoo a neck of, 53. Ditto breast, several ways, 54. Fillet, 55. To stew a knuckle, two ways, 59. A fillet, ib. Shoulder with ragoo of turnips, 74. A la Bourgeoise, 78. Leg of, disguised, and bacon, ib. Loin en epigram, ib. Porcupine of a breast, 79. Pillaw, ib. Fricando, 80. Bombarded, ib. Rolls, ib. Olives, 81. Ditto French way, ib. Bianquets, ib. Shoulder à la Piedmontese, 82. Cold, to fry, 142. To toss up white, ib. To mince, 143 Florentine, ib. Gravy, 178. To make a very fine sweet veal pie, 191. Savoury ditto, 192. To boil a scrag, 264. To mince for the sick, 267. To make marble veal, 289. Veal hams, 295.

Vegetable pie, 259.

Venison, to choose, 10. To roast, 19. How to keep venison sweet, and make it fresh when it stinks, 20. Different sorts of sauce for, 33. To hash, 47. To dress a leg of mutton to eat like, 72, 92. Pretty dish of a breast, 91. To boil a neck or haunch, ib. To hash mutton like, 142. Pasty, 197. Sea venison, 277. To pot, two ways, 283. To pot beef like, 285.

Vermicelli, soup, 178. Pudding, 190, 254. To make, 371.

Vine-leaf fritters, 216.

Vinegar, to make, 375.

Uxbridge cakes, 315.

W.

Wafer pancakes, 219. Fruit wafers of codlins, plums, 336. White, ib. Brown, ib. Gooseberry, ib. Orange, 337.

Walnuts, to pickle green, 297. Ditto white, 298. Black, ib. To preserve white, 362. Green, ib. To keep all the year, 374. To make walnut water, 376.

Water, to make water-sokey, 159. Tansey, 223. Chicken, 267, 268. Buttered, 269. Seed, ib. Barley, 270. Walnut, 376. Treacle, 377. Black cherry, 378. Hysterical, ib. Plague, ib. Surfeit, 379. Milk, ib. Stag's heart, 380. Angelica, ib. Cordial poppy, 381.

Weaver-fish, to broil, 156.

Welch rabbit, 230.

Westminster fool, 212.

Westphalia. See *Hams*.

Wheat, buttered, 213.

Wheat ears, how to choose, 11.

Whipt cream, 325. Syllabubs, 327.

White bait, to dress, 173.

White fish sauce, to make, 176 Pot, 211. Rice ditto, 212. Fritters, 216. Of eggs, pretty dish of, 237. Plums to pickle, 302. Wafers, 336. Cakes, like China dishes, 338. Bread, London way, 351.

Whitings, to choose, 13. To broil, 155.

Wigeons, to choose, 12. To roast, 21.

Wigs, to make, 314. Light wigs, ib. Very good, ib.

Wine, to make raisin wine, two ways, 342. Blackberry, 343. Elder, ib. Orange, 344. Ditto with raisins, ib. Elder-flower, ib. Gooseberry, 345. Currant,

Currant, 345. White ditto, ib. Cherry, ib. Quince, ib. Turnip, 347. Birch, 346. Cowslip, ib. Raspberry, ib.

Woodcocks, to choose, 12. To roast, 22. To hash, 48. To falmec, 123. In a surtout, ib. To boil, 124. To pot, 286. To thigh, 382.

Y.

Yam pudding, 254.

Yeast dumplings, 256. To preserve yeast for several months, 353.

Yellow varnish, to make, 387.

Yorkshire pudding, 190. Christmas pie, 196. Yorkshire, why famous for ham, 282.

THE END.

ERRATA.

Page 150. line 11. *for* beu *read* bleu.
    290. — 11. *for* callar *read* collar.
    381. — 4 *from the bottom, for* mullard *read* mallard.

Bringing Classics to Life # BOOK JUNGLE

www.bookjungle.com *email: sales@bookjungle.com fax: 630-214-0564 mail: Book Jungle PO Box 2226 Champaign, IL 61825*

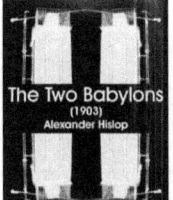

The Two Babylons
Alexander Hislop
QTY

You may be surprised to learn that many traditions of Roman Catholicism in fact don't come from Christ's teachings but from an ancient Babylonian "Mystery" religion that was centered on Nimrod, his wife Semiramis, and a child Tammuz. This book shows how this ancient religion transformed itself as it incorporated Christ into its teachings....

Religion/History   **Pages:358**

ISBN: *1-59462-010-5*   **MSRP** *$22.95*

The Power Of Concentration
Theron Q. Dumont

It is of the utmost value to learn how to concentrate. To make the greatest success of anything you must be able to concentrate your entire thought upon the idea you are working on. The person that is able to concentrate utilizes all constructive thoughts and shuts out all destructive ones...

Self Help/Inspirational   **Pages:196**

ISBN: *1-59462-141-1*   **MSRP** *$14.95*

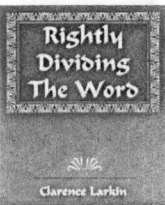

Rightly Dividing The Word
Clarence Larkin

The "Fundamental Doctrines" of the Christian Faith are clearly outlined in numerous books on Theology, but they are not available to the average reader and were mainly written for students. The Author has made it the work of his ministry to preach the "Fundamental Doctrines." To this end he has aimed to express them in the simplest and clearest manner..

Religion   **Pages:352**

ISBN: *1-59462-334-1*   **MSRP** *$23.45*

The Law of Psychic Phenomena
Thomson Jay Hudson

"I do not expect this book to stand upon its literary merits; for if it is unsound in principle, felicity of diction cannot save it, and if sound, homeliness of expression cannot destroy it. My primary object in offering it to the public is to assist in bringing Psychology within the domain of the exact sciences. That this has never been accomplished..."

New Age   **Pages:420**

ISBN: *1-59462-124-1*   **MSRP** *$29.95*

Beautiful Joe
Marshall Saunders

When Marshall visited the Moore family in 1892, she discovered Joe, a dog they had nursed back to health from his previous abusive home to live a happy life. So moved was she, that she wrote this classic masterpiece which won accolades and was recognized as a heartwarming symbol for humane animal treatment...

Fiction   **Pages:256**

ISBN: *1-59462-261-2*   **MSRP** *$18.45*

Bringing Classics to Life BOOK JUNGLE

www.bookjungle.com *email: sales@bookjungle.com fax: 630-214-0564 mail: Book Jungle PO Box 2226 Champaign, IL 61825*

The Go-Getter
Kyne B. Peter

QTY

The Go Getter is the story of William Peck. He was a war veteran and amputee who will not be refused what he wants. Peck not only fights to find employment but continually proves himself more than competent at the many difficult test that are throw his way in the course of his early days with the Ricks Lumber Company...

Business/Self Help/Inspirational   Pages:68

ISBN: *1-59462-186-1*   MSRP *$8.95*

Self Mastery
Emile Coue

Emile Coue came up with novel way to improve the lives of people. He was a pharmacist by trade and often saw ailing people. This lead him to develop autosuggestion, a form of self-hypnosis. At the time his theories weren't popular but over the years evidence is mounting that he was indeed right all along...

New Age/Self Help   Pages:98

ISBN: *1-59462-189-6*   MSRP *$7.95*

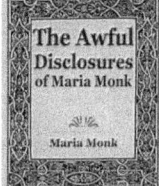

The Awful Disclosures Of Maria Monk

"I cannot banish the scenes and characters of this book from my memory. To me it can never appear like an amusing fable, or lose its interest and importance. The story is one which is continually before me, and must return fresh to my mind with painful emotions as long as I live..."

Religion   Pages:232

ISBN: *1-59462-160-8*   MSRP *$17.95*

As a Man Thinketh
James Allen

"This little volume (the result of meditation and experience) is not intended as an exhaustive treatise on the much-written-upon subject of the power of thought. It is suggestive rather than explanatory, its object being to stimulate men and women to the discovery and perception of the truth that by virtue of the thoughts which they choose and encourage..."

Inspirational/Self Help   Pages:80

ISBN: *1-59462-231-0*   MSRP *$9.45*

The Enchanted April
Elizabeth Von Arnim

It began in a woman's club in London on a February afternoon, an uncomfortable club, and a miserable afternoon when Mrs. Wilkins, who had come down from Hampstead to shop and had lunched at her club, took up The Times from the table in the smoking-room...

Fiction   Pages:368

ISBN: *1-59462-150-0*   MSRP *$23.45*

Bringing Classics to Life # BOOK JUNGLE

www.bookjungle.com email: sales@bookjungle.com fax: 630-214-0564 mail: Book Jungle PO Box 2226 Champaign, IL 61825

The Codes Of Hammurabi And Moses - W. W. Davies

The discovery of the Hammurabi Code is one of the greatest achievements of archaeology, and is of paramount interest, not only to the student of the Bible, but also to all those interested in ancient history...

Religion Pages: 132
ISBN: *1-59462-338-4*   MSRP *$12.95*

The Thirty-Six Dramatic Situations
Georges Polti

An incredibly useful guide for aspiring authors and playwrights. This volume categorizes every dramatic situation which could occur in a story and describes them in a list of 36 situations. A great aid to help inspire or formalize the creative writing process...

Self Help/Reference Pages: 204
ISBN: *1-59462-134-9*   MSRP *$15.95*

Holland - The History Of Netherlands
Thomas Colley Grattan

Thomas Grattan was a prestigious writer from Dublin who served as British Consul to the US. Among his works is an authoritative look at the history of Holland. A colorful and interesting look at history....

History/Politics Pages: 408
ISBN: *1-59462-137-3*   MSRP *$26.95*

A Concise Dictionary of Middle English
A. L. Mayhew
Walter W. Skeat

The present work is intended to meet, in some measure, the requirements of those who wish to make some study of Middle-English, and who find a difficulty in obtaining such assistance as will enable them to find out the meanings and etymologies of the words most essential to their purpose...

Reference/History Pages: 332
ISBN: *1-59462-119-5*   MSRP *$29.95*

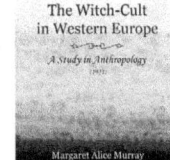

The Witch-Cult in Western Europe
Margaret Murray

QTY

The mass of existing material on this subject is so great that I have not attempted to make a survey of the whole of European "Witchcraft" but have confined myself to an intensive study of the cult in Great Britain. In order, however, to obtain a clearer understanding of the ritual and beliefs I have had recourse to French and Flemish sources...

Occult Pages: 308
ISBN: *1-59462-126-8*   MSRP *$22.45*

BOOK JUNGLE

Bringing Classics to Life

www.bookjungle.com *email:* sales@bookjungle.com *fax:* 630-214-0564 *mail:* Book Jungle PO Box 2226 Champaign, IL 61825

Name	
Email	
Telephone	
Address	
City, State ZIP	

☐ **Credit Card** ☐ **Check / Money Order**

Credit Card Number	
Expiration Date	
Signature	

Please Mail to: Book Jungle
　　　　　　　　　 PO Box 2226
　　　　　　　　　 Champaign, IL 61825
or Fax to:　　　 630-214-0564

ORDERING INFORMATION

web: *www.bookjungle.com*
email: *sales@bookjungle.com*
fax: *630-214-0564*
mail: *Book Jungle PO Box 2226 Champaign, IL 61825*
or PayPal *to sales@bookjungle.com*

Please contact us for bulk discounts
DIRECT-ORDER TERMS

**20% Discount if You Order
Two or More Books**
Free Domestic Shipping!

www.ingramcontent.com/pod-product-compliance
Lightning Source LLC
Chambersburg PA
CBHW082032230426
43670CB00016B/2635